GMAT

Prep Course

with Software
and
Online Course

JEFF KOLBY

Additional educational titles from Nova Press (available at novapress.net):

GRE Prep Course (624 pages, includes software, online course)

Master The LSAT (608 pages, includes 4 official LSAT exams!)

The MCAT Physics Book (444 pages)

The MCAT Chemistry Book (480 pages)

The MCAT Biology Book (416 pages)

SAT Prep Course (640 pages, includes software)

Law School Basics: A Preview of Law School and Legal Reasoning (224 pages)

Vocabulary 4000: The 4000 Words Essential for an Educated Vocabulary (160 pages)

11659 Mayfield Avenue
Los Angeles, CA 90049

Phone: 1-800-949-6175
E-mail: info@novapress.net
Website: www.novapress.net

ABOUT THIS BOOK

If you don't have a pencil in your hand, get one now! Don't just read this book—write on it, study it, scrutinize it! In short, for the next six weeks, this book should be a part of your life. When you have finished the book, it should be marked-up, dog-eared, tattered and torn.

Although the GMAT is a difficult test, it is a *very* learnable test. This is not to say that the GMAT is "beatable." There is no bag of tricks that will show you how to master it overnight. You probably have already realized this. Some books, nevertheless, offer "inside stuff" or "tricks" which they claim will enable you to beat the test. These include declaring that answer-choices B, C, or D are more likely to be correct than choices A or E. This tactic, like most of its type, does not work. It is offered to give the student the feeling that he or she is getting the scoop on the test.

The GMAT cannot be "beaten." But it can be mastered—through hard work, analytical thought, and by training yourself to think like a test writer.

This book will introduce you to numerous analytic techniques that will help you immensely, not only on the GMAT but in business school as well. For this reason, studying for the GMAT can be a rewarding and satisfying experience.

Although the quick-fix method is not offered in this book, about 15% of the material is dedicated to studying how the questions are constructed. Knowing how the problems are written and how the test writers think will give you useful insight into the problems and make them less mysterious. Moreover, familiarity with the GMAT's structure will help reduce your anxiety. The more you know about this test, the less anxious you will be the day you take it.

ACKNOWLEDGMENT

Behind any successful test-prep book, there is more than just the author's efforts.

I would like to thank Scott Thornburg for his meticulous editing of the manuscript and for his continued support and inspiration. I would also like to thank Kathleen Pierce for contributing the Writing Assessment section, Alex Kwon for the cover design, and Susan Shankin for the interior design.

This book is dedicated to my parents

David and Mary Kolby

To whom I owe more than words can express.

Reading passages were drawn from the following sources:

The Two Faces of Eastern Europe, © 1990 Adam Michnik.

Deschooling Society, © 1971 Harper & Row, by Ivan Illich.

The Cult of Multiculturalism, © 1991 Fred Siegel.

Ways of Seeing, © 1972 Penguin Books Limited, by John Berger.

Placebo Cures for the Incurable, Journal of Irreproducible Results, © 1985 Thomas G. Kyle.

Women, Fire, and Dangerous Things, © George Lakoff.

Screening Immigrants and International Travelers for the Human Immunodeficiency Virus, © 1990 New England Journal of Medicine.

The Perry Scheme and the Teaching of Writing, © 1986 Christopher Burnham.

Man Bites Shark, © 1990 Scientific American.

Hemingway: The Writer as Artist, © 1952 Carlos Baker.

The Stars in Their Courses, © 1931 James Jeans.

CONTENTS

Part Two: VERBAL

ORIENTATION

- **WHAT DOES THE GMAT MEASURE?**

- **FORMAT OF THE GMAT**

- **THE CAT AND THE PAPER & PENCIL TEST**

- **PACING**

- **SCORING THE GMAT**

- **GUESSING**

- **ORDER OF DIFFICULTY**

- **THE "2 OUT OF 5" RULE**

- **COMPUTER SCREEN OPTIONS**

- **TEST DAY**

- **HOW TO USE THIS BOOK**
  Shortened Study Plan

- **QUESTIONS AND ANSWERS**

What Does the GMAT Measure?

The GMAT is an aptitude test. Like all aptitude tests, it must choose a medium in which to measure intellectual ability. The GMAT has chosen math, English, and logic.

OK, the GMAT is an aptitude test. The question is—does it measure aptitude for business school? The GMAT's ability to predict performance in school is as poor as the SAT's. This is to be expected since the problems on the tests are quite similar (though the formats are different). However, the GMAT also includes two types of questions—Arguments and Data Sufficiency—that the SAT does not. Many students struggle with these questions because they are unlike any material they have studied in school. However, the argument and data sufficiency questions are not inherently hard, and with sufficient study you can raise your performance on these questions significantly.

No test can measure all aspects of intelligence. Thus any admission test, no matter how well written, is inherently inadequate. Nevertheless, some form of admission testing is necessary. It would be unfair to base acceptance to business school solely on grades; they can be misleading. For instance, would it be fair to admit a student with an A average earned in easy classes over a student with a B average earned in difficult classes? A school's reputation is too broad a measure to use as admission criteria: many students seek out easy classes and generous instructors, in hopes of inflating their GPA. Furthermore, a system that would monitor the academic standards of every class would be cost prohibitive and stifling. So until a better system is proposed, the admission test is here to stay.

Format of the GMAT

The GMAT is a three-and-one-half hour computer adaptive test (CAT). There are four sections in the test.

Section	Type	Questions	Time
1	Analysis of Issue Essay		30 minutes
2	Analysis of Argument Essay		30 minutes
3	Math	37	75 minutes
4	Verbal	41	75 minutes

The writing sections begin the test. You will type your essay on the computer, using a very basic word processor.

Each question must be answered before you can go to the next question. Further, you cannot return to a question once you go to the next question.

The GMAT is a standardized test. Each time it is offered, the test has, as close as possible, the same level of difficulty as every previous test. Maintaining this consistency is very difficult—hence the experimental questions (questions that are not scored). The effectiveness of each question must be assessed before it can be used on the GMAT. A problem that one person finds easy another person may find hard, and vice versa. The experimental questions measure the relative difficulty of potential questions; if responses to a question do not perform to strict specifications, the question is rejected.

About one quarter of the questions are experimental. The experimental questions can be standard math, data sufficiency, reading comprehension, arguments, or sentence correction. You won't know which questions are experimental.

Because the "bugs" have not been worked out of the experimental questions—or, to put it more directly, because you are being used as a guinea pig to work out the "bugs"—these unscored questions are often more difficult and confusing than the scored questions.

This brings up an ethical issue: How many students have run into experimental questions early in the test and have been confused and discouraged by them? Crestfallen by having done poorly on a few experimental questions, they lose confidence and perform below their ability on the other parts of the test. Some testing companies are becoming more enlightened in this regard and are administering experimental questions as separate practice tests. Unfortunately, the GMAT has yet to see the light.

Knowing that the experimental questions can be disproportionately difficult, if you do poorly on a particular question you can take some solace in the hope that it may have been experimental. In other words, do not allow a few difficult questions to discourage your performance on the rest of the test.

The CAT and the Paper & Pencil Test

The computerized GMAT uses the same type of questions as did the old Paper & Pencil Test. The only thing that has changed is medium, that is the way the questions are presented.

There are advantages and disadvantages to the CAT. Probably the biggest advantages are that you can take the CAT just about any time and you can take it in a small room with just a few other people—instead of in a large auditorium with hundreds of other stressed people. One the other hand, you cannot return to previous questions, it is easier to misread a computer screen than it is to misread printed material, and it can be distracting looking back and forth from the computer screen to your scratch paper.

Pacing

Although time is limited on the GMAT, working too quickly can damage your score. Many problems hinge on subtle points, and most require careful reading of the setup. Because undergraduate school puts such heavy reading loads on students, many will follow their academic conditioning and read the questions quickly, looking only for the gist of what the question is asking. Once they have found it, they mark their answer and move on, confident they have answered it correctly. Later, many are startled to discover that they missed questions because they either misread the problems or overlooked subtle points.

To do well in your undergraduate classes, you had to attempt to solve every, or nearly every, problem on a test. Not so with the GMAT. For the vast majority of people, the key to performing well on the GMAT is not the number of questions they solve, within reason, but the percentage they solve correctly.

Scoring the GMAT

The two major parts of the test are scored independently. You will receive a verbal score (0 to 60) and a math score (0 to 60). You will also receive a total score (200 to 800), and a writing score (0 to 6). The average Verbal score is about 27, the average Math score is about 31, and the average total score is about 500.

In addition, you will be assigned a percentile ranking, which gives the percentage of students with scores below yours.

Guessing

On the CAT, you cannot skip questions; each question must be answered before moving on to the next question. However, if you can eliminate even one of the answer-choices, guessing can be advantageous. We'll talk more about this later. Unfortunately, you cannot return to previously answered questions.

On the test, your first question will be of medium difficulty. If you answer it correctly, the next question will be a little harder. If you again answer it correctly, the next question will be harder still, and so on. If your GMAT skills are strong and you are not making any mistakes, you should reach the medium-hard or hard problems by about the fifth problem. Although this is not very precise, it can be quite helpful. Once you have passed the fifth question, you should be alert to subtleties in any seemingly simple problems.

Often students become obsessed with a particular problem and waste time trying to solve it. To get a top score, learn to cut your losses and move on. The exception to this rule is the first five questions of each section. Because of the importance of the first five questions to your score, you should read and solve these questions slowly and carefully.

Because the total number of questions answered contributes to the calculation of your score, you should answer ALL the questions—even if this means guessing randomly before time runs out.

Order of Difficulty

Most standardized paper-&-pencil tests list problems in ascending order of difficulty. However, on a CAT, the first question will be of medium difficulty. If you answer it correctly, the next question will be a little harder. If you answer it incorrectly, the next question will be a little easier. Because the GMAT "adapts" to your performance, early questions are more important than later ones.

The "2 out of 5" Rule

It is significantly harder to create a good but incorrect answer-choice than it is to produce the correct answer. For this reason usually only two attractive answer-choices are offered. One correct; the other either intentionally misleading or only partially correct. The other three answer-choices are usually fluff. This makes educated guessing on the GMAT immensely effective. If you can dismiss the three fluff choices, your probability of answering the question successfully will increase from 20% to 50%.

Example: *"2 out of 5" rule*

During the late seventies when Japan was rapidly expanding its share of the American auto market, GM surveyed owners of GM cars and asked, "Would you be more willing to buy a large, powerful car or a small, economical car?" Seventy percent of those who responded said that they would prefer a large car. On the basis of this survey, GM decided to continue building large cars. Yet during the '80s, GM lost even more of the market to the Japanese.

Which one of the following, if it were determined to be true, would best explain this discrepancy?

(A)   Only 10 percent of those who were polled replied.
(B)   Ford which conducted a similar survey with similar results continued to build large cars and also lost more of their market to the Japanese.
(C)   The surveyed owners who preferred big cars also preferred big homes.
(D)   GM determined that it would be more profitable to make big cars.
(E)   Eighty percent of the owners who wanted big cars and only 40 percent of the owners who wanted small cars replied to the survey.

Only two answer-choices have any real merit—(A) and (E). The argument generalizes from the survey to the general car-buying population, so the reliability of the projection depends on how representative the sample is. At first glance choice (A) seems rather good, because 10 percent does not seem large enough. However, political opinion polls typically are based on only .001 percent of the population. More importantly, we don't know what percentage of GM car owners received the survey. Choice (E), on the other hand, points out that the survey did not represent the entire public, so it is the answer.

The other choices can be quickly dismissed. Choice (B) simply states that Ford made the same mistake that GM did. Choice (C) is irrelevant. Finally, choice (D), rather than explaining the discrepancy, would give even more reason for GM to continue making large cars.

Computer Screen Options

When taking the test, you will have six on-screen options/buttons:

Quit   Section   Time   Help   Next   Confirm

Unless you just cannot stand it any longer, never select Quit or Section. If you finish a section early, just relax while the time runs out. If you're not pleased with your performance on the test, you can always cancel it at the end.

The Time button allows you to display or hide the time. During the last five minutes, the time display cannot be hidden and it will also display the seconds remaining.

The Help button will present a short tutorial showing how to use the program.

You select an answer-choice by clicking the small oval next to it.

To go to the next question, click the Next button. You will then be asked to confirm your answer by clicking the Confirm button. Then the next question will be presented.

Test Day

- Bring a photo ID.
- Bring a list of schools that you wish to send your scores to.
- Arrive at the test center 30 minutes before your test appointment. If you arrive late, you might not be admitted and your fee will be forfeited.
- You will be provided with scratch paper. Do not bring your own, and do not remove scratch paper from the testing room.
- You cannot bring testing aids in to the testing room. This includes pens, calculators, watch calculators, books, rulers, cellular phones, watch alarms, and any electronic or photographic devices.
- You may be photographed and videotaped at the test center.

How to Use this Book

The six parts of this book—(1) Standard Math, (2) Data Sufficiency, (3) Reading Comprehension, (4) Arguments, (5) Sentence Correction, and (6) Writing Assessment—are independent of one another. However, to take full advantage of the system presented in the book, it is best to tackle each part in the order given.

This book contains the equivalent of a 6-week, 50-hour course. Ideally you have bought the book at least four weeks before your scheduled test date. However, if the test is only a week or two away, there is still a truncated study plan that will be useful.

Shortened Study Plan

Standard Math
Study: Substitution
           Math Notes
           Number Theory
           Geometry
           Elimination Strategies

Data Sufficiency
Study: All

Reading Comprehension
Study: The Six Questions
           Pivotal Words

Arguments
Study: Logic I
           Logic II (Diagramming)
           Classification

Sentence Correction
Study: All

The GMAT is not easy—nor is this book. To improve your GMAT score, you must be willing to work; if you study hard and master the techniques in this book, your score will improve—significantly.

Questions and Answers

When is the GMAT given?
The test is given year round during normal business hours. There is often one week during each month in which the test is not offered.

How important is the GMAT and how is it used?
It is crucial! Although business schools may consider other factors, the vast majority of admission decisions are based on only two criteria: your GMAT score and your GPA.

How many times should I take the GMAT?
Most people are better off preparing thoroughly for the test, taking it once and getting their top score. You can take the test at most once a month and at most five times in any one year period, but some business schools will average your scores. You should call the schools to which you are applying to find out their policy. Then plan your strategy accordingly.

Can I cancel my score?
Yes. When you finish the test, the computer will offer the option of canceling the test or accepting it. If you cancel the test, neither you nor any school will see your score. If you accept the test, the computer will display your score and it will be available to all schools.

Where can I get the registration forms?

Most colleges and universities have the forms. You can also get them directly from the Graduate Management Admission Council by writing to:

> Pearson VUE
> Attention: GMAT Program
> PO Box 581907
> Minneapolis, MN 55458-1907
>
> Or calling, 1-800-717-4628
>
> Or online: www.mba.com

Part One
MATH

STANDARD MATH

- **TYPES OF MATH QUESTIONS**
- **GMAT VS. SAT**
- **SUBSTITUTION**
- **MATH NOTES**
- **DEFINED FUNCTIONS**
- **NUMBER THEORY**
- **GEOMETRY**
- **COORDINATE GEOMETRY**
- **ELIMINATION STRATEGIES**
- **INEQUALITIES**
- **FRACTIONS & DECIMALS**
- **EQUATIONS**
- **AVERAGES**
- **RATIO & PROPORTION**
- **EXPONENTS & ROOTS**
- **FACTORING**
- **ALGEBRAIC EXPRESSIONS**
- **PERCENTS**
- **GRAPHS**
- **WORD PROBLEMS**
- **SEQUENCES & SERIES**
- **COUNTING**
- **PROBABILITY & STATISTICS**
- **SUMMARY OF MATH PROPERTIES**

Types of Math Questions

The Math section consists of 37 multiple-choice questions. The questions come in two formats: the standard multiple-choice question which we will study in this section and the Data Sufficiency question which we will study in the next section. The math section is designed to test your ability to solve problems, not to test your mathematical knowledge.

GMAT VS. SAT

GMAT math is very similar to SAT math, though slightly harder. The mathematical skills tested are very basic: only first year high school algebra and geometry (no proofs). However, this does not mean that the math section is easy. The medium of basic mathematics is chosen so that everyone taking the test will be on a fairly even playing field. Although the questions require only basic mathematics and **all** have **simple** solutions, it can require considerable ingenuity to find the simple solution. If you have taken a course in calculus or another advanced math topic, don't assume that you will find the math section easy. Other than increasing your mathematical maturity, little you learned in calculus will help on the GMAT.

As mentioned above, every GMAT math problem has a simple solution, but finding that simple solution may not be easy. The intent of the math section is to test how skilled you are at finding the simple solutions. The premise is that if you spend a lot of time working out long solutions you will not finish as much of the test as students who spot the short, simple solutions. So if you find yourself performing long calculations or applying advanced mathematics—stop. You're heading in the wrong direction.

To insure that you perform at your expected level on the actual GMAT, you need to develop a level of mathematical skill that is greater than what is tested on the GMAT. Hence, about 10% of the math problems in this book are harder than actual GMAT math problems.

Substitution

Substitution is a very useful technique for solving GMAT math problems. It often reduces hard problems to routine ones. In the substitution method, we choose numbers that have the properties given in the problem and plug them into the answer-choices. A few examples will illustrate.

Example 1: If n is an odd integer, which one of the following is an even integer?

(A) n^3
(B) $n/4$
(C) $2n + 3$
(D) $n(n + 3)$
(E) $\sqrt{n}$

We are told that n is an odd integer. So choose an odd integer for n, say, 1 and substitute it into each answer-choice. Now, n^3 becomes $1^3 = 1$, which is not an even integer. So eliminate (A). Next, $n/4 = 1/4$ is not an even integer—eliminate (B). Next, $2n + 3 = 2 \cdot 1 + 3 = 5$ is not an even integer—eliminate (C). Next, $n(n + 3) = 1(1 + 3) = 4$ is even and hence the answer is possibly (D). Finally, $\sqrt{n} = \sqrt{1} = 1$, which is not even—eliminate (E). The answer is (D).

- When using the substitution method, be sure to check every answer-choice because the number you choose may work for more than one answer-choice. If this does occur, then choose another number and plug it in, and so on, until you have eliminated all but the answer. This may sound like a lot of computing, but the calculations can usually be done in a few seconds.

Example 2: If n is an integer, which of the following CANNOT be an even integer?

(A) $2n + 2$
(B) $n - 5$
(C) $2n$
(D) $2n + 3$
(E) $5n + 2$

Choose n to be 1. Then $2n + 2 = 2(1) + 2 = 4$, which is even. So eliminate (A). Next, $n - 5 = 1 - 5 = -4$. Eliminate (B). Next, $2n = 2(1) = 2$. Eliminate (C). Next, $2n + 3 = 2(1) + 3 = 5$ is not even—it *may* be our answer. However, $5n + 2 = 5(1) + 2 = 7$ is not even as well. So we choose another number, say, 2. Then $5n + 2 = 5(2) + 2 = 12$ is even, which eliminates (E). Thus, choice (D), $2n + 3$, is the answer.

Example 3:   If $\dfrac{x}{y}$ is a fraction greater than 1, then which of the following must be less than 1?

(A) $\dfrac{3y}{x}$

(B) $\dfrac{x}{3y}$

(C) $\sqrt{\dfrac{x}{y}}$

(D) $\dfrac{y}{x}$

(E) y

We must choose x and y so that $\dfrac{x}{y} > 1$. So choose $x = 3$ and $y = 2$. Now, $\dfrac{3y}{x} = \dfrac{3 \cdot 2}{3} = 2$ is greater than 1, so eliminate (A). Next, $\dfrac{x}{3y} = \dfrac{3}{3 \cdot 2} = \dfrac{1}{2}$, which is less than 1—it may be our answer. Next, $\sqrt{\dfrac{x}{y}} = \sqrt{\dfrac{3}{2}} > 1$; eliminate (C). Now, $\dfrac{y}{x} = \dfrac{2}{3} < 1$. So it too may be our answer. Next, $y = 2 > 1$; eliminate (E). Hence, we must decide between answer-choices (B) and (D). Let $x = 6$ and $y = 2$. Then $\dfrac{x}{3y} = \dfrac{6}{3 \cdot 2} = 1$, which eliminates (B). Therefore, the answer is (D).

Problem Set A: Solve the following problems by using substitution. Solutions begin on page 155.

1.   If n is an odd integer, which of the following must be an even integer?

(A) $n/2$
(B) $4n + 3$ 4 +3
(C) $2n$
(D) n^4
(E) $\sqrt{n}$

2.   If x and y are perfect squares, then which of the following is not necessarily a perfect square?

(A) x^2
(B) xy
(C) $4x$
(D) $x + y$
(E) x^5

3.   If y is an even integer and x is an odd integer, which of the following expressions could be an even integer?

(A) $3x + \dfrac{y}{2}$

(B) $\dfrac{x + y}{2}$

(C) $x + y$

(D) $\dfrac{x}{4} - \dfrac{y}{2}$

(E) $x^2 + y^2$

4.   If $0 < k < 1$, then which of the following must be less than k?

(A) $\dfrac{3}{2}k$

(B) $\dfrac{1}{k}$

(C) $|k|$

(D) $\sqrt{k}$

(E) k^2

5. Suppose you begin reading a book on page h and end on page k. If you read each page completely and the pages are numbered and read consecutively, then how many pages have you read?

   (A) $h + k$
   (B) $h - k$
   (C) $k - h + 2$
   (D) $k - h - 1$
   (E) $k - h + 1$

6. If m is an even integer, then which of the following is the sum of the next two even integers greater than $4m + 1$?

   (A) $8m + 2$
   (B) $8m + 4$
   (C) $8m + 6$
   (D) $8m + 8$
   (E) $8m + 10$

7. If x^2 is even, which of the following must be true?

   I. x is odd.
   II. x is even.
   III. x^3 is odd.

   (A) I only
   (B) II only
   (C) III only
   (D) I and II only
   (E) II and III only

8. Suppose x is divisible by 8 but not by 3. Then which of the following CANNOT be an integer?

   (A) $\dfrac{x}{2}$ (B) $\dfrac{x}{4}$ (C) $\dfrac{x}{6}$ (D) $\dfrac{x}{8}$ (E) x

9. If p and q are positive integers, how many integers are larger than pq and smaller than $p(q + 2)$?

   (A) 3
   (B) $p + 2$
   (C) $p - 2$
   (D) $2p - 1$
   (E) $2p + 1$

10. If x and y are prime numbers, then which one of the following cannot equal $x - y$?

    (A) 1 (B) 2 (C) 13 (D) 14 (E) 20

11. If x is an integer, then which of the following is the product of the next two integers greater than $2(x + 1)$?

    (A) $4x^2 + 14x + 12$
    (B) $4x^2 + 12$
    (C) $x^2 + 14x + 12$
    (D) $x^2 + x + 12$
    (E) $4x^2 + 14x$

12. If the integer x is divisible by 3 but not by 2, then which one of the following expressions is NEVER an integer?

    (A) $\dfrac{x + 1}{2}$

    (B) $\dfrac{x}{7}$

    (C) $\dfrac{x^2}{3}$

    (D) $\dfrac{x^3}{3}$

    (E) $\dfrac{x}{24}$

13. If both x and y are positive even integers, then which of the following expressions must also be even?

    I. y^{x-1} II. $y - 1$ III. $x/2$

    (A) I only
    (B) II only
    (C) III only
    (D) I and III only
    (E) I, II, and III

14. Which one of the following is a solution to the equation $x^4 - 2x^2 = -1$?

    (A) 0   (B) 1   (C) 2   (D) 3   (E) 4

15. If $x \neq 3/4$, which one of the following will equal -2 when multiplied by $\dfrac{3 - 4x}{5}$?

    (A) $\dfrac{5 - 4x}{4}$

    (B) $\dfrac{10}{3 - 4x}$

    (C) $\dfrac{10}{4x - 3}$

    (D) $\dfrac{3 - 4x}{5}$

    (E) $\dfrac{4x - 3}{10}$

Substitution (Plugging In): Sometimes instead of making up numbers to substitute into the problem, we can use the actual answer-choices. This is called Plugging In. It is a very effective technique but not as common as Substitution.

Example 1:   The digits of a three-digit number add up to 18. If the ten's digit is twice the hundred's digit and the hundred's digit is 1/3 the unit's digit, what is the number?

  (A)   246
  (B)   369
  (C)   531
  (D)   855
  (E)   893

First, check to see which of the answer-choices has a sum of digits equal to 18. For choice (A), $2 + 4 + 6 \neq 18$. Eliminate. For choice (B), $3 + 6 + 9 = 18$. This may be the answer. For choice (C), $5 + 3 + 1 \neq 18$. Eliminate. For choice (D), $8 + 5 + 5 = 18$. This too may be the answer. For choice (E), $8 + 9 + 3 \neq 18$. Eliminate. Now, in choice (D), the ten's digit is <u>not</u> twice the hundred's digit, $5 \neq 2 \cdot 8$. Hence, by process of elimination, the answer is (B). Note that we did not need the fact that the hundred's digit is 1/3 the unit's digit.

Problem Set B: Use the method of Plugging In to solve the following problems. Solutions begin on page 160.

1.   The ten's digit of a two-digit number is twice the unit's digit. Reversing the digits yields a new number that is 27 less than the original number. Which one of the following is the original number?

  (A)   12
  (B)   21
  (C)   43
  (D)   63
  (E)   83

2.   If $\dfrac{N + N}{N^2} = 1$, then $N =$

  (A)   1/6
  (B)   1/3
  (C)   1
  (D)   2
  (E)   3

3.   Suppose half the people on a bus exit at each stop and no additional passengers board the bus. If on the third stop the next to last person exits the bus, then how many people were on the bus?

  (A) 20   (B) 16   (C) 8   (D) 6   (E) 4

4.   The sum of the digits of a two-digit number is 12, and the ten's digit is one-third the unit's digit. What is the number?

  (A)   93
  (B)   54
  (C)   48
  (D)   39
  (E)   31

5.   If $\dfrac{x^6 - 5x^3 - 16}{8} = 1$, then x could be

  (A)   1
  (B)   2
  (C)   3
  (D)   5
  (E)   8

6.   Which one of the following is a solution to the equation $x^4 - 2x^2 = -1$?

  (A)   0
  (B)   1
  (C)   2
  (D)   3
  (E)   4

Math Notes

1. **To compare two fractions, cross-multiply. The larger product will be on the same side as the larger fraction.**

   Example: Given $\dfrac{5}{6}$ vs. $\dfrac{6}{7}$. Cross-multiplying gives $5\cdot 7$ vs. $6\cdot 6$, or 35 vs. 36. Now 36 is larger than 35, so $\dfrac{6}{7}$ is larger than $\dfrac{5}{6}$.

2. **Taking the square root of a fraction between 0 and 1 makes it larger.**

   Example: $\sqrt{\dfrac{1}{4}} = \dfrac{1}{2}$ and $\dfrac{1}{2}$ is greater than $\dfrac{1}{4}$.

   Caution: This is not true for fractions greater than 1. For example, $\sqrt{\dfrac{9}{4}} = \dfrac{3}{2}$. But $\dfrac{3}{2} < \dfrac{9}{4}$.

3. **Squaring a fraction between 0 and 1 makes it smaller.**

   Example: $\left(\dfrac{1}{2}\right)^2 = \dfrac{1}{4}$ and $\dfrac{1}{4}$ is less than $\dfrac{1}{2}$.

4. $ax^2 \neq (ax)^2$. **In fact,** $a^2x^2 = (ax)^2$.

   Example: $3\cdot 2^2 = 3\cdot 4 = 12$. But $(3\cdot 2)^2 = 6^2 = 36$. This mistake is often seen in the following form: $-x^2 = (-x)^2$. To see more clearly why this is wrong, write $-x^2 = (-1)x^2$, which is negative. But $(-x)^2 = (-x)(-x) = x^2$, which is positive.

   Example: $-5^2 = (-1)5^2 = (-1)25 = -25$. But $(-5)^2 = (-5)(-5) = 5\cdot 5 = 25$.

5. $\dfrac{1/a}{b} \neq \dfrac{1}{a/b}$. **In fact,** $\dfrac{1/a}{b} = \dfrac{1}{ab}$ **and** $\dfrac{1}{a/b} = \dfrac{b}{a}$.

   Example: $\dfrac{1/2}{3} = \dfrac{1}{2}\cdot\dfrac{1}{3} = \dfrac{1}{6}$. But $\dfrac{1}{2/3} = 1\cdot\dfrac{3}{2} = \dfrac{3}{2}$.

6. $-(a + b) \neq -a + b$. **In fact,** $-(a + b) = -a - b$.

   Example: $-(2 + 3) = -5$. But $-2 + 3 = 1$.

   Example: $-(2 + x) = -2 - x$.

7. **Memorize the following factoring formulas—they occur frequently on the GMAT.**

   A. $a^2 - b^2 = (a - b)(a + b)$

   B. $x^2 \pm 2xy + y^2 = (x \pm y)^2$

   C. $a(b + c) = ab + ac$

Problem Set C: Use the properties and techniques on the previous page to solve the following problems. Solutions begin on page 161.

1. $2x^2 + (2x)^2 =$

   (A) $4x^2$ (B) $4x^4$ (C) $8x^2$ (D) $6x^4$ (E) $6x^2$

2.   Which of the following fractions is greatest?

   (A) $15/16$ (B) $7/9$ (C) $13/15$ (D) $8/9$ (E) $10/11$

3. $1 + \dfrac{1}{1 - \dfrac{1}{2}} =$

   (A) $-1/2$ (B) $1/2$ (C) $3/2$ (D) 2 (E) 3

4.   If the ratio of $\dfrac{1}{5}$ to $\dfrac{1}{4}$ is equal to the ratio of $\dfrac{1}{4}$ to x, then what is the value of x?

   (A) $\dfrac{1}{20}$ (B) $\dfrac{1}{5}$ (C) $\dfrac{5}{16}$ (D) $\dfrac{4}{5}$ (E) 5

5.   Which of the following are true?

   I. $\dfrac{\sqrt{\dfrac{7}{8}}}{\left(\dfrac{7}{8}\right)^2} > 1$

   II. $\dfrac{\sqrt{\dfrac{7}{8}}}{\left(\dfrac{8}{7}\right)^2} > 1$

   III. $\sqrt{\dfrac{\dfrac{7}{8}}{\sqrt{\dfrac{7}{8}}}} > 1$

   (A) I only   (B) II only   (C) I and II only   (D) I and III only   (E) I, II, and III

6.   If $a \# b$ is defined by the expression $a \# b = -b^4$, what is the value of $x \# (-y)$?

   (A) y^4 (B) $-x^4$ (C) $-(xy)^4$ (D) x^4 (E) $-y^4$

7. $\dfrac{1}{1 - (.2)^2} =$

   (A) $-\dfrac{1}{2}$ (B) $\dfrac{1}{4}$ (C) $\dfrac{1}{2}$ (D) $\dfrac{25}{24}$ (E) 4

8.   If $0 < x < 1$, which of the following expressions is greatest?

(A) $\dfrac{1}{\sqrt{x}}$ (B) $\sqrt{x}$ (C) $\dfrac{1}{\pi}x$ (D) x^3 (E) x^4

9.   If $x > y > 0$, which of the following are true?

I. $\dfrac{x+1}{y+1} > \dfrac{x}{y}$

II. $\dfrac{x+1}{y+1} = \dfrac{x}{y}$

III. $\dfrac{x+1}{y+1} > 1$

(A) I only   (B) II only   (C) III only   (D) I and III only   (E) II and III only

10. If $rs = 4$ and $st = 10$, then $\dfrac{\frac{4}{r}}{\frac{10}{t}} =$

(A) $1/10$ (B) 1 (C) $5/2$ (D) 8 (E) 40

---

8.   **Know these rules for radicals:**

$$\sqrt{x}\,\sqrt{y} = \sqrt{xy} \qquad\qquad \sqrt{\dfrac{x}{y}} = \dfrac{\sqrt{x}}{\sqrt{y}}$$

9.   **Pythagorean Theorem (For right triangles only):**

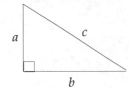

$$c^2 = a^2 + b^2$$

Example: What is the area of the triangle to the right?

(A) 6   (B) 7   (C) 8   (D) 10   (E) 16

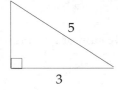

Solution: Since the triangle is a right triangle, the Pythagorean Theorem applies: $h^2 + 3^2 = 5^2$, where h is the height of the triangle. Solving for h yields $h = 4$. Hence, the area of the triangle is $\dfrac{1}{2}(base)(height) = \dfrac{1}{2}(3)(4) = 6$. The answer is (A).

10. **When parallel lines are cut by a transversal, three important angle relationships are formed:**

Alternate interior angles are equal.

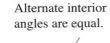

Corresponding angles are equal.

Interior angles on the same side of the transversal are supplementary.

$a + b = 180°$

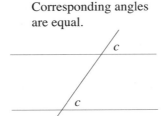

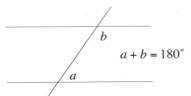

11. **In a triangle, an exterior angle is equal to the sum of its remote interior angles and therefore greater than either of them.**

$e = a + b$ and $e > a$ and $e > b$

12. **A central angle has by definition the same measure as its intercepted arc.**

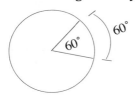

13. **An inscribed angle has one-half the measure of its intercepted arc.**

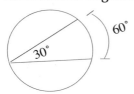

14. **There are 180° in a straight angle.**

$x + y = 180°$

15. **The angle sum of a triangle is 180°.**

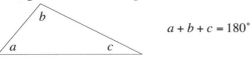

$a + b + c = 180°$

Example: What is the degree measure of angle c in the triangle to the right?

(A) 30   (B) 35   (C) 40   (D) 41   (E) 45

Solution: Since a triangle has 180°, we get $100 + 50 + c = 180$. Solving for c yields $c = 30$. Hence, the answer is (A).

16. **Consecutive integers are written x, x + 1, x + 2, ... Consecutive even or odd integers are written x, x + 2, x + 4, ...**

17. **To find the percentage increase, find the absolute increase and divide by the original amount.**

    Example: If a shirt selling for $18 is marked up to $20, then the absolute increase is 20 – 18 = 2. Thus, the percentage increase is $\dfrac{increase}{original\ amount} = \dfrac{2}{18} = \dfrac{1}{9} \approx 11\%$.

18. **Systems of simultaneous equations can most often be solved by merely adding or subtracting the equations.**

    Example: If $4x + y = 14$ and $3x + 2y = 13$, then $x - y =$

    Solution: We merely subtract the second equation from the first:

    $$\begin{array}{r} 4x + y = 14 \\ (-) \quad 3x + 2y = 13 \\ \hline x - y = 1 \end{array}$$

19. **When counting elements that are in overlapping sets, the total number will equal the number in one group plus the number in the other group minus the number common to both groups. Venn diagrams are very helpful with these problems.**

    Example: If in a certain school 20 students are taking math and 10 are taking history and 7 are taking both, how many students are there?

    Solution:

    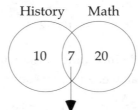

    History   Math

    10 7 20

    Both History and Math

    By the principle stated above, we add 10 and 20 and then subtract 7 from the result. Thus, there are $(10 + 20) - 7 = 23$ students.

20. **The number of integers between two integers inclusive is one more than their difference.**

    For example: The number of integers between 49 and 101 inclusive is $(101 - 49) + 1 = 53$. To see this more clearly, choose smaller numbers, say, 9 and 11. The difference between 9 and 11 is 2. But there are three numbers between them inclusive—9, 10, and 11—one more than their difference.

21. **Rounding Off:** The convention used for rounding numbers is *"if the following digit is less than five, then the preceding digit is not changed. But if the following digit is greater than or equal to five, then the preceding digit is increased by one."*

    Example: 65,439 —> 65,000 (following digit is 4)
                5.5671 —> 5.5700 (dropping the unnecessary zeros gives 5.57)

Defined Functions

Defined functions are common on the GMAT, and most students struggle with them. Yet once you get used to them, defined functions can be some of the easiest problems on the test. In these problems, you are given a symbol and a mathematical expression or description that defines the symbol. Some examples will illustrate.

Example 1: Define $x \nabla y$ by the equation $x \nabla y = xy - y$. Then $2 \nabla 3 =$

(A) 1   (B) 3   (C) 12   (D) 15   (E) 18

From the above definition, we know that $x \nabla y = xy - y$. So we merely replace x with 2 and y with 3 in the definition: $2 \nabla 3 = 2 \cdot 3 - 3 = 3$. Hence, the answer is (B).

Example 2: If $a \Delta b$ is defined to be a^2, then what is the value of $\dfrac{z \Delta 2}{z \Delta 3}$?

(A) $\dfrac{2}{3}$ (B) 1   (C) $\dfrac{3}{2}$ (D) 2   (E) 3

Most students who are unfamiliar with defined functions are unable to solve this problem. Yet it is actually quite easy. By the definition above, Δ merely squares the first term. So $z \Delta 2 = z^2$, and $z \Delta 3 = z^2$. Forming the fraction yields $\dfrac{z \Delta 2}{z \Delta 3} = \dfrac{z^2}{z^2} = 1$. Hence, the answer is (B).

Example 3: The operation @ is defined for all non-zero x and y by the equation $x @ y = x^y$. Then the expression $(x @ y) @ z$ is equal to

(A) x^{y^z}
(B) xyz
(C) $(xy)^z$
(D) $x^y z$
(E) $\left(x^y\right)^z$

$(x @ y) @ z = \left(x^y\right) @ z = \left(x^y\right)^z$. Hence, the answer is (E). Note, though it may appear that choices (A) and (E) are equivalent, they are not: $\left(x^y\right)^z = x^{yz}$, which is not equal to x^{y^z}.

Example 4:   For all real numbers x and y, let $x \# y = (xy)^2 - x + y^2$. What is the value of y that makes $x \# y$ equal to $-x$ for all values of x ?

(A) 0   (B) 2   (C) 5   (D) 7   (E) 10

Setting $x \# y$ equal to $-x$ yields $(xy)^2 - x + y^2 = -x$

Canceling $-x$ from both sides of the equation yields $(xy)^2 + y^2 = 0$

Expanding the first term yields $x^2 y^2 + y^2 = 0$

Factoring out y^2 yields $y^2(x^2 + 1) = 0$

Setting each factor equal to zero yields $y^2 = 0$ or $x^2 + 1 = 0$

Now, $x^2 + 1$ is greater than or equal to 1 (why?). Hence, $y^2 = 0$

Taking the square root of both sides of this equation yields $y = 0$

Hence, the answer is (A).

Example 5:   If $\boxed{x}$ denotes the area of a square with sides of length x, then which of the following is equal to $\boxed{9} \div \boxed{3}$?

(A) $\boxed{\sqrt{3}}$ (B) $\boxed{3}$ (C) $\boxed{\sqrt{27}}$ (D) $\boxed{27}$ (E) $\boxed{81}$

The area of a square with sides of length x is x^2. This formula yields $\boxed{9} \div \boxed{3} = 9^2 \div 3^2 = 81 \div 9 = 9$. Now, $\boxed{3} = 3^2 = 9$. Hence, the answer is (B).

Example 6:   If x is a positive integer, define: $\boxed{x} = \sqrt{x}$, if x is even;

$\boxed{x} = 4x$, if x is odd.

If k is a positive integer, which of the following equals $\boxed{2k - 1}$?

(A) $\sqrt{2k - 1}$
(B) $k - 1$
(C) $8k - 4$
(D) $\sqrt{8k - 4}$
(E) $8k - 1$

First, we must determine whether $2k - 1$ is odd or even. (It cannot be both—why?) To this end, let $k = 1$. Then $2k - 1 = 2 \cdot 1 - 1 = 1$, which is an odd number. Therefore, we use the bottom-half of the definition given above. That is, $\boxed{2k - 1} = 4(2k - 1) = 8k - 4$. The answer is (C).

You may be wondering how defined functions differ from the functions, $f(x)$, you studied in Intermediate Algebra and more advanced math courses. They *don't* differ. They are the same old concept you dealt with in your math classes. The function in Example 6 could just as easily be written $f(x) = \sqrt{x}$ and $f(x) = 4x$. The purpose of defined functions is to see how well you can adapt unusual structures. Once you realize that defined functions are evaluated and manipulated just as regular functions, they become much less daunting.

Example 7:   Define x^* by the equation $x^* = \pi - x$. Then $((-\pi)^*)^* =$

(A) -2π (B) -1 (C) $-\pi$ (D) 2π (E) 4π

Working from the inner parentheses out, we get

$$((-\pi)^*)^* = (\pi - (-\pi))^* = (\pi + \pi)^* = (2\pi)^* = \pi - 2\pi = -\pi.$$

Hence, the answer is (C).

Method II: We can rewrite this problem using ordinary function notation. Replacing the odd symbol x^* with $f(x)$ gives $f(x) = \pi - x$. Now, the expression $((-\pi)^*)^*$ becomes the ordinary composite function $f(f(-\pi)) = f(\pi - (-\pi)) = f(\pi + \pi) = f(2\pi) = \pi - 2\pi = -\pi$.

Example 8:   If x is an integer, define: $\boxed{x} = 5$, if x is odd;

$\qquad\qquad\qquad\qquad\qquad\qquad\quad \boxed{x} = 10$, if x is even.

If u and v are integers, and both $3u$ and $7 - v$ are odd, then $\boxed{u} - \boxed{v} =$

(A) -5 (B) 0 (C) 5 (D) 10 (E) 15

Since $3u$ is odd, u is odd. (Proof: Suppose u were even, then $3u$ would be even as well. But we are given that $3u$ is odd. Hence, u must be odd.) Since $7 - v$ is odd, v must be even. (Proof: Suppose v were odd, then $7 - v$ would be even [the difference of two odd numbers is an even number]. But we are given that $7 - v$ is odd. Hence, v must be even.)
    Since u is odd, the top part of the definition gives $\boxed{u} = 5$. Since v is even, the bottom part of the definition gives $\boxed{v} = 10$. Hence, $\boxed{u} - \boxed{v} = 5 - 10 = -5$. The answer is (A).

Example 9:   For all real numbers a and b, where $a \cdot b \neq 0$, let $a \lozenge b = a^b$. Then which of the following must be true?

   I. $a \lozenge b = b \lozenge a$

   II. $(-a) \lozenge (-a) = \dfrac{(-1)^{-a}}{a^a}$

   III. $(a \lozenge b) \lozenge c = a \lozenge (b \lozenge c)$

(A)   I only
(B)   II only
(C)   III only
(D)   I and II only
(E)   II and III only

Statement I is false. For instance, $1 \lozenge 2 = 1^2 = 1$, but $2 \lozenge 1 = 2^1 = 2$. This eliminates (A) and (D).

Statement II is true: $(-a) \lozenge (-a) = (-a)^{-a} = (-1 \cdot a)^{-a} = (-1)^{-a}(a)^{-a} = \dfrac{(-1)^{-a}}{a^a}$. This eliminates (C).

Unfortunately, we have to check Statement III. It is false: $(2 \lozenge 2) \lozenge 3 = 2^2 \lozenge 3 = 4 \lozenge 3 = 4^3 = 64$ and $2 \lozenge (2 \lozenge 3) = 2 \lozenge 2^3 = 2 \lozenge 8 = 2^8 = 256$. This eliminates (E), and the answer is (B). Note: The expression $a \cdot b \neq 0$ insures that neither a nor b equals 0: if $a \cdot b = 0$, then either $a = 0$ or $b = 0$, or both. This prevents division by zero from occurring in the problem, otherwise if $a = 0$ and $b = -1$, then $0 \lozenge (-1) = 0^{-1} = \dfrac{1}{0}$.

Problem Set D: Solutions begin on page 164.

1. For all $p \neq 2$ define p^* by the equation $p^* = \dfrac{p+5}{p-2}$. If $p = 3$, then $p^* =$

   (A)   8/5
   (B)   8/3
   (C)   4
   (D)   5
   (E)   8

2. Let $\boxed{x}$ be defined by the equation $\boxed{x} = \dfrac{x^2}{2}$. Then which of the following equals 2 ?

   (A) $\boxed{2}$
   (B) $\boxed{4}$
   (C) $\boxed{6}$
   (D) $\boxed{8}$
   (E) $\boxed{10}$

3. For all a and b, define $a \# b$ to be $-\sqrt{(a+b)^2}$. What is the value of $(2\#3)(0\#1)$?

   (A)   –2
   (B)   0
   (C)   5
   (D)   6
   (E)   9

4. If $\bigcirc\!\!\!d$ denotes the area of a circle with diameter d, then which of the following is equal to $\textbf{4} \cdot \textbf{6}$?

   (A) $\textbf{10}$
   (B) $\textbf{12}$
   (C) $\textbf{24}$
   (D) $\pi \cdot \textbf{12}$
   (E) $\pi \cdot \textbf{24}$

5. For all real numbers x, y, and z, let $\overleftrightarrow{x, y, z} = (x-y)z$. For what value of a is $\overleftrightarrow{0, 1, a}$ equal to $\overleftrightarrow{1, a, 0}$?

   (A)   –1
   (B)   0
   (C)   1
   (D)   5
   (E)   All values of a.

6. Let $\boxed{x} = x^2 - 2$. If $\boxed{2} - \boxed{x} = x^2$, then $x =$

   (A) $\sqrt{2}$
   (B) $\sqrt{3}$
   (C)   2
   (D)   4
   (E)   8

7. For all real numbers a and b, where $a \cdot b \neq 0$, let $a \Diamond b = ab - \dfrac{a}{b}$. Then which of the following must be true?

   I. $a \Diamond b = b \Diamond a$
   II. $a \Diamond a = (a+1)(a-1)$
   III. $(a \Diamond b) \Diamond c = a \Diamond (b \Diamond c)$

   (A)   I only
   (B)   II only
   (C)   III only
   (D)   I and II only
   (E)   I, II, and III

8. The operation * is defined for all non-zero x and y by the equation $x * y = \dfrac{x}{y}$. Then the expression $(x * y) * z$ is equal to

   (A) $\dfrac{z}{xy}$
   (B) $\dfrac{y}{xz}$
   (C) xyz
   (D) $\dfrac{xz}{y}$
   (E) $\dfrac{x}{yz}$

9. Let $x \ominus y = x\sqrt{y} - y - 2x$. For what value of x does $x \ominus y = -y$ for all values of y?

    (A) 0
    (B) $\dfrac{2}{\sqrt{3}}$
    (C) $\sqrt{3}$
    (D) 2
    (E) 4

10. For all positive numbers n, $n^* = \dfrac{\sqrt{n}}{2}$.

    What is the value of $\left(64^*\right)^*$?

    (A) 1
    (B) 2
    (C) $\dfrac{\sqrt{32}}{2}$
    (D) 4
    (E) 16

11. If $\boxed{x} = (x+2)x$, for all x, what is the value of $\boxed{x+2} - \boxed{x-2}$?

    (A) -2
    (B) $x+4$
    (C) 0
    (D) x^2
    (E) $8(x+1)$

12. For all numbers N, let $\overset{\infty}{N}$ denote the least integer greater than or equal to N.

    What is the value of $\overset{\infty}{-2.1}$?

    (A) -4
    (B) -3
    (C) -2
    (D) -1
    (E)   0

Questions 13–14 refer to the following definition:

Define the symbol # by the following equations:

$x \mathbin{\#} y = (x-y)^2$, if $x > y$.

$x \mathbin{\#} y = x + \dfrac{y}{4}$, if $x \le y$.

13. $4 \mathbin{\#} 12 =$

    (A) 4
    (B) 7
    (C) 8
    (D) 13
    (E) 64

14. If $x \mathbin{\#} y = -1$, which of the following could be true?

    I. $x = y$
    II. $x > y$
    III. $x < y$

    (A) I only
    (B) II only
    (C) III only
    (D) I and III only
    (E) I, II, and III

Questions 15–16 refer to the following definition:

Define the symbol * by the following equation: $x^* = 2 - x$, for all non-negative x.

15. $(a + b^*)^* =$

    (A) $b - a$
    (B) $a - b - 4$
    (C) $b - a + 4$
    (D) $a + b - 2$
    (E) $a - b$

16. If $(2 - x)^* = (x - 2)^*$, then $x =$

    (A) 0
    (B) 1
    (C) 2
    (D) 4
    (E) 6

Number Theory

This broad category is a popular source for GMAT questions. At first, students often struggle with these problems since they have forgotten many of the basic properties of arithmetic. So before we begin solving these problems, let's review some of these basic properties.

- *"The remainder is r when p is divided by q"* **means** $p = qz + r$; **the integer z is called the quotient. For instance,** *"The remainder is 1 when 7 is divided by 3"* **means** $7 = 3 \cdot 2 + 1$.

Example 1: When the integer n is divided by 2, the quotient is u and the remainder is 1. When the integer n is divided by 5, the quotient is v and the remainder is 3. Which one of the following must be true?

    (A) $2u + 5v = 4$
    (B) $2u - 5v = 2$
    (C) $4u + 5v = 2$
    (D) $4u - 5v = 2$
    (E) $3u - 5v = 2$

Translating *"When the integer n is divided by 2, the quotient is u and the remainder is 1"* into an equation gives

$$n = 2u + 1$$

Translating *"When the integer n is divided by 5, the quotient is v and the remainder is 3"* into an equation gives

$$n = 5v + 3$$

Since both expressions equal n, we can set them equal to each other:

$$2u + 1 = 5v + 3$$

Rearranging and then combining like terms yields

$$2u - 5v = 2$$

The answer is (B).

- **A number n is even if the remainder is zero when n is divided by 2:** $n = 2z + 0$, **or** $n = 2z$.

- **A number n is odd if the remainder is one when n is divided by 2:** $n = 2z + 1$.

- **The following properties for odd and even numbers are very useful—you should memorize them:**

$$even \times even = even$$
$$odd \times odd = odd$$
$$even \times odd = even$$

$$even + even = even$$
$$odd + odd = even$$
$$even + odd = odd$$

Example 2: Suppose p is even and q is odd. Then which of the following CANNOT be an integer?

  I. $\dfrac{p+q}{p}$

  II. $\dfrac{pq}{3}$

  III. $\dfrac{q}{p^2}$

  (A) I only   (B) II only   (C) III only   (D) I and II only   (E) I and III only

For a fractional expression to be an integer, the denominator must divide evenly into the numerator. Now, Statement I cannot be an integer. Since q is odd and p is even, $p + q$ is odd. Further, since $p + q$ is odd, it cannot be divided evenly by the even number p. Hence, $\dfrac{p+q}{p}$ cannot be an integer. Next, Statement II can be an integer. For example, if $p = 2$ and $q = 3$, then $\dfrac{pq}{3} = \dfrac{2 \cdot 3}{3} = 2$. Finally, Statement III cannot be an integer. $p^2 = p \cdot p$ is even since it is the product of two even numbers. Further, since q is odd, it cannot be divided evenly by the even integer p^2. The answer is (E).

- **Consecutive integers are written as $x, x + 1, x + 2, \ldots$**

- **Consecutive even or odd integers are written as $x, x + 2, x + 4, \ldots$**

- **The integer zero is neither positive nor negative, but it is even: $0 = 2 \cdot 0$.**

- **A *prime number* is an integer that is divisible only by itself and 1.**

  The prime numbers are 2, 3, 5, 7, 11, 13, 17, 19, 23, 29, 31, 37, 41, . . .

- **A number is divisible by 3 if the sum of its digits is divisible by 3.**

  For example, 135 is divisible by 3 because the sum of its digits (1 + 3 + 5 = 9) is divisible by 3.

- **The absolute value of a number, $|\ |$, is always positive. In other words, the absolute value symbol eliminates negative signs.**

  For example, $|-7| = 7$ and $|-\pi| = \pi$. Caution, the absolute value symbol acts only on what is inside the symbol, $|\ |$. For example, $-|-(7 - \pi)| = -(7 - \pi)$. Here, only the negative sign inside the absolute value symbol but outside the parentheses is eliminated.

Example 3:   If a, b, and c are consecutive integers and $a < b < c$, which of the following must be true?

      I. $b - c = 1$

      II. $\dfrac{abc}{3}$ is an integer.

      III. $a + b + c$ is even.

      (A)   I only
      (B)   II only
      (C)   III only
      (D)   I and II only
      (E)   II and III only

Let x, $x + 1$, $x + 2$ stand for the consecutive integers a, b, and c, in that order. Plugging this into Statement I yields

$$b - c = (x + 1) - (x + 2) = -1$$

Hence, Statement I is false.

As to Statement II, since a, b, and c are three consecutive integers, one of them must be divisible by 3. Hence, $\dfrac{abc}{3}$ is an integer, and Statement II is true.

As to Statement III, suppose a is even, b is odd, and c is even. Then $a + b$ is odd since

$$even + odd = odd$$

Hence,

$$a + b + c = (a + b) + c = (odd) + even = odd$$

Thus, Statement III is not necessarily true. The answer is (B).

Example 4:   If both x and y are prime numbers, which of the following CANNOT be the difference of x and y?

      (A) 1   (B) 3   (C) 9   (D) 15   (E) 23

Both 3 and 2 are prime, and $3 - 2 = 1$. This eliminates (A). Next, both 5 and 2 are prime, and $5 - 2 = 3$. This eliminates (B). Next, both 11 and 2 are prime, and $11 - 2 = 9$. This eliminates (C). Next, both 17 and 2 are prime, and $17 - 2 = 15$. This eliminates (D). Hence, by process of elimination, the answer is (E).

Example 5:   If $-x = -\left|-(-2 + 5)\right|$, then $x =$

      (A) –7   (B) –3   (C) 3   (D) 7   (E) 9

Working from the innermost parentheses out, we get

$$-x = -\left|-(-2 + 5)\right|$$
$$-x = -\left|-3\right|$$
$$-x = -(+3)$$
$$-x = -3$$
$$x = 3$$

The answer is (C).

Problem Set E: Solutions begin on page 169.

1. If the remainder is 1 when m is divided by 2 and the remainder is 3 when n is divided by 4, which of the following must be true?

    (A) m is even   (B) n is even   (C) $m + n$ is even   (D) mn is even   (E) m/n is even

2. If x and y are both prime and greater than 2, then which of the following CANNOT be a divisor of xy?

    (A) 2   (B) 3   (C) 11   (D) 15   (E) 17

3. If 2 is the greatest number that will divide evenly into both x and y, what is the greatest number that will divide evenly into both $5x$ and $5y$?

    (A) 2   (B) 4   (C) 6   (D) 8   (E) 10

4. If the average of the consecutive even integers a, b, and c is less than $\frac{1}{3}a$, which of the following best describes the value of a?

    (A) a is prime   (B) a is odd   (C) a is zero   (D) a is positive   (E) a is negative

5. If $\dfrac{x+5}{y}$ is a prime integer, which of the following must be true?

    I. $y = 5x$
    II. y is a prime integer.
    III. $\dfrac{x+5}{y}$ is odd.

    (A) None   (B) I only   (C) II only   (D) I and II only   (E) II and III only

6. If x is both the cube and the square of an integer and x is between 2 and 200, what is the value of x?

    (A) 8   (B) 16   (C) 64   (D) 125   (E) 169

7. In the two-digit number x, both the sum and the difference of its digits is 4. What is the value of x?

    (A) 13   (B) 31   (C) 40   (D) 48   (E) 59

8. If p divided by 9 leaves a remainder of 1, which of the following must be true?

    I. p is even.
    II. p is odd.
    III. $p = 3 \cdot z + 1$ for some integer z.

    (A) I only   (B) II only   (C) III only   (D) I and II only   (E) I and III only

9. p and q are integers. If p is divided by 2, the remainder is 1; and if q is divided by 6, the remainder is 1. Which of the following must be true.

    I. $pq + 1$ is even.
    II. $\dfrac{pq}{2}$ is an integer.
    III. pq is a multiple of 12.

    (A) I only   (B) II only   (C) III only   (D) I and II only   (E) I and III only

10. The smallest prime number greater than 53 is

   (A) 54   (B) 55   (C) 57   (D) 59   (E) 67

11. Which one of the following numbers is the greatest positive integer x such that 3^x is a factor of 27^5?

   (A) 5   (B) 8   (C) 10   (D) 15   (E) 19

12. If x, y, and z are consecutive integers in that order, which of the following must be true?

   I. xy is even.
   II. $x - z$ is even.
   III. x^z is even.

   (A) I only   (B) II only   (C) III only   (D) I and II only   (E) I and III only

13. If $-x - 2 = -|-(6 - 2)|$, then $x =$

   (A) –5   (B) –2   (C) 0   (D) 2   (E) 5

14. If the sum of two prime numbers x and y is odd, then the product of x and y must be divisible by

   (A) 2   (B) 3   (C) 4   (D) 5   (E) 8

15. If $\dfrac{x + y}{x - y} = 3$ and x and y are integers, then which one of the following must be true?

   (A) x is divisible by 4
   (B) y is an odd number
   (C) y is an even integer
   (D) x is an even number
   (E) x is an irreducible fraction

16. A two-digit even number is such that reversing its digits creates an odd number greater than the original number. Which one of the following cannot be the first digit of the original number?

   (A) 1   (B) 3   (C) 5   (D) 7   (E) 9

17. Let a, b, and c be three integers, and let a be a perfect square. If $a/b = b/c$, then which one of the following statements must be true?

   (A) c must be an even number
   (B) c must be an odd number
   (C) c must be a perfect square
   (D) c must not be a perfect square
   (E) c must be a prime number

18. If n > 2, then the sum, S, of the integers from 1 through n can be calculated by the following formula: $S = n(n + 1)/2$. Which one of the following statements about S must be true?

   (A) S is always odd.
   (B) S is always even.
   (C) S must be a prime number.
   (D) S must not be a prime number.
   (E) S must be a perfect square.

Which one of the following could be the difference between two numbers both of which are divisible by 2, 3 and 4?

(A) 71   (B) 72   (C) 73   (D) 74   (E) 75

20. A number, when divided by 12, gives a remainder of 7. If the same number is divided by 6, then the remainder must be

(A) 1   (B) 2   (C) 3   (D) 4   (E) 5

21. Let x be a two-digit number. If the sum of the digits of x is 9, then the sum of the digits of the number $(x + 10)$ is

(A) 1   (B) 8   (C) 10   (D) either 8 or 10   (E) either 1 or 10

22. $\dfrac{39693}{3} =$

(A) 33231   (B) 13231   (C) 12331   (D) 23123   (E) 12321

23. If n^3 is an odd integer, which one of the following expressions is an even integer?

(A) $2n^2 + 1$ (B) n^4 (C) $n^2 + 1$ (D) $n(n + 2)$ (E) n

24. If the product of two integers is odd, then the sum of those two integers must be

(A) odd
(B) even
(C) prime
(D) divisible by the difference of the two numbers
(E) a perfect square

25. If the sum of three consecutive integers is odd, then the first and the last integers must be

(A) odd, even   (B) odd, odd   (C) even, odd   (D) even, even   (E) none of the above

26. If l, m, and n are positive integers such that $l < m < n$ and $n < 4$, then $m =$

(A) 0   (B) 1   (C) 2   (D) 3   (E) 4

27. If two non-zero positive integers p and q are such that $p = 4q$ and $p < 8$, then $q =$

(A) 1   (B) 2   (C) 3   (D) 4   (E) 5

28. If n is an integer, then which one of the following expressions must be even?

(A) $n^2 + 1$ (B) $n(n + 2)$ (C) $n(n + 1)$ (D) $n(n + 4)$ (E) $(n + 1)(n + 3)$

29. The sum of three consecutive positive integers must be divisible by which of the following?

(A) 2   (B) 3   (C) 4   (D) 5   (E) 6

Geometry

One-fifth of the math problems on the GMAT involve geometry. (There are no proofs.) Fortunately, except for Data Sufficiency questions, the figures on the GMAT are usually drawn to scale. Hence, you can check your work and in some cases even solve a problem by "eyeballing" the drawing. We'll discuss this technique in detail later.

Following is a discussion of the basic properties of geometry. You probably know many of these properties. Memorize any that you do not know.

Lines & Angles

When two straight lines meet at a point, they form an angle. The point is called the vertex of the angle, and the lines are called the sides of the angle.

The angle to the right can be identified in three ways:

1. $\angle x$
2. $\angle B$
3. $\angle ABC$ or $\angle CBA$

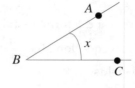

When two straight lines meet at a point, they form four angles. The angles opposite each other are called vertical angles, and they are congruent (equal). In the figure to the right, $a = b$, and $c = d$.

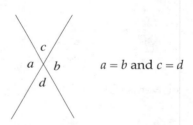

$a = b$ and $c = d$

Angles are measured in degrees, °. By definition, a circle has 360°. So an angle can be measured by its fractional part of a circle. For example, an angle that is $\dfrac{1}{360}$ of the arc of a circle is 1°. And an angle that is $\dfrac{1}{4}$ of the arc of a circle is $\dfrac{1}{4} \times 360 = 90$.

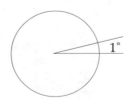

1/360 of an arc
of a circle

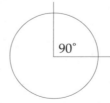

1/4 of an arc
of a circle

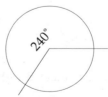

2/3 of an arc
of a circle

There are four major types of angle measures:

An **acute angle** has measure less than 90°:

A **right angle** has measure 90°:

90°

An **obtuse angle** has measure greater than 90°:

A **straight angle** has measure 180°:

$y°$ $x°$ $x + y = 180°$

Example: In the figure to the right, if the quotient of a and b is $7/2$, then $b =$

$a°$ $b°$

(A) 30   (B) 35   (C) 40   (D) 46   (E) 50

Since a and b form a straight angle, $a + b = 180$. Now, translating "the quotient of a and b is $7/2$" into an equation gives $\dfrac{a}{b} = \dfrac{7}{2}$. Solving for a yields $a = \dfrac{7}{2}b$. Plugging this into the equation $a + b = 180$ yields

$$\frac{7}{2}b + b = 180$$
$$7b + 2b = 360$$
$$9b = 360$$
$$b = 40$$

The answer is (C).

Two angles are supplementary if their angle sum is 180°:

45°   135°

45 + 135 = 180

Two angles are complementary if their angle sum is 90°:

60°
30°

30 + 60 = 90

Perpendicular lines meet at right angles:

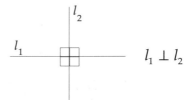

l_2

l_1 $l_1 \perp l_2$

Two lines in the same plane are parallel if they never intersect. Parallel lines have the same slope.

When parallel lines are cut by a transversal, three important angle relationships exist:

Alternate interior angles are equal.

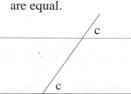

Corresponding angles are equal.

Interior angles on the same side of the transversal are supplementary.

$a + b = 180°$

The shortest distance from a point to a line is along a new line that passes through the point and is perpendicular to the original line.

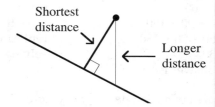

Shortest distance

Longer distance

Triangles

A triangle containing a right angle is called a *right triangle*. The right angle is denoted by a small square:

A triangle with two equal sides is called *isosceles*. The angles opposite the equal sides are called the base angles, and they are congruent (equal). A triangle with all three sides equal is called *equilateral*, and each angle is 60°. A triangle with no equal sides (and therefore no equal angles) is called *scalene*:

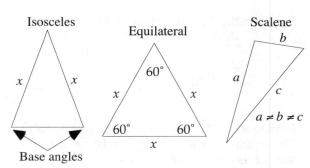

Isosceles

Equilateral

Scalene

Base angles

The altitude to the base of an isosceles or equilateral triangle bisects the base and bisects the vertex angle:

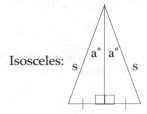

Isosceles:

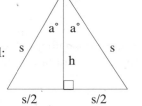

Equilateral:

$$h = \frac{s\sqrt{3}}{2}$$

memorize

The angle sum of a triangle is 180°:

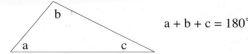

$a + b + c = 180°$

Example: In the figure to the right, $w =$
            (A) 30   (B) 32   (C) 40   (D) 52   (E) 60

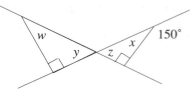

$x + 150 = 180$	since x and 150 form a straight angle
$x = 30$	solving for x
$z + x + 90 = 180$	since the angle sum of a triangle is 180°
$z + 30 + 90 = 180$	replacing x with 30
$z = 60$	solving for z
$z = y = 60$	since y and z are vertical angles
$w + y + 90 = 180$	since the angle sum of a triangle is 180°
$w + 60 + 90 = 180$	replacing y with 60
$w = 30$	solving for w

The answer is (A).

The area of a triangle is $\frac{1}{2}bh$, where b is the base and h is the height. Sometimes the base must be extended in order to draw the altitude, as in the third drawing immediately below:

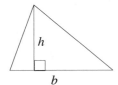 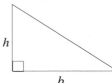 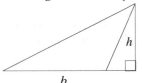 $A = \frac{1}{2}bh$

In a triangle, the longer side is opposite the larger angle, and vice versa:

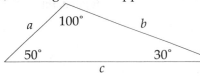   50° is larger than 30°, so side b is longer than side a.

Pythagorean Theorem (right triangles only): The square of the hypotenuse is equal to the sum of the squares of the legs.

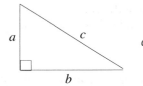 $c^2 = a^2 + b^2$

Pythagorean triples: The numbers 3, 4, and 5 can always represent the sides of a right triangle and they appear very often: $5^2 = 3^2 + 4^2$. Another, but less common, Pythagorean Triple is 5, 12, 13: $13^2 = 5^2 + 12^2$.

Two triangles are similar (same shape and usually different sizes) if their corresponding angles are equal. If two triangles are similar, their corresponding sides are proportional:

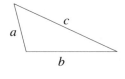 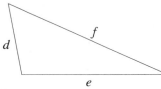

$$\frac{a}{d} = \frac{b}{e} = \frac{c}{f}$$

If two angles of a triangle are congruent to two angles of another triangle, the triangles are similar.

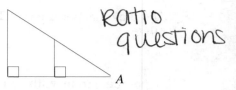

In the figure to the right, the large and small triangles are similar because both contain a right angle and they share $\angle A$.

Two triangles are congruent (identical) if they have the same size and shape.

In a triangle, an exterior angle is equal to the sum of its remote interior angles and is therefore greater than either of them:

$e = a + b$ and $e > a$ and $e > b$

In a triangle, the sum of the lengths of any two sides is greater than the length of the remaining side:

$x + y > z$
$y + z > x$
$x + z > y$

$2x+60 = x+90$
$x = 30$

Example: In the figure to the right, what is the value of x ?

(A) 30
(B) 32
(C) 35
(D) 40
(E) 47

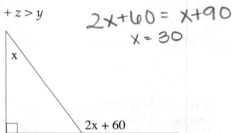

Since $2x + 60$ is an exterior angle, it is equal to the sum of the remote interior angles. That is, $2x + 60 = x + 90$. Solving for x gives $x = 30$. The answer is (A).

In a 30°–60°–90° triangle, the sides have the following relationships:

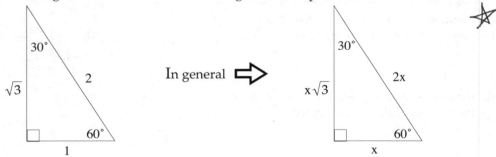

In general ⟹

Quadrilaterals

A _quadrilateral_ is a four-sided closed figure, where each side is a straight line.

The angle sum of a quadrilateral is 360°. You can view a quadrilateral as being composed of two 180-degree triangles:

A _parallelogram_ is a quadrilateral in which the opposite sides are both parallel and congruent. Its area is _base × height_:

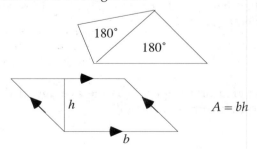

$A = bh$

The diagonals of a parallelogram bisect each other:

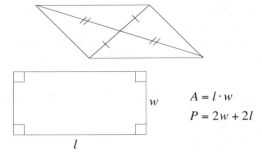

A parallelogram with four right angles is a *rectangle*. If w is the width and l is the length of a rectangle, then its area is $A = l \cdot w$ and its perimeter is $P = 2w + 2l$.

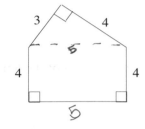

$A = l \cdot w$

$P = 2w + 2l$

Example: In the figure to the right, what is the perimeter of the pentagon?
(A)   12
(B)   13
(C)   17
(D)   20
(E)   25

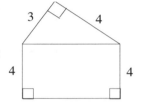

Add the following line to the figure:

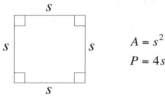

Since the legs of the right triangle formed are of lengths 3 and 4, the triangle must be a 3-4-5 right triangle. Hence, the added line has length 5. Since the bottom figure is a rectangle, the length of the base of the figure is also 5. Hence, the perimeter of the pentagon is $3 + 4 + 4 + 5 + 4 = 20$. The answer is (D).

If the opposite sides of a rectangle are equal, it is a square and its area is $A = s^2$ and its perimeter is $P = 4s$, where s is the length of a side:

$A = s^2$

$P = 4s$

The diagonals of a square bisect each other and are perpendicular to each other:

A quadrilateral with only one pair of parallel sides is a *trapezoid*. The parallel sides are called *bases*, and the non-parallel sides are called *legs*:

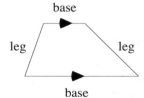

The area of a trapezoid is the average of the two bases times the height:

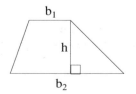

$A = \left(\dfrac{b_1 + b_2}{2} \right) h$

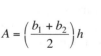

Volume

The volume of a rectangular solid (a box) is the product of the length, width, and height. The surface area is the sum of the area of the six faces:

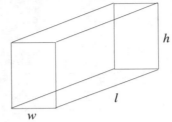

$$V = l \cdot w \cdot h$$
$$S = 2wl + 2hl + 2wh$$

If the length, width, and height of a rectangular solid (a box) are the same, it is a cube. Its volume is the cube of one of its sides, and its surface area is the sum of the areas of the six faces:

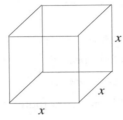

$$V = x^3$$
$$S = 6x^2$$

Example: The volume of the cube to the right is x and its surface area is x. What is the length of an edge of the cube?

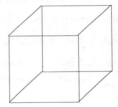

(A)   6
(B)   10
(C)   18
(D)   36
(E)   48

Let e be the length of an edge of the cube. Recall that the volume of a cube is e^3 and its surface area is $6e^2$. Since we are given that both the volume and the surface area are x, these expressions are equal:

$$e^3 = 6e^2$$
$$e^3 - 6e^2 = 0$$
$$e^2(e - 6) = 0$$
$$e^2 = 0 \ \text{ or } \ e - 6 = 0$$
$$e = 0 \ \text{ or } \ e = 6$$

We reject $e = 0$ since in that case no cube would exist. Hence, $e = 6$ and the answer is (A).

The volume of a cylinder is $V = \pi r^2 h$, and the lateral surface (excluding the top and bottom) is $S = 2\pi rh$, where r is the radius and h is the height:

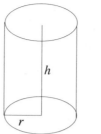

$$V = \pi r^2 h$$
$$S = 2\pi rh + 2\pi r^2$$

Circles

A circle is a set of points in a plane equidistant from a fixed point (the center of the circle). The perimeter of a circle is called the *circumference*.

A line segment from a circle to its center is a *radius*.

A line segment with both end points on a circle is a *chord*.

A chord passing though the center of a circle is a *diameter*.

A diameter can be viewed as two radii, and hence a diameter's length is twice that of a radius.

A line passing through two points on a circle is a *secant*.

A piece of the circumference is an *arc*.

The area bounded by the circumference and an angle with vertex at the center of the circle is a *sector*.

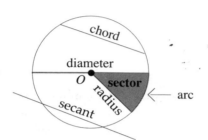

A tangent line to a circle intersects the circle at only one point. The radius of the circle is perpendicular to the tangent line at the point of tangency:

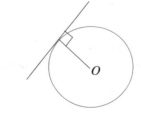

Two tangents to a circle from a common exterior point of the circle are congruent:

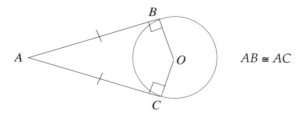

$AB \cong AC$

An angle inscribed in a semicircle is a right angle:

A central angle has by definition the same measure as its intercepted arc:

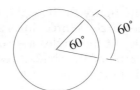

An inscribed angle has one-half the measure of its intercepted arc:

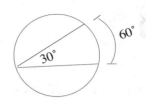

The area of a circle is πr^2, and its circumference (perimeter) is $2\pi r$, where r is the radius:

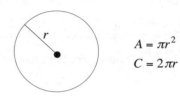

$$A = \pi r^2$$
$$C = 2\pi r$$

On the GMAT, $\pi \approx 3$ is a sufficient approximation for π. You don't need $\pi \approx 3.14$.

Example: In the figure to the right, the circle has center O and its radius is 2. What is the length of arc ACB ?

(A) $\dfrac{\pi}{3}$ (B) $\dfrac{2\pi}{3}$ (C) π (D) $\dfrac{4\pi}{3}$ (E) $\dfrac{7\pi}{3}$

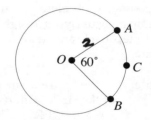

The circumference of the circle is $2\pi r = 2\pi(2) = 4\pi$. A central angle has by definition the same degree measure as its intercepted arc. Hence, arc ACB is also 60°. Now, the circumference of the circle has 360°. So arc ACB is $\dfrac{1}{6}$ (= 60/360) of the circle's circumference. Hence, arc ACB = $\dfrac{1}{6}(4\pi) = \dfrac{2}{3}\pi$. The answer is (B).

Shaded Regions

To find the area of the shaded region of a figure, subtract the area of the unshaded region from the area of the entire figure.

Example: What is the area of the shaded region formed by the circle and the rectangle in the figure to the right?
(A) $15 - 2\pi$
(B) $15 - \pi$
(C)   14
(D) $16 - \pi$
(E) 15π

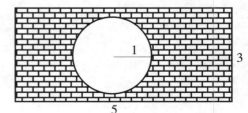

To find the area of the shaded region subtract the area of the circle from the area of the rectangle:

area of rectangle	–	area of circle
$3 \cdot 5$	–	$\pi \cdot 1^2$
15	–	π

The answer is (B).

Example: In the figure to the right, the radius of the larger circle is three times that of the smaller circle. If the circles are concentric, what is the ratio of the shaded region's area to the area of the smaller circle?

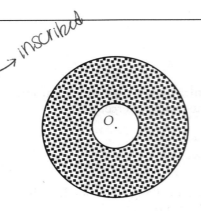

inscribed

    (A)   10:1
    (B)   9:1
    (C)   8:1
    (D)   3:1
    (E)   5:2

Since we are not given the radii of the circles, we can choose any two positive numbers such that one is three times the other. Let the outer radius be 3 and the inner radius be 1. Then the area of the outer circle is $\pi 3^2 = 9\pi$, and the area of the inner circle is $\pi 1^2 = \pi$. So the area of the shaded region is $9\pi - \pi = 8\pi$. Hence, the ratio of the area of the shaded region to the area of the smaller circle is $\dfrac{8\pi}{\pi} = \dfrac{8}{1}$. Therefore, the answer is (C).

$r_s = x$

$r_L = 3x$

$a = \pi x^2$

$a = 9x^2\pi$

compare shaded to smaller

shaded

$\dfrac{9x^2\pi - \pi x^2 = 8x^2\pi}{x^2}$

"Birds-Eye" View

Most geometry problems on the GMAT require straightforward calculations. However, some problems measure your insight into the basic rules of geometry. For this type of problem, you should step back and take a "birds-eye" view of the problem. The following example will illustrate.

Example: In the figure to the right, O is both the center of the circle with radius 2 and a vertex of the square OPRS. What is the length of diagonal PS?

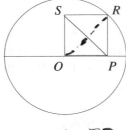

    (A) $1/2$
    (B) $\dfrac{\sqrt{2}}{2}$
    (C) 4
    (D) 2
    (E) $2\sqrt{5}$

OR = PS

The diagonals of a square are equal. Hence, line segment OR (not shown) is equal to SP. Now, OR is a radius of the circle and therefore OR = 2. Hence, SP = 2 as well, and the answer is (D).

Problem Set F: Solutions begin on page 177.

1. In the triangle to the right, what is the value of y?

    (A) 3
    (B) $\sqrt{18}$
    (C) $\sqrt{27}$
    (D) 9
    (E) 27

2. In the figure to the right, circle P has diameter 2 and circle Q has diameter 1. What is the area of the shaded region?

    (A) $3\pi/4$
    (B) 3π
    (C) $7\pi/2$
    (D) 5π
    (E) 6π

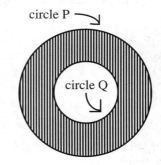

3. In the figure to the right, $QRST$ is a square. If the shaded region is bounded by arcs of circles with centers at Q, R, S, and T, then the area of the shaded region is

    (A) 9
    (B) 36
    (C) $36 - 9\pi$
    (D) $36 - \pi$
    (E) $9 - 3\pi$

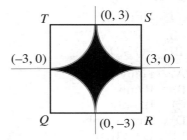

4. In the figure to the right, QRST is a square. If the area of each circle is 2π, then the area of square QRST is

    (A) $\sqrt{2}$
    (B) 4
    (C) $\sqrt{2}\pi$
    (D) $4\sqrt{2}$
    (E) 32

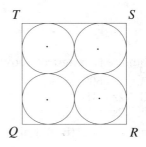

5. In the figure to the right, if O is the center of the circle, then $y =$

    (A) 75
    (B) 76
    (C) 77
    (D) 78
    (E) 79

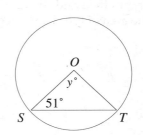

6.   In the figure to the right, the value of $a + b$ is

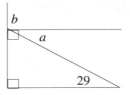

    (A)   118
    (B)   119
    (C)   120
    (D)   121
    (E)   122

7.   If $l_1 \| l_2$ in the figure to the right, what is the value of x?

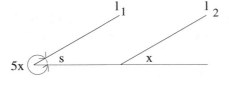

    (A)   30
    (B)   45
    (C)   60
    (D)   72
    (E)   90

8.   For the figure to the right, which of the following are true?

    I. $OP = OQ$
    II. $\sqrt{PQ} < \sqrt{OP}$
    III. $PQ > OQ$

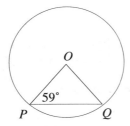

    (A)   I only
    (B)   II only
    (C)   III only
    (D)   I and II only
    (E)   I and III only

O is the center of the circle.

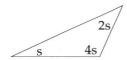

9.   From the two figures above, which of the following can be determined?

    I. $x = 60°$
    II. $7s = 180°$
    III. $2s < x$

(A) I only   (B) II only   (C) III only   (D) I and II only   (E) I, II, and III

10.   In the figure to the right, x is both the radius of the larger circle and the diameter of the smaller circle. The area of the shaded region is

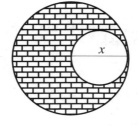

    (A) $\dfrac{3}{4}\pi x^2$

    (B) $\dfrac{\pi}{3}$

    (C) $\dfrac{4}{3}\pi x^2$

    (D) $\dfrac{3}{5}\pi x^2$

    (E) πx^2

11. In the figure to the right, the circle with center O is inscribed in the square PQRS. The combined area of the shaded regions is

(A) $36 - 9\pi$

(B) $36 - \dfrac{9}{2}\pi$

(C) $\dfrac{36 - 9\pi}{2}$

(D) $18 - 9\pi$

(E) $9 - \dfrac{9}{4}\pi$

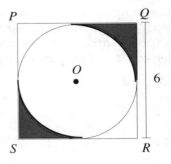

12. In the figure to the right, the length of QS is

(A) $\sqrt{51}$

(B) $\sqrt{61}$

(C) $\sqrt{69}$

(D) $\sqrt{77}$

(E) $\sqrt{89}$

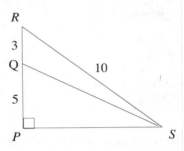

13. For the figure to the right, which of the following best describes the value of y?

(A) $y < 50$

(B) $y < 55$

(C) $y > 35$

(D) $y > 55$

(E) $y < 35$

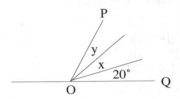

$\angle\,POQ = 70°$ and $x > 15$

14. In the figure to the right, if $l \| k$, then what is the value of y ?

(A) 20

(B) 45

(C) 55

(D) 75

(E) 110

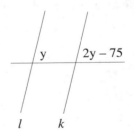

15. In the figure to the right, both triangles are right triangles. The area of the shaded region is

(A) 1/2

(B) 2/3

(C) 7/8

(D) 3/2

(E) 5/2

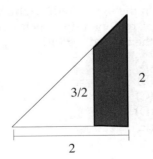

16. In the figure to the right, the radius of the larger circle is twice that of the smaller circle. If the circles are concentric, what is the ratio of the shaded region's area to the area of the smaller circle?

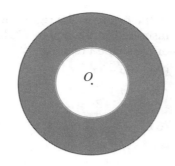

(A)   10:1
(B)   9:1
(C)   3:1
(D)   2:1
(E)   1:1

17. In the figure to the right, $\triangle PST$ is an isosceles right triangle, and $PS = 2$. What is the area of the shaded region $URST$?

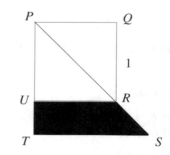

(A)   4
(B)   2
(C)   5/4
(D)   5/6
(E)   1/2

18. In the figure to the right, the area of $\triangle PQR$ is 40. What is the area of $\triangle QRS$?

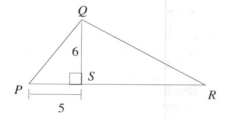

(A)   10
(B)   15
(C)   20
(D)   25
(E)   45

19. In the figure to the right, $PQRS$ is a square and M and N are midpoints of their respective sides. What is the area of quadrilateral $PMRN$?

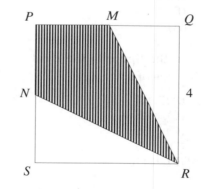

(A)   8
(B)   10
(C)   12
(D)   14
(E)   16

20. In the figure to the right, what is the greatest number of regions into which two straight lines will divide the shaded region?

(A)   1
(B)   2
(C)   3
(D)   4
(E)   5

21. In the figure to the right, O is the center of the circle. If the area of the circle is 9π, then the perimeter of the sector *PRQO* is

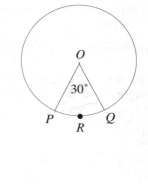

(A) $\dfrac{\pi}{2} + 18$

(B) $\dfrac{\pi}{2} + 6$

(C) $\dfrac{3}{4}\pi + 6$

(D) $\dfrac{3}{4}\pi + 18$

(E) $\dfrac{\pi}{2} - 6$

22. Let A denote the area of a circular region. Which of the following denotes the circumference of that circular region?

(A) $\sqrt{\dfrac{A}{\pi}}$ (B) $2\dfrac{A}{\sqrt{\pi}}$ (C) $2\pi\sqrt{A}$ (D) $2\sqrt{\dfrac{A}{\pi}}$ (E) $2\pi\sqrt{\dfrac{A}{\pi}}$

23. Ship X and ship Y are 5 miles apart and are on a collision course. Ship X is sailing directly north, and ship Y is sailing directly east. If the point of impact is 1 mile closer to the current position of ship X than to the current position of ship Y, how many miles away from the point of impact is ship Y at this time?

(A) 1   (B) 2   (C) 3   (D) 4   (E) 5

24. The figure to the right represents a square with sides of length 4 surmounted by a circle with center O. What is the outer perimeter of the figure?

(A) $\dfrac{49}{9}\pi + 12$

(B) $\dfrac{20}{3}\pi + 12$

(C) $\dfrac{5}{6}\pi + 12$

(D) $\pi + 12$

(E) $9\pi + 12$

25. The perimeter of a square is equal to the perimeter of a rectangle whose length and width are $6m$ and $4m$, respectively. The side of the square is

(A) $3m$ (B) $4m$ (C) $5m$ (D) $6m$ (E) $7m$

26. If the circumference of a circle is $4m$, then the ratio of circumference of the circle to the diameter of the circle is

(A) π (B) 4   (C) 2π (D) 4π (E) 16

27. In Triangle *ABC*, $\angle A$ is 10 degrees greater than $\angle B$, and $\angle B$ is 10 degrees greater than $\angle C$. The value of angle B is

(A) 30   (B) 40   (C) 50   (D) 60   (E) 70

28. Two squares each with sides of length s are joined to form a rectangle. The area of the rectangle is

(A) s^2 (B) $2s^2$ (C) $4s^2$ (D) $8s^2$ (E) $16s^2$

29.   A person travels 16 miles due north and then 12 miles due east. How far is the person from his initial location?

    (A) 4 miles   (B) 8 miles   (C) 14 miles   (D) 20 miles   (E) 28 miles

30.   The area of Triangle PQR is 6. If $PR = 4$, then the length of the hypotenuse QR is

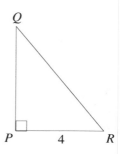

    (A)   1
    (B)   2
    (C)   3
    (D)   4
    (E)   5

31.   In the figure, the equation of line AB is $y = -\dfrac{5}{3}x + 10$. The area of the shaded portion is

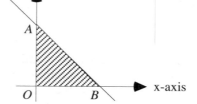

    (A)   12
    (B)   30
    (C)   100/3
    (D)   60
    (E)   100

32.   In the figure, if $x = 54°$ and $y = 72°$, then $z =$

    (A)   54°
    (B)   56°
    (C)   72°
    (D)   76°
    (E)   98°

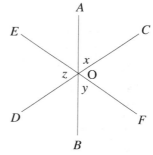

O is the point of intersection of the three lines in the figure.

33.   If one of the sides of the rectangle shown in the figure has a length of 3, then the area of the rectangle is
    (A)   9
    (B)   13.5
    (C)   18
    (D)   27
    (E)   54

34.   The value of $x + y + z =$

    (A)   120°
    (B)   160°
    (C)   180°
    (D)   270°
    (E)   360°

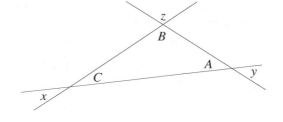

35. In the figure, what is the area of Triangle *ABC* ?

    (A) 25
    (B) 50
    (C) $100/\sqrt{2}$
    (D) 100
    (E) $100\sqrt{2}$

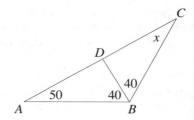

36. In the figure, what is the value of *x*?

    (A) 20°
    (B) 30°
    (C) 40°
    (D) 50°
    (E) 60°

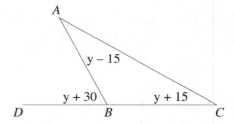

37. The area of the Triangle *ABC* shown in the figure is 30. The area of Triangle *ADC* is

    (A) 5
    (B) 10
    (C) 15
    (D) 20
    (E) 25

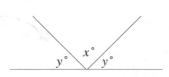

38. In the figure, what is the value of *y* ?

    (A) 7.5
    (B) 15
    (C) 30
    (D) 40
    (E) 45

39. A circle is depicted in the rectangular coordinate system as shown. The value of *x* is

    (A) 4
    (B) 6
    (C) 8
    (D) 10
    (E) 12

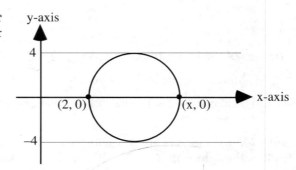

40. In the figure, the ratio of *x* to *y* is 2. What is the value of *y* ?

    (A) 108
    (B) 90
    (C) 68
    (D) 45
    (E) 36

EYE-BALLING

Surprisingly, on the GMAT you can often solve geometry problems by merely "eye-balling" the given drawing. Even on problems whose answers you can't get directly by looking, you often can eliminate a couple of the answer-choices.

Unless stated otherwise, all figures on Standard Math questions are drawn exactly to scale. Hence, if an angle looks like it's about 90°, it is; if a line segment looks like it's about 2 units long, it is; if one figure looks like it's about twice as large as another figure, it is. **Caution:** The figures in Data Sufficiency questions are not necessarily drawn to scale. Hence, you cannot use the methods of this section on Data Sufficiency problems. All the problems in this section were solved before. Now, we will solve them by eye-balling the drawings.

Example 1:   In the figure to the right, if $l \| k$, then what is the value of y?

  (A)   20
  (B)   45
  (C)   55
  (D)   75
  (E)   110

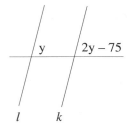

By eye-balling the drawing, we can see that y is less than 90°. It appears to be somewhere between 65° and 85°. But 75° is the only answer-choice in that range. Hence, the answer is (D).

Example 2:   In the figure to the right, the area of the shaded region is

  (A)   1/2
  (B)   2/3
  (C)   7/8
  (D)   3/2
  (E)   5/2

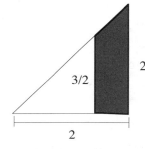

The area of the larger triangle is $A = \dfrac{1}{2}bh = \dfrac{1}{2} \cdot 2 \cdot 2 = 2$. Now, by eye-balling the drawing, the area of the shaded region looks to be about half that of the larger triangle. Therefore, the answer should be about $\dfrac{1}{2} \cdot 2 = 1$. The closest answer-choice to 1 is 7/8. The answer is (C).

Note: On the GMAT, answer-choices are listed in order of size: usually from smallest to largest (unless the question asks for the smallest or largest). Hence, in the previous example, 2/3 is smaller than 7/8 because it comes before 7/8.

Problem Set G: Solutions begin on page 193.

The following problems have been solved before. Now, solve them by eye-balling the figures.

1. In the figure to the right, the radius of the larger circle is twice that of the smaller circle. If the circles are concentric, what is the ratio of the shaded region's area to the area of the smaller circle?

   (A) 10:1
   (B) 9:1
   (C) 3:1
   (D) 2:1
   (E) 1:1

2. In the figure to the right, ΔPST is an isosceles right triangle, and $PS = 2$. What is the area of the shaded region $URST$?

   (A) 4
   (B) 2
   (C) 5/4
   (D) 5/6
   (E) 1/2

3. In the figure to the right, the area of ΔPQR is 40. What is the area of ΔQRS?

   (A) 10
   (B) 15
   (C) 20
   (D) 25
   (E) 45

4. In the figure to the right, $PQRS$ is a square and M and N are midpoints of their respective sides. What is the area of quadrilateral $PMRN$?

   (A) 8
   (B) 10
   (C) 12
   (D) 14
   (E) 16

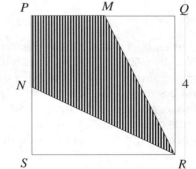

Coordinate Geometry

On a number line, the numbers increase in size to the right and decrease to the left:

If we draw a line through the point 0 perpendicular to the number line, we will form a grid:

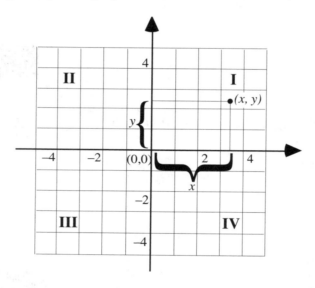

The thick horizontal line in the above diagram is called the x-axis, and the thick vertical line is called the y-axis. The point at which the axes meet, $(0, 0)$, is called the origin. On the x-axis, positive numbers are to the right of the origin and increase in size to the right; further, negative numbers are to the left of the origin and decrease in size to the left. On the y-axis, positive numbers are above the origin and ascend in size; further, negative numbers are below the origin and descend in size. As shown in the diagram, the point represented by the ordered pair (x, y) is reached by moving x units along the x-axis from the origin and then moving y units vertically. In the ordered pair (x, y), x is called the *abscissa* and y is called the *ordinate*; collectively they are called coordinates. The x and y axes divide the plane into four quadrants, numbered I, II, III, and IV counterclockwise. Note, if $x \neq y$, then (x, y) and (y, x) represent different points on the coordinate system. The points $(2, 3)$, $(-3, 1)$, $(-4, -4)$, and $(4, -2)$ are plotted in the following coordinate system:

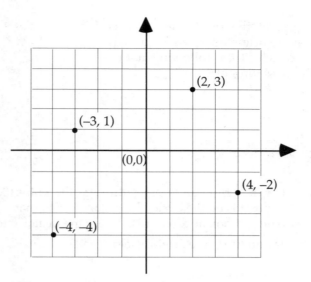

Example: In the figure to the right, polygon *ABCO* is a square. If the coordinates of *B* are $(h, 4)$, what is the value of *h* ?

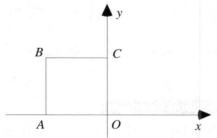

(A)   4

(B) $4\sqrt{2}$

(C) $-4\sqrt{2}$

(D) -4

(E)   not enough information

Since the *y*-coordinate of point *B* is 4, line segment *CO* has length 4. Since figure *ABCO* is a square, line segment *AO* also has length 4. Since point *B* is in the second quadrant, the *x*-coordinate of *B* is –4. The answer is (D). Be careful not to choose 4. *h* is the *x*-coordinate of point *B*, not the length of the square's side.

Distance Formula:

The distance formula is derived by using the Pythagorean theorem. Notice in the figure below that the distance between the points (x, y) and (a, b) is the hypotenuse of a right triangle. The difference $y - b$ is the measure of the height of the triangle, and the difference $x - a$ is the length of base of the triangle. Applying the Pythagorean theorem yields

$$d^2 = (x - a)^2 + (y - b)^2$$

Taking the square root of both sides this equation yields

$$\boxed{d = \sqrt{(x - a)^2 + (y - b)^2}}$$

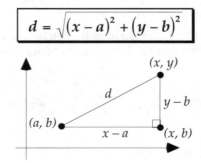

Example: In the figure to the right, the circle is centered at the origin and passes through point *P*. Which of the following points does it also pass through?

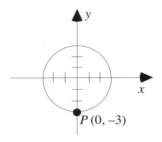

(A)   (3, 3)
(B) $(-2\sqrt{2}, -1)$
(C)   (2, 6)
(D) $(-\sqrt{3}, \sqrt{3})$
(E)   (−3, 4)

Since the circle is centered at the origin and passes through the point (0, −3), the radius of the circle is 3. Now, if any other point is on the circle, the distance from that point to the center of the circle (the radius) must also be 3. Look at choice (B). Using the distance formula to calculate the distance between $\left(-2\sqrt{2}, -1\right)$ and (0, 0) (the origin) yields

$$d = \sqrt{\left(-2\sqrt{2} - 0\right)^2 + \left(-1 - 0\right)^2} = \sqrt{\left(-2\sqrt{2}\right)^2 + \left(-1\right)^2} = \sqrt{8 + 1} = \sqrt{9} = 3$$

Hence, $\left(-2\sqrt{2}, -1\right)$ is on the circle, and the answer is (B).

Midpoint Formula:

The midpoint M between points (*x*, *y*) and (*a*, *b*) is given by

$$M = \left(\frac{x + a}{2}, \frac{y + b}{2}\right)$$

In other words, to find the midpoint, simply average the corresponding coordinates of the two points.

Example: In the figure to the right, polygon *PQRO* is a square and *T* is the midpoint of side *QR*. What are the coordinates of *T* ?

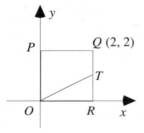

(A)   (1, 1)
(B)   (1, 2)
(C)   (1.5, 1.5)
(D)   (2, 1)
(E)   (2, 3)

Since point *R* is on the *x*-axis, its *y*-coordinate is 0. Further, since *PQRO* is a square and the *x*-coordinate of *Q* is 2, the *x*-coordinate of *R* is also 2. Since *T* is the midpoint of side *QR*, the midpoint formula yields

$$T = \left(\frac{2 + 2}{2}, \frac{2 + 0}{2}\right) = \left(\frac{4}{2}, \frac{2}{2}\right) = (2, 1)$$

The answer is (D).

Slope Formula:

The slope of a line measures the inclination of the line. By definition, it is the ratio of the vertical change to the horizontal change (see figure below). The vertical change is called the *rise*, and the horizontal change is called the *run*. Thus, the slope is the *rise over the run*.

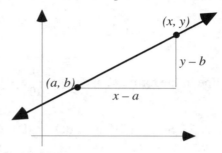

Forming the *rise over the run* in the above figure yields

$$m = \frac{y - b}{x - a}$$

Example: In the figure to the right, what is the slope of line passing through the two points?

(A) 1/4
(B) 1
(C) 1/2
(D) 3/2
(E) 2

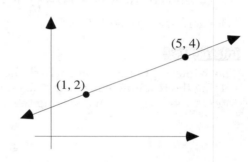

The slope formula yields $m = \dfrac{4 - 2}{5 - 1} = \dfrac{2}{4} = \dfrac{1}{2}$. The answer is (C).

Slope-Intercept Form:

Multiplying both sides of the equation $m = \dfrac{y - b}{x - a}$ by x–a yields

$$y - b = m(x - a)$$

Now, if the line passes through the y-axis at $(0, b)$, then the equation becomes

$$y - b = m(x - 0)$$

or

$$y - b = mx$$

or

$$y = mx + b$$

This is called the slope-intercept form of the equation of a line, where m is the slope and b is the y-intercept. This form is convenient because it displays the two most important bits of information about a line: its slope and its y-intercept.

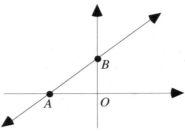

Example: The equation of the line in the figure above is $y = \dfrac{9}{10}x + k$. Which one of the following is true?

    (A) $AO > BO$ (B) $AO < BO$ (C) $AO = BO$ (D) $AO = 2$ (E) $BO = 2$

Since $y = \dfrac{9}{10}x + k$ is in slope-intercept form, we know the slope of the line is $9/10$. Now, the ratio of BO to AO is the slope of the line (rise over run). Hence, $\dfrac{BO}{AO} = \dfrac{9}{10}$. Multiplying both sides of this equation by AO yields $BO = \dfrac{9}{10}AO$. In other words, BO is $9/10$ the length of AO. Hence, AO is longer. The answer is (A).

Intercepts:

The x-intercept is the point where the line crosses the x-axis. It is found by setting $y = 0$ and solving the resulting equation. The y-intercept is the point where the line crosses the y-axis. It is found by setting $x = 0$ and solving the resulting equation.

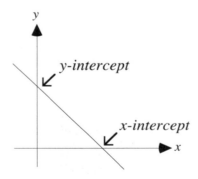

Example: Graph the equation $x - 2y = 4$.

Solution: To find the x-intercept, set $y = 0$. This yields $x - 2 \cdot 0 = 4$, or $x = 4$. So the x-intercept is $(4, 0)$. To find the y-intercept, set $x = 0$. This yields $0 - 2y = 4$, or $y = -2$. So the y-intercept is $(0, -2)$. Plotting these two points and connecting them with a straight line yields

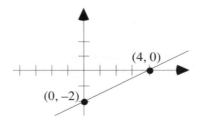

Areas and Perimeters:

Often, you will be given a geometric figure drawn on a coordinate system and will be asked to find its area or perimeter. In these problems, use the properties of the coordinate system to deduce the dimensions of the figure and then calculate the area or perimeter. For complicated figures, you may need to divide the figure into simpler forms, such as squares and triangles. A couple examples will illustrate:

Example: What is the area of the quadrilateral in the coordinate system to the right?

(A)   2
(B)   4
(C)   6
(D)   8
(E)   11

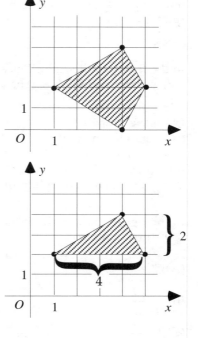

If the quadrilateral is divided horizontally through the line $y = 2$, two congruent triangles are formed. As the figure to the right shows, the top triangle has height 2 and base 4. Hence, its area is

$$A = \frac{1}{2}bh = \frac{1}{2} \cdot 4 \cdot 2 = 4$$

The area of the bottom triangle is the same, so the area of the quadrilateral is $4 + 4 = 8$. The answer is (D).

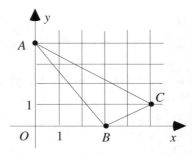

Example: What is the perimeter of Triangle ABC in the figure to the right?

(A) $5 + \sqrt{5} + \sqrt{34}$
(B) $10 + \sqrt{34}$
(C) $5 + \sqrt{5} + \sqrt{28}$
(D) $2\sqrt{5} + \sqrt{34}$
(E) $\sqrt{5} + \sqrt{28}$

Point A has coordinates $(0, 4)$, point B has coordinates $(3, 0)$, and point C has coordinates $(5, 1)$. Using the distance formula to calculate the distances between points A and B, A and C, and B and C yields

$$\overline{AB} = \sqrt{(0-3)^2 + (4-0)^2} = \sqrt{9+16} = \sqrt{25} = 5$$
$$\overline{AC} = \sqrt{(0-5)^2 + (4-1)^2} = \sqrt{25+9} = \sqrt{34}$$
$$\overline{BC} = \sqrt{(5-3)^2 + (1-0)^2} = \sqrt{4+1} = \sqrt{5}$$

Adding these lengths gives the perimeter of Triangle ABC:

$$\overline{AB} + \overline{AC} + \overline{BC} = 5 + \sqrt{34} + \sqrt{5}$$

The answer is (A).

Problem Set H: Solutions begin on page 195.

1.   In the figure to the right, O is the center of the circle. What is the area of the circle?

   (A) 2π
   (B) 3π
   (C) 5.5π
   (D) 7π
   (E) 9π

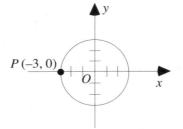

2.   In the figure to the right, P is a point in the coordinate system and $OP = 6$. The y-coordinate of point P is

   (A)   less than OP
   (B)   greater than OP
   (C)   equal to OP
   (D)   equal to 5
   (E)   there is not enough information to decide

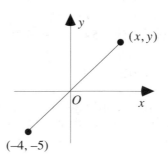

3.   In the figure to the right, if the equation of the line is $y = px + a$, then $p =$

   (A) $\dfrac{b}{a}$

   (B) $\dfrac{-b}{a}$

   (C) $\dfrac{-a}{b}$

   (D) $\dfrac{a}{b}$

   (E)   there is not enough information to decide

4.   For the figure to the right, which of the following must be true?

   (A) $x > y$
   (B) $y > x$
   (C) $x = y$
   (D) $x = 2$
   (E)   there is not enough information to decide

5.   In the figure to the right, a is the x-coordinate of point P and b is the y-coordinate of point Q. In which quadrant is the point (a, b) ?

   (A)   I
   (B)   II
   (C)   III
   (D)   IV
   (E)   cannot be determined from the information given

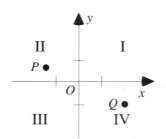

6. In the figure to the right, if $x = 4$, then $y =$

    (A) 1
    (B) 2
    (C) 3
    (D) 4
    (E) 5.1

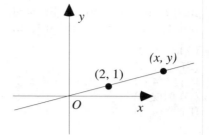

7. In the figure to the right, which of the following could be the coordinates of a point in the shaded region?

    (A) (1, 2)
    (B) (−2, 3)
    (C) (3, −5)
    (D) (−5, 1)
    (E) (−1, −6)

8. In the figure to the right, which of the following points lies within the circle?

    (A) (3.5, 9.5)
    (B) (−7, 7)
    (C) (−10, 1)
    (D) (0, 11)
    (E) (5.5, 8.5)

9. For the figure to the right, which of the following statements about −3a and 3b must be true?

    (A) −3a = 3b
    (B) −3a > 3b
    (C) −3a < 3b
    (D) −3a ≠ 3b
    (E) there is not enough information to decide

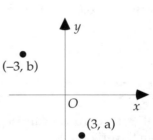

Note: Figure not drawn to scale

10. In the figure to the right, the grid consists of unit squares. What is the area of the polygon?

    (A) 7
    (B) 9
    (C) 10
    (D) 12
    (E) 15

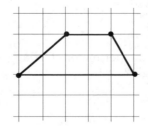

11. In the figure to the right, which of the following points is three times as far from *P* as from *Q*?

   (A)   (0, 3)
   (B)   (1, 1)
   (C)   (4, 5)
   (D)   (2, 3)
   (E)   (4, 1)

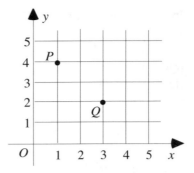

12. In the figure to the right, what is the area of quadrilateral *ABCO* ?

   (A)   3
   (B)   5
   (C)   6.5
   (D)   8
   (E)   13

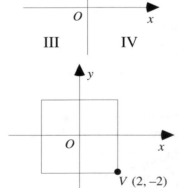

13. In the figure to the right, which quadrants contain points (x, y) such that $xy = -2$?

   (A)   I only
   (B)   II only
   (C)   III and IV only
   (D)   II and IV only
   (E)   II, III, and IV

14. If the square in the figure to the right is rotated clockwise about the origin until vertex *V* is on the negative *y*-axis, then the new *y*-coordinate of *V* is

   (A)   –2
   (B) $-2\sqrt{2}$
   (C)   –4
   (D) $-3\sqrt{2}$
   (E)   –8

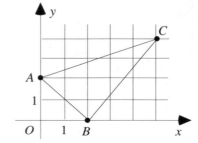

15. In the standard coordinate system, which of the following points is the greatest distance from the origin:

   (A)   (–4, –1)
   (B)   (–3, 3)
   (C)   (4, 0)
   (D)   (2, 3)
   (E)   (0, 4)

16. What is the perimeter of Triangle *ABC* in the figure to the right?

   (A) $5 + \sqrt{2} + \sqrt{29}$
   (B) $5 + 2\sqrt{2} + \sqrt{29}$
   (C) $5 + 4\sqrt{2} + \sqrt{29}$
   (D) $3\sqrt{2} + \sqrt{34}$
   (E) $4\sqrt{2} + \sqrt{34}$

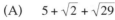

Elimination Strategies

 On hard problems, if you are asked to find the least (or greatest) number, then eliminate the least (or greatest) answer-choice.

This rule also applies to easy and medium problems. When people guess on these types of problems, they most often choose either the least or the greatest number. But if the least or the greatest number were the answer, most people would answer the problem correctly, and it therefore would not be a hard problem.

Example: What is the maximum number of points common to the intersection of a square and a triangle if no two sides coincide?

(A) 4   (B) 5   (C) 6   (D) 8   (E) 9

By the above rule, we eliminate answer-choice (E).

 On hard problems, eliminate the answer-choice "not enough information."

When people cannot solve a problem, they most often choose the answer-choice "not enough information." But if this were the answer, then it would not be a "hard" problem.

 On hard problems, eliminate answer-choices that <u>merely</u> repeat numbers from the problem.

Example: If the sum of x and 20 is 8 more than the difference of 10 and y, what is the value of $x + y$?

    (A)   –2
    (B)   8
    (C)   9
    (D)   28
    (E)   not enough information

By the above rule, we eliminate choice (B) since it merely repeats the number 8 from the problem. By Strategy 2, we would also eliminate choice (E). **Caution:** If choice (B) contained more than the number 8, say, $8 + \sqrt{2}$, then it would not be eliminated by the above rule.

On hard problems, eliminate answer-choices that can be derived from elementary operations.

Example: In the figure to the right, what is the perimeter of parallelogram ABCD?

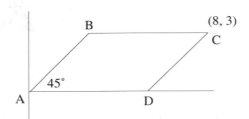

(A)   12
(B) $10 + 6\sqrt{2}$
(C) $20 + \sqrt{2}$
(D)   24
(E)   not enough information

Using the above rule, we eliminate choice (D) since $24 = 8 \cdot 3$. Further, using Strategy 2, eliminate choice (E). Note, 12 was offered as an answer-choice because some people will interpret the drawing as a rectangle tilted halfway on its side and therefore expect it to have one-half its original area.

After you have eliminated as many answer-choices as you can, choose from the more complicated or more unusual answer-choices remaining.

Example: Suppose you were offered the following answer-choices:

(A) $4 + \sqrt{3}$ (B) $4 + 2\sqrt{3}$ (C) 8   (D) 10   (E) 12

Then you would choose either (A) or (B).

We have been discussing hard problems but have not mentioned how to identify a hard problem. Most of the time, we have an intuitive feel for whether a problem is hard or easy. But on tricky problems (problems that appear easy but are actually hard) our intuition can fail us.

On the test, your first question will be of medium difficulty. If you answer it correctly, the next question will be a little harder. If you again answer it correctly, the next question will be harder still, and so on. If your math skills are strong and you are not making any mistakes, you should reach the medium-hard or hard problems by about the fifth problem. Although this is not very precise, it can be quite helpful. Once you have passed the fifth question, you should be alert to subtleties in any seemingly simple problems.

Problem Set I: Solutions begin on page 201.

1.   What is the maximum number of 3x3 squares that can be formed from the squares in the 6x6 checker board to the right?

(A)   4
(B)   6
(C)   12
(D)   16
(E)   24

2. Let P stand for the product of the first 5 positive integers. What is the greatest possible value of m if $\dfrac{P}{10^m}$ is an integer?

    (A) 1   (B) 2   (C) 3   (D) 5   (E) 10

3. After being marked down 20 percent, a calculator sells for $10. The original selling price was

    (A) $20   (B) $12.5   (C) $12   (D) $9   (E) $7

4. The distance between cities A and B is 120 miles. A car travels from A to B at 60 miles per hour and returns from B to A along the same route at 40 miles per hour. What is the average speed for the round trip?

    (A) 48   (B) 50   (C) 52   (D) 56   (E) 58

5. If **w** is 10 percent less than **x,** and **y** is 30 percent less than **z,** then **wy** is what percent less than **xz**?

    (A) 10%   (B) 20%   (C) 37%   (D) 40%   (E) 100%

6. In the game of chess, the Knight can make any of the moves displayed in the diagram to the right. If a Knight is the only piece on the board, what is the greatest number of spaces from which not all 8 moves are possible?

    (A)   8
    (B)   24
    (C)   38
    (D)   48
    (E)   56

    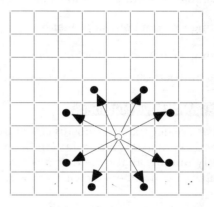

7. How many different ways can 3 cubes be painted if each cube is painted one color and only the 3 colors red, blue, and green are available? (Order is not considered, for example, green, green, blue is considered the same as green, blue, green.)

    (A) 2   (B) 3   (C) 9   (D) 10   (E) 27

8. What is the greatest prime factor of $\left(2^4\right)^2 - 1$?

    (A) 3   (B) 5   (C) 11   (D) 17   (E) 19

9. Suppose five circles, each 4 inches in diameter, are cut from a rectangular strip of paper 12 inches long. If the least amount of paper is to be wasted, what is the width of the paper strip?

    (A) 5   (B) $4 + 2\sqrt{3}$ (C) 8 ·   (D) $4\left(1 + \sqrt{3}\right)$ (E) not enough information

10. Let C and K be constants. If $x^2 + Kx + 5$ factors into $(x + 1)(x + C)$, the value of K is

    (A) 0   (B) 5   (C) 6   (D) 8   (E) not enough information

Inequalities

Inequalities are manipulated algebraically the same way as equations with one exception:

 Multiplying or dividing both sides of an inequality by a negative number reverses the inequality. That is, if $x > y$ and $c < 0$, then $cx < cy$.

Example: For which values of x is $4x + 3 > 6x - 8$?

As with equations, our goal is to isolate x on one side:

Subtracting $6x$ from both sides yields $\qquad\qquad\qquad\qquad\qquad$ $-2x + 3 > -8$

Subtracting 3 from both sides yields $\qquad\qquad\qquad\qquad\qquad$ $-2x > -11$

Dividing both sides by –2 and reversing the inequality yields $\quad$ $x < 11/2$

Positive & Negative Numbers

A number greater than 0 is positive. On the number line, positive numbers are to the right of 0. A number less than 0 is negative. On the number line, negative numbers are to the left of 0. Zero is the only number that is neither positive nor negative; it divides the two sets of numbers. On the number line, numbers increase to the right and decrease to the left.

The expression $x > y$ means that x is greater than y. In other words, x is to the right of y on the number line:

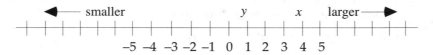

We usually have no trouble determining which of two numbers is larger when both are positive or one is positive and the other negative (e.g., $5 > 2$ and $3.1 > -2$). However, we sometimes hesitate when both numbers are negative (e.g., $-2 > -4.5$). When in doubt, think of the number line: if one number is to the right of the number, then it is larger. As the number line below illustrates, –2 is to the right of –4.5. Hence, –2 is larger than –4.5.

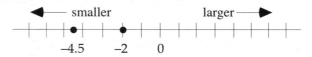

74

Miscellaneous Properties of Positive and Negative Numbers

1. The product (quotient) of positive numbers is positive.

2. The product (quotient) of a positive number and a negative number is negative.

3. The product (quotient) of an even number of negative numbers is positive.

4. The product (quotient) of an odd number of negative numbers is negative.

5. The sum of negative numbers is negative.

6. A number raised to an even exponent is greater than or equal to zero.

Example: If $xy^2z < 0$, then which one of the following statements must also be true?

    I. $xz < 0$

   II. $z < 0$

  III. $xyz < 0$

  (A) None   (B) I only   (C) III only   (D) I and II   (E) II and III

Since a number raised to an even exponent is greater than or equal to zero, we know that y^2 is positive (it cannot be zero because the product xy^2z would then be zero). Hence, we can divide both sides of the inequality $xy^2z < 0$ by y^2:

$$\frac{xy^2z}{y^2} < \frac{0}{y^2}$$

Simplifying yields $\qquad\qquad\qquad\qquad xz < 0$

Therefore, I is true, which eliminates (A), (C), and (E). Now, the following illustrates that $z < 0$ is not necessarily true:

$$-1 \cdot 2^2 \cdot 3 = -12 < 0$$

This eliminates (D). Hence, the answer is (B).

Absolute Value

The absolute value of a number is its distance on the number line from 0. Since distance is a positive number, absolute value of a number is positive. Two vertical bars denote the absolute value of a number: $|x|$. For example, $|3| = 3$ and $|-3| = 3$. This can be illustrated on the number line:

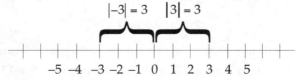

Students rarely struggle with the absolute value of numbers: if the number is negative, simply make it positive; and if it is already positive, leave it as is. For example, since –2.4 is negative, $|-24| = 2.4$ and since 5.01 is positive $|5.01| = 5.01$.

Further, students rarely struggle with the absolute value of positive variables: if the variable is positive, simply drop the absolute value symbol. For example, if $x > 0$, then $|x| = x$.

However, negative variables can cause students much consternation. If x is negative, then $|x| = -x$. This often confuses students because the absolute value is positive but the $-x$ appears to be negative. It is actually positive—it is the negative of a negative number, which is positive. To see this more clearly let $x = -k$, where k is a <u>positive</u> number. Then x is a negative number. So

$|x| = -x = -(-k) = k$.   Since k is positive so is $-x$.   Another way to view this is $|x| = -x = (-1) \cdot x = (-1)(\text{a negative number}) = \text{a positive number}$.

Example: If $x = \pm|x|$, then which one of the following statements could be true?

    I. $x = 0$

    II. $x < 0$

    III. $x > 0$

    (A) None   (B) I only   (C) III only   (D) I and II   (E) II and III

Statement I could be true because $\pm|0| = -(+0) = -(0) = 0$.   Statement II could be true because the right side of the equation is always negative $[\pm|x| = -(\text{a positive number}) = \text{a negative number}]$. Now, if one side of an equation is always negative, then the other side must always be negative, otherwise the opposite sides of the equation would not be equal. Since Statement III is the opposite of Statement II, it must be false. But let's show this explicitly: Suppose x were positive. Then $|x| = x$, and the equation $x = \pm|x|$ becomes $x = -x$. Dividing both sides of this equation by x yields $1 = -1$. This is contradiction. Hence, x cannot be positive. The answer is (D).

Higher Order Inequalities

These inequalities have variables whose exponents are greater than 1. For example, $x^2 + 4 < 2$ and $x^3 - 9 > 0$. The number line is often helpful in solving these types of inequalities.

Example: For which values of x is $x^2 > -6x - 5$?

First, replace the inequality symbol with an equal symbol: $x^2 = -6x - 5$

Adding $6x$ and 5 to both sides yields $x^2 + 6x + 5 = 0$

Factoring yields (see General Trinomials in the chapter Factoring) $(x + 5)(x + 1) = 0$

Setting each factor to 0 yields $x + 5 = 0$ and $x + 1 = 0$

Or $x = -5$ and $x = -1$

Now, the only numbers at which the expression can change sign are –5 and –1. So –5 and –1 divide the number line into three intervals. Let's set up a number line and choose test points in each interval:

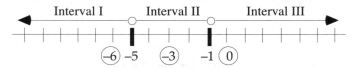

When $x = -6$, $x^2 > -6x - 5$ becomes $36 > 31$. This is true. Hence, all numbers in Interval I satisfy the inequality. That is, $x < -5$. When $x = -3$, $x^2 > -6x - 5$ becomes $9 > 13$. This is false. Hence, no numbers in Interval II satisfy the inequality. When $x = 0$, $x^2 > -6x - 5$ becomes $0 > -5$. This is true. Hence, all numbers in Interval III satisfy the inequality. That is, $x > -1$. The graph of the solution follows:

Note, if the original inequality had included the greater-than-or-equal symbol, $\geq$, the solution set would have included both –5 and –1. On the graph, this would have been indicated by filling in the circles above –5 and –1. The open circles indicate that –5 and –1 are not part of the solution.

Summary of steps for solving higher order inequalities:

1. Replace the inequality symbol with an equal symbol.
2. Move all terms to one side of the equation (usually the left side).
3. Factor the equation.
4. Set the factors equal to 0 to find zeros.
5. Choose test points on either side of the zeros.
6. If a test point satisfies the original inequality, then all numbers in that interval satisfy the inequality. Similarly, if a test point does not satisfy the inequality, then no numbers in that interval satisfy the inequality.

Transitive Property

$$\boxed{\text{If } x < y \text{ and } y < z, \text{ then } x < z}$$

Example: If $\dfrac{1}{Q} > 1$, which of the following must be true?

(A) $1 < Q^2$ (B) $\dfrac{1}{Q^2} > 2$ (C) $1 > Q^2$ (D) $\dfrac{1}{Q^2} < 1$ (E) $Q < Q^2$

Since $\dfrac{1}{Q} > 1$ and $1 > 0$, we know from the transitive property that $\dfrac{1}{Q}$ is positive. Hence, Q is positive. Therefore, we can multiply both sides of $\dfrac{1}{Q} > 1$ by Q without reversing the inequality:

$$Q \cdot \dfrac{1}{Q} > 1 \cdot Q$$

Reducing yields $1 > Q$

Multiplying both sides again by Q yields $Q > Q^2$

Using the transitive property to combine the last two inequalities yields $1 > Q^2$

The answer is (C).

Like Inequalities Can Be Added

$$\boxed{\text{If } x < y \text{ and } w < z, \text{ then } x + w < y + z}$$

Example: If $2 < x < 5$ and $3 < y < 5$, which of the following best describes $x - y$?
  (A) $-3 < x - y < 2$
  (B) $-3 < x - y < 5$
  (C) $0 < x - y < 2$
  (D) $3 < x - y < 5$
  (E) $2 < x - y < 5$

Multiplying both sides of $3 < y < 5$ by -1 yields $-3 > -y > -5$. Now, we usually write the smaller number on the left side of the inequality. So $-3 > -y > -5$ becomes $-5 < -y < -3$. Add this inequality to the like inequality $2 < x < 5$:

$$
\begin{array}{r}
2 < x < 5 \\
(+) \quad -5 < -y < -3 \\
\hline
-3 < x - y < 2
\end{array}
$$

The answer is (A).

Problem Set J: Solutions begin on page 207.

1. If $1 < x < y$, which of the following must be true?

    (A) $-x^2 < -y^2$ (B) $\dfrac{x}{y} < \dfrac{y}{x}$ (C) $\dfrac{y}{x} < \dfrac{x}{y}$ (D) $\dfrac{-x}{y} < \dfrac{-y}{x}$ (E) $x^2 > y^2$

2. If $-3 < x < -1$ and $3 < y < 7$, which of the following best describes $\dfrac{x-y}{2}$?

    (A) $-5 < \dfrac{x-y}{2} < -2$

    (B) $-3 < \dfrac{x-y}{2} < -1$

    (C) $-2 < \dfrac{x-y}{2} < 0$

    (D) $2 < \dfrac{x-y}{2} < 5$

    (E) $3 < \dfrac{x-y}{2} < 7$

3. If x is an integer and $y = -2x - 8$, what is the least value of x for which y is less than 9?
    (A) -9 (B) -8 (C) -7 (D) -6 (E) -5

4. Which one of the following could be the graph of $3 - 6x \le \dfrac{4x + 2}{-2}$?

    (A)

    (B)

    (C)

    (D)

    (E)

5. If line segment AD has midpoint M_1 and line segment M_1D has midpoint M_2, what is the value of $\dfrac{M_1D}{AM_2}$?
    (A) $1/2$ (B) $2/3$ (C) $3/4$ (D) $4/5$ (E) $5/6$

6. If $x < y < -1$, which of the following must be true?

    (A) $\dfrac{x}{y} > xy$ (B) $\dfrac{y}{x} > x + y$ (C) $\dfrac{y}{x} > xy$ (D) $\dfrac{y}{x} < x + y$ (E) $\dfrac{y}{x} > \dfrac{x}{y}$

7. Which of the following represents all solutions of the inequality $x^2 < 2x$?
    (A) $-1 < x < 1$ (B) $0 < x < 2$ (C) $1 < x < 3$ (D) $2 < x < 4$ (E) $4 < x < 6$

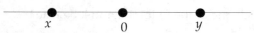

8. Given the positions of numbers x and y on the number line above, which of the following must be true?

   I. $xy > 0$

   II. $\dfrac{x}{y} < 0$

   III. $x - y > 0$

   (A) I only   (B) II only   (C) III only   (D) I and II only   (E) I, II, and III

9. If $\begin{array}{l} x^4 y < 0 \\ xy^4 > 0 \end{array}$, which of the following must be true?

   (A) $x > y$ (B) $y > x$ (C) $x = y$ (D) $x < 0$ (E) $y > 0$

10. If n is an integer, what is the least value of n such that $\dfrac{1}{3^n} < 0.01$?

    (A) 2   (B) 3   (C) 4   (D) 5   (E) 6

11. If the average of 10, 14, and n is greater than or equal to 8 and less than or equal to 12, what is the least possible value of n ?

    (A) –12   (B) –6   (C) 0   (D) 6   (E) 12

12. If $\begin{array}{l} 3x + y < 4 \\ x > 3 \end{array}$, which of the following must be true?

    (A) $y < -5$ (B) $y < -10$ (C) $x = y$ (D) $x < 3$ (E) $y > 0$

$$2 - 3x \text{ ? } 5$$

13. Of the following symbols, which one can be substituted for the question mark in the above expression to make a true statement for all values of x such that $-1 < x \le 2$?

    (A) $=$ (B) $<$ (C) $\ge$ (D) $>$ (E) $\le$

14. Let x, y, z be three different positive integers each less than 20. What is the smallest possible value of expression $\dfrac{x - y}{-z}$?

    (A) –18   (B) –17   (C) –14   (D) –11   (E) –9

15. If $x > 0$ and $|x| = \dfrac{1}{x}$, then $x =$

    (A) –1   (B) 0   (C) 1   (D) 2   (E) 3

16. Four letters—a, b, c, and d—represent one number each from one through four. No two letters represent the same number. It is known that $c > a$ and $a > d$. If $b = 2$, then $a =$

    (A)   1
    (B)   2
    (C)   3
    (D)   4
    (E)   Not enough information to decide.

17.   If $r > t$ and $r < 1$ and $rt = 1$, then which one of the following must be true?

   (A) $r > 0$ and $t < -1$
   (B) $r > -1$ and $t < -1$
   (C) $r < -1$ and $t > -1$
   (D) $r < 1$ and $t > 1$
   (E) $r > 1$ and $t < 0$

18.   If $x > y > 0$ and $p > q > 0$, then which one of the following expressions must be greater than 1?

   (A) $\dfrac{x + p}{y + q}$

   (B) $\dfrac{x + q}{y + p}$

   (C) $\dfrac{x}{p}$

   (D) $\dfrac{xq}{yp}$

   (E) $\dfrac{yq}{xp}$

19.   If $2x + y > m$ and $2y + x < n$, then $x - y$ must be greater than

   (A) $m + n$
   (B) $m - n$
   (C) mn
   (D) $2m + n$
   (E) $n - m$

20.   If $p > 2$, then which one of the following inequalities must be false?

   (A) $2p > 7$
   (B) $3p < 7$
   (C) $p < 3$
   (D) $p > 4$
   (E) $3p < 6$

Fractions & Decimals

Fractions

A fraction consists of two parts: a numerator and a denominator.

$$\frac{numerator}{denominator}$$

If the numerator is smaller than the denominator, the fraction is called *proper* and is less than one. For example: $\frac{1}{2}$, $\frac{4}{5}$, and $\frac{3}{\pi}$ are all proper fractions and therefore less than 1.

If the numerator is larger than the denominator, the fraction is called *improper* and is greater than 1. For example: $\frac{3}{2}$, $\frac{5}{4}$, and $\frac{\pi}{3}$ are all improper fractions and therefore greater than 1.

An improper fraction can be converted into a *mixed fraction* by dividing its denominator into its numerator. For example, since 2 divides into 7 three times with a remainder of 1, we get

$$\frac{7}{2} = 3\frac{1}{2}$$

To convert a mixed fraction into an improper fraction, multiply the denominator and the integer and then add the numerator. Then, write the result over the denominator. For example, $5\frac{2}{3} = \frac{3 \cdot 5 + 2}{3} = \frac{17}{3}$.

In a negative fraction, the negative symbol can be written on the top, in the middle, or on the bottom; however, when a negative symbol appears on the bottom, it is usually moved to the top or the middle: $\frac{5}{-3} = \frac{-5}{3} = -\frac{5}{3}$. If both terms in the denominator of a fraction are negative, the negative symbol is often factored out and moved to the top or middle of the fraction: $\frac{1}{-x-2} = \frac{1}{-(x+2)} = -\frac{1}{x+2}$ or $\frac{-1}{x+2}$.

 To compare two fractions, cross-multiply. The larger number will be on the same side as the larger fraction.

Example: Which of the following fractions is larger?

$$\frac{9}{10} \qquad\qquad \frac{10}{11}$$

Cross-multiplying gives $9 \cdot 11$ versus $10 \cdot 10$, which reduces to 99 versus 100. Now, 100 is greater than 99. Hence, $\frac{10}{11}$ is greater than $\frac{9}{10}$.

 Always reduce a fraction to its lowest terms.

Example: If $x \neq -1$, then $\dfrac{2x^2 + 4x + 2}{(x+1)^2} =$

      (A) 0   (B) 1   (C) 2   (D) 4   (E) 6

Factor out the 2 in the expression: $\dfrac{2\left(x^2 + 2x + 1\right)}{(x+1)^2}$

Factor the quadratic expressions: $\dfrac{2(x+1)(x+1)}{(x+1)(x+1)}$

Finally, canceling the $(x + 1)$'s gives 2. The answer is (C).

- **To solve a fractional equation, multiply both sides by the LCD (lowest common denominator) to clear fractions.**

Example: If $\dfrac{x+3}{x-3} = y$, what is the value of x in terms of y?

      (A) $3 - y$ (B) $\dfrac{3}{y}$ (C) $\sqrt{y+12}$ (D) $\dfrac{-3y-3}{1-y}$ (E) $3y^2$

First, multiply both sides of the equation by $x -3$: $(x-3)\dfrac{x+3}{x-3} = (x-3)y$

Cancel the $(x - 3)$'s on the left side of the equation: $x + 3 = (x-3)y$

Distribute the y: $x + 3 = xy - 3y$

Subtract xy and 3 from both sides: $x - xy = -3y - 3$

Factor out the x on the left side of the equation: $x(1 - y) = -3y - 3$

Finally, divide both sides of the equation by $1 - y$: $x = \dfrac{-3y-3}{1-y}$

Hence, the answer is (D).

- **Complex Fractions: When dividing a fraction by a whole number (or vice versa), you must keep track of the main division bar:**

$$\frac{a}{\dfrac{b}{c}} = a \cdot \frac{c}{b} = \frac{ac}{b}. \text{ But } \frac{\dfrac{a}{b}}{c} = \frac{a}{b} \cdot \frac{1}{c} = \frac{a}{bc}.$$

Example: $\dfrac{1 - \dfrac{1}{2}}{3} =$

      (A) 6   (B) 3   (C) $\dfrac{1}{3}$ (D) $\dfrac{1}{6}$ (E) $\dfrac{1}{8}$

Solution: $\dfrac{1 - \dfrac{1}{2}}{3} = \dfrac{\dfrac{2}{2} - \dfrac{1}{2}}{3} = \dfrac{\dfrac{2-1}{2}}{3} = \dfrac{\dfrac{1}{2}}{3} = \dfrac{1}{2} \cdot \dfrac{1}{3} = \dfrac{1}{6}$. The answer is (D).

Example: If $z \neq 0$ and $yz \neq 1$, then $\dfrac{1}{y - \dfrac{1}{z}} =$

      (A) $\dfrac{yz}{zy-1}$ (B) $\dfrac{y-z}{z}$ (C) $\dfrac{yz-z}{z-1}$ (D) $\dfrac{z}{zy-1}$ (E) $\dfrac{y-z}{zy-1}$

Solution: $\dfrac{1}{y - \dfrac{1}{z}} = \dfrac{1}{\dfrac{z}{z}y - \dfrac{1}{z}} = \dfrac{1}{\dfrac{zy-1}{z}} = 1 \cdot \dfrac{z}{zy-1} = \dfrac{z}{zy-1}$. The answer is (D).

- Multiplying fractions is routine: merely multiply the numerators and multiply the denominators: $\dfrac{a}{b} \cdot \dfrac{c}{d} = \dfrac{ac}{bd}$. For example, $\dfrac{1}{2} \cdot \dfrac{3}{4} = \dfrac{1 \cdot 3}{2 \cdot 4} = \dfrac{3}{8}$.

- Two fractions can be added quickly by cross-multiplying: $\dfrac{a}{b} \pm \dfrac{c}{d} = \dfrac{ad \pm bc}{bd}$

Example: $\dfrac{1}{2} - \dfrac{3}{4} =$

(A) $-\dfrac{5}{4}$ (B) $-\dfrac{2}{3}$ (C) $-\dfrac{1}{4}$ (D) $\dfrac{1}{2}$ (E) $\dfrac{2}{3}$

Cross multiplying the expression $\dfrac{1}{2} - \dfrac{3}{4}$ yields $\dfrac{1 \cdot 4 - 2 \cdot 3}{2 \cdot 4} = \dfrac{4 - 6}{8} = \dfrac{-2}{8} = -\dfrac{1}{4}$. Hence, the answer is (C).

Example: Which of the following equals the average of x and $\dfrac{1}{x}$?

(A) $\dfrac{x + 2}{x}$ (B) $\dfrac{x^2 + 1}{2x}$ (C) $\dfrac{x + 1}{x^2}$ (D) $\dfrac{2x^2 + 1}{x}$ (E) $\dfrac{x + 1}{x}$

The average of x and $\dfrac{1}{x}$ is $\dfrac{x + \dfrac{1}{x}}{2} = \dfrac{\dfrac{x^2 + 1}{x}}{2} = \dfrac{x^2 + 1}{x} \cdot \dfrac{1}{2} = \dfrac{x^2 + 1}{2x}$. Hence, the answer is (B).

- **To add three or more fractions with different denominators, you need to form a common denominator of all the fractions.**

For example, to add the fractions in the expression $\dfrac{1}{3} + \dfrac{1}{4} + \dfrac{1}{18}$, we have to change the denominator of each fraction into the common denominator 36 (note, 36 is a common denominator because 3, 4, and 18 all divide into it evenly). This is done by multiply the top and bottom of each fraction by an appropriate number (this does not change the value of the expression because any number divided by itself equals 1):

$$\dfrac{1}{3}\left(\dfrac{12}{12}\right) + \dfrac{1}{4}\left(\dfrac{9}{9}\right) + \dfrac{1}{18}\left(\dfrac{2}{2}\right) = \dfrac{12}{36} + \dfrac{9}{36} + \dfrac{2}{36} = \dfrac{12 + 9 + 2}{36} = \dfrac{23}{36}$$

You may remember from algebra that to find a common denominator of a set of fractions, you prime factor the denominators and then select each factor the greatest number of times it occurs in any of the factorizations. That is too cumbersome, however. A better way is to simply add the largest denominator to itself until all the other denominators divide into it evenly. In the above example, we just add 18 to itself to get the common denominator 36.

- **To find a common denominator of a set of fractions, simply add the largest denominator to itself until all the other denominators divide into it evenly.**

- **Fractions often behave in unusual ways: Squaring a fraction makes it smaller, and taking the square root of a fraction makes it larger. (Caution:** This is true only for proper fractions, that is, fractions between 0 and 1.)

Example: $\left(\dfrac{1}{3}\right)^2 = \dfrac{1}{9}$ and $\dfrac{1}{9}$ is less than $\dfrac{1}{3}$. Also $\sqrt{\dfrac{1}{4}} = \dfrac{1}{2}$ and $\dfrac{1}{2}$ is greater than $\dfrac{1}{4}$.

- **You can cancel only over multiplication, not over addition or subtraction.**

For example, the c's in the expression $\dfrac{c+x}{c}$ cannot be canceled. However, the c's in the

expression $\dfrac{cx+c}{c}$ can be canceled as follows: $\dfrac{cx+c}{c} = \dfrac{\cancel{c}(x+1)}{\cancel{c}} = x+1$.

Decimals

If a fraction's denominator is a power of 10, it can be written in a special form called a *decimal fraction*. Some common decimals are $\dfrac{1}{10} = .1$, $\dfrac{2}{100} = .02$, $\dfrac{3}{1000} = .003$. Notice that the number of decimal places corresponds to the number of zeros in the denominator of the fraction. Also note that the value of the decimal place decreases to the right of the decimal point:

$$\underset{\text{tenths}}{.1}\ \ \underset{\text{hundredths}}{2}\ \ \underset{\text{thousandths}}{3}\ \ \underset{\text{ten-thousandths}}{4}$$

This decimal can be written in expanded form as follows:

$$.1234 = \frac{1}{10} + \frac{2}{100} + \frac{3}{1000} + \frac{4}{10000}$$

Sometimes a zero is placed before the decimal point to prevent misreading the decimal as a whole number. The zero has no affect on the value of the decimal. For example, $.2 = 0.2$.

Fractions can be converted to decimals by dividing the denominator into the numerator. For example, to convert 5/8 to a decimal, divide 8 into 5 (note, a decimal point and as many zeros as necessary are added after the 5):

$$
\begin{array}{r}
.625 \\
8\overline{)5.000} \\
\underline{48} \\
20 \\
\underline{16} \\
40 \\
\underline{40} \\
0
\end{array}
$$

The procedures for adding, subtracting, multiplying, and dividing decimals are the same as for whole numbers, except for a few small adjustments.

- **Adding and Subtracting Decimals:** To add or subtract decimals, merely align the decimal points and then add or subtract as you would with whole numbers.

$$
\begin{array}{r}
1.369 \\
+\ \ 9.7 \\
\hline
11.069
\end{array}
\qquad
\begin{array}{r}
12.45 \\
-\ \ 6.367 \\
\hline
6.083
\end{array}
$$

- **Multiplying Decimals:** Multiply decimals as you would with whole numbers. The answer will have as many decimal places as the sum of the number of decimal places in the numbers being multiplied.

$$
\begin{array}{r}
1.23 \\
\times\ \ 2.4 \\
\hline
492 \\
246 \\
\hline
2.952
\end{array}
\qquad
\begin{array}{l}
\text{2 decimal places} \\[4pt]
\text{1 decimal place} \\[20pt]
\text{3 decimal places}
\end{array}
$$

• **Dividing Decimals:** Before dividing decimals, move the decimal point of the divisor all the way to the right and move the decimal point of the dividend the same number of spaces to the right (adding zeros if necessary). Then divide as you would with whole numbers.

$$.24\overline{).6} = \quad 24\overline{)60.0}$$

$$\begin{array}{r} 2.5 \\ \hline 48 \\ \hline 120 \\ 120 \\ \hline 0 \end{array}$$

Example: $\frac{1}{5}$ of .1 percent equals:

    (A) 2   (B) .2   (C) .02   (D) .002   (E) .0002

Recall that percent means to divide by 100. So .1 percent equals $\frac{.1}{100} = .001$. To convert $\frac{1}{5}$ to a decimal, divide 5 into 1:

$$\begin{array}{r} .2 \\ 5\overline{)1.0} \\ \underline{10} \\ 0 \end{array}$$

In percent problems, "of" means multiplication. So multiplying .2 and .001 yields

$$\begin{array}{r} .001 \\ \times \quad .2 \\ \hline .0002 \end{array}$$

Hence, the answer is (E). Note, you may be surprised to learn that the GMAT would consider this to be a hard problem.

Example: The decimal .1 is how many times greater than the decimal $(.001)^3$?

    (A) 10   (B) 10^2 (C) 10^5 (D) 10^8 (E) 10^{10}

Converting .001 to a fraction gives $\frac{1}{1000}$. This fraction, in turn, can be written as $\frac{1}{10^3}$, or 10^{-3}. Cubing this expression yields $(.001)^3 = \left(10^{-3}\right)^3 = 10^{-9}$. Now, dividing the larger number, .1, by the smaller number, $(.001)^3$, yields

$$\frac{.1}{(.001)^3} = \frac{10^{-1}}{10^{-9}} = 10^{-1-(-9)} = 10^{-1+9} = 10^8$$

Hence, .1 is 10^8 times as large as $(.001)^3$. The answer is (D).

Example: Let $x = .99$, $y = \sqrt{.99}$, and $z = (.99)^2$. Then which of the following is true?

    (A) $x < z < y$ (B) $z < y < x$ (C) $z < x < y$ (D) $y < x < z$ (E) $y < z < x$

Converting .99 into a fraction gives $\frac{99}{100}$. Since $\frac{99}{100}$ is between 0 and 1, squaring it will make it smaller and taking its square root will make it larger. Hence, $(.99)^2 < .99 < \sqrt{.99}$. The answer is (C). Note, this property holds for all proper decimals (decimals between 0 and 1) just as it does for all proper fractions.

Problem Set K: Solutions begin on page 213.

1. Which one of the following fractions is greatest?

   (A) 5/6   (B) 4/5   (C) 1/2   (D) 2/3   (E) 3/4

2. If $x \neq \pm 3$, then $\dfrac{x^2 + 6x + 9}{x + 3} \cdot \dfrac{x^2 - 9}{x - 3} =$

   (A) $\dfrac{x+3}{x-3}$ (B) -1 (C) $(x+3)^2$ (D) $\left(\dfrac{x+3}{x-3}\right)^2$ (E) 1

3. $\dfrac{\dfrac{1}{4}}{\dfrac{4}{3} - 1} =$

   (A) $-1/3$ (B) $-1/4$ (C) $3/4$ (D) 3   (E) $9/2$

4. If $0 < x < 1$, which of the following must be true?

   I. $x^2 < x$ II. $x < \dfrac{1}{x^2}$ III. $\sqrt{x} < x$

   (A) I only   (B) II only   (C) III only   (D) I and II only   (E) I, II, and III

5. In the following pairs of numbers, which are reciprocals of each other?

   I. 1 and 1   II. $\dfrac{1}{11}$ and -11 III. $\sqrt{5}$ and $\dfrac{\sqrt{5}}{5}$

   (A) I only   (B) II only   (C) I and II only   (D) I and III only   (E) II and III only

6. $\dfrac{6^4 - 6^3}{5} =$

   (A) $\dfrac{1}{5}$ (B) 6^3 (C) $\dfrac{6}{5}$ (D) 6^4 (E) $\dfrac{6^3}{5}$

7. $\dfrac{1}{1 - \dfrac{1}{1 - \dfrac{1}{2}}} =$

   (A) -2 (B) -1 (C) $3/2$ (D) 2   (E) 4

8. If $\left(x^2 - 4\right)\left(\dfrac{4}{x} - 5\right) = 0$, then $x =$

   (A) -4 (B) -1 (C) $-4/5$ (D) $4/5$ (E) 4

9. $\dfrac{1}{10^9} - \dfrac{1}{10^{10}} =$

   (A) $-\dfrac{1}{10}$ (B) $-\dfrac{1}{10^9}$ (C) $-\dfrac{1}{10^{19}}$ (D) $\dfrac{9}{10^{10}}$ (E) $\dfrac{9}{10}$

10. If $x \neq \pm 1$, then $\dfrac{\dfrac{2x^2 - 2}{x - 1}}{2(x + 1)} =$

(A) $x + 1$ (B) 1 (C) $x^2 - 1$ (D) $x - 1$ (E) 2

11. If $z \neq 0$ and $yz \neq 1$, then $x - \dfrac{1}{y - \dfrac{1}{z}} =$

(A) $\dfrac{xyz}{zy - 1}$ (B) $\dfrac{y - x - z}{z}$ (C) $\dfrac{xyz - x - z}{z - 1}$ (D) $\dfrac{xyz - x - z}{zy - 1}$ (E) $\dfrac{x - y - z}{zy - 1}$

12. If $\sqrt{\dfrac{\dfrac{1}{x}}{\dfrac{1}{y}}} = \dfrac{1}{2}$, then which of the following statements must be true?

I. $\dfrac{x}{y} > \dfrac{y}{x}$ II. $\dfrac{x}{y} < \dfrac{y}{x}$ III. $\dfrac{x}{y} = \dfrac{y}{x}$

(A) I only   (B) II only   (C) I and II only   (D) I and III only   (E) II and III only

13. For all $p \neq \dfrac{1}{4}$ define p^* by the equation $p^* = \dfrac{\dfrac{p}{2}}{4p - 1}$. If $q = 1^*$, then $q^* =$

(A) $-5/7$ (B) $-1/3$ (C) $-1/4$ (D) $2/3$ (E) $3/4$

14. If $\dfrac{1}{x} + \dfrac{1}{y} \neq 0$, then which one of the following is equal to the negative reciprocal of $\dfrac{1}{x} + \dfrac{1}{y}$?

(A) $\dfrac{xy}{x + y}$ (B) $-\dfrac{x + y}{xy}$ (C) $-(x + y)$ (D) $\dfrac{x - y}{xy}$ (E) $\dfrac{-xy}{x + y}$

$$\dfrac{v + w}{x / yz}$$

15. To halve the value of the expression above by doubling exactly one of the variables, one must double which of the following variables?

(A) v (B) w (C) x (D) y (E) z

16. The picture above represents 4,250 apples. How many apples does each 🍎 stand for?

(A) 400   (B) 450   (C) 500   (D) 625   (E) 710

Equations

When simplifying algebraic expressions, we perform operations within parentheses first and then exponents and then multiplication and then division and then addition and lastly subtraction. This can be remembered by the mnemonic:

PEMDAS
Please Excuse My Dear Aunt Sally

When solving equations, however, we apply the mnemonic in reverse order: **SADMEP**. This is often expressed as follows: inverse operations in inverse order. The goal in solving an equation is to isolate the variable on one side of the equal sign (usually the left side). This is done by identifying the main operation—addition, multiplication, etc.—and then performing the opposite operation.

Example: Solve the following equation for x: $2x + y = 5$

Solution: The main operation is addition (remember addition now comes before multiplication, SADMEP), so subtracting y from both sides yields

$$2x + y - y = 5 - y$$

Simplifying yields $\qquad 2x = 5 - y$

The only operation remaining on the left side is multiplication. Undoing the multiplication by dividing both sides by 2 yields

$$\frac{2x}{2} = \frac{5-y}{2}$$

Canceling the 2 on the left side yields $\qquad x = \dfrac{5-y}{2}$

Example: Solve the following equation for x: $3x - 4 = 2(x - 5)$

Solution: Here x appears on both sides of the equal sign, so let's move the x on the right side to the left side. But the x is trapped inside the parentheses. To release it, distribute the 2:

$$3x - 4 = 2x - 10$$

Now, subtracting $2x$ from both sides yields[*]

$$x - 4 = -10$$

Finally, adding 4 to both sides yields

$$x = -6$$

---

[*] Note, students often mistakenly add $2x$ to both sides of this equation because of the minus symbol between $2x$ and 10. But $2x$ is positive, so we subtract it. This can be seen more clearly by rewriting the right side of the equation as $-10 + 2x$.

We often manipulate equations without thinking about what the equations actually say. The GMAT likes to test this oversight. Equations are packed with information. Take for example the simple equation $3x + 2 = 5$. Since 5 is positive, the expression $3x + 2$ must be positive as well. An equation means that the terms on either side of the equal sign are equal in every way. Hence, any property one side of an equation has the other side will have as well. Following are some immediate deductions that can be made from simple equations.

Equation	Deduction
$y - x = 1$	$y > x$
$y^2 = x^2$	$y = \pm x$, or $\lvert y \rvert = \lvert x \rvert$. That is, x and y can differ only in sign.
$y^3 = x^3$	$y = x$
$y = x^2$	$y \geq 0$
$\dfrac{y}{x^2} = 1$	$y > 0$
$\dfrac{y}{x^3} = 2$	Both x and y are positive or both x and y are negative.
$x^2 + y^2 = 0$	$y = x = 0$
$3y = 4x$ and $x > 0$	$y > x$ and y is positive.
$3y = 4x$ and $x < 0$	$y < x$ and y is negative.
$y = \sqrt{x + 2}$	$y \geq 0$ and $x \geq -2$
$y = 2x$	y is even
$y = 2x + 1$	y is odd
$yx = 0$	$y = 0$ or $x = 0$, or both

 Note! In Algebra, you solve an equation for, say, y by isolating y on one side of the equality symbol. On the GMAT, however, you are often asked to solve for an entire term, say, $3 - y$ by isolating it on one side.

Example: If $a + 3a$ is 4 less than $b + 3b$, then $a - b =$
     (A) -4 (B) -1 (C) $1/5$ (D) $1/3$ (E) 2

Translating the sentence into an equation gives	$a + 3a = b + 3b - 4$
Combining like terms gives	$4a = 4b - 4$
Subtracting $4b$ from both sides gives	$4a - 4b = -4$
Finally, dividing by 4 gives	$a - b = -1$

Hence, the answer is (B).

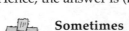 **Note!** Sometimes on the GMAT, a system of 3 equations will be written as one long "triple" equation. For example, the three equations $x = y$, $y = z$, $x = z$, can be written more compactly as $x = y = z$.

Example: If $w \neq 0$ and $w = 2x = \sqrt{2}y$, what is the value of $w - x$ in terms of y ?

     (A) $2y$ (B) $\dfrac{\sqrt{2}}{2}y$ (C) $\sqrt{2y}$ (D) $\dfrac{4}{\sqrt{2}}y$ (E) y

The equation $w = 2x = \sqrt{2}y$ stands for three equations: $w = 2x$, $2x = \sqrt{2}y$, and $w = \sqrt{2}y$. From the last equation, we get $w = \sqrt{2}y$, and from the second equation we get $x = \dfrac{\sqrt{2}}{2}y$. Hence,

$$w - x = \sqrt{2}y - \frac{\sqrt{2}}{2}y = \frac{2}{2}\sqrt{2}y - \frac{\sqrt{2}}{2}y = \frac{2\sqrt{2}y - \sqrt{2}y}{2} = \frac{\sqrt{2}y}{2}.$$ Hence, the answer is (B).

Note! Often on the GMAT, you can solve a system of two equations in two unknowns by merely adding or subtracting the equations—instead of solving for one of the variables and then substituting it into the other equation.

Example : If p and q are positive, $p^2 + q^2 = 16$, and $p^2 - q^2 = 8$, then $q =$

(A) 2   (B) 4   (C) 8   (D) $2\sqrt{2}$ (E) $2\sqrt{6}$

Subtract the second equation from the first:

$$p^2 + q^2 = 16$$
$$(-) \quad p^2 - q^2 = 8$$
$$2q^2 = 8$$

Dividing both sides of the equation by 2 gives $q^2 = 4$

Finally, taking the square root of both sides gives $q = \pm 2$

Hence, the answer is (A).

METHOD OF SUBSTITUTION (Four-Step Method)

Although on the GMAT you can usually solve a system of two equations in two unknowns by merely adding or subtracting the equations, you still need to know a standard method for solving these types of systems.

The four-step method will be illustrated with the following system:

$$2x + y = 10$$
$$5x - 2y = 7$$

1) *Solve one of the equations for one of the variables*:
    Solving the top equation for y yields $y = 10 - 2x$.

2) *Substitute the result from Step 1 into the other equation*:
    Substituting $y = 10 - 2x$ into the bottom equation yields $5x - 2(10 - 2x) = 7$.

3) *Solve the resulting equation*:

$$5x - 2(10 - 2x) = 7$$
$$5x - 20 + 4x = 7$$
$$9x - 20 = 7$$
$$9x = 27$$
$$x = 3$$

4) *Substitute the result from Step 3 into the equation derived in Step 1*:
    Substituting $x = 3$ into $y = 10 - 2x$ yields $y = 10 - 2(3) = 10 - 6 = 4$.

Hence, the solution of the system of equations is the ordered pair (3, 4).

Problem Set L: Solutions begin on page 218.

1. If $a > 0$ and $6a = 5b$, which of the following must be true?

    (A) $a = \dfrac{6}{5}b$ (B) $ab < 0$ (C) $a > b$ (D) $b = \dfrac{5}{6}a$ (E) $b > a$

2. If $p - q + r = 4$ and $p + q + r = 8$, then $p + r =$
    (A) 2   (B) 4   (C) 6   (D) 8   (E) 10

3. Suppose $x = y - 2 = \dfrac{y + 5}{2}$. Then x equals

    (A) $\dfrac{1}{3}$ (B) 1   (C) $\dfrac{7}{6}$ (D) 2   (E) 7

4. Let $p = 3^{q+1}$ and $q = 2r$. Then $\dfrac{p}{3^2} =$

    (A) 3^{2r-1} (B) 3^{2r} (C) 3   (D) r (E) 3^{2r+1}

5. k is a constant in the equation $\dfrac{u - v}{k} = 8$. If $u = 18$ when $v = 2$, then what is the value of u when $v = 4$?
    (A) –3   (B) 0   (C) 10   (D) 23/2   (E) 20

6. If $x = 3y = 4z$, which of the following must equal $6x$?

    I. $18y$ II. $3y + 20z$ III. $\dfrac{4y + 10z}{3}$

    (A) I only   (B) II only   (C) III only   (D) I and II only   (E) I and III only

7. Let $P = (x + y)k$. If $P = 10$ and $k = 3$, what is the average of x and y?
    (A) 0   (B) 1/2   (C) 5/3   (D) 10/3   (E) 7/2

8. Let $\dfrac{x}{y} + \dfrac{w}{z} = 2$. Then the value of $\dfrac{y}{x} + \dfrac{z}{w}$ is

    (A) $\dfrac{1}{2}$

    (B) $\dfrac{3}{4}$

    (C) 1
    (D) 5
    (E) It cannot be determined from the information given.

9. If 4 percent of $(p + q)$ is 8 and p is a positive integer, what is the greatest possible value of q?
    (A) 196   (B) 197   (C) 198   (D) 199   (E) 200

10. If $x^5 = 4$ and $x^4 = \dfrac{7}{y}$, then what is the value of x in terms of y?

    (A) $\dfrac{7}{4}y$ (B) $\dfrac{4}{7}y$ (C) $\dfrac{1}{7}y$ (D) $7y$ (E) $7 + \dfrac{5}{y}$

11. $2x + y = 3$

                                 $3y = 9 - 6x$

How many solutions does the above system of equations have?

(A)   None
(B)   One
(C)   Two
(D)   Four
(E)   An infinite number

12. If $\dfrac{p}{19}$ is 1 less than 3 times $\dfrac{q}{19}$, then p equals which of the following expressions?

(A) $3q + 19$ (B) $3q + 38$ (C) $19/2$ (D) $3q - 38$ (E) $3q - 19$

13. If n is a number such that $(-8)^{2n} = 2^{8+2n}$, then $n =$

(A) $1/2$ (B) 2   (C) $3/2$ (D) 4   (E) 5

14. If $s + S \neq 0$ and $\dfrac{1}{3} = \dfrac{1}{4}\dfrac{s - S}{s + S}$, then what is s in terms of S ?

(A) $s = S + 3$ (B) $s = 4S$ (C) $s = \dfrac{S}{12}$ (D) $s = -7S$ (E) $s = 4S - 6$

15. If $3^x = 81$, then $\left(3^{x+3}\right)\left(4^{x+1}\right) =$

(A) $5(7)^5$ (B) $9(7)^5$ (C) $2(12)^4$ (D) $9(12)^5$ (E) $2(12)^7$

16. If $x = y/2$ and $y = z/2$, then $\sqrt{x/z} =$

(A) 4   (B) 2   (C) 1   (D) $1/2$ (E) $1/4$

17. If $a = b/c$ and $b = a/c$, then $c =$

(A) b/a (B) a/b (C) -1 (D) a (E) $-b$

18. If $x + 3y = 5$ and $3x + y = 7$, then $x + y =$

(A) 1   (B) 2   (C) 3   (D) 4   (E) 5

19. If $7x - y = 23$ and $7y - x = 31$, then $x + y =$

(A) 4   (B) 6   (C) 7   (D) 8   (E) 9

20. If $x + y = 4a/5$, $y + z = 7a/5$ and $z + x = 9a/5$, then $x + y + z =$

(A) $7a/15$ (B) a (C) $2a$ (D) $3a$ (E) $4a$

Averages

Problems involving averages are very common on the GMAT. They can be classified into four major categories as follows.

 The average of N numbers is their sum divided by N, that is, $average = \dfrac{sum}{N}$.

Example 1: What is the average of x, $2x$, and 6?

(A) $x/2$

(B) $2x$

(C) $\dfrac{x+2}{6}$

(D) $x+2$

(E) $\dfrac{x+2}{3}$

By the definition of an average, we get $\dfrac{x+2x+6}{3} = \dfrac{3x+6}{3} = \dfrac{3(x+2)}{3} = x+2$. The answer is (D).

 Weighted average: The average between two sets of numbers is closer to the set with more numbers.

Example 2: If on a test three people answered 90% of the questions correctly and two people answered 80% correctly, then the average for the group is not 85% but rather $\dfrac{3 \cdot 90 + 2 \cdot 80}{5} = \dfrac{430}{5} = 86$. Here, 90 has a weight of 3—it occurs 3 times. Whereas 80 has a weight of 2—it occurs 2 times. So the average is closer to 90 than to 80 as we have just calculated.

 Using an average to find a number.

Sometimes you will be asked to find a number by using a given average. An example will illustrate.

Example 3: If the average of five numbers is –10, and the sum of three of the numbers is 16, then what is the average of the other two numbers?

(A) –33   (B) –1   (C) 5   (D) 20   (E) 25

Let the five numbers be a, b, c, d, e. Then their average is $\dfrac{a+b+c+d+e}{5} = -10$. Now three of the numbers have a sum of 16, say, $a+b+c = 16$. So substitute 16 for $a+b+c$ in the average above: $\dfrac{16+d+e}{5} = -10$. Solving this equation for $d+e$ gives $d+e = -66$. Finally, dividing by 2 (to form the average) gives $\dfrac{d+e}{2} = -33$. Hence, the answer is (A).

Note! $Average\ Speed = \dfrac{Total\ Distance}{Total\ Time}$

Although the formula for average speed is simple, few people solve these problems correctly because most fail to find both the <u>total distance</u> and the <u>total time</u>.

Example 4:   In traveling from city A to city B, John drove for 1 hour at 50 mph and for 3 hours at 60 mph. What was his average speed for the whole trip?

(A)   50
(B) $53\frac{1}{2}$
(C)   55
(D)   56
(E) $57\frac{1}{2}$

The total distance is $1 \cdot 50 + 3 \cdot 60 = 230$. And the total time is 4 hours. Hence,

$$Average\ Speed = \frac{Total\ Distance}{Total\ Time} = \frac{230}{4} = 57\frac{1}{2}$$

The answer is (E). Note, the answer is not the mere average of 50 and 60. Rather the average is closer to 60 because he traveled longer at 60 mph (3 hrs) than at 50 mph (1 hr).

Problem Set M: Solutions begin on page 225.

1.   If the average of p and $4p$ is 10, then $p =$

(A) 1   (B) 3   (C) 4   (D) 10   (E) 18

2.   The average of six consecutive integers in increasing order of size is $9\frac{1}{2}$. What is the average of the last three integers?

(A) 8   (B) $9\frac{1}{2}$ (C) 10   (D) 11   (E) 19

3.   If S denotes the sum and A the average of the consecutive positive integers 1 through n, then which of the following must be true?

I. $A = \dfrac{S}{n}$

II. $S = \dfrac{A}{n}$

III. $A - S = n$

(A) I only   (B) II only   (C) III only   (D) I and II only   (E) I, II, and III

4.   Cars X and Y leave City A at the same time and travel the same route to City B. Car X takes 30 minutes to complete the trip and car Y takes 20 minutes. Which of the following must be true?

I.   The average miles per hour at which car X traveled was greater than the average miles per hour at which car Y traveled.

II.   The distance between the cities is 30 miles.

III.   The average miles per hour at which car Y traveled was greater than the average miles per hour at which car X traveled.

(A) I only   (B) II only   (C) III only   (D) I and II only   (E) I and III only

5. If $p + q = r$, what is the average of p, q, and r ?

    (A) $\dfrac{r}{3}$ (B) $\dfrac{p+q}{3}$ (C) $\dfrac{2r}{3}$ (D) $\dfrac{r}{2}$ (E) $\dfrac{p+q}{2}$

6. Suppose a train travels x miles in y hours and 15 minutes. Its average speed in miles per hour is

    (A) $\dfrac{y+15}{x}$ (B) $x\left(y-\dfrac{1}{4}\right)$ (C) $\dfrac{x}{y+\dfrac{1}{4}}$ (D) $\dfrac{x}{y+15}$ (E) $\dfrac{y+\dfrac{1}{4}}{x}$

7. The average of five numbers is 6.9. If one of the numbers is deleted, the average of the remaining numbers is 4.4. What is the value of the number deleted?

    (A) 6.8
    (B) 7.4
    (C) 12.5
    (D) 16.9
    (E) 17.2

8. The average of two numbers is $\pi/2$, and one of the numbers is x. What is the other number in terms of x?

    (A) $\dfrac{\pi}{2} - x$ (B) $\dfrac{\pi}{2} + x$ (C) $\pi - x$ (D) $\pi + x$ (E) $2\pi + x$

9. A shopper spends \$25 to purchase floppy disks at 50¢ each. The next day, the disks go on sale for 30¢ each and the shopper spends \$45 to purchase more disks? What was the average price per disk purchased?

    (A) 25¢   (B) 30¢   (C) 35¢   (D) 40¢   (E) 45¢

10. The average of 8 numbers is A, and one of the numbers is 14. If 14 is replaced with 28, then what is the new average in terms of A ?

    (A) $A + \dfrac{7}{4}$ (B) $A + \dfrac{1}{2}$ (C) $A + 2$ (D) $2A + 1$ (E) $A + 4$

Ratio & Proportion

RATIO

A ratio is simply a fraction. The following notations all express the ratio of x to y: $x:y$, $x \div y$, or $\frac{x}{y}$. Writing two numbers as a ratio provides a convenient way to compare their sizes. For example, since $\frac{3}{\pi} < 1$, we know that 3 is less than π. A ratio compares two numbers. Just as you cannot compare apples and oranges, so to must the numbers you are comparing have the same units. For example, you cannot form the ratio of 2 feet to 4 yards because the two numbers are expressed in different units—feet vs. yards. It is quite common for the GMAT to ask for the ratio of two numbers with different units. Before you form any ratio, make sure the two numbers are expressed in the same units.

Example 1: What is the ratio of 2 feet to 4 yards?

(A) 1:9   (B) 1:8   (C) 1:7   (D) 1:6   (E) 1:5

The ratio cannot be formed until the numbers are expressed in the same units. Let's turn the yards into feet. Since there are 3 feet in a yard, 4 yards = 4 × 3 feet = 12 feet. Forming the ratio yields

$$\frac{2 \; feet}{12 \; feet} = \frac{1}{6} \; or \; 1:6$$

The answer is (D).

Note, taking the reciprocal of a fraction usually changes its size. For example, $\frac{3}{4} \neq \frac{4}{3}$. So order is important in a ratio: $3:4 \neq 4:3$.

PROPORTION

A proportion is simply an equality between two ratios (fractions). For example, the ratio of x to y is equal to the ratio of 3 to 2 is translated as

$$\frac{x}{y} = \frac{3}{2}$$

or in ratio notation,

$$x:y::3:2$$

Two variables are *directly proportional* if one is a constant multiple of the other:

$$y = kx$$

where k is a constant.

The above equation shows that as x increases (or decreases) so does y. This simple concept has numerous applications in mathematics. For example, in constant velocity problems, distance is directly proportional to time: $d = vt$, where v is a constant. Note, sometimes the word *directly* is suppressed.

Example 2:   If the ratio of y to x is equal to 3 and the sum of y and x is 80, what is the value of y?

   (A) –10   (B) –2   (C) 5   (D) 20   (E) 60

Translating *"the ratio of y to x is equal to 3"* into an equation yields

$$\frac{y}{x} = 3$$

Translating *"the sum of y and x is 80"* into an equation yields

$$y + x = 80$$

Solving the first equation for y gives $y = 3x$. Substituting this into the second equation yields

$$3x + x = 80$$
$$4x = 80$$
$$x = 20$$

Hence, $y = 3x = 3(20) = 60$. The answer is (E).

In many word problems, as one quantity increases (decreases), another quantity also increases (decreases). This type of problem can be solved by setting up a *direct* proportion.

Example 3:   If Biff can shape 3 surfboards in 50 minutes, how many surfboards can he shape in 5 hours?

   (A) 16   (B) 17   (C) 18   (D) 19   (E) 20

As time increases so does the number of shaped surfboards. Hence, we set up a direct proportion. First, convert 5 hours into minutes: *5 hours = 5 × 60 minutes = 300 minutes*. Next, let x be the number of surfboards shaped in 5 hours. Finally, forming the proportion yields

$$\frac{3}{50} = \frac{x}{300}$$

$$\frac{3 \cdot 300}{50} = x$$

$$18 = x$$

The answer is (C).

Example 4: On a map, 1 inch represents 150 miles. What is the actual distance between two cities if they are $3\frac{1}{2}$ inches apart on the map?

(A) 225   (B) 300   (C) 450   (D) 525   (E) 600

As the distance on the map increases so does the actual distance. Hence, we set up a direct proportion. Let x be the actual distance between the cities. Forming the proportion yields

$$\frac{1\,in}{150\,mi} = \frac{3\frac{1}{2}\,in}{x\,mi}$$

$$x = 3\frac{1}{2} \times 150$$

$$x = 525$$

The answer is (D).

Note, you need not worry about how you form the direct proportion so long as the order is the same on both sides of the equal sign. The proportion in Example 4 could have been written as $\frac{1\,in}{3\frac{1}{2}\,in} = \frac{150\,mi}{x\,mi}$. In this case, the order is inches to inches and miles to miles. However, the following is not a direct proportion because the order is not the same on both sides of the equal sign: $\frac{1\,in}{150\,mi} = \frac{x\,mi}{3\frac{1}{2}\,in}$. In this case, the order is inches to miles on the left side of the equal sign but miles to inches on the right side.

If one quantity increases (or decreases) while another quantity decreases (or increases), the quantities are said to be *inversely* proportional. The statement "y is inversely proportional to x" is written as

$$y = \frac{k}{x}$$

where k is a constant.

Multiplying both sides of $y = \frac{k}{x}$ by x yields

$$yx = k$$

Hence, in an inverse proportion, the product of the two quantities is constant. Therefore, instead of setting ratios equal, we set products equal.

In many word problems, as one quantity increases (decreases), another quantity decreases (increases). This type of problem can be solved by setting up a product of terms.

Example 5:   If 7 workers can assemble a car in 8 hours, how long would it take 12 workers to assemble the same car?

(A) 3 hrs   (B) $3\frac{1}{2}$ hrs   (C) $4\frac{2}{3}$ hrs   (D) 5 hrs   (E) $6\frac{1}{3}$ hrs

As the number of workers increases, the amount time required to assemble the car decreases. Hence, we set the products of the terms equal. Let x be the time it takes the 12 workers to assemble the car. Forming the equation yields

$$7 \cdot 8 = 12 \cdot x$$

$$\frac{56}{12} = x$$

$$4\frac{2}{3} = x$$

The answer is (C).

To summarize: if one quantity increases (decreases) as another quantity also increases (decreases), set ratios equal. If one quantity increases (decreases) as another quantity decreases (increases), set products equal.

The concept of proportion can be generalized to three or more ratios. A, B, and C are in the ratio 3:4:5 means $\frac{A}{B} = \frac{3}{4}$, $\frac{A}{C} = \frac{3}{5}$, and $\frac{B}{C} = \frac{4}{5}$.

Example 6:   In the figure to the right, the angles A, B, C of the triangle are in the ratio 5:12:13. What is the measure of angle A?

(A)   15
(B)   27
(C)   30
(D)   34
(E)   40

Since the angle sum of a triangle is $180°$, $A + B + C = 180$. Forming two of the ratios yields

$$\frac{A}{B} = \frac{5}{12} \qquad \frac{A}{C} = \frac{5}{13}$$

Solving the first equation for B yields $B = \frac{12}{5}A$

Solving the second equation for C yields $C = \frac{13}{5}A$

Hence, $180 = A + B + C = A + \frac{12}{5}A + \frac{13}{5}A = 6A$. Therefore, $180 = 6A$, or $A = 30$. The answer is (C).

Problem Set N: Solutions begin on page 229.

1. What is the ratio of 2 ft. 3 in. to 2 yds?

    (A) 1/4   (B) 1/3   (C) 3/8   (D) 1/2   (E) 3/4

2. The ratio of two numbers is 10 and their difference is 18. What is the value of the smaller number?

    (A) 2   (B) 5   (C) 10   (D) 21   (E) 27

3. If the degree measures of two angles of an isosceles triangle are in the ratio 1:3, what is the degree measure of the largest angle if it is not a base angle?

    (A) 26°   (B) 36°   (C) 51°   (D) 92°   (E) 108°

4. A jet uses 80 gallons of fuel to fly 320 miles. At this rate, how many gallons of fuel are needed for a 700 mile flight?

    (A) 150   (B) 155   (C) 160   (D) 170   (E) 175

5. Two boys can mow a lawn in 2 hours and 30 minutes If they are joined by three other boys, how many hours will it take to mow the lawn?

    (A) 1 hr.   (B) $1\frac{1}{4}$ hrs.   (C) $1\frac{1}{2}$ hrs.   (D) $1\frac{3}{4}$ hrs.   (E) 2 hrs.

6. A recipe requires $\frac{1}{2}$ lb. of shortening and 14 oz. of flour. If the chef accidentally pours in 21 oz. of flour, how many ounces of shortening should be added?

    (A) 9   (B) 10   (C) 11   (D) 12   (E) 13

7. If w widgets cost d dollars, then at this rate how many dollars will 2000 widgets cost?

    (A) $\dfrac{wd}{2000}$ (B) $\dfrac{2000w}{d}$ (C) $\dfrac{2000d}{w}$ (D) $\dfrac{d}{2000w}$ (E) $\dfrac{2000}{wd}$

8. In the system of equations to the right, $z \neq 0$. What is ratio of x to z?

    $$x + 2y - z = 1$$
    $$3x - 2y - 8z = -1$$

    (A) –9/4   (B) –1/3   (C) 1/3   (D) 4/9   (E) 9/4

9. If a sprinter takes 30 steps in 9 seconds, how many steps does he take in 54 seconds?

    (A) 130   (B) 170   (C) 173   (D) 180   (E) 200

10. If $5x = 6y$, then the ratio of x to y is

    (A) 5:11   (B) 5:6   (C) 1:1   (D) 6:5   (E) 11:6

Exponents & Roots

EXPONENTS

Exponents afford a convenient way of expressing long products of the same number. The expression b^n is called a power and it stands for $b \times b \times b \times \cdots \times b$, where there are n factors of b. b is called the base, and n is called the exponent. By definition, $b^0 = 1$[*]

There are six rules that govern the behavior of exponents:

Rule 1: $x^a \cdot x^b = x^{a+b}$ Example, $2^3 \cdot 2^2 = 2^{3+2} = 2^5 = 32$. Caution, $x^a + x^b \neq x^{a+b}$

Rule 2: $\left(x^a\right)^b = x^{ab}$ Example, $\left(2^3\right)^2 = 2^{3\cdot2} = 2^6 = 64$

Rule 3: $\left(xy\right)^a = x^a \cdot y^a$ Example, $\left(2y\right)^3 = 2^3 \cdot y^3 = 8y^3$

Rule 4: $\left(\dfrac{x}{y}\right)^a = \dfrac{x^a}{y^a}$ Example, $\left(\dfrac{x}{3}\right)^2 = \dfrac{x^2}{3^2} = \dfrac{x^2}{9}$

Rule 5: $\dfrac{x^a}{x^b} = x^{a-b}$, if $a > b$.   Example, $\dfrac{2^6}{2^3} = 2^{6-3} = 2^3 = 8$

$\dfrac{x^a}{x^b} = \dfrac{1}{x^{b-a}}$, if $b > a$.   Example, $\dfrac{2^3}{2^6} = \dfrac{1}{2^{6-3}} = \dfrac{1}{2^3} = \dfrac{1}{8}$

Rule 6: $x^{-a} = \dfrac{1}{x^a}$ Example, $z^{-3} = \dfrac{1}{z^3}$ Caution, a negative exponent does not make the number negative; it merely indicates that the base should be reciprocated. For example, $3^{-2} \neq -\dfrac{1}{3^2}$ or $-\dfrac{1}{9}$.

Problems involving these six rules are common on the GMAT, and they are often listed as hard problems. However, the process of solving these problems is quite mechanical: simply apply the six rules until they can no longer be applied.

Example 1:   If $x \neq 0$, $\dfrac{x\left(x^5\right)^2}{x^4} =$

(A) x^5 (B) x^6 (C) x^7 (D) x^8 (E) x^9

First, apply the rule $\left(x^a\right)^b = x^{ab}$ to the expression $\dfrac{x\left(x^5\right)^2}{x^4}$:

---

[*] Any term raised to the zero power equals 1, no matter how complex the term is. For example, $\left(\dfrac{x + 5\pi}{y}\right)^0 = 1$.

$$\frac{x \cdot x^{5 \cdot 2}}{x^4} = \frac{x \cdot x^{10}}{x^4}$$

Next, apply the rule $x^a \cdot x^b = x^{a+b}$:

$$\frac{x \cdot x^{10}}{x^4} = \frac{x^{11}}{x^4}$$

Finally, apply the rule $\frac{x^a}{x^b} = x^{a-b}$:

$$\frac{x^{11}}{x^4} = x^{11-4} = x^7$$

The answer is (C).

Note: Typically, there are many ways of solving these types of problems. For this example, we could have begun with Rule 5, $\frac{x^a}{x^b} = \frac{1}{x^{b-a}}$:

$$\frac{x\left(x^5\right)^2}{x^4} = \frac{\left(x^5\right)^2}{x^{4-1}} = \frac{\left(x^5\right)^2}{x^3}$$

Then apply Rule 2, $\left(x^a\right)^b = x^{ab}$:

$$\frac{\left(x^5\right)^2}{x^3} = \frac{x^{10}}{x^3}$$

Finally, apply the other version of Rule 5, $\frac{x^a}{x^b} = x^{a-b}$:

$$\frac{x^{10}}{x^3} = x^7$$

Example 2: $\dfrac{3 \cdot 3 \cdot 3 \cdot 3}{9 \cdot 9 \cdot 9 \cdot 9} =$

(A) $\left(\dfrac{1}{3}\right)^4$ (B) $\left(\dfrac{1}{3}\right)^3$ (C) $\dfrac{1}{3}$ (D) $\dfrac{4}{9}$ (E) $\dfrac{4}{3}$

Canceling the common factor 3 yields $\dfrac{1 \cdot 1 \cdot 1 \cdot 1}{3 \cdot 3 \cdot 3 \cdot 3}$, or $\dfrac{1}{3} \cdot \dfrac{1}{3} \cdot \dfrac{1}{3} \cdot \dfrac{1}{3}$. Now, by the definition of a power,

$\dfrac{1}{3} \cdot \dfrac{1}{3} \cdot \dfrac{1}{3} \cdot \dfrac{1}{3} = \left(\dfrac{1}{3}\right)^4$ Hence, the answer is (A).

Example 3: $\dfrac{6^4}{3^2} =$

(A) 2^4 (B) $2^3 \cdot 3$ (C) 6^2 (D) $2^4 \cdot 3^2$ (E) $2^2 \cdot 3^4$

First, factor the top of the fraction:

$$\frac{(2 \cdot 3)^4}{3^2}$$

Next, apply the rule $(xy)^a = x^a \cdot y^a$:

$$\frac{2^4 \cdot 3^4}{3^2}$$

Finally, apply the rule $\frac{x^a}{x^b} = x^{a-b}$:

$$2^4 \cdot 3^2$$

Hence, the answer is (D).

ROOTS

The symbol $\sqrt[n]{b}$ is read the nth root of b, where n is called the index, b is called the base, and $\sqrt{}$ is called the radical. $\sqrt[n]{b}$ denotes that number which raised to the nth power yields b. In other words, a is the nth root of b if $a^n = b$. For example, $\sqrt{9} = 3^*$ because $3^2 = 9$, and $\sqrt[3]{-8} = -2$ because $(-2)^3 = -8$. Even roots occur in pairs: both a positive root and a negative root. For example, $\sqrt[4]{16} = 2$ since $2^4 = 16$, and $\sqrt[4]{16} = -2$ since $(-2)^4 = 16$. Odd roots occur alone and have the same sign as the base: $\sqrt[3]{-27} = -3$ since $(-3)^3 = -27$. If given an even root, you are to assume it is the positive root. However, if you introduce even roots by solving an equation, then you <u>must</u> consider both the positive and negative roots:

$$x^2 = 9$$
$$\sqrt{x^2} = \pm\sqrt{9}$$
$$x = \pm 3$$

Square roots and cube roots can be simplified by removing perfect squares and perfect cubes, respectively. For example,

$$\sqrt{8} = \sqrt{4 \cdot 2} = \sqrt{4}\sqrt{2} = 2\sqrt{2}$$
$$\sqrt[3]{54} = \sqrt[3]{27 \cdot 2} = \sqrt[3]{27}\sqrt[3]{2} = 3\sqrt[3]{2}$$

There are only two rules for roots that you need to know for the GMAT:

$$\sqrt[n]{xy} = \sqrt[n]{x}\sqrt[n]{y} \qquad \text{For example, } \sqrt{3x} = \sqrt{3}\sqrt{x}.$$

$$\sqrt[n]{\frac{x}{y}} = \frac{\sqrt[n]{x}}{\sqrt[n]{y}} \qquad \text{For example, } \sqrt[3]{\frac{x}{8}} = \frac{\sqrt[3]{x}}{\sqrt[3]{8}} = \frac{\sqrt[3]{x}}{2}.$$

Caution: $\sqrt[n]{x+y} \neq \sqrt[n]{x} + \sqrt[n]{y}$. For example, $\sqrt{x+5} \neq \sqrt{x} + \sqrt{5}$. Also, $\sqrt{x^2 + y^2} \neq x + y$. This common mistake occurs because it is similar to the following valid property: $\sqrt{(x+y)^2} = x + y$ (If $x + y$ can be negative, then it must be written with the absolute value symbol: $|x + y|$). Note, in the valid formula, it's the whole term, $x + y$, that is squared, not the individual x and y.

To add two roots, both the index and the base must be the same. For example, $\sqrt[3]{2} + \sqrt[4]{2}$ cannot be added because the indices are different, nor can $\sqrt{2} + \sqrt{3}$ be added because the bases are different. However, $\sqrt[3]{2} + \sqrt[3]{2} = 2\sqrt[3]{2}$. In this case, the roots can be added because both the indices and bases are the same. Sometimes radicals with different bases can actually be added once they have been simplified to look alike. For example, $\sqrt{28} + \sqrt{7} = \sqrt{4 \cdot 7} + \sqrt{7} = \sqrt{4}\sqrt{7} + \sqrt{7} = 2\sqrt{7} + \sqrt{7} = 3\sqrt{7}$.

You need to know the approximations of the following roots:

$$\sqrt{2} \approx 1.4 \qquad \sqrt{3} \approx 1.7 \qquad \sqrt{5} \approx 2.2$$

---

* With square roots, the index is not written, $\sqrt[2]{9} = \sqrt{9}$.

Example 4: Given the system $\begin{array}{c} x^2 = 4 \\ y^3 = -8 \end{array}$, which of the following is NOT necessarily true?

(A) $y < 0$ (B) $x < 5$ (C) y is an integer   (D) $x > y$ (E) $\dfrac{x}{y}$ is an integer

$y^3 = -8$ yields one cube root, $y = -2$. However, $x^2 = 4$ yields two square roots, $x = \pm 2$. Now, if $x = 2$, then $x > y$; but if $x = -2$, then $x = y$. Hence, choice (D) is not necessarily true. The answer is (D).

Example 5: If $x < 0$ and y is 5 more than the square of x, which one of the following expresses x in terms of y?

(A) $x = \sqrt{y - 5}$ (B) $x = -\sqrt{y - 5}$ (C) $x = \sqrt{y + 5}$ (D) $x = \sqrt{y^2 - 5}$ (E) $x = -\sqrt{y^2 - 5}$

Translating the expression *"y is 5 more than the square of x"* into an equation yields:

$$y = x^2 + 5$$

$$y - 5 = x^2$$

$$\pm\sqrt{y - 5} = x$$

Since we are given that $x < 0$, we take the negative root, $-\sqrt{y - 5} = x$. The answer is (B).

RATIONALIZING

A fraction is not considered simplified until all the radicals have been removed from the denominator. If a denominator contains a single term with a square root, it can be rationalized by multiplying both the numerator and denominator by that square root. If the denominator contains square roots separated by a plus or minus sign, then multiply both the numerator and denominator by the conjugate, which is formed by merely changing the sign between the roots.

Example: Rationalize the fraction $\dfrac{2}{3\sqrt{5}}$.

Multiply top and bottom of the fraction by $\sqrt{5}$:

$$\dfrac{2}{3\sqrt{5}} \cdot \dfrac{\sqrt{5}}{\sqrt{5}} = \dfrac{2\sqrt{5}}{3 \cdot \sqrt{25}} = \dfrac{2\sqrt{5}}{3 \cdot 5} = \dfrac{2\sqrt{5}}{15}$$

Example: Rationalize the fraction $\dfrac{2}{3 - \sqrt{5}}$.

Multiply top and bottom of the fraction by the conjugate $3 + \sqrt{5}$:

$$\dfrac{2}{3 - \sqrt{5}} \cdot \dfrac{3 + \sqrt{5}}{3 + \sqrt{5}} = \dfrac{2\left(3 + \sqrt{5}\right)}{3^2 + 3\sqrt{5} - 3\sqrt{5} - \left(\sqrt{5}\right)^2} = \dfrac{2\left(3 + \sqrt{5}\right)}{9 - 5} = \dfrac{2\left(3 + \sqrt{5}\right)}{4} = \dfrac{3 + \sqrt{5}}{2}$$

Problem Set O: Solutions begin on page 232.

1. If $x \neq 0$, $\left(\dfrac{2y^3}{x^2}\right)^4 \cdot x^{10} =$

   (A) $16y^{12}x^2$ (B) $8y^7x^2$ (C) $16\dfrac{y^{12}}{x^8}$ (D) $8\dfrac{y^{12}}{x^8}$ (E) $\dfrac{y^{12}}{16x^8}$

2. $\sqrt{(31-6)(16+9)} =$

   (A) 5 (B) 10 (C) 25 (D) 50 (E) 625

3. What is the largest integer n such that 2^n is a factor of 20^8?

   (A) 1 (B) 2 (C) 4 (D) 8 (E) 16

4. $\dfrac{55^5}{5^{55}} =$

   (A) $\dfrac{11}{5^{50}}$ (B) $\dfrac{11}{5^{55}}$ (C) $\dfrac{11^5}{5^{50}}$ (D) $\dfrac{11^5}{5^5}$ (E) $\dfrac{11^5}{5}$

5. If $x = \dfrac{1}{9}$, then $\sqrt{x} - x^2 =$

   (A) 0 (B) 1/9 (C) 26/81 (D) 1/3 (E) 1

6. $\left(9^x\right)^3 =$

   (A) 3^{3x} (B) 3^{2+3x} (C) 3^{6x} (D) $729x^3$ (E) 9^{x^3}

7. If $x = 4$, then $-2^{2\sqrt{x}} + 2 =$

   (A) -14 (B) -8 (C) -2 (D) 0 (E) 18

8. $\sqrt{\dfrac{25 + 10x + x^2}{2}} =$

   (A) $\dfrac{\sqrt{2}(5-x)}{2}$ (B) $\dfrac{\sqrt{5+x}}{\sqrt{2}}$ (C) $\dfrac{\sqrt{2}(5+x)}{2}$ (D) $\dfrac{5+x}{2}$ (E) $\dfrac{5-x}{2}$

9. $\dfrac{2+\sqrt{5}}{2-\sqrt{5}} =$

   (A) $-9 - 4\sqrt{5}$ (B) $-1 - \dfrac{4}{9}\sqrt{5}$ (C) $1 + \dfrac{4}{9}\sqrt{5}$ (D) $9 + 4\sqrt{5}$ (E) 20

10. $2^{12} + 2^{12} + 2^{12} + 2^{12} =$

    (A) 4^{12} (B) 2^{14} (C) 2^{16} (D) 4^{16} (E) 2^{48}

11. $\left(\dfrac{\left(x^2y\right)^3 z}{xyz}\right)^3 =$

    (A) x^8y^5 (B) xy^6 (C) $x^{15}y^6z$ (D) x^3y^6 (E) $x^{15}y^6$

Factoring

To factor an algebraic expression is to rewrite it as a product of two or more expressions, called factors. In general, any expression on the GMAT that can be factored should be factored, and any expression that can be unfactored (multiplied out) should be unfactored.

DISTRIBUTIVE RULE

The most basic type of factoring involves the distributive rule:

$$ax + ay = a(x + y)$$

When this rule is applied from left to right, it is called factoring. When the rule is applied from right to left, it is called distributing.

For example, $3h + 3k = 3(h + k)$, and $5xy + 45x = 5xy + 9 \cdot 5x = 5x(y + 9)$. The distributive rule can be generalized to any number of terms. For three terms, it looks like $ax + ay + az = a(x + y + z)$. For example, $2x + 4y + 8 = 2x + 2 \cdot 2y + 2 \cdot 4 = 2(x + 2y + 4)$. For another example, $x^2y^2 + xy^3 + y^5 = y^2(x^2 + xy + y^3)$.

Example 1: If $x - y = 9$, then $\left(x - \dfrac{y}{3} \right) - \left(y - \dfrac{x}{3} \right) =$

  (A) –4   (B) –3   (C) 0   (D) 12   (E) 27

$$\left(x - \frac{y}{3} \right) - \left(y - \frac{x}{3} \right) =$$

$$x - \frac{y}{3} - y + \frac{x}{3} = \qquad \text{by distributing the negative sign}$$

$$\frac{4}{3}x - \frac{4}{3}y = \qquad \text{by combining the fractions}$$

$$\frac{4}{3}(x - y) = \qquad \text{by factoring out the common factor } \frac{4}{3}$$

$$\frac{4}{3}(9) = \qquad \text{since } x - y = 9$$

$$12$$

The answer is (D).

106

Example 2: $\dfrac{2^{20} - 2^{19}}{2^{11}} =$

(A) $2^9 - 2^{19}$ (B) $\dfrac{1}{2^{11}}$ (C) 2^8 (D) 2^{10} (E) 2^{28}

$$\dfrac{2^{20} - 2^{19}}{2^{11}} = \dfrac{2^{19+1} - 2^{19}}{2^{11}} =$$

$$\dfrac{2^{19} \cdot 2^1 - 2^{19}}{2^{11}} = \qquad \text{by the rule } x^a \cdot x^b = x^{a+b}$$

$$\dfrac{2^{19}(2 - 1)}{2^{11}} = \qquad \text{by the distributive property } ax + ay = a(x + y)$$

$$\dfrac{2^{19}}{2^{11}} =$$

$$2^8 \qquad \text{by the rule } \dfrac{x^a}{x^b} = x^{a-b}$$

The answer is (C).

DIFFERENCE OF SQUARES

One of the most important formulas on the GMAT is the difference of squares:

$$x^2 - y^2 = (x + y)(x - y)$$

Example 3:   If $x \neq -2$, then $\dfrac{8x^2 - 32}{4x + 8} =$

(A) $2(x - 2)$ (B) $2(x - 4)$ (C) $8(x + 2)$ (D) $x - 2$ (E) $x + 4$

In most algebraic expressions involving multiplication or division, you won't actually multiply or divide, rather you will factor and cancel, as in this problem.

$$\dfrac{8x^2 - 32}{4x + 8} =$$

$$\dfrac{8(x^2 - 4)}{4(x + 2)} = \qquad \text{by the distributive property } ax + ay = a(x + y)$$

$$\dfrac{8(x + 2)(x - 2)}{4(x + 2)} = \qquad \text{by the difference of squares } x^2 - y^2 = (x + y)(x - y)$$

$$2(x - 2) \qquad \text{by canceling common factors}$$

The answer is (A).

PERFECT SQUARE TRINOMIALS

Like the difference of squares formula, perfect square trinomial formulas are very common on the GMAT.

$$x^2 + 2xy + y^2 = (x + y)^2$$
$$x^2 - 2xy + y^2 = (x - y)^2$$

For example, $x^2 + 6x + 9 = x^2 + 2(3x) + 3^2 = (x + 3)^2$. Note, in a perfect square trinomial, the middle term is twice the product of the square roots of the outer terms.

Example 4:   If $r^2 - 2rs + s^2 = 4$, then $(r - s)^6 =$

        (A) –4   (B) 4   (C) 8   (D) 16   (E) 64

$$r^2 - 2rs + s^2 = 4$$

$$(r - s)^2 = 4 \qquad \text{by the formula } x^2 - 2xy + y^2 = (x - y)^2$$

$$\left[(r - s)^2\right]^3 = 4^3 \qquad \text{by cubing both sides of the equation}$$

$$(r - s)^6 = 64 \qquad \text{by the rule } \left(x^a\right)^b = x^{ab}$$

The answer is (E).

GENERAL TRINOMIALS

$$x^2 + (a + b)x + ab = (x + a)(x + b)$$

The expression $x^2 + (a + b)x + ab$ tells us that we need two numbers whose product is the last term and whose sum is the coefficient of the middle term. Consider the trinomial $x^2 + 5x + 6$. Now, two factors of 6 are 1 and 6, but $1 + 6 \neq 5$. However, 2 and 3 are also factors of 6, and $2 + 3 = 5$. Hence, $x^2 + 5x + 6 = (x + 2)(x + 3)$.

Example 5:   Which of the following could be a solution of the equation $x^2 - 7x - 18 = 0$?
        (A) –1   (B) 0   (C) 2   (D) 7   (E) 9

Now, both 2 and –9 are factors of 18, and $2 + (-9) = -7$. Hence, $x^2 - 7x - 18 = (x + 2)(x - 9) = 0$. Setting each factor equal to zero yields $x + 2 = 0$ and $x - 9 = 0$. Solving these equations yields $x = -2$ and 9. The answer is (E).

COMPLETE FACTORING

When factoring an expression, first check for a common factor, then check for a difference of squares, then for a perfect square trinomial, and then for a general trinomial.

Example 6:   Factor the expression $2x^3 - 2x^2 - 12x$ completely.

Solution: First check for a common factor: $2x$ is common to each term. Factoring $2x$ out of each term yields $2x\left(x^2 - x - 6\right)$. Next, there is no difference of squares, and $x^2 - x - 6$ is not a perfect square trinomial since x does not equal twice the product of the square roots of x^2 and 6. Now, –3 and 2 are factors of –6 whose sum is –1. Hence, $2x\left(x^2 - x - 6\right)$ factors into $2x(x - 3)(x + 2)$.

Problem Set P: Solutions begin on page 235.

1. If $3y + 5 = 7x$, then $21y - 49x =$

   (A) –40   (B) –35   (C) –10   (D) 0   (E) 15

2. If $x - y = p$, then $2x^2 - 4xy + 2y^2 =$

   (A) p (B) $2p$ (C) $4p$ (D) p^2 (E) $2p^2$

3. If $p \neq 0$ and $p = \sqrt{2pq - q^2}$, then in terms of q, $p =$

   (A) q (B) q^2 (C) $2q$ (D) $-2q$ (E) $\dfrac{q}{4}$

4. If $\dfrac{x^2 + 2x - 10}{5} = 1$, then x could equal

   (A) –5   (B) –3   (C) 0   (D) 10   (E) 15

5. What is the absolute value of twice the difference of the roots of the equation $5y^2 - 20y + 15 = 0$?

   (A) 0   (B) 1   (C) 2   (D) 3   (E) 4

6. If $x \neq -2$, then $\dfrac{7x^2 + 28x + 28}{(x + 2)^2} =$

   (A) 7   (B) 8   (C) 9   (D) 10   (E) 11

7. $\dfrac{7^9 + 7^8}{8} =$

   (A) $\dfrac{1}{8}$ (B) $\dfrac{7}{8}$ (C) $\dfrac{7^7}{8}$ (D) 7^8 (E) 7^9

8. If $x + y = 10$ and $x - y = 5$, then $x^2 - y^2 =$

   (A) 50   (B) 60   (C) 75   (D) 80   (E) 100

9. $x(x - y) - z(x - y) =$

   (A) $x - y$ (B) $x - z$ (C) $(x - y)(x - z)$ (D) $(x - y)(x + z)$ (E) $(x - y)(z - x)$

10. If $(x - y)^2 = x^2 + y^2$, then which one of the following statements must also be true?

    I. $x = 0$ II. $y = 0$ III. $xy = 0$

    (A) None   (B) I only   (C) II only   (D) III only   (E) II and III only

11. If x and y are prime numbers such that $x > y > 2$, then $x^2 - y^2$ must be divisible by which one of the following numbers?

    (A) 3   (B) 4   (C) 5   (D) 9   (E) 12

12. If $\dfrac{x + y}{x - y} = \dfrac{1}{2}$, then $\dfrac{xy + x^2}{xy - x^2} =$

    (A) –4.2   (B) –1/2   (C) 1.1   (D) 3   (E) 5.3

Algebraic Expressions

A mathematical expression that contains a variable is called an algebraic expression. Some examples of algebraic expressions are x^2, $3x - 2y$, $2z(y^3 - \frac{1}{z^2})$. Two algebraic expressions are called like terms if both the variable parts and the exponents are identical. That is, the only parts of the expressions that can differ are the coefficients. For example, $5y^3$ and $\frac{3}{2}y^3$ are like terms, as are $x + y^2$ and $-7(x + y^2)$. However, x^3 and y^3 are not like terms, nor are $x - y$ and $2 - y$.

ADDING & SUBTRACTING ALGEBRAIC EXPRESSIONS

Only like terms may be added or subtracted. To add or subtract like terms, merely add or subtract their coefficients:

$x^2 + 3x^2 = (1 + 3)x^2 = 4x^2$

$2\sqrt{x} - 5\sqrt{x} = (2 - 5)\sqrt{x} = -3\sqrt{x}$

$.5\left(x + \frac{1}{y}\right)^2 + .2\left(x + \frac{1}{y}\right)^2 = (.5 + .2)\left(x + \frac{1}{y}\right)^2 = .7\left(x + \frac{1}{y}\right)^2$

$\left(3x^3 + 7x^2 + 2x + 4\right) + \left(2x^2 - 2x - 6\right) = 3x^3 + (7 + 2)x^2 + (2 - 2)x + (4 - 6) = 3x^3 + 9x^2 - 2$

You may add or multiply algebraic expressions in any order. This is called the commutative property:

$$\boxed{x + y = y + x}$$
$$\boxed{xy = yx}$$

For example, $-2x + 5x = 5x + (-2x) = (5 - 2)x = 3x$ and $(x - y)(-3) = (-3)(x - y) = (-3)x - (-3)y = -3x + 3y$.

Caution: the commutative property does not apply to division or subtraction: $2 = 6 \div 3 \neq 3 \div 6 = \frac{1}{2}$ and $-1 = 2 - 3 \neq 3 - 2 = 1$.

When adding or multiplying algebraic expressions, you may regroup the terms. This is called the associative property:

$$\boxed{x + (y + z) = (x + y) + z}$$
$$\boxed{x(yz) = (xy)z}$$

Notice in these formulas that the variables have not been moved, only the way they are grouped has changed: on the left side of the formulas the last two variables are grouped together, and on the right side of the formulas the first two variables are grouped together.

For example, $(x - 2x) + 5x = (x + [-2x]) + 5x = x + (-2x + 5x) = x + 3x = 4x$
and
$$2(12x) = (2 \cdot 12)x = 24x$$

The associative property doesn't apply to division or subtraction: $4 = 8 \div 2 = 8 \div (4 \div 2) \neq (8 \div 4) \div 2 = 2 \div 2 = 1$ and $-6 = -3 - 3 = (-1 - 2) - 3 \neq -1 - (2 - 3) = -1 - (-1) = -1 + 1 = 0$.

Notice in the first example that we changed the subtraction into negative addition: $(x - 2x) = (x + [-2x])$. This allowed us to apply the associative property over addition.

PARENTHESES

When simplifying expressions with nested parentheses, work from the inner most parentheses out:

$$5x + (y - (2x - 3x)) = 5x + (y - (-x)) = 5x + (y + x) = 6x + y$$

Sometimes when an expression involves several pairs of parentheses, one or more pairs are written as brackets. This makes the expression easier to read:

$$2x(x - [y + 2(x - y)]) =$$
$$2x(x - [y + 2x - 2y]) =$$
$$2x(x - [2x - y]) =$$
$$2x(x - 2x + y) =$$
$$2x(-x + y) =$$
$$-2x^2 + 2xy$$

ORDER OF OPERATIONS: (PEMDAS)

When simplifying algebraic expressions, perform operations within parentheses first and then exponents and then multiplication and then division and then addition and lastly subtraction. This can be remembered by the mnemonic:

PEMDAS
Please Excuse My Dear Aunt Sally

This mnemonic isn't quite precise enough. Multiplication and division are actually tied in order of operation, as is the pair addition and subtraction. When multiplication and division, or addition and subtraction, appear at the same level in an expression, perform the operations from left to right. For example, $6 \div 2 \times 4 = (6 \div 2) \times 4 = 3 \times 4 = 12$. To emphasize this left-to-right order, we can use parentheses in the mnemonic: **PE(MD)(AS)**.

Example 1: $\quad 2 - \left(5 - 3^3\left[4 \div 2 + 1\right]\right) =$

(A) –21   (B) 32   (C) 45   (D) 60   (E) 78

$2 - \left(5 - 3^3\left[4 \div 2 + 1\right]\right) =$	
$2 - \left(5 - 3^3\left[2 + 1\right]\right) =$	By performing the division within the innermost parentheses
$2 - \left(5 - 3^3\left[3\right]\right) =$	By performing the addition within the innermost parentheses
$2 - (5 - 27[3]) =$	By performing the exponentiation
$2 - (5 - 81) =$	By performing the multiplication within the parentheses
$2 - (-76) =$	By performing the subtraction within the parentheses
$2 + 76 =$	By multiplying the two negatives
78	

The answer is (E).

FOIL MULTIPLICATION

You may recall from algebra that when multiplying two expressions you use the FOIL method: First, Outer, Inner, Last:

$$(x + y)(x + y) = xx + xy + xy + yy$$

Simplifying the right side yields $(x + y)(x + y) = x^2 + 2xy + y^2$. For the product $(x - y)(x - y)$ we get $(x - y)(x - y) = x^2 - 2xy + y^2$. These types of products occur often, so it is worthwhile to memorize the formulas. Nevertheless, you should still learn the FOIL method of multiplying because the formulas do not apply in all cases.

Examples (FOIL):

$$(2 - y)\left(x - y^2\right) = 2x - 2y^2 - xy + yy^2 = 2x - 2y^2 - xy + y^3$$

$$\left(\frac{1}{x} - y\right)\left(x - \frac{1}{y}\right) = \frac{1}{x}x - \frac{1}{x}\frac{1}{y} - xy + y\frac{1}{y} = 1 - \frac{1}{xy} - xy + 1 = 2 - \frac{1}{xy} - xy$$

$$\left(\frac{1}{2} - y\right)^2 = \left(\frac{1}{2} - y\right)\left(\frac{1}{2} - y\right) = \left(\frac{1}{2}\right)^2 - 2\left(\frac{1}{2}\right)y + y^2 = \frac{1}{4} - y + y^2$$

DIVISION OF ALGEBRAIC EXPRESSIONS

When dividing algebraic expressions, the following formula is useful:

$$\frac{x + y}{z} = \frac{x}{z} + \frac{y}{z}$$

This formula generalizes to any number of terms.

Examples:

$$\frac{x^2 + y}{x} = \frac{x^2}{x} + \frac{y}{x} = x^{2-1} + \frac{y}{x} = x + \frac{y}{x}$$

$$\frac{x^2 + 2y - x^3}{x^2} = \frac{x^2}{x^2} + \frac{2y}{x^2} - \frac{x^3}{x^2} = x^{2-2} + \frac{2y}{x^2} - x^{3-2} = x^0 + \frac{2y}{x^2} - x = 1 + \frac{2y}{x^2} - x$$

When there is more than a single variable in the denominator, we usually factor the expression and then cancel, instead of using the above formula.

Example 2: $\dfrac{x^2 - 2x + 1}{x - 1} =$

       (A) $x + 1$ (B) $-x - 1$ (C) $-x + 1$ (D) $x - 1$ (E) $x - 2$

$\dfrac{x^2 - 2x + 1}{x - 1} = \dfrac{(x - 1)(x - 1)}{x - 1} = x - 1$. The answer is (D).

Problem Set Q: Solutions begin on page 239.

1. $\left(x^2 + 2\right)\left(x - x^3\right) =$

    (A) $x^4 - x^2 + 2$ (B) $-x^5 - x^3 + 2x$ (C) $x^5 - 2x$ (D) $3x^3 + 2x$ (E) $x^5 + x^3 + 2x$

2. $-2\left(3 - x\left[\dfrac{5 + y - 2}{x}\right] - 7 + 2 \cdot 3^2\right) =$

    (A) $2y - 11$ (B) $2y + 1$ (C) $x - 2$ (D) $x + 22$ (E) $2y - 22$

3. For all real numbers a and b, $a \cdot b \neq 0$, let $a \lozenge b = ab - 1$. Which of the following must be true?

    I. $a \lozenge b = b \lozenge a$

    II. $\dfrac{a \lozenge a}{a} = 1 \lozenge 1$

    III. $\left(a \lozenge b\right) \lozenge c = a \lozenge \left(b \lozenge c\right)$

    (A) I only   (B) II only   (C) III only   (D) I and II only   (E) I and III only

4. $\left(x + \dfrac{1}{2}\right)^2 - \left(2x - 4\right)^2 =$

    (A) $-3x^2 - 15x + \dfrac{65}{4}$ (B) $3x^2 + 16x$ (C) $-3x^2 + 17x - \dfrac{63}{4}$ (D) $5x^2 + \dfrac{65}{4}$ (E) $3x^2$

5. If $x = 2$ and $y = -3$, then $y^2 - \left(x - \left[y + \dfrac{1}{2}\right]\right) - 2 \cdot 3 =$

    (A) $-39/2$ (B) $-3/2$ (C) 0 (D) 31 (E) 43

6. $4(xy)^3 + \left(x^3 - y^3\right)^2 =$

    (A) $x^3 - y^3$ (B) $\left(x^2 + y^2\right)^3$ (C) $\left(x^3 + y^3\right)^3$ (D) $\left(x^3 - y^3\right)^2$ (E) $\left(x^3 + y^3\right)^2$

7. If $\dfrac{a}{b} = -\dfrac{2}{3}$, then $\dfrac{b - a}{a} =$

    (A) $-5/2$ (B) $-5/3$ (C) $-1/3$ (D) 0 (E) 7

8. The operation $*$ is defined for all non-zero x and y by the equation $x * y = \dfrac{x}{y}$. Then the expression $(x - 2)^2 * x$ is equal to

    (A) $x - 4 + \dfrac{4}{x}$ (B) $4 + \dfrac{4}{x}$ (C) $\dfrac{4}{x}$ (D) $1 + \dfrac{4}{x}$ (E) $1 - 4x + \dfrac{4}{x}$

9. $\left(2 + \sqrt{7}\right)\left(4 - \sqrt{7}\right)(-2x) =$

    (A) $78x - 4x\sqrt{7}$ (B) $\sqrt{7}x$ (C) $-2x - 4x\sqrt{7}$ (D) $-2x$ (E) $4x\sqrt{7}$

10. If the operation $*$ is defined for all non-zero x and y by the equation $x * y = (xy)^2$, then $(x * y) * z =$

    (A) $x^2y^2z^2$ (B) $x^4y^4z^2$ (C) $x^2y^4z^2$ (D) $x^4y^2z^2$ (E) $x^4y^4z^4$

11. If $p = z + 1/z$ and $q = z - 1/z$, where z is a real number not equal to zero, then $(p + q)(p - q) =$

   (A)   2
   (B)   4
   (C) z^2
   (D) $\dfrac{1}{z^2}$
   (E) $z^2 - \dfrac{1}{z^2}$

12. If $x^2 + y^2 = xy$, then $(x + y)^4 =$

   (A) xy
   (B) $x^2 y^2$
   (C) $9x^2 y^2$
   (D) $\left(x^2 + y^2\right)^2$
   (E) $x^4 + y^4$

13. $(2 + x)(2 + y) - (2 + x) - (2 + y) =$

   (A) $2y$
   (B) xy
   (C) $x + y$
   (D) $x - y$
   (E) $x + y + xy$

14. If $x^2 + y^2 = 2ab$ and $2xy = a^2 + b^2$, with $a, b, x, y > 0$, then $x + y =$

   (A) ab
   (B) $a - b$
   (C) $a + b$
   (D) $\sqrt{a^2 + b^2}$
   (E) $\sqrt{a^2 - b^2}$

Percents

Problems involving percent are common on the GMAT. The word *percent* means "divided by one hundred." When you see the word "percent," or the symbol %, remember it means 1/100. For example,

$$25 \text{ percent}$$
$$\downarrow \quad \downarrow$$
$$25 \times \frac{1}{100} = \frac{1}{4}$$

To convert a decimal into a percent, move the decimal point two places to the right. For example,

$$0.25 = 25\%$$
$$0.023 = 2.3\%$$
$$1.3 = 130\%$$

Conversely, to convert a percent into a decimal, move the decimal point two places to the left. For example,

$$47\% = .47$$
$$3.4\% = .034$$
$$175\% = 1.75$$

To convert a fraction into a percent, first change it into a decimal (by dividing the denominator [bottom] into the numerator [top]) and then move the decimal point two places to the right. For example,

$$\frac{7}{8} = 0.875 = 87.5\%$$

Conversely, to convert a percent into a fraction, first change it into a decimal and then change the decimal into a fraction. For example,

$$80\% = .80 = \frac{80}{100} = \frac{4}{5}$$

Following are the most common fractional equivalents of percents:

$$33\frac{1}{3}\% = \frac{1}{3} \qquad\qquad 20\% = \frac{1}{5}$$

$$66\frac{1}{3}\% = \frac{2}{3} \qquad\qquad 40\% = \frac{2}{5}$$

$$25\% = \frac{1}{4} \qquad\qquad 60\% = \frac{3}{5}$$

$$50\% = \frac{1}{2} \qquad\qquad 80\% = \frac{4}{5}$$

Percent problems often require you to translate a sentence into a mathematical equation.

Example 1:   What percent of 25 is 5?

     (A) 10%   (B) 20%   (C) 30%   (D) 35%   (E) 40%

Translate the sentence into a mathematical equation as follows:

$$
\begin{array}{cccccc}
\text{What} & \text{percent} & \text{of} & 25 & \text{is} & 5 \\
\downarrow & \downarrow & \downarrow & \downarrow & \downarrow & \downarrow \\
x & \dfrac{1}{100} & \cdot & 25 & = & 5
\end{array}
$$

$$\frac{25}{100}x = 5$$

$$\frac{1}{4}x = 5$$

$$x = 20$$

The answer is (B).

Example 2:   2 is 10% of what number

     (A) 10   (B) 12   (C) 20   (D) 24   (E) 32

Translate the sentence into a mathematical equation as follows:

$$
\begin{array}{cccccc}
2 & \text{is} & 10 & \% & \text{of} & \underline{\text{what number}} \\
\downarrow & \downarrow & \downarrow & \downarrow & \downarrow & \downarrow \\
2 & = & 10 & \dfrac{1}{100} & \cdot & x
\end{array}
$$

$$2 = \frac{10}{100}x$$

$$2 = \frac{1}{10}x$$

$$20 = x$$

The answer is (C).

Example 3:   What percent of a is $3a$?

     (A) 100%   (B) 150%   (C) 200%   (D) 300%   (E) 350%

Translate the sentence into a mathematical equation as follows:

$$
\begin{array}{cccccc}
\text{What} & \text{percent} & \text{of} & a & \text{is} & 3a \\
\downarrow & \downarrow & \downarrow & \downarrow & \downarrow & \downarrow \\
x & \dfrac{1}{100} & \cdot & a & = & 3a
\end{array}
$$

$$\frac{x}{100} \cdot a = 3a$$

$$\frac{x}{100} = 3 \quad \text{(by canceling the } a\text{'s)}$$

$$x = 300$$

The answer is (D).

Example 4:   If there are 15 boys and 25 girls in a class, what percent of the class is boys?

(A)   10%
(B)   15%
(C)   18%
(D)   25%
(E)   37.5%

The total number of students in the class is 15 + 25 = 40. Now, translate the main part of the sentence into a mathematical equation:

what	percent	of	the class	is	boys
↓	↓	↓	↓	↓	↓
x	$\dfrac{1}{100}$	$\cdot$	40	=	15

$$\frac{40}{100}x = 15$$

$$\frac{2}{5}x = 15$$

$$2x = 75$$

$$x = 37.5$$

The answer is (E).

 Often you will need to find the percent of increase (or decrease). To find it, calculate the increase (or decrease) and divide it by the original amount:

Percent of change: $\dfrac{Amount\ of\ change}{Original\ amount} \times 100\%$

Example 5:   The population of a town was 12,000 in 1980 and 16,000 in 1990. What was the percent increase in the population of the town during this period?

(A) $33\dfrac{1}{3}\%$
(B)   50%
(C)   75%
(D)   80%
(E)   120%

The population increased from 12,000 to 16,000. Hence, the change in population was 4,000. Now, translate the main part of the sentence into a mathematical equation:

Percent of change: $\dfrac{Amount\ of\ change}{Original\ amount} \times 100\% =$

$$\frac{4000}{12000} \times 100\% =$$

$$\frac{1}{3} \times 100\% =   \text{(by canceling 4000)}$$

$$33\frac{1}{3}\%$$

The answer is (A).

Problem Set R: Solutions begin on page 244.

1. John spent $25, which is 15 percent of his monthly wage. What is his monthly wage?

    (A) $80   (B) 166\frac{2}{3}$ (C) $225   (D) $312.5   (E) $375

2. If $a = 4b$, what percent of $2a$ is $2b$?

    (A) 10%   (B) 20%   (C) 25%   (D) 26%   (E) 40%

3. If $p = 5q > 0$, then 40 percent of $3p$ equals

    (A) $6q$ (B) $5.52q$ (C) $13.3q$ (D) $9q$ (E) $20.1q$

4. A jar contains 24 blue balls and 40 red balls. Which one of the following is 50% of the blue balls?

    (A) 10   (B) 11   (C) 12   (D) 13   (E) 14

5. In a company with 180 employees, 108 of the employees are female. What percent of the employees are male?

    (A) 5%   (B) 25%   (C) 35%   (D) 40%   (E) 60%

6. John bought a shirt, a pair of pants, and a pair of shoes, which cost $10, $20, and $30, respectively. What percent of the total expense was spent for the pants?

    (A) $16\frac{2}{3}$%   (B) 20%   (C) 30%   (D) $33\frac{1}{3}$%   (E) 60%

7. Last year Jenny was 5 feet tall, and this year she is 5 feet 6 inches. What is the percent increase of her height?

    (A) 5%   (B) 10%   (C) 15%   (D) 20%   (E) 40%

8. Last month the price of a particular pen was $1.20. This month the price of the same pen is $1.50. What is the percent increase in the price of the pen?

    (A) 5%   (B) 10%   (C) 25%   (D) 30%   (E) $33\frac{1}{3}$%

9. Stella paid $1,500 for a computer after receiving a 20 percent discount. What was the price of the computer before the discount?

    (A) $300   (B) $1,500   (C) $1,875   (D) $2,000   (E) $3,000

10. A town has a population growth rate of 10% per year. The population in 1990 was 2000. What was the population in 1992?

    (A) 1600   (B) 2200   (C) 2400   (D) 2420   (E) 4000

11. In a class of 200 students, forty percent are girls. Twenty-five percent of the boys and 10 percent of the girls signed up for a tour to Washington DC. What percent of the class signed up for the tour?

    (A) 19%   (B) 23%   (C) 25%   (D) 27%   (E) 35%

12. If 15% of a number is 4.5, then 45% of the same number is

    (A) 1.5   (B) 3.5   (C) 13.5   (D) 15   (E) 45

13. A 30% discount reduces the price of a commodity by $90. If the discount is reduced to 20%, then the price of the commodity will be

    (A) $180   (B) $210   (C) $240   (D) $270   (E) $300

Graphs

Questions involving graphs rarely involve any significant calculating. Usually, the solution is merely a matter of interpreting the graph.

Questions 1-4 refer to the following graphs.

SALES AND EARNINGS OF CONSOLIDATED CONGLOMERATE

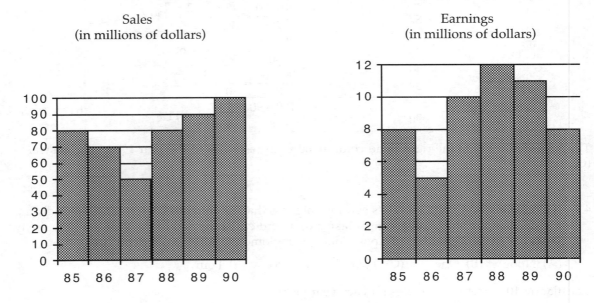

Sales
(in millions of dollars)

Earnings
(in millions of dollars)

Note: Figure drawn to scale.

1.   During what two-year period did the company's earnings increase the greatest?

(A) 85–87   (B) 86–87   (C) 86–88   (D) 87–89   (E) 88–90

Reading from the graph, the company's earnings increased from $5 million in 1986 to $10 million in 1987, and then to $12 million in 1988. The two-year increase from '86 to '88 was $7 million—clearly the largest on the graph. The answer is (C).

2.   During the years 1986 through 1988, what were the average earnings per year?

(A) 6 million   (B) 7.5 million   (C) 9 million   (D) 10 million   (E) 27 million

The graph yields the following information:

Year	Earnings
1986	$5 million
1987	$10 million
1988	$12 million

Forming the average yields $\dfrac{5+10+12}{3} = \dfrac{27}{3} = 9$. The answer is (C).

3. In which year did sales increase by the greatest percentage over the previous year?

(A) 86   (B) 87   (C) 88   (D) 89   (E) 90

To find the percentage increase (or decrease), divide the numerical change by the original amount. This yields

Year	Percentage increase
86	$\dfrac{70-80}{80} = \dfrac{-10}{80} = \dfrac{-1}{8} = -12.5\%$
87	$\dfrac{50-70}{70} = \dfrac{-20}{70} = \dfrac{-2}{7} \approx -29\%$
88	$\dfrac{80-50}{50} = \dfrac{30}{50} = \dfrac{3}{5} = 60\%$
89	$\dfrac{90-80}{80} = \dfrac{10}{80} = \dfrac{1}{8} = 12.5\%$
90	$\dfrac{100-90}{90} = \dfrac{10}{90} = \dfrac{1}{9} \approx 11\%$

The largest number in the right-hand column, 60%, corresponds to the year 1988. The answer is (C).

4. If Consolidated Conglomerate's earnings are less than or equal to 10 percent of sales during a year, then the stockholders must take a dividend cut at the end of the year. In how many years did the stockholders of Consolidated Conglomerate suffer a dividend cut?

(A) None   (B) One   (C) Two   (D) Three   (E) Four

Calculating 10 percent of the sales for each year yields

Year	10% of Sales (millions)	Earnings (millions)
85	$.10 \times 80 = 8$	8
86	$.10 \times 70 = 7$	5
87	$.10 \times 50 = 5$	10
88	$.10 \times 80 = 8$	12
89	$.10 \times 90 = 9$	11
90	$.10 \times 100 = 10$	8

Comparing the right columns shows that earnings were 10 percent or less of sales in 1985, 1986, and 1990. The answer is (D).

Problem Set S: Solutions begin on page 250.

Questions 1–5 refer to the following graphs.

PROFIT AND REVENUE DISTRIBUTION FOR ZIPPY PRINTING, 1990–1993, COPYING AND PRINTING.

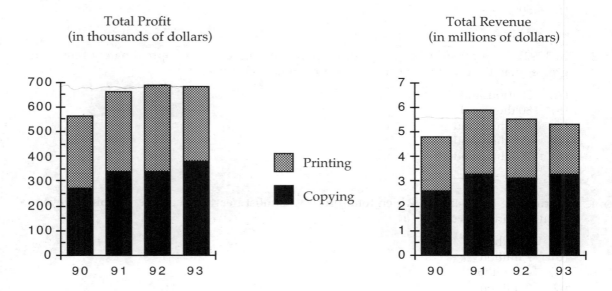

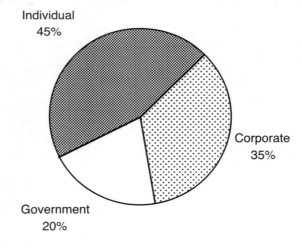

Distribution of Profit from Copying, 1992
(in thousands of dollars)

1.   In 1993, the total profit was approximately how much greater than the total profit in 1990?

    (A)   50 thousand
    (B)   75 thousand
    (C)   120 thousand
    (D)   200 thousand
    (E)   350 thousand

2. In 1990, the profit from copying was approximately what percent of the revenue from copying?

    (A)   2%
    (B)   10%
    (C)   20%
    (D)   35%
    (E)   50%

3. In 1992, the profit from copying for corporate customers was approximately how much greater than the profit from copying for government customers?

    (A)   50 thousand
    (B)   80 thousand
    (C)   105 thousand
    (D)   190 thousand
    (E)   260 thousand

4. During the two years in which total profit was most nearly equal, the combined revenue from printing was closest to

    (A)   1 million
    (B)   2 million
    (C)   4.5 million
    (D)   6 million
    (E)   6.5 million

5. The amount of profit made from government copy sales in 1992 was

    (A)   70 thousand
    (B)   100 thousand
    (C)   150 thousand
    (D)   200 thousand
    (E)   350 thousand

Questions 6–10 refer to the following graphs.

DISTRIBUTION OF CRIMINAL ACTIVITY BY CATEGORY OF CRIME FOR COUNTRY X IN 1990 AND PROJECTED FOR 2000.

Criminal Population: 10 million

Criminal Population: 20 million

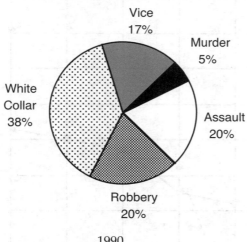

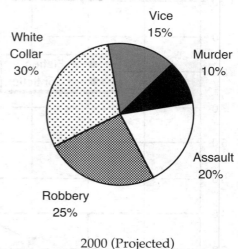

1990

2000 (Projected)

6. What is the projected number of white-collar criminals in 2000?

(A) 1 million
(B) 3.8 million
(C) 6 million
(D) 8 million
(E) 10 million

7. The ratio of the number of robbers in 1990 to the number of projected robbers in 2000 is

(A) 2/5   (B) 3/5   (C) 1   (D) 3/2   (E) 5/2

8. From 1990 to 2000, there is a projected decrease in the number of criminals for which of the following categories?

  I. Vice
 II. Assault
III. White Collar

(A) None
(B) I only
(C) II only
(D) II and III only
(E) I, II, and III

9. What is the approximate projected percent increase between 1990 and 2000 in the number of criminals involved in vice?

(A) 25%   (B) 40%   (C) 60%   (D) 75%   (E) 85%

10. The projected number of Robbers in 2000 will exceed the number of white-collar criminals in 1990 by

(A) 1.2 million   (B) 2.3 million   (C) 3.4 million   (D) 5.8 million   (E) 7.2 million

Questions 11–15 refer to the following graph.

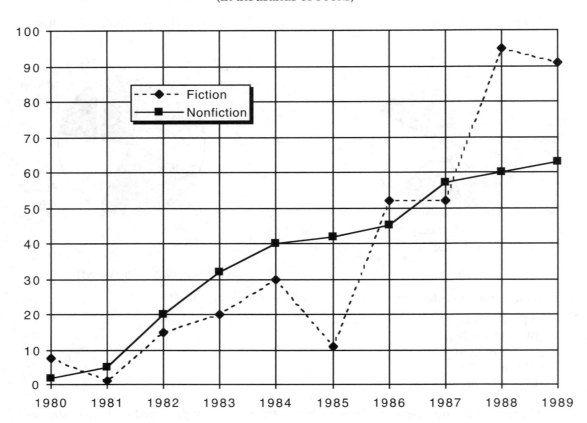

SALES BY CATEGORY FOR GRAMMERCY PRESS, 1980–1989
(in thousands of books)

11. In how many years did the sales of nonfiction titles exceed the sales of fiction titles ?

(A) 2   (B) 3   (C) 4   (D) 5   (E) 6

12. Which of the following best approximates the amount by which the increase in sales of fiction titles from 1985 to 1986 exceeded the increase in sales of fiction titles from 1983 to 1984?

(A)   31.5   thousand
(B)   40   thousand
(C)   49.3   thousand
(D)   50.9   thousand
(E)   68   thousand

13. Which of the following periods showed a continual increase in the sales of fiction titles?

(A) 1980–1982   (B) 1982–1984   (C) 1984–1986   (D) 1986–1988   (E) 1987–1989

14. What was the approximate average number of sales of fiction titles from 1984 to 1988?

(A) 15 thousand   (B) 30 thousand   (C) 40 thousand   (D) 48 thousand   (E) 60 thousand

15. By approximately what percent did the sale of nonfiction titles increase from 1984 to 1987?

(A) 42%   (B) 50%   (C) 70%   (D) 90%   (E) 110%

Questions 16–20 refer to the following graph.

AUTOMOBILE ACCIDENTS IN COUNTRY X: 1990 TO 1994
(in ten thousands)

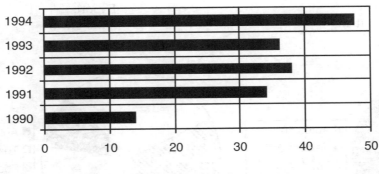

CARS IN COUNTRY X
(in millions)

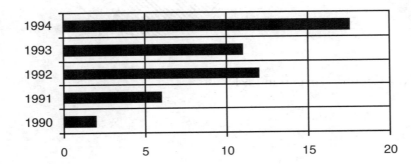

16. Approximately how many millions of cars were in Country X in 1994?

(A) 1.0   (B) 4.7   (C) 9.0   (D) 15.5   (E) 17.5

17. The amount by which the number of cars in 1990 exceeded the number of accidents in 1991 was approximately

(A) 0.3 million   (B) 0.7 million   (C) 1.0 million   (D) 1.7 million   (E) 2.5 million

18. The number of accidents in 1993 was approximately what percentage of the number of cars?

(A) 1%   (B) 1.5%   (C) 3%   (D) 5%   (E) 10%

19. In which of the following years will the number of accidents exceed 500 thousand?

(A)   1994
(B)   1995
(C)   1998
(D)   2000
(E)   It cannot be determined from the information given.

20. If no car in 1993 was involved in more than four accidents, what is the minimum number of cars that could have been in accidents in 1993?

(A) 50 thousand   (B) 60 thousand   (C) 70 thousand   (D) 80 thousand   (E) 90 thousand

<u>Questions 21–25</u> refer to the following graphs.

DISTRIBUTION OF IMPORTS AND EXPORTS FOR COUNTRY X IN 1994.

Imports
200 million items

Exports
100 million items

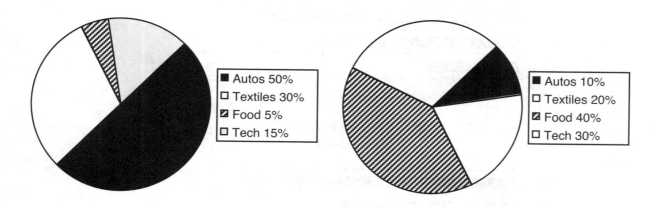

- ■ Autos 50%
- □ Textiles 30%
- ▨ Food 5%
- □ Tech 15%

- ■ Autos 10%
- □ Textiles 20%
- ▨ Food 40%
- □ Tech 30%

21. How many autos did Country X export in 1994?

   (A)   10 million
   (B)   15 million
   (C)   16 million
   (D)   20 million
   (E)   30 million

22. In how many categories did the total number of items (import and export) exceed 75 million?

   (A) 1   (B) 2   (C) 3   (D) 4   (E) none

23. The ratio of the number of technology items imported in 1994 to the number of textile items exported in 1994 is

   (A) 1/3   (B) 3/5   (C) 1   (D) 6/5   (E) 3/2

24. If in 1995 the number of autos exported was 16 million, then the percent increase from 1994 in the number of autos exported is

   (A) 40%   (B) 47%   (C) 50%   (D) 60%   (E) 65%

25. In 1994, if twice as many autos imported to Country X broke down as autos exported from Country X and 20 percent of the exported autos broke down, what percent of the imported autos broke down?

   (A) 1%   (B) 1.5%   (C) 2%   (D) 4%   (E) 5.5%

Word Problems

Before we begin solving word problems, we need to be very comfortable with translating words into mathematical symbols. Following is a partial list of words and their mathematical equivalents.

Concept	Symbol	Words	Example	Translation
equality	=	is	2 plus 2 is 4	$2 + 2 = 4$
		equals	x minus 5 equals 2	$x - 5 = 2$
		is the same as	multiplying x by 2 is the same as dividing x by 7	$2x = x/7$
addition	+	sum	the sum of y and π is 20	$y + \pi = 20$
		plus	x plus y equals 5	$x + y = 5$
		add	how many marbles must John add to collection P so that he has 13 marbles	$x + P = 13$
		increase	a number is increased by 10%	$x + 10\%x$
		more	the perimeter of the square is 3 more than the area	$P = 3 + A$
subtraction	−	minus	x minus y	$x - y$
		difference	the difference of x and y is 8	$|x - y| = 8$
		subtracted	x subtracted from y	$y - x$ *
		less than	the circumference is 5 less than the area	$C = A - 5$
multiplication	× or •	times	the acceleration is 5 times the velocity	$a = 5v$
		product	the product of two consecutive integers	$x(x + 1)$
		of	x is 125% of y	$x = 125\%y$
division	÷	quotient	the quotient of x and y is 9	$x \div y = 9$
		divided	if x is divided by y, the result is 4	$x \div y = 4$

Although exact steps for solving word problems cannot be given, the following guidelines will help:

(1) First, choose a variable to stand for the least unknown quantity, and then try to write the other unknown quantities in terms of that variable. *most known quantity*

For example, suppose we are given that Sue's age is 5 years less than twice Jane's and the sum of their ages is 16. Then Jane's age would be the least unknown, and we let $x = Jane's\ age$. Expressing Sue's age in terms of x gives $Sue's\ age = 2x - 5$.

(2) Second, write an equation that involves the expressions in Step 1. Most (though not all) word problems pivot on the fact that two quantities in the problem are equal. Deciding which two quantities should be set equal is usually the hardest part in solving a word problem since it can require considerable ingenuity to discover which expressions are equal.

For the example above, we would get $(2x - 5) + x = 16$.

(3) Third, solve the equation in Step 2 and interpret the result.

For the example above, we would get by adding the x's: $3x - 5 = 16$

Then adding 5 to both sides gives $\qquad 3x = 21$

---

* Notice that with "minus" and "difference" the terms are subtracted in the same order as they are written, from left to right (x minus $y \longrightarrow x - y$). However, with "subtracted" and "less than," the order of subtraction is reversed (x subtracted from $y \longrightarrow y - x$). Many students translate "subtracted from" in the wrong order.

Finally, dividing by 3 gives $x = 7$

Hence, Jane is 7 years old and Sue is $2x - 5 = 2 \cdot 7 - 5 = 9$ years old.

MOTION PROBLEMS

Virtually, all motion problems involve the formula *Distance = Rate × Time* , or

$$D = R \times T$$

Overtake: In this type of problem, one person catches up with or overtakes another person. The key to these problems is that at the moment one person overtakes the other they have traveled the same distance.

Example: Scott starts jogging from point X to point Y. A half-hour later his friend Garrett who jogs 1 mile per hour slower than twice Scott's rate starts from the same point and follows the same path. If Garrett overtakes Scott in 2 hours, how many miles will Garrett have covered?

(A) $2\frac{1}{5}$ (B) $3\frac{1}{3}$ (C) 4   (D) 6   (E) $6\frac{2}{3}$

Following Guideline 1, we let $r =$ *Scott's rate*. Then $2r - 1 =$ *Garrett's rate*. Turning to Guideline 2, we look for two quantities that are equal to each other. When Garrett overtakes Scott, they will have traveled the same distance. Now, from the formula $D = R \times T$, Scott's distance is

$$D = r \times 2\frac{1}{2}$$

and Garrett's distance is $D = (2r - 1)2 = 4r - 2$

Setting these expressions equal to each other gives $4r - 2 = r \times 2\frac{1}{2}$

Solving this equation for r gives $r = \frac{4}{3}$

Hence, Garrett will have traveled $D = 4r - 2 = 4\left(\frac{4}{3}\right) - 2 = 3\frac{1}{3}$ miles. The answer is (B).

Opposite Directions: In this type of problem, two people start at the same point and travel in opposite directions. The key to these problems is that the total distance traveled is the sum of the individual distances traveled.

Example: Two people start jogging at the same point and time but in opposite directions. If the rate of one jogger is 2 mph faster than the other and after 3 hours they are 30 miles apart, what is the rate of the faster jogger?

(A) 3   (B) 4   (C) 5   (D) 6   (E) 7

Let r be the rate of the slower jogger. Then the rate of the faster jogger is $r + 2$. Since they are jogging for 3 hours, the distance traveled by the slower jogger is $D = rt = 3r$, and the distance traveled by the faster jogger is $3(r + 2)$. Since they are 30 miles apart, adding the distances traveled gives

$$3r + 3(r + 2) = 30$$
$$3r + 3r + 6 = 30$$
$$6r + 6 = 30$$
$$6r = 24$$
$$r = 4$$

Hence, the rate of the faster jogger is $r + 2 = 4 + 2 = 6$. The answer is (D).

Round Trip: The key to these problems is that the distance going is the same as the distance returning.

Example: A cyclist travels 20 miles at a speed of 15 miles per hour. If he returns along the same path and the entire trip takes 2 hours, at what speed did he return?

      (A) 15 mph   (B) 20 mph   (C) 22 mph   (D) 30 mph   (E) 34 mph

Solving the formula $D = R \times T$ for T yields $T = \dfrac{D}{R}$. For the first half of the trip, this yields $T = \dfrac{20}{15} = \dfrac{4}{3}$ hours. Since the entire trip takes 2 hours, the return trip takes $2 - \dfrac{4}{3}$ hours, or $\dfrac{2}{3}$ hours. Now, the return trip is also 20 miles, so solving the formula $D = R \times T$ for R yields $R = \dfrac{D}{T} = \dfrac{20}{\frac{2}{3}} = 20 \cdot \dfrac{3}{2} = 30$. The answer is (D).

Compass Headings: In this type of problem, typically two people are traveling in perpendicular directions. The key to these problems is often the Pythagorean Theorem.

Example: At 1 PM, Ship A leaves port heading due west at x miles per hour. Two hours later, Ship B is 100 miles due south of the same port and heading due north at y miles per hour. At 5 PM, how far apart are the ships?

      (A) $\sqrt{(4x)^2 + (100 + 2y)^2}$

      (B) $x + y$

      (C) $\sqrt{x^2 + y^2}$

      (D) $\sqrt{(4x)^2 + (2y)^2}$

      (E) $\sqrt{(4x)^2 + (100 - 2y)^2}$

Since Ship A is traveling at x miles per hour, its distance traveled at 5 PM is $D = rt = 4x$. The distance traveled by Ship B is $D = rt = 2y$. This can be represented by the following diagram:

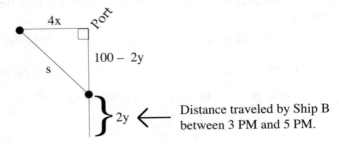

Applying the Pythagorean Theorem yields $s^2 = (4x)^2 + (100 - 2y)^2$. Taking the square root of this equation gives $s = \sqrt{(4x)^2 + (100 - 2y)^2}$. The answer is (E).

Circular Motion: In this type of problem, the key is often the arc length formula $S = R\theta$, where S is the arc length (or distance traveled), R is the radius of the circle, and θ is the angle.

Example: The figure to the right shows the path of a car moving around a circular racetrack. How many miles does the car travel in going from point A to point B ?

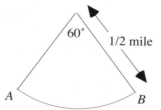

(A) $\dfrac{\pi}{6}$ (B) $\dfrac{\pi}{3}$ (C) π (D) 30   (E) 60

When calculating distance, degree measure must be converted to radian measure. To convert degree measure to radian measure, multiply by the conversion factor $\dfrac{\pi}{180}$. Multiplying 60° by $\dfrac{\pi}{180}$ yields $60 \cdot \dfrac{\pi}{180} = \dfrac{\pi}{3}$. Now, the length of arc traveled by the car in moving from point A to point B is S. Plugging this information into the formula $S = R\theta$ yields $S = \dfrac{1}{2} \cdot \dfrac{\pi}{3} = \dfrac{\pi}{6}$. The answer is (A).

Example: If a wheel is spinning at 1200 revolutions per minute, how many revolutions will it make in t seconds?

(A) $2t$ (B) $10t$ (C) $20t$ (D) $48t$ (E) $72t$

Since the question asks for the number of revolutions in t seconds, we need to find the number of revolutions per second and multiply that number by t. Since the wheel is spinning at 1200 revolutions per minute and there are 60 seconds in a minute, we get $\dfrac{1200 \text{ revolutions}}{60 \text{ seconds}} = 20\,\text{rev/sec}$. Hence, in t seconds, the wheel will make $20t$ revolutions. The answer is (C).

WORK PROBLEMS

The formula for work problems is *Work = Rate × Time*, or $W = R \times T$. The amount of work done is usually 1 unit. Hence, the formula becomes $1 = R \times T$. Solving this for R gives $R = \dfrac{1}{T}$.

Example: If Johnny can mow the lawn in 30 minutes and with the help of his brother, Bobby, they can mow the lawn 20 minutes, how long would it take Bobby working alone to mow the lawn?

(A) 1/2 hour   (B) 3/4 hour   (C) 1 hour   (D) 3/2 hours   (E) 2 hours

Let $r = \dfrac{1}{t}$ be Bobby's rate. Now, the rate at which they work together is merely the sum of their rates:

Total Rate = Johnny@ Rate + Bobby@ Rate

$$\frac{1}{20} = \frac{1}{30} + \frac{1}{t}$$

$$\frac{1}{20} - \frac{1}{30} = \frac{1}{t}$$

$$\frac{30 - 20}{30 \cdot 20} = \frac{1}{t}$$

$$\frac{1}{60} = \frac{1}{t}$$

$$t = 60$$

Hence, working alone, Bobby can do the job in 1 hour. The answer is (C).

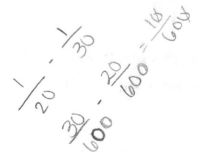

Example: A tank is being drained at a constant rate. If it takes 3 hours to drain $\frac{6}{7}$ of its capacity, how much longer will it take to drain the tank completely?

(A) 1/2 hour   (B) 3/4 hour   (C) 1 hour   (D) 3/2 hours   (E) 2 hours

Since $\frac{6}{7}$ of the tank's capacity was drained in 3 hours, the formula $W = R \times T$ becomes $\frac{6}{7} = R \times 3$. Solving for R gives $R = \frac{2}{7}$. Now, since $\frac{6}{7}$ of the work has been completed, $\frac{1}{7}$ of the work remains. Plugging this information into the formula $W = R \times T$ gives $\frac{1}{7} = \frac{2}{7} \times T$. Solving for T gives $T = \frac{1}{2}$. The answer is (A).

MIXTURE PROBLEMS

The key to these problems is that the combined total of the concentrations in the two parts must be the same as the whole mixture.

Example: How many ounces of a solution that is 30 percent salt must be added to a 50-ounce solution that is 10 percent salt so that the resulting solution is 20 percent salt?

(A) 20   (B) 30   (C) 40   (D) 50   (E) 60

Let x be the ounces of the 30 percent solution. Then $30\%x$ is the amount of salt in that solution. The final solution will be $50 + x$ ounces, and its concentration of salt will be $20\%(50 + x)$. The original amount of salt in the solution is $10\% \cdot 50$. Now, the concentration of salt in the original solution plus the concentration of salt in the added solution must equal the concentration of salt in the resulting solution:

$$10\% \cdot 50 + 30\%x = 20\%(50 + x)$$

Multiply this equation by 100 to clear the percent symbol and then solving for x yields $x = 50$. The answer is (D).

COIN PROBLEMS

The key to these problems is to keep the quantity of coins distinct from the value of the coins. An example will illustrate.

Example: Laura has 20 coins consisting of quarters and dimes. If she has a total of $3.05, how many dimes does she have?

(A) 3   (B) 7   (C) 10   (D) 13   (E) 16

Let D stand for the number of dimes, and let Q stand for the number of quarters. Since the total number of coins in 20, we get $D + Q = 20$, or $Q = 20 - D$. Now, each dime is worth 10¢, so the value of the dimes is $10D$. Similarly, the value of the quarters is $25Q = 25(20 - D)$. Summarizing this information in a table yields

	Dimes	Quarters	Total
Number	D	$20 - D$	20
Value	$10D$	$25(20 - D)$	305

Notice that the total value entry in the table was converted from $3.05 to 305¢. Adding up the value of the dimes and the quarters yields the following equation:

$$10D + 25(20 - D) = 305$$

$$10D + 500 - 25D = 305$$
$$-15D = -195$$
$$D = 13$$

Hence, there are 13 dimes, and the answer is (D).

AGE PROBLEMS

Typically, in these problems, we start by letting x be a person's current age and then the person's age a years ago will be $x - a$ and the person's age a years in future will be $x + a$. An example will illustrate.

Example: John is 20 years older than Steve. In 10 years, Steve's age will be half that of John's. What is Steve's age?

(A) 2   (B) 8   (C) 10   (D) 20   (E) 25

Steve's age is the most unknown quantity. So we let x = Steve's age and then $x + 20$ is John's age. Ten years from now, Steve and John's ages will be $x + 10$ and $x + 30$, respectively. Summarizing this information in a table yields

	Age now	Age in 10 years
Steve	x	$x + 10$
John	$x + 20$	$x + 30$

Since "in 10 years, Steve's age will be half that of John's," we get

$$\frac{1}{2}(x + 30) = x + 10$$
$$x + 30 = 2(x + 10)$$
$$x + 30 = 2x + 20$$
$$x = 10$$

Hence, Steve is 10 years old, and the answer is (C).

INTEREST PROBLEMS

These problems are based on the formula

$$\text{INTEREST} = \text{AMOUNT} \times \text{TIME} \times \text{RATE}$$

Often, the key to these problems is that the interest earned from one account plus the interest earned from another account equals the total interest earned:

Total Interest = (Interest from first account) + (Interest from second account)

An example will illustrate.

Example: A total of $1200 is deposited in two savings accounts for one year, part at 5% and the remainder at 7%. If $72 was earned in interest, how much was deposited at 5%?

(A) 410   (B) 520   (C) 600   (D) 650   (E) 760

Let x be the amount deposited at 5%. Then $1200 - x$ is the amount deposited at 7%. The interest on these investments is $.05x$ and $.07(1200 - x)$. Since the total interest is $72, we get

$$.05x + .07(1200 - x) = 72$$
$$.05x + 84 - .07x = 72$$
$$-.02x + 84 = 72$$
$$-.02x = -12$$
$$x = 600$$

The answer is (C).

Problem Set T: Solutions begin on page 260.

1. Jennifer and Alice are 4 miles apart. If Jennifer starts walking toward Alice at 3 miles per hour and at the same time Alice starts walking toward Jennifer at 2 miles per hour, how much time will pass before they meet?

   (A) 20 minutes   (B) 28 minutes   (C) 43 minutes   (D) 48 minutes   (E) 60 minutes

2. If Robert can assemble a model car in 30 minutes and Craig can assemble the same model car in 20 minutes, how long would it take them, working together, to assemble the model car?

   (A) 12 minutes   (B) 13 minutes   (C) 14 minutes   (D) 15 minutes   (E) 16 minutes

3. How many ounces of nuts costing 80 cents a pound must be mixed with nuts costing 60 cents a pound to make a 10-ounce mixture costing 70 cents a pound?

   (A) 3   (B) 4   (C) 5   (D) 7   (E) 8

4. Tom is 10 years older than Carrie. However, 5 years ago Tom was twice as old as Carrie. How old is Carrie?

   (A) 5   (B) 10   (C) 12   (D) 15   (E) 25

5. Two cars start at the same point and travel in opposite directions. If one car travels at 45 miles per hour and the other at 60 miles per hour, how much time will pass before they are 210 miles apart?

   (A) .5 hours   (B) 1 hour   (C) 1.5 hours   (D) 2 hours   (E) 2.5 hours

6. If the value of x quarters is equal to the value of $x + 32$ nickels, $x =$

   (A) 8   (B) 11   (C) 14   (D) 17   (E) 20

7. Steve has $5.25 in nickels and dimes. If he has 15 more dimes than nickels, how many nickels does he have?

   (A) 20   (B) 25   (C) 27   (D) 30   (E) 33

8. Cathy has equal numbers of nickels and quarters worth a total of $7.50. How many coins does she have?

   (A) 20   (B) 25   (C) 50   (D) 62   (E) 70

9. Richard leaves to visit his friend who lives 200 miles down Interstate 10. One hour later his friend Steve leaves to visit Richard via Interstate 10. If Richard drives at 60 mph and Steve drives at 40 mph, how many miles will Steve have driven when they cross paths?

   (A) 56   (B) 58   (C) 60   (D) 65   (E) 80

10. At 1 PM, Ship A leaves port traveling 15 mph. Three hours later, Ship B leaves the same port in the same direction traveling 25 mph. At what time does Ship B pass Ship A?

    (A) 8:30 PM   (B) 8:35 PM   (C) 9 PM   (D) 9:15 PM   (E) 9:30 PM

11. In x hours and y minutes a car traveled z miles. What is the car's speed in miles per hour?

    (A) $\dfrac{z}{60 + y}$ (B) $\dfrac{60z}{60x + y}$ (C) $\dfrac{60}{60 + y}$ (D) $\dfrac{z}{x + y}$ (E) $\dfrac{60 + y}{60z}$

12. In a class of 40 students, the number of students who passed the math exam is equal to half the number of students who passed the science exam. Each student in the class passed at least one of the two exams. If 5 students passed both exams, then the number of students who passed the math exam is

   (A) 5
   (B) 10
   (C) 15
   (D) 20
   (E) 25

13. A train of length l, traveling at a constant velocity, passes a pole in t seconds. If the same train traveling at the same velocity passes a platform in $3t$ seconds, then the length of the platform is

   (A) $0.5l$
   (B) l
   (C) $1.5l$
   (D) $2l$
   (E) $3l$

14. If two workers can assemble a car in 8 hours and a third worker can assemble the same car in 12 hours, then how long would it take the three workers together to assemble the car?

   (A) $\dfrac{5}{12}$ hrs
   (B) $2\dfrac{2}{5}$ hrs
   (C) $2\dfrac{4}{5}$ hrs
   (D) $3\dfrac{1}{2}$ hrs
   (E) $4\dfrac{4}{5}$ hrs

15. The age of B is half the sum of the ages of A and C. If B is 2 years younger than A and C is 32 years old, then the age of B must be

   (A) 28
   (B) 30
   (C) 32
   (D) 34
   (E) 36

16. The ages of three people are such that the age of one person is twice the age of the second person and three times the age of the third person. If the sum of the ages of the three people is 33, then the age of the youngest person is

   (A) 3
   (B) 6
   (C) 9
   (D) 11
   (E) 18

Sequences & Series

SEQUENCES

A sequence is an ordered list of numbers. The following is a sequence of odd numbers:

$$1, 3, 5, 7, \ldots$$

A term of a sequence is identified by its position in the sequence. In the above sequence, 1 is the first term, 3 is the second term, etc. The ellipsis symbol (...) indicates that the sequence continues forever.

Example 1: In sequence S, the 3rd term is 4, the 2nd term is three times the 1st, and the 3rd term is four times the 2nd. What is the 1st term in sequence S?

    (A) 0   (B) 1/3   (C) 1   (D) 3/2   (E) 4

We know *"the 3rd term of S is 4,"* and that *"the 3rd term is four times the 2nd."* This is equivalent to saying the 2nd term is 1/4 the 3rd term: $\frac{1}{4} \cdot 4 = 1$. Further, we know *"the 2nd term is three times the 1st."* This is equivalent to saying the 1st term is 1/3 the 2nd term: $\frac{1}{3} \cdot 1 = \frac{1}{3}$. Hence, the first term of the sequence is fully determined:

$$\frac{1}{3}, 1, 4$$

The answer is (B).

Example 2: Except for the first two numbers, every number in the sequence –1, 3, –3, ... is the product of the two immediately preceding numbers. How many numbers of this sequence are odd?

    (A) one   (B) two   (C) three   (D) four   (E) more than four

Since *"every number in the sequence –1, 3, –3, ... is the product of the two immediately preceding numbers,"* the forth term of the sequence is –9 = 3(–3). The first 6 terms of this sequence are

$$-1, 3, -3, -9, 27, -243, \ldots$$

At least six numbers in this sequence are odd: –1, 3, –3, –9, 27, –243. The answer is (E).

Arithmetic Progressions

An arithmetic progression is a sequence in which the difference between any two consecutive terms is the same. This is the same as saying: each term exceeds the previous term by a fixed amount. For example, 0, 6, 12, 18, ... is an arithmetic progression in which the common difference is 6. The sequence 8, 4, 0, –4, ... is arithmetic with a common difference of –4.

Example 3: The seventh number in a sequence of numbers is 31 and each number after the first number in the sequence is 4 less than the number immediately preceding it. What is the fourth number in the sequence?

(A) 15   (B) 19   (C) 35   (D) 43   (E) 51

Since each number *"in the sequence is 4 less than the number immediately preceding it,"* the sixth term is 31 + 4 = 35; the fifth number in the sequence is 35 + 4 = 39; and the fourth number in the sequence is 39 + 4 = 43. The answer is (D). Following is the sequence written out:

$$55, 51, 47, 43, 39, 35, 31, 27, 23, 19, 15, 11, \ldots$$

Advanced concepts: (Sequence Formulas)

Students with strong backgrounds in mathematics may prefer to solve sequence problems by using formulas. Note, none of the formulas in this section are necessary to answer questions about sequences on the GMAT.

Since each term of an arithmetic progression *"exceeds the previous term by a fixed amount,"* we get the following:

first term	$a + 0d$	where a is the first term and d is the common difference
second term	$a + 1d$	
third term	$a + 2d$	
fourth term	$a + 3d$	

$$\ldots$$

nth term	$a + (n-1)d$	This formula generates the nth term

The sum of the first n terms of an arithmetic sequence is

$$\frac{n}{2}\big[2a + (n-1)d\big]$$

Geometric Progressions

A geometric progression is a sequence in which the ratio of any two consecutive terms is the same. Thus, each term is generated by multiplying the preceding term by a fixed number. For example, –3, 6, –12, 24, . . . is a geometric progression in which the common ratio is –2. The sequence 32, 16, 8, 4, . . . is geometric with common ratio 1/2.

Example 4: What is the sixth term of the sequence $90, -30, 10, -\dfrac{10}{3}, \ldots$?

(A) 1/3   (B) 0   (C) –10/27   (D) –3   (E) –100/3

Since the common ratio between any two consecutive terms is $-\dfrac{1}{3}$, the fifth term is $\dfrac{10}{9} = \left(-\dfrac{1}{3}\right) \cdot \left(-\dfrac{10}{3}\right)$. Hence, the sixth number in the sequence is $-\dfrac{10}{27} = \left(-\dfrac{1}{3}\right) \cdot \left(\dfrac{10}{9}\right)$. The answer is (C).

Advanced concepts: (Sequence Formulas)

Note, none of the formulas in this section are necessary to answer questions about sequences on the GMAT.

Since each term of a geometric progression *"is generated by multiplying the preceding term by a fixed number,"* we get the following:

first term a

second term ar^1 where r is the common ratio

third term ar^2

fourth term ar^3

. . .

nth term $a_n = ar^{n-1}$ This formula generates the nth term

The sum of the first n terms of an geometric sequence is

$$\frac{a\left(1 - r^n\right)}{1 - r}$$

SERIES

A series is simply the sum of the terms of a sequence. The following is a series of even numbers formed from the sequence 2, 4, 6, 8, . . . :

$$2 + 4 + 6 + 8 + \cdots$$

A term of a series is identified by its position in the series. In the above series, 2 is the first term, 4 is the second term, etc. The ellipsis symbol (. . .) indicates that the series continues forever.

Example 5: The sum of the squares of the first n positive integers $1^2 + 2^2 + 3^2 + \ldots + n^2$ is $\frac{n(n+1)(2n+1)}{6}$. What is the sum of the squares of the first 9 positive integers?

(A) 90   (B) 125   (C) 200   (D) 285   (E) 682

We are given a formula for the sum of the squares of the first n positive integers. Plugging $n = 9$ into this formula yields

$$\frac{n(n+1)(2n+1)}{6} = \frac{9(9+1)(2\cdot 9 + 1)}{6} = \frac{9(10)(19)}{6} = 285$$

The answer is (D).

Example 6: For all integers $x > 1$, $\langle x \rangle = 2x + (2x - 1) + (2x - 2) + \ldots + 2 + 1$. What is the value of $\langle 3 \rangle \cdot \langle 2 \rangle$?

(A) 60   (B) 116   (C) 210   (D) 263   (E) 478

$\langle 3 \rangle = 2(3) + (2\cdot 3 - 1) + (2\cdot 3 - 2) + (2\cdot 3 - 3) + (2\cdot 3 - 4) + (2\cdot 3 - 5) = 6 + 5 + 4 + 3 + 2 + 1 = 21$

$\langle 2 \rangle = 2(2) + (2\cdot 2 - 1) + (2\cdot 2 - 2) + (2\cdot 2 - 3) = 4 + 3 + 2 + 1 = 10$

Hence, $\langle 3 \rangle \cdot \langle 2 \rangle = 21\cdot 10 = 210$, and the answer is (C).

Problem Set U: Solutions begin on page 266.

1. By dividing 21 into 1, the fraction $\frac{1}{21}$ can be written as a repeating decimal: 0.476190476190 . . . where the block of digits 476190 repeats. What is the 54th digit following the decimal point?

    (A) 0   (B) 4   (C) 6   (D) 7   (E) 9

2. The positive integers *P, Q, R, S,* and *T* increase in order of size such that the value of each successive integer is one more than the preceding integer and the value of *T* is 6. What is the value of *R*?

    (A) 0   (B) 1   (C) 2   (D) 3   (E) 4

3. Let *u* represent the sum of the integers from 1 through 20, and let *v* represent the sum of the integers from 21 through 40. What is the value of *v – u* ?

    (A) 21   (B) 39   (C) 200   (D) 320   (E) 400

4. In the pattern of dots to the right, each row after the first row has two more dots than the row immediately above it. Row 6 contains how many dots?

    (A) 6   (B) 8   (C) 10   (D) 11   (E) 12

5. In sequence S, all odd numbered terms are equal and all even numbered terms are equal. The first term in the sequence is $\sqrt{2}$ and the second term is –2. What is approximately the sum of two consecutive terms of the sequence?

    (A) –2   (B) –0.6   (C) 0   (D) 2   (E) 0.8

6. The sum of the first *n* even, positive integers is $2 + 4 + 6 + \cdots + 2n$ is $n(n + 1)$. What is the sum of the first 20 even, positive integers?

    (A) 120   (B) 188   (C) 362   (D) 406   (E) 420

7. In the array of numbers to the right, each number above the bottom row is equal to three times the number immediately below it. What is value of *x + y* ?

27	*x*	81	–108
9	–18	27	–36
3	–6	*y*	–12
1	–2	3	–4

    (A) –45   (B) –15   (C) –2   (D) 20   (E) 77

8. The first term of a sequence is 2. All subsequent terms are found by adding 3 to the immediately preceding term and then multiplying the sum by 2. Which of the following describes the terms of the sequence?

    (A) Each term is odd   (B) Each term is even   (C) The terms are: even, odd, even, odd...
    (D) The terms are: even, odd, odd, odd...   (E) The terms are: even, odd, odd, even, odd, odd...

9. Except for the first two numbers, every number in the sequence –1, 3, 2, . . . is the sum of the two immediately preceding numbers. How many numbers of this sequence are even?

    (A) none   (B) one   (C) two   (D) three   (E) more than three

10. In the sequence w, x, y, 30, adding any one of the first three terms to the term immediately following it yields *w*/2. What is the value of *w* ?

    (A) –60   (B) –30   (C) 0   (D) 5   (E) 25

Counting

Counting may have been one of humankind's first thought processes; nevertheless, counting can be deceptively hard. In part, because we often forget some of the principles of counting, but also because counting can be inherently difficult.

 When counting elements that are in overlapping sets, the total number will equal the number in one group plus the number in the other group minus the number common to both groups. Venn diagrams are very helpful with these problems.

Example 1: If in a certain school 20 students are taking math and 10 are taking history and 7 are taking both, how many students are taking either math or history?

(A) 20 (B) 22 (C) 23 (D) 25 (E) 29

Solution:

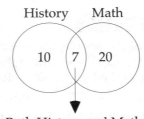

By the principle stated above, we add 10 and 20 and then subtract 7 from the result. Thus, there are $(10 + 20) - 7 = 23$ students. The answer is (C).

 The number of integers between two integers _inclusive_ is one more than their difference.

Example 2: How many integers are there between 49 and 101, inclusive?

(A) 50 (B) 51 (C) 52 (D) 53 (E) 54

By the principle stated above, the number of integers between 49 and 101 inclusive is $(101 - 49) + 1 = 53$. The answer is (D). To see this more clearly, choose smaller numbers, say, 9 and 11. The difference between 9 and 11 is 2. But there are three numbers between them inclusive—9, 10, and 11—one more than their difference.

 Fundamental Principle of Counting: **If an event occurs _m_ times, and each of the _m_ events is followed by a second event which occurs _k_ times, then the first event follows the second event _m · k_ times.**

The following diagram illustrates the fundamental principle of counting for an event that occurs 3 times with each occurrence being followed by a second event that occurs 2 times for a total of $3 \cdot 2 = 6$ events:

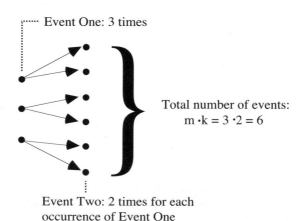

Event One: 3 times

Total number of events:
$m \cdot k = 3 \cdot 2 = 6$

Event Two: 2 times for each
occurrence of Event One

Example 3:　A drum contains 3 to 5 jars each of which contains 30 to 40 marbles. If 10 percent of the marbles are flawed, what is the greatest possible number of flawed marbles in the drum?

(A) 51　　(B) 40　　(C) 30　　(D) 20　　(E) 12

There is at most 5 jars each of which contains at most 40 marbles; so by the fundamental counting principle, there is at most $5 \cdot 40 = 200$ marbles in the drum. Since 10 percent of the marbles are flawed, there is at most $20 = 10\% \cdot 200$ flawed marbles. The answer is (D).

MISCELLANEOUS COUNTING PROBLEMS

Example 4:　In a legislative body of 200 people, the number of Democrats is 50 less than 4 times the number of Republicans. If one fifth of the legislators are neither Republican nor Democrat, how many of the legislators are Republicans?

(A) 42　　(B) 50　　(C) 71　　(D) 95　　(E) 124

Let D be the number of Democrats and let R be the number of Republicans. "One fifth of the legislators are neither Republican nor Democrat," so there are $\frac{1}{5} \cdot 200 = 40$ legislators who are neither Republican nor Democrat. Hence, there are $200 - 40 = 160$ Democrats and Republicans, or $D + R = 160$. Translating the clause "the number of Democrats is 50 less than 4 times the number of Republicans" into an equation yields $D = 4R - 50$. Plugging this into the equation $D + R = 160$ yields

$$4R - 50 + R = 160$$
$$5R - 50 = 160$$
$$5R = 210$$
$$R = 42$$

The answer is (A).

Example 5:　Speed bumps are being placed at 20 foot intervals along a road 1015 feet long. If the first speed bump is placed at one end of the road, how many speed bumps are needed?

(A) 49　　(B) 50　　(C) 51　　(D) 52　　(E) 53

Since the road is 1015 feet long and the speed bumps are 20 feet apart, there are $\frac{1015}{20} = 50.75$, or 50 full sections in the road. If we ignore the first speed bump and associate the speed bump at the end of each section with that section, then there are 50 speed bumps (one for each of the fifty full sections). Counting the first speed bump gives a total of 51 speed bumps. The answer is (C).

Problem Set V: Solutions begin on page 269.

1. The number of integers between 29 and 69, inclusive is

   (A) 39   (B) 40   (C) 41   (D) 42   (E) 43

2. A school has a total enrollment of 150 students. There are 63 students taking French, 48 taking chemistry, and 21 taking both. How many students are taking <u>neither</u> French nor chemistry?

   (A) 60   (B) 65   (C) 71   (D) 75   (E) 97

3. The number of minutes in $1\frac{1}{3}$ hours is

   (A) 60   (B) 65   (C) 71   (D) 80   (E) 97

4. A web press prints 5 pages every 2 seconds. At this rate, how many pages will the press print in 7 minutes?

   (A) 350   (B) 540   (C) 700   (D) 950   (E) 1050

5. A school has a total enrollment of 90 students. There are 30 students taking physics, 25 taking English, and 13 taking both. What percentage of the students are taking either physics or English?

   (A) 30%   (B) 36%   (C) 47%   (D) 51%   (E) 58%

6. Callers 49 through 91 to a radio show won a prize. How many callers won a prize?

   (A) 42   (B) 43   (C) 44   (D) 45   (E) 46

7. A rancher is constructing a fence by stringing wire between posts 20 feet apart. If the fence is 400 feet long, how many posts must the rancher use?

   (A) 18   (B) 19   (C) 20   (D) 21   (E) 22

8. The number of marbles in x jars, each containing 15 marbles, plus the number of marbles in $3x$ jars, each containing 20 marbles is

   (A) $65x$ (B) $70x$ (C) $75x$ (D) $80x$ (E) $85x$

9. The number of integers from 2 to 10^3, inclusive is

   (A) 997   (B) 998   (C) 999   (D) 1000   (E) 1001

10. In a small town, 16 people own Fords and 11 people own Toyotas. If exactly 15 people own only one of the two types of cars, how many people own both types of cars.

    (A) 2   (B) 6   (C) 7   (D) 12   (E) 14

Probability & Statistics

PROBABILITY

We know what probability means, but what is its formal definition? Let's use our intuition to define it. If there is no chance that an event will occur, then its probability of occurring should be 0. On the other extreme, if an event is certain to occur, then its probability of occurring should be 100%, or 1. Hence, our *probability* should be a number between 0 and 1, inclusive. But what kind of number? Suppose your favorite actor has a 1 in 3 chance of winning the Oscar for best actor. This can be measured by forming the fraction 1/3. Hence, a *probability* is a fraction where the top is the number of ways an event can occur and the bottom is the total number of possible events:

$$P = \frac{Number\ of\ ways\ an\ event\ can\ occur}{Number\ of\ total\ possible\ events}$$

Example: *Flipping a coin*

What's the probability of getting heads when flipping a coin?

There is only one way to get heads in a coin toss. Hence, the top of the probability fraction is 1. There are two possible results: heads or tails. Forming the probability fraction gives 1/2.

Example: *Tossing a die*

What's the probability of getting a 3 when tossing a die?

A die (a cube) has six faces, numbered 1 through 6. There is only one way to get a 3. Hence, the top of the fraction is 1. There are 6 possible results: 1, 2, 3, 4, 5, and 6. Forming the probability fraction gives 1/6.

Example: *Drawing a card from a deck*

What's the probability of getting a king when drawing a card from a deck of cards?

A deck of cards has four kings, so there are 4 ways to get a king. Hence, the top of the fraction is 4. There are 52 total cards in a deck. Forming the probability fraction gives 4/52, which reduces to 1/13. Hence, there is 1 chance in 13 of getting a king.

Example: *Drawing marbles from a bowl*

What's the probability of drawing a blue marble from a bowl containing 4 red marbles, 5 blue marbles, and 5 green marbles?

There are five ways of drawing a blue marble. Hence, the top of the fraction is 5. There are 14 (= 4 + 5 + 5) possible results. Forming the probability fraction gives 5/14.

Example: *Drawing marbles from a bowl (second drawing)*

What's the probability of drawing a red marble from the same bowl, given that the first marble drawn was blue and was not placed back in the bowl?

There are four ways of drawing a red marble. Hence, the top of the fraction is 4. Since the blue marble from the first drawing was not replaced, there are only 4 blue marbles remaining. Hence, there are 13 (= 4 + 4 + 5) possible results. Forming the probability fraction gives 4/13.

Consecutive Probabilities

What's the probability of getting heads twice in a row when flipping a coin twice? Previously we calculated the probability for the first flip to be 1/2. Since the second flip is not affected by the first (these are called *mutually exclusive* events), its probability is also 1/2. Forming the product yields the probability of two heads in a row: $\frac{1}{2} \times \frac{1}{2} = \frac{1}{4}$.

What's the probability of drawing a blue marble and then a red marble from a bowl containing 4 red marbles, 5 blue marbles, and 5 green marbles? (Assume that the marbles are not replaced after being selected.) As calculated before, there is a 5/14 likelihood of selecting a blue marble first and a 4/13 likelihood of selecting a red marble second. Forming the product yields the probability of a blue marble immediately followed by a red marble: $\frac{5}{14} \times \frac{4}{13} = \frac{20}{182} = \frac{10}{91}$.

These two examples can be generalized into the following rule for calculating consecutive probabilities:

> **To calculate consecutive probabilities, multiply the individual probabilities.**

This rule applies to two, three, or any number of consecutive probabilities.

Either-Or Probabilities

What's the probability of getting either heads or tails when flipping a coin once? Since the only possible outcomes are heads or tails, we expect the probability to be 100%, or 1: $\frac{1}{2} + \frac{1}{2} = 1$. Note that the events heads and tails are mutually exclusive. That is, if heads occurs, then tails cannot (and vice versa).

What's the probability of drawing a red marble or a green marble from a bowl containing 4 red marbles, 5 blue marbles, and 5 green marbles? There are 4 red marbles out of 14 total marbles. So the probability of selecting a red marble is 4/14 = 2/7. Similarly, the probability of selecting a green marble is 5/14. So the probability of selecting a red or green marble is $\frac{2}{7} + \frac{5}{14} = \frac{9}{14}$. Note again that the events are mutually exclusive. For instance, if a red marble is selected, then neither a blue marble nor a green marble is selected.

These two examples can be generalized into the following rule for calculating *either-or* probabilities:

> **To calculate *either-or* probabilities, add the individual probabilities (only if the events are mutually exclusive).**

The probabilities in the two immediately preceding examples can be calculated more naturally by adding up the events that occur and then dividing by the total number of possible events. For the coin example, we get 2 events (heads or tails) divided by the total number of possible events, 2 (heads and tails): 2/2 = 1. For the marble example, we get 9 (= 4 + 5) ways the event can occur divided by 14 (= 4 + 5 + 5) possible events: 9/14.

If it's more natural to calculate the *either-or* probabilities above by adding up the events that occur and then dividing by the total number of possible events, why did we introduce a second way of calculating the probabilities? Because in some cases, you may have to add the individual probabilities. For example, you may be given the individual probabilities of two mutually exclusive events and be asked for the probability that either could occur. You now know to merely add their individual probabilities.

STATISTICS

Statistics is the study of the patterns and relationships of numbers and data. There are four main concepts that may appear on the test:

Median

When a set of numbers is arranged in order of size, the *median* is the middle number. For example, the median of the set {8, 9, 10, 11, 12} is 10 because it is the middle number. In this case, the median is also the mean (average). But this is usually not the case. For example, the median of the set {8, 9, 10, 11, 17} is 10 because it is the middle number, but the mean is $11 = \dfrac{8 + 9 + 10 + 11 + 17}{5}$. If a set contains an even number of elements, then the median is the average of the two middle elements. For example, the median of the set {1, 5, 8, 20} is $6.5 \left(= \dfrac{5 + 8}{2} \right)$.

Example: What is the median of 0, –2, 256 , 18, $\sqrt{2}$?

Arranging the numbers from smallest to largest (we could also arrange the numbers from the largest to smallest; the answer would be the same), we get –2, 0, $\sqrt{2}$, 18, 256. The median is the middle number, $\sqrt{2}$.

Mode

The *mode* is the number or numbers that appear most frequently in a set. Note that this definition allows a set of numbers to have more than one mode.

Example: What is the mode of 3, –4, 3 , 7, 9, 7.5 ?

The number 3 is the mode because it is the only number that is listed more than once.

Example: What is the mode of 2, π, 2 , –9, π, 5 ?

Both 2 and π are modes because each occurs twice, which is the greatest number of occurrences for any number in the list.

Range

The *range* is the distance between the smallest and largest numbers in a set. To calculate the range, merely subtract the smallest number from the largest number.

Example: What is the range of 2, 8, 1 , –6, π, 1/2 ?

The largest number in this set is 8, and the smallest number is –6. Hence, the range is 8 – (–6) = 8 + 6 = 14.

Standard Deviation

On the test, you are not expected to know the definition of standard deviation. However, you may be presented with the definition of standard deviation and then be asked a question based on the definition. To make sure we cover all possible bases, we'll briefly discuss this concept.

Standard deviation measures how far the numbers in a set vary from the set's mean. If the numbers are scattered far from the set's mean, then the standard deviation is large. If the numbers are bunched up near the set's mean, then the standard deviation is small.

Example: Which of the following sets has the larger standard deviation?

$$A = \{1, 2, 3, 4, 5\}$$
$$B = \{1, 4, 15, 21, 27\}$$

All the numbers in Set A are within 2 units of the mean, 3. All the numbers in Set B are greater than 5 units from the mean, 15. Hence, the standard deviation of Set B is greater.

Problem Set W: Solutions begin on page 271.

1. The median is larger than the average for which one of the following sets of integers?

    (A) {8, 9, 10, 11, 12}
    (B) {8, 9, 10, 11, 13}
    (C) {8, 10, 10, 10, 12}
    (D) {10, 10, 10, 10, 10}
    (E) {7, 9, 10, 11, 12}

2. A hat contains 15 marbles, and each marble is numbered with one and only one of the numbers 1, 2, 3. From a group of 15 people, each person selects exactly 1 marble from the hat.

Numbered Marble	Number of People Who Selected The Marble
1	4
2	5
3	6

    What is the probability that a person selected at random picked a marble numbered 2 or greater?

    (A) 5/15   (B) 9/15   (C) 10/15   (D) 11/15   (E) 1

3. Sarah cannot completely remember her four-digit ATM pin number. She does remember the first two digits, and she knows that each of the last two digits is greater than 5. The ATM will allow her three tries before it blocks further access. If she randomly guesses the last two digits, what is the probability that she will get access to her account?

    (A) 1/2   (B) 1/4   (C) 3/16   (D) 3/18   (E) 1/32

4. If $x < y < z$, $z = ky$, $x = 0$, and the average of the numbers x, y, and z is 3 times the median, what is the value of k?

    (A) –2   (B) 3   (C) 5.5   (D) 6   (E) 8

5. Three positive numbers x, y, and z have the following relationships $y = x + 2$ and $z = y + 2$. When the median of x, y, and z is subtracted from the product of the smallest number and the median, the result is 0. What is the value of the largest number?

    (A) –2   (B) π (C) 5   (D) 8   (E) 21/2

6. A jar contains only three types of objects: red, blue, and silver paper clips. The probability of selecting a red paper clip is 1/4, and the probability of selecting a blue paper clip is 1/6. What is the probability of selecting a silver paper clip?

    (A) 5/12   (B) 1/2   (C) 7/12   (D) 3/4   (E) 11/12

7. A bowl contains one marble labeled 0, one marble labeled 1, one marble labeled 2, and one marble labeled 3. The bowl contains no other objects. If two marbles are drawn randomly without replacement, what is the probability that they will add up to 3?

    (A) 1/12   (B) 1/8   (C) 1/6   (D) 1/4   (E) 1/3

8. A housing subdivision contains only two types of homes: ranch-style homes and townhomes. There are twice as many townhomes as ranch-style homes. There are 3 times as many townhomes with pools than without pools. What is the probability that a home selected at random from the subdivision will be a townhome with a pool?

    (A) 1/6   (B) 1/5   (C) 1/4   (D) 1/3   (E) 1/2

Summary of Math Properties

Arithmetic

1. A *prime number* is an integer that is divisible only by itself and 1.
2. An even number is divisible by 2, and can be written as $2x$.
3. An odd number is not divisible by 2, and can be written as $2x + 1$.
4. Division by zero is undefined.
5. Perfect squares: 1, 4, 9, 16, 25, 36, 49, 64, 81 . . .
6. Perfect cubes: 1, 8, 27, 64, 125 . . .
7. If the last digit of a integer is 0, 2, 4, 6, or 8, then it is divisible by 2.
8. An integer is divisible by 3 if the sum of its digits is divisible by 3.
9. If the last digit of a integer is 0 or 5, then it is divisible by 5.
10. Miscellaneous Properties of Positive and Negative Numbers:

    A. The product (quotient) of positive numbers is positive.
    B. The product (quotient) of a positive number and a negative number is negative.
    C. The product (quotient) of an even number of negative numbers is positive.
    D. The product (quotient) of an odd number of negative numbers is negative.
    E. The sum of negative numbers is negative.
    F. A number raised to an even exponent is greater than or equal to zero.

$$even \times even = even$$
$$odd \times odd = odd$$
$$even \times odd = even$$

$$even + even = even$$
$$odd + odd = even$$
$$even + odd = odd$$

11. Consecutive integers are written as $x, x + 1, x + 2, \ldots$
12. Consecutive even or odd integers are written as $x, x + 2, x + 4, \ldots$
13. The integer zero is neither positive nor negative, but it is even: $0 = 2 \cdot 0$.
14. Commutative property: $x + y = y + x$. Example: $5 + 4 = 4 + 5$.
15. Associative property: $(x + y) + z = x + (y + z)$. Example: $(1 + 2) + 3 = 1 + (2 + 3)$.
16. Order of operations: Parentheses, Exponents, Multiplication, Division, Addition, Subtraction.
17. $-\dfrac{x}{y} = \dfrac{-x}{y} = \dfrac{x}{-y}$. Example: $-\dfrac{2}{3} = \dfrac{-2}{3} = \dfrac{2}{-3}$

18.

$$33\frac{1}{3}\% = \frac{1}{3} \qquad 20\% = \frac{1}{5}$$

$$66\frac{2}{3}\% = \frac{2}{3} \qquad 40\% = \frac{2}{5}$$

$$25\% = \frac{1}{4} \qquad 60\% = \frac{3}{5}$$

$$50\% = \frac{1}{2} \qquad 80\% = \frac{4}{5}$$

19.

$$\frac{1}{100} = .01 \qquad \frac{1}{10} = .1 \qquad \frac{2}{5} = .4$$

$$\frac{1}{50} = .02 \qquad \frac{1}{5} = .2 \qquad \frac{1}{2} = .5$$

$$\frac{1}{25} = .04 \qquad \frac{1}{4} = .25 \qquad \frac{2}{3} = .666\ldots$$

$$\frac{1}{20} = .05 \qquad \frac{1}{3} = .333\ldots \qquad \frac{3}{4} = .75$$

20. Common measurements:
    1 foot = 12 inches
    1 yard = 3 feet
    1 mile = 5,280 feet
    1 quart = 2 pints
    1 gallon = 4 quarts
    1 pound = 16 ounces
    1 ton = 2,000 pounds
    1 year = 365 days
    1 year = 52 weeks

21. Important approximations: $\sqrt{2} \approx 1.4 \qquad \sqrt{3} \approx 1.7 \qquad \pi \approx 3.14$

22. *"The remainder is r when p is divided by q"* means $p = qz + r$; the integer z is called the quotient. For instance, *"The remainder is 1 when 7 is divided by 3"* means $7 = 3 \cdot 2 + 1$.

23. $Probability = \dfrac{number\ of\ outcomes}{total\ number\ of\ possible\ outcomes}$

Algebra

24. Multiplying or dividing both sides of an inequality by a negative number reverses the inequality. That is, if $x > y$ and $c < 0$, then $cx < cy$.

25. Transitive Property: If $x < y$ and $y < z$, then $x < z$.

26. Like Inequalities Can Be Added: If $x < y$ and $w < z$, then $x + w < y + z$.

27. Rules for exponents:

$$x^a \cdot x^b = x^{a+b} \qquad \text{Caution, } x^a + x^b \neq x^{a+b}$$

$$\left(x^a\right)^b = x^{ab}$$

$$(xy)^a = x^a \cdot y^a$$

$$\left(\frac{x}{y}\right)^a = \frac{x^a}{y^a}$$

$$\frac{x^a}{x^b} = x^{a-b}, \text{ if } a > b. \qquad \frac{x^a}{x^b} = \frac{1}{x^{b-a}}, \text{ if } b > a.$$

$$x^0 = 1$$

28. There are only two rules for roots that you need to know for the test:

$$\sqrt[n]{xy} = \sqrt[n]{x}\sqrt[n]{y} \qquad\qquad \text{For example, } \sqrt{3x} = \sqrt{3}\sqrt{x}.$$

$$\sqrt[n]{\frac{x}{y}} = \frac{\sqrt[n]{x}}{\sqrt[n]{y}} \qquad\qquad \text{For example, } \sqrt[3]{\frac{x}{8}} = \frac{\sqrt[3]{x}}{\sqrt[3]{8}} = \frac{\sqrt[3]{x}}{2}.$$

$$\text{Caution: } \sqrt[n]{x+y} \neq \sqrt[n]{x} + \sqrt[n]{y}.$$

29.   Factoring formulas:

$$x(y + z) = xy + xz$$
$$x^2 - y^2 = (x + y)(x - y)$$
$$(x - y)^2 = x^2 - 2xy + y^2$$
$$(x + y)^2 = x^2 + 2xy + y^2$$
$$-(x - y) = y - x$$

30.   Adding, multiplying, and dividing fractions:

$$\frac{x}{y} + \frac{z}{y} = \frac{x + z}{y} \quad \text{and} \quad \frac{x}{y} - \frac{z}{y} = \frac{x - z}{y}$$
Example: $\dfrac{2}{4} + \dfrac{3}{4} = \dfrac{2 + 3}{4} = \dfrac{5}{4}$.

$$\frac{w}{x} \cdot \frac{y}{z} = \frac{wy}{xz}$$
Example: $\dfrac{1}{2} \cdot \dfrac{3}{4} = \dfrac{1 \cdot 3}{2 \cdot 4} = \dfrac{3}{8}$.

$$\frac{w}{x} \div \frac{y}{z} = \frac{w}{x} \cdot \frac{z}{y}$$
Example: $\dfrac{1}{2} \div \dfrac{3}{4} = \dfrac{1}{2} \cdot \dfrac{4}{3} = \dfrac{4}{6} = \dfrac{2}{3}$.

31. $x\% = \dfrac{x}{100}$

32.   Quadratic Formula: $x = \dfrac{-b \pm \sqrt{b^2 - 4ac}}{2a}$ are the solutions of the equation $ax^2 + bx + c = 0$.

Geometry

33.   There are four major types of angle measures:

An **acute angle** has measure less than 90°:

A **right angle** has measure 90°:

90°

An **obtuse angle** has measure greater than 90°:

A **straight angle** has measure 180°:

y°   x°   x + y = 180°

34.   Two angles are supplementary if their angle sum is 180°:

45°   135°

45 + 135 = 180

35.   Two angles are complementary if their angle sum is 90°:

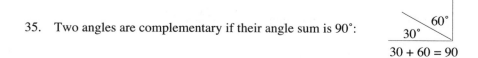

60°

30°

30 + 60 = 90

36. Perpendicular lines meet at right angles:

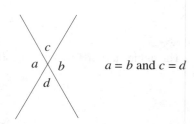

$l_1 \perp l_2$

37. When two straight lines meet at a point, they form four angles. The angles opposite each other are called vertical angles, and they are congruent (equal). In the figure to the right, $a = b$, and $c = d$.

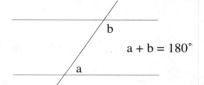

$a = b$ and $c = d$

38. When parallel lines are cut by a transversal, three important angle relationships exist:

Alternate interior angles are equal.

Corresponding angles are equal.

Interior angles on the same side of the transversal are supplementary.

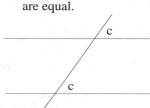

$a + b = 180°$

39. The shortest distance from a point not on a line to the line is along a perpendicular line.

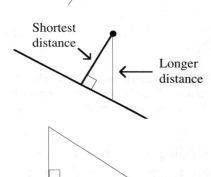

Shortest distance

Longer distance

40. A triangle containing a right angle is called a *right triangle*. The right angle is denoted by a small square:

41. A triangle with two equal sides is called isosceles. The angles opposite the equal sides are called the base angles:

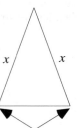

Base angles

42. In an equilateral triangle, all three sides are equal and each angle is 60°:

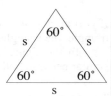

43.   The altitude to the base of an isosceles or equilateral triangle bisects the base and bisects the vertex angle:

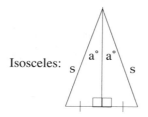 Isosceles: Equilateral: $h = \dfrac{s\sqrt{3}}{2}$

44.   The angle sum of a triangle is 180°:

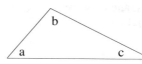 $a + b + c = 180°$

45.   The area of a triangle is $\dfrac{1}{2}bh$, where b is the base and h is the height.

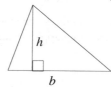 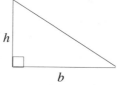 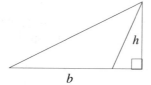 $A = \dfrac{1}{2}bh$

46.   In a triangle, the longer side is opposite the larger angle, and vice versa:

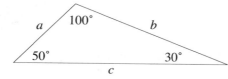   50° is larger than 30°, so side b is longer than side a.

47.   Pythagorean Theorem (right triangles only): The square of the hypotenuse is equal to the sum of the squares of the legs.

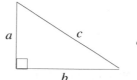 $c^2 = a^2 + b^2$

48.   A Pythagorean triple: the numbers 3, 4, and 5 can always represent the sides of a right triangle and they appear very often: $5^2 = 3^2 + 4^2$.

49.   Two triangles are similar (same shape and usually different size) if their corresponding angles are equal. If two triangles are similar, their corresponding sides are proportional:

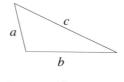 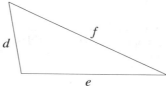

$$\dfrac{a}{d} = \dfrac{b}{e} = \dfrac{c}{f}$$

50.   If two angles of a triangle are congruent to two angles of another triangle, the triangles are similar.

   In the figure to the right, the large and small triangles are similar because both contain a right angle and they share $\angle A$.

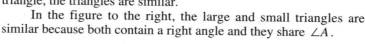

51.   Two triangles are congruent (identical) if they have the same size and shape.

52. In a triangle, an exterior angle is equal to the sum of its remote interior angles and is therefore greater than either of them:

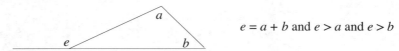

$e = a + b$ and $e > a$ and $e > b$

53. In a triangle, the sum of the lengths of any two sides is greater than the length of the remaining side:

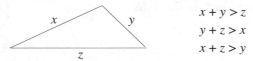

$x + y > z$

$y + z > x$

$x + z > y$

54. In a 30°–60°–90° triangle, the sides have the following relationships:

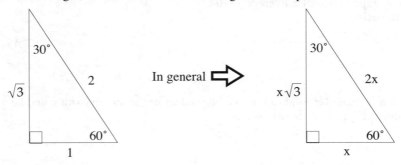

In general

55. In a 45°–45°–90° triangle, the sides have the following relationships:

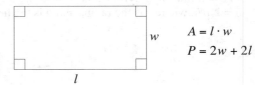

56. Opposite sides of a parallelogram are both parallel and congruent:

57. The diagonals of a parallelogram bisect each other:

58. A parallelogram with four right angles is a *rectangle*. If w is the width and l is the length of a rectangle, then its area is $A = lw$ and its perimeter is $P = 2w + 2l$:

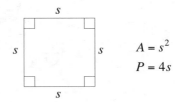

$A = l \cdot w$

$P = 2w + 2l$

59. If the opposite sides of a rectangle are equal, it is a square and its area is $A = s^2$ and its perimeter is $P = 4s$, where s is the length of a side:

$A = s^2$

$P = 4s$

60. The diagonals of a square bisect each other and are perpendicular to each other:

61. A quadrilateral with only one pair of parallel sides is a *trapezoid*. The parallel sides are called *bases*, and the non-parallel sides are called *legs*:

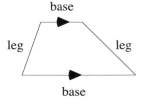

62. The area of a trapezoid is the average of the bases times the height:

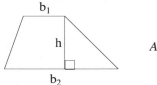

$$A = \left(\frac{b_1 + b_2}{2} \right) h$$

63. The volume of a rectangular solid (a box) is the product of the length, width, and height. The surface area is the sum of the area of the six faces:

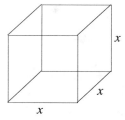

$$V = l \cdot w \cdot h$$
$$S = 2wl + 2hl + 2wh$$

64. If the length, width, and height of a rectangular solid (a box) are the same, it is a cube. Its volume is the cube of one of its sides, and its surface area is the sum of the areas of the six faces:

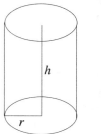

$$V = x^3$$
$$S = 6x^2$$

65. The volume of a cylinder is $V = \pi r^2 h$, and the lateral surface (excluding the top and bottom) is $S = 2\pi rh$, where r is the radius and h is the height:

$$V = \pi r^2 h$$
$$S = 2\pi rh + 2\pi r^2$$

66.   A line segment form the circle to its center is a *radius*.
      A line segment with both end points on a circle is a *chord*.
      A chord passing though the center of a circle is a *diameter*.
      A diameter can be viewed as two radii, and hence a diameter's
      length is twice that of a radius.
      A line passing through two points on a circle is a *secant*.
      A piece of the circumference is an *arc*.
      The area bounded by the circumference and an angle with vertex
      at the center of the circle is a *sector*.

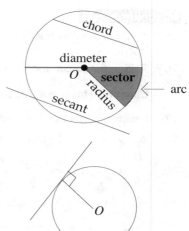

67.   A tangent line to a circle intersects the circle at only one point.
      The radius of the circle is perpendicular to the tangent line at the
      point of tangency:

68.   Two tangents to a circle from a common
      exterior point of the circle are congruent:

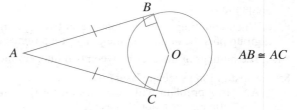

$AB \cong AC$

69.   An angle inscribed in a semicircle is a right angle:

70.   A central angle has by definition the same measure as its intercepted arc.

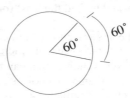

71.   An inscribed angle has one-half the measure of its intercepted arc.

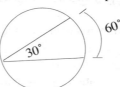

72.   The area of a circle is πr^2, and its circumference
      (perimeter) is $2\pi r$, where r is the radius:

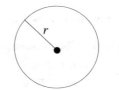

$A = \pi r^2$

$C = 2\pi r$

73.   To find the area of the shaded region of a figure, subtract the area of the unshaded region from the
      area of the entire figure.

74.   When drawing geometric figures, don't forget extreme cases.

Miscellaneous

75. To compare two fractions, cross-multiply. The larger product will be on the same side as the larger fraction.

76. Taking the square root of a fraction between 0 and 1 makes it larger.

    Caution: This is not true for fractions greater than 1. For example, $\sqrt{\dfrac{9}{4}} = \dfrac{3}{2}$. But $\dfrac{3}{2} < \dfrac{9}{4}$.

77. Squaring a fraction between 0 and 1 makes it smaller.

78. $ax^2 \neq (ax)^2$. In fact, $a^2x^2 = (ax)^2$.

79. $\dfrac{1/a}{b} \neq \dfrac{1}{a/b}$. In fact, $\dfrac{1/a}{b} = \dfrac{1}{ab}$ and $\dfrac{1}{a/b} = \dfrac{b}{a}$.

80. $-(a + b) \neq -a + b$. In fact, $-(a + b) = -a - b$.

81. $percentage\ increase = \dfrac{increase}{original\ amount}$

82. Systems of simultaneous equations can most often be solved by merely adding or subtracting the equations.

83. When counting elements that are in overlapping sets, the total number will equal the number in one group plus the number in the other group minus the number common to both groups.

84. The number of integers between two integers <u>inclusive</u> is one more than their difference.

85. Substitution (Special Cases):
    A. In a problem with two variables, say, x and y, you must check the case in which $x = y$. (This often gives a double case.)
    B. When you are given that $x < 0$, you must plug in negative whole numbers, negative fractions, and -1. (Choose the numbers -1, -2, and $-1/2$, in that order.)
    C. Sometimes you have to plug in the first three numbers (but never more than three) from a class of numbers.

86. Elimination strategies:
    A. On hard problems, if you are asked to find the least (or greatest) number, then eliminate the least (or greatest) answer-choice.
    B. On hard problems, eliminate the answer-choice "not enough information."
    C. On hard problems, eliminate answer-choices that <u>merely</u> repeat numbers from the problem.
    D. On hard problems, eliminate answer-choices that can be derived from elementary operations.
    E. After you have eliminated as many answer-choices as you can, choose from the more complicated or more unusual answer-choices remaining.

87. To solve a fractional equation, multiply both sides by the LCD (lowest common denominator) to clear fractions.

88. You can cancel only over multiplication, not over addition or subtraction. For example, the c's in the expression $\dfrac{c + x}{c}$ cannot be canceled.

89. Often you can solve a system of two equations in two unknowns by merely adding or subtracting the equations.

90. The average of N numbers is their sum divided by N, that is, $average = \dfrac{sum}{N}$.

91. *Weighted average:* The average between two sets of numbers is closer to the set with more numbers.

92. $Average\ Speed = \dfrac{Total\ Distance}{Total\ Time}$

93. Distance = Rate × Time

94. $Work = Rate \times Time$, or $W = R \times T$. The amount of work done is usually 1 unit. Hence, the formula becomes $1 = R \times T$. Solving this for R gives $R = \dfrac{1}{T}$.

95. *Interest = Amount × Time × Rate*

SOLUTIONS TO PROBLEMS

Problem Set A:

1. If n is an odd integer, which of the following must be an even integer?

    (A) $n/2$
    (B) $4n + 3$
    (C) $2n$
    (D) n^4
    (E) $\sqrt{n}$

Choose $n = 1$. Then $n/2 = 1/2$, which is not even—eliminate (A). Next, $4n + 3 = 4 \cdot 1 + 3 = 7$, which is not even—eliminate (B). Next, $2n = 2 \cdot 1 = 2$, which is even and may therefore be the answer. Next, both (D) and (E) equal 1, which is not even. Hence, the answer is (C).

2. If x and y are perfect squares, then which of the following is <u>not</u> necessarily a perfect square?

    (A) x^2
    (B) xy
    (C) $4x$
    (D) $x + y$
    (E) x^5

Choose $x = 4$ and $y = 9$. Then $x^2 = 4^2 = 16$, which is a perfect square. (Note, we cannot eliminate x^2 because it may not be a perfect square for another choice of x.) Next, $xy = 4 \cdot 9 = 36$, which is a perfect square. Next, $4x = 4 \cdot 4 = 16$, which is a perfect square. Next, $x + y = 4 + 9 = 13$, which is <u>not</u> a perfect square. Hence, the answer is (D).

3. If y is an even integer and x is an odd integer, which of the following expressions could be an even integer?

    (A) $3x + \dfrac{y}{2}$
    (B) $\dfrac{x + y}{2}$
    (C) $x + y$
    (D) $\dfrac{x}{4} - \dfrac{y}{2}$
    (E) $x^2 + y^2$

Choose $x = 1$ and $y = 2$. Then $3x + \dfrac{y}{2} = 3 \cdot 1 + \dfrac{2}{2} = 4$, which is even. The answer is (A). Note: We don't need to check the other answer-choices because the problem asked for the expression that *could be* even. Thus, the first answer-choice that turns out even is the answer.

4.   If $0 < k < 1$, then which of the following must be less than k?

   (A) $\dfrac{3}{2}k$

   (B) $\dfrac{1}{k}$

   (C) $|k|$

   (D) $\sqrt{k}$

   (E) k^2

Choose $k = 1/4$. Then $\dfrac{3}{2}k = \dfrac{3}{2} \cdot \dfrac{1}{4} = \dfrac{3}{8} > \dfrac{1}{4}$; eliminate (A).   Next, $\dfrac{1}{k} = \dfrac{1}{1/4} = 4 > \dfrac{1}{4}$; eliminate (B).

Next, $|k| = \left|\dfrac{1}{4}\right| = \dfrac{1}{4}$; eliminate (C).   Next, $\sqrt{k} = \sqrt{\dfrac{1}{4}} = \dfrac{1}{2} > \dfrac{1}{4}$; eliminate (D).   Thus, by process of elimination, the answer is (E).

5.   Suppose you begin reading a book on page h and end on page k. If you read each page completely and the pages are numbered and read consecutively, then how many pages have you read?

   (A) $h + k$
   (B) $h - k$
   (C) $k - h + 2$
   (D) $k - h - 1$
   (E) $k - h + 1$

Without substitution, this is a hard problem. With substitution, it's quite easy. Suppose you begin reading on page 1 and stop on page 2. Then you will have read 2 pages. Now, merely substitute $h = 1$ and $k = 2$ into the answer-choices to see which one(s) equal 2. Only $k - h + 1 = 2 - 1 + 1 = 2$ does. (Verify this.) The answer is (E).

6.   If m is an even integer, then which of the following is the sum of the next two even integers greater than $4m + 1$?

   (A) $8m + 2$
   (B) $8m + 4$
   (C) $8m + 6$
   (D) $8m + 8$
   (E) $8m + 10$

Suppose $m = 2$, an even integer. Then $4m + 1 = 9$, which is odd. Hence, the next even integer greater than 9 is 10. And the next even integer after 10 is 12. Now, $10 + 12 = 22$. So look for an answer-choice which equals 22 when $m = 2$.

   Begin with choice (A). Since $m = 2$, $8m + 2 = 18$—eliminate (A). Next, $8m + 4 = 20$—eliminate (B). Next, $8m + 6 = 22$. Hence, the answer is (C).

7.   If x^2 is even, which of the following must be true?

    I. x is odd.

    II. x is even.

    III. x^3 is odd.

    (A)   I only
    (B)   II only
    (C)   III only
    (D)   I and II only
    (E)   II and III only

Suppose $x^2 = 4$. Then $x = 2$ or $x = -2$. In either case, x is even. Hence, Statement I need not be true, which eliminates (A) and (D). Further, $x^3 = 8$ or $x^3 = -8$. In either case, x^3 is even. Hence, Statement III need not be true, which eliminates (C) and (E). Therefore, by process of elimination, the answer is (B).

8.   Suppose x is divisible by 8 but not by 3. Then which of the following CANNOT be an integer?

    (A) $\dfrac{x}{2}$ (B) $\dfrac{x}{4}$ (C) $\dfrac{x}{6}$ (D) $\dfrac{x}{8}$ (E) x

Suppose $x = 8$. Then x is divisible by 8 and is not divisible by 3. Now, $x/2 = 4$, $x/4 = 2$, $x/8 = 1$, and $x = 8$, which are all integers—eliminate (A), (B), (D), and (E). Hence, by process of elimination, the answer is (C).

9.   If p and q are positive integers, how many integers are larger than pq and smaller than $p(q + 2)$?

    (A)   3
    (B) $p + 2$
    (C) $p - 2$
    (D) $2p - 1$
    (E) $2p + 1$

Let $p = 1$ and $q = 2$. Then $pq = 2$ and $p(q + 2) = 4$. This scenario has one integer, 3, greater than pq and less than $p(q + 2)$. Now, we plug $p = 1$ and $q = 2$ into the answer-choices until we find one that has the value 1. Look at choice (D): $2p - 1 = (2)(1) - 1 = 1$. Thus, the answer is (D).

10.   If x and y are prime numbers, then which one of the following cannot equal $x - y$?

    (A) 1 (B) 2 (C) 13 (D) 14 (E) 20

If $x = 3$ and $y = 2$, then $x - y = 3 - 2 = 1$. This eliminates (A). If $x = 5$ and $y = 3$, then $x - y = 5 - 3 = 2$. This eliminates (B). If $x = 17$ and $y = 3$, then $x - y = 17 - 3 = 14$. This eliminates (D). If $x = 23$ and $y = 3$, then $x - y = 23 - 3 = 20$. This eliminates (E). Hence, by process of elimination, the answer is (C).

    Method II (without substitution): Suppose $x - y = 13$. Now, let x and y be distinct prime numbers, both greater than 2. Then both x and y are odd numbers since the only even prime is 2. Hence, $x = 2k + 1$, and $y = 2h$ k and h. And $x - y = (2k + 1) - (2h + 1) = 2k - 2h = 2(k - h)$. Hence, $x - y$ is even. This contradicts the assumption that $x - y = 13$, an odd number. Hence, x and y cannot both be greater than 2. Next, suppose $y = 2$, then $x - y = 13$ becomes $x - 2 = 13$. Solving yields $x = 15$. But 15 is not prime. Hence, there does not exist prime numbers x and y such that $x - y = 13$. The answer is (C).

11. If x is an integer, then which of the following is the product of the next two integers greater than $2(x + 1)$?

(A) $4x^2 + 14x + 12$
(B) $4x^2 + 12$
(C) $x^2 + 14x + 12$
(D) $x^2 + x + 12$
(E) $4x^2 + 14x$

Suppose $x = 1$, an integer. Then $2(x + 1) = 2(1 + 1) = 4$. The next two integers greater than 4 are 5 and 6, and their product is 30. Now, check which of the answer-choices equal 30 when $x = 1$. Begin with (A): $4x^2 + 14x + 12 = 4(1)^2 + 14 \cdot 1 + 12 = 30$. No other answer-choice equals 30 when $x = 1$. Hence, the answer is (A).

12. If the integer x is divisible by 3 but not by 2, then which one of the following expressions is NEVER an integer?

(A) $\dfrac{x + 1}{2}$

(B) $\dfrac{x}{7}$

(C) $\dfrac{x^2}{3}$

(D) $\dfrac{x^3}{3}$

(E) $\dfrac{x}{24}$

The number 3 itself is divisible by 3 but not by 2. With this value for x, Choice (A) becomes $\dfrac{3 + 1}{2} = \dfrac{4}{2} = 2$, eliminate; Choice (C) becomes $\dfrac{3^2}{3} = \dfrac{9}{3} = 3$, eliminate; Choice (D) becomes $\dfrac{3^3}{3} = \dfrac{27}{3} = 9$, eliminate. Next, if $x = 21$, then Choice (B) becomes $\dfrac{21}{7} = 3$, eliminate. Hence, by process of elimination, the answer is (E).

13. If both x and y are positive even integers, then which of the following expressions must also be even?

I. y^{x-1} II. $y - 1$ III. $x/2$

(A)   I only
(B)   II only
(C)   III only
(D)   I and III only
(E)   I, II, and III

If $x = y = 2$, then $y^{x-1} = 2^{2-1} = 2^1 = 2$, which is even. But $y - 1 = 2 - 1 = 1$ is odd, and $x/2 = 2/2 = 1$ is also odd. This eliminates choices (B), (C), (D), and (E). The answer is (A).

14. Which one of the following is a solution to the equation $x^4 - 2x^2 = -1$?

(A)   0   (B)   1   (C)   2   (D)   3   (E)   4

We could solve the equation, but it is much faster to just plug in the answer-choices. Begin with 0: $x^4 - 2x^2 = 0^4 - 2 \cdot 0^2 = 0 - 0 = 0$. Hence, eliminate (A). Next, plug in 1: $x^4 - 2x^2 = 1^4 - 2 \cdot 1^2 = 1 - 2 = -1$. Hence, the answer is (B).

15. If $x \neq 3/4$ which one of the following will equal -2 when multiplied by $\dfrac{3-4x}{5}$?

    (A) $\dfrac{5-4x}{4}$

    (B) $\dfrac{10}{3-4x}$

    (C) $\dfrac{10}{4x-3}$

    (D) $\dfrac{3-4x}{5}$

    (E) $\dfrac{4x-3}{10}$

If $x = 0$, then $\dfrac{3-4x}{5}$ becomes $3/5$ and the answer-choices become

(A) $5/4$
(B) $10/3$
(C) $-10/3$
(D) $3/5$
(E) $-3/10$

Multiplying Choice (C) by $3/5$, gives $\left(\dfrac{3}{5}\right)\left(-\dfrac{10}{3}\right) = -2$. The answer is (C).

Problem Set B:

1. The ten's digit of a two-digit number is twice the unit's digit. Reversing the digits yields a new number that is 27 less than the original number. Which one of the following is the original number?

    (A)   12   (B)   21   (C)   43   (D)   63   (E)   83

The ten's digit must be twice the unit's digit. This eliminates (A), (C), and (E). Now reversing the digits in choice (B) yields 12. But $21 - 12 \neq 27$ This eliminates (B). Hence, by process of elimination, the answer is (D). $(63 - 36 = 27.)$

2. If $\dfrac{N + N}{N^2} = 1$, then $N =$

    (A) $\dfrac{1}{6}$ (B) $\dfrac{1}{3}$ (C)   1   (D)   2   (E)   3

Here we need only plug in answer-choices until we find the one that yields a result of 1. Start with 1, the easiest number to calculate with. $\dfrac{1+1}{1^2} = 2 \neq 1$. Eliminate (C). Next, choosing $N = 2$, we get $\dfrac{2+2}{2^2} = \dfrac{4}{4} = 1$. The answer is (D).

3. Suppose half the people on a bus exit at each stop and no additional passengers board the bus. If on the third stop the next to last person exits the bus, then how many people were on the bus?

    (A)   20   (B)   16   (C)   8   (D)   6   (E)   4

Suppose there were 8 people on the bus—choice (C). Then after the first stop, there would be 4 people left on the bus. After the second stop, there would 2 people left on the bus. After the third stop, there would be only one person left on the bus. Hence, on the third stop the next to last person would have exited the bus. The answer is (C).

4. The sum of the digits of a two-digit number is 12, and the ten's digit is one-third the unit's digit. What is the number?

    (A)   93   (B)   54   (C)   48   (D)   39   (E)   31

In choice (D), $3 + 9 = 12$ and $3 = \dfrac{1}{3} \cdot 9$. Hence, the answer is (D).

5. If $\dfrac{x^6 - 5x^3 - 16}{8} = 1$, then x could be
    (A) 1   (B) 2   (C) 3   (D) 5   (E) 8

We could solve the equation, but it is much faster to just plug in the answer-choices. Begin with 1: $\dfrac{1^6 - 5(1)^3 - 16}{8} = \dfrac{1 - 5 - 16}{8} = \dfrac{-20}{8}$. Hence, eliminate (A). Next, plug in 2: $\dfrac{2^6 - 5(2)^3 - 16}{8} = \dfrac{64 - 5(8) - 16}{8} = \dfrac{64 - 40 - 16}{8} = \dfrac{8}{8} = 1$. The answer is (B).

6. Which one of the following is a solution to the equation $x^4 - 2x^2 = -1$?
    (A) 0   (B) 1   (C) 2   (D) 3   (E) 4

Begin with 0: $x^4 - 2x^2 = 0^4 - 2 \cdot 0^2 = 0 - 0 = 0$. Hence, eliminate (A). Next, plug in 1: $x^4 - 2x^2 = 1^4 - 2 \cdot 1^2 = 1 - 2 = -1$. Hence, the answer is (B).

Problem Set C:

1. $2x^2 + (2x)^2 =$

    (A) $4x^2$ (B) $4x^4$ (C) $8x^2$ (D) $6x^4$ (E) $6x^2$

From the formula $a^2x^2 = (ax)^2$, we see that $(2x)^2 = 2^2 \cdot x^2 = 4x^2$. Plugging this result into the expression $2x^2 + (2x)^2$ yields

$$2x^2 + 4x^2$$

Combining like terms gives

$$6x^2$$

The answer is (E).

2. Which of the following fractions is greatest?

    (A) 15/16   (B) 7/9   (C) 13/15   (D) 8/9   (E) 10/11

Begin by comparing 15/16 to each of the other answer-choices. Cross-multiplying 15/16 and 7/9 gives

$$135 \text{ vs. } 112$$

Now, 135 is greater than 112, so 15/16 is greater than 7/9. Using this procedure to compare 15/16 to each of the remaining answer-choices shows that 15/16 is the greatest fraction listed. The answer is (A).

3. $1 + \dfrac{1}{1 - \dfrac{1}{2}} =$

    (A) $-\dfrac{1}{2}$ (B) $\dfrac{1}{2}$ (C) $\dfrac{3}{2}$ (D) 2   (E) 3

$1 + \dfrac{1}{1 - \dfrac{1}{2}} = 1 + \dfrac{1}{1/2} = 1 + 2 = 3$. The answer is (E).

4. If the ratio of $\dfrac{1}{5}$ to $\dfrac{1}{4}$ is equal to the ratio of $\dfrac{1}{4}$ to x, then what is the value of x?

    (A) $\dfrac{1}{20}$ (B) $\dfrac{1}{5}$ (C) $\dfrac{5}{16}$ (D) $\dfrac{4}{5}$ (E) 5

"The ratio of $\dfrac{1}{5}$ to $\dfrac{1}{4}$ is equal to the ratio of $\dfrac{1}{4}$ to x" means

$$\frac{1/5}{1/4} = \frac{1/4}{x}$$

or

$$\frac{1}{5} \cdot \frac{4}{1} = \frac{1}{4} \cdot \frac{1}{x}$$

This in turn reduces to

$$\frac{4}{5} = \frac{1}{4x}$$

Cross-multiplying yields

$$16x = 5$$

dividing by 16 gives

$$x = \frac{5}{16}$$

The answer is (C).

5.   Which of the following are true?

I. $\dfrac{\sqrt{\dfrac{7}{8}}}{\left(\dfrac{7}{8}\right)^2} > 1$

II. $\dfrac{\sqrt{\dfrac{7}{8}}}{\left(\dfrac{8}{7}\right)^2} > 1$

III. $\sqrt{\dfrac{\dfrac{7}{8}}{\sqrt{\dfrac{7}{8}}}} > 1$

(A) I only   (B) II only   (C) I and II only   (D) I and III only   (E) I, II, and III

Squaring a fraction between 0 and 1 makes it smaller, and taking the square root of it makes it larger. Therefore, Statement I is true since the top part of the fraction is larger than the bottom. This eliminates (B). Next, Statement II is false. Squaring a fraction makes it smaller only if the fraction is between 0 and 1. This eliminates (C) and (E). Finally, Statement III is false. Since $\frac{7}{8} < \sqrt{\frac{7}{8}}$, we get

$$\frac{\dfrac{7}{8}}{\sqrt{\dfrac{7}{8}}} < 1$$

Although taking the square root of this expression will make it larger, it will still be less than 1. The answer is (A).

6.   If $a \# b$ is defined by the expression $a \# b = -b^4$, what is the value of $x \# (-y)$?

(A) y^4 (B) $-x^4$ (C) $-(xy)^4$ (D) x^4 (E) $-y^4$

$x \# (-y) = -(-y)^4 = -y^4$. Note: The exponent applies only to the negative inside the parentheses. The answer is (E).

7. $\dfrac{1}{1-(.2)^2} =$

   (A) $-1/2$ (B) $1/4$ (C) $1/2$ (D) $25/24$ (E) 4

$\dfrac{1}{1-(.2)^2} = \dfrac{1}{1-.04} = \dfrac{1}{.96} = \dfrac{1}{96\big/100} = 1 \cdot \dfrac{100}{96} = \dfrac{100}{96} = \dfrac{25}{24}$. The answer is (D).

8.   If $0 < x < 1$, which of the following expressions is greatest?

   (A) $\dfrac{1}{\sqrt{x}}$ (B) $\sqrt{x}$ (C) $\dfrac{1}{\pi}x$ (D) x^3 (E) x^4

Since x is a fraction between 0 and 1, $\sqrt{x}$ is greater than either x^3 or x^4. It's also greater than $\dfrac{1}{\pi}x$ since $\dfrac{1}{\pi}x$ is less than x. To tell which is greater between $\sqrt{x}$ and $\dfrac{1}{\sqrt{x}}$, let $x = \dfrac{1}{4}$ and plug it into each expression: $\sqrt{x} = \sqrt{\dfrac{1}{4}} = \dfrac{1}{2}$ and $\dfrac{1}{\sqrt{x}} = \dfrac{1}{\sqrt{1/4}} = \dfrac{1}{1/2} = 2$. Hence, $\dfrac{1}{\sqrt{x}}$ is greater than $\sqrt{x}$. The answer is (A).

9.   If $x > y > 0$, which of the following are true?

   I. $\dfrac{x+1}{y+1} > \dfrac{x}{y}$

   II. $\dfrac{x+1}{y+1} = \dfrac{x}{y}$

   III. $\dfrac{x+1}{y+1} > 1$

   (A) I only   (B) II only   (C) III only   (D) I and III only   (E) II and III only

Statement I is not necessarily true. For example, if $x = 2$ and $y = 1$, then

$$\dfrac{x+1}{y+1} = \dfrac{2+1}{1+1} = \dfrac{3}{2} \neq 2 = \dfrac{2}{1} = \dfrac{x}{y}$$

This is also a counterexample to Statement II. Hence, we can eliminate (A), (B), (D), and (E). Thus, by process of elimination, the answer is (C).

   However, it is instructive to prove that Statement III is true. From the expression $x > y > 0$, we get

$$x + 1 > y + 1$$

Since $y + 1 > 0$, dividing both sides of the above expression will not reverse the inequality:

$$\dfrac{x+1}{y+1} > 1$$

Hence, Statement III is necessarily true.

10.   If $rs = 4$ and $st = 10$, then $\dfrac{\frac{4}{r}}{\frac{10}{t}} =$

   (A) $1/10$ (B) 1   (C) $5/2$ (D) 8   (E) 40

Solving the equation $rs = 4$ for s gives $s = \dfrac{4}{r}$. Solving the equation $st = 10$ for s gives $s = \dfrac{10}{t}$.

Hence, $\dfrac{\frac{4}{r}}{\frac{10}{t}} = \dfrac{s}{s} = 1$. The answer is (B).

Problem Set D:

1.   For all $p \neq 2$ define p^* by the equation $p^* = \dfrac{p+5}{p-2}$. If $p = 3$, then $p^* =$

   (A) $8/5$
   (B) $8/3$
   (C)   4
   (D)   5
   (E)   8

Substituting $p = 3$ into the equation $p^* = \dfrac{p+5}{p-2}$ gives $3^* = \dfrac{3+5}{3-2} = \dfrac{8}{1} = 8$. The answer is (E).

2.   Let $\boxed{x}$ be defined by the equation $\boxed{x} = \dfrac{x^2}{2}$. Then which of the following equals 2 ?

   (A) $\boxed{2}$
   (B) $\boxed{4}$
   (C) $\boxed{6}$
   (D) $\boxed{8}$
   (E) $\boxed{10}$

GMAT answer-choices are usually listed in ascending order of size—occasionally they are listed in descending order. Hence, start with choice (C). If it is less than 2, then turn to choice (D). If it is greater than 2, then turn to choice (B).

   Now, $\boxed{6} = \dfrac{6^2}{2} = \dfrac{36}{2} = 18$, which is greater than 2. So we next check choice (B). Now,

$\boxed{4} = \dfrac{4^2}{2} = \dfrac{16}{2} = 8$, which is greater than 2. Therefore, by process of elimination, the answer is (A).

Let's verify this: $\boxed{2} = \dfrac{2^2}{2} = \dfrac{4}{2} = 2$.

3.   For all a and b, define $a \# b$ to be $-\sqrt{(a+b)^2}$. What is the value of $(2 \# 3)(0 \# 1)$?

   (A) -2   (B) 0   (C) 5   (D) 6   (E) 9

$(2 \# 3)(0 \# 1) = \left(-\sqrt{(2+3)^2}\right)\left(-\sqrt{(0+1)^2}\right) = \left(-\sqrt{5^2}\right)\left(-\sqrt{1^2}\right) = (-5)(-1) = 5$. The answer is (C).

4. If $\left(\!d\!\right)$ denotes the area of a circle with diameter d, then which of the following is equal to $\left(\!4\!\right) \cdot \left(\!6\!\right)$?

    (A) $\left(\!10\!\right)$

    (B) $\left(\!12\!\right)$

    (C) $\left(\!24\!\right)$

    (D) $\pi \cdot \left(\!12\!\right)$

    (E) $\pi \cdot \left(\!24\!\right)$

The area of a circle is πr^2 (where r is the radius), or $\pi\!\left(\dfrac{d}{2}\right)^{\!2}$ (where d is the diameter). This formula yields $\left(\!4\!\right) \cdot \left(\!6\!\right) = \pi\!\left(\dfrac{4}{2}\right)^{\!2} \cdot \pi\!\left(\dfrac{6}{2}\right)^{\!2} = \pi 4 \cdot \pi 9 = 36\pi^2$. Now, $\pi \cdot \left(\!12\!\right) = \pi \cdot \pi\!\left(\dfrac{12}{2}\right)^{\!2} = \pi^2 6^2 = 36\pi^2$. Hence, the answer is (D).

5. For all real numbers x, y, and z, let $\overleftrightarrow{x,\,y,\,z} = (x-y)z$. For what value of a is $\overleftrightarrow{0,\,1,\,a}$ equal to $\overleftrightarrow{1,\,a,\,0}$?

    (A) -1 (B) 0 (C) 1 (D) 5 (E) All values of a.

$\overleftrightarrow{0,\,1,\,a} = (0-1)a = -a$, and $\overleftrightarrow{1,\,a,\,0} = (1-a)0 = 0$. Setting these expressions equal to each other gives $-a = 0$, which reduces to $a = 0$. The answer is (B).

6. Let $\boxed{x} = x^2 - 2$. If $\boxed{2} - \boxed{x} = x^2$, then $x =$

    (A) $\sqrt{2}$
    (B) $\sqrt{3}$
    (C) 2
    (D) 4
    (E) 8

$\boxed{2} = 2^2 - 2 = 2$, and $\boxed{x} = x^2 - 2$. Substituting these values into the equation $\boxed{2} - \boxed{x} = x^2$ yields

$$2 - \left(x^2 - 2\right) = x^2$$
$$2 - x^2 + 2 = x^2$$
$$4 - x^2 = x^2$$
$$4 = 2x^2$$
$$2 = x^2$$
$$\sqrt{2} = x$$

The answer is (A).

7.   For all real numbers a and b, where $a \cdot b \neq 0$, let $a \Diamond b = ab - \dfrac{a}{b}$. Then which of the following must be true?

    I. $a \Diamond b = b \Diamond a$
   II. $a \Diamond a = (a + 1)(a - 1)$
  III. $(a \Diamond b) \Diamond c = a \Diamond (b \Diamond c)$

    (A)   I only
    (B)   II only
    (C)   III only
    (D)   I and II only
    (E)   I, II, and III

Statement I is false. For instance, $1 \Diamond 2 = 1 \cdot 2 - \dfrac{1}{2} = \dfrac{3}{2}$, but $2 \Diamond 1 = 2 \cdot 1 - \dfrac{2}{1} = 0$. This eliminates (A), (D), and (E).

Statement II is true: $a \Diamond a = aa - \dfrac{a}{a} = a^2 - 1 = (a+1)(a-1)$. This eliminates (C). Hence, by process of elimination, the answer is (B).

Note: The expression $a \cdot b \neq 0$ insures that neither a nor b equals 0: if $a \cdot b = 0$, then either $a = 0$ or $b = 0$, or both.

8.   The operation $*$ is defined for all non-zero x and y by the equation $x * y = \dfrac{x}{y}$. Then the expression $(x * y) * z$ is equal to

    (A) $\dfrac{z}{xy}$

    (B) $\dfrac{y}{xz}$

    (C) xyz

    (D) $\dfrac{xz}{y}$

    (E) $\dfrac{x}{yz}$

$$(x * y) * z = \left(\dfrac{x}{y}\right) * z = \dfrac{\left(\dfrac{x}{y}\right)}{z} = \dfrac{x}{y} \cdot \dfrac{1}{z} = \dfrac{x}{yz}.$$ Hence, the answer is (E).

9.   Let $x \Theta y = x\sqrt{y} - y - 2x$. For what value of x does $x \Theta y = -y$ for all values of y?

    (A)   0

    (B) $\dfrac{2}{\sqrt{3}}$

    (C) $\sqrt{3}$

    (D)   2

    (E)   4

From the equation $x \Theta y = -y$, we get

$$x\sqrt{y} - y - 2x = -y$$

$$x\sqrt{y} - 2x = 0$$

$$x\left(\sqrt{y} - 2\right) = 0$$

Now, if $x = 0$, then $x\left(\sqrt{y} - 2\right) = 0$ will be true regardless the value of y since the product of zero and any number is zero. The answer is (A).

10. For all positive numbers n, $n^{*} = \dfrac{\sqrt{n}}{2}$. What is the value of $\left(64^{*}\right)^{*}$?

    (A)   1
    (B)   2
    (C) $\dfrac{\sqrt{32}}{2}$
    (D)   4
    (E)   16

$\left(64^{*}\right)^{*} = \left(\dfrac{\sqrt{64}}{2}\right)^{*} = \left(\dfrac{8}{2}\right)^{*} = 4^{*} = \dfrac{\sqrt{4}}{2} = \dfrac{2}{2} = 1$. The answer is (A).

11. If $\boxed{x} = (x + 2)x$, for all x, what is the value of $\boxed{x + 2} - \boxed{x - 2}$?

    (A) -2
    (B) $x + 4$
    (C)   0
    (D) x^{2}
    (E) $8(x + 1)$

$$\boxed{x + 2} - \boxed{x - 2} = \left([x + 2] + 2\right)[x + 2] - \left([x - 2] + 2\right)[x - 2]$$
$$= (x + 4)[x + 2] - x[x - 2]$$
$$= x^{2} + 6x + 8 - \left(x^{2} - 2x\right)$$
$$= x^{2} + 6x + 8 - x^{2} + 2x$$
$$= 8x + 8$$
$$= 8(x + 1)$$

The answer is (E).

12. For all numbers N, let $\overset{\infty}{N}$ denote the least integer greater than or equal to N. What is the value of $\overset{\infty}{-2.1}$?

    (A) -4
    (B) -3
    (C) -2
    (D) -1
    (E)   0

Following is the set of all integers greater than -2.1:

$$\{-2, -1, 0, 1, 2, \ldots\}$$

The least integer in this set is -2. The answer is (C).

<u>Questions 13–14</u> refer to the following definition:

Define the symbol # by the following equations:

$x \# y = (x - y)^2$, if $x > y$.

$x \# y = x + \dfrac{y}{4}$, if $x \leq y$.

13.　4 # 12 =

　　(A)　4
　　(B)　7
　　(C)　8
　　(D)　13
　　(E)　64

Since $4 < 12$, we use the bottom half of the definition of #:

$$4 \# 12 = 4 + \frac{12}{4} = 4 + 3 = 7$$

The answer is (B).

14.　If $x \# y = -1$, which of the following could be true?

　　　I.　$x = y$
　　　II.　$x > y$
　　　III.　$x < y$

　　(A)　I only
　　(B)　II only
　　(C)　III only
　　(D)　I and III only
　　(E)　I, II, and III

Statement I is possible: $\left(-\dfrac{4}{5}\right) \# \left(-\dfrac{4}{5}\right) = -\dfrac{4}{5} + \dfrac{(-4/5)}{4} = -\dfrac{4}{5} - \dfrac{1}{5} = -\dfrac{5}{5} = -1$. Statement II is not possible: since $x > y$, the top part of the definition of # applies. But a square cannot be negative (i.e., cannot equal –1). Statement III is possible: $-1 < 0$. So by the bottom half of the definition, $-1 \# 0 = -1 + \dfrac{0}{4} = -1$. The answer is (D).

15.　$(a + b^*)^* =$

　　(A)　$b - a$
　　(B)　$a - b - 4$
　　(C)　$b - a + 4$
　　(D)　$a + b - 2$
　　(E)　$a - b$

$(a + b^*)^* = (a + [2 - b])^* = (a + 2 - b)^* = 2 - (a + 2 - b) = 2 - a - 2 + b = -a + b = b - a$. The answer is (A).

16. If $(2 - x)^* = (x - 2)^*$, then $x =$
   (A) 0
   (B) 1
   (C) 2
   (D) 4
   (E) 6

$$(2 - x)^* = (x - 2)^*$$
$$2 - (2 - x) = 2 - (x - 2)$$
$$2 - 2 + x = 2 - x + 2$$
$$x = 4 - x$$
$$2x = 4$$
$$x = 2$$

The answer is (C).

Problem Set E:

1. If the remainder is 1 when m is divided by 2 and the remainder is 3 when n is divided by 4, which of the following must be true?

   (A) m is even   (B) n is even   (C) $m + n$ is even   (D) mn is even   (E) m/n is even

The statement *"the remainder is 1 when m is divided by 2"* translates into

$$m = 2u + 1$$

The statement *"the remainder is 3 when n is divided by 4"* translates into

$$n = 4v + 3$$

Forming the sum of m and n gives

$$m + n = 2u + 1 + 4v + 3 = 2u + 4v + 4 = 2(u + 2v + 2)$$

Since we have written $m + n$ as a multiple of 2, it is even. The answer is (C).

Method II (Substitution)

Let $m = 3$ and $n = 7$. Then

$$3 = 2 \cdot 1 + 1$$

and

$$7 = 4 \cdot 1 + 3$$

Now, both 3 and 7 are odd, which eliminates (A) and (B). Further, $3 \cdot 7 = 21$ is odd, which eliminates (D). Finally, 3/7 is not an integer, which eliminates (E). Hence, by process of elimination, the answer is (C).

2. If x and y are both prime and greater than 2, then which of the following CANNOT be a divisor of xy?
   (A) 2   (B) 3   (C) 11   (D) 15   (E) 17

Since x and y are prime and greater than 2, xy is the product of two odd numbers and is therefore odd. Hence, 2 cannot be a divisor of xy. The answer is (A).

3. If 2 is the greatest number that will divide evenly into both x and y, what is the greatest number that will divide evenly into both $5x$ and $5y$?
   (A) 2   (B) 4   (C) 6   (D) 8   (E) 10

Since 2 divides evenly into x, we get $x = 2z$. Hence, $5x = 5(2z) = 10z$. In other words, $5x$ is divisible by 10. A similar analysis shows that $5y$ is also divisible by 10. Since 10 is the greatest number listed, the answer is (E).

4.   If the average of the consecutive even integers a, b, and c is less than $\frac{1}{3}a$, which of the following best describes the value of a?

(A) a is prime   (B) a is odd   (C) a is zero   (D) a is positive   (E) a is negative

Let a, $a + 2$, $a + 4$ stand for the consecutive even integers a, b, and c, in that order. Forming the average of a, b, and c yields

$$\frac{a+b+c}{3} = \frac{a+a+2+a+4}{3} = \frac{3a+6}{3} = a+2$$

Setting this less than $\frac{1}{3}a$ gives

$$a+2 < \frac{1}{3}a$$

Multiplying by 3 yields $3a + 6 < a$

Subtracting 6 and a from both sides yields $2a < -6$

Dividing by 2 yields $a < -3$

Hence, a is negative, and the best answer is (E).

5.   If $\dfrac{x+5}{y}$ is a prime integer, which of the following must be true?

I. $y = 5x$
II. y is a prime integer.
III. $\dfrac{x+5}{y}$ is odd.

(A) None   (B) I only   (C) II only   (D) I and II only   (E) II and III only

If $x = 1$ and $y = 3$, then

$$y \neq 5x$$

and

$$\frac{x+5}{y} = \frac{1+5}{3} = \frac{6}{3} = 2,$$

which is prime and not odd. Hence, I and III are not necessarily true. Next, let $x = 3$ and $y = 4$. Then y is not prime and

$$\frac{x+5}{y} = \frac{3+5}{4} = \frac{8}{4} = 2,$$

which is prime. Hence, II is not necessarily true. The answer is (A).

6.   If x is both the cube and the square of an integer and x is between 2 and 200, what is the value of x?

(A) 8   (B) 16   (C) 64   (D) 125   (E) 169

Since x is both a cube and between 2 and 200, we are looking at the integers:

$$2^3,\ 3^3,\ 4^3,\ 5^3$$

which reduce to

$$8, 27, 64, 125$$

There is only one perfect square, $64 = 8^2$, in this set. The answer is (C).

7. In the two-digit number x, both the sum and the difference of its digits is 4. What is the value of x?

(A) 13   (B) 31   (C) 40   (D) 48   (E) 59

Since the sum of the digits is 4, x must be 13, 22, 31, or 40. Further, since the difference of the digits is 4, x must be 40, 51, 15, 62, 26, 73, 37, 84, 48, 95, or 59. We see that 40 and only 40 is common to the two sets of choices for x. Hence, x must be 40. The answer is (C).

8. If p divided by 9 leaves a remainder of 1, which of the following must be true?

   I. p is even.
   II. p is odd.
   III. $p = 3 \cdot z + 1$ for some integer z.

(A) I only   (B) II only   (C) III only   (D) I and II only   (E) I and III only

First, let's briefly review the concept of division. "Seven divided by 3 leaves a remainder of 1" means that $7 = 3 \cdot 2 + 1$. By analogy, "x divided by y leaves a remainder of 1" means that $x = y \cdot q + 1$, where q is an integer.

Hence, *"p divided by 9 leaves a remainder of 1"* translates into $p = 9 \cdot q + 1$. If $q = 1$, then $p = 10$ which is even. But if $q = 2$, then $p = 19$ which is odd. Hence, neither Statement I nor Statement II need be true. This eliminates (A), (B), (D), and (E). Hence, the answer is (C).

Let's verify that Statement III is true. $p = 9 \cdot q + 1 = 3(3q) + 1 = 3z + 1$, where $z = 3q$.

9. p and q are integers. If p is divided by 2, the remainder is 1; and if q is divided by 6, the remainder is 1. Which of the following must be true.

   I. $pq + 1$ is even.

   II. $\dfrac{pq}{2}$ is an integer.

   III. pq is a multiple of 12.

(A) I only   (B) II only   (C) III only   (D) I and II only   (E) I and III only

Statement I is true: From *"If p is divided by 2, the remainder is 1,"* $p = 2u + 1$; and from *"if q is divided by 6, the remainder is 1,"* $q = 6v + 1$. Hence, $pq + 1 =$

$$(2u + 1)(6v + 1) + 1 =$$
$$12uv + 2u + 6v + 1 + 1 =$$
$$12uv + 2u + 6v + 2 =$$
$$2(6uv + u + 3v + 1)$$

Since we have written $pq + 1$ as a multiple of 2, it is even.

Method II

Since p and q each leave a remainder of 1 when divided by an even number, both are odd. Now, the product of two odd numbers is another odd number. Hence, pq is odd, and therefore $pq + 1$ is even.

Now, since $pq + 1$ is even, pq is odd. Hence, $pq/2$ is not an integer, and Statement II is not necessarily true. Next, Statement III is not necessarily true. For example, if $p = 3$ and $q = 7$, then $pq = 21$, which is not a multiple of 12. The answer is (A).

10. The smallest prime number greater than 53 is

(A) 54   (B) 55   (C) 57   (D) 59   (E) 67

Since the question asks for the *smallest* prime greater than 53, we start with the smallest answer-choice. 54 is not prime since $54 = 2(27)$. 55 is not prime since $55 = 5(11)$. 57 is not prime since $57 = 3(19)$. Now, 59 *is* prime. Hence, the answer is (D).

11.   Which one of the following numbers is the greatest positive integer x such that 3^x is a factor of 27^5?

(A) 5   (B) 8   (C) 10   (D) 15   (E) 19

$27^5 = \left(3^3\right)^5 = 3^{15}$. Hence, $x = 15$ and the answer is (D).

12.   If x, y, and z are consecutive integers in that order, which of the following must be true?

   I. xy is even.
   II. $x - z$ is even.
   III. x^z is even.

(A) I only   (B) II only   (C) III only   (D) I and II only   (E) I and III only

Since x and y are consecutive integers, one of them must be even. Hence, the product xy is even and Statement I is true. As to Statement II, suppose z is odd, then x must be odd as well. Now, the difference of two odd numbers is an even number. Next, suppose z is even, then x must be even as well. Now, the difference of two even numbers is again an even number. Hence, Statement II is true. As to Statement III, let $x = 1$, then $z = 3$ and $x^z = 1^3 = 1$, which is odd. Thus, Statement III is not necessarily true. The answer is (D).

13.   If $-x - 2 = -\left|-(6 - 2)\right|$, then $x =$

(A) –5   (B) –2   (C) 0   (D) 2   (E) 5

Working from the innermost parentheses out, we get

$$-x - 2 = -\left|-(6 - 2)\right|$$
$$-x - 2 = -\left|-4\right|$$
$$-x - 2 = -(+4)$$
$$-x - 2 = -4$$
$$-x = -2$$
$$x = 2$$

The answer is (D).

14.   If the sum of two prime numbers x and y is odd, then the product of x and y must be divisible by

(A) 2   (B) 3   (C) 4   (D) 5   (E) 8

We are told that the sum of the prime numbers x and y is odd. For a sum of two numbers to be odd, one number must be odd and another even. There is only one even prime number—2; all others are odd. Hence, either x or y must be 2. Thus, the product of x and y is a multiple of 2 and therefore is divisible by 2. The answer is (A).

15. If $\dfrac{x+y}{x-y} = 3$ and x and y are integers, then which one of the following must be true?

   (A) x is divisible by 4
   (B) y is an odd number
   (C) y is an even integer
   (D) x is an even number
   (E) x is an irreducible fraction

Solution: $\dfrac{x+y}{x-y} = 3$. Multiplying both sides of this equation by $(x - y)$ yields

$$x + y = 3(x - y)$$
$$x + y = 3x - 3y$$
$$-2x = -4y$$
$$x = 2y$$

Since we have expressed x as 2 times an integer, it is even. The answer is (D).

16. A two-digit even number is such that reversing its digits creates an odd number greater than the original number. Which one of the following cannot be the first digit of the original number?

   (A) 1   (B) 3   (C) 5   (D) 7   (E) 9

Let the original number be represented by xy. (Note: here xy does not denote multiplication, but merely the position of the digits: x first, then y.). Reversing the digits of xy gives yx. We are told that $yx > xy$. This implies that $y > x$. (For example, $73 > 69$ because $7 > 6$.) If $x = 9$, then the condition $y > x$ cannot be satisfied. Hence, x cannot equal 9. The answer is (E).

Method II:
Let the original number be represented by xy. In expanded form, xy can be written as $10x + y$. For example, $53 = 5(10) + 3$. Similarly, $yx = 10y + x$. Since $yx > xy$, we get $10y + x > 10x + y$. Subtracting x and y from both sides of this equation yields $9y > 9x$. Dividing this equation by 9 yields $y > x$. Now, if $x = 9$, then the inequality $y > x$ cannot be satisfied. The answer is (E).

17. Let a, b, and c be three integers, and let a be a perfect square. If $a/b = b/c$, then which one of the following statements must be true?

   (A) c must be an even number
   (B) c must be an odd number
   (C) c must be a perfect square
   (D) c must not be a perfect square
   (E) c must be a prime number

Cross multiplying the equation $a/b = b/c$ yields

$$ac = b^2$$

Dividing by a yields $\qquad\qquad c = b^2/a$

We are given that a is a perfect square. Hence, $a = k^2$, for some number k. Replacing a in the bottom equation with k^2, we get $c = b^2/k^2 = (b/k)^2$. Since we have written c as the square of a number, it is a perfect square. The answer is (C).

18. If n > 2, then the sum, S, of the integers from 1 through n can be calculated by the following formula: $S = n(n + 1)/2$. Which one of the following statements about S must be true?

   (A) S is always odd.
   (B) S is always even.
   (C) S must be a prime number.
   (D) S must not be a prime number.
   (E) S must be a perfect square.

Observe that n and $(n + 1)$ are consecutive integers. Hence, one of the numbers is even. Therefore, the 2 in the denominator divides evenly into either n or $(n + 1)$, eliminating 2 from the denominator. Thus, S can be reduced to a product of two integers. Remember, a prime number cannot be written as the product of two integers (other than itself and 1). Hence, S is not a prime number, and the answer is (D).

19.   Which one of the following could be the difference between two numbers both of which are divisible by 2, 3 and 4?

   (A) 71   (B) 72   (C) 73   (D) 74   (E) 75

A number divisible by all three numbers 2, 3, and 4 is also divisible by 12. Hence, each number can be written as a multiple of 12. Let the first number be represented as $12a$ and the second number as $12b$. Assuming $a > b$, the difference between the two numbers is $12a - 12b = 12(a - b)$. Observe that this number is also a multiple of 12. Hence, the answer must also be divisible by 12. Since 72 is the only answer-choice divisible by 12, the answer is (B).

20.   A number, when divided by 12, gives a remainder of 7. If the same number is divided by 6, then the remainder must be

   (A) 1   (B) 2   (C) 3   (D) 4   (E) 5

We are told that the remainder is 7 when the number is divided by 12. Hence, we can represent the number as $12x + 7$. Now, 7 can be written as $6 + 1$. Plugging this into the expression yields

$$12x + (6 + 1) =$$
$$(12x + 6) + 1 = \quad \text{by regrouping}$$
$$6(2x + 1) + 1 \quad \text{by factoring 6 out of the first two terms}$$

This shows that the remainder is 1 when the expression $12x + 7$ is divided by 6. The answer is (A).

Method II (Substitution):
Choose the number 19, which gives a remainder of 7 when divided by 12. Now, divide 19 by 6:

$$\frac{19}{6} = 3\frac{1}{6}$$

This shows that 6 divides into 19 with a remainder of 1. The answer is (A).

21.   Let x be a two-digit number. If the sum of the digits of x is 9, then the sum of the digits of the number $(x + 10)$ is

   (A) 1   (B) 8   (C) 10   (D) either 8 or 10   (E) either 1 or 10

Let's take a two-digit number whose digits add up to 9, say, 72. Adding 10 to this number gives 82. The sum of the digits of this number is 10. Now, let's choose another two-digit number whose digits add up to 9, say, 90. Then $x + 10 = 90 + 10 = 100$. The sum of the digits of this number is 1. Hence, the sum of the numbers is either 1 or 10. The answer is (E).

22. $\dfrac{39693}{3} =$

    (A) 33231   (B) 13231   (C) 12331   (D) 23123   (E) 12321

Observe that all the digits of the dividend 39693 are divisible by 3. So 3 will divide the dividend into such a number that each of its digits will be 1/3 the corresponding digit in the dividend (i.e., 39693). For example, the third digit in the dividend is 6, and hence the third digit in the quotient will be 2, which is 1/3 of 6. Applying the same process to all digits gives the quotient 13231. The answer is (B).

23. If n^3 is an odd integer, which one of the following expressions is an even integer?

    (A) $2n^2 + 1$ (B) n^4 (C) $n^2 + 1$ (D) $n(n + 2)$ (E) n

Suppose $n = 1$. Then $n^3 = 1^3 = 1$, which is odd. Now, we plug this value for n into each of the answer-choices to see which ones are even. Thus, $2n^2 + 1$ becomes $2(1)^2 + 1 = 3$, which is not even. So eliminate (A). Next, $n^4 = 1^4 = 1$ is not even—eliminate (B). Next, $n^2 + 1 = 1^2 + 1 = 2$ is even, so the answer is possibly (C). Next, $n(n + 2) = 1(1 + 2) = 3$ is not even—eliminate (D). Finally, $n = 1$, which is not even—eliminate (E). Hence, by the process of elimination, the answer is (C).

24. If the product of two integers is odd, then the sum of those two integers must be

    (A) odd
    (B) even
    (C) prime
    (D) divisible by the difference of the two numbers
    (E) a perfect square

If the product of the two numbers is odd, then each number in the product must be odd. Recall that the sum of two odd numbers is an even number. The answer is (B).

25. If the sum of three consecutive integers is odd, then the first and the last integers must be

    (A) odd, even   (B) odd, odd   (C) even, odd   (D) even, even   (E) none of the above

Let the three consecutive integers be x, $x + 1$, and $x + 2$. The sum of these integers is $3x + 3$. According to the question, this sum is odd. Hence $3x + 3$ is odd. Recall that if the sum of two integers is odd, then one of the integers is odd and the other one is even. Since 3 in the expression $3x + 3$ is odd, $3x$ must be even. Now, recall that the product of two numbers is odd only when one of the numbers is odd and the other is even. So x must be even. If x is an even number, then $x + 2$ is also even. Thus, the first and the last integers must both be even. The answer is (D).

26. If l, m, and n are positive integers such that $l < m < n$ and $n < 4$, then $m =$

    (A) 0   (B) 1   (C) 2   (D) 3   (E) 4

We are given that l, m, and n are three positive integers such that $l < m < n$. This implies that l, m, and n are each greater than zero and not equal to each other. Since n is less than 4, the numbers l, m, and n must have the values 1, 2, and 3, respectively. Hence, the answer is (C).

27. If two non-zero positive integers p and q are such that $p = 4q$ and $p < 8$, then $q =$

(A) 1   (B) 2   (C) 3   (D) 4   (E) 5

Dividing both sides of the equation $p = 4q$ by 4, we get $q = p/4$. We are also given that $p < 8$. Dividing both sides of this inequality by 4 yields, $p/4 < 8/4$. Simplifying it, we get $p/4 < 2$. But $q = p/4$. Hence, $q < 2$. The only non-zero positive integer less than 2 is 1. Hence, $q = 1$. The answer is (A).

28. If n is an integer, then which one of the following expressions must be even?

(A) $n^2 + 1$ (B) $n(n + 2)$ (C) $n(n + 1)$ (D) $n(n + 4)$ (E) $(n + 1)(n + 3)$

Answer-choice (C) consists of the product of two consecutive integers. Now, of any two consecutive integers, one of the integers must be even. Hence, their product must be even. The answer is (C).

29. The sum of three consecutive positive integers must be divisible by which of the following?

(A) 2   (B) 3   (C) 4   (D) 5   (E) 6

Let the three consecutive positive integers be n, $n + 1$, and $n + 2$. The sum of these three positive integers is

$$n + (n + 1) + (n + 2) =$$
$$3n + 3 =$$
$$3(n + 1)$$

Since we have written the sum as a multiple of 3, it is divisible by 3. The answer is (B).

Problem Set F:

1. In the triangle to the right, what is the value of y?

(A) 3
(B) $\sqrt{18}$
(C) $\sqrt{27}$
(D) 9
(E) 27

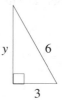

Since we have a right triangle, the Pythagorean Theorem yields $y^2 + 3^2 = 6^2$

Simplifying yields $y^2 + 9 = 36$

Subtracting 9 from both sides yields $y^2 = 27$

Taking the square root of both sides yields $y = \sqrt{27}$

The answer is (C).

2. In the figure to the right, circle P has diameter 2 and circle Q has diameter 1. What is the area of the shaded region?

(A) $3\pi/4$
(B) 3π
(C) $7\pi/2$
(D) 5π
(E) 6π

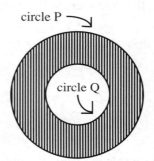

Since the diameter of circle P is 2, its radius is 1. So the area of circle P is $\pi(1)^2 = \pi$. Since the diameter of circle Q is 1, its radius is 1/2. So the area of circle Q is $\pi\left(\dfrac{1}{2}\right)^2 = \dfrac{1}{4}\pi$. The area of the shaded region is the difference between the area of circle P and the area of circle Q: $\pi - \dfrac{1}{4}\pi = \dfrac{3}{4}\pi$. The answer is (A).

3. In the figure to the right, $QRST$ is a square. If the shaded region is bounded by arcs of circles with centers at Q, R, S, and T, then the area of the shaded region is

(A) 9
(B) 36
(C) $36 - 9\pi$
(D) $36 - \pi$
(E) $9 - 3\pi$

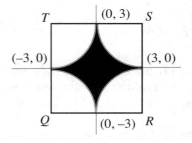

Each arc forms a quarter of a circle. Taken together the four arcs constitute one whole circle. From the drawing, we see that the radii of the arcs are each length 3, so the area of the four arcs together is $\pi(3)^2 = 9\pi$. Since the square has sides of length 6, its area is 36. Hence, the area of the shaded region is $36 - 9\pi$. The answer is (C).

4. In the figure to the right, QRST is a square. If the area of each circle is 2π, then the area of square QRST is

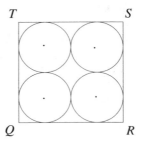

(A) $\sqrt{2}$
(B)   4
(C) $\sqrt{2}\pi$
(D) $4\sqrt{2}$
(E)   32

Setting the area of a circle equal to 2π gives $\qquad$ $\pi r^2 = 2\pi$

Dividing both sides of this equation by π gives $\qquad$ $r^2 = 2$

Taking the square root of both sides gives $\qquad$ $r = \sqrt{2}$

Hence, the diameter of each circle is $\qquad$ $d = 2r = 2\sqrt{2}$

Adding the diameters to the diagram gives

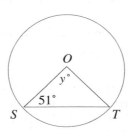

Clearly, in this diagram, the sides of the square are length $2\sqrt{2} + 2\sqrt{2} = 4\sqrt{2}$. Hence, the area of the square is $4\sqrt{2} \cdot 4\sqrt{2} = 16 \cdot 2 = 32$. The answer is (E).

5. In the figure to the right, if O is the center of the circle, then $y =$

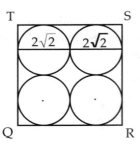

(A)   75
(B)   76
(C)   77
(D)   78
(E)   79

OS and OT are equal since they are radii of the circle. Hence, ΔSOT is isosceles. Therefore, $S = T = 51°$. Recalling that the angle sum of a triangle is 180°, we get $S + T + y = 51° + 51° + y = 180°$. Solving for y gives $y = 78°$. The answer is (D).

6. In the figure to the right, the value of $a + b$ is

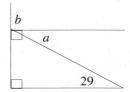

(A)   118
(B)   119
(C)   120
(D)   121
(E)   122

Since the two horizontal lines are parallel (Why?), angle a and the angle with measure 29 are alternate interior angles and therefore are equal. Further, from the drawing, angle b is 90°. Hence, $a + b = 29 + 90 = 119$. The answer is (B).

7.   If $l_1 \| l_2$ in the figure to the right, what is the value of x?

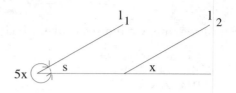

    (A)   30
    (B)   45
    (C)   60
    (D)   72
    (E)   90

Since $l_1 \| l_2$, s and x are corresponding angles and therefore are congruent.

Now, about any point there are 360°. Hence,	$5x + s = 360$
Substituting x for s in this equation gives	$5x + x = 360$
Combining like terms gives	$6x = 360$
Dividing by 6 gives	$x = 60$

The answer is (C).

8.   For the figure to the right, which of the following are true?

    I. $OP = OQ$
   II. $\sqrt{PQ} < \sqrt{OP}$
  III. $PQ > OQ$

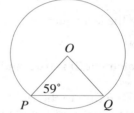

O is the center of the circle.

    (A)   I only
    (B)   II only
    (C)   III only
    (D)   I and II only
    (E)   I and III only

Since OP and OQ are radii of the circle, they are equal and Statement I is true. This eliminates (B) and (C). Since 2 sides of $\triangle OPQ$ are equal, the triangle is isosceles with $P = Q = 59°$. Now, the angle sum of a triangle is 180. So

	$O + P + Q = 180.$
Substituting $P = Q = 59°$ into this equation gives	$O + 59 + 59 = 180.$
Solving for O gives	$O = 62.$

Now, since O is the largest angle in $\triangle OPQ$, the side opposite it, PQ, is the longest side of the triangle. Therefore, $PQ > OQ$ and Statement III is true. This eliminates, (A) and (D). Hence, by process of elimination, the answer is (E).

9.   From the two figures above, which of the following can be determined?

    I. $x = 60°$
    II. $7s = 180°$
    III. $2s < x$

    (A)   I only
    (B)   II only
    (C)   III only
    (D)   I and II only
    (E)   I, II, and III

The second triangle is equilateral.

Hence, $x = 60°$

Thus, Statement I is true.

The angle sum of the first triangle is $s + 2s + 4s = 180°$

Combining like terms yields $7s = 180°$

Thus, Statement II is true.

Dividing the last equation by 7 gives $s = \dfrac{180°}{7} < 30°$

So $2s < 60° = x$

Thus, Statement III is true, and the answer is (E).

10.   In the figure to the right, x is both the radius of the larger circle and the diameter of the smaller circle. The area of the shaded region is

    (A) $\dfrac{3}{4}\pi x^2$

    (B) $\dfrac{\pi}{3}$

    (C) $\dfrac{4}{3}\pi x^2$

    (D) $\dfrac{3}{5}\pi x^2$

    (E) πx^2

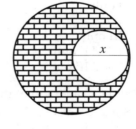

Since x is the radius of the larger circle, the area of the larger circle is πx^2. Since x is the diameter of the smaller circle, the radius of the smaller circle is $\dfrac{x}{2}$. Therefore, the area of the smaller circle is $\pi\left(\dfrac{x}{2}\right)^2 = \pi\dfrac{x^2}{4}$. Subtracting the area of the smaller circle from the area of the larger circle gives

$$\pi x^2 - \pi\dfrac{x^2}{4} = \dfrac{4}{4}\pi x^2 - \pi\dfrac{x^2}{4} = \dfrac{4\pi x^2 - \pi x^2}{4} = \dfrac{3\pi x^2}{4}$$ The answer is (A).

11. In the figure to the right, the circle with center O is inscribed in the square PQRS. The combined area of the shaded regions is

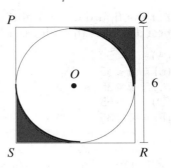

(A) $36 - 9\pi$

(B) $36 - \dfrac{9}{2}\pi$

(C) $\dfrac{36 - 9\pi}{2}$

(D) $18 - 9\pi$

(E) $9 - \dfrac{9}{4}\pi$

The area of square PQRS is $6^2 = 36$. Now, the radius of the circle is 3. (Why?) So the area of the circle is $\pi(3)^2 = 9\pi$. Subtracting the area of the circle from the area of the square yields $36 - 9\pi$. This is the combined area of the regions outside the circle and inside the square. Dividing this quantity by 2 gives $\dfrac{36 - 9\pi}{2}$. The answer is (C).

12. In the figure to the right, the length of QS is

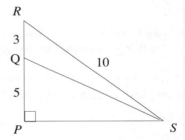

(A) $\sqrt{51}$

(B) $\sqrt{61}$

(C) $\sqrt{69}$

(D) $\sqrt{77}$

(E) $\sqrt{89}$

The length of PR is $PR = 3 + 5 = 8$. Applying the Pythagorean Theorem to triangle PRS yields

$$8^2 + (PS)^2 = 10^2$$

Squaring yields

$$64 + (PS)^2 = 100$$

Subtracting 64 from both sides yields

$$(PS)^2 = 36$$

Taking the square root of both sides yields

$$PS = \sqrt{36} = 6$$

Now, applying the Pythagorean Theorem to triangle PQS yields

$$(QS)^2 = 5^2 + 6^2$$

Squaring and adding yields

$$(QS)^2 = 61$$

Taking the square root of both sides yields

$$QS = \sqrt{61}$$

The answer is (B).

13. For the figure to the right, which of the following
    best describes the value of y?

    (A) $y < 50$
    (B) $y < 55$
    (C) $y > 35$
    (D) $y > 55$
    (E) $y < 35$

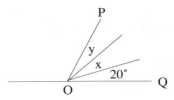

$\angle$ POQ = 70° and x > 15

Since $\angle$ POQ = 70° we get $x + y + 20 = 70$. Solving this equation for y yields $y = 50 - x$. Now, we are given that $x > 15$. Hence, the expression $50 - x$ must be less than 35. The answer is (E).

14. In the figure to the right, if $l \| k$, then what is the
    value of y ?

    (A)   20
    (B)   45
    (C)   55
    (D)   75
    (E)   110

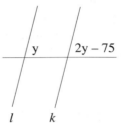

Since lines l and k are parallel, we know that the corresponding angles are equal. Hence, $y = 2y - 75$. Solving this equation for y gives $y = 75$. The answer is (D).

15. In the figure to the right, both triangles are right
    triangles. The area of the shaded region is

    (A)   1/2
    (B)   2/3
    (C)   7/8
    (D)   3/2
    (E)   5/2

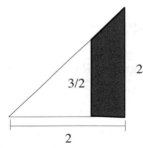

Since the height and base of the larger triangle are the same, the slope of the hypotenuse is 45°. Hence, the base of the smaller triangle is the same as its height, 3/2. Thus, the area of the shaded region = (area of the larger triangle) – (area of the smaller triangle) =

$$\left(\frac{1}{2} \cdot 2 \cdot 2\right) - \left(\frac{1}{2} \cdot \frac{3}{2} \cdot \frac{3}{2}\right) = 2 - \frac{9}{8} = \frac{7}{8}$$

The answer is (C).

16. In the figure to the right, the radius of the larger circle is twice that of the smaller circle. If the circles are concentric, what is the ratio of the shaded region's area to the area of the smaller circle?

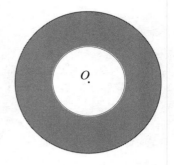

    (A)   10:1
    (B)   9:1
    (C)   3:1
    (D)   2:1
    (E)   1:1

Suppose the radius of the larger circle is 2 and the radius of the smaller circle is 1. Then the area of the larger circle is $\pi r^2 = \pi(2)^2 = 4\pi$, and the area of the smaller circle is $\pi r^2 = \pi(1)^2 = \pi$. Hence, the area of the shaded region is $4\pi - \pi = 3\pi$. Now, $\dfrac{\textit{area of shaded region}}{\textit{area of smaller circle}} = \dfrac{3\pi}{\pi} = \dfrac{3}{1}$. The answer is (C).

17. In the figure to the right, $\triangle PST$ is an isosceles right triangle, and $PS = 2$. What is the area of the shaded region $URST$?

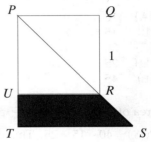

    (A)   4
    (B)   2
    (C)   5/4
    (D)   5/6
    (E)   1/2

Let x stand for the distances TP and TS. Applying the Pythagorean Theorem to the right triangle PST gives

$$TP^2 + TS^2 = PS^2$$

Substituting x for TP and TS and substituting 2 for PS gives

$$x^2 + x^2 = 2^2$$

Squaring and combining like terms gives

$$2x^2 = 4$$

Dividing by 2 gives

$$x^2 = 2$$

Finally, taking the square root gives

$$x = \sqrt{2}$$

Adding this information to the diagram gives

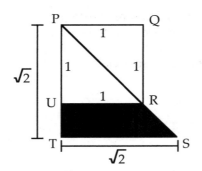

Now, the area of the shaded region equals *(area of triangle PST)* − *(area of triangle PRU)* =

$\left(\frac{1}{2}\cdot\sqrt{2}\cdot\sqrt{2}\right)-\left(\frac{1}{2}\cdot1\cdot1\right)=\left(\frac{1}{2}\cdot2\right)-\left(\frac{1}{2}\right)=1-\frac{1}{2}=\frac{1}{2}$. The answer is (E).

18.   In the figure to the right, the area of $\triangle PQR$ is 40. What is the area of $\triangle QRS$?

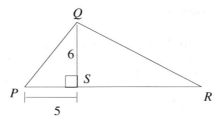

(A)   10
(B)   15
(C)   20
(D)   25
(E)   45

The area of triangle PQS is $\frac{1}{2}\cdot5\cdot6=15$. Now, (the area of $\triangle QRS$) = (the area of $\triangle PQR$) − (the area of $\triangle PQS$) = 40 − 15 = 25. The answer is (D).

19.   In the figure to the right, $PQRS$ is a square and M and N are midpoints of their respective sides. What is the area of quadrilateral $PMRN$?

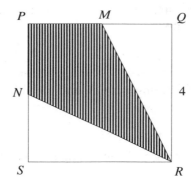

(A)   8
(B)   10
(C)   12
(D)   14
(E)   16

Since M is the midpoint of side PQ, the length of MQ is 2. Hence, the area of triangle MQR is $\frac{1}{2}\cdot2\cdot4=4$. A similar analysis shows that the area of triangle NSR is 4. Thus, the unshaded area of the figure is 4 + 4 = 8. Subtracting this from the area of the square gives 16 − 8 = 8. The answer is (A).

20. In the figure to the right, what is the greatest number of regions into which two straight lines will divide the shaded region?

(A) 1
(B) 2
(C) 3
(D) 4
(E) 5

Most people will draw one or the other of the two following drawings:

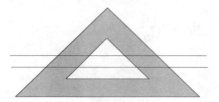   

In each case, four separate shaded regions are formed. But these drawings are too ordinary, too easy. There must be a way to draw the lines to form more than four regions. Try to draw it before looking at the answer below.

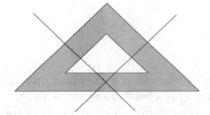

The lines must intersect in the shaded region.

The answer is (E).

21. In the figure to the right, O is the center of the circle. If the area of the circle is 9π, then the perimeter of the sector $PRQO$ is

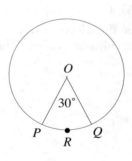

(A) $\dfrac{\pi}{2} + 18$

(B) $\dfrac{\pi}{2} + 6$

(C) $\dfrac{3}{4}\pi + 6$

(D) $\dfrac{3}{4}\pi + 18$

(E) $\dfrac{\pi}{2} - 6$

Since the area of the circle is 9π, we get

$$\pi r^2 = 9\pi$$
$$r^2 = 9$$
$$r = 3$$

Now, the circumference of the circle is

$$C = 2\pi r = 2\pi 3 = 6\pi$$

Since the central angle is 30°, the length of arc PRQ is

$$\frac{30}{360}C = \frac{1}{12}\cdot 6\pi = \frac{1}{2}\pi$$

Hence, the perimeter of the sector is

$$\frac{1}{2}\pi + 3 + 3 = \frac{1}{2}\pi + 6$$

The answer is (B).

22. Let A denote the area of a circular region. Which of the following denotes the circumference of that circular region?

(A) $\sqrt{\dfrac{A}{\pi}}$ (B) $2\dfrac{A}{\sqrt{\pi}}$ (C) $2\pi\sqrt{A}$ (D) $2\sqrt{\dfrac{A}{\pi}}$ (E) $2\pi\sqrt{\dfrac{A}{\pi}}$

Since A denotes the area of the circular region, we get

$$A = \pi r^2$$

$$\frac{A}{\pi} = r^2$$

$$\sqrt{\frac{A}{\pi}} = r$$

Hence, the circumference is $C = 2\pi r = 2\pi\sqrt{\dfrac{A}{\pi}}$

The answer is (E).

23. Ship X and ship Y are 5 miles apart and are on a collision course. Ship X is sailing directly north, and ship Y is sailing directly east. If the point of impact is 1 mile closer to the current position of ship X than to the current position of ship Y, how many miles away from the point of impact is ship Y at this time?

(A) 1   (B) 2   (C) 3   (D) 4   (E) 5

Let d be the distance ship Y is from the point of collision. Then the distance ship X is from the point of collision is $d - 1$. The following diagram depicts the situation:

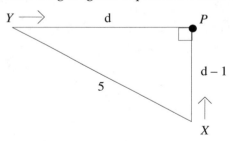

Applying the Pythagorean Theorem to the diagram yields

$$d^2 + (d-1)^2 = 5^2$$

$$d^2 + d^2 - 2d + 1 = 25$$

$$2d^2 - 2d - 24 = 0$$

$$d^2 - d - 12 = 0$$

$$(d-4)(d+3) = 0$$

$$d = 4 \quad \text{or} \quad d = -3$$

Since d denotes distance, we reject $d = -3$. Hence, $d = 4$ and the answer is (D).

24. The figure to the right represents a square with sides of length 4 surmounted by a circle with center O. What is the outer perimeter of the figure?

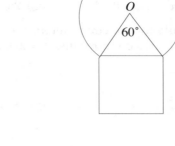

(A) $\dfrac{49}{9}\pi + 12$

(B) $\dfrac{20}{3}\pi + 12$

(C) $\dfrac{5}{6}\pi + 12$

(D) $\pi + 12$

(E) $9\pi + 12$

Since two sides of the triangle are radii of the circle, they are equal. Hence, the triangle is isosceles, and the base angles are equal:

Since the angle sum of a triangle is 180, we get

$$x + x + 60 = 180$$
$$2x = 120$$
$$x = 60$$

Hence, the triangle is equilateral. Therefore, the radius of the circle is 4, and the circumference is $C = 2\pi r = 2\pi 4 = 8\pi$. Now, the portion of the perimeter formed by the circle has length $\dfrac{360 - 60}{360} \cdot C = \dfrac{5}{6} \cdot 8\pi = \dfrac{20}{3}\pi$. Adding the three sides of the square to this expression gives $\dfrac{20}{3}\pi + 12$. The answer is (B).

25. The perimeter of a square is equal to the perimeter of a rectangle whose length and width are $6m$ and $4m$, respectively. The side of the square is

(A) $3m$ (B) $4m$ (C) $5m$ (D) $6m$ (E) $7m$

The length of the rectangle is $6m$ and the width of the rectangle is $4m$. From the standard formula for the perimeter of a rectangle, we get

$$P = 2L + 2W = 2(6m) + 2(4m) = 20m$$

Now, the formula for the perimeter of a square is $4x$, where x represents the length of a side of the square. Since we are given that the perimeter of the square is equal to that of the rectangle, we write

$$4x = 20m$$

$$x = \frac{20m}{4} = 5m$$

The answer is (C).

26. If the circumference of a circle is $4m$, then the ratio of circumference of the circle to the diameter of the circle is

(A) π (B) 4   (C) 2π (D) 4π (E) 16

The formula for the circumference of a circle with diameter d is $C = 2\pi r = \pi(2r) = \pi d$ (since the diameter is twice the radius, $d = 2r$). Hence, the ratio of the circumference of the circle to its diameter is

$$\frac{C}{d} = \frac{\pi d}{d} = \pi$$

The answer is (A).

Note: The fact that the circumference of the circle is $4m$ was not used in solving the problem. Thus, the answer is independent of the size of the circle. In other words, the ratio of the circumference of a circle to its diameter is always π.

27. In Triangle ABC, $\angle A$ is 10 degrees greater than $\angle B$, and $\angle B$ is 10 degrees greater than $\angle C$. The value of angle B is

(A) 30   (B) 40   (C) 50   (D) 60   (E) 70

We are given that $\angle A$ is 10 degrees greater than $\angle B$. Expressing this as an equation gives

$$\angle A = \angle B + 10$$

We are also given that $\angle B$ is 10 degrees greater than $\angle C$. Expressing this as an equation gives

$$\angle B = \angle C + 10$$

In a triangle, the sum of the three angles is 180 degrees. Expressing this as an equation gives

$$\angle A + \angle B + \angle C = 180$$

Solving these three equations for $\angle B$, we get $\angle B = 60$ degrees. The answer is (D).

28. Two squares each with sides of length s are joined to form a rectangle. The area of the rectangle is

(A) s^2 (B) $2s^2$ (C) $4s^2$ (D) $8s^2$ (E) $16s^2$

The area of a square with side s is s^2. On joining two such squares, the resulting area will be twice the area of either square: $2s^2$. The answer is (B).

29. A person travels 16 miles due north and then 12 miles due east. How far is the person from his initial location?

(A) 4 miles   (B) 8 miles   (C) 14 miles   (D) 20 miles   (E) 28 miles

Solution:

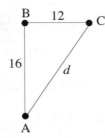

A: Initial position
B: Second position
C: Final position

The path taken by the person can be represented diagrammatically as shown. Let d be the distance between his initial location and his final location. Since a person traveling due north has to turn 90 degrees to travel due east, the Angle ABC is a right angle. Hence, we can apply the Pythagorean Theorem to the triangle, which yields

$$d^2 = 12^2 + 16^2$$
$$d^2 = 400$$
$$d = \sqrt{400}$$
$$d = 20$$

The answer is (D).

30. The area of Triangle PQR is 6. If $PR = 4$, then the length of the hypotenuse QR is

(A) 1
(B) 2
(C) 3
(D) 4
(E) 5

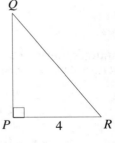

Triangle PQR is a right triangle with the base PR equal to 4 and height PQ. The area of Triangle PQR is $\frac{1}{2}bh = 6$. Substituting the known quantities into this formula yields $\frac{1}{2}(4)(PQ) = 6$. Solving this equation for PQ yields $PQ = 3$. Applying the Pythagorean Theorem to the triangle yields

$$(PQ)^2 + (PR)^2 = (QR)^2$$
$$3^2 + 4^2 = (QR)^2 \qquad \text{by substitution}$$
$$25 = (QR)^2$$
$$5 = QR \qquad \text{by taking the square root of both sides}$$

The answer is (E).

31. In the figure, the equation of line $A\,B$ is $y = -\dfrac{5}{3}x + 10$. The area of the shaded portion is

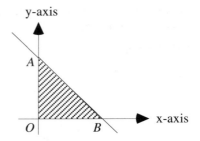

(A) 12
(B) 30
(C) 100/3
(D) 60
(E) 100

To find the y-intercept of a line, we set $x = 0$: $y = -\dfrac{5}{3}(0) + 10 = 10$. Hence, the height of the triangle is 10. To find the x-intercept of a line, we set $y = 0$: $-\dfrac{5}{3}x + 10 = 0$. Solving this equation for x yields $x = 6$. Hence, the base of the triangle is 6. Therefore, the area of shaded portion (which is a triangle) is $\dfrac{1}{2} \cdot 6 \cdot 10 = 30$. The answer is (B).

32. In the figure, if $x = 54°$ and $y = 72°$, then $z =$

(A) 54°
(B) 56°
(C) 72°
(D) 76°
(E) 98°

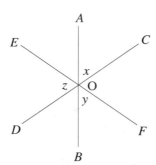

O is the point of intersection of the three lines in the figure.

From the figure, observe that $\angle AOC$ and $\angle BOD$ are vertical angles between the lines AB and CD. Hence, $\angle AOC = \angle BOD = x$. Since a straight angle has 180°, we get the following equation:

$$\angle EOD + \angle BOD + \angle BOF = 180$$
$$z + x + y = 180 \qquad \text{since } \angle EOD = z, \angle BOD = x, \angle BOF = y$$
$$z + 54 + 72 = 180 \qquad \text{since } x = 54° \text{ and } y = 72°$$
$$z = 180 - 54 - 72 = 54$$

The answer is (A)

33. If one of the sides of the rectangle shown in the figure has a length of 3, then the area of the rectangle is
(A) 9
(B) 13.5
(C) 18
(D) 27
(E) 54

We are given that one of the sides of the rectangle has length 3. This implies that either x or $x + 6$ equals 3. If $x + 6$ equals 3, then x must be -3, which is impossible since a length cannot be negative. Hence, $x = 3$ and $x + 6 = 3 + 6 = 9$. The area of the rectangle, being the product of two adjacent sides of the rectangle, is $x(x + 6) = 3(9) = 27$. The answer is (D).

34. The value of $x + y + z =$

    (A) 120°
    (B) 160°
    (C) 180°
    (D) 270°
    (E) 360°

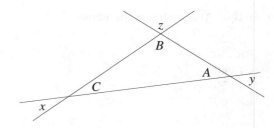

Since angles A, B, and C are the interior angles of the triangle, their angle sum is 180°. Hence, $A + B + C = 180$. Since A and y are vertical angles, they are equal. This is also true for angles B and z and angles C and x. Substituting these values into the equation yields $y + z + x = 180$. The answer is (C).

35. In the figure, what is the area of Triangle ABC ?

    (A) 25
    (B) 50
    (C) $100/\sqrt{2}$
    (D) 100
    (E) $100\sqrt{2}$

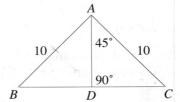

In a triangle, the sum of the interior angles is 180 degrees. Applying this to Triangle ADC yields

$$\angle DAC + \angle C + \angle CDA = 180$$
$$45 + \angle C + 90 = 180 \qquad \text{since } \angle DAC = 45° \text{ and } \angle CDA = 90°$$
$$\angle C = 180 - 90 - 45 = 45$$

In Triangle ABC, $AB = AC$. Recall that angles opposite equal sides of a triangle are equal. Hence, $\angle B = \angle C$. We have already derived that $\angle C = 45°$. Hence, $\angle B = \angle C = 45°$. Again, the sum of the interior angles of a triangle is 180 degrees. Applying this to Triangle ABC yields

$$\angle A + \angle B + \angle C = 180$$
$$\angle A + 45 + 45 = 180$$
$$\angle A = 90$$

This implies that Triangle ABC is a right triangle with right angle at A. Hence, the area of the triangle is

$$\frac{1}{2}\left(\text{the product of the sides containing the right angle}\right) =$$

$$\frac{1}{2} AB \cdot AC =$$

$$\frac{1}{2} 10 \cdot 10 =$$

$$50$$

The answer is (B).

36. In the figure, what is the value of x?

  (A) 20°
  (B) 30°
  (C) 40°
  (D) 50°
  (E) 60°

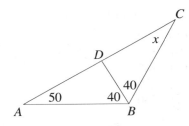

In the figure, $\angle B$ is the sum of $\angle ABD$ and $\angle DBC$. So, $\angle B = \angle ABD + \angle DBC = 40 + 40 = 80$. Now, recall that the sum of the angles in a triangle is 180°. Hence,

$$\angle A + \angle B + \angle C = 180$$
$$50 + 80 + x = 180 \qquad \text{since } \angle A = 50 \text{ and } \angle B = 80$$
$$130 + x = 180$$
$$x = 50$$

The answer is (D).

37. The area of the Triangle ABC shown in the figure is 30. The area of Triangle ADC is

  (A) 5
  (B) 10
  (C) 15
  (D) 20
  (E) 25

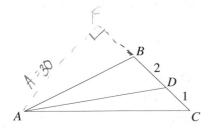

Let's add an altitude to Triangle ABC by extending side BC as shown in the figure below.

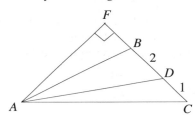

The formula for the area of a triangle is $A = (1/2)(\text{base})(\text{height})$. Hence, the area of Triangle $ABC = (1/2)(BC)(AF) = (1/2)(2 + 1)(AF) = (3/2)(AF) = 30$ (the area of Triangle ABC is given to be 30). Solving this equation for AF yields $AF = 20$. Now, the area of Triangle $ADC = (1/2)(DC)(AF) = (1/2)(1)(20) = 10$. The answer is (B).

38. In the figure, what is the value of y ?

  (A) 7.5
  (B) 15
  (C) 30
  (D) 40
  (E) 45

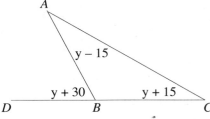

Observe that $\angle DBA$ is an exterior angle of Triangle ABC. Applying the exterior angle theorem yields

$$\angle DBA = \angle A + \angle C$$
$$y + 30 = (y - 15) + (y + 15)$$
$$y + 30 = 2y \qquad \text{by adding like terms}$$
$$30 = y \qquad \text{by subtracting } y \text{ from both sides}$$

The answer is (C).

39. A circle is depicted in the rectangular coordinate system as shown. The value of x is

    (A) 4
    (B) 6
    (C) 8
    (D) 10
    (E) 12

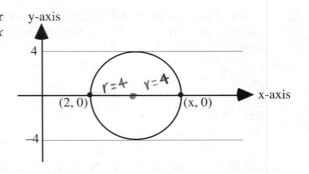

The figure shows that the circle is located between the lines $y = 4$ and $y = -4$ and that the circle is symmetric to the x-axis. From this, we make two observations: 1) The center of the circle is on the x-axis. 2) The diameter of the circle is 8. Since the center of the circle is on the x-axis, the points $(2, 0)$ and $(x, 0)$ must be diametrically opposite points of the circle. That is, they are end points of a diameter of the circle. Hence, the distance between the two points, $x - 2$, must equal the length of the diameter. Hence, $x - 2 = 8$. Adding 2 to both sides of this equation, we get $x = 10$. The answer is (D).

40. In the figure, the ratio of x to y is 2. What is the value of y ?

    (A) 108
    (B) 90
    (C) 68
    (D) 45
    (E) 36

Since the ratio of x to y is 2, we get $x/y = 2$. Solving this equation for x yields $x = 2y$. Since the sum of the angles made by a line is 180°, $y + x + y = 180$. Substituting $2y$ for x in this equation yields

$$y + 2y + y = 180$$
$$4y = 180$$
$$y = 45$$

The answer is (D).

Problem Set G:

1. In the figure to the right, the radius of the larger circle is twice that of the smaller circle. If the circles are concentric, what is the ratio of the shaded region's area to the area of the smaller circle?

    (A) 10:1
    (B) 9:1
    (C) 3:1
    (D) 2:1
    (E) 1:1

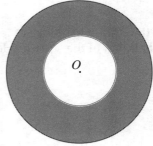

The area of the shaded region appears to be about three times the area of the smaller circle, so the answer should be (C). Let's verify this. Suppose the radius of the larger circle is 2 and the radius of the smaller circle is 1. Then the area of the larger circle is $\pi r^2 = \pi(2)^2 = 4\pi$, and the area of the smaller circle is $\pi r^2 = \pi(1)^2 = \pi$. Hence, the area of the shaded region is $4\pi - \pi = 3\pi$. Now, $\dfrac{area\ of\ shaded\ region}{area\ of\ smaller\ circle} = \dfrac{3\pi}{\pi} = \dfrac{3}{1}$. The answer is (C).

2. In the figure to the right, $\triangle PST$ is an isosceles right triangle, and $PS = 2$. What is the area of the shaded region $URST$?

    (A) 4
    (B) 2
    (C) 5/4
    (D) 5/6
    (E) 1/2

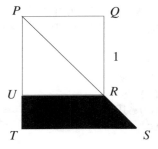

The area of the square is $1^2 = 1$. Now, the area of the shaded region appears to be about half that of the square. Hence, the area of the shaded region is about $1/2$. The answer is (E).

3. In the figure to the right, the area of $\triangle PQR$ is 40. What is the area of $\triangle QRS$?

    (A) 10
    (B) 15
    (C) 20
    (D) 25
    (E) 45

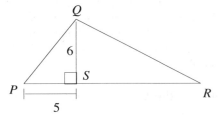

Clearly from the drawing, the area of $\triangle QRS$ is greater than half the area of $\triangle PQR$. This eliminates (A), (B), and (C). Now, the area of $\triangle QRS$ cannot be greater than the area of $\triangle PQR$. This eliminates (E). The answer is (D).

4. In the figure to the right, $PQRS$ is a square and M and N are midpoints of their respective sides. What is the area of quadrilateral $PMRN$?

    (A) 8
    (B) 10
    (C) 12
    (D) 14
    (E) 16

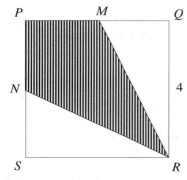

Since the square has sides of length 4, its area is 16. Now, the area of the shaded region appears to be half that of the square. Hence, its area is 8. The answer is (A).

Problem Set H:

1. In the figure to the right, O is the center of the circle. What is the area of the circle?

    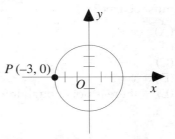

    (A) 2π
    (B) 3π
    (C) 5.5π
    (D) 7π
    (E) 9π

Since the circle is centered at the origin and passes through the point $(-3, 0)$, the radius of the circle is 3. Hence, the area is $A = \pi r^2 = \pi 3^2 = 9\pi$. The answer is (E).

2. In the figure to the right, P is a point in the coordinate system and $OP = 6$. The y-coordinate of point P is

    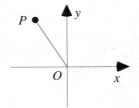

    (A) less than OP
    (B) greater than OP
    (C) equal to OP
    (D) equal to 5
    (E) there is not enough information to decide

Whatever the coordinates of P are, the line OP is the hypotenuse of a right triangle with sides being the absolute value of the x and y coordinates. Hence, OP is greater than the y-coordinate of point P. The answer is (A).

This problem brings up the issue of how much you can assume when viewing a diagram. We are told that P is a point in the coordinate system and that it appears in the second quadrant. Could P be on one of the axes or in another quadrant? No. Although P could be anywhere in Quadrant II (not necessarily where it is displayed), P could not be on the y-axis because the "position of points, angles, regions, etc. can be assumed to be in the order shown." If P were on the y-axis, then it would not be to the left of the y-axis, as it is in the diagram. That is, the order would be different. [By the way, if P could also be on the axes, the answer would be (E). Why?]

3. In the figure to the right, if the equation of the line is $y = px + a$, then $p =$

    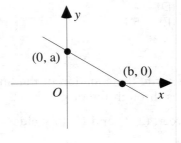

    (A) $\dfrac{b}{a}$

    (B) $\dfrac{-b}{a}$

    (C) $\dfrac{-a}{b}$

    (D) $\dfrac{a}{b}$

    (E) there is not enough information to decide

Since $(b, 0)$ is the x-intercept of the line, it must satisfy the equation: $\qquad 0 = pb + a$

Subtracting a from both sides yields $\qquad\qquad\qquad\qquad\qquad -a = pb$

Dividing both sides by b yields $\qquad\qquad\qquad\qquad\qquad\quad \dfrac{-a}{b} = p$

Hence, the answer is (C).

4. For the figure to the right, which of the following must be true?

    (A) $x > y$
    (B) $y > x$
    (C) $x = y$
    (D) $x = 2$
    (E) there is not enough information to decide

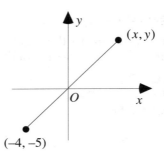

Since the line passes through (–4, –5) and (0, 0), its slope is $m = \dfrac{rise}{run} = \dfrac{-5-0}{-4-0} = \dfrac{5}{4}$. Notice that the rise, 5, is larger than the run, 4. Hence, the y-coordinate will always be larger in absolute value than the x-coordinate. The answer is (B).

5. In the figure to the right, a is the x-coordinate of point P and b is the y-coordinate of point Q. In which quadrant is the point (a, b) ?

    (A) I
    (B) II
    (C) III
    (D) IV
    (E) cannot be determined from the information given

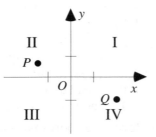

Since P is in Quadrant II, its x-coordinate is negative. That is, a is negative. Since Q is in Quadrant IV, its y-coordinate is negative. That is, b is negative. Hence, (a, b) is in Quadrant III. The answer is (C).

6. In the figure to the right, if $x = 4$, then $y =$

    (A) 1
    (B) 2
    (C) 3
    (D) 4
    (E) 5.1

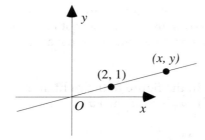

Let's write the equation of the line, using the slope-intercept form, $y = mx + b$. Since the line passes through the origin, $b = 0$. This reduces the equation to $y = mx$. Calculating the slope between (2, 1) and (0, 0) yields $m = \dfrac{1-0}{2-0} = \dfrac{1}{2}$. Plugging this into the equation yields $y = \dfrac{1}{2}x$.

Since $x = 4$, we get $y = \dfrac{1}{2} \cdot 4 = 2$. The answer is (B).

7. In the figure to the right, which of the following could be the coordinates of a point in the shaded region?

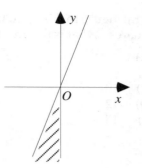

    (A)   (1, 2)
    (B)   (–2, 3)
    (C)   (3, –5)
    (D)   (–5, 1)
    (E)   (–1, –6)

The shaded region is entirely within the third quadrant. Now, both coordinates of any point in Quadrant III are negative. The only point listed with both coordinates negative is (–1, –6). The answer is (E).

8. In the figure to the right, which of the following points lies within the circle?

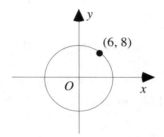

    (A)   (3.5, 9.5)
    (B)   (–7, 7)
    (C)   (–10, 1)
    (D)   (0, 11)
    (E)   (5.5, 8.5)

For a point to be within a circle, its distance from the center of the circle must be less than the radius of the circle. The distance from (6, 8) to (0, 0) is the radius of the circle: $R = \sqrt{(6-0)^2 + (8-0)^2} = \sqrt{36 + 64} = \sqrt{100} = 10$. Now, let's calculate the distance between (–7, 7) and (0, 0): $R = \sqrt{(-7-0)^2 + (7-0)^2} = \sqrt{49 + 49} = \sqrt{98} < 10$. The answer is (B).

9. For the figure to the right, which of the following statements about –3a and 3b must be true?

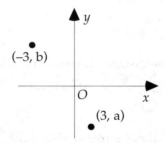

    (A) $-3a = 3b$
    (B) $-3a > 3b$
    (C) $-3a < 3b$
    (D) $-3a \neq 3b$
    (E)   there is not enough information to decide

Note: Figure not drawn to scale

Since b is the y-coordinate of a point in Quadrant II, it is positive. Since a is the y-coordinate of a point in Quadrant IV, it is negative and therefore –3a is positive. However, since the point (–3, b) could be anywhere in Quadrant II and the point (3, a) could be anywhere in Quadrant IV, we cannot deduce anything more about the relative sizes of –3a and 3b. The answer is (E).

10.   In the figure to the right, the grid consists of unit
      squares. What is the area of the polygon?

      (A)   7
      (B)   9
      (C)   10
      (D)   12
      (E)   15

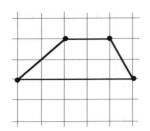

Dividing the polygon into triangles and squares yields

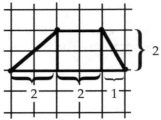

The triangle furthest to the left has area $A = \dfrac{1}{2}bh = \dfrac{1}{2} \cdot 2 \cdot 2 = 2$.   The square has area
$A = s^2 = 2^2 = 4$. The triangle furthest to the right has area $A = \dfrac{1}{2} \cdot 1 \cdot 2 = 1$. The sum of the areas of
these three figures is $2 + 4 + 1 = 7$. The answer is (A).

11.   In the figure to the right, which of the following
      points is three times as far from P as from Q?

      (A)   (0, 3)
      (B)   (1, 1)
      (C)   (4, 5)
      (D)   (2, 3)
      (E)   (4, 1)

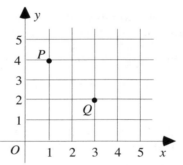

From the distance formula, the distance between (4, 1) and Q is $\sqrt{2}$, and the distance between
(4, 1) and P is $\sqrt{(4-1)^2 + (1-4)^2} = \sqrt{3^2 + (-3)^2} = \sqrt{2 \cdot 3^2} = 3\sqrt{2}$. The answer is (E).

12.   In the figure to the right, what is the area of
      quadrilateral $ABCO$?

      (A)   3
      (B)   5
      (C)   6.5
      (D)   8
      (E)   13

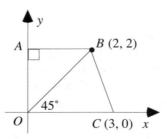

Dropping a vertical line from point B perpendicular to the x-axis will form a square and a
triangle:

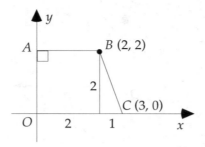

From the figure, we see that the square has area $s^2 = 2^2 = 4$, and the triangle has area $\frac{1}{2}bh = \frac{1}{2} \cdot 1 \cdot 2 = 1$. Hence, the area of the quadrilateral is $4 + 1 = 5$. The answer is (B). Note, with this particular solution, we did not need to use the properties of the diagonal line in the original diagram.

13. In the figure to the right, which quadrants contain points (x, y) such that $xy = -2$?

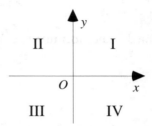

    (A)   I only
    (B)   II only
    (C)   III and IV only
    (D)   II and IV only
    (E)   II, III, and IV

If the product of two numbers is negative, the numbers must have opposite signs. Now, only the coordinates of points in quadrants II and IV have opposite signs. The following diagram illustrates the sign pattern of points for all four quadrants. The answer is (D).

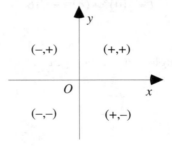

14. If the square in the figure to the right is rotated clockwise about the origin until vertex V is on the negative y-axis, then the new y-coordinate of V is

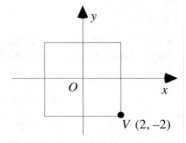

    (A) -2
    (B) $-2\sqrt{2}$
    (C) -4
    (D) $-3\sqrt{2}$
    (E) -8

Calculating the distance between V and the origin yields $\sqrt{(2-0)^2 + (-2-0)^2} = \sqrt{4+4} = \sqrt{8} = 2\sqrt{2}$. Since the square is rotated about the origin, the distance between the origin and V is fix. Hence, the new y-coordinate of V is $-2\sqrt{2}$. The following diagram illustrates the position of V after the rotation. The answer is (B).

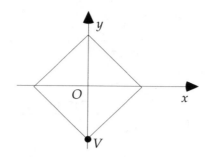

15. In the standard coordinate system, which of the following points is the greatest distance from the origin:

    (A)   (–4, –1)
    (B)   (–3, 3)
    (C)   (4, 0)
    (D)   (2, 3)
    (E)   (0, 4)

Using the distance formula to calculate the distance of each point from the origin yields

$$d = \sqrt{(-4)^2 + (-1)^2} = \sqrt{17}$$

$$d = \sqrt{(-3)^2 + (3)^2} = \sqrt{18}$$

$$d = \sqrt{(4)^2 + (0)^2} = \sqrt{16}$$

$$d = \sqrt{(2)^2 + (3)^2} = \sqrt{13}$$

$$d = \sqrt{(0)^2 + (4)^2} = \sqrt{16}$$

The answer is (B).

16. What is the perimeter of Triangle *ABC* in the figure to the right?

    (A) $5 + \sqrt{2} + \sqrt{29}$
    (B) $5 + 2\sqrt{2} + \sqrt{29}$
    (C) $5 + 4\sqrt{2} + \sqrt{29}$
    (D) $3\sqrt{2} + \sqrt{34}$
    (E) $4\sqrt{2} + \sqrt{34}$

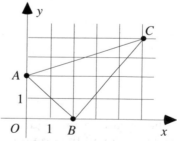

Point *A* has coordinates (0, 2), point *B* has coordinates (2, 0), and point *C* has coordinates (5, 4). Using the distance formula to calculate the distances between points *A* and *B*, *A* and *C*, and *B* and *C* yields

$$\overline{AB} = \sqrt{(0-2)^2 + (2-0)^2} = \sqrt{4+4} = \sqrt{8} = 2\sqrt{2}$$

$$\overline{AC} = \sqrt{(0-5)^2 + (2-4)^2} = \sqrt{25+4} = \sqrt{29}$$

$$\overline{BC} = \sqrt{(2-5)^2 + (0-4)^2} = \sqrt{9+16} = 5$$

Adding these lengths gives the perimeter of Triangle *ABC*:

$$\overline{AB} + \overline{AC} + \overline{BC} = 2\sqrt{2} + \sqrt{29} + 5$$

The answer is (B).

Problem Set I:

1. What is the maximum number of 3x3 squares that can be formed from the squares in the 6x6 checker board to the right?

    (A) 4
    (B) 6
    (C) 12
    (D) 16
    (E) 24

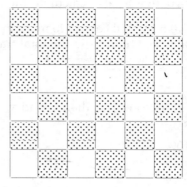

Clearly, there are more than four 3x3 squares in the checker board—eliminate (A). Next, eliminate (B) since it merely repeats a number from the problem. Further, eliminate (E) since it is the greatest. This leaves choices (C) and (D). If you count carefully, you will find sixteen 3x3 squares in the checker board. The answer is (D).

2. Let P stand for the product of the first 5 positive integers. What is the greatest possible value of m if $\dfrac{P}{10^m}$ is an integer?

    (A) 1   (B) 2   (C) 3   (D) 5   (E) 10

Since we are to find the greatest value of m, we eliminate (E)—the greatest. Also, eliminate 5 because it is repeated from the problem. Now, since we are looking for the largest number, start with the greatest number remaining and work toward the smallest number. The first number that works will be the answer. To this end, let $m = 3$. Then $\dfrac{P}{10^m} = \dfrac{1 \cdot 2 \cdot 3 \cdot 4 \cdot 5}{10^3} = \dfrac{120}{1000} = \dfrac{3}{25}$. This is not an integer, so eliminate (C). Next, let $m = 2$. Then $\dfrac{P}{10^m} = \dfrac{1 \cdot 2 \cdot 3 \cdot 4 \cdot 5}{10^2} = \dfrac{120}{100} = \dfrac{6}{5}$. This still is not an integer, so eliminate (B). Hence, by process of elimination, the answer is (A).

3. After being marked down 20 percent, a calculator sells for $10. The original selling price was

    (A) $20   (B) $12.5   (C) $12   (D) $9   (E) $7

Twenty dollars is too large. The discount was only 20 percent—eliminate (A). Both (D) and (E) are impossible since they are less than the selling price—eliminate. 12 is the eye-catcher: 20% of 10 is 2 and 10 + 2 = 12. This is too easy for a hard problem—eliminate. Thus, by process of elimination, the answer is (B).

4. The distance between cities A and B is 120 miles. A car travels from A to B at 60 miles per hour and returns from B to A along the same route at 40 miles per hour. What is the average speed for the round trip?

    (A) 48
    (B) 50
    (C) 52
    (D) 56
    (E) 58

We can eliminate 50 (the mere average of 40 and 60) since that would be too elementary. Now, the average must be closer to 40 than to 60 because the car travels for a longer time at 40 mph. But 48 is the only number given that is closer to 40 than to 60. The answer is (A).

It's instructive to also calculate the answer. *Average Speed* = $\dfrac{\text{Total Distance}}{\text{Total Time}}$. Now, a car traveling at 40 mph will cover 120 miles in 3 hours. And a car traveling at 60 mph will cover the same 120 miles in 2 hours. So the total traveling time is 5 hours. Hence, for the round trip, the average speed $= \dfrac{120 + 120}{5} = 48$.

5.   If **w** is 10 percent less than **x**, and **y** is 30 percent less than **z**, then **wy** is what percent less than **xz**?

   (A)   10%
   (B)   20%
   (C)   37%
   (D)   40%
   (E)   100%

We eliminate (A) since it repeats the number 10 from the problem. We can also eliminate choices (B), (D), and (E) since they are derivable from elementary operations:

$$20 = 30 - 10$$
$$40 = 30 + 10$$
$$100 = 10 \cdot 10$$

This leaves choice (C) as the answer.
   Let's also solve this problem directly. The clause

w is 10 percent less than x

translates into

$w = x - .10x$

Simplifying yields

1) $w = .9x$

Next, the clause

y is 30 percent less than **z**

translates into

$y = z - .30z$

Simplifying yields

2) $y = .7z$

Multiplying 1) and 2) gives

$$wy = (.9x)(.7z) = .63xz = xz - .37xz$$

Hence, **wy** is 37 percent less than **xz**. The answer is (C).

6. In the game of chess, the Knight can make any of the moves displayed in the diagram to the right. If a Knight is the only piece on the board, what is the greatest number of spaces from which not all 8 moves are possible?

    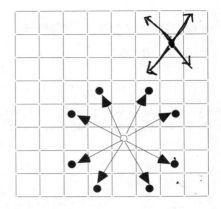

    (A) 8
    (B) 24
    (C) 38
    (D) 48
    (E) 56

Since we are looking for the <u>greatest</u> number of spaces from which not all 8 moves are possible, we can eliminate the greatest number, 56. Now, clearly not all 8 moves are possible from the outer squares, and there are 28 outer squares—not 32. Also, not all 8 moves are possible from the next to outer squares, and there are 20 of them—not 24. All 8 moves are possible from the remaining squares. Hence, the answer is 28 + 20 = 48. The answer is (D). Notice that 56, (32 + 24), is given as an answer-choice to catch those who don't add carefully.

7. How many different ways can 3 cubes be painted if each cube is painted one color and only the 3 colors red, blue, and green are available? (Order is not considered, for example, green, green, blue is considered the same as green, blue, green.)

    (A) 2   (B) 3   (C) 9   (D) 10   (E) 27

Clearly, there are more than 3 color combinations possible. This eliminates (A) and (B). We can also eliminate (C) and (E) because they are both multiples of 3, and that would be too ordinary, too easy, to be the answer. Hence, by process of elimination, the answer is (D).

   Let's also solve this problem directly. The following list displays all 27 (= 3·3·3) color combinations possible (without restriction):

RRR	BBB	GGG
RRB	BBR	GGR
RRG	BBG	GGB
RBR	BRB	GRG
RBB	BRR	GRR
RBG	BRG	GRB
RGR	BGB	GBG
RGB	BGR	GBR
RGG	BGG	GBB

If order is not considered, then there are 10 distinct color combinations in this list. You should count them.

8.   What is the greatest prime factor of $\left(2^4\right)^2 - 1$?

(A) 3   (B) 5   (C) 11   (D) 17   (E) 19

$\left(2^4\right)^2 - 1 = (16)^2 - 1 = 256 - 1 = 255$.   Since the question asks for the <u>greatest</u> prime factor, we eliminate 19, the greatest number. Now, we start with the next largest number and work our way up the list; the first number that divides into 255 evenly will be the answer. Dividing 17 into 255 gives

$$17\overline{)255} = 15$$

Hence, 17 is the largest prime factor of $\left(2^4\right)^2 - 1$. The answer is (D).

9.   Suppose five circles, each 4 inches in diameter, are cut from a rectangular strip of paper 12 inches long. If the least amount of paper is to be wasted, what is the width of the paper strip?

(A)   5
(B) $4 + 2\sqrt{3}$
(C)   8
(D) $4\left(1 + \sqrt{3}\right)$
(E)   not enough information

Since this is a hard problem, we can eliminate (E), "not enough information." And because it is too easily derived, we can eliminate (C), (8 = 4 + 4). Further, we can eliminate (A), 5, because answer-choices (B) and (D) form a more complicated set. At this stage we cannot apply any more elimination rules; so if we could not solve the problem, we would guess either (B) or (D).

Let's solve the problem directly. The drawing below shows the position of the circles so that the paper width is a minimum.

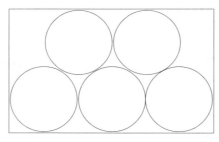

Now, take three of the circles in isolation, and connect the centers of these circles to form a triangle:

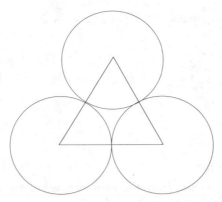

Since the triangle connects the centers of circles of diameter 4, the triangle is equilateral with sides of length 4.

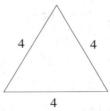

Drawing an altitude gives

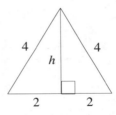

Applying the Pythagorean Theorem to either right triangle gives $\qquad$ $h^2 + 2^2 = 4^2$

Squaring yields $\qquad$ $h^2 + 4 = 16$

Subtracting 4 from both sides of this equation yields $\qquad$ $h^2 = 12$

Taking the square root of both sides yields $\qquad$ $h = \sqrt{12} = \sqrt{4 \cdot 3}$

Removing the perfect square 4 from the radical yields $\qquad$ $h = 2\sqrt{3}$

Summarizing gives

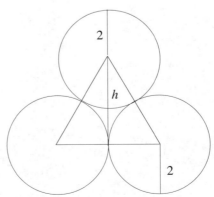

Adding to the height, $h = 2\sqrt{3}$, the distance above the triangle and the distance below the triangle to the edges of the paper strip gives

$$width = (2+2) + 2\sqrt{3} = 4 + 2\sqrt{3}$$

The answer is (B).

10.   Let C and K be constants. If $x^2 + Kx + 5$ factors into $(x+1)(x+C)$, the value of K is

(A)   0
(B)   5
(C)   6
(D)   8
(E)   not enough information

Since the number 5 is merely repeated from the problem, we eliminate (B). Further, since this is a hard problem, we eliminate (E), "not enough information."

Now, since 5 is prime, its only factors are 1 and 5. So the constant C in the expression $(x + 1)(x + C)$ must be 5:

$$(x + 1)(x + 5)$$

Multiplying out this expression yields

$$(x+1)(x+5) = x^2 + 5x + x + 5$$

Combining like terms yields

$$(x+1)(x+5) = x^2 + 6x + 5$$

Hence, $K = 6$, and the answer is (C).

Problem Set J:

1. If $1 < x < y$, which of the following must be true?

    (A) $-x^2 < -y^2$ (B) $\dfrac{x}{y} < \dfrac{y}{x}$ (C) $\dfrac{y}{x} < \dfrac{x}{y}$ (D) $\dfrac{-x}{y} < \dfrac{-y}{x}$ (E) $x^2 > y^2$

From $1 < x < y$, we know that both x and y are positive. So dividing both sides of $x < y$ by x yields $1 < \dfrac{y}{x}$; and dividing both sides of $x < y$ by y yields $\dfrac{x}{y} < 1$. Hence, $\dfrac{x}{y} < 1 < \dfrac{y}{x}$. By the transitive property of inequalities, $\dfrac{x}{y} < \dfrac{y}{x}$. The answer is (B).

2. If $-3 < x < -1$ and $3 < y < 7$, which of the following best describes $\dfrac{x-y}{2}$?

    (A) $-5 < \dfrac{x-y}{2} < -2$

    (B) $-3 < \dfrac{x-y}{2} < -1$

    (C) $-2 < \dfrac{x-y}{2} < 0$

    (D) $2 < \dfrac{x-y}{2} < 5$

    (E) $3 < \dfrac{x-y}{2} < 7$

Multiplying both sides of $3 < y < 7$ by -1 yields $-3 > -y > -7$. Now, we usually write the smaller number on the left side of an inequality. So $-3 > -y > -7$ becomes $-7 < -y < -3$. Add this inequality to the like inequality $-3 < x < -1$:

$$\begin{array}{r} -3 < x < -1 \\ (+) \quad \underline{-7 < -y < -3} \\ -10 < x - y < -4 \end{array}$$

Dividing $-10 < x - y < -4$ by 2 yields $\dfrac{-10}{2} < \dfrac{x-y}{2} < \dfrac{-4}{2}$, or $-5 < \dfrac{x-y}{2} < -2$. The answer is (A).

3. If x is an integer and $y = -2x - 8$, what is the least value of x for which y is less than 9?

    (A) -9 (B) -8 (C) -7 (D) -6 (E) -5

Since y is less than 9 and $y = -2x - 8$, we get $\quad\quad\quad -2x - 8 < 9$
Adding 8 to both sides of this inequality yields $\quad\quad\quad -2x < 17$

Dividing by -2 and reversing the inequality yields $\quad\quad\quad x > -\dfrac{17}{2} = -8.5$

Since x is an integer and is to be as small as possible, $\quad\quad\quad x = -8$
The answer is (B).

4.   Which one of the following could be the graph of $3 - 6x \le \dfrac{4x + 2}{-2}$?

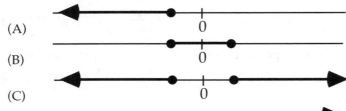

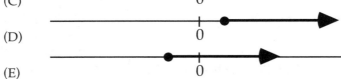

Multiplying both sides of the inequality by –2 yields	$-2(3 - 6x) \ge 4x + 2$
Distributing the –2 yields	$-6 + 12x \ge 4x + 2$
Subtracting $4x$ and adding 6 to both sides yields	$8x \ge 8$
Dividing both sides of the inequality by 8 yields	$x \ge 1$

The answer is (D).

5.   If line segment AD has midpoint M_1 and line segment M_1D has midpoint M_2, what is the value of $\dfrac{M_1D}{AM_2}$?

   (A) $\dfrac{1}{2}$ (B) $\dfrac{2}{3}$ (C) $\dfrac{3}{4}$ (D) $\dfrac{4}{5}$ (E) $\dfrac{5}{6}$

Let 4 be the length of line segment AD. Since M_1 is the midpoint of AD, this yields

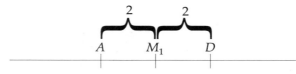

Now, since M_2 is the midpoint of M_1D, this yields

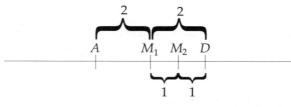

From the diagram, we see that $M_1D = 2$ and $AM_2 = 3$. Hence, $\dfrac{M_1D}{AM_2} = \dfrac{2}{3}$. The answer is (B).

6.   If $x < y < -1$, which of the following must be true?

   (A) $\dfrac{x}{y} > xy$ (B) $\dfrac{y}{x} > x + y$ (C) $\dfrac{y}{x} > xy$ (D) $\dfrac{y}{x} < x + y$ (E) $\dfrac{y}{x} > \dfrac{x}{y}$

Since the sum of negative numbers is negative, $x + y$ is negative. Since the quotient of an even number of negative numbers is positive, $\dfrac{y}{x}$ is positive. Hence, $\dfrac{y}{x} > x + y$. The answer is (B).

7.   Which of the following represents all solutions of the inequality $x^2 < 2x$?

    (A) $-1 < x < 1$ (B) $0 < x < 2$ (C) $1 < x < 3$ (D) $2 < x < 4$ (E) $4 < x < 6$

Forming an equation from $x^2 < 2x$ yields $x^2 = 2x$

Subtracting $2x$ from both sides yields $x^2 - 2x = 0$

Factoring yields $x(x - 2) = 0$

Setting each factor to zero yields $x = 0$ and $x - 2 = 0$

Solving yields $x = 0$ and $x = 2$

Setting up a number line and choosing test points (the circled numbers on the number line below) yields

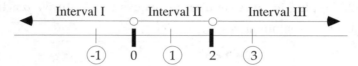

Now, if $x = -1$, the inequality $x^2 < 2x$ becomes $(-1)^2 < 2(-1)$, or $1 < -2$. This is false. Hence, Interval I is not a solution. If $x = 1$, the inequality $x^2 < 2x$ becomes $1^2 < 2(1)$, or $1 < 2$. This is true. Hence, Interval II is a solution. If $x = 3$, the inequality $x^2 < 2x$ becomes $3^2 < 2(3)$, or $9 < 6$. This is false. Hence, Interval III is not a solution. Thus, only Interval II is a solution:

The answer is (B).

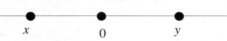

8.   Given the positions of numbers x and y on the number line above, which of the following must be true?

    I. $xy > 0$ II. $\dfrac{x}{y} < 0$ III. $x - y > 0$

    (A) I only   (B) II only   (C) III only   (D) I and II only   (E) I, II, and III

Since x is to the left of zero on the number line, it's negative. Since y is to the right of zero, it's positive. Now, the product or quotient of a positive number and a negative number is negative. Hence, Statement I is false and Statement II is true. Regarding Statement III, since x is to the left of y on the number line, $x < y$. Subtracting y from both sides of this inequality yields $x - y < 0$. Hence, Statement III is false. Therefore, the answer is (B).

9.   If $\begin{array}{c} x^4 y < 0 \\ xy^4 > 0 \end{array}$, which of the following must be true?

    (A) $x > y$ (B) $y > x$ (C) $x = y$ (D) $x < 0$ (E) $y > 0$

Since x is raised to an even exponent, it is greater than or equal to zero. Further, since $x^4 y \neq 0$, we know that neither x nor y is zero (otherwise $x^4 y = 0$). Hence, we may divide $x^4 y < 0$ by x^4 without reversing the inequality:

$$\frac{x^4 y}{x^4} < \frac{0}{x^4}$$

Simplifying yields $y < 0$

A similar analysis of the inequality $xy^4 > 0$ shows that $x > 0$. Hence, $x > y$. The answer is (A).

10.   If n is an integer, what is the least value of n such that $\dfrac{1}{3^n} < 0.01$?

   (A) 2   (B) 3   (C) 4   (D) 5   (E) 6

Replacing 0.01 with its fractional equivalent, $\dfrac{1}{100}$, yields $\dfrac{1}{3^n} < \dfrac{1}{100}$

Multiplying both sides by 3^n and 100 and then simplifying yields $100 < 3^n$

Beginning with $n = 2$, we plug in larger and larger values of n until we reach one that makes $100 < 3^n$ true. The table below summarizes the results:

n	$100 < 3^n$	
2	$100 < 3^2 = 9$	False
3	$100 < 3^3 = 27$	False
4	$100 < 3^4 = 81$	False
5	$100 < 3^5 = 243$	True

Since 5 is the first integer to work, the answer is (D).

11.   If the average of 10, 14, and n is greater than or equal to 8 and less than or equal to 12, what is the least possible value of n ?

   (A) −12   (B) −6   (C) 0   (D) 6   (E) 12

Translating the clause "the average of 10, 14, and n is greater than or equal to 8 and less than or equal to 12" into an inequality yields

$$8 \le \frac{10 + 14 + n}{3} \le 12$$

Adding 10 and 14 yields $8 \le \dfrac{24 + n}{3} \le 12$

Multiplying <u>each</u> term by 3 yields $24 \le 24 + n \le 36$

Subtracting 24 from each term yields $0 \le n \le 12$

Hence, the least possible value of n is 0. The answer is (C).

12.   If $\begin{array}{l} 3x + y < 4 \\ x > 3 \end{array}$, which of the following must be true?

   (A) $y < -5$ (B) $y < -10$ (C) $x = y$ (D) $x < 3$ (E) $y > 0$

Subtracting $3x$ from both sides of $3x + y < 4$ yields $y < 4 - 3x$. Now, multiplying both sides of $x > 3$ by -3 yields $-3x < -9$. Adding 4 to both sides yields $4 - 3x < -5$. Now, using the transitive property to combine $y < 4 - 3x$ and $4 - 3x < -5$ yields $y < 4 - 3x < -5$. Hence, $y < -5$. The answer is (A).

$$2 - 3x \; ? \; 5$$

13.   Of the following symbols, which one can be substituted for the question mark in the above expression to make a true statement for all values of x such that $-1 < x \le 2$?

   (A) $=$ (B) $<$ (C) $\ge$ (D) $>$ (E) $\le$

Multiply each term of the inequality $-1 < x \le 2$ by -3 (this is done because the original expression involves $-3x$): $3 > -3x \ge -6$.

Add 2 to each term of this inequality (this is done because the original expression adds 2 and $-3x$): $5 > 2 - 3x \geq -4$.

Rewrite the inequality in standard form (with the smaller number on the left and the larger number on the right): $-4 \leq 2 - 3x < 5$.

The answer is (B).

14. Let x, y, z be three different positive integers each less than 20. What is the smallest possible value of expression $\dfrac{x - y}{-z}$ is

(A) -18 (B) -17 (C) -14 (D) -11 (E) -9

First, bring the negative symbol in the expression $\dfrac{x - y}{-z}$ to the top:

$$\frac{-(x - y)}{z}$$

Then distribute the negative symbol:

$$\frac{y - x}{z}$$

To make this expression as small as possible, we need to make both the $y - x$ and z as small as possible. To make $y - x$ as small as possible, let $y = 1$ and $x = 19$. Then $y - x = 1 - 19 = -18$. With these choices for y and x, the smallest remaining value for z is 2. This gives

$$\frac{y - x}{z} = \frac{1 - 19}{2} = \frac{-18}{2} = -9$$

In this case, we made the numerator as small as possible. Now, let's make the denominator as small as possible. To that end, chose $z = 1$ and $y = 2$ and $x = 19$. This gives

$$\frac{y - x}{z} = \frac{2 - 19}{1} = \frac{-17}{1} = -17$$

The answer is (B).

15. If $x > 0$ and $|x| = \dfrac{1}{x}$, then $x =$

(A) -1 (B) 0 (C) 1 (D) 2 (E) 3

Since $x > 0$, $|x| = x$. And the equation $|x| = \dfrac{1}{x}$ becomes $x = \dfrac{1}{x}$. Multiplying both sides of this equation by x yields $x^2 = 1$. Taking the square root of both sides gives $x = \pm 1$. Since we are given that $x > 0$, x must equal 1. The answer is (C).

16. Four letters—a, b, c, and d—represent one number each from one through four. No two letters represent the same number. It is known that $c > a$ and $a > d$. If $b = 2$, then $a =$

(A) 1
(B) 2
(C) 3
(D) 4
(E) Not enough information to decide.

Combining the inequalities $c > a$ and $a > d$ gives $c > a > d$. Since $b = 2$, a, c, and d must represent the remaining numbers 1, 3, and 4—not necessarily in that order. In order to satisfy the condition $c > a > d$, c must be 4, a must be 3, and d must be 1. The answer is (C).

17. If $r > t$ and $r < 1$ and $rt = 1$, then which one of the following must be true?

   (A) $r > 0$ and $t < -1$
   (B) $r > -1$ and $t < -1$
   (C) $r < -1$ and $t > -1$
   (D) $r < 1$ and $t > 1$
   (E) $r > 1$ and $t < 0$

Note that the product of r and t is 1. The product of two numbers is positive only if both numbers are positive or both numbers are negative. Since $rt = 1$ and $r > t$, there are two possibilities:

$$\text{Case I (both negative): } -1 < r < 0 \text{ and } t < -1$$
$$\text{Case II (both positive): } 0 < t < 1 \text{ and } r > 1$$

The second case violates the condition $r < 1$. Hence, Case I is true, and the answer is (B).

18. If $x > y > 0$ and $p > q > 0$, then which one of the following expressions must be greater than 1?

   (A) $\dfrac{x + p}{y + q}$

   (B) $\dfrac{x + q}{y + p}$

   (C) $\dfrac{x}{p}$

   (D) $\dfrac{xq}{yp}$

   (E) $\dfrac{yq}{xp}$

Adding the given inequalities $x > y > 0$ and $p > q > 0$ yields

$$x + p > y + q > 0$$

Since $y + q$ is positive, dividing the inequality by $y + q$ will not reverse the inequality:

$$\frac{x + p}{y + q} > \frac{y + q}{y + q}$$

$$\frac{x + p}{y + q} > 1$$

Hence, the answer is (A).

19. If $2x + y > m$ and $2y + x < n$, then $x - y$ must be greater than

   (A) $m + n$
   (B) $m - n$
   (C) mn
   (D) $2m + n$
   (E) $n - m$

Aligning the system of inequalities vertically yields

$$2x + y > m$$
$$2y + x < n$$

Multiplying both sides of the bottom inequality by –1 and flipping the direction of the inequality yields

$$-2y - x > -n$$

Adding this inequality to the top inequality yields

$$(2x + y) + (-2y - x) > m - n$$
$$(2x - x) + (-2y + y) > m - n$$
$$x - y > m - n$$

The answer is (B).

20. If $p > 2$, then which one of the following inequalities must be false?

  (A) $2p > 7$
  (B) $3p < 7$
  (C) $p < 3$
  (D) $p > 4$
  (E) $3p < 6$

We are given that $p > 2$. Multiplying both sides of this inequality by 3 yields $3p > 6$. The answer is (E).

Problem Set K:

1. Which one of the following fractions is greatest?

  (A) $\dfrac{5}{6}$ (B) $\dfrac{4}{5}$ (C) $\dfrac{1}{2}$ (D) $\dfrac{2}{3}$ (E) $\dfrac{3}{4}$

Begin with $\dfrac{5}{6}$ and $\dfrac{4}{5}$. Cross-multiplying gives 25 versus 24. Hence, $\dfrac{5}{6} > \dfrac{4}{5}$. Continuing in this manner will show that $\dfrac{5}{6}$ is the greatest fraction listed. The answer is (A).

2. If $x \neq \pm 3$, then $\dfrac{x^2 + 6x + 9}{x + 3} \cdot \dfrac{x^2 - 9}{x - 3} =$

  (A) $\dfrac{x + 3}{x - 3}$ (B) -1 (C) $(x + 3)^2$ (D) $\left(\dfrac{x + 3}{x - 3}\right)^2$ (E) 1

First, factor the expression $\dfrac{x^2 + 6x + 9}{x + 3} \cdot \dfrac{x^2 - 9}{x - 3}$:

$$\dfrac{(x + 3)(x + 3)}{x + 3} \cdot \dfrac{(x + 3)(x - 3)}{x - 3}$$

Next, cancel the $x + 3$ and the $x - 3$:

$$(x + 3) \cdot (x + 3)$$

or

$$(x + 3)^2$$

The answer is (C).

3. $\dfrac{1}{\dfrac{4}{3} - 1} =$

   (A) $-\dfrac{1}{3}$ (B) $-\dfrac{1}{4}$ (C) $\dfrac{3}{4}$ (D) 3   (E) $\dfrac{9}{2}$

$\dfrac{1}{\dfrac{4}{3} - 1} = \dfrac{1}{\dfrac{4}{3} - \dfrac{3}{3}} = \dfrac{1}{\dfrac{1}{3}} = 3$. The answer is (D).

4. If $0 < x < 1$, which of the following must be true?

   I. $x^2 < x$ II. $x < \dfrac{1}{x^2}$ III. $\sqrt{x} < x$

   (A) I only   (B) II only   (C) III only   (D) I and II only   (E) I, II, and III

Since squaring a fraction between 0 and 1 makes it smaller, we know Statement I is true. This eliminates both (B) and (C).

Also, since taking the square root of a fraction between 0 and 1 makes it larger, we know Statement III is false. This eliminates (E).

To analyze Statement II, we'll use substitution. Since $0 < x < 1$, we need only check one fraction, say, $x = \dfrac{1}{2}$. Then $\dfrac{1}{x^2} = \dfrac{1}{\left(\dfrac{1}{2}\right)^2} = \dfrac{1}{\left(\dfrac{1}{4}\right)} = 1 \cdot \dfrac{4}{1} = 4$. Now, $\dfrac{1}{2} < 4$. Hence, Statement II is true,

and the answer is (D).

5. In the following pairs of numbers, which are reciprocals of each other?

   I. 1 and 1   II. $\dfrac{1}{11}$ and -11 III. $\sqrt{5}$ and $\dfrac{\sqrt{5}}{5}$

   (A) I only   (B) II only   (C) I and II only   (D) I and III only   (E) II and III only

Let's take the first number in each pair, form its reciprocal, and then try to reduce it to the second number. Now, $1 \Rightarrow \dfrac{1}{1} = 1$. Hence the pair 1 and 1 are reciprocals of each other. Next, $\dfrac{1}{11} \Rightarrow \dfrac{1}{\dfrac{1}{11}} = 1 \cdot \dfrac{11}{1} = 11 \neq -11$. Hence, the pair $\dfrac{1}{11}$ and -11 are not reciprocals of each other. Finally, $\sqrt{5} \Rightarrow \dfrac{1}{\sqrt{5}} = \dfrac{1}{\sqrt{5}} \cdot \dfrac{\sqrt{5}}{\sqrt{5}} = \dfrac{\sqrt{5}}{5}$. Hence, the pair $\sqrt{5}$ and $\dfrac{\sqrt{5}}{5}$ are reciprocals of each other. The answer is (D).

6. $\dfrac{6^4 - 6^3}{5} =$

   (A) $\dfrac{1}{5}$ (B) 6^3 (C) $\dfrac{6}{5}$ (D) 6^4 (E) $\dfrac{6^3}{5}$

$\dfrac{6^4 - 6^3}{5} = \dfrac{6^3(6-1)}{5} = \dfrac{6^3 \cdot 5}{5} = 6^3$. The answer is (B).

7. $\dfrac{1}{1-\dfrac{1}{1-\dfrac{1}{2}}} =$

    (A) –2   (B) –1   (C) $\dfrac{3}{2}$ (D) 2   (E) 4

$\dfrac{1}{1-\dfrac{1}{1-\dfrac{1}{2}}} = \dfrac{1}{1-\dfrac{1}{\dfrac{2}{2}-\dfrac{1}{2}}} = \dfrac{1}{1-\dfrac{1}{\dfrac{1}{2}}} = \dfrac{1}{1-2} = \dfrac{1}{-1} = -1.$ The answer is (B).

8. If $\left(x^2 - 4\right)\left(\dfrac{4}{x} - 5\right) = 0$, then $x =$

    (A) –4   (B) –1   (C) $-\dfrac{4}{5}$ (D) $\dfrac{4}{5}$ (E) 4

From the equation $\left(x^2 - 4\right)\left(\dfrac{4}{x} - 5\right) = 0$, we get $x^2 - 4 = 0$ or $\dfrac{4}{x} - 5 = 0$. Consider the equation $x^2 - 4 = 0$ first. Factoring gives

$$(x + 2)(x - 2) = 0$$

Setting each factor to zero gives

$$x + 2 = 0 \quad \text{or} \quad x - 2 = 0$$

Hence, $x = 2$ or $x = -2$. But neither number is offered as an answer-choice. So we turn to the equation $\dfrac{4}{x} - 5 = 0$. Adding 5 to both sides yields

$$\frac{4}{x} = 5$$

Multiplying both sides by x gives

$$4 = 5x$$

Dividing both sides by 5 gives

$$\frac{4}{5} = x$$

The answer is (D).

9. $\dfrac{1}{10^9} - \dfrac{1}{10^{10}} =$

    (A) $-\dfrac{1}{10}$ (B) $-\dfrac{1}{10^9}$ (C) $-\dfrac{1}{10^{19}}$ (D) $\dfrac{9}{10^{10}}$ (E) $\dfrac{9}{10}$

$\dfrac{1}{10^9} - \dfrac{1}{10^{10}} = \dfrac{1}{10^9} - \dfrac{1}{10^9}\cdot\dfrac{1}{10} = \dfrac{1}{10^9}\left(1 - \dfrac{1}{10}\right) = \dfrac{1}{10^9}\left(\dfrac{9}{10}\right) = \dfrac{9}{10^{10}}.$ The answer is (D).

10. If $x \neq \pm 1$, then $\dfrac{\dfrac{2x^2 - 2}{x - 1}}{2(x + 1)} =$

    (A) $x + 1$ (B) 1   (C) $x^2 - 1$ (D) $x - 1$ (E) 2

$\dfrac{\dfrac{2x^2 - 2}{x - 1}}{2(x + 1)} = \dfrac{2x^2 - 2}{x - 1}\cdot\dfrac{1}{2(x + 1)} = \dfrac{2\left(x^2 - 1\right)}{x - 1}\cdot\dfrac{1}{2(x + 1)} = \dfrac{2(x + 1)(x - 1)}{x - 1}\cdot\dfrac{1}{2(x + 1)} = \dfrac{2}{2}\cdot\dfrac{x + 1}{x + 1}\cdot\dfrac{x - 1}{x - 1} = 1.$

The answer is (B).

11. If $z \neq 0$ and $yz \neq 1$, then $x - \dfrac{1}{y - \dfrac{1}{z}} =$

(A) $\dfrac{xyz}{zy - 1}$ (B) $\dfrac{y - x - z}{z}$ (C) $\dfrac{xyz - x - z}{z - 1}$ (D) $\dfrac{xyz - x - z}{zy - 1}$ (E) $\dfrac{x - y - z}{zy - 1}$

$$x - \dfrac{1}{y - \dfrac{1}{z}} = x - \dfrac{1}{\dfrac{z}{z}y - \dfrac{1}{z}} = x - \dfrac{1}{\dfrac{zy - 1}{z}} = x - \dfrac{z}{zy - 1} = \dfrac{zy - 1}{zy - 1}x - \dfrac{z}{zy - 1} = \dfrac{(zy - 1)x - z}{zy - 1} = \dfrac{xyz - x - z}{zy - 1}$$

The answer is (D).

12. If $\sqrt{\dfrac{\dfrac{1}{x}}{\dfrac{1}{y}}} = \dfrac{1}{2}$, then which of the following statements must be true?

I. $\dfrac{x}{y} > \dfrac{y}{x}$ II. $\dfrac{x}{y} < \dfrac{y}{x}$ III. $\dfrac{x}{y} = \dfrac{y}{x}$

(A) I only (B) II only (C) I and II only (D) I and III only (E) II and III only

$$\sqrt{\dfrac{\dfrac{1}{x}}{\dfrac{1}{y}}} = \dfrac{1}{2}$$

$$\sqrt{\dfrac{1}{x} \cdot \dfrac{y}{1}} = \dfrac{1}{2}$$

$$\sqrt{\dfrac{y}{x}} = \dfrac{1}{2}$$

$$\left(\sqrt{\dfrac{y}{x}}\right)^2 = \left(\dfrac{1}{2}\right)^2$$

$$\dfrac{y}{x} = \dfrac{1}{4}$$

Reciprocating both sides of this final equation yields $\dfrac{x}{y} = 4$. Hence, $4 = \dfrac{x}{y} > \dfrac{y}{x} = \dfrac{1}{4}$. The answer is (A).

13. For all $p \neq \frac{1}{4}$ define p^* by the equation $p^* = \dfrac{\frac{p}{2}}{4p-1}$. If $q = 1^*$, then $q^* =$

(A) $-\dfrac{5}{7}$　　(B) $-\dfrac{1}{3}$　　(C) $-\dfrac{1}{4}$　　(D) $\dfrac{2}{3}$　　(E) $\dfrac{3}{4}$

$$q = 1^* = \frac{\frac{1}{2}}{4 \cdot 1 - 1} = \frac{\frac{1}{2}}{3} = \frac{1}{2} \cdot \frac{1}{3} = \frac{1}{6}$$

Hence, $q^* = \dfrac{\frac{\frac{1}{6}}{2}}{4 \cdot \frac{1}{6} - 1} = \dfrac{\frac{1}{6} \cdot \frac{1}{2}}{\frac{2}{3} - 1} = \dfrac{\frac{1}{12}}{-\frac{1}{3}} = \frac{1}{12}\left(-\frac{3}{1}\right) = -\frac{3}{12} = -\frac{1}{4}$

The answer is (C).

14. If $\dfrac{1}{x} + \dfrac{1}{y} \neq 0$, then which one of the following is equal to the negative reciprocal of $\dfrac{1}{x} + \dfrac{1}{y}$?

(A) $\dfrac{xy}{x+y}$　　　(B) $-\dfrac{x+y}{xy}$　　　(C) $-(x+y)$　　　(D) $\dfrac{x-y}{xy}$　　　(E) $\dfrac{-xy}{x+y}$

Forming the negative reciprocal of $\dfrac{1}{x} + \dfrac{1}{y}$ yields

$$\dfrac{-1}{\frac{1}{x} + \frac{1}{y}}$$

Adding the fractions in the denominator yields

$$\dfrac{-1}{\frac{y+x}{xy}}$$

Reciprocating the denominator yields

$$-1 \cdot \dfrac{xy}{x+y}$$

Or

$$\dfrac{-xy}{x+y}$$

The answer is (E).

15. To halve the value of the expression above $\dfrac{\frac{v+w}{x}}{yz}$ by doubling exactly one of the variables, one must double which of the following variables?

(A) v　　　　(B) w　　　　(C) x　　　　(D) y　　　　(E) z

Doubling the x in the expression yields $\dfrac{\frac{v+w}{2x}}{yz} = \dfrac{1}{2}\left(\dfrac{\frac{v+w}{x}}{yz}\right)$. Since we have written the expression

as $1/2$ times the original expression, doubling the x halved the original expression. The answer is (C).

16. The picture above represents 4,250 apples. How many apples does each 🍎 stand for?

(A) 400　　　(B) 450　　　(C) 500　　　(D) 625　　　(E) 710

There are 8.5 apples in the picture. Dividing the total number of apples by 8.5 yields $\dfrac{4,250}{8.5} = 500$. The answer is (C).

Problem Set L:

1. If $a > 0$ and $6a = 5b$, which of the following must be true?

    (A) $a = \dfrac{6}{5}b$ (B) $ab < 0$ (C) $a > b$ (D) $b = \dfrac{5}{6}a$ (E) $b > a$

Dividing both sides of the equation $6a = 5b$ by 6 gives $a = \dfrac{5}{6}b$. That is, a is a fraction of b. But b is greater than zero and therefore b is greater than a. (Note, had we been given that a was less than zero, then a would have been greater than b.) The answer is (E).

2. If $p - q + r = 4$ and $p + q + r = 8$, then $p + r =$
    (A) 2   (B) 4   (C) 6   (D) 8   (E) 10

Adding the two equations $\begin{array}{l} p - q + r = 4 \\ p + q + r = 8 \end{array}$ gives $2p + 2r = 12$

Then dividing by 2 gives $p + r = 6$

Hence, the answer is (C).

3. Suppose $x = y - 2 = \dfrac{y + 5}{2}$. Then x equals

    (A) $\dfrac{1}{3}$ (B) 1   (C) $\dfrac{7}{6}$ (D) 2   (E) 7

Clearing fractions in the equation $y - 2 = \dfrac{y + 5}{2}$ gives $2(y - 2) = y + 5$

Distributing the 2 gives $2y - 4 = y + 5$
Subtracting y and adding 4 to both sides gives $y = 9$
Now, replacing y with 9 in the equation $x = y - 2$ gives $x = y - 2 = 9 - 2 = 7$
Hence, the answer is (E).

4. Let $p = 3^{q+1}$ and $q = 2r$. Then $\dfrac{p}{3^2} =$

    (A) 3^{2r-1} (B) 3^{2r} (C) 3   (D) r (E) 3^{2r+1}

Replacing p with 3^{q+1} in the expression $\dfrac{p}{3^2}$ gives $\dfrac{p}{3^2} = \dfrac{3^{q+1}}{3^2} = 3^{q+1-2} = 3^{q-1}$

Now, replacing q with $2r$ in the expression 3^{q-1} gives $3^{q-1} = 3^{2r-1}$

Hence, the answer is (A).

5. k is a constant in the equation $\dfrac{u-v}{k} = 8$. If $u = 18$ when $v = 2$, then what is the value of u when $v = 4$?

    (A) –3   (B) 0   (C) 10   (D) $\dfrac{23}{2}$ (E) 20

Substituting $u = 18$ and $v = 2$ into the equation $\dfrac{u-v}{k} = 8$ gives

$$\dfrac{18-2}{k} = 8$$

Subtracting gives

$$\dfrac{16}{k} = 8$$

Multiplying both sides of this equation by k gives

$$16 = 8k$$

Dividing by 8 gives

$$2 = k$$

With this value for k, the original equation becomes

$$\dfrac{u-v}{2} = 8$$

Now, we are asked to find u when $v = 4$.

Replacing v with 4 in the equation $\dfrac{u-v}{2} = 8$ gives

$$\dfrac{u-4}{2} = 8$$

Multiplying by 2 gives

$$u - 4 = 16$$

Adding 4 gives

$$u = 20$$

Hence, the answer is (E).

6. If $x = 3y = 4z$, which of the following must equal $6x$?

    I. $18y$ II. $3y + 20z$ III. $\dfrac{4y + 10z}{3}$

    (A) I only   (B) II only   (C) III only   (D) I and II only   (E) I and III only

The equation $x = 3y = 4z$ contains three equations:

$$x = 3y$$
$$3y = 4z$$
$$x = 4z$$

Multiplying both sides of the equation $x = 3y$ by 6 gives $6x = 18y$. Hence, Statement I is true. This eliminates (B) and (C). Next, $3y + 20z = 3y + 5(4z)$. Substituting x for $3y$ and for $4z$ in this equation gives $3y + 20z = 3y + 5(4z) = x + 5x = 6x$. Hence, Statement II is true. This eliminates (A) and (E). Hence, by process of elimination, the answer is (D).

7. Let $P = (x + y)k$. If $P = 10$ and $k = 3$, what is the average of x and y?

    (A) 0   (B) $\dfrac{1}{2}$ (C) $\dfrac{5}{3}$ (D) $\dfrac{10}{3}$ (E) $\dfrac{7}{2}$

Plugging $P = 10$ and $k = 3$ into the equation $P = (x + y)k$ gives $10 = (x + y)3$. Dividing by 3 gives $x + y = \dfrac{10}{3}$. Finally, to form the average, divide both sides of this equation by 2: $\dfrac{x+y}{2} = \dfrac{10}{6} = \dfrac{5}{3}$. Hence, the answer is (C).

8.   Let $\dfrac{x}{y} + \dfrac{w}{z} = 2$. Then the value of $\dfrac{y}{x} + \dfrac{z}{w}$ is

    (A) $\dfrac{1}{2}$

    (B) $\dfrac{3}{4}$

    (C)   1

    (D)   5

    (E)   It cannot be determined from the information given.

There are many different values for w, x, y, and z such that $\dfrac{x}{y} + \dfrac{w}{z} = 2$. Two particular cases are listed below:

If $x = y = w = z = 1$, then $\dfrac{x}{y} + \dfrac{w}{z} = \dfrac{1}{1} + \dfrac{1}{1} = 1 + 1 = 2$ and $\dfrac{y}{x} + \dfrac{z}{w} = \dfrac{1}{1} + \dfrac{1}{1} = 1 + 1 = 2$.

If $x = 3$, $y = 2$, $w = 1$, and $z = 2$, then $\dfrac{x}{y} + \dfrac{w}{z} = \dfrac{3}{2} + \dfrac{1}{2} = \dfrac{3+1}{2} = \dfrac{4}{2} = 2$ and $\dfrac{y}{x} + \dfrac{z}{w} = \dfrac{2}{3} + \dfrac{2}{1} = \dfrac{2}{3} + \dfrac{2}{1} \cdot \dfrac{3}{3} =$

$\dfrac{2}{3} + \dfrac{6}{3} = \dfrac{2+6}{3} = \dfrac{8}{3}$

This is a double case. Hence, the answer is (E).

9.   If 4 percent of $(p + q)$ is 8 and p is a positive integer, what is the greatest possible value of q?
    (A) 196   (B) 197   (C) 198   (D) 199   (E) 200

Translating the clause "4 percent of $(p + q)$ is 8" into a mathematical expression yields

$$.04(p + q) = 8$$

Dividing both sides of this equation by .04 yields

$$p + q = \dfrac{8}{.04} = 200$$

Subtracting p from both sides yields

$$q = 200 - p$$

This expression will be greatest when p is as small as possible. This is when $p = 1$:

$$q = 200 - 1 = 199$$

The answer is (D).

10.   If $x^5 = 4$ and $x^4 = \dfrac{7}{y}$, then what is the value of x in terms of y?

    (A) $\dfrac{7}{4}y$ (B) $\dfrac{4}{7}y$ (C) $\dfrac{1}{7}y$ (D) $7y$ (E) $7 + \dfrac{5}{y}$

The expression $x^5 = 4$ can be rewritten as $x \cdot x^4 = 4$

Replacing x^4 in this expression with $\dfrac{7}{y}$ yields $x \cdot \dfrac{7}{y} = 4$

Multiplying both sides of this equation by y gives $x \cdot 7 = 4 \cdot y$

Dividing both sides of this equation by 7 yields $x = \dfrac{4}{7} \cdot y$

Hence, the answer is (B).

11.

$$2x + y = 3$$
$$3y = 9 - 6x$$

How many solutions does the above system of equations have?

(A) None
(B) One
(C) Two
(D) Four
(E) An infinite number

Start with the bottom equation $3y = 9 - 6x$:

Dividing by 3 yields $\qquad\qquad\qquad\qquad y = 3 - 2x$

Adding $2x$ yields $\qquad\qquad\qquad\qquad 2x + y = 3$

Notice that this is the top equation in the system. Hence, the system is only one equation in two different forms. Thus, there are an infinite number of solutions. For example, the pair $x = 2$, $y = -1$ is a solution as is the pair $x = 0$, $y = 3$. The answer is (E).

12. If $\frac{p}{19}$ is 1 less than 3 times $\frac{q}{19}$, then p equals which of the following expressions?

(A) $3q + 19$ (B) $3q + 38$ (C) $\frac{19}{2}$ (D) $3q - 38$ (E) $3q - 19$

The clause " $\frac{p}{19}$ is 1 less than 3 times $\frac{q}{19}$ " translates into:

$$\frac{p}{19} = 3 \cdot \frac{q}{19} - 1$$

Multiplying both sides of this equation by 19 gives

$$p = 3 \cdot q - 19$$

The answer is (E).

13. If n is a number such that $(-8)^{2n} = 2^{8+2n}$, then $n =$

(A) $\frac{1}{2}$ (B) 2 (C) $\frac{3}{2}$ (D) 4 (E) 5

Since the right side of the equation is positive, the left side must also be positive. Thus, $(-8)^{2n}$ is equal to 8^{2n}

This in turn can be written as $\qquad\qquad\qquad\qquad\qquad\qquad\qquad\qquad\qquad \left(2^3\right)^{2n}$

Multiplying the exponents gives $\qquad\qquad\qquad\qquad\qquad\qquad\qquad\qquad 2^{6n}$

Plugging this into the original equation gives $\qquad\qquad\qquad\qquad\qquad 2^{6n} = 2^{8+2n}$

Now, since the bases are the same, the exponents must be equal: $\qquad 6n = 8 + 2n$

Solving this equation gives $\qquad\qquad\qquad\qquad\qquad\qquad\qquad\qquad n = 2$

The answer is (B).

14.   If $s + S \neq 0$ and $\dfrac{1}{3} = \dfrac{1}{4}\dfrac{s - S}{s + S}$, then what is s in terms of S ?

(A) $s = S + 3$ (B) $s = 4S$ (C) $s = \dfrac{S}{12}$ (D) $s = -7S$ (E) $s = 4S - 6$

First, clear fractions by multiplying both sides by $12(s + S)$: $4(s + S) = 3(s - S)$

Next, distribute the 3 and 4: $4s + 4S = 3s - 3S$

Finally, subtract $3s$ and $4S$ from both sides: $s = -7S$

The answer is (D).

15.   If $3^x = 81$, then $\left(3^{x+3}\right)\left(4^{x+1}\right) =$

(A) $5(7)^5$ (B) $9(7)^5$ (C) $2(12)^4$ (D) $9(12)^5$ (E) $2(12)^7$

$3^x = 81 = 3^4$. Hence, $x = 4$. Replacing x with 4 in the expression $\left(3^{x+3}\right)\left(4^{x+1}\right)$ yields

$$\left(3^{4+3}\right)\left(4^{4+1}\right) =$$

$$3^7 \cdot 4^5 =$$

$$3^2 \cdot 3^5 \cdot 4^5 =$$

$$3^2(3 \cdot 4)^5 =$$

$$9(12)^5$$

The answer is (D).

16.   If $x = y/2$ and $y = z/2$, then $\sqrt{x/z} =$

(A)   4
(B)   2
(C)   1
(D)   1/2
(E)   1/4

We are given the equations: $x = y/2$
                                 $y = z/2$

Solving the bottom equation for z yields $z = 2y$. Replacing x and z in the expression $\sqrt{x/z}$ with $y/2$ and $2y$, respectively, yields

$$\sqrt{x/z} = \sqrt{\dfrac{y/2}{2y}} = \sqrt{\dfrac{y}{2} \cdot \dfrac{1}{2y}} = \sqrt{\dfrac{1}{4}} = \dfrac{1}{2}$$

The answer is (D).

17. If $a = b/c$ and $b = a/c$, then $c =$

    (A) b/a
    (B) a/b
    (C) -1
    (D) a
    (E) $-b$

We are given

$$a = b/c$$
$$b = a/c$$

Replacing b in the top equation with a/c (since $b = a/c$ according to the bottom equation) yields

$$a = \frac{a/c}{c}$$
$$a = \frac{a}{c} \cdot \frac{1}{c}$$
$$a = \frac{a}{c^2}$$
$$1 = \frac{1}{c^2} \qquad \text{(by canceling } a \text{ from both sides)}$$
$$c^2 = 1$$
$$c = \pm\sqrt{1} = \pm 1$$

Since one of the two possible answers is -1, the answer is (C).

18. If $x + 3y = 5$ and $3x + y = 7$, then $x + y =$

    (A)   1
    (B)   2
    (C)   3
    (D)   4
    (E)   5

Forming a system from the two given equations yields

$$x + 3y = 5$$
$$3x + y = 7$$

Adding the two equations yields

$$4x + 4y = 12$$
$$4(x + y) = 12 \qquad \text{by factoring out 4}$$
$$x + y = 12/4 = 3 \qquad \text{by dividing by 4}$$

The answer is (C).

19.   If $7x - y = 23$ and $7y - x = 31$, then $x + y =$

(A)   4
(B)   6
(C)   7
(D)   8
(E)   9

Aligning the system of equations vertically yields

$$7x - y = 23$$
$$7y - x = 31$$

Adding the system of equations yields

$(7x - y) + (7y - x) = 23 + 31$	
$(7x - x) + (7y - y) = 54$	by collecting like terms
$6x + 6y = 54$	by adding like terms
$6(x + y) = 54$	by factoring out 6
$x + y = 9$	by dividing both sides by 6

The answer is (E).

20.   If $x + y = 4a/5$, $y + z = 7a/5$ and $z + x = 9a/5$, then $x + y + z =$

(A) $7a/15$
(B) a
(C) $2a$
(D) $3a$
(E) $4a$

Writing the system of given equations vertically yields

$$x + y = 4a/5$$
$$y + z = 7a/5$$
$$z + x = 9a/5$$

Adding the three equations yields

$(x + y) + (y + z) + (z + x) = 4a/5 + 7a/5 + 9a/5$	
$2x + 2y + 2z = 20a/5$	by adding like terms
$2(x + y + z) = 4a$	
$x + y + z = 2a$	by dividing both sides by 2

The answer is (C).

Problem Set M:

1. If the average of p and $4p$ is 10, then $p =$

    (A) 1
    (B) 3
    (C) 4
    (D) 10
    (E) 18

Since the average of p and $4p$ is 10, we get $\dfrac{p+4p}{2}=10$

Combining the p's gives $\dfrac{5p}{2}=10$

Multiplying by 2 yields $5p=20$

Finally, dividing by 5 gives $p=4$

The answer is (C).

2. The average of six consecutive integers in increasing order of size is $9\frac{1}{2}$. What is the average of the last three integers?

    (A) 8
    (B) $9\frac{1}{2}$
    (C) 10
    (D) 11
    (E) 19

We have six consecutive integers whose average is $9\frac{1}{2}$, so we have the first three integers less than $9\frac{1}{2}$ and the first three integers greater than $9\frac{1}{2}$. That is, we are dealing with the numbers 7, 8, 9, 10, 11, 12. Clearly, the average of the last three numbers in this list is 11. Hence, the answer is (D).

3. If S denotes the sum and A the average of the consecutive positive integers 1 through n, then which of the following must be true?

    I. $A = \dfrac{S}{n}$

    II. $S = \dfrac{A}{n}$

    III. $A - S = n$

    (A) I only
    (B) II only
    (C) III only
    (D) I and II only
    (E) I, II, and III

The average of the consecutive positive integers 1 through n is $A = \dfrac{1+2+\ldots+n}{n}$. Now, we are given that S denotes the sum of the consecutive positive integers 1 through n, that is, $S = 1 + 2 + \cdots + n$. Plugging this into the formula for the average gives $A = \dfrac{S}{n}$. Hence, Statement I is true, which eliminates (B) and (C). Next, solving the equation $A = \dfrac{S}{n}$ for S yields $S = A \cdot n$. Thus, Statement II is false, which eliminates (D) and (E). Therefore, the answer is (A).

4.   Cars X and Y leave City A at the same time and travel the same route to City B. Car X takes 30 minutes to complete the trip and car Y takes 20 minutes. Which of the following must be true?

   I.   The average miles per hour at which car X traveled was greater than the average miles per hour at which car Y traveled.

   II. The distance between the cities is 30 miles.

   III. The average miles per hour at which car Y traveled was greater than the average miles per hour at which car X traveled.

   (A)   I only
   (B)   II only
   (C)   III only
   (D)   I and II only
   (E)   I and III only

The average speed at which car X traveled is $\dfrac{Total\ Distance}{30}$.

The average speed at which car Y traveled is $\dfrac{Total\ Distance}{20}$.

The two fractions have the same numerators, and the denominator for car Y is smaller. Hence, the average miles per hour at which car Y traveled is greater than the average miles per hour at which car X traveled. Thus, Statement I is false and Statement III is true. As to Statement II, we do not have enough information to calculate the distance between the cities. Hence, Statement II need not be true. The answer is (C).

5.   If $p + q = r$, what is the average of p, q, and r ?

   (A) $\dfrac{r}{3}$

   (B) $\dfrac{p+q}{3}$

   (C) $\dfrac{2r}{3}$

   (D) $\dfrac{r}{2}$

   (E) $\dfrac{p+q}{2}$

The average of p, q, and r is $\dfrac{p+q+r}{3}$. Replacing $p + q$ with r gives $\dfrac{r+r}{3} = \dfrac{2r}{3}$. The answer is (C).

6. Suppose a train travels x miles in y hours and 15 minutes. Its average speed in miles per hour is

(A) $\dfrac{y+15}{x}$

(B) $x\left(y-\dfrac{1}{4}\right)$

(C) $\dfrac{x}{y+\dfrac{1}{4}}$

(D) $\dfrac{x}{y+15}$

(E) $\dfrac{y+\dfrac{1}{4}}{x}$

Often on the GMAT you will be given numbers in different units. When this occurs, you must convert the numbers into the same units. (This is obnoxious but it does occur on the GMAT, so be alert to it.) In this problem, we must convert 15 minutes into hours: $15\cdot\dfrac{1}{60}=\dfrac{1}{4}hr$. Hence, the average speed is $\dfrac{\textit{Total Distance}}{\textit{Total Time}}=\dfrac{x}{y+\dfrac{1}{4}}$. The answer is (C).

7. The average of five numbers is 6.9. If one of the numbers is deleted, the average of the remaining numbers is 4.4. What is the value of the number deleted?

(A) 6.8
(B) 7.4
(C) 12.5
(D) 16.9
(E) 17.2

Forming the average of five numbers gives

$$\frac{v+w+x+y+z}{5}=6.9$$

Let the deleted number be z. Then forming the average of the remaining four numbers gives

$$\frac{v+w+x+y}{4}=4.4$$

Multiplying both sides of this equation by 4 gives $\qquad v+w+x+y=17.6$

Plugging this value into the original average gives $\qquad \dfrac{17.6+z}{5}=6.9$

Solving this equation for z gives $\qquad z=16.9$

The answer is (D).

8. The average of two numbers is $\dfrac{\pi}{2}$, and one of the numbers is x. What is the other number in terms of x?

(A) $\dfrac{\pi}{2} - x$ (B) $\dfrac{\pi}{2} + x$ (C) $\pi - x$ (D) $\pi + x$ (E) $2\pi + x$

Let the other number be y. Since the average of the two numbers is $\dfrac{\pi}{2}$, we get

$$\frac{x + y}{2} = \frac{\pi}{2}$$

Multiplying both sides of this equation by 2 yields $x + y = \pi$
Subtracting x from both sides of this equation yields $y = \pi - x$

The answer is (C).

9. A shopper spends \$25 to purchase floppy disks at 50¢ each. The next day, the disks go on sale for 30¢ each and the shopper spends \$45 to purchase more disks. What was the average price per disk purchased?

(A) 25¢   (B) 30¢   (C) 35¢   (D) 40¢   (E) 45¢

This is a weighted-average problem because more disks were purchased on the second day. Let x be the number of disks purchased on the first day. Then $.50x = 25$. Solving for x yields $x = 50$. Let y be the number of disks purchased on the second day. Then $.30y = 45$. Solving for y yields $y = 150$. Forming the weighted average, we get

$$Average\ Cost = \frac{Total\ Cost}{Total\ Number} = \frac{25 + 45}{50 + 150} = \frac{70}{200} = .35$$

The answer is (C).

10. The average of 8 numbers is A, and one of the numbers is 14. If 14 is replaced with 28, then what is the new average in terms of A?

(A) $A + \dfrac{7}{4}$ (B) $A + \dfrac{1}{2}$ (C) $A + 2$ (D) $2A + 1$ (E) $A + 4$

Let the seven unknown numbers be represented by $x_1, x_2, \cdots, x_7$. Forming the average of the eight numbers yields

$$\frac{x_1 + x_2 + \cdots + x_7 + 14}{8} = A$$

Replacing 14 with 28 (= 14+14), and forming the average yields

$$\frac{x_1 + x_2 + \cdots + x_7 + (14 + 14)}{8}$$

Separating the fraction into the sum of two fractions yields $\dfrac{x_1 + x_2 + \cdots + x_7 + 14}{8} + \dfrac{14}{8}$

Since $\dfrac{x_1 + x_2 + \cdots + x_7 + 14}{8} = A$, this becomes $A + \dfrac{14}{8}$

Reducing the fraction yields $A + \dfrac{7}{4}$

The answer is (A).

Problem Set N:

1. What is the ratio of 2 ft. 3 in. to 2 yds?

    (A) $\dfrac{1}{4}$ (B) $\dfrac{1}{3}$ (C) $\dfrac{3}{8}$ (D) $\dfrac{1}{2}$ (E) $\dfrac{3}{4}$

First change all the units to inches: 2 ft. 3 in. = 27 in., and 2 yds. = 72 in. Forming the ratio yields

$$\frac{2\,ft.\,3\,in.}{2\,yds.} = \frac{27\,in.}{72\,in.} = \frac{3}{8}$$

The answer is (C).

2. The ratio of two numbers is 10 and their difference is 18. What is the value of the smaller number?

    (A) 2   (B) 5   (C) 10   (D) 21   (E) 27

Let x and y denote the numbers. Then $\dfrac{x}{y} = 10$ and $x - y = 18$. Solving the first equation for x and plugging it into the second equation yields

$$10y - y = 18$$

$$9y = 18$$

$$y = 2$$

Plugging this into the equation $x - y = 18$ yields $x = 20$. Hence, y is the smaller number. The answer is (A).

3. If the degree measures of two angles of an isosceles triangle are in the ratio 1:3, what is the degree measure of the largest angle if it is not a base angle?

    (A) 26°   (B) 36°   (C) 51°   (D) 92°   (E) 108°

Let x and y denote the angles:  Then $\dfrac{x}{y} = \dfrac{1}{3}$ and since the angle sum of a triangle is 180°, $x + x + y = 180$. Solving the first equation for y and plugging it into the second equation yields

$$2x + 3x = 180$$

$$5x = 180$$

$$x = 36$$

Plugging this into the equation $\dfrac{x}{y} = \dfrac{1}{3}$ yields $y = 108$. The answer is (E).

4.   A jet uses 80 gallons of fuel to fly 320 miles. At this rate, how many gallons of fuel are needed for a 700 mile flight?

(A) 150   (B) 155   (C) 160   (D) 170   (E) 175

This is a direct proportion: as the distance increases, the gallons of fuel consumed also increases. Setting ratios equal yields

$$\frac{80 \, gal.}{320 \, mi.} = \frac{x \, gal.}{700 \, mi.}$$

$$\frac{700 \cdot 80}{320} = x$$

$$175 = x$$

The answer is (E).

5.   Two boys can mow a lawn in 2 hours and 30 minutes If they are joined by three other boys, how many hours will it take to mow the lawn?

(A) 1 hr.   (B) $1\frac{1}{4}$ hrs.   (C) $1\frac{1}{2}$ hrs.   (D) $1\frac{3}{4}$ hrs.   (E) 2 hrs.

This is an inverse proportion: as the number of boys increases the time required to complete the job decreases. Setting products equal yields

$$2 \times 2.5 = 5 \times t$$

$$1 = t$$

The answer is (A).

6.   A recipe requires $\frac{1}{2}$ lb. of shortening and 14 oz. of flour. If the chef accidentally pours in 21 oz. of flower, how many ounces of shortening should be added?

(A) 9   (B) 10   (C) 11   (D) 12   (E) 13

This is a direct proportion: as the amount of flour increases so must the amount of shortening. First change $\frac{1}{2}$ lb. into 8 oz., Setting ratios equal yields

$$\frac{8}{14} = \frac{x}{21}$$

$$\frac{21 \cdot 8}{14} = x$$

$$12 = x$$

The answer is (D).

7. If w widgets cost d dollars, then at this rate how many dollars will 2000 widgets cost?

    (A) $\dfrac{wd}{2000}$ (B) $\dfrac{2000w}{d}$ (C) $\dfrac{2000d}{w}$ (D) $\dfrac{d}{2000w}$ (E) $\dfrac{2000}{wd}$

Most students struggle with this type of problem, and the GMAT considers them to be difficult. However, if you can identify whether a problem is a direct proportion or an inverse proportion, then it is not so challenging. In this problem, as the number of widgets increases so does the absolute cost. This is a direct proportion, and therefore we set ratios equal:

$$\frac{w}{d} = \frac{2000}{x}$$

Cross multiplying yields $w \cdot x = 2000 \cdot d$

Dividing by w yields $x = \dfrac{2000d}{w}$

The answer is (C).

8. In the system of equations to the right, $z \neq 0$. What is ratio of x to z? $\begin{aligned} x + 2y - z &= 1 \\ 3x - 2y - 8z &= -1 \end{aligned}$

    (A) $-\dfrac{9}{4}$ (B) $-\dfrac{1}{3}$ (C) $\dfrac{1}{3}$ (D) $\dfrac{4}{9}$ (E) $\dfrac{9}{4}$

This is considered to be a hard problem. Begin by adding the two equations:

$$\begin{aligned} x + 2y - z &= 1 \\ \underline{3x - 2y - 8z} &= \underline{-1} \\ 4x - 9z &= 0 \\ 4x &= 9z \\ \frac{x}{z} &= \frac{9}{4} \end{aligned}$$

The answer is (E).

9. If a sprinter takes 30 steps in 9 seconds, how many steps does he take in 54 seconds?

    (A) 130   (B) 170   (C) 173   (D) 180   (E) 200

This is a direct proportion: as the time increases so does the number of steps that the sprinter takes. Setting ratios equal yields

$$\frac{30}{9} = \frac{x}{54}$$

$$\frac{30 \cdot 54}{9} = x$$

$$180 = x$$

The answer is (D).

10. If $5x = 6y$, then the ratio of x to y is

    (A) 5:11   (B) 5:6   (C) 1:1   (D) 6:5   (E) 11:6

Dividing the equation $5x = 6y$ by $5y$ yields

$$\frac{x}{y} = \frac{6}{5} \qquad \text{ratio of } x \text{ to } y$$

or in ratio notation $x : y = 6 : 5$

The answer is (D).

Problem Set O:

1. If $x \neq 0$, $\left(\dfrac{2y^3}{x^2}\right)^4 \cdot x^{10} =$

    (A) $16y^{12}x^2$ (B) $8y^7x^2$ (C) $16\dfrac{y^{12}}{x^8}$ (D) $8\dfrac{y^{12}}{x^8}$ (E) $\dfrac{y^{12}}{16x^8}$

$$\left(\frac{2y^3}{x^2}\right)^4 \cdot x^{10} = \frac{\left(2y^3\right)^4}{\left(x^2\right)^4} \cdot x^{10} = \qquad \text{by the rule } \left(\frac{x}{y}\right)^a = \frac{x^a}{y^a}$$

$$\frac{2^4 \cdot \left(y^3\right)^4}{\left(x^2\right)^4} \cdot x^{10} = \qquad \text{by the rule } (xy)^a = x^a \cdot y^a$$

$$\frac{2^4 \cdot y^{12}}{x^8} \cdot x^{10} = \qquad \text{by the rule } \left(x^a\right)^b = x^{ab}$$

$$2^4 \cdot y^{12} \cdot x^2 = \qquad \text{by the rule } \frac{x^a}{x^b} = x^{a-b}$$

$$16 \cdot y^{12} \cdot x^2$$

The answer is (A).

2. $\sqrt{(31-6)(16+9)} =$

    (A) 5   (B) 10   (C) 25   (D) 50   (E) 625

$\sqrt{(31-6)(16+9)} = \sqrt{25 \cdot 25} = \sqrt{25}\sqrt{25} = 5 \cdot 5 = 25.$ The answer is (C).

3. What is the largest integer n such that 2^n is a factor of 20^8?

    (A) 1   (B) 2   (C) 4   (D) 8   (E) 16

Begin by completely factoring 20:

$$20^8 = (2 \cdot 2 \cdot 5)^8 =$$

$$2^8 \cdot 2^8 \cdot 5^8 = \qquad \text{by Rule 3, } (xy)^a = x^a \cdot y^{a*}$$

$$2^{16} \cdot 5^8 \qquad \text{by Rule 1, } x^a \cdot x^b = x^{a+b}$$

The expression 2^{16} represents all the factors of 20^8 of the form 2^n. Hence, 16 is the largest such number, and the answer is (E).

---

* Note, Rule 3 can be extended to any number of terms by repeatedly applying the rule. For example, $(xyz)^a = \left([xy]z\right)^a = [xy]^a \cdot z^a = x^a y^a z^a$.

4. $\dfrac{55^5}{5^{55}} =$

(A) $\dfrac{11}{5^{50}}$ (B) $\dfrac{11}{5^{55}}$ (C) $\dfrac{11^5}{5^{50}}$ (D) $\dfrac{11^5}{5^5}$ (E) $\dfrac{11^5}{5}$

Begin by factoring 55 in the top of the fraction:

$$\frac{55^5}{5^{55}} = \frac{(5 \cdot 11)^5}{5^{55}} =$$

$$\frac{5^5 \cdot 11^5}{5^{55}} = \qquad \text{by Rule 3, } (xy)^a = x^a \cdot y^a$$

$$\frac{11^5}{5^{50}} \qquad \text{by Rule 5, } \frac{x^a}{x^b} = \frac{1}{x^{b-a}}$$

The answer is (C).

5. If $x = \dfrac{1}{9}$, then $\sqrt{x} - x^2 =$

(A) 0 (B) $\dfrac{1}{9}$ (C) $\dfrac{26}{81}$ (D) $\dfrac{1}{3}$ (E) 1

$$\sqrt{x} - x^2 = \sqrt{\frac{1}{9}} - \left(\frac{1}{9}\right)^2 = \frac{1}{3} - \frac{1}{81} = \frac{27}{27} \cdot \frac{1}{3} - \frac{1}{81} = \frac{27-1}{81} = \frac{26}{81}$$

The answer is (C).

6. $\left(9^x\right)^3 =$

(A) 3^{3x} (B) 3^{2+3x} (C) 3^{6x} (D) $729x^3$ (E) 9^{x^3}

$$\left(9^x\right)^3 = 9^{3x} = \qquad \text{by the rule } \left(x^a\right)^b = x^{ab}$$

$$\left(3^2\right)^{3x} = \qquad \text{since } 9 = 3^2$$

$$3^{6x} \qquad \text{again by the rule } \left(x^a\right)^b = x^{ab}$$

The answer is (C). Note, this is considered to be a hard problem.

7. If $x = 4$, then $-2^{2\sqrt{x}} + 2 =$

(A) -14 (B) -8 (C) -2 (D) 0 (E) 18

Plugging $x = 4$ into the expression $-2^{2\sqrt{x}} + 2$ yields

$$-2^{2\sqrt{4}} + 2 = -2^{2 \cdot 2} + 2 = -2^4 + 2 = -16 + 2 = -14$$

The answer is (A).

8. $\sqrt{\dfrac{25 + 10x + x^2}{2}} =$

(A) $\dfrac{\sqrt{2}(5-x)}{2}$ (B) $\dfrac{\sqrt{5+x}}{\sqrt{2}}$ (C) $\dfrac{\sqrt{2}(5+x)}{2}$ (D) $\dfrac{5+x}{2}$ (E) $\dfrac{5-x}{2}$

$\sqrt{\dfrac{25+10x+x^2}{2}} = \sqrt{\dfrac{(5+x)^2}{2}} =$ since $25 + 10x + x^2$ factors into $(5+x)^2$

$\dfrac{\sqrt{(5+x)^2}}{\sqrt{2}} =$ by the rule $\sqrt[n]{\dfrac{x}{y}} = \dfrac{\sqrt[n]{x}}{\sqrt[n]{y}}$

$\dfrac{5+x}{\sqrt{2}} =$ since $\sqrt{x^2} = x$

$\dfrac{\sqrt{2}}{\sqrt{2}} \cdot \dfrac{5+x}{\sqrt{2}} =$ rationalizing the denominator

$\dfrac{\sqrt{2}(5+x)}{2}$

Hence, the answer is (C).

9. $\dfrac{2+\sqrt{5}}{2-\sqrt{5}} =$

(A) $-9-4\sqrt{5}$ (B) $-1-\dfrac{4}{9}\sqrt{5}$ (C) $1+\dfrac{4}{9}\sqrt{5}$ (D) $9+4\sqrt{5}$ (E) 20

$\dfrac{2+\sqrt{5}}{2-\sqrt{5}} = \dfrac{2+\sqrt{5}}{2-\sqrt{5}} \cdot \dfrac{2+\sqrt{5}}{2+\sqrt{5}} = \dfrac{4+4\sqrt{5}+5}{4-5} = \dfrac{9+4\sqrt{5}}{-1} = -9-4\sqrt{5}$

Hence, the answer is (A).

10. $2^{12} + 2^{12} + 2^{12} + 2^{12} =$

(A) 4^{12} (B) 2^{14} (C) 2^{16} (D) 4^{16} (E) 2^{48}

$2^{12} + 2^{12} + 2^{12} + 2^{12} = 4 \cdot 2^{12} = 2^2 \cdot 2^{12} = 2^{2+12} = 2^{14}$. The answer is (B).

11. $\left(\dfrac{\left(x^2 y\right)^3 z}{xyz} \right)^2 =$

(A) $x^8 y^5$ (B) xy^6 (C) $x^{15}y^6 z$ (D) $x^3 y^6$ (E) $x^{15}y^6$

$\left(\dfrac{\left(x^2 y\right)^3 z}{xyz} \right)^3 = \left(\dfrac{\left(x^2 y\right)^3}{xy} \right)^3 = \left(\dfrac{\left(x^2\right)^3 y^3}{xy} \right)^3 = \left(\dfrac{x^6 y^3}{xy} \right)^3 = \left(x^5 y^2\right)^3 = \left(x^5\right)^3 \left(y^2\right)^3 = x^{15} y^6$

Hence, the answer is (E).

Problem Set P:

1.   If $3y + 5 = 7x$, then $21y - 49x =$

   (A) -40 (B) -35 (C) -10 (D) 0 (E) 15

First, interchanging 5 and $7x$ in the expression $3y + 5 = 7x$ yields $3y - 7x = -5$. Next, factoring $21y - 49x$ yields

$$21y - 49x =$$
$$7 \cdot 3y - 7 \cdot 7x =$$
$$7(3y - 7x) =$$
$$7(-5) = \qquad \text{since } 3y - 7x = -5$$
$$-35$$

The answer is (B).

2.   If $x - y = p$, then $2x^2 - 4xy + 2y^2 =$

   (A) p (B) $2p$ (C) $4p$ (D) p^2 (E) $2p^2$

$$2x^2 - 4xy + 2y^2 =$$
$$2\left(x^2 - 2xy + y^2\right) = \qquad \text{by factoring out the common factor 2}$$
$$2(x - y)^2 = \qquad \text{by the formula } x^2 - 2xy + y^2 = (x - y)^2$$
$$2p^2 \qquad \text{since } x - y = p$$

The answer is (E).

3.   If $p \neq 0$ and $p = \sqrt{2pq - q^2}$, then in terms of q, $p =$

   (A) q (B) q^2 (C) $2q$ (D) $-2q$ (E) $\dfrac{q}{4}$

$$p = \sqrt{2pq - q^2}$$
$$p^2 = 2pq - q^2 \qquad \text{by squaring both sides}$$
$$p^2 - 2pq + q^2 = 0 \qquad \text{by subtracting } 2pq \text{ and adding } q^2 \text{ to both sides}$$
$$(p - q)^2 = 0 \qquad \text{by the formula } x^2 - 2xy + y^2 = (x - y)^2$$
$$p - q = 0 \qquad \text{by taking the square root of both sides}$$
$$p = q \qquad \text{by adding } q \text{ to both sides}$$

The answer is (A).

4.   If $\dfrac{x^2 + 2x - 10}{5} = 1$, then x could equal

   (A) -5 (B) -3 (C) 0 (D) 10 (E) 15

$$\frac{x^2 + 2x - 10}{5} = 1$$
$$x^2 + 2x - 10 = 5 \qquad \text{by multiplying both sides by 5}$$
$$x^2 + 2x - 15 = 0 \qquad \text{by subtracting 5 from both sides}$$
$$(x + 5)(x - 3) = 0 \qquad \text{since } 5 \cdot 3 = 15 \text{ and } 5 - 3 = 2$$
$$x + 5 = 0 \text{ and } x - 3 = 0 \qquad \text{by setting each factor equal to zero}$$
$$x = -5 \text{ and } x = 3$$

The answer is (A).

5. What is the absolute value of twice the difference of the roots of the equation $5y^2 - 20y + 15 = 0$?

    (A) 0   (B) 1   (C) 2   (D) 3   (E) 4

Begin by factoring out the common factor in the equation $5y^2 - 20y + 15 = 0$:

$$5\left(y^2 - 4y + 3\right) = 0$$

Dividing both sides of this equation by 5 yields $\qquad\qquad\qquad$ $y^2 - 4y + 3 = 0$

Since $3 + 1 = 4$, the trinomial factors into $\qquad\qquad\qquad$ $(y - 3)(y - 1) = 0$

Setting each factor equal to zero yields $\qquad\qquad\qquad$ $y - 3 = 0$ and $y - 1 = 0$

Solving these equations yields $y = 3$ and $y = 1$. Now, the difference of 3 and 1 is 2 and twice 2 is 4. Further, the difference of 1 and 3 is –2 and twice –2 is –4. Now, the absolute value of both 4 and –4 is 4. The answer is (E).

6. If $x \neq -2$, then $\dfrac{7x^2 + 28x + 28}{(x + 2)^2} =$

    (A) 7   (B) 8   (C) 9   (D) 10   (E) 11

$$\dfrac{7x^2 + 28x + 28}{(x + 2)^2} =$$

$$\dfrac{7\left(x^2 + 4x + 4\right)}{(x + 2)^2} = \qquad \text{by factoring out 7}$$

$$\dfrac{7(x + 2)^2}{(x + 2)^2} = \qquad \text{by the formula } x^2 + 2xy + y^2 = (x + y)^2$$

$$7 \qquad \text{by canceling the common factor } (x + 2)^2$$

The answer is (A).

7. $\dfrac{7^9 + 7^8}{8} =$

    (A) $\dfrac{1}{8}$ (B) $\dfrac{7}{8}$ (C) $\dfrac{7^7}{8}$ (D) 7^8 (E) 7^9

$$\dfrac{7^9 + 7^8}{8} =$$

$$\dfrac{7^8 \cdot 7 + 7^8}{8} = \qquad \text{since } 7^9 = 7^8 \cdot 7$$

$$\dfrac{7^8(7 + 1)}{8} = \qquad \text{by factoring out the common factor } 7^8$$

$$\dfrac{7^8(8)}{8} =$$

$$7^8$$

Hence, the answer is (D). Note, this is considered to be a very hard problem.

8.   If $x + y = 10$ and $x - y = 5$, then $x^2 - y^2 =$

   (A) 50   (B) 60   (C) 75   (D) 80   (E) 100

$$x^2 - y^2 =$$
$$(x + y)(x - y) = \qquad \text{since } x^2 - y^2 \text{ is a difference of squares}$$
$$(10)(5) = \qquad \text{since } x + y = 10 \text{ and } x - y = 5$$
$$50$$

The answer is (A). This problem can also be solved by adding the two equations. However, that approach will lead to long, messy fractions. Writers of the GMAT put questions like this one on the GMAT to see whether you will discover the short cut. The premise being that those students who do not see the short cut will take longer to solve the problem and therefore will have less time to finish the test.

9. $x(x - y) - z(x - y) =$

   (A) $x - y$ (B) $x - z$ (C) $(x - y)(x - z)$ (D) $(x - y)(x + z)$ (E) $(x - y)(z - x)$

Noticing that $x - y$ is a common factor, we factor it out:

$$x(x - y) - z(x - y) = (x - y)(x - z)$$

The answer is (C).

Method II

Sometimes a complicated expression can be simplified by making a substitution. In the expression $x(x - y) - z(x - y)$ replace $x - y$ with w:

$$xw - zw$$

Now, the structure appears much simpler. Factoring out the common factor w yields

$$w(x - z)$$

Finally, re-substitute $x - y$ for w:

$$(x - y)(x - z)$$

10.   If $(x - y)^2 = x^2 + y^2$, then which one of the following statements must also be true?

   I. $x = 0$ II. $y = 0$ III. $xy = 0$

   (A) None   (B) I only   (C) II only   (D) III only   (E) II and III only

$$(x - y)^2 = x^2 + y^2$$
$$x^2 - 2xy + y^2 = x^2 + y^2 \quad \text{by the formula } x^2 - 2xy + y^2 = (x - y)^2$$
$$-2xy = 0 \qquad\qquad \text{by subtracting } x^2 \text{ and } y^2 \text{ from both sides of the equation}$$
$$xy = 0 \qquad\qquad \text{by dividing both sides of the equation by } -2$$

Hence, Statement III is true, which eliminates choices (A), (B), and (C). However, Statement II is false. For example, if $y = 5$ and $x = 0$, then $xy = 0 \cdot 5 = 0$. A similar analysis shows that Statement I is false. The answer is (D).

11. If x and y are prime numbers such that $x > y > 2$, then $x^2 - y^2$ must be divisible by which one of the following numbers?

(A) 3   (B) 4   (C) 5   (D) 9   (E) 12

The Difference of Squares formula yields $x^2 - y^2 = (x + y)(x - y)$. Now, both x and y must be odd because 2 is the only even prime and $x > y > 2$. Remember that the sum (or difference) of two odd numbers is even. Hence, $(x + y)(x - y)$ is the product of two even numbers and therefore is divisible by 4. To show this explicitly, let $x + y = 2p$ and let $x - y = 2q$. Then $(x + y)(x - y) = 2p \cdot 2q = 4pq$. Since we have written $(x + y)(x - y)$ as a multiple of 4, it is divisible by 4. The answer is (B).

Method II (substitution):

Let $x = 5$ and $y = 3$, then $x > y > 2$ and $x^2 - y^2 = 5^2 - 3^2 = 25 - 9 = 16$. Since 4 is the only number listed that divides evenly into 16, the answer is (B).

12. If $\dfrac{x+y}{x-y} = \dfrac{1}{2}$, then $\dfrac{xy + x^2}{xy - x^2} =$

(A) –4.2   (B) –1/2   (C) 1.1   (D) 3   (E) 5.3

Solution:

$$\frac{xy + x^2}{xy - x^2} =$$

$$\frac{x(y + x)}{x(y - x)} = \quad \text{by factoring out } x \text{ from both the top and bottom expressions}$$

$$\frac{y + x}{y - x} = \quad \text{by canceling the common factor } x$$

$$\frac{x + y}{-(x - y)} = \quad \text{by factoring out the negative sign in the bottom and then rearranging}$$

$$-\frac{x + y}{x - y} = \quad \text{by recalling that a negative fraction can be written three ways: } \frac{a}{-b} = -\frac{a}{b} = \frac{-a}{b}$$

$$-\frac{1}{2} \quad \text{by replacing } \frac{x + y}{x - y} \text{ with } \frac{1}{2}$$

The answer is (B).

Problem Set Q:

1. $\left(x^2 + 2\right)\left(x - x^3\right) =$

    (A) $x^4 - x^2 + 2$ (B) $-x^5 - x^3 + 2x$ (C) $x^5 - 2x$ (D) $3x^3 + 2x$ (E) $x^5 + x^3 + 2x$

    $\left(x^2 + 2\right)\left(x - x^3\right) = x^2 x - x^2 x^3 + 2x - 2x^3 = x^3 - x^5 + 2x - 2x^3 = -x^5 - x^3 + 2x$. Thus, the answer is (B).

2. $-2\left(3 - x\left[\dfrac{5 + y - 2}{x}\right] - 7 + 2 \cdot 3^2\right) =$

    (A) $2y - 11$ (B) $2y + 1$ (C) $x - 2$ (D) $x + 22$ (E) $2y - 22$

    $$-2\left(3 - x\left[\frac{5 + y - 2}{x}\right] - 7 + 2 \cdot 3^2\right) =$$
    $$-2\left(3 - x\left[\frac{3 + y}{x}\right] - 7 + 2 \cdot 3^2\right) =$$
    $$-2\left(3 - [3 + y] - 7 + 2 \cdot 3^2\right) =$$
    $$-2\left(3 - 3 - y - 7 + 2 \cdot 3^2\right) =$$
    $$-2(3 - 3 - y - 7 + 2 \cdot 9) =$$
    $$-2(3 - 3 - y - 7 + 18) =$$
    $$-2(-y + 11) =$$
    $$2y - 22$$

    The answer is (E).

3. For all real numbers a and b, $a \cdot b \neq 0$, let $a \Diamond b = ab - 1$. Which of the following must be true?

    I. $a \Diamond b = b \Diamond a$

    II. $\dfrac{a \Diamond a}{a} = 1 \Diamond 1$

    III. $\left(a \Diamond b\right) \Diamond c = a \Diamond \left(b \Diamond c\right)$

    (A) I only   (B) II only   (C) III only   (D) I and II only   (E) I and III only

    $a \Diamond b = ab - 1 = ba - 1 = b \Diamond a$. Thus, I is true, which eliminates (B) and (C).

    $\dfrac{a \Diamond a}{a} = \dfrac{aa - 1}{a} \neq 1 \cdot 1 - 1 = 1 - 1 = 0 = 1 \Diamond 1$. Thus, II is false, which eliminates (D).

    $\left(a \Diamond b\right) \Diamond c = (ab - 1) \Diamond c = (ab - 1)c - 1 = abc - c - 1 \neq a \Diamond (bc - 1) = a(bc - 1) - 1 = abc - a - 1 = a \Diamond \left(b \Diamond c\right)$.
    Thus, III is false, which eliminates (E). Hence, the answer is (A).

4. $\left(x + \dfrac{1}{2}\right)^2 - (2x - 4)^2 =$

(A) $-3x^2 - 15x + \dfrac{65}{4}$ (B) $3x^2 + 16x$ (C) $-3x^2 + 17x - \dfrac{63}{4}$ (D) $5x^2 + \dfrac{65}{4}$ (E) $3x^2$

$$\left(x + \dfrac{1}{2}\right)^2 - (2x - 4)^2 =$$

$$x^2 + 2x\dfrac{1}{2} + \left(\dfrac{1}{2}\right)^2 - \left[(2x)^2 - 2(2x)4 + 4^2\right] =$$

$$x^2 + x + \dfrac{1}{4} - 4x^2 + 16x - 16 =$$

$$-3x^2 + 17x - \dfrac{63}{4}$$

Hence, the answer is (C).

5. If $x = 2$ and $y = -3$, then $y^2 - \left(x - \left[y + \dfrac{1}{2}\right]\right) - 2 \cdot 3 =$

(A) $-\dfrac{39}{2}$ (B) $-\dfrac{3}{2}$ (C) 0 (D) 31 (E) 43

$$y^2 - \left(x - \left[y + \dfrac{1}{2}\right]\right) - 2 \cdot 3 =$$

$$(-3)^2 - \left(2 - \left[-3 + \dfrac{1}{2}\right]\right) - 2 \cdot 3 =$$

$$(-3)^2 - \left(2 - \left[-\dfrac{5}{2}\right]\right) - 2 \cdot 3 =$$

$$(-3)^2 - \left(2 + \dfrac{5}{2}\right) - 2 \cdot 3 =$$

$$(-3)^2 - \dfrac{9}{2} - 2 \cdot 3 =$$

$$9 - \dfrac{9}{2} - 2 \cdot 3 =$$

$$9 - \dfrac{9}{2} - 6 =$$

$$3 - \dfrac{9}{2} =$$

$$-\dfrac{3}{2}$$

The answer is (B).

6. $4(xy)^3 + (x^3 - y^3)^2 =$

    (A) $x^3 - y^3$ (B) $(x^2 + y^2)^3$ (C) $(x^3 + y^3)^3$ (D) $(x^3 - y^3)^2$ (E) $(x^3 + y^3)^2$

$4(xy)^3 + (x^3 - y^3)^2 =$

$$4x^3y^3 + (x^3)^2 - 2x^3y^3 + (y^3)^2 =$$

$$(x^3)^2 + 2x^3y^3 + (y^3)^2 =$$

$$(x^3 + y^3)^2$$

The answer is (E).

7. If $\dfrac{a}{b} = -\dfrac{2}{3}$, then $\dfrac{b - a}{a} =$

    (A) $-\dfrac{5}{2}$ (B) $-\dfrac{5}{3}$ (C) $-\dfrac{1}{3}$ (D) 0   (E) 7

$\dfrac{b - a}{a} = \dfrac{b}{a} - \dfrac{a}{a} = \dfrac{b}{a} - 1 = \dfrac{-3}{2} - 1 = \dfrac{-3}{2} - \dfrac{2}{2} = \dfrac{-3-2}{2} = \dfrac{-5}{2}$. The answer is (A).

8. The operation $*$ is defined for all non-zero x and y by the equation $x * y = \dfrac{x}{y}$. Then the expression $(x - 2)^2 * x$ is equal to

    (A) $x - 4 + \dfrac{4}{x}$ (B) $4 + \dfrac{4}{x}$ (C) $\dfrac{4}{x}$ (D) $1 + \dfrac{4}{x}$ (E) $1 - 4x + \dfrac{4}{x}$

$(x - 2)^2 * x = \dfrac{(x-2)^2}{x} = \dfrac{x^2 - 4x + 4}{x} = \dfrac{x^2}{x} - \dfrac{4x}{x} + \dfrac{4}{x} = x - 4 + \dfrac{4}{x}$. The answer is (A).

9. $(2 + \sqrt{7})(4 - \sqrt{7})(-2x) =$

    (A) $78x - 4x\sqrt{7}$ (B) $\sqrt{7}x$ (C) $-2x - 4x\sqrt{7}$ (D) $-2x$ (E) $4x\sqrt{7}$

$(2 + \sqrt{7})(4 - \sqrt{7})(-2x) =$

$$(2 \cdot 4 - 2\sqrt{7} + 4\sqrt{7} - \sqrt{7}\sqrt{7})(-2x) =$$

$$(8 + 2\sqrt{7} - 7)(-2x) =$$

$$(1 + 2\sqrt{7})(-2x) =$$

$$1(-2x) + 2\sqrt{7}(-2x) =$$

$$-2x - 4x\sqrt{7}$$

The answer is (C).

10. If the operation $*$ is defined for all non-zero x and y by the equation $x*y = (xy)^2$, then $(x*y)*z =$

(A) $x^2y^2z^2$ (B) $x^4y^4z^2$ (C) $x^2y^4z^2$ (D) $x^4y^2z^2$ (E) $x^4y^4z^4$

$(x*y)*z = (xy)^2 *z = \left((xy)^2 z\right)^2 = \left((xy)^2\right)^2 z^2 = (xy)^4 z^2 = x^4y^4z^2$. The answer is (B).

11. If $p = z + 1/z$ and $q = z - 1/z$, where z is a real number not equal to zero, then $(p+q)(p-q) =$

(A) 2
(B) 4
(C) z^2
(D) $\dfrac{1}{z^2}$
(E) $z^2 - \dfrac{1}{z^2}$

Since we are given that $p = z + 1/z$ and $q = z - 1/z$,

$$p + q = (z + 1/z) + (z - 1/z) = z + 1/z + z - 1/z = 2z.$$
$$p - q = (z + 1/z) - (z - 1/z) = z + 1/z - z + 1/z = 2/z.$$

Therefore, $(p+q)(p-q) = (2z)(2/z) = 4$. The answer is (B).

12. If $x^2 + y^2 = xy$, then $(x+y)^4 =$

(A) xy
(B) x^2y^2
(C) $9x^2y^2$
(D) $\left(x^2 + y^2\right)^2$
(E) $x^4 + y^4$

Adding $2xy$ to both sides of the equation $x^2 + y^2 = xy$ yields

$$x^2 + y^2 + 2xy = 3xy$$
$$(x+y)^2 = 3xy \qquad \text{from the formula } (x+y)^2 = x^2 + 2xy + y^2$$

Squaring on both sides of this equation yields

$$(x+y)^4 = (3xy)^2 = 9x^2y^2$$

The answer is (C).

13. $(2 + x)(2 + y) - (2 + x) - (2 + y) =$

(A) $2y$
(B) xy
(C) $x + y$
(D) $x - y$
(E) $x + y + xy$

Solution:

$$(2 + x)(2 + y) - (2 + x) - (2 + y) =$$
$$4 + 2y + 2x + xy - 2 - x - 2 - y =$$
$$x + y + xy$$

The answer is (E).

14. If $x^2 + y^2 = 2ab$ and $2xy = a^2 + b^2$, with $a, b, x, y > 0$, then $x + y =$

(A) ab
(B) $a - b$
(C) $a + b$
(D) $\sqrt{a^2 + b^2}$
(E) $\sqrt{a^2 - b^2}$

Writing the system of equations vertically yields

$$x^2 + y^2 = 2ab$$
$$2xy = a^2 + b^2$$

Adding the equations yields

$$x^2 + 2xy + y^2 = a^2 + 2ab + b^2$$

Applying the Perfect Square Trinomial formula to both the sides of the equation yields

$$(x + y)^2 = (a + b)^2$$
$$x + y = a + b \qquad \text{by taking the square root of both sides and noting all numbers are positive}$$

The answer is (C).

Problem Set R:

1.   John spent $25, which is 15 percent of his monthly wage. What is his monthly wage?

   (A) $80   (B) 166\frac{2}{3}$ (C) $225   (D) $312.5   (E) $375

Consider the first sentence: John spent $25, which is 15 percent of his monthly wage. Now, translate the main part of the sentence into a mathematical equation as follows:

$$\begin{array}{ccccccc} 25 & \text{is} & 15 & \% & \text{of} & & \underline{\text{his monthly wage}} \\ \downarrow & \downarrow & \downarrow & \downarrow & \downarrow & & \downarrow \\ 25 & = & 15 & \dfrac{1}{100} & \cdot & & x \end{array}$$

$$25 = \frac{15}{100}x$$

$$2500 = 15x$$

$$x = \frac{2500}{15} = \frac{500}{3} = 166\frac{2}{3}$$

The answer is (B).

2.   If a = 4b, what percent of 2a is 2b?

   (A) 10%   (B) 20%   (C) 25%   (D) 26%   (E) 40%

Translate the main part of the sentence into a mathematical equation as follows:

$$\begin{array}{cccccc} \text{What} & \text{percent} & \text{of} & 2a & \text{is} & 2b \\ \downarrow & \downarrow & \downarrow & \downarrow & \downarrow & \downarrow \\ x & \dfrac{1}{100} & \cdot & 2a & = & 2b \end{array}$$

$$\frac{x}{100} \cdot 2a = 2b$$

$$\frac{x}{100} \cdot 2(4b) = 2b \qquad \text{(substituting } a = 4b\text{)}$$

$$\frac{x}{100} \cdot 8 = 2 \qquad \text{(canceling } b \text{ from both sides)}$$

$$\frac{8x}{100} = 2$$

$$8x = 200$$

$$x = 25$$

The answer is (C).

Remark: You can substitute $b = a/4$ instead of $a = 4b$. Whichever letter you substitute, you will get the same answer. However, depending on the question, one substitution may be easier than another.

3. If $p = 5q > 0$, then 40 percent of $3p$ equals

    (A) $6q$ (B) $5.52q$ (C) $13.3q$ (D) $9q$ (E) $20.1q$

Since more than one letter is used in this question, we need to substitute one of the letters for the other to minimize the number of unknown quantities (letters).

40	percent	of	$3p$
↓	↓	↓	↓
40	$\dfrac{1}{100}$	×	$3p$

$$= \frac{40}{100} \times 3p$$
$$= \frac{40}{100} \times 3(5q) \qquad \text{(substituting } p = 5q)$$
$$= \frac{600q}{100}$$
$$= 6q$$

The answer is (A).

4. A jar contains 24 blue balls and 40 red balls. Which one of the following is 50% of the blue balls?

    (A) 10   (B) 11   (C) 12   (D) 13   (E) 14

50	%	of	the blue balls
↓	↓	↓	↓
50	$\dfrac{1}{100}$	×	24

$$= \frac{50 \times 24}{100}$$
$$= \frac{1200}{100}$$
$$= 12$$

The answer is (C).

5. In a company with 180 employees, 108 of the employees are female. What percent of the employees are male?

    (A) 5%   (B) 25%   (C) 35%   (D) 40%   (E) 60%

Since female employees are 108 out of 180, there are $180 - 108 = 72$ male employees. Now, translate the main part of the sentence into a mathematical equation as follows:

What	percent	of	the employees	are	male
↓	↓	↓	↓	↓	↓
x	$\dfrac{1}{100}$	·	180	=	72

$$\frac{180}{100}x = 72$$
$$\frac{100}{180} \times \frac{180}{100}x = \frac{100}{180} \times 72$$
$$x = 40$$

The answer is (D).

6.   John bought a shirt, a pair of pants, and a pair of shoes, which cost $10, $20, and $30, respectively. What percent of the total expense was spent for the pants?

   (A) $16\frac{2}{3}\%$ (B) 20%   (C) 30%   (D) $33\frac{1}{3}\%$ (E) 60%

The total expense is the sum of expenses for the shirt, pants, and shoes, which is $10 + $20 + $30 = $60.
Now, translate the main part of the sentence into a mathematical equation:

What	percent	of	the total expense	was spent for	the pants
↓	↓	↓	↓	↓	↓
x	$\frac{1}{100}$	·	60	=	20

$\frac{60}{100}x = 20$

$60x = 2000$ (by multiplying both sides of the equation by 100)

$x = \frac{2000}{60}$ (by dividing both sides of the equation by 60)

$x = \frac{100}{3} = 33\frac{1}{3}$

The answer is (D).

7.   Last year Jenny was 5 feet tall, and this year she is 5 feet 6 inches. What is the percent increase of her height?

   (A) 5%   (B) 10%   (C) 15%   (D) 20%   (E) 40%

First, express all the numbers in the same units (inches):

The original height is $5\ feet = 5\ feet \times \frac{12\ inches}{1\ feet} = 60\ inches$

The change in height is (5 *feet* 6 *inches*) − (5 *feet*) = 6 *inches*.
Now, use the formula for percent of change.

Percent of change: $\frac{Amount\ of\ change}{Original\ amount} \times 100\% =$

$\frac{6}{60} \times 100\% =$

$\frac{1}{10} \times 100\% =$ (by canceling 6)

10%

The answer is (B).

8. Last month the price of a particular pen was \$1.20. This month the price of the same pen is \$1.50. What is the percent increase in the price of the pen?

    (A) 5%   (B) 10%   (C) 25%   (D) 30%   (E) $33\frac{1}{3}\%$

The change in price is \$1.50 – \$1.20 = \$.30. Now, use the formula for percent of change.

$$\frac{Amount\ of\ change}{Original\ amount} \times 100\% =$$

$$\frac{.30}{1.20} \times 100\% =$$

$$\frac{1}{4} \times 100\% =$$

$$25\%$$

The answer is (C).

9. Stella paid \$1,500 for a computer after receiving a 20 percent discount. What was the price of the computer before the discount?

    (A) \$300   (B) \$1,500   (C) \$1,875   (D) \$2,000   (E) \$3,000

Let x be the price before the discount. Since Stella received a 20 percent discount, she paid 80 percent of the original price. Thus, 80 percent of the original price is \$1,500. Now, translate this sentence into a mathematical equation:

80	percent	of	the original price	is	\$1,500
↓	↓	↓	↓	↓	↓
80	$\frac{1}{100}$	·	x	=	1500

$$\frac{80}{100}x = 1500$$

$$\frac{100}{80}\frac{80}{100}x = \frac{100}{80}1500 \qquad \text{(by multiplying both sides by the reciprocal of } \frac{80}{100}\text{)}$$

$$x = 1875$$

The answer is (C).

10. A town has a population growth rate of 10% per year. The population in 1990 was 2000. What was the population in 1992?

    (A) 1600   (B) 2200   (C) 2400   (D) 2420   (E) 4000

Since the population increased at a rate of 10% per year, the population of any year is the population of the previous year + 10% of that same year. Hence, the population in 1991 is the population of 1990 + 10% of the population of 1990:

$$2000 + 10\% \text{ of } 2000 =$$

$$2000 + 200 =$$

$$2200$$

Similarly, the population in 1992 is the population of 1991 + 10% of the population of 1991:

$$2200 + 10\% \text{ of } 2200 =$$

$$2200 + 220 =$$

$$2420$$

Hence, the answer is (D).

11. In a class of 200 students, forty percent are girls. Twenty-five percent of the boys and 10 percent of the girls signed up for a tour to Washington DC. What percent of the class signed up for the tour?

(A) 19%   (B) 23%   (C) 25%   (D) 27%   (E) 35%

Let g be the number of girls, and b the number of boys. Calculate the number of girls in the class:

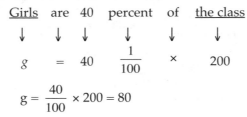

$$g = \frac{40}{100} \times 200 = 80$$

The number of boys equals the total number of students minus the number of girls:

$$b = 200 - 80 = 120$$

Next, calculate the number of boys and girls who signed up for the tour:

25 percent of boys ($\frac{25}{100} \times 120 = 30$) and 10 percent of girls ($\frac{10}{100} \times 80 = 8$) signed up for the tour.

Thus, $30 + 8 = 38$ students signed up. Now, translate the main part of the question with a little modification into a mathematical equation:

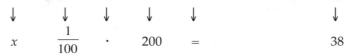

$$\frac{200}{100}x = 38$$

$x = 19$

The answer is (A).

12. If 15% of a number is 4.5, then 45% of the same number is

(A) 1.5
(B) 3.5
(C) 13.5
(D) 15
(E) 45

Let x be the number of which the percentage is being calculated. Then 15% of the number x is $.15x$. We are told this is equal to 4.5. Hence,

$$.15x = 4.5$$

Solving this equation by dividing both sides by .15 yields

$$x = \frac{4.5}{.15} = 30$$

Now, 45% of 30 is

$$.45(30)$$

Multiplying out this expression gives 13.5. The answer is (C).

13. A 30% discount reduces the price of a commodity by $90. If the discount is reduced to 20%, then the price of the commodity will be
   (A) $180
   (B) $210
   (C) $240
   (D) $270
   (E) $300

Let the original price of the commodity be x. The reduction in price due to the 30% discount is $0.3x$. It is given that the 30% discount reduced the price of the commodity by $90. Expressing this as an equation yields

$$0.3x = 90$$

Solving for x yields

$$x = 300$$

Hence, the original price of the commodity was $300. The value of a 20% discount on $300 is

$$.20(300) = 60$$

Hence, the new selling price of the commodity is

$$\$300 - \$60 = \$240$$

The answer is (C).

Problem Set S:

Questions 1–5 refer to the following graphs.

PROFIT AND REVENUE DISTRIBUTION FOR ZIPPY PRINTING, 1990–1993, COPYING AND PRINTING.

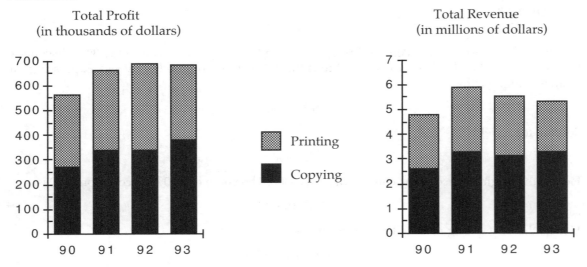

Distribution of Profit from Copying, 1992
(in thousands of dollars)

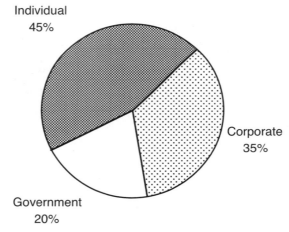

1.   In 1993, the total profit was approximately how much greater than the total profit in 1990?

   (A)   50 thousand
   (B)   75 thousand
   (C)   120 thousand
   (D)   200 thousand
   (E)   350 thousand

Remember, rarely does a graph question involve significant computation. For this question, we need merely to read the bar graph. The Total Profit graph shows that in 1993 approximately 680 thousand was earned, and in 1990 approximately 560 thousand was earned. Subtracting these numbers yields

$$680 - 560 = 120$$

The answer is (C).

2. In 1990, the profit from copying was approximately what percent of the revenue from copying?

(A) 2%
(B) 10%
(C) 20%
(D) 35%
(E) 50%

The Total Revenue graph indicates that in 1990 the revenue from copying was about $2,600,000. The Total Profit graph shows the profit from copying in that same year was about $270,000. The profit margin is

$$\frac{\text{Profit}}{\text{Revenue}} = \frac{270,000}{2,600,000} \approx 10\%$$

The answer is (B).

3. In 1992, the profit from copying for corporate customers was approximately how much greater than the profit from copying for government customers?

(A) 50 thousand
(B) 80 thousand
(C) 105 thousand
(D) 190 thousand
(E) 260 thousand

From the chart, the profit in 1992 for copying was approximately $340,000 of which 35% x $340,000 = $119,000 was from corporate customers and 20% x $340,000 = $68,000 was from government customers. Subtracting these amounts yields

$$\$119,000 - \$68,000 = \$51,000$$

The answer is (A).

4. During the two years in which total profit was most nearly equal, the combined revenue from printing was closest to

(A) 1 million
(B) 2 million
(C) 4.5 million
(D) 6 million
(E) 6.5 million

The Total Profit graph shows that 1992 and 1993 are clearly the two years in which total profit was most nearly equal. Turning to the Total Revenue graph, we see that in 1992 the revenue from printing sales was approximately 2.5 million, and that in 1993 the revenue from printing sales was approximately 2 million. This gives a total of 4.5 million in total printing sales revenue for the period. The answer is (C).

5.   The amount of profit made from government copy sales in 1992 was

   (A)   70 thousand
   (B)   100 thousand
   (C)   150 thousand
   (D)   200 thousand
   (E)   350 thousand

The Total Profit graph shows that Zippy Printing earned about $340,000 from copying in 1992. The Pie Chart indicates that 20% of this was earned from government sales. Multiplying these numbers gives

$$\$340,000 \times 20\% \approx \$70,000$$

The answer is (A).

Questions 6–10 refer to the following graphs.

DISTRIBUTION OF CRIMINAL ACTIVITY BY CATEGORY OF CRIME FOR COUNTRY X IN 1990 AND PROJECTED FOR 2000.

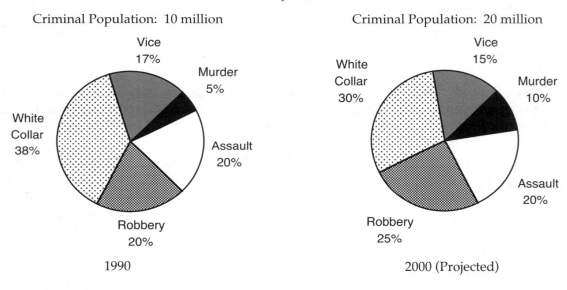

6.   What is the projected number of white-collar criminals in 2000?

   (A)   1 million
   (B)   3.8 million
   (C)   6 million
   (D)   8 million
   (E)   10 million

From the projected-crime graph, we see that the criminal population will be 20 million and of these 30 percent are projected to be involved in white-collar crime. Hence, the number of white-collar criminals is

$$(30\%)(20 \text{ million}) = (.30)(20 \text{ million}) = 6 \text{ million}$$

The answer is (C).

7. The ratio of the number of robbers in 1990 to the number of projected robbers in 2000 is

    (A) 2/5   (B) 3/5   (C) 1   (D) 3/2   (E) 5/2

In 1990, there were 10 million criminals and 20% were robbers. Thus, the number of robbers in 1990 was

$$(20\%)(10 \text{ million}) = (.20)(10 \text{ million}) = 2 \text{ million}$$

In 2000, there are projected to be 20 million criminals of which 25% are projected to be robbers. Thus, the number of robbers in 2000 is projected to be

$$(25\%)(20 \text{ million}) = (.25)(20 \text{ million}) = 5 \text{ million}$$

Forming the ratio of the above numbers yields

$$\frac{number\ of\ robbers\ in\ 1990}{number\ of\ robbers\ in\ 2000} = \frac{2}{5}$$

The answer is (A).

8. From 1990 to 2000, there is a projected decrease in the number of criminals for which of the following categories?

    I.   Vice
    II. Assault
    III. White Collar

    (A) None
    (B) I only
    (C) II only
    (D) II and III only
    (E) I, II, and III

The following table lists the number of criminals by category for 1990 and 2000 and the projected increase or decrease:

Category	Number in 1990 (millions)	Number in 2000 (millions)	Projected increase (millions)	Projected decrease (millions)
Vice	1.7	3	1.3	None
Assault	2	4	2	None
White Collar	3.8	6	2.2	None

As the table displays, there is a projected increase (not decrease) in all three categories. Hence, the answer is (A).

9. What is the approximate projected percent increase between 1990 and 2000 in the number of criminals involved in vice?

    (A) 25%   (B) 40%   (C) 60%   (D) 75%   (E) 85%

Remember, to calculate the percentage increase, find the absolute increase and divide it by the original number. Now, in 1990, the number of criminals in vice was 1.7 million, and in 2000 it is projected to be 3 million. The absolute increase is thus:

$$3 - 1.7 = 1.3$$

Hence the projected percent increase in the number of criminals in vice is

$$\frac{absolute\ increase}{original\ number} = \frac{1.3}{1.7} \approx 75\%.$$

The answer is (D).

10. The projected number of Robbers in 2000 will exceed the number of white-collar criminals in 1990 by

(A) 1.2 million   (B) 2.3 million   (C) 3.4 million   (D) 5.8 million   (E) 7.2 million

In 1990, the number of white-collar criminals was (38%)(10 million) = 3.8 million. From the projected-crime graph, we see that the criminal population in the year 2000 will be 20 million and of these (25%)(20 million) = 5 million will be robbers. Hence, the projected number of Robbers in 2000 will exceed the number of white-collar criminals in 1990 by 5 – 3.8 = 1.2 million. The answer is (A).

Questions 11–15 refer to the following graph.

SALES BY CATEGORY FOR GRAMMERCY PRESS, 1980–1989
(in thousands of books)

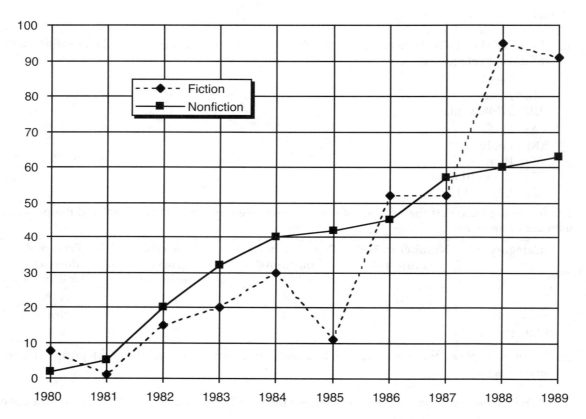

11. In how many years did the sales of nonfiction titles exceed the sales of fiction titles ?

(A) 2   (B) 3   4   (D) 5   (E) 6

The graph shows that nonfiction sales exceeded fiction sales in '81, '82, '83, '84, '85, and '87. The answer is (E).

12. Which of the following best approximates the amount by which the increase in sales of fiction titles from 1985 to 1986 exceeded the increase in sales of fiction titles from 1983 to 1984?
    (A) 31.5 thousand
    (B)   40 thousand
    (C) 49.3 thousand
    (D) 50.9 thousand
    (E)   68 thousand

The graph shows that the increase in sales of fiction titles from 1985 to 1986 was approximately 40 thousand and the increase in sales of fiction titles from 1983 to 1984 was approximately 10 thousand. Hence, the difference is

$$40 - 10 = 30$$

Choice (A) is the only answer-choice close to 30 thousand.

13. Which of the following periods showed a continual increase in the sales of fiction titles?
    (A) 1980–1982   (B) 1982–1984   (C) 1984–1986   (D) 1986–1988   (E) 1987–1989

According to the chart, sales of fiction increased from 15,000 to 20,000 to 30,000 between 1982 and 1984. The answer is (B).

14. What was the approximate average number of sales of fiction titles from 1984 to 1988?
    (A) 15 thousand   (B) 30 thousand   (C) 40 thousand   (D) 48 thousand   (E) 60 thousand

The following chart summarizes the sales for the years 1984 to 1988:

Year	Sales
1984	30 thousand
1985	11 thousand
1986	52 thousand
1987	52 thousand
1988	95 thousand

Forming the average yields:

$$\frac{30 + 11 + 52 + 52 + 95}{5} = 48$$

The answer is (D).

Note, it is important to develop a feel for how the writers of the GMAT approximate when calculating. We used 52 thousand to calculate the sales of fiction in 1986, which is the actual number. But from the chart, it is difficult to tell whether the actual number is 51, 52, or 53 thousand. However, using any of the these numbers, the average would still be nearer to 40 than to any other answer-choice.

15. By approximately what percent did the sale of nonfiction titles increase from 1984 to 1987?
    (A) 42%   (B) 50%   (C) 70%   (D) 90%   (E) 110%

Recall that the percentage increase (decrease) is formed by dividing the absolute increase (decrease) by the original amount:

$$\frac{57 - 40}{40} = .425$$

The answer is (A).

Questions 16–20 refer to the following graph.

AUTOMOBILE ACCIDENTS IN COUNTRY X: 1990 TO 1994
(in ten thousands)

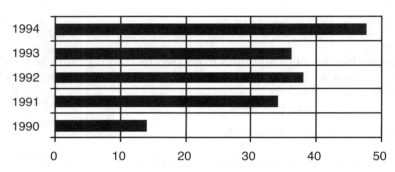

CARS IN COUNTRY X
(in millions)

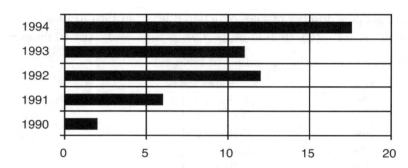

16. Approximately how many millions of cars were in Country X in 1994?

    (A) 1.0   (B) 4.7   (C) 9.0   (D) 15.5   (E) 17.5

In the bottom chart, the bar for 1994 ends half way between 15 and 20. Thus, there were about 17.5 million cars in 1994. The answer is (E).

17. The amount by which the number of cars in 1990 exceeded the number of accidents in 1991 was approximately

    (A) 0.3 million   (B) 0.7 million   (C) 1.0 million   (D) 1.7 million   (E) 2.5 million

From the bottom chart, there were 2 million cars in 1990; and from the top chart, there were 340 thousand accidents in 1991. Forming the difference yields

$$2,000,000 - 340,000 = 1,660,000$$

Rounding 1.66 million off yields 1.7 million. The answer is (D).

18. The number of accidents in 1993 was approximately what percentage of the number of cars?

(A) 1%   (B) 1.5%   (C) 3%   (D) 5%   (E) 10%

From the charts, the number of accidents in 1993 was 360,000 and the number of cars was 11,000,000. Forming the percentage yields

$$\frac{360,000}{11,000,000} \approx 3\%$$

The answer is (C).

19. In which of the following years will the number of accidents exceed 500 thousand?

(A)   1994
(B)   1995
(C)   1998
(D)   2000
(E)   It cannot be determined from the information given.

From the graphs, there is no way to predict what will happen in the future. The number of accidents could continually decrease after 1994. The answer is (E).

20. If no car in 1993 was involved in more than four accidents, what is the minimum number of cars that could have been in accidents in 1993?

(A) 50 thousand   (B) 60 thousand   (C) 70 thousand   (D) 80 thousand   (E) 90 thousand

The number of cars involved in accidents will be minimized when each car has exactly 4 accidents. Now, from the top chart, there were 360,000 accidents in 1993. Dividing 360,000 by 4 yields

$$\frac{360,000}{4} = 90,000$$

The answer is (E).

<u>Questions 21–25</u> refer to the following graphs.

DISTRIBUTION OF IMPORTS AND EXPORTS FOR COUNTRY X IN 1994.

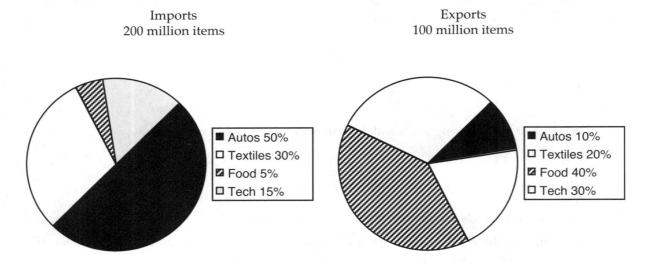

21. How many autos did Country X export in 1994?

    (A)   10 million
    (B)   15 million
    (C)   16 million
    (D)   20 million
    (E)   30 million

The graph shows that 100 million items were exported in 1994 and 10% were autos. Hence, 10 million autos were exported. The answer is (A).

22. In how many categories did the total number of items (import and export) exceed 75 million?

    (A) 1   (B) 2   (C) 3   (D) 4   (E) none

The following chart summarizes the items imported and exported:

	Imports	Exports	Total
Autos	100	10	110
Textiles	60	20	80
Food	10	40	50
Tech	30	30	60

The chart shows that only autos and textiles exceeded 75 million total items. The answer is (B).

23. The ratio of the number of technology items imported in 1994 to the number of textile items exported in 1994 is

    (A) 1/3   (B) 3/5   (C) 1   (D) 6/5   (E) 3/2

In 1994, there were 200 million items imported of which 15% were technology items. Thus, the number of technology items imported was

$$(15\%)(200 \text{ million}) = (.15)(200 \text{ million}) = 30 \text{ million}$$

In 1994, there were 100 million items exported of which 20% were textile items. Thus, the number of textile items exported was

$$(20\%)(100 \text{ million}) = (.20)(100 \text{ million}) = 20 \text{ million}$$

Forming the ratio of the above numbers yields

$$\frac{number\ of\ technology\ items\ imported}{number\ of\ textile\ items\ \exp orted} = \frac{30}{20} = \frac{3}{2}$$

The answer is (E).

24. If in 1995 the number of autos exported was 16 million, then the percent increase from 1994 in the number of autos exported is

    (A) 40%   (B) 47%   (C) 50%   (D) 60%   (E) 65%

Remember, to calculate the percentage increase, find the absolute increase and divide it by the original number. Now, in 1994, the number of autos exported was 10 million (100x10%), and in 1995 it was 16 million. The absolute increase is thus:

$$16 - 10 = 6$$

Hence the percent increase in the number of autos exported is

$$\frac{absolute\ increase}{original\ number} = \frac{6}{10} = 60\%$$

The answer is (D).

25. In 1994, if twice as many autos imported to Country X broke down as autos exported from Country X and 20 percent of the exported autos broke down, what percent of the imported autos broke down?

    (A) 1%   (B) 1.5%   (C) 2%   (D) 4%   (E) 5.5%

If 20% of the exports broke down, then 2 million autos broke down (20%x10). Since "twice as many autos imported to Country X broke down as autos exported from Country X," 4 million imported autos broke down. Further, Country X imported 100 million autos (50%x200). Forming the percentage yields

$$\frac{4}{100} = 0.04 = 4\%$$

The answer is (D).

Problem Set T:

1. Jennifer and Alice are 4 miles apart. If Jennifer starts walking toward Alice at 3 miles per hour and at the same time Alice starts walking toward Jennifer at 2 miles per hour, how much time will pass before they meet?

    (A) 20 minutes   (B) 28 minutes   (C) 43 minutes   (D) 48 minutes   (E) 60 minutes

Let the distance Jennifer walks be x. Then since they are 4 miles apart, Alice will walk $4 - x$ miles. The key to this problem is that when they meet each person will have walked for an equal amount of time. Solving the equation $D = R \times T$ for T yields $T = \dfrac{D}{R}$. Hence,

$$\frac{x}{3} = \frac{4-x}{2}$$
$$2x = 3(4-x)$$
$$2x = 12 - 3x$$
$$5x = 12$$
$$x = \frac{12}{5}$$

Therefore, the time that Jennifer walks is $T = \dfrac{D}{R} = \dfrac{12/5}{3} = \dfrac{12}{5} \times \dfrac{1}{3} = \dfrac{4}{5}$ of an hour. Converting this into minutes gives $\dfrac{4}{5} \times 60 = 48$ minutes. The answer is (D).

2. If Robert can assemble a model car in 30 minutes and Craig can assemble the same model car in 20 minutes, how long would it take them, working together, to assemble the model car?

    (A) 12 minutes   (B) 13 minutes   (C) 14 minutes   (D) 15 minutes   (E) 16 minutes

Let t be the time it takes the boys, working together, to assemble the model car. Then their combined rate is $\dfrac{1}{t}$, and their individual rates are $\dfrac{1}{30}$ and $\dfrac{1}{20}$. Now, their combined rate is merely the sum of their individual rates:

$$\frac{1}{t} = \frac{1}{30} + \frac{1}{20}$$

Solving this equation for t yields $t = 12$. The answer is (A).

3. How many ounces of nuts costing 80 cents a pound must be mixed with nuts costing 60 cents a pound to make a 10-ounce mixture costing 70 cents a pound?

    (A) 3   (B) 4   (C) 5   (D) 7   (E) 8

Let x be the amount of nuts at 80 cents a pound. Then $10 - x$ is the amount of nuts at 60 cents a pound. The cost of the 80-cent nuts is $80x$, the cost of the 60-cent nuts is $60(10 - x)$, and the cost of the mixture is $70(10)$ cents. Since the cost of the mixture is the sum of the costs of the 70- and 80-cent nuts, we get

$$80x + 60(10 - x) = 70(10)$$

Solving this equation for x yields $x = 5$. The answer is (C).

4. Tom is 10 years older than Carrie. However, 5 years ago Tom was twice as old as Carrie. How old is Carrie?

 (A) 5   (B) 10   (C) 12   (D) 15   (E) 25

Let C be Carrie's age. Then Tom's age is $C + 10$. Now, 5 years ago, Carrie's age was $C - 5$ and Tom's age was $(C + 10) - 5 = C + 5$. Since at that time, Tom was twice as old as Carrie, we get $5 + C = 2(C - 5)$. Solving this equation for C yields $C = 15$. The answer is (D).

5. Two cars start at the same point and travel in opposite directions. If one car travels at 45 miles per hour and the other at 60 miles per hour, how much time will pass before they are 210 miles apart?

 (A) .5 hours   (B) 1 hour   (C) 1.5 hours   (D) 2 hours   (E) 2.5 hours

Since the cars start at the same time, the time each has traveled is the same. Let t be the time when the cars are 210 miles apart. From the equation $D = R \times T$, we get

$$210 = 45 \cdot t + 60 \cdot t$$
$$210 = 105 \cdot t$$
$$2 = t$$

The answer is (D).

6. If the value of x quarters is equal to the value of $x + 32$ nickels, $x =$

 (A) 8   (B) 11   (C) 14   (D) 17   (E) 20

The value of the x quarters is $25x$, and the value of the $x + 32$ nickels is $5(x + 32)$. Since these two quantities are equal, we get

$$25x = 5(x + 32)$$
$$25x = 5x + 160$$
$$20x = 160$$
$$x = 8$$

The answer is (A).

7. Steve has \$5.25 in nickels and dimes. If he has 15 more dimes than nickels, how many nickels does he have?

 (A) 20   (B) 25   (C) 27   (D) 30   (E) 33

Let N stand for the number of nickels. Then the number of dimes is $N + 15$. The value of the nickels is $5N$, and the value of the dimes is $10(N + 15)$. Since the total value of the nickels and dimes is 525¢, we get

$$5N + 10(N + 15) = 525$$
$$15N + 150 = 525$$
$$15N = 375$$
$$N = 25$$

Hence, there are 25 nickels, and the answer is (B).

8.   Cathy has equal numbers of nickels and quarters worth a total of $7.50. How many coins does she have?

(A) 20   (B) 25   (C) 50   (D) 62   (E) 70

Let x stand for both the number of nickels and the number of quarters. Then the value of the nickels is $5x$ and the value of the quarters is $25x$. Since the total value of the coins is $7.50, we get

$$5x + 25x = 750$$
$$30x = 750$$
$$x = 25$$

Hence, she has $x + x = 25 + 25 = 50$ coins. The answer is (C).

9.   Richard leaves to visit his friend who lives 200 miles down Interstate 10. One hour later his friend Steve leaves to visit Richard via Interstate 10. If Richard drives at 60 mph and Steve drives at 40 mph, how many miles will Steve have driven when they cross paths?

(A) 56   (B) 58   (C) 60   (D) 65   (E) 80

Let t be time that Steve has been driving. Then $t + 1$ is time that Richard has been driving. Now, the distance traveled by Steve is $D = rt = 40t$, and Richard's distance is $60(t + 1)$. At the moment they cross paths, they will have traveled a combined distance of 200 miles. Hence,

$$40t + 60(t + 1) = 200$$
$$40t + 60t + 60 = 200$$
$$100t + 60 = 200$$
$$100t = 140$$
$$t = 1.4$$

Therefore, Steve will have traveled $D = rt = 40(1.4) = 56$ miles. The answer is (A).

10.   At 1 PM, Ship A leaves port traveling 15 mph. Three hours later, Ship B leaves the same port in the same direction traveling 25 mph. At what time does Ship B pass Ship A?

(A) 8:30 PM   (B) 8:35 PM   (C) 9 PM   (D) 9:15 PM   (E) 9:30 PM

Let t be time that Ship B has been traveling. Then $t + 3$ is time that Ship A has been traveling. The distance traveled by Ship B is $D = rt = 25t$, and Ship A's distance is $15(t + 3)$. At the moment Ship B passes Ship A, they will have traveled the same distance. Hence,

$$25t = 15(t + 3)$$
$$25t = 15t + 45$$
$$10t = 45$$
$$t = 4.5$$

Since Ship B left port at 4 PM and overtook Ship A in 4.5 hours, it passed Ship A at 8:30 PM. The answer is (A).

11. In x hours and y minutes a car traveled z miles. What is the car's speed in miles per hour?

(A) $\dfrac{z}{60+y}$ (B) $\dfrac{60z}{60x+y}$ (C) $\dfrac{60}{60+y}$ (D) $\dfrac{z}{x+y}$ (E) $\dfrac{60+y}{60z}$

Since the time is given in mixed units, we need to change the minutes into hours. Since there are 60 minutes in an hour, y minutes is equivalent to $\dfrac{y}{60}$ hours. Hence, the car's travel time, "x hours and y minutes," is $x+\dfrac{y}{60}$ hours. Plugging this along with the distance traveled, z, into the formula $d = rt$ yields

$$z = r\left(x+\frac{y}{60}\right)$$
$$z = r\left(\frac{60}{60}x+\frac{y}{60}\right)$$
$$z = r\left(\frac{60x+y}{60}\right)$$
$$\frac{60z}{60x+y} = r$$

The answer is (B).

12. In a class of 40 students, the number of students who passed the math exam is equal to half the number of students who passed the science exam. Each student in the class passed at least one of the two exams. If 5 students passed both exams, then the number of students who passed the math exam is

(A) 5
(B) 10
(C) 15
(D) 20
(E) 25

Let x represent the number of students in the class who passed the math exam. Since it is given that the number of students who passed the math exam is half the number of students who passed the science exam, the number of students in the class who passed the science exam is $2x$. It is given that 5 students passed both exams. Hence, the number of students who passed only the math exam is $(x-5)$, and the number of students who passed only the science exam is $(2x-5)$. Since it is given that each student in the class passed at least one of the two exams, the number of students who failed both exams is 0.

We can divide the class into four groups:
1) Group of students who passed only the math exam: $(x-5)$
2) Group of students who passed only the science exam: $(2x-5)$
3) Group of students who passed both exams: 5
4) Group of students who failed both exams: 0

The sum of the number of students from each of these four categories is equal to the number of students in the class—40. Expressing this as an equation yields

$$(x-5)+(2x-5)+5+0 = 40$$
$$3x-5 = 40$$
$$3x = 45$$
$$x = 15$$

Thus, the number of students who passed the math exam is 15. The answer is (C).

13. A train of length *l*, traveling at a constant velocity, passes a pole in *t* seconds. If the same train traveling at the same velocity passes a platform in 3*t* seconds, then the length of the platform is

   (A) 0.5*l*
   (B) *l*
   (C) 1.5*l*
   (D) 2*l*
   (E) 3*l*

The distance traveled by the train while passing the pole is *l* (which is the length of the train). The train takes *t* seconds to pass the pole. Recall the formula velocity = distance/time. Applying this formula, we get

$$\text{velocity} = \frac{l}{t}$$

While passing the platform, the train travels a distance of *l* + *x*, where *x* is the length of the platform. The train takes 3*t* seconds at the velocity of *l*/*t* to cross the platform. Recalling the formula distance = velocity × time and substituting the values for the respective variables, we get

$$l + x = \frac{l}{t} \times 3t \qquad \text{by substitution}$$
$$l + x = 3l \qquad \text{by canceling } t$$
$$x = 2l \qquad \text{by subtracting } l \text{ from both sides}$$

Hence, the length of the platform is 2*l*. The answer is (D).

14. If two workers can assemble a car in 8 hours and a third worker can assemble the same car in 12 hours, then how long would it take the three workers together to assemble the car?

   (A) $\dfrac{5}{12}$ hrs

   (B) $2\dfrac{2}{5}$ hrs

   (C) $2\dfrac{4}{5}$ hrs

   (D) $3\dfrac{1}{2}$ hrs

   (E) $4\dfrac{4}{5}$ hrs

The fraction of work done in 1 hour by the first two people working together is 1/8. The fraction of work done in 1 hour by the third person is 1/12. When the three people work together, the total amount of work done in 1 hour is 1/8 + 1/12 = 5/24. The time taken by the people working together to complete the job is

$$\frac{1}{\text{fraction of work done per unit time}} =$$

$$\frac{1}{5/24} =$$

$$\frac{24}{5} =$$

$$4\frac{4}{5}$$

The answer is (E).

15. The age of B is half the sum of the ages of A and C. If B is 2 years younger than A and C is 32 years old, then the age of B must be

   (A) 28
   (B) 30
   (C) 32
   (D) 34
   (E) 36

Let a represent the age of A and let c represent the age of C. If b represents the age of B, then according to the question $b = \dfrac{a+c}{2}$. We are told that B is 2 years younger than A. This generates the equation $a = b + 2$. We know that the age of C is 32. Substituting these values into the equation $b = \dfrac{a+c}{2}$ yields $b = \dfrac{(b+2)+32}{2}$. Solving this equation for b yields $b = 34$. The answer is (D).

16. The ages of three people are such that the age of one person is twice the age of the second person and three times the age of the third person. If the sum of the ages of the three people is 33, then the age of the youngest person is

   (A) 3
   (B) 6
   (C) 9
   (D) 11
   (E) 18

Let a represent the age of the oldest person, b the age of the age of second person, and c the age of youngest person. The age of first person is twice the age of the second person and three times the age of the third person. This can be expressed as $a = 2b$ and $a = 3c$. Solving these equations for b and c yields $b = a/2$ and $c = a/3$. The sum of the ages of the three people is $a + b + c = 33$. Substituting for b and c in this equation, we get

$$a + a/2 + a/3 = 33$$
$$6a + 3a + 2a = 198 \qquad \text{by multiplying both sides by 6}$$
$$11a = 198$$
$$a = 198/11 = 18 \qquad \text{by dividing both sides by 11}$$

Since $c = a/3$, we get

$$c = a/3 = 18/3 = 6$$

The answer is (B).

Problem Set U:

1. By dividing 21 into 1, the fraction $\frac{1}{21}$ can be written as a repeating decimal: 0.476190476190 . . . where the block of digits 476190 repeats. What is the 54th digit following the decimal point?

    (A) 0   (B) 4   (C) 6   (D) 7   (E) 9

The sixth digit following the decimal point is the number zero: 0.476190476190 . . . Since the digits repeat in blocks of six numbers, 0 will appear in the space for all multiplies of six. Since 54 is a multiple of six, the 54th digit following the decimal point is 0. The answer is (A).

2. The positive integers *P, Q, R, S,* and *T* increase in order of size such that the value of each successive integer is one more than the preceding integer and the value of *T* is 6. What is the value of *R*?

    (A) 0   (B) 1   (C) 2   (D) 3   (E) 4

We know that *T* is 6; and therefore from the fact that *"each successive integer is one more than the preceding integer"* we see that *S* is 5. Continuing in this manner yields the following unique sequence:

$$\begin{array}{ccccc} P & Q & R & S & T \\ 2 & 3 & 4 & 5 & 6 \end{array}$$

Hence, the value of *R* is 4. The answer is (E).

3. Let *u* represent the sum of the integers from 1 through 20, and let *v* represent the sum of the integers from 21 through 40. What is the value of $v - u$?

    (A) 21   (B) 39   (C) 200   (D) 320   (E) 400

Forming the series for *u* and *v* yields

$$u = 1 + 2 + \cdots + 19 + 20$$
$$v = 21 + 22 + \cdots + 39 + 40$$

Subtracting the series for *u* from the series for *v* yields

$$v - u = \underbrace{20 + 20 + \cdots + 20 + 20}_{20 \text{ times}} = 20 \cdot 20 = 400$$

The answer is (E).

4. In the pattern of dots to the right, each row after the first row has two more dots than the row immediately above it. Row 6 contains how many dots?

    (A) 6   (B) 8   (C) 10   (D) 11   (E) 12

Extending the dots to six rows yields

Row 6 has twelve dots. Hence, the answer is (E).

5. In sequence S, all odd numbered terms are equal and all even numbered terms are equal. The first term in the sequence is $\sqrt{2}$ and the second term is –2. What is approximately the sum of two consecutive terms of the sequence?

    (A) –2   (B) –0.6   (C) 0   (D) 2   (E) 0.8

Since the *"the first term in the sequence is $\sqrt{2}$"* and *"all odd numbered terms are equal,"* all odd numbered terms equal $\sqrt{2}$. Since the *"the second term is –2"* and *"all even numbered terms are equal,"* all even numbered terms equal –2. Hence, the sum of any two consecutive terms of the sequence is $\sqrt{2} + (-2) \approx -0.6$ (remember, $\sqrt{2} \approx 1.4$). The answer is (B).

6. The sum of the first *n* even, positive integers is $2 + 4 + 6 + \cdots + 2n$ is $n(n + 1)$. What is the sum of the first 20 even, positive integers?

    (A) 120   (B) 188   (C) 362   (D) 406   (E) 420

We are given a formula for the sum of the first *n* even, positive integers. Plugging *n* = 20 into this formula yields

$$n(n + 1) = 20(20 + 1) = 20(21) = 420$$

The answer is (E).

7. In the array of numbers to the right, each number above the bottom row is equal to three times the number immediately below it. What is value of $x + y$?

27	x	81	–108
9	–18	27	–36
3	–6	y	–12
1	–2	3	–4

    (A) –45   (B) –15   (C) –2   (D) 20   (E) 77

Since *"each number above the bottom row is equal to three times the number immediately below it,"* $x = 3(-18) = -54$ and $y = 3(3) = 9$. Hence, $x + y = -54 + 9 = -45$. The answer is (A).

8. The first term of a sequence is 2. All subsequent terms are found by adding 3 to the immediately preceding term and then multiplying the sum by 2. Which of the following describes the terms of the sequence?

    (A) Each term is odd   (B) Each term is even   (C) The terms are: even, odd, even, odd, etc.
    (D) The terms are: even, odd, odd, odd, etc.   (E) The terms are: even, odd, odd, even, odd, odd, etc.

The first term is even, and all subsequent terms are found by multiplying a number by 2. Hence, all terms of the sequence are even. The answer is (B). Following is the sequence:

$$2, 10, 26, 58, \ldots$$

9. Except for the first two numbers, every number in the sequence –1, 3, 2, . . . is the sum of the two immediately preceding numbers. How many numbers of this sequence are even?

    (A) none   (B) one   (C) two   (D) three   (E) more than three

Since *"every number in the sequence –1, 3, 2, . . . is the sum of the two immediately preceding numbers,"* the forth term of the sequence is $5 = 3 + 2$. The first 12 terms of this sequence are

$$-1, 3, 2, 5, 7, 12, 19, 31, 50, 81, 131, 212, \ldots$$

At least four numbers in this sequence are even: 2, 12, 50, and 212. The answer is (E).

10. In the sequence w, x, y, 30, adding any one of the first three terms to the term immediately following it yields $\dfrac{w}{2}$. What is the value of w?

(A) –60   (B) –30   (C) 0   (D) 5   (E) 25

Since "*adding any one of the first three terms to the term immediately following it yields $\dfrac{w}{2}$*," we get

$$w + x = \frac{w}{2}$$

$$x + y = \frac{w}{2}$$

$$y + 30 = \frac{w}{2}$$

Subtracting the last equation from the second equation yields $x - 30 = 0$. That is $x = 30$. Plugging $x = 30$ into the first equation yields

$$w + 30 = \frac{w}{2}$$

Multiplying both sides by 2 yields $2w + 60 = w$
Subtracting w from both sides yields $w + 60 = 0$
Finally, subtracting 60 from both sides yields $w = -60$

The answer is (A).

Problem Set V:

1. The number of integers between 29 and 69, inclusive is

   (A) 39   (B) 40   (C) 41   (D) 42   (E) 43

Since the number of integers between two integers inclusive is one more than their difference, we get $69 - 29 + 1 = 41$ integers. The answer is (C).

2. A school has a total enrollment of 150 students. There are 63 students taking French, 48 taking chemistry, and 21 taking both. How many students are taking <u>neither</u> French nor chemistry?

   (A) 60   (B) 65   (C) 71   (D) 75   (E) 97

French   Chemistry

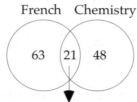

Both French and Chemistry

Adding the number of students taking French and the number of students taking chemistry and then subtracting the number of students taking both yields $(63 + 48) - 21 = 90$. This is the number of students enrolled in *either* French or chemistry or both. Since the total school enrollment is 150, there are $150 - 90 = 60$ students enrolled in *neither* French nor chemistry. The answer is (A).

3. The number of minutes in $1\frac{1}{3}$ hours is

   (A) 60   (B) 65   (C) 71   (D) 80   (E) 97

There are 60 minutes in an hour. Hence, there are $1\frac{1}{3} \cdot 60 = 80$ minutes in $1\frac{1}{3}$ hours. The answer is (D).

4. A web press prints 5 pages every 2 seconds. At this rate, how many pages will the press print in 7 minutes?

   (A) 350   (B) 540   (C) 700   (D) 950   (E) 1050

Since there are 60 seconds in a minute and the press prints 5 pages every 2 seconds, the press prints $5 \cdot 30 = 150$ pages in one minute. Hence, in 7 minutes, the press will print $7 \cdot 150 = 1050$ pages. The answer is (E).

5. A school has a total enrollment of 90 students. There are 30 students taking physics, 25 taking English, and 13 taking both. What percentage of the students are taking either physics or English?

   (A) 30%   (B) 36%   (C) 47%   (D) 51%   (E) 58%

Physics   English

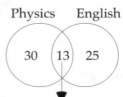

Both Physics and English

Adding the number of students taking physics and the number of students taking English and then subtracting the number of students taking both yields $(30 + 25) - 13 = 42$. This is the number of students enrolled in *either* physics or English or both. The total school enrollment is 90, so forming the ratio yields

$$\frac{physics\ or\ math\ enrollment}{total\ enrollment} = \frac{42}{90} \approx .47 = 47\%$$

The answer is (C).

6.   Callers 49 through 91 to a radio show won a prize. How many callers won a prize?

   (A) 42   (B) 43   (C) 44   (D) 45   (E) 46

Since the number of integers between two integers inclusive is one more than their difference, $(91 - 49) + 1 = 43$ callers won a prize. The answer is (B).

7.   A rancher is constructing a fence by stringing wire between posts 20 feet apart. If the fence is 400 feet long, how many posts must the rancher use?

   (A) 18   (B) 19   (C) 20   (D) 21   (E) 22

Since the fence is 400 feet long and the posts are 20 feet apart, there are $\frac{400}{20} = 20$ sections in the fence. Now, if we ignore the first post and associate the post at the end of each section with that section, then there are 20 posts (one for each of the twenty sections). Counting the first post gives a total of 21 posts. The answer is (D).

8.   The number of marbles in x jars , each containing 15 marbles, plus the number of marbles in $3x$ jars , each containing 20 marbles is

   (A) $65x$ (B) $70x$ (C) $75x$ (D) $80x$ (E) $85x$

The x jars have $15x$ marbles, and the $3x$ jars have $20 \cdot 3x = 60x$ marbles. Hence, there are a total of $15x + 60x = 75x$ marbles. The answer is (C).

9.   The number of integers from 2 to 10^3, inclusive is

   (A) 997   (B) 998   (C) 999   (D) 1000   (E) 1001

Since the number of integers between two integers inclusive is one more than their difference, we have $\left(10^3 - 2\right) + 1 = (1000 - 2) + 1 = 999$ integers. The answer is (C).

10.   In a small town, 16 people own Fords and 11 people own Toyotas. If exactly 15 people own only one of the two types of cars, how many people own both types of cars.

   (A) 2   (B) 6   (C) 7   (D) 12   (E) 14

This is a hard problem. Let x be the number of people who own both types of cars. Then the number of people who own only Fords is $16 - x$, and the number of people who own only Toyotas is $11 - x$. Adding these two expressions gives the number of people who own only one of the two types of cars, which we are told is 15:

$$(16 - x) + (11 - x) = 15$$

Add like terms: $27 - 2x = 15$
Subtract 27 from both sides of the equation: $-2x = -12$
Finally, divide both sides of the equation by –2: $x = 6$
The answer is (B).

Problem Set W:

1. The median is larger than the average for which one of the following sets of integers?

    (A) {8, 9, 10, 11, 12}
    (B) {8, 9, 10, 11, 13}
    (C) {8, 10, 10, 10, 12}
    (D) {10, 10, 10, 10, 10}
    (E) {7, 9, 10, 11, 12}

The median in all five answer-choices is 10. By symmetry, the average in answer-choices (A), (C), and (D) is 10 as well. The average in choice (B) is larger than 10 because 13 is further away from 10 than 8 is. Similarly, the average in choice (E) is smaller than 10 because 7 is further away from 10 than 12 is. The exact average is $\dfrac{7+9+10+11+12}{5} = \dfrac{49}{5} < 10$. The answer is (E).

2. A hat contains 15 marbles, and each marble is numbered with one and only one of the numbers 1, 2, 3. From a group of 15 people, each person selects exactly 1 marble from the hat.

Numbered Marble	Number of People Who Selected The Marble
1	4
2	5
3	6

    What is the probability that a person selected at random picked a marble numbered 2 or greater?

    (A) 5/15   (B) 9/15   (C) 10/15   (D) 11/15   (E) 1

There are 11 (= 5 + 6) people who selected a number 2 or number 3 marble, and there are 15 total people. Hence, the probability of selecting a number 2 or number 3 marble is 11/15, and the answer is (D).

3. Sarah cannot completely remember her four-digit ATM pin number. She does remember the first two digits, and she knows that each of the last two digits is greater than 5. The ATM will allow her three tries before it blocks further access. If she randomly guesses the last two digits, what is the probability that she will get access to her account?

    (A) 1/2   (B) 1/4   (C) 3/16   (D) 3/18   (E) 1/32

Randomly guessing either of the last two digits does not affect the choice of the other, which means that these events are mutually exclusive and we are dealing with consecutive probabilities. Since each of the last two digits is greater than 5, Sarah has four digits to choose from: 6, 7, 8, 9. Her chance of guessing correctly on the first choice is 1/4, and on the second choice also 1/4. Her chance of guessing correctly on both choices is

$$\frac{1}{4} \cdot \frac{1}{4} = \frac{1}{16}$$

Since she gets three tries, the total probability is $\dfrac{1}{16} + \dfrac{1}{16} + \dfrac{1}{16} = \dfrac{3}{16}$. The answer is (C).

4. If $x < y < z$, $z = ky$, $x = 0$, and the average of the numbers x, y, and z is 3 times the median, what is the value of k?

    (A) –2   (B) 3   (C) 5.5   (D) 6   (E) 8

Since y is the middle number, it is the median. Forming the average of x, y, and z and setting it equal to 3 times the median yields

$$\frac{x+y+z}{3} = 3y$$

Replacing x with 0 and z with ky yields

$$\frac{0+y+ky}{3} = 3y$$

Multiplying both sides of this equation by 3 yields

$$y + ky = 9y$$

Subtracting $9y$ from both sides yields

$$-8y + ky = 0$$

Factoring out y yields

$$y(-8 + k) = 0$$

Since $y \neq 0$ (why?), $-8 + k = 0$. Hence, $k = 8$ and the answer is (E).

5. Three positive numbers x, y, and z have the following relationships $y = x + 2$ and $z = y + 2$. When the median of x, y, and z is subtracted from the product of the smallest number and the median, the result is 0. What is the value of the largest number?

   (A) –2   (B) π (C) 5   (D) 8   (E) 21/2

Plugging $y = x + 2$ into the equation $z = y + 2$ gives $z = (x + 2) + 2 = x + 4$. Hence, in terms of x, the three numbers x, y, and z are

$$x, x + 2, x + 4$$

Clearly, x is the smallest number. Further, since $x + 2$ is smaller than $x + 4$, $x + 2$ is the median. Subtracting the median from the product of the smallest number and the median and setting the result equal to 0 yields

$$x(x + 2) - (x + 2) = 0$$

Factoring out the common factor $x + 2$ yields

$$(x + 2)(x - 1) = 0$$

Setting each factor equal to 0 yields

$$x + 2 = 0 \ \text{ or } \ x - 1 = 0$$

Hence, $x = -2$ or $x = 1$. Since the three numbers are positive, x must be 1. Hence, the largest number is $x + 4 = 1 + 4 = 5$. The answer is (C).

6. A jar contains only three types of objects: red, blue, and silver paper clips. The probability of selecting a red paper clip is $1/4$, and the probability of selecting a blue paper clip is $1/6$. What is the probability of selecting a silver paper clip?

   (A) 5/12   (B) 1/2   (C) 7/12   (D) 3/4   (E) 11/12

First, let's calculate the probability of selecting a red or a blue paper clip. This is an either-or probability and is therefore the sum of the individual probabilities:

$$1/4 + 1/6 = 5/12$$

Now, since there are only three types of objects, the sum of their probabilities must be 1 (Remember that the sum of the probabilities of all possible outcomes is always 1):

$$P(r) + P(b) + P(s) = 1,$$

where *r* stands for red, *b* stands for blue, and *s* stands for silver.

Replacing $P(r) + P(b)$ with $5/12$ yields $\qquad\qquad 5/12 + P(s) = 1$

Subtracting $5/12$ from both sides of this equation yields $\qquad P(s) = 1 - 5/12$

Performing the subtraction yields $\qquad\qquad\qquad P(s) = 7/12$

The answer is (C).

7. A bowl contains one marble labeled 0, one marble labeled 1, one marble labeled 2, and one marble labeled 3. The bowl contains no other objects. If two marbles are drawn randomly without replacement, what is the probability that they will add up to 3?

(A) 1/12 (B) 1/8 (C) 1/6 (D) 1/4 (E) 1/3

The following list shows all 12 ways of selecting the two marbles:

(0, 1)	(1, 0)	(2, 0)	**(3, 0)**
(0, 2)	**(1, 2)**	**(2, 1)**	(3, 1)
(0, 3)	(1, 3)	(2, 3)	(3, 2)

The four pairs in bold are the only ones whose sum is 3. Hence, the probability that two randomly drawn marbles will have a sum of 3 is

$$4/12 = 1/3$$

The answer is (E).

8. A housing subdivision contains only two types of homes: ranch-style homes and townhomes. There are twice as many townhomes as ranch-style homes. There are 3 times as many townhomes with pools than without pools. What is the probability that a home selected at random from the subdivision will be a townhome with a pool?

(A) 1/6 (B) 1/5 (C) 1/4 (D) 1/3 (E) 1/2

Since there are twice as many townhomes as ranch-style homes, the probability of selecting a townhome is $2/3$.[*] Now, "there are 3 times as many townhomes with pools than without pools." So the probability that a townhome will have a pool is $3/4$. Hence, the probability of selecting a townhome with a pool is

$$\frac{2}{3} \cdot \frac{3}{4} = \frac{1}{2}$$

The answer is (E).

---

[*] Caution: Were you tempted to choose $1/2$ for the probability because there are "twice" as many townhomes? One-half (= 50%) would be the probability if there were an equal number of townhomes and ranch-style homes. Remember the probability of selecting a townhome is not the ratio of townhomes to ranch-style homes, but the ratio of townhomes to the total number of homes. To see this more clearly, suppose there are 3 homes in the subdivision. Then 2 would be townhomes and 1 would be a ranch-style home. So the ratio of townhomes to total homes would be $2/3$.

Diagnostic/Review Math Test

This diagnostic test appears at the end of the math section because it is probably best for you to use it a review test. Unless your math skills are very strong, you should thoroughly study every math chapter. Afterwards, you can use this diagnostic/review test to determine which math chapters you need to work on more. If you do not have much time to study, this test can also be used to concentrate your studies on your weakest areas.

1. If $3x + 9 = 15$, then $x + 2 =$

    (A) 2
    (B) 3
    (C) 4
    (D) 5
    (E) 6

2. If $a = 3b$, $b^2 = 2c$, $9c = d$, then $\dfrac{a^2}{d} =$

    (A) 1/2
    (B) 2
    (C) 10/3
    (D) 5
    (E) 6

$$a + b + c/2 = 60$$
$$-a - b + c/2 = -10$$

3. In the system of equations above, what is the value of b ?

    (A) 8
    (B) 20
    (C) 35
    (D) 50
    (E) Not enough information to decide.

4. $3 - (2^3 - 2[3 - 16 \div 2]) =$

    (A) −15
    (B) −5
    (C) 1
    (D) 2
    (E) 30

5. $(x - 2)(x + 4) - (x - 3)(x - 1) = 0$

    (A) −5
    (B) −1
    (C) 0
    (D) 1/2
    (E) 11/6

6. $-2^4 - \left(x^2 - 1\right)^2 =$

    (A) $-x^4 + 2x^2 + 15$
    (B) $-x^4 - 2x^2 + 17$
    (C) $-x^4 + 2x^2 - 17$
    (D) $-x^4 + 2x^2 - 15$
    (E) $-x^4 + 2x^2 + 17$

7. The smallest prime number greater than 48 is

    (A) 49
    (B) 50
    (C) 51
    (D) 52
    (E) 53

8. If a, b, and c are consecutive integers and $a < b < c$, which of the following must be true?

    (A) b^2 is a prime number
    (B) $\dfrac{a + c}{2} = b$
    (C) $a + b$ is even
    (D) $\dfrac{ab}{3}$ is an integer
    (E) $c - a = b$

9. $\sqrt{(42 - 6)(20 + 16)} =$

    (A) 2
    (B) 20
    (C) 28
    (D) 30
    (E) 36

10. $\left(4^x\right)^2 =$

    (A) 2^{4x}
    (B) 4^{x+2}
    (C) 2^{2x+2}
    (D) 4^{x^2}
    (E) 2^{2x^2}

11. If $8^{13} = 2^z$, then $z =$

    (A) 10
    (B) 13
    (C) 19
    (D) 26
    (E) 39

12. 1/2 of 0.2 percent equals

    (A) 1
    (B) 0.1
    (C) 0.01
    (D) 0.001
    (E) 0.0001

13. $\dfrac{4}{\dfrac{1}{3} + 1} =$

    (A) 1
    (B) 1/2
    (C) 2
    (D) 3
    (E) 4

14. If $x + y = k$, then $3x^2 + 6xy + 3y^2 =$

   (A) k
   (B) $3k$
   (C) $6k$
   (D) k^2
   (E) $3k^2$

15. $8x^2 - 18 =$

   (A) $8(x^2 - 2)$
   (B) $2(2x + 3)(2x - 3)$
   (C) $2(4x + 3)(4x - 3)$
   (D) $2(2x + 9)(2x - 9)$
   (E) $2(4x + 3)(x - 3)$

16. For which values of x is the following inequality true: $x^2 < 2x$.

   (A) $x < 0$
   (B) $0 < x < 2$
   (C) $-2 < x < 2$
   (D) $x < 2$
   (E) $x > 2$

17. If x is an integer and $y = -3x + 7$, what is the least value of x for which y is less than 1?

   (A) 1
   (B) 2
   (C) 3
   (D) 4
   (E) 5

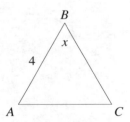

Note, figure not drawn to scale

18. In the figure above, triangle ABC is isosceles with base AC. If $x = 60°$, then $AC =$

   (A) 2
   (B) 3
   (C) 4
   (D) 14/3
   (E) $\sqrt{30}$

19. A unit square is circumscribed about a circle. If the circumference of the circle is $q\pi$, what is the value of q?

   (A) 1
   (B) 2
   (C) π
   (D) 2π
   (E) 5π

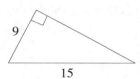

20. What is the area of the triangle above?

   (A) 20
   (B) 24
   (C) 30
   (D) 54
   (E) 64

21. If the average of $2x$ and $4x$ is 12, then $x =$

   (A) 1
   (B) 2
   (C) 3
   (D) 4
   (E) 24

22. The average of x, y, and z is 8 and the average of y and z is 4. What is the value of x?

   (A) 4
   (B) 9
   (C) 16
   (D) 20
   (E) 24

23. If the ratio of two numbers is 6 and their sum is 21, what is the value of the larger number?

   (A) 1
   (B) 5
   (C) 12
   (D) 17
   (E) 18

24. What percent of $3x$ is $6y$ if $x = 4y$?

   (A) 50%
   (B) 40%
   (C) 30%
   (D) 20%
   (E) 18%

25. If $y = 3x$, then the value of 10% of y is

    (A) $.003x$
    (B) $.3x$
    (C) $3x$
    (D) $30x$
    (E) $300x$

26. How many ounces of water must be added to a 30-ounce solution that is 40 percent alcohol to dilute the solution to 25 percent alcohol?

    (A) 9
    (B) 10
    (C) 15
    (D) 16
    (E) 18

27. What is the value of the 201st term of a sequence if the first term of the sequence is 2 and each successive term is 4 more than the term immediately preceding it?

    (A) 798
    (B) 800
    (C) 802
    (D) 804
    (E) 806

28. A particular carmaker sells four models of cars, and each model comes with 5 options. How many different types of cars does the carmaker sell?

    (A) 15
    (B) 16
    (C) 17
    (D) 18
    (E) 20

29. Define a @ b to be $a^3 - 1$. What is the value of x @ 1 ?

    (A) 0
    (B) a^3
    (C) $x^3 - 1$
    (D) $x^3 + 1$
    (E) 2

30. Define the symbol * by the following equation: $x* = 1 - x$, for all non-negative x. If $\left((1-x)*\right)* = (1-x)*$, then $x =$

    (A) 1/2
    (B) 3/4
    (C) 1
    (D) 2
    (E) 3

1. Dividing both sides of the equation by 3 yields

$$x + 3 = 5$$

Subtracting 1 from both sides of this equation (because we are looking for $x + 2$) yields

$$x + 2 = 4$$

The answer is (C).

2.

$$\frac{a^2}{d} =$$

$$\frac{(3b)^2}{9c} = \qquad \text{since } a = 3b \text{ and } 9c = d$$

$$\frac{9b^2}{9c} =$$

$$\frac{b^2}{c} =$$

$$\frac{2c}{c} = \qquad \text{since } b^2 = 2c$$

$$2$$

The answer is (B).

3. Merely adding the two equations yields

$$c = 50$$

Next, multiplying the bottom equation by -1 and then adding the equations yields

$$\begin{array}{r} a + b + c/2 = 60 \\ (+) \quad a + b - c/2 = 10 \\ \hline 2a + 2b = 70 \end{array}$$

Dividing this equation by 2 yields

$$a + b = 35$$

This equation does not allow us to determine the value of b. For example, if $a = 0$, then $b = 35$. Now suppose, is $a = -15$, then $b = 50$. This is a double case and therefore the answer is (E), not enough information to decide.

4.

$$3 - (2^3 - 2[3 - 16 \div 2]) = \qquad \text{Within the innermost parentheses, division is performed before subtraction:}$$

$$3 - (2^3 - 2[3 - 8]) =$$

$$3 - (2^3 - 2[-5]) =$$

$$3 - (8 - 2[-5]) =$$

$$3 - (8 + 10) =$$

$$3 - 18 =$$

$$-15$$

The answer is (A).

5. Multiplying (using foil multiplication) both terms in the expression yields

$$x^2 + 4x - 2x - 8 - (x^2 - x - 3x + 3) = 0$$

(Notice that parentheses are used in the second expansion but not in the first. Parentheses must be used in the second expansion because the negative sign must be distributed to *every* term within the parentheses.)

Combining like terms yields

$$x^2 + 2x - 8 - (x^2 - 4x + 3) = 0$$

Distributing the negative sign to every term within the parentheses yields

$$x^2 + 2x - 8 - x^2 + 4x - 3 = 0$$

(Note, although distributing the negative sign over the parentheses is an elementary operation, many, if not most, students will apply the negative sign to only the first term:

$$-x^2 - 4x + 3$$

The writers of the test are aware of this common mistake and structure the test so that there are many opportunities to make this mistake.)

Grouping like terms together yields

$$(x^2 - x^2) + (2x + 4x) + (-8 - 3) = 0$$

Combining the like terms yields

$$6x - 11 = 0$$
$$6x = 11$$
$$x = 11/6$$

The answer is (E).

6.
$$-2^4 - (x^2 - 1)^2 =$$
$$-16 - [(x^2)^2 - 2x^2 + 1] =$$
$$-16 - [x^4 - 2x^2 + 1] =$$
$$-16 - x^4 + 2x^2 - 1 =$$
$$-x^4 + 2x^2 - 17$$

The answer is (C).

Notice that $-2^4 = -16$, not 16. This is one of the most common mistakes on the test. To see why $-2^4 = -16$ more clearly, rewrite -2^4 as follows:

$$-2^4 = (-1)2^4$$

In this form, it is clearer that the exponent, 4, applies only to the number 2, not to the number -1. So $-2^4 = (-1)2^4 = (-1)16 = -16$.

To make the answer positive 16, the -2 could be placed in parentheses:

$$(-2)^4 = [(-1)2]^4 = (-1)^4\, 2^4 = (+1)16 = 16$$

7. Since the question asks for the *smallest* prime greater then 48, we start with the smallest answer-choice. Now, 49 is not prime since $49 = 7 \cdot 7$. Next, 50 is not prime since $50 = 5 \cdot 10$. Next, 51 is not prime since $51 = 3 \cdot 17$. Next, 52 is not prime since $52 = 2 \cdot 26$. Finally, 53 *is* prime since it is divisible by only itself and 1. The answer is (E).

Note, an integer is prime if it greater than 1 and divisible by only itself and 1. The number 2 is the smallest prime (and the only even prime) because the only integers that divide into it evenly are 1 and 2. The number 3 is the next larger prime. The number 4 is not prime because $4 = 2 \cdot 2$. Following is a partial list of the prime numbers. You should memorize it.

$$2, 3, 5, 7, 11, 13, 17, 19, 23, 29, 31, \ldots$$

8. Recall that an integer is prime if it is divisible by only itself and 1. In other words, an integer is prime if it cannot be written as a product of two other integers, other than itself and 1. Now, $b^2 = bb$. Since b^2 can be written as a product of b and b, it is not prime. Statement (A) is false.

Turning to Choice (B), since a, b, and c are consecutive integers, in that order, b is one unit larger than a: $b = a + 1$, and c is one unit larger than b: $c = b + 1 = (a + 1) + 1 = a + 2$. Now, plugging this information into the expression $\dfrac{a+c}{2}$ yields

$$\frac{a+c}{2} =$$
$$\frac{a+(a+2)}{2} =$$
$$\frac{2a+2}{2} =$$
$$\frac{2a}{2} + \frac{2}{2} =$$
$$a + 1 =$$
$$b$$

The answer is (B).

Regarding the other answer-choices, Choice (C) is true in some cases and false in others. To show that it can be false, let's plug in some numbers satisfying the given conditions. How about $a = 1$ and $b = 2$. In this case, $a + b = 1 + 2 = 3$, which is odd, not even. This eliminates Choice (C). Notice that to show a statement is false, we need only find one exception. However, to show a statement is true by plugging in numbers, you usually have to plug in more than one set of numbers because the statement may be true for one set of numbers but not for another set. We'll discuss in detail later the conditions under which you can say that a statement is true by plugging in numbers.

Choice (D) is not necessarily true. For instance, let $a = 1$ and $b = 2$. Then $\dfrac{ab}{3} = \dfrac{1 \cdot 2}{3} = \dfrac{2}{3}$, which is not an integer. This eliminates Choice (D).

Finally, $c - a = b$ is not necessarily true. For instance, let $a = 2$, $b = 3$, and $c = 4$. Then $c - a = 4 - 2 = 2 \neq 3$. This eliminates Choice (E).

9.
$$\sqrt{(42-6)(20+16)} =$$
$$\sqrt{(36)(36)} =$$
$$\sqrt{36}\sqrt{36} = \qquad \text{from the rule } \sqrt{xy} = \sqrt{x}\sqrt{y}$$
$$6 \cdot 6 =$$
$$36$$

The answer is (E).

10.
$$\left(4^x\right)^2 =$$
$$4^{2x} = \qquad \text{by the rule } \left(x^a\right)^b = x^{ab}$$
$$\left(2^2\right)^{2x} = \qquad \text{by replacing 4 with } 2^2$$
$$(2)^{4x} \qquad \text{by the rule } \left(x^a\right)^b = x^{ab}$$

The answer is (A). Note, this is considered to be a hard problem.

As to the other answer-choices, Choice (B) wrongly adds the exponents x and 2. The exponents are added when the same bases are multiplied:

$$a^x a^y = a^{x+y}$$

For example: $2^3 2^2 = 2^{3+2} = 2^5 = 32$. Be careful not to multiply unlike bases. For example, do not add exponents in the following expression: $2^3 4^2$. The exponents cannot be added here because the bases, 2 and 4, are not the same.

Choice (C), first changes 4 into 2^2, and then correctly multiplies 2 and x: $\left(2^2\right)^x = 2^{2x}$. However, it then errs in adding $2x$ and 2: $\left(2^{2x}\right)^2 \neq 2^{2x+2}$.

Choice (D) wrongly squares the x. When a power is raised to another power, the powers are multiplied:

$$\left(x^a\right)^b = x^{ab}$$

So $\left(4^x\right)^2 = 4^{2x}$.

Choice (E) makes the same mistake as in Choice (D).

11. The number 8 can be written as 2^3. Plugging this into the equation $8^{13} = 2^z$ yields

$$\left(2^3\right)^{13} = 2^z$$

Applying the rule $\left(x^a\right)^b = x^{ab}$ yields

$$2^{39} = 2^z$$

Since the bases are the same, the exponents must be the same. Hence, $z = 39$, and the answer is (E).

12. Recall that percent means to divide by 100. So .2 percent equals $.2/100 = .002$. (Recall that the decimal point is moved to the left one space for each zero in the denominator.) Now, as a decimal $1/2 = .5$.

In percent problems, "of" means multiplication. So multiplying .5 and .002 yields

$$
\begin{array}{r}
.002 \\
\times \quad .5 \\
\hline
.001
\end{array}
$$

Hence, the answer is (D).

13.

$$\frac{4}{\frac{1}{3}+1} =$$

$$\frac{4}{\frac{1}{3}+\frac{3}{3}} = \qquad \text{by creating a common denominator of 3}$$

$$\frac{4}{\frac{1+3}{3}} =$$

$$\frac{4}{\frac{4}{3}} =$$

$$4 \cdot \frac{3}{4} = \qquad \text{Recall: "to divide" means to invert and multiply}$$

$$3 \qquad \text{by canceling the 4's}$$

Hence, the answer is (D).

14. $\quad 3x^2 + 6xy + 3y^2 =$

$3(x^2 + 2xy + y^2) = \qquad$ by factoring out the common factor 3

$3(x + y)^2 = \qquad$ by the perfect square trinomial formula $x^2 + 2xy + y^2 = (x + y)^2$

$3k^2$

Hence, the answer is (E).

15. $8x^2 - 18 =$

        $2(4x^2 - 9) =$ by the distributive property $ax + ay = a(x + y)$

        $2(2^2x^2 - 3^2) =$

        $2([2x]^2 - 3^2) =$

        $2(2x + 3)(2x - 3)$ by the difference of squares formula $x^2 - y^2 = (x + y)(x - y)$

The answer is (B).

It is common for students to wrongly apply the difference of squares formula to a perfect square:

$$(x - y)^2 \neq (x + y)(x - y)$$

The correct formulas follow. Notice that the first formula is the square of a difference, and the second formula is the difference of two squares.

Perfect square trinomial: $(x - y)^2 = x^2 - 2xy + y^2$

Difference of squares: $x^2 - y^2 = (x + y)(x - y)$

It is also common for students to wrongly distribute the 2 in a perfect square:

$$(x - y)^2 \neq x^2 - y^2$$

Note, there is no factoring formula for a sum of squares: $x^2 + y^2$. It cannot be factored.

16. First, replace the inequality symbol with an equal symbol: $x^2 = 2x$

Subtracting $2x$ from both sides yields $x^2 - 2x = 0$

Factoring by the distributive rule yields $x(x - 2) = 0$

Setting each factor to 0 yields $x = 0$ and $x - 2 = 0$

Or $x = 0$ and $x = 2$

Now, the only numbers at which the expression can change sign are 0 and 2. So 0 and 2 divide the number line into three intervals. Let's set up a number line and choose test points in each interval:

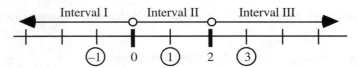

When $x = -1$, $x^2 < 2x$ becomes $1 < -2$. This is false. Hence, no numbers in Interval I satisfy the inequality. When $x = 1$, $x^2 < 2x$ becomes $1 < 2$. This is true. Hence, all numbers in Interval II satisfy the inequality. That is, $0 < x < 2$. When $x = 3$, $x^2 < 2x$ becomes $9 < 6$. This is false. Hence, no numbers in Interval III satisfy the inequality. The answer is (B). The graph of the solution follows:

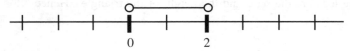

17. Since y is lto be ess than 1 and $y = -3x + 7$, we get

      $-3x + 7 < 1$

      $-3x < -6$ by subtracting 7 from both sides of the inequality

      $x > 2$ by dividing both sides of the inequality by -3

(Note that the inequality changes direction when we divide both sides by a negative number. This is also the case if you multiply both sides of an inequality by a negative number.)

Since x is an integer and is to be as small as possible, $x = 3$. The answer is (C).

18. Since the triangle is isosceles, with base AC, the base angles are congruent (equal). That is, $A = C$. Since the angle sum of a triangle is 180, we get

$$A + C + x = 180$$

Replacing C with A and x with 60 gives

$$A + A + 60 = 180$$
$$A + A + 60 = 180$$
$$2A + 60 = 180$$
$$2A = 120$$
$$A = 60$$

Hence, the triangle is equilateral (all three sides are congruent). Since we are given that side AB has length 4, side AC also has length 4. The answer is (C).

19. Since the unit square is circumscribed about the circle, the diameter of the circle is 1 and the radius of the circle is r = d/2 = 1/2. This is illustrated in the following figure:

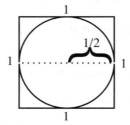

Now, the circumference of a circle is given by the formula $2\pi r$. For this circle the formula becomes $2\pi r = 2\pi(1/2) = \pi$. We are told that the circumference of the circle is $q\pi$. Setting these two expressions equal yields

$$\pi = q\pi$$

Dividing both sides of this equation by π yields

$$1 = q$$

The answer is (A).

20. Let x be the unknown side of the triangle. Applying the Pythagorean Theorem yields

$9^2 + x^2 = 15^2$

$81 + x^2 = 225$ by squaring the terms

$x^2 = 144$ by subtracting 81 from both sides of the equation

$x = \pm\sqrt{144}$ by taking the square root of both sides of the equation

$x = 12$ since we are looking for a length, we take the positive root

In a right triangle, the legs are the base and the height of the triangle. Hence, $A = \dfrac{1}{2}bh = \dfrac{1}{2} \cdot 9 \cdot 12 = 54$. The answer is (D).

21. Since the average of $2x$ and $4x$ is 12, we get

$$\frac{2x + 4x}{2} = 12$$
$$\frac{6x}{2} = 12$$
$$3x = 12$$
$$x = 4$$

The answer is (D).

22. Recall that the average of N numbers is their sum divided by N. That is, average = sum/N. Since the average of x, y, and z is 8 and the average of y and z is 4, this formula yields

$$\frac{x + y + z}{3} = 8$$

$$\frac{y + z}{2} = 4$$

Solving the bottom equation for $y + z$ yields $y + z = 8$. Plugging this into the top equation gives

$$\frac{x + 8}{3} = 8$$

$$x + 8 = 24$$

$$x = 16$$

The answer is (C).

23. Let the two numbers be x and y. Now, a ratio is simply a fraction. Forming the fraction yields $x/y = 6$, and forming the sum yields $x + y = 21$. Solving the first equation for x yields $x = 6y$. Plugging this into the second equation yields

$$6y + y = 21$$

$$7y = 21$$

$$y = 3$$

Plugging this into the equation $x = 6y$ yields

$$x = 6(3) = 18$$

The answer is (E).

24. Let $z\%$ represent the unknown percent. Now, when solving percent problems, "of" means times. Translating the statement "What percent of $3x$ is $6y$" into an equation yields

$$z\%(3x) = 6y$$

Substituting $x = 4y$ into this equation yields

$$z\%(3 \cdot 4y) = 6y$$

$$z\%(12y) = 6y$$

$$z\% = \frac{6y}{12y}$$

$$z\% = 1/2 = .50 = 50\%$$

The answer is (A).

25. The percent symbol, %, means to divide by 100. So $10\% = 10/100 = .10$. Hence, the expression 10% of y tranlsates into $.10y$. Since $y = 3x$, this becomes $.10y = .10(3x) = .30x$. The answer is (B).

26. Let x be the amount of water added. Since there is no alcohol in the water, the percent of alcohol in the water is $0\%x$. The amount of alcohol in the original solution is $40\%(30)$, and the amount of alcohol in the final solution will be $25\%(30 + x)$. Now, the concentration of alcohol in the original solution plus the concentration of alcohol in the added solution (water) must equal the concentration of alcohol in the resulting solution:

$$40\%(30) + 0\%x = 25\%(30 + x)$$

Multiplying this equation by 100 to clear the percent symbol yields

$$40(30) + 0 = 25(30 + x)$$

$$1200 = 750 + 25x$$

$$450 = 25x$$

$$18 = x$$

The answer is (E).

27. Except for the first term, each term of the sequence is found by adding 4 to the term immediately preceding it. In other words, we are simply adding 4 to the sequence 200 times. This yields

$$4 \cdot 200 = 800$$

Adding the 2 in the first term gives $800 + 2 = 802$. The answer is (C).

We can also solve this problem formally. The first term of the sequence is 2, and since each successive term is 4 more than the term immediately preceding it, the second term is $2 + 4$, and the third term is $(2 + 4) + 4$, and the fourth term is $[(2 + 4) + 4] + 4$, etc. Regrouping yields (note that we rewrite the first term as $2 + 4(0)$. You'll see why in a moment.)

$$2 + 4(0), \, 2 + 4(1), \, 2 + 4(2), \, 2 + 4(3), \ldots$$

Notice that the number within each pair of parentheses is 1 less than the numerical order of the term. For instance, the *first* term has a 0 within the parentheses, the *second* term has a 1 within the parentheses, etc. Hence, the nth term of the sequence is

$$2 + 4(n - 1)$$

Using this formula, the 201st term is $2 + 4(201 - 1) = 2 + 4(200) = 2 + 800 = 802$.

28. For the first model, there are 5 options. So there are 5 different types of cars in this model. For the second model, there are the same number of different types of cars. Likewise, for the other two types of models. Hence, there are $5 + 5 + 5 + 5 = 20$ different types of cars. The answer is (E).

This problem illustrates the *Fundamental Principle of Counting*:

If an event occurs m times, and each of the m events is followed by a second event which occurs k times, then the first event follows the second event $m \cdot k$ times.

29. This is considered to be a hard problem. However, it is actually quite easy. By the definition given, the function @ merely cubes the term on the left and then subtracts 1 from it (the value of the term on the right is irrelevant). The term on the left is x. Hence, $x @ 1 = x^3 - 1$, and the answer is (C).

30.

$$\left((1 - x)* \right)* = (1 - x)*$$
$$\left(1 - (1 - x) \right)* = (1 - x)*$$
$$(1 - 1 + x)* = (1 - x)*$$
$$(x)* = (1 - x)*$$
$$1 - x = 1 - (1 - x)$$
$$1 - x = 1 - 1 + x$$
$$1 - x = x$$
$$1 = 2x$$
$$1/2 = x$$

The answer is (A).

Study Plan

Use the list below to review the appropriate chapters for any questions you missed.

Equations: Page 88
Questions: 1, 2, 3

Factoring: Page 106
Questions: 14, 15

Percents: Page 115
Questions: 24, 25

Algebraic Expressions: Page 110
Questions: 4, 5, 6

Inequalities: Page 74
Questions: 16, 17

Word Problems: Page 127
Question: 26

Number Theory: Page 37
Questions: 7, 8

Geometry: Page 43
Questions: 18, 19, 20

Sequences & Series: Page 135
Question: 27

Exponents & Roots: Page 101
Questions: 9, 10, 11

Averages: Page 93
Questions: 21, 22

Counting: Page 139
Question: 28

Fractions & Decimals: Page 81
Questions: 12, 13

Ratio & Proportion: Page 96
Question: 23

Defined Functions: Page 32
Questions: 29, 30

DATA SUFFICIENCY

- **FORMAT OF DATA SUFFICIENCY QUESTIONS**

- **THE DIRECTIONS**

- **ELIMINATION**

- **UNWARRANTED ASSUMPTIONS/TRICKY PROBLEMS**

- **CHECKING EXTREME CASES**

Format of Data Sufficiency Questions

Most people have much more difficulty with the Data Sufficiency problems than with the Standard Math problems. However, the mathematical knowledge and skill required to solve Data Sufficiency problems is no greater than that required to solve standard math problems. What makes Data Sufficiency problems appear harder at first is the complicated directions. But once you become familiar with the directions, you'll find these problems no harder than standard math problems. In fact, people usually become proficient more quickly on Data Sufficiency problems.

The Directions

The directions for Data Sufficiency questions are rather complicated. Before reading any further, take some time to learn the directions cold. Some of the wording in the directions below has been changed from the GMAT to make it clearer. You should never have to look at the instructions during the test.

<u>Directions:</u> Each of the following Data Sufficiency problems contains a question followed by two statements, numbered (1) and (2). You need not solve the problem; rather you must decide whether the information given is <u>sufficient</u> to solve the problem.

The correct answer to a question is

    A   if statement (1) ALONE is sufficient to answer the question but statement (2) alone is not sufficient;

    B   if statement (2) ALONE is sufficient to answer the question but statement (1) alone is not sufficient;

    C   if the two statements TAKEN TOGETHER are sufficient to answer the question, but NEITHER statement ALONE is sufficient;

    D   if EACH statement ALONE is sufficient to answer the question;

    E   if the two statements TAKEN TOGETHER are still NOT sufficient to answer the question.

<u>Numbers:</u>   Only real numbers are used. That is, there are no complex numbers.

<u>Drawings:</u>   The drawings are drawn to scale according to the information given in the question, but may conflict with the information given in statements (1) and (2).

You can assume that a line that appears straight is straight and that angle measures cannot be zero.

You can assume that the relative positions of points, angles, and objects are as shown.

All drawings lie in a plane unless stated otherwise.

<u>Example:</u>

In $\triangle ABC$ to the right, what is the value of y?

(1) $AB = AC$
(2) $x = 30$

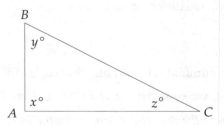

Explanation: By statement (1), $\triangle ABC$ is isosceles. Hence, its base angles are equal: $y = z$. Since the angle sum of a triangle is $180°$, we get $x + y + z = 180$. Replacing z with y in this equation and then simplifying yields $x + 2y = 180$. Since statement (1) does not give a value for x, we cannot determine the value of y from statement (1) alone. By statement (2), $x = 30$. Hence, $x + y + z = 180$ becomes $30 + y + z = 180$, or $y + z = 150$. Since statement (2) does not give a value for z, we cannot determine the value of y from statement (2) alone. However, using both statements in combination, we can find both x and z and therefore y. Hence, the answer is C.

Notice in the above example that the triangle appears to be a right triangle. However, that cannot be assumed: angle A may be $89°$ or $91°$, we can't tell from the drawing. **You must be very careful not to assume any more than what is explicitly given in a Data Sufficiency problem.**

Elimination

Data Sufficiency questions provide fertile ground for elimination. In fact, it is rare that you won't be able to eliminate some answer-choices. Remember, if you can eliminate at least one answer choice, the odds of gaining points by guessing are in your favor.

The following table summarizes how elimination functions with Data Sufficiency problems.

Statement	Choices Eliminated
(1) is sufficient	B, C, E
(1) is not sufficient	A, D
(2) is sufficient	A, C, E
(2) is not sufficient	B, D
(1) is not sufficient and (2) is not sufficient	A, B, D

Example 1:   What is the 1st term in sequence S?

   (1)   The 3rd term of S is 4.
   (2)   The 2nd term of S is three times the 1st, and the 3rd term is four times the 2nd.

(1) is no help in finding the first term of S. For example, the following sequences each have 4 as their third term, yet they have different first terms:

$$0, 2, 4$$
$$-4, 0, 4$$

This eliminates choices A and D. Now, even if we are unable to solve this problem, we have significantly increased our chances of guessing correctly—from 1 in 5 to 1 in 3.

Turning to (2), we <u>completely</u> ignore the information in (1). Although (2) contains a lot of information, it also is not sufficient. For example, the following sequences each satisfy (2), yet they have different first terms:

$$1, 3, 12$$
$$3, 9, 36$$

This eliminates B, and our chances of guessing correctly have increased to 1 in 2.

Next, we consider (1) and (2) together. From (1), we know *"the 3rd term of S is 4."* From (2), we know *"the 3rd term is four times the 2nd."* This is equivalent to saying the 2nd term is $\frac{1}{4}$ the 3rd term: $\frac{1}{4} \cdot 4 = 1$. Further, from (2), we know *"the 2nd term is three times the 1st."* This is equivalent to saying the 1st term is $\frac{1}{3}$ the 2nd term: $\frac{1}{3} \cdot 1 = \frac{1}{3}$. Hence, the first term of the sequence is fully determined:

$$\frac{1}{3}, 1, 4$$

The answer is C.

Example 2: In the figure to the right, what is the area of the triangle?

(1) $c^2 = 6^2 + 8^2$
(2) $x = 90$

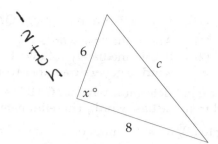

Recall that a triangle is a right triangle if and only if the square of the longest side is equal to the sum of the squares of the shorter sides (Pythagorean Theorem). Hence, (1) implies that the triangle is a right triangle. So the area of the triangle is $\frac{1}{2} \cdot 6 \cdot 8$. Note, there is no need to calculate the area—we just need to know that the area *can be* calculated. Hence, the answer is either A or D.

Turning to (2), we see immediately that we have a right triangle. Hence, again the area can be calculated. The answer is D.

Example 3: What is the value of $x - y$?

(1) $x + y = 3y - x$
(2) $x + y = x^3 + y^3$

Start with (1): $x + y = 3y - x$

Subtract $3y$ and add x to both sides of the equation: $2x - 2y = 0$

Divide by 2: $x - y = 0$

Hence, (1) is sufficient to determine the value of $x - y$, and therefore the answer is either A or D.

Turning to (2), we suspect there is not enough information since there are no like terms that can be combined as in (1). So use substitution to look for a counterexample. Let $x = y = 0$. Then $0 + 0 = 0^3 + 0^3$ and $x - y = 0$. However, if $x = 1$ and $y = 0$, then $1 + 0 = 1^3 + 0^3$ and $x - y = 1$. This shows that there are different pairs of numbers which satisfy (2) yet yield different values for $x - y$. Hence, (2) is not sufficient to determine the value of $x - y$. The answer is A. (Note, for the information to be sufficient, it is not enough to find *a* value of $x - y$; there must be a *unique* value.)

Example 4: If x is both the cube of an integer and between 2 and 200, what is the value of x?

(1) x is odd.
(2) x is the square of an integer.

Since x is both a cube and between 2 and 200, we are looking at the integers:

$$2^3, \ 3^3, \ 4^3, \ 5^3$$

which reduce to

$$8, 27, 64, 125$$

Since there are two odd integers in this set, (1) is not sufficient to uniquely determine the value of x. This eliminates choices A and D.

Next, there is only one perfect square, $64 = 8^2$, in the set. Hence, (2) is sufficient to determine the value of x. The answer is B.

Example 5:   Is CAB a code word in language Q?

(1)   ABC is the base word.

(2)   If C immediately follows B, then C can be moved to the front of the code word to generate another word.

From (1), we cannot determine whether CAB is a code word since (1) gives no rule for generating another word from the base word. This eliminates A and D.

Turning to (2), we still cannot determine whether CAB is a code word since now we have no word to apply this rule to. This eliminates B.

However, if we consider (1) and (2) together, then we can determine whether CAB is a code word:

From (1), ABC is a code word.

From (2), the C in the code word ABC can be moved to the front of the word: CAB.

Hence, CAB is a code word and the answer is C.

Example 6:   If x and y are positive integers, is $\sqrt{2xy}$ an integer?

(1) $y - x = 0$

(2) $xy = 1$ for some positive integer y.

From $y - x = 0$, we get $y = x$. Plug this into the expression $\sqrt{2xy}$:

$$\sqrt{2xx} = \sqrt{2x^2} = \sqrt{2}x$$

Since $\sqrt{2}$ is not an integer, $\sqrt{2xy}$ is not an integer. Hence, (1) is sufficient to answer the question.

Next, dividing both sides of $xy = 1$ by x yields $y = 1/x$. Plugging this into the expression $\sqrt{2xy}$ yields

$$\sqrt{2x\left(\frac{1}{x}\right)} = \sqrt{2}$$

Since $\sqrt{2}$ is not an integer, $\sqrt{2xy}$ is not an integer. Hence, (2) is also sufficient to answer the question. The answer is D.

Example 7:   What is the value of $\dfrac{3 + 2p}{3p}$?

(1) $p^2 - 5p + 4 = 0$.

(2)   The value of $\dfrac{1}{p} + \dfrac{2}{3}$ is -2.

Factoring (1) gives $(p - 1)(p - 4) = 0$.

Hence, $p - 1 = 0$ or $p - 4 = 0$.

So, $p = 1$ or $p = 4$.

However, if $p = 1$, then $\dfrac{3 + 2p}{3p} = \dfrac{5}{3}$. But if $p = 4$, then $\dfrac{3 + 2p}{3p} = \dfrac{11}{12}$. Therefore, (1) is not sufficient.

Translating (2) into an equation gives $\dfrac{1}{p} + \dfrac{2}{3} = -2$.

Adding the fractions on the left side gives $\dfrac{3+2p}{3p}=-2$. Hence, (2) is sufficient to answer the question. The answer is B.

Example 8:   If $x \neq -1$ and $y \neq \pm1$, then what is the value of $\dfrac{xy-x}{(x+1)(y-1)}$?

> (1) $x = 5$
> (2) $y = 4$

Begin by factoring the expression: $\dfrac{x(y-1)}{(x+1)(y-1)}$

Next, cancel the term $(y-1)$: $\dfrac{x}{x+1}$

Since x is the only variable left in the expression and (1) gives a value for x, we can calculate the value of the expression. Hence, (1) is sufficient to determine the value of the expression, and the answer is A or D.

Next, (2) is insufficient to determine the value of the expression since the value of x is not given. The answer is A.

Note, the value of y is not needed to determine the value of the expression since all the y's can be canceled from the expression; however, the value of x is needed since not all the x's can be canceled.

Unwarranted Assumptions

With data sufficiency problems, be careful not to read any more into a statement than what is given.

- **The main purpose of some difficult problems is to lure you into making an unwarranted assumption.**

If you avoid the temptation, these problems can become routine.

Example 6:   Did Incumbent _I_ get over 50% of the vote?

> (1)   Challenger _C_ got 49% of the vote.
> (2)   Incumbent _I_ got 25,000 of the 100,000 votes cast.

If you did not make any unwarranted assumptions, you probably did not find this to be a hard problem. What makes a problem difficult is not necessarily its underlying complexity; rather a problem is classified as difficult if many people miss it. A problem may be simple yet contain a psychological trap that causes people to answer it incorrectly.

The above problem is difficult because many people subconsciously assume that there are only two candidates. They then figure that since the challenger received 49% of the vote the incumbent received 51% of the vote. This would be a valid deduction if _C_ were the only challenger[*]. But we cannot assume that. There may be two or more challengers. Hence, (1) is insufficient.

---

[*] You might ask, "What if some people voted for none-of-the-above?" But don't get carried away with finding exceptions. The writers of the GMAT would not set a trap that subtle.

Now, consider (2) alone. Since Incumbent *I* received 25,000 of the 100,000 votes cast, *I* necessarily received 25% of the vote. Hence, the answer to the question is "No, the incumbent did not receive over 50% of the vote." Therefore, (2) is sufficient to answer the question. The answer is B.

Note, some people have trouble with (2) because they feel that the question asks for a "yes" answer. But on Data Sufficiency questions, a "no" answer is just as valid as a "yes" answer. What we're looking for is a *definite* answer.

Checking Extreme Cases

 When Drawing a Geometric Figure or Checking a Given One, Be Sure to Include Drawings of Extreme Cases As Well As Ordinary Ones.

Tip!

Example 1: In the figure to the right, *AC* is a chord and *B* is a point on the circle. What is the measure of angle x?

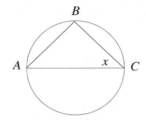

Although in the drawing *AC* looks to be a diameter, that cannot be assumed. All we know is that *AC* is a chord. Hence, numerous cases are possible, three of which are illustrated below:

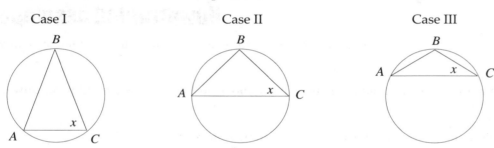

In Case I, x is greater than 45 degrees; in Case II, x equals 45 degrees; in Case III, x is less than 45 degrees. Hence, the given information is not sufficient to answer the question.

Example 2: Three rays emanate from a common point and form three angles with measures *p*, *q*, and *r*. What is the measure of *q* + *r* ?

It is natural to make the drawing symmetric as follows:

In this case, *p* = *q* = *r* = 120°, so *q* + *r* = 240°. However, there are other drawings possible. For example:

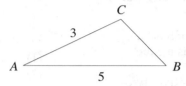

In this case, $q + r = 180°$. Hence, the given information is not sufficient to answer the question.

Example 3: In triangle ABC, $AB = 5$ and $AC = 3$. Is $BC < 7$?

The most natural drawing is the following:

In this case, BC is less than 7. However, there is another drawing possible, as follows:

In this case, BC is greater than 7. Hence, the given information is not sufficient to answer the question.

Example 4: In the figure to the right, what is the area of triangle $\triangle ABC$?

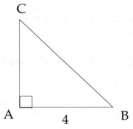

Although the drawing looks to be an isosceles triangle, that cannot be assumed. We are not given the length of side AC: it could be 4 units long or 100 units long, we don't know. Hence, the given information is not sufficient to answer the question.

Problem Set A: Solutions begin on page 304.

1. Is $p > q$?

    (1) $0 < p < 0.5$
    (2) $0.4 < q < 1$

2. What is the remainder if the positive integer y is divided by 3?

    (1) y is an even integer.
    (2) y is a multiple of 6.

3. What is the volume of rectangular box S?

    (1)   The total surface area of S is 22.
    (2)   The rectangular box S is a cube.

4. What is the value of the positive, two-digit number x?

    (1)   The sum of its digits is 4.
    (2)   The difference of its digits is 4.

5. How many students are enrolled in Math?

    (1)   There are 72 students enrolled in History.
    (2)   There are 40 students enrolled in both History and Math.

6. If ◊ is a function, is the value of $u \lozenge v$ less than 9?

    (1) $x \lozenge y = \sqrt{xy}$ for all x and y.
    (2) $u = 3$ and $v = 4$.

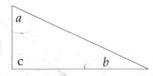

7. What is the area of the triangle above?

    (1) $a = x$, $b = 2x$, and $c = 3x$.
    (2)   The side opposite a is 4 and the side opposite b is 3.

8. Is 500 the average (arithmetic mean) score on the GMAT?

    (1)   Half of the people who take the GMAT score above 500 and half of the people score below 500.
    (2)   The highest GMAT score is 800 and the lowest score is 200.

9. Is $-x - y > -u - v$?

    (1) $x < u$ and $y < v$.
    (2) $x = 3$, $y = 4$, $u = 7$, and $v = 9$

10. If bowl S contains only marbles, how many marbles are in the bowl?

    (1)   If 1/4 of the marbles were removed, the bowl would be filled to 1/2 of its capacity.
    (2)   If 100 marbles were added to the bowl, it would be full.

11. Is x an odd integer?

    (1) x is the square root of an integer.
    (2) x is the square of an integer.

12. If Scott is 5 years older than Kathy, how old is Scott?

    (1)   Seven years ago, Scott was 3 times as old as Kathy was at that time.
    (2)   Kathy and Scott were born on the same day of the month.

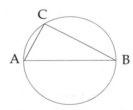

13. Triangle ABC is inscribed in a circle as shown above. What is the radius of the circle?

    (1) AB is a diameter of the circle.
    (2) $AC = 3$ and $BC = 4$.

14. Does $x - y = 0$?

    (1) $\dfrac{x}{y} > 0$
    (2) $x^2 = y^2$

15. If p is a positive integer, is p even?

    (1) p divided by 3 leaves a remainder of 1.
    (2) p divided by 4 leaves a remainder of 1.

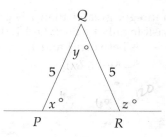

16. In the figure above, the circle is inscribed in the square. What is the area of the shaded region?

    (1) The area of the square is 16 square feet.
    (2) The area of the circle is 1.21π square feet.

17. If the positive integers $P, Q, R, S,$ and T increase in order of size, what is the value of R?

    (1) The value of T is 6.
    (2) The value of each successive integer is one more than the preceding integer.

18. If $x \neq 0, -1$, then is $\dfrac{1}{x}$ greater than $\dfrac{1}{x+1}$?

    (1) $x < 1$
    (2) $x > 1$

19. Does $z = 3$?

    (1) z is a solution of $z^2 - 2z - 3 = 0$.
    (2) z is a solution of $z^2 - 3z = 0$.

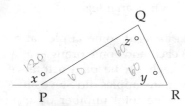

20. In the triangle above is $RP > PQ$?

    (1) $y = 180 - x$
    (2) $y = z = 60$

21. How many minutes are there in time period T?

    (1) Time period T extends from 12:00 midnight to 12:00 noon.
    (2) Time period T is 2 hours and 180 seconds long.

22. If $x \neq -1$ and $y \neq \pm 1$, then what is the value of $\dfrac{(xy)^2 - x^2}{(x+1)(y^2 - 1)}$?

    (1) $x = \dfrac{3}{2}$
    (2) $y = 2$

23. A dress was initially listed at a price that would have given the store a profit of 20 percent of the wholesale cost. What was the wholesale cost of the dress?

    (1) After reducing the asking price by 10 percent, the dress sold for a net profit of 10 dollars.
    (2) The dress sold for 50 dollars.

24. The set S of numbers has the following properties:

    I) If x is in S, then $\dfrac{1}{x}$ is in S.

    II) If both x and y are in S, then so is $x + y$.

    Is 3 in S?

    (1) $\dfrac{1}{3}$ is in S.
    (2) 1 is in S.

25. In $\triangle PQR$ above, what is the value of y?

    (1) $x = 60$
    (2) $y + z = 150$

Problem Set B: Solutions begin on page 316.

1. A certain brand of computer can be bought with or without a hard drive. What is the cost of the hard drive?
    (1)   The computer with the hard-drive costs 2,900 dollars.
    (2)   The computer without the hard drive costs 1,950 dollars more than the hard drive alone.

2. If $x = 3y$, what is the value of $x + y$?
    (1) $3y = 4x + 21$
    (2) $x > y$

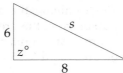

3. What is the area of the triangle above?
    (1) $z < 90$
    (2) $s^2 - 36 = 64$

4. The capacity of glass X is 80 percent of the capacity of glass Y. Glass X contains how many more ounces of punch than glass Y?
    (1)   Glass X contains 6 ounces of punch and is half-full, while glass Y is 75 percent full.
    (2)   Glass X is 70 percent full, and glass Y is 30 percent full.

5. An integer greater than 1 is prime if it is divisible only by itself and 1. Is n prime?
    (1) n is between 1 and 4.
    (2) $n^2 - 5n + 6 = 0$

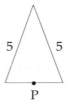

6. If point P (shown above) makes one complete revolution around the triangle, what is the length of the path traveled by P?
    (1)   The point P moves in a counter-clockwise direction at 1 unit per second and completes one revolution around the triangle in 15 seconds.
    (2)   The height of the triangle is 4.

7. If ϕ is a function, does $a \phi 1 = 1$ for all a?
    (1) $1 \phi a = 1$ for all a.
    (2) $a \phi b = b \phi a$ for all a and b.

8. S is a sequence such that each term is 3 more than the preceding term. What is the third term of S?
    (1)   The middle term of S is 11.
    (2)   The first term of S is 0.

9. Car X traveled from city A to city B in 30 minutes. What was the average speed of car X?
    (1)   Half the distance of the trip was covered at 50 miles per hour, and the other half of the distance was covered at 60 miles per hour.
    (2)   Car X traveled 30 miles during the trip.

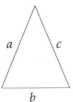

10. Is the triangle above isosceles?
    (1) $a = b$
    (2) $c \neq b$

11. Is the integer n greater than 3?
    (1) $2n$ is a positive integer.
    (2) $\sqrt{n}$ is an integer.

12. Steve bought some apples at a cost of \$.60 each and some oranges at a cost of \$.50 each. If he paid a total of \$4.10, how many apples did Steve buy?
    (1)   The total number of apples and oranges Steve bought was 8.
    (2)   Steve bought seven times as many oranges as apples.

13. If $x \neq 0$, is $|x| > 1$?
    (1) $x^4 < 1$
    (2) $\dfrac{|x|}{x} = 1$

14. If p and q are integers, is $pq + 1$ even?
    (1) If p is divided by 2, the remainder is 1.
    (2) If q is divided by 6, the remainder is 1.

15. If Q is a quadrilateral, is Q a rectangle?
    (1) Opposite sides of Q are parallel.
    (2) One of the four angles of Q is 90 degrees.

16. Cyclist M leaves point P at 12 noon and travels at constant velocity in a straight path. Cyclist N leaves point P at 2 PM, travels the same path at a constant velocity, and overtakes M at 4 PM. What was the average speed of N?
    (1) The velocity of Cyclist M was 20 miles per hour.
    (2) When Cyclist N overtook Cyclist M, both had traveled 60 miles.

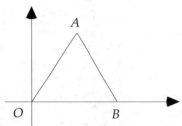

17. In the above figure, what is the area of $\triangle ABO$?
    (1) The coordinates of A are $(3, \sqrt{3})$.
    (2) $\triangle ABO$ is equilateral.

18. Does $x^2 = \sqrt{xy}$?
    (1) $\dfrac{y}{x^3} = 1$
    (2) $x^2 + y^2 = (x - y)^2$

19. If $\sqrt{a}$ is an integer, what is the value of a?
    (1) $\dfrac{1}{4} < \dfrac{1}{\sqrt{a}} < \dfrac{2}{3}$
    (2) The integer a is odd.

20. n is an integer between 1 and 84. What is the value of n?
    (1) The square root of n is divisible by 5.
    (2) n is both the square of an integer and the cube of an integer.

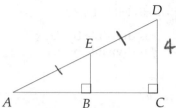

21. If E is the midpoint of AD, what is the length of EB?
    (1) $\angle D = 60°$
    (2) $DC = 4$

22. If $x, y \neq 0$, is $\dfrac{x}{y}$ an integer?
    (1) x is prime.
    (2) y is even.

23. Is $x^2 - y^2$ even?
    (1) $x + y$ is odd.
    (2) $x - y$ is odd.

24. If both x and y are integers, is $\sqrt{x^2 - y^2}$ an integer?
    (1) $x + y = 0$
    (2) $x^2 - y^2$ equals the cube of an integer.

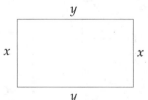

25. If the sides x of the rectangle above are increased by 3 units, what was the original area?
    (1) The resulting area is 20.
    (2) The resulting figure is a square.

Problem Set C: Solutions begin on page 330.

1. Suppose $3p + 4q = 11$. Then what is the value of q?

   (1) p is prime.
   (2) $q = -2p$

2. Is $x - y$ divisible by 5?

   (1) x is divisible by 5.
   (2) y is divisible by 5.

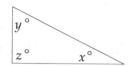

3. In the triangle above, what is the value of y?

   (1) $x = 90$
   (2) $y + z = 90$

4. A pair of pants and matching shirt cost $52. What is the cost of the shirt alone?

   (1) The pants cost $32.95.
   (2) The pants cost two and a half times as much as the shirt.

5. Is $p < q$?

   (1) $\dfrac{1}{3}p < \dfrac{1}{3}q$
   (2) $-p + x > -q + x$

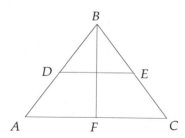

6. What is the perimeter of $\triangle ABC$ above?

   (1) The ratio of DE to BF is $1:3$.
   (2) D and E are midpoints of sides AB and CB, respectively.

7. A group of 50 people, all of who voted in the last Presidential election, were polled. How many men voted for the Democratic candidate?

   (1) Fifty percent of the men in the group voted for the Democratic candidate.
   (2) Twenty-five people in the group voted for the Democratic candidate.

8. Is the integer x even?

   (1) x is divisible by 5.
   (2) x is divisible by 7.

9. If x is a prime integer, does $x = 7$?

   (1) $x = \sqrt{n} + 1$, where n is an integer.
   (2) $x^2 - 11x + 28 = 0$

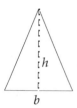

10. Let h denote the height and b the base of the triangle above. What is the area of the triangle?

    (1) $2b + h = 6$
    (2) $(bh)^2 = 16$

11. If $x \neq 0$, what is the value of $\sqrt{\dfrac{x^u}{x^v}}$?

    (1) $u = v$
    (2) x is a perfect square.

12. If a marble is selected at random from a bag containing only red and black marbles, what is the probability that the marble will be red?

    (1) There are 9 marbles in the bag.
    (2) There are 3 red marbles in the bag.

13. Is the negative number x less than -1?

   (1) $\dfrac{1}{x} < \dfrac{1}{2}$

   (2) $\dfrac{1}{x^2} < \dfrac{1}{2}$

14. What is the volume of a given cube?

   (1)   The ratio of an edge of the cube and the greatest distance between two points on the cube is $1:\sqrt{3}$.

   (2)   The length of the diagonal across a face of the cube is 2.

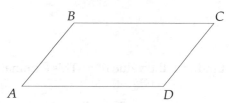

15. In the parallelogram above, what is the measure of $\angle ABC$?

   (1) $\angle BAD + \angle BCD = 140$

   (2) $\angle BAD = 140$

16. What is the value of $p^3 + 2p$?

   (1) $p^2 - 5p + 4 = 0$.

   (2)   The value of $p^2 + \dfrac{1}{p}$ is -2.

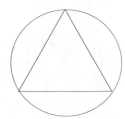

17. An equilateral triangle is inscribed in a circle, as shown above. What is the area of the triangle?

   (1)   The radius of the circle is 2.

   (2)   The ratio of the radius of the circle to a side of the triangle is $1:\sqrt{3}$.

18. If $2x + y = -31$, what is the value of x?

   (1) $(y - 2)\cdot(y - 2) - 4 = 0$

   (2) $y = 2$

19. The symbol Θ denotes one of the operations: addition, subtraction, multiplication, or division. What is the value of $\pi \Theta \sqrt{2}$?

   (1) $1 \Theta 1 = 1$

   (2) $0 \Theta 0 = 0$

20. Let ∇ denote a mathematical operation. Is it true that $x \nabla y = y \nabla x$ for all x and y?

   (1) $x \nabla y = \dfrac{1}{x} + \dfrac{1}{y}$

   (2) $x \nabla y = x - y$

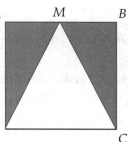

21. The triangle above has side DC of the square as its base. What is the area of the shaded region?

   (1) $DM = 5$

   (2) M is the midpoint of side AB.

22. If p and q are consecutive even integers, is $p > q$?

   (1) $p - 2$ and $q + 2$ are consecutive even integers.

   (2) p is prime.

23. S is a set of integers such that

   I)   If x is in S, then $-x$ is in S.

   II)   If both x and y are in S, then so is $x + y$.

   Is -2 in S?

   (1)   1 is in S.

   (2)   0 is in S.

24. If $m = 3^{n-1}$, what is the value of $\dfrac{m}{n}$?

   (1) $3^{4n-1} = 27$

   (2) $m = 3^{3n+1}$

25. If x is an integer, is $\sqrt{x^2 + y^2}$ an integer?

   (1) $x^2 - y^2 = 0$

   (2) $x^2 - k^2 = -y^2$ for some positive integer k.

Answers and Solutions to Problems

Answers Set A

1.	E	6.	C	11.	E	16.	D	21.	B
2.	B	7.	C	12.	A	17.	C	22.	A
3.	C	8.	E	13.	C	18.	B	23.	A
4.	C	9.	D	14.	C	19.	C	24.	D
5.	E	10.	C	15.	B	20.	B	25.	D

Solutions Set A

1. Is $p > q$?

    (1) $0 < p < 0.5$
    (2) $0.4 < q < 1$

(1) is not sufficient to answer the question since it does not indicate the value of q. This eliminates A and D.

Likewise, (2) is not sufficient since it does not indicate the value of p. This eliminates B.

Since the range of p and the range of q overlap, (1) and (2) together are still insufficient to answer the question. For example, if $p = 0.49$ and $q = 0.45$, then $p > q$. However, if $p = 0.49$ and $q = 0.9$, then $p < q$. The answer is E.

A number line will make the situation clearer:

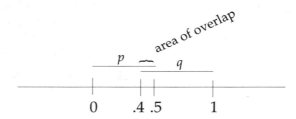

2. What is the remainder if the positive integer y is divided by 3?

    (1) y is an even integer.
    (2) y is a multiple of 6.

(1) is not sufficient to answer the question. For example,

$$4 \div 3 \text{ leaves a remainder of } 1.$$
$$6 \div 3 \text{ leaves a remainder of } 0.$$

However, (2) is sufficient to answer the question. If a number is a multiple of 6, then it is necessarily a multiple of 3; therefore, the remainder when the number is divided by 3 is 0. The answer is B.

3.   What is the volume of rectangular box S?

    (1)   The total surface area of S is 22.
    (2)   The rectangular box S is a cube.

(1) is not sufficient to determine the volume of box S since the dimensions of S can vary. The diagram below shows two boxes with different volumes yet both have surface area 22. This eliminates A and D.

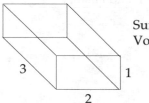

Surface area: 22
Volume: 1x2x3=6

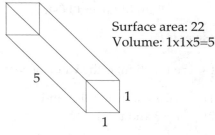

Surface area: 22
Volume: 1x1x5=5

(2) alone is not sufficient since the cube could be small, medium, or large. This eliminates B.

Next, consider (1) and (2) together. Since the total surface area of the cube is 22 and each of the cube's six faces has the same area, the area of each face is 22/6, or 11/3. Now, each face of the cube is a square with area 11/3, so the length of a side of the cube is $\sqrt{\dfrac{11}{3}}$. Hence, the volume of the cube is $\sqrt{\dfrac{11}{3}} \cdot \sqrt{\dfrac{11}{3}} \cdot \sqrt{\dfrac{11}{3}}$. Thus, (1) and (2) together are sufficient to find the volume. The answer is C.

4.   What is the value of the positive, two-digit number x?

    (1)   The sum of its digits is 4.
    (2)   The difference of its digits is 4.

Considering (1) only, x must be 13, 22, 31, or 40. Hence, (1) is not sufficient to determine the value of x.

Considering (2) only, x must be 40, 51, 15, 62, 26, 73, 37, 84, 48, 95, or 59. Hence, (2) is not sufficient to determine the value of x.

Considering (1) and (2) together, we see that 40 and only 40 is common to the two sets of choices for x. Hence, x must be 40. Thus, together (1) and (2) are sufficient to uniquely determine the value of x. The answer is C.

5.   How many students are enrolled in Math?

    (1)   There are 72 students enrolled in History.
    (2)   There are 40 students enrolled in both History and Math.

(1) tells us nothing about the number of people enrolled in Math. This eliminates A and D.

Although (2) tells us that there are at least 40 students enrolled in Math, there could be more. This eliminates B.

Taken together, (1) and (2) do tell us the number of History students who are not taking Math—32; however, the statements still do not tell us the number of students enrolled in Math.

The following Venn diagrams show two scenarios that satisfy both (1) and (2) yet have different numbers of students enrolled in Math:

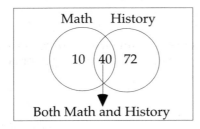

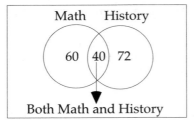

The answer is E.

6. If ◊ is a function, is the value of $u◊v$ less than 9?

(1) $x◊y = \sqrt{xy}$ for all x and y.
(2) $u = 3$ and $v = 4$.

(1) is not sufficient to answer the question since while it defines the function, it does not tell us the values of u and v. Next, (2) does tell us the values of u and v, but now we don't know the function. However, together (1) and (2) describe both the function and the values of u and v. Therefore, we can calculate the value of $u◊v$:

$$u◊v = 3◊4 = \sqrt{3 \cdot 4} = \sqrt{12} < 9$$

The answer is C.

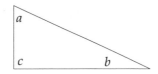

7. What is the area of the triangle above?

(1) $a = x$, $b = 2x$, and $c = 3x$.
(2) The side opposite a is 4 and the side opposite b is 3.

From (1) we can determine the measures of the angles:

$$a + b + c = x + 2x + 3x = 6x = 180$$

Dividing the last equation by 6 gives

$$x = 30$$

Hence, $a = 30$, $b = 60$, and $c = 90$. However, different size triangles can have these angle measures, as the diagram below illustrates:

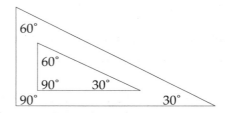

Hence, (1) is not sufficient to determine the area of the triangle.

Turning to (2), be careful not to assume that c is a right angle. Although from the diagram c appears to be a right angle, it could be 91° or 89°—we can't tell. Hence, (2) is not sufficient to determine the area of the triangle.

However, with both (1) and (2), c is a right angle and the area of the triangle is $\frac{1}{2} \cdot base \cdot height = \frac{1}{2} \cdot 4 \cdot 3$. The answer is C.

8.   Is 500 the average (arithmetic mean) score on the GMAT?

    (1)   Half of the people who take the GMAT score above 500 and half of the people score below 500.

    (2)   The highest GMAT score is 800 and the lowest score is 200.

Many students mistakenly think that (1) implies the average is 500. Suppose just 2 people take the test and one scores 700 (above 500) and the other scores 400 (below 500). Clearly, the average score for the two test-takers is not 500. (2) is less tempting. Knowing the highest and lowest scores tells us nothing about the other scores. Finally, (1) and (2) together do not determine the average since together they still don't tell us the distribution of most of the scores. The answer is E.

9.   Is $-x - y > -u - v$?

    (1) $x < u$ and $y < v$.

    (2) $x = 3, y = 4, u = 7$, and $v = 9$

Remember, multiplying both sides of an inequality by a negative number reverses the direction of the inequality. Multiplying both sides of $x < u$ and $y < v$ by –1 gives

$$-x > -u$$

$$-y > -v$$

Adding these inequalities yields

$$-x - y > -u - v$$

Hence, (1) is sufficient to answer the question.

As to (2), clearly by plugging in the given numbers we can answer the question. Hence, (2) is also sufficient. The answer, therefore, is D.

10.   If bowl S contains only marbles, how many marbles are in the bowl?

    (1)   If 1/4 of the marbles were removed, the bowl would be filled to 1/2 of its capacity.

    (2)   If 100 marbles were added to the bowl, it would be full.

(1) alone is insufficient to answer the question since we don't know the capacity of the bowl.

(2) alone is also insufficient to answer the question since we still don't know the capacity of the bowl.

However, (1) and (2) together are sufficient to answer the question: Let n be the number of marbles in the bowl, and let c be the capacity of the bowl. Then from (1), $n - \frac{1}{4}n = \frac{1}{2}c$, or $\frac{3}{2}n = c$. Next, from (2), $100 + n = c$. Hence, we have the system:

$$\frac{3}{2}n = c$$
$$100 + n = c$$

This system can be solved for n. Hence, the number of marbles in the bowl can be calculated, and the answer is C.

11.   Is x an odd integer?

   (1) x is the square root of an integer.
   (2) x is the square of an integer.

(1) alone is insufficient to answer the question. For example, consider $x = 2 = \sqrt{4}$ and $x = 3 = \sqrt{9}$; in one case x is even, in the other case x is odd.

   (2) alone is also insufficient. For example, $x = 4 = 2^2$ or $x = 9 = 3^2$; in one case x is even, in the other case x is odd.

   (1) and (2) taken together are still insufficient to determine whether x is odd. For example, both 9 (odd) and 16 (even) are squares of integers, fulfilling (2). As to (1), clearly both numbers are square roots of integers, namely 81 and 256, respectively. The answer is E.

12.   If Scott is 5 years older than Kathy, how old is Scott?

   (1)   Seven years ago, Scott was 3 times as old as Kathy was at that time.
   (2)   Kathy and Scott were born on the same day of the month.

Let S be Scott's age and K be Kathy's age. Then from the question setup, $S = K + 5$. Considering (1) alone, Scott's age 7 years ago can be represented as $S - 7$, and Kathy's age can be represented as $K - 7$. Translating (1) into an equation gives

$$S - 7 = 3(K - 7)$$

Combining this equation with $S = K + 5$ yields the system:

$$S - 7 = 3(K - 7)$$
$$S = K + 5$$

By solving this system, we can determine S. Hence, (1) is sufficient to determine Scott's age. This eliminates B, C, and E.

   Considering (2) alone, clearly the fact that they were born on the same day of the month does not determine Scott's age. For example, Scott could be 20 and Kathy 15, or Scott could be 30 and Kathy 25; yet in both cases they could be born on the same day of the month, but of course in different years. This eliminates D. Hence, the answer is A.

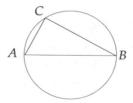

13.   Triangle *ABC* is inscribed in a circle as shown above. What is the radius of the circle?

   (1)   *AB* is a diameter of the circle.
   (2) $AC = 3$ and $BC = 4$.

(1) is insufficient since the circle can be small or large:

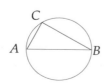
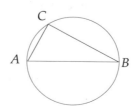

(2) is insufficient since the lengths of two sides of a triangle will determine the length of the third side only in special cases (for example, in a right triangle).

However, (1) and (2) taken together will determine the radius of the circle. Recall from geometry that a triangle inscribed in a semicircle is a right triangle. Hence, we can use the Pythagorean Theorem to calculate the length of AB:

$$AC^2 + BC^2 = AB^2$$

or

$$3^2 + 4^2 = AB^2$$

or

$$25 = AB^2$$

or

$$5 = AB$$

Hence, the radius of the circle is $\dfrac{diameter}{2} = \dfrac{5}{2}$. The answer is C.

14. Does $x - y = 0$?

    (1) $\dfrac{x}{y} > 0$

    (2) $x^2 = y^2$

Asking whether $x - y = 0$ is equivalent to asking whether $x = y$. Now, if $\dfrac{x}{y} > 0$, then both x and y are positive or both are negative. But this tells us nothing about their relative value. For example, $\dfrac{3}{2} > 0$ and $3 \ne 2$, and $\dfrac{2}{\sqrt{4}} > 0$ and $2 = \sqrt{4}$. Thus, (1) is insufficient, which eliminates A and D.

$x^2 = y^2$ implies that $x = \pm y$. Hence, we cannot determine whether $x = y$. Therefore, (2) is insufficient, which eliminates B.

However, together (1) and (2) are sufficient to determine whether $x = y$. From (1), x and y must both be positive or both negative, so we need to consider two cases:

Case I x and y are positive.	Case II x and y are negative.
From (2), we know that $x = \pm y$. But if $x = -y$, then x would be negative—contradicting our assumption that x is positive. Hence, $x = y$.	Again, from (2), we know that $x = \pm y$. But if $x = -y$, then x would be positive[*] —contradicting our assumption that x is negative. Hence, $x = y$.

The answer is C.

---

[*] Remember, y itself is negative. Hence, $-y$ is positive.

15. If p is a positive integer, is p even?

    (1) p divided by 3 leaves a remainder of 1.

    (2) p divided by 4 leaves a remainder of 1.

First, let's briefly review the concept of division. "Seven divided by 3 leaves a remainder of 1" means that $7 = 3 \cdot 2 + 1$. By analogy, "x divided by y leaves a remainder of 1" means that $x = y \cdot z + 1$, where z is an integer.

    Hence, (1) translates into $p = 3 \cdot z + 1$. If $z = 1$, then $p = 4$ which is even. But if $z = 2$, then $p = 7$ which is odd. Hence, (1) is insufficient to answer the question. This eliminates A and D.

    Now, (2) translates into $p = 4 \cdot z + 1$. The expression $4 \cdot z + 1$ is odd since it is 1 more than the even expression $4 \cdot z$[†]. Hence, (2) alone is sufficient to determine whether p is even. The answer is B.

16. In the figure above, the circle is inscribed in the square. What is the area of the shaded region?

    (1)   The area of the square is 16 square feet.

    (2)   The area of the circle is 1.21π square feet.

Consider (1) alone. Since the area of the square is 16, the length of a side is

$$\sqrt{16} = 4$$

Since the circle is inscribed in the square, a diameter of the circle has the same length as a side of the square. Hence, the radius of the circle is

$$\frac{diameter}{2} = \frac{4}{2} = 2$$

Therefore, the area of the circle is

$$\pi \cdot 2^2 = 4\pi$$

and the area of the shaded region is

$$16 - 4\pi$$

So the answer must be A or D.

    Next, consider (2) alone. Since the area of the circle is 1.21π, we get

$$\pi r^2 = 1.21\pi$$

Dividing by π yields

$$r^2 = 1.21$$

Taking the square root of both sides gives

$$r = 1.1$$

[†] $4 \cdot z$ is even since is a multiple of 2: $4 \cdot z = 2(2z)$.

So the diameter of the circle is

$$d = 2r = 2(1.1) = 2.2$$

Hence, a side of the square has length 2.2, and the area of the square is

$$(2.2)^2 = 4.84$$

Therefore, the area of the shaded region is

$$4.84 - 1.21\pi$$

The answer is D.

17. If the positive integers *P, Q, R, S,* and *T* increase in order of size, what is the value of *R*?

    (1)   The value of *T* is 6.
    (2)   The value of each successive integer is one more than the preceding integer.

Considering (1) alone, there are several possible sequences:

P	Q	R	S	T		P	Q	R	S	T
1	2	3	4	6		2	3	4	5	6

In the first sequence, *R* is 3, but in the second sequence *R* is 4. Hence, (1) is not sufficient to determine the value of *R*. This eliminates A and D.

    Considering (2) alone, there are many possible sequences:

P	Q	R	S	T		P	Q	R	S	T
1	2	3	4	5		10	11	12	13	14

Hence, (2) is not sufficient to determine the value of *R*. This eliminates B.

    Considering (1) and (2) together, there is sufficient information to determine the value of *R*. From (1), we know that *T* is 6; and therefore from (2), we see that *S* is 5. Continuing in this manner yields the following unique sequence:

P	Q	R	S	T
2	3	4	5	6

Hence, the value of *R* is 4. The answer is C.

18. If $x \neq 0, -1$, then is $\dfrac{1}{x}$ greater than $\dfrac{1}{x+1}$?

    (1) $x < 1$
    (2) $x > 1$

The key to this problem is to note that *x* can be negative. Consider (1) alone. If $x = \dfrac{1}{2}$, then $\dfrac{1}{x} = \dfrac{1}{\frac{1}{2}} = 1 \cdot \dfrac{2}{1} = 2$ and $\dfrac{1}{x+1} = \dfrac{1}{\frac{1}{2}+1} = \dfrac{1}{\frac{3}{2}} = \dfrac{2}{3}$. In this case, $\dfrac{1}{x}$ is greater than $\dfrac{1}{x+1}$. But if $x = -\dfrac{1}{2}$, then $\dfrac{1}{x} = \dfrac{1}{-\frac{1}{2}} = -2$ and $\dfrac{1}{x+1} = \dfrac{1}{-\frac{1}{2}+1} = \dfrac{1}{\frac{1}{2}} = 2$. In this case, $\dfrac{1}{x+1}$ is greater than $\dfrac{1}{x}$. Hence, (1) alone is insufficient to answer the question.

Consider (2) alone. Now, $x < x + 1$; and since $x > 1$, it is positive. Hence, dividing both sides of $x < x + 1$ by $x(x + 1)$ will not reverse the inequality:

$$\frac{x}{x(x+1)} < \frac{x+1}{x(x+1)}$$

Canceling yields

$$\frac{1}{x+1} < \frac{1}{x}$$

Hence, (2) is sufficient to answer the question. The answer is B.

19.   Does $z = 3$?

   (1) z is a solution of $z^2 - 2z - 3 = 0$.
   (2) z is a solution of $z^2 - 3z = 0$.

Factoring $z^2 - 2z - 3$ yields

$$(z + 1)(z - 3) = 0$$

Hence, $z = -1$ or $z = 3$. Therefore, (1) is insufficient to answer the question.

   Next, factoring $z^2 - 3z = 0$ yields

$$z(z - 3) = 0$$

Hence, $z = 0$ or $z = 3$. Therefore, (2) is also insufficient to answer the question.

   Next, considering (1) and (2) together, we see that only $z = 3$ is a solution of both $z^2 - 2z - 3 = 0$ and $z^2 - 3z = 0$. Hence, $z = 3$ and the answer is C.

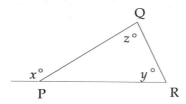

20.   In the triangle above is $RP > PQ$?

   (1) $y = 180 - x$
   (2) $y = z = 60$

The supplement of angle x is $180 - x$, which by (1) is also the value of y. Hence, we have an isosceles triangle:

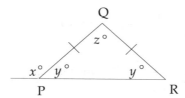

In this drawing, $RP > PQ$. However, this is not always the case. The triangle could be taller:

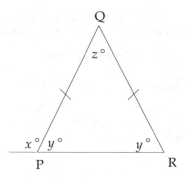

In this case, $RP < PQ$. Hence, (1) is not sufficient to answer the question.

Next, if $y = z = 60$, then the triangle is equilateral (remember, the angle sum of a triangle is 180°). Hence, in this case, RP is equal to PQ and so is not greater than PQ. Thus, (2) is sufficient, and the answer is B.

21. How many minutes are there in time period T?

  (1) Time period T extends from 12:00 midnight to 12:00 noon.
  (2) Time period T is 2 hours and 180 seconds long.

This is an easy question—provided you do not make any unwarranted assumptions. (1) is not sufficient since we do not know whether the time period T occurs entirely within one day. For instance, time period T could begin Monday at 12:00 midnight and end Tuesday at 12:00 noon. (2) is sufficient since it indicates that time period T is 123 minutes long. The answer is B.

22. If $x \ne -1$ and $y \ne \pm 1$, then what is the value of $\dfrac{(xy)^2 - x^2}{(x+1)(y^2-1)}$?

  (1) $x = \dfrac{3}{2}$
  (2) $y = 2$

Begin by simplifying the expression $\dfrac{(xy)^2 - x^2}{(x+1)(y^2-1)}$:

$$\frac{x^2 y^2 - x^2}{(x+1)(y^2-1)}$$

$$\frac{x^2(y^2-1)}{(x+1)(y^2-1)}$$

$$\frac{x^2}{x+1}$$

Since x is the only variable left in the expression and (1) gives a value for x, we can calculate the value of the expression. Hence, (1) is sufficient to determine the value of the expression, and the answer is A or D.

Next, (2) is insufficient to determine the value of the expression since the value of x is not given. The answer is A.

Note, the value of y is not needed to determine the value of the expression since all the y's can be canceled from the expression; however, the value of x is needed since not all the x's can be canceled.

23.   A dress was initially listed at a price that would have given the store a profit of 20 percent of the wholesale cost. What was the wholesale cost of the dress?

   (1)   After reducing the asking price by 10 percent, the dress sold for a net profit of 10 dollars.
   (2)   The dress sold for 50 dollars.

Consider just the question setup. Since the store would have made a profit of 20 percent on the wholesale cost, the original price P of the dress was 120 percent of the cost: $P = 1.2C$. Now, translating (1) into an equation yields:

$$P - .1P = C + 10$$

Simplifying gives

$$.9P = C + 10$$

Solving for P yields

$$P = \frac{C + 10}{.9}$$

Plugging this expression for P into $P = 1.2C$ gives

$$\frac{C + 10}{.9} = 1.2C$$

Since we now have only one equation involving the cost, we can determine the cost by solving for C. Hence, the answer is A or D.

   (2) is insufficient since it does not relate the selling price to any other information. Note, the phrase "initially listed" implies that there was more than one asking price. If it wasn't for that phrase, (2) would be sufficient. The answer is A.

24.   The set S of numbers has the following properties:

   I)   If x is in S, then $\dfrac{1}{x}$ is in S.

   II)   If both x and y are in S, then so is $x + y$.

   Is 3 in S?

   (1) $\dfrac{1}{3}$ is in S.
   (2)   1 is in S.

Consider (1) alone. Since $\dfrac{1}{3}$ is in S, we know from Property I that $\dfrac{1}{\diagup{}^{1}\!/_{3}} = 3$ is in S. Hence, (1) is sufficient.

   Consider (2) alone. Since 1 is in S, we know from Property II that $1 + 1 = 2^{*}$ is in S. Applying Property II again shows that $1 + 2 = 3$ is in S. Hence, (2) is also sufficient. The answer is D.

---

[*]   Note, nothing in Property II prevents x and y from standing for the same number. In this case both stand for 1.

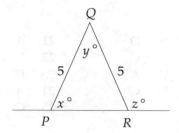

25. In $\triangle PQR$ above, what is the value of y?

    (1) $x = 60$
    (2) $y + z = 150$

Consider (1) alone. Since $\triangle PQR$ is isosceles, its base angles are equal:

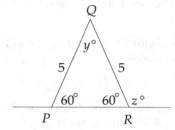

Remembering that the angle sum of a triangle is 180°, we see y is also 60°. Hence, (1) is sufficient to determine the value of y, and the answer must be A or D.

Next, consider (2) alone. Again since the base angles of an isosceles triangle are equal, the diagram becomes

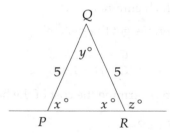

Since x and z form a straight angle, $x + z = 180$. Hence, we have the system:

$$x + z = 180$$
$$y + z = 150$$

Subtracting these equations yields $x - y = 30$. Since there are two variables and only one equation, we need another equation in order to determine y. However, since the angle sum of a triangle is 180°, $x + x + y = 180$, or $2x + y = 180$. This yields the system:

$$x - y = 30$$
$$2x + y = 180$$

Adding the equations gives $3x = 210$. Hence, $x = 70$. Plugging this value for x back into either equation gives $y = 40$. Thus, (2) alone is also sufficient to determine the value of y, and the answer is D.

Answers Set B

1.	**C**	6.	**D**	11.	**E**	16.	**D**	21.	**B**
2.	**A**	7.	**C**	12.	**D**	17.	**C**	22.	**E**
3.	**B**	8.	**B**	13.	**A**	18.	**A**	23.	**D**
4.	**A**	9.	**D**	14.	**C**	19.	**C**	24.	**A**
5.	**D**	10.	**A**	15.	**C**	20.	**D**	25.	**C**

Solutions Set B

1.   A certain brand of computer can be bought with or without a hard drive. What is the cost of the hard drive?

   (1)   The computer with the hard drive costs 2,900 dollars.
   (2)   The computer without the hard drive costs 1,950 dollars more than the hard drive alone.

Let C be the cost of the computer without the hard drive, and let H be the cost of the hard drive. Then translating (1) into an equation yields

$$C + H = 2,900$$

Since we don't know the value of C, we cannot determine the cost of the hard drive from this equation. Hence, (1) is insufficient, which eliminates A and D.

   Translating (2) into an equation yields

$$C = H + 1,950$$

As before, we cannot determine the cost of the hard drive since we still don't know the value of C. Hence, (2) is also insufficient, which eliminates B.

   Considering (1) and (2) together, we get the system:

$$C + H = 2,900$$
$$C = H + 1,950$$

By solving this system for H, we can determine the cost of the hard drive. The answer is C.

2.   If $x = 3y$, what is the value of $x + y$?

   (1) $3y = 4x + 21$
   (2) $x > y$

Considering (1) alone yields the following system:

$$3y = 4x + 21$$
$$x = 3y$$

By solving this system, we can determine the value of both x and y and therefore the value of $x + y$. Hence, (1) is sufficient, and the answer is either A or D.

   Considering (2) alone, we don't have enough information to determine the value of $x + y$. For example, if $x = 9$ and $y = 3$, then $x = 3y$ is satisfied ($9 = 3 \cdot 3$) and $x > y$ is also satisfied ($9 > 3$). In this case, $x + y = 9 + 3 = 12$. However, if $x = 3$ and $y = 1$, then $x = 3y$ is again satisfied ($3 = 3 \cdot 1$) and $x > y$ is also satisfied ($3 > 1$). In this case, $x + y = 3 + 1 = 4$. Since the value of $x + y$ is not unique, (2) is insufficient. The answer is A.

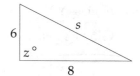

3.   What is the area of the triangle above?

(1) $z < 90$

(2) $s^2 - 36 = 64$

Consider (1) alone. Since we do not know the value of z, the triangle can vary in size. The two triangles illustrated below both satisfy (1) yet have different areas:

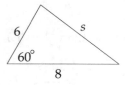
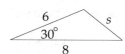

Hence, (1) is insufficient.

Consider (2) alone. The expression $s^2 - 36 = 64$ can be rewritten as follows:

$$s^2 = 6^2 + 8^2$$

You should recognize this as the Pythagorean Theorem. Hence, we have a right triangle, and we can calculate the area:

$$\frac{1}{2} \cdot base \cdot height = \frac{1}{2} \cdot 8 \cdot 6$$

Hence, (2) is sufficient and the answer is B.

4.   The capacity of glass X is 80 percent of the capacity of glass Y. Glass X contains how many more ounces of punch than glass Y?

(1)   Glass X contains 6 ounces of punch and is half-full, while glass Y is 75 percent full.
(2)   Glass X is 70 percent full, and glass Y is 30 percent full.

Since "_the capacity of glass X is 80 percent of the capacity of glass Y,_" we get

$$X = .8Y$$

Translating (1) into an equation yields

$$.5X = 6$$

By solving the system of two equations above, we can determine the values of both X and Y and therefore how many more ounces of punch glass X contains than glass Y. Hence, (1) is sufficient and the answer is A or D.

Next, (2) is not sufficient since it does not provide any absolute numbers. The following diagram shows two situations: one in which Glass X contains 5.2 more ounces of punch than glass Y, and one in which Glass X contains 2.6 more ounces than glass Y.

Scenario I (Glass X contains 5.2 more ounces than glass Y.)

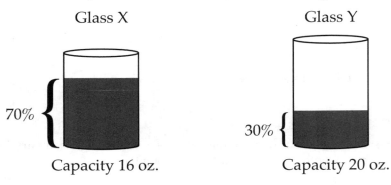

Scenario II (Glass X contains 2.6 more ounces than glass Y.)

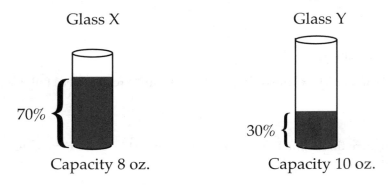

The answer is A.

5.   An integer greater than 1 is prime if it is divisible only by itself and 1. Is n prime?

   (1) n is between 1 and 4.

   (2) $n^2 - 5n + 6 = 0$

Consider (1) alone. The only integers between 1 and 4 are 2 and 3, and both are prime. Hence, from (1) we can determine that n is prime, and the answer is A or D.

Consider (2) alone. Solving the equation $n^2 - 5n + 6 = 0$ for n gives

$$(n - 2)(n - 3) = 0$$

or

$$n - 2 = 0 \quad \text{or} \quad n - 3 = 0$$

Hence, $n = 2$ or $n = 3$. Again, both 2 and 3 are prime. Hence, (2) is also sufficient, and the answer is D.

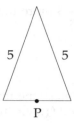

6. If point P (shown above) makes one complete revolution around the triangle, what is the length of the path traveled by P?

    (1) The point P moves in a counterclockwise direction at 1 unit per second and completes one revolution around the triangle in 15 seconds.
    (2) The height of the triangle is 4.

Consider (1) alone. Since P moves at 1 unit per second and travels around the triangle in 15 seconds, the perimeter of the triangle is 15. Hence, (1) is sufficient.

Consider (2) alone. Add the height to the diagram:

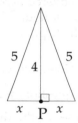

Applying the Pythagorean Theorem to either of the right triangles formed above yields
$$x^2 + 4^2 = 5^2$$
Solving for x yields

$$x = 3$$

Hence, the base of the triangle is $2x = 2 \cdot 3 = 6$, and therefore the perimeter is $5 + 5 + 6 = 16$. Thus, (2) is also sufficient. The answer is D.

7. If ϕ is a function, does $a \phi 1 = 1$ for all a?

    (1) $1 \phi a = 1$ for all a.
    (2) $a \phi b = b \phi a$ for all a and b.

(1) gives us no device for moving a to the front of the function. Hence, we cannot determine whether $a \phi 1 = 1$ from (1) alone.

(2) gives us a device for moving a to the front of the function, but now we are not given any values for $a \phi b$. Hence, (2) is also insufficient.

However, together (1) and (2) are sufficient to determine whether $a \phi 1 = 1$:

$$a \phi 1 =$$

$$1 \phi a = \qquad \text{[By statement (2)]}$$

$$1 \qquad \text{[By statement (1)]}$$

The answer is C.

8. S is a sequence such that each term is 3 more than the preceding term. What is the third term of S?

   (1) The middle term of S is 11.
   (2) The first term of S is 0.

Considered alone, (1) is not sufficient to determine the third term. For example, the following sequences satisfy both the question setup and (1), yet they have different third terms:

$$8, 11, \textcircled{14}$$

$$5, 8, \textcircled{11}, 14, 17$$

Considered alone, (2) is sufficient to determine the third term. Since the first term is 0, the second term must be $0 + 3 = 3$ and the third term must be $3 + 3 = 6$. The answer is B.

9. Car X traveled from city A to city B in 30 minutes. What was the average speed of car X?

   (1) Half the distance of the trip was covered at 50 miles per hour, and the other half of the distance was covered at 60 miles per hour.
   (2) Car X traveled 30 miles during the trip.

Recall that *Average Speed* $= \dfrac{\text{Total Distance}}{\text{Total Time}}$. Now, the setup to the question gives the total time for the trip—30 minutes. Hence, to answer the question, we need to find the distance of the trip.

Consider (1) alone. Let t equal the time for the first half of the trip. Then since the whole trip took 30 minutes (or $\dfrac{1}{2}$ hour), the second half of the trip took $\dfrac{1}{2} - t$ hours. Now, from the formula Distance = Rate × Time, we get for the first half of the trip:

$$\frac{d}{2} = 50 \cdot t$$

And for the second half of the trip, we get

$$\frac{d}{2} = 60\left(\frac{1}{2} - t\right)$$

By solving the above system, we can determine the distance d between the cities. Therefore, (1) is sufficient to answer the question.

Consider (2) alone. Since (2) gives the distance of the trip—30 miles, we can immediately conclude that (2) is also sufficient to answer the question. The answer is D.

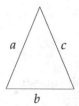

10. Is the triangle above isosceles?

(1) $a = b$
(2) $c \neq b$

By definition, a triangle with two equal sides is isosceles. Hence, (1) is sufficient to answer the question.

However, (2) is not sufficient to answer the question since a *could* equal b or c but it may not, as the following diagrams illustrate:

$a = b$ $a = c$ $a \neq b, c$

Isosceles   Isosceles   Not Isosceles

 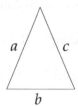 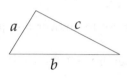

The answer is A.

11. Is the integer n greater than 3?

(1) $2n$ is a positive integer.
(2) $\sqrt{n}$ is an integer.

(1) is not sufficient to answer the question. For example, $2 \cdot 1 = 2$ is a positive integer and $1 < 3$. Further, $2 \cdot 4 = 8$ is a positive integer and $4 > 3$.

(2) is also insufficient. For example, $\sqrt{1} = 1$ is an integer and $1 < 3$. Further, $\sqrt{16} = 4$ is an integer and $16 > 3$.

Since together (1) and (2) do not put any further restrictions on n than does (2) alone, taken together they are still insufficient to answer the question. The answer is E.

12. Steve bought some apples at a cost of $.60 each and some oranges at a cost of $.50 each. If he paid a total of $4.10, how many apples did Steve buy?

(1) The total number of apples and oranges Steve bought was 8.
(2) Steve bought seven times as many oranges as apples.

Let x denote the number of apples bought, and let y denote the number of oranges bought. Then, translating the question setup into an equation yields

$$.60x + .50y = 4.10$$

Since there are two variables and only one equation, the key to this problem is finding a second equation that relates x and y. From (1), we get

$$x + y = 8$$

Since this equation relates x and y, (1) is sufficient to answer the question.

Next, from (2), we get

$$y = 7x$$

Since this equation also relates x and y, (2) is again sufficient to answer the question. The answer is D.

13.   If $x \neq 0$, is $|x| > 1$?

   (1) $x^4 < 1$

   (2) $\dfrac{|x|}{x} = 1$

Consider (1) alone. The only numbers raised to the fourth power that are less than 1 are numbers between -1 and 1. Now, the absolute value of any number between -1 and 1 is less than 1. Hence, (1) is sufficient to answer the question.

Consider (2) alone. The expression $\dfrac{|x|}{x} = 1$ tells us only that x is positive. Hence, (2) is insufficient to answer the question. For example, if $x = 1$, then $\dfrac{|x|}{x} = \dfrac{|1|}{1} = \dfrac{1}{1} = 1$ and $|x| = 1 \not> 1$. However, if $x = 2$, then $\dfrac{|x|}{x} = \dfrac{|2|}{2} = \dfrac{2}{2} = 1$ and $|x| = 2 > 1$. The answer is A.

14.   If p and q are integers, is $pq + 1$ even?

   (1)   If p is divided by 2, the remainder is 1.
   (2)   If q is divided by 6, the remainder is 1.

(1) is insufficient. For example, suppose $p = 3 = 2 \cdot 1 + 1$. Now, if $q = 1$, then $pq + 1 = 3 \cdot 1 + 1 = 4$—which is even. However, if $q = 2$, then $pq + 1 = 3 \cdot 2 + 1 = 7$—which is odd. A similar analysis shows that (2) is also insufficient.

Taken together, however, (1) and (2) are sufficient: From (1), $p = 2u + 1$; and from (2), $q = 6v + 1$, where u and v are integers. Hence, $pq + 1 =$

$$(2u + 1)(6v + 1) + 1 =$$

$$12uv + 2u + 6v + 1 + 1 =$$

$$12uv + 2u + 6v + 2 =$$

$$2(6uv + u + 3v + 1)$$

Since we have written $pq + 1$ as a multiple of 2, it is even. The answer is C.

Method II

Since both p and q leave remainders of 1 when divided by an even number, both are odd. Now, the product of two odd numbers is another odd number. Hence, pq is odd, and therefore $pq + 1$ is even.

15. If Q is a quadrilateral, is Q a rectangle?
    (1)   Opposite sides of Q are parallel.
    (2)   One of the four angles of Q is 90 degrees.

Note, a quadrilateral is a closed figure formed by four straight lines. (1) is not sufficient, as the diagrams below illustrate:

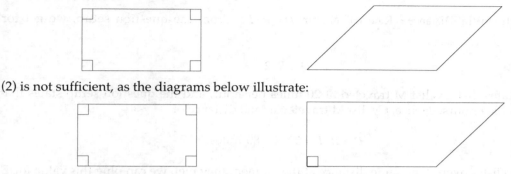

(2) is not sufficient, as the diagrams below illustrate:

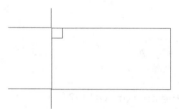

Now, (1) and (2) together generate the following diagram:

Here, our goal is to show that the other three angles are also 90 degrees. It will help to extend the sides as follows:

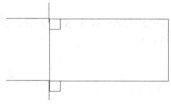

Since corresponding angles are congruent, we get

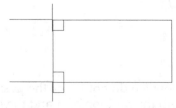

Or

Continuing in this manner will show that the other two angles are also 90 degrees. Hence, Q is a rectangle, and the answer is C.

16. Cyclist M leaves point P at 12 noon and travels at constant velocity in a straight path. Cyclist N leaves point P at 2 PM, travels the same path at a constant velocity, and overtakes M at 4 PM. What was the average speed of N?

(1)   The velocity of Cyclist M was 20 miles per hour.
(2)   When Cyclist N overtook Cyclist M, both had traveled 60 miles.

Recall the formula Distance = Rate × Time, or $D = R \cdot T$. From the question setup, we get for Cyclist N:

$$D = R \cdot 2$$

Now, (1) states that Cyclist M traveled at 20 miles per hour, and the question setup states that Cyclist M took 4 hours. Hence, Cyclist M traveled a total distance of

$$D = R \cdot T = 20 \cdot 4 = 80 \text{ miles}$$

Since the cyclists covered the same distance at the moment they met, we can plug this value for D into the equation $D = R \cdot 2$ and thereby determine the rate of Cyclist N. Hence, (1) is sufficient.

(2) states that the distance the cyclists traveled was 60 miles. Hence, we can plug this value for D into the equation $D = R \cdot 2$ and thereby determine the rate of Cyclist N. So (2) is also sufficient, and the answer is D.

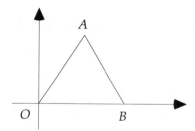

17. In the above figure, what is the area of $\triangle ABO$?

(1)   The coordinates of A are $(3, \sqrt{3})$.
(2) $\triangle ABO$ is equilateral.

(1) is insufficient to determine the area since we have no means of determining the length of OB. For example, each diagram below is possible:

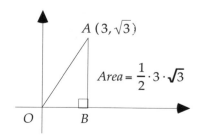 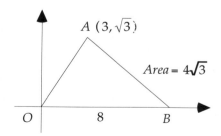

(2) is also insufficient since now we do not know the position of A. Together, however, (1) and (2) are sufficient since now both the position of A and the length of OB are known. Drawing an altitude yields

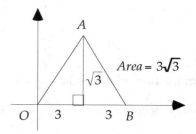

The answer is C.

18. Does $x^2 = \sqrt{xy}$?

(1) $\dfrac{y}{x^3} = 1$

(2) $x^2 + y^2 = (x - y)^2$

Consider (1) alone. Solving the equation $\dfrac{y}{x^3} = 1$ for y gives

$$y = x^3$$

Plugging this into the expression $\sqrt{xy}$ yields

$$\sqrt{x \cdot x^3}$$

Adding exponents gives

$$\sqrt{x^4}$$

Taking the square root yields

$$x^2$$

Hence, from (1) alone, we can determine that x^2 does equal $\sqrt{xy}$.

  Consider (2) alone. Multiplying out the expression on the right side of $x^2 + y^2 = (x - y)^2$ gives

$$x^2 + y^2 = x^2 - 2xy + y^2$$

Subtracting x^2 and y^2 from both sides of the equation yields

$$0 = -2xy$$

Dividing by –2 gives

$$0 = xy$$

Hence, $x = 0$ or $y = 0$ or both. If $x = 0$, then $x^2 = \sqrt{xy}$ becomes

$$0^2 = \sqrt{0 \cdot y}$$

This in turn reduces to

$$0 = 0$$

Hence, if $x = 0$, then we can determine that x^2 does equal $\sqrt{xy}$.

However, if $y = 0$, then $x^2 = \sqrt{xy}$ becomes

$$x^2 = \sqrt{x \cdot 0}$$

or

$$x^2 = 0$$

But this equation is true only if $x = 0$, which is not required. Hence, (2) is insufficient. The answer is A.

19.   If $\sqrt{a}$ is an integer, what is the value of a?

   (1) $\dfrac{1}{4} < \dfrac{1}{\sqrt{a}} < \dfrac{2}{3}$

   (2)   The integer a is odd.

(1) is not sufficient since two integers, 4 and 9, satisfy the inequality $\dfrac{1}{4} < \dfrac{1}{\sqrt{a}} < \dfrac{2}{3}$:

$$\frac{1}{4} < \left(\frac{1}{\sqrt{4}} = \frac{1}{2} \right) < \frac{2}{3} \qquad \frac{1}{4} < \left(\frac{1}{\sqrt{9}} = \frac{1}{3} \right) < \frac{2}{3}$$

Clearly, (2) is not sufficient. However, together (1) and (2) determine that $a = 9$ since 4 is even. The answer is C.

20. n is an integer between 1 and 84. What is the value of n?

   (1)   The square root of n is divisible by 5.
   (2) n is both the square of an integer and the cube of an integer.

Consider (1) alone. Twenty-five is the only integer between 1 and 84 whose square root is divisible by 5. Hence, (1) is sufficient.

   Consider (2) alone. Below is a list of all cubes between 1 and 84:

8, 27, 64

Now, 64 is the only number in this list that is also a square, $64 = 8^2$. Hence, (2) is also sufficient. The answer is D.

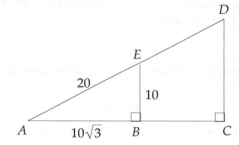

21. If *E* is the midpoint of *AD*, what is the length of *EB*?

(1)   ∠*D* = 60°
(2)   *DC* = 4

Recall from geometry that if two angles of one triangle are equal to two angles of another triangle then the triangles are similar. Hence, Δ*ACD* is similar to Δ*ABE* since they share angle *A* and both are right triangles.

Consider (1) alone. Since angle *D* is 60°, angle *A* is 30° (*A* + *C* + *D* = *A* + 90 + 60 = 180). Hence, both Δ*ACD* and Δ*ABE* are 30°–60°–90° triangles. However, unless we know the length of at least one of the sides, we cannot calculate the length of *EB*. For example, in the following diagram each drawing satisfies both the question setup and Statement (1) yet each has a different length for *EB*:

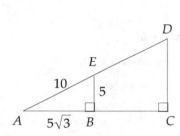 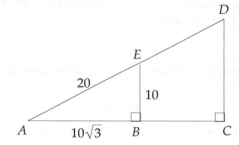

Hence, (1) is insufficient.

Before we consider (2), let's calculate the relative sizes of *EB* and *DC*. Since *E* is the midpoint of *AD*, the diagram becomes

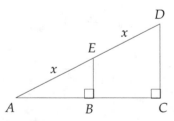

Since Δ*ABE* and Δ*ACD* are similar, their corresponding sides are proportional:

$$\frac{EB}{EA} = \frac{DC}{DA}$$

or

$$\frac{EB}{x} = \frac{DC}{2x}$$

Solving for *EB* yields

$$EB = \frac{1}{2}DC$$

Now from (2), *DC* = 4. Hence, $EB = \frac{1}{2} \cdot 4 = 2$. Thus, (2) is sufficient and the answer is B.

22. If $x, y \neq 0$, is $\dfrac{x}{y}$ an integer?

   (1) x is prime.
   (2) y is even.

(1) is not sufficient since we don't know the value of y. Similarly, (2) is not sufficient.
Furthermore, (1) and (2) together are still insufficient since there is an even prime number—2.
For example, let x be the prime number 2, and let y be the even number 2 (don't forget that
different variables can stand for the same number). Then $\dfrac{x}{y} = \dfrac{2}{2} = 1$, which is an integer. For all

other values of x and y, $\dfrac{x}{y}$ is not an integer. (Plug in a few values to verify this.) The answer is E.

23. Is $x^2 - y^2$ even?

   (1) $x + y$ is odd.
   (2) $x - y$ is odd.

Consider (1): $x + y$ is odd. For two numbers to produce an odd sum, one number must be odd
and the other even. In such a case, the difference of the two numbers will also be odd. Hence,
$x - y$ is also odd and

$$x^2 - y^2 = (x + y)(x - y) = odd \times odd = odd$$

   A similar analysis using (2) alone gives the same result. The answer is D.

24. If both x and y are integers, is $\sqrt{x^2 - y^2}$ an integer?

   (1) $x + y = 0$
   (2) $x^2 - y^2$ equals the cube of an integer.

If $x + y = 0$, then $y = -x$. Substituting this into the expression $\sqrt{x^2 - y^2}$ yields

$$\sqrt{x^2 - (-x)^2}$$

or

$$\sqrt{x^2 - x^2}$$

or

$$\sqrt{0} = 0$$

Since 0 is an integer, (1) is sufficient.

   However, (2) is not sufficient. For example, if $x = 3$ and $y = 1$, then $x^2 - y^2 = 3^2 - 1^2 = 9 - 1 = 8$,
which is a cube. But $\sqrt{8}$ is not an integer. On the other hand, if $x = 1$ and $y = 0$, then
$x^2 - y^2 = 1^2 - 0^2 = 1$—which is a cube. But now $\sqrt{1} = 1$ is an integer. The answer is A.

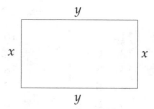

25. If the sides x of the rectangle above are increased by 3 units, what was the original area?

(1)　The resulting area is 20.
(2)　The resulting figure is a square.

The area of the original rectangle is $A = xy$. So the goal in this problem is to find the values of x and y.

Lengthening side x of the original figure by 3 units yields

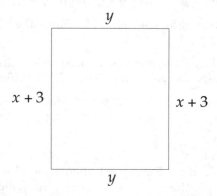

From (1), the area of this figure is $y(x + 3) = 20$. Since we have two variables and only one equation, we cannot find the values of x and y. Hence, (1) is not sufficient.

If the resulting figure is a square, then $y = x + 3$. Again, since we have two variables and only one equation, we cannot find the values of x and y. Hence, (2) is not sufficient.

However, (1) and (2) together form the system:

$$y(x + 3) = 20$$
$$y = x + 3$$

From this system, we can determine the values of both x and y, and therefore calculate the area of the original rectangle. The answer is C.

Answers Set C

1.	**B**	6.	**E**	11.	**A**	16.	**B**	21.	**C**
2.	**C**	7.	**E**	12.	**C**	17.	**A**	22.	**A**
3.	**E**	8.	**E**	13.	**B**	18.	**B**	23.	**A**
4.	**D**	9.	**B**	14.	**B**	19.	**C**	24.	**D**
5.	**D**	10.	**B**	15.	**D**	20.	**D**	25.	**D**

Solutions Set C

1.   Suppose $3p + 4q = 11$. Then what is the value of q?

   (1) p is prime.
   (2) $q = -2p$

(1) is insufficient. For example, if $p = 3$ and $q = \dfrac{1}{2}$, then $3p + 4q = 3(3) + 4\left(\dfrac{1}{2}\right) = 11$. However, if $p = 5$ and $q = -1$, then $3p + 4q = 3(5) + 4(-1) = 11$. Since the value of q is not unique, (1) is insufficient.

   Turning to (2), we now have a system of two equations in two unknowns. Hence, the system can be solved to determine the value of q. Thus, (2) is sufficient, and the answer is B.

2.   Is $x - y$ divisible by 5?

   (1) x is divisible by 5.
   (2) y is divisible by 5.

(1) is not sufficient. For example, if $x = 5$ and $y = 1$, then $x - y = 5 - 1 = 4$, which is not divisible by 5. However, if $x = 5$ and $y = -5$, then $x - y = 5 - (-5) = 10$, which is divisible by 5. A similar analysis shows that (2) is not sufficient.

   However, together, (1) and (2) are sufficient. Since both x and y are now divisible by 5, we can set $x = 5u$ and $y = 5v$. So $x - y = 5u - 5v = 5(u - v)$. Since $x - y$ can be written as a multiple of 5, it too is divisible by 5. The answer is C.

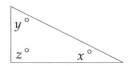

3.   In the triangle above, what is the value of y?

   (1) $x = 90$
   (2) $y + z = 90$

(1) is insufficient since we don't know the value of z. Similarly, (2) is insufficient since a variety of values of y and z can add up to 90. For example, $y + z = 45 + 45 = 90$ and $y + z = 60 + 30 = 90$. Together, (1) and (2) are still insufficient to determine y. For example, $x + (y + z) = 90 + (45 + 45) = 180$ and $x + (y + z) = 90 + (60 + 30) = 180$. The answer is E.

4.   A pair of pants and matching shirt cost $52. What is the cost of the shirt alone?

   (1)   The pants cost $32.95.
   (2)   The pants cost two and a half times as much as the shirt.

Let p denote the cost of the pants, and let s denote the cost of the shirt. Then from the question setup, $p + s = 52$. Since we have one equation in two unknowns, the goal in this problem is to find another equation relating p and s.

Clearly, (1) is sufficient: we can subtract the cost of the pants from the total bill to obtain the cost of the shirt. (2) is also sufficient. Translating (2) into an equation gives $p = 2.5s$. We now have a system of two equations in two unknowns, so the cost of the shirt can be determined. The answer is D.

5.   Is $p < q$?

(1) $\frac{1}{3}p < \frac{1}{3}q$

(2) $-p + x > -q + x$

Multiplying both sides of $\frac{1}{3}p < \frac{1}{3}q$ by 3 yields

$$p < q$$

Hence, (1) is sufficient. As to (2), subtract x from both sides of $-p + x > -q + x$:

$$-p > -q$$

Multiply both sides of this inequality by -1, and recall that multiplying both sides of an inequality by a negative number reverses the inequality:

$$p < q$$

Hence, (2) is also sufficient. The answer is D.

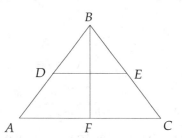

6.   What is the perimeter of $\triangle ABC$ above?

(1)   The ratio of DE to BF is $1:3$.
(2) D and E are midpoints of sides AB and CB, respectively.

Since we do not even know whether BF is an altitude, nothing can be determined from (1). More importantly, there is no information telling us the absolute size of the triangle.

As to (2), although from geometry we know that $DE = \frac{1}{2}AC$, this relationship holds for any size triangle. Hence, (2) is also insufficient.

Together, (1) and (2) are also insufficient since we still don't have information about the size of the triangle, so we can't determine the perimeter. The answer is E.

7.   A group of 50 people, all of who voted in the last Presidential election, were polled. How many men voted for the Democratic candidate?

(1)   Fifty percent of the men in the group voted for the Democratic candidate.
(2)   Twenty-five people in the group voted for the Democratic candidate.

Since from (1) alone we cannot determine the total number of men polled, (1) is not sufficient.

(2) is also insufficient. While we know twenty-five people voted Democratic, we have no information whatsoever about how many of them were men.

Together (1) and (2) are still insufficient. For example, the group could have 30 men 15 of who voted Democratic and 20 women 10 of who voted Democratic Or the numbers of men and women could be switched. Thus, we still cannot determine the number of men in the group. The answer is E.

8.   Is the integer x even?

   (1) x is divisible by 5.
   (2) x is divisible by 7.

(1) is not sufficient since both 5 (odd) and 10 (even) are divisible by 5. Similarly, (2) is not sufficient since both 7 and 14 are divisible by 7. Together (1) and (2) are still not sufficient since 35 is divisible by both 5 and 7 as is 70. The answer is E.

9.   If x is a prime integer, does $x = 7$?

   (1) $x = \sqrt{n} + 1$, where n is an integer.
   (2) $x^2 - 11x + 28 = 0$

Both 3 and 7 are prime, and $3 = \sqrt{4} + 1$ while $7 = \sqrt{36} + 1$. Hence, (1) is not sufficient. Consider (2) alone. Factoring the equation $x^2 - 11x + 28 = 0$ gives

$$(x - 4)(x - 7) = 0$$
$$x - 4 = 0 \quad \text{or} \quad x - 7 = 0$$

Hence, $x = 4$ or $x = 7$. But 4 is not prime. Therefore, $x = 7$, and the answer is B.

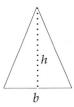

10.   Let h denote the height and b the base of the triangle above. What is the area of the triangle?

   (1) $2b + h = 6$
   (2) $(bh)^2 = 16$

The area of a triangle is $\frac{1}{2} base \times height$. For the given triangle, this becomes

$$Area = \frac{1}{2} b \times h$$

Solving the equation $2b + h = 6$ for h gives $h = 6 - 2b$. Plugging this into the area formula gives

$$Area = \frac{1}{2} b(6 - 2b)$$

Since the value of b is not given, we cannot determine the area. Hence, (1) is not sufficient.

Taking the square root of both sides of the equation $(bh)^2 = 16$ gives

$$bh = 4$$

Plugging this into the area formula gives

$$Area = \frac{1}{2} \cdot 4 = 2$$

Hence, (2) is sufficient to determine the area. The answer is B.

11. If $x \neq 0$, what is the value of $\sqrt{\dfrac{x^u}{x^v}}$?

   (1) $u = v$

   (2) x is a perfect square.

Plugging $u = v$ into the expression $\sqrt{\dfrac{x^u}{x^v}}$ gives

$$\sqrt{\dfrac{x^v}{x^v}} =$$

$$\sqrt{1} =$$

$$1$$

Hence, (1) is sufficient. However, (2) is not sufficient. For example, let $x = 4$ and $u = v = 1$. Then $\sqrt{\dfrac{x^u}{x^v}} = \sqrt{\dfrac{4^1}{4^1}} = \sqrt{1} = 1$. But if $u = 3$ and $v = 1$, then $\sqrt{\dfrac{4^3}{4^1}} = \sqrt{4^2} = 4$. The answer is A.

12. If a marble is selected at random from a bag containing only red and black marbles, what is the probability that the marble will be red?

   (1)   There are 9 marbles in the bag.

   (2)   There are 3 red marbles in the bag.

(1) is not sufficient since there could be 8 red marbles and 1 black, or 7 red marbles and 2 black, etc. (2) is not sufficient since along with the 3 red marbles there could be 1 black, 2 black, 3 black, etc. However, together (1) and (2) are sufficient since now there are 3 red and 6 black marbles in the bag. Hence, the probability of selecting a red marble is $\dfrac{3}{9} = \dfrac{1}{3}$. The answer is C.

13. Is the negative number x less than -1?

   (1) $\dfrac{1}{x} < \dfrac{1}{2}$

   (2) $\dfrac{1}{x^2} < \dfrac{1}{2}$

(1) is not sufficient. For example, if $x = -1$, then $\dfrac{1}{x} = \dfrac{1}{-1} = -1 < \dfrac{1}{2}$. But if $x = -2$, then $\dfrac{1}{x} = -\dfrac{1}{2} < \dfrac{1}{2}$. Hence, (1) is insufficient since different values of x satisfy (1), some less than -1 and some not less than -1.

Considering (2), since x^2 is positive, multiplying both sides of $\dfrac{1}{x^2} < \dfrac{1}{2}$ by $2x^2$ will not reverse the inequality:

$$2x^2 \cdot \dfrac{1}{x^2} < 2x^2 \cdot \dfrac{1}{2}$$

$$2 < x^2$$

$$x < -\sqrt{2} \quad \text{or} \quad x > \sqrt{2}$$

Since we are given that x is negative, we reject the inequality $x > \sqrt{2}$. From $x < -\sqrt{2}$, we can conclude that x is less than -1. Hence, (2) is sufficient, and the answer is B.

14. What is the volume of a given cube?

    (1)   The ratio of an edge of the cube and the greatest distance between two points on the cube is $1:\sqrt{3}$.

    (2)   The length of the diagonal across a face of the cube is 2.

(1) is not sufficient since different size cubes all have the ratio $1:\sqrt{3}$.

Ratio: $\dfrac{2}{2\sqrt{3}} = \dfrac{1}{\sqrt{3}}$

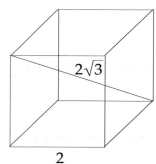

Ratio: $\dfrac{1}{\sqrt{3}}$

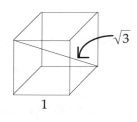

A diagram illustrating (2) is shown below:

Looking at the face in isolation gives

Applying the Pythagorean Theorem to this diagram gives

$$x^2 + x^2 = 2^2$$

$$2x^2 = 4$$

$$x^2 = 2$$

$$x = \sqrt{2}$$

Hence, the volume of the cube is $x^3 = \left(\sqrt{2}\right)^3$. Thus, (2) is sufficient, and the answer is B.

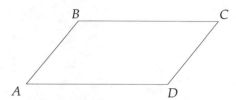

15. In the parallelogram above, what is the measure of $\angle ABC$?

    (1) $\angle BAD + \angle BCD = 140$

    (2) $\angle BAD = 140$

Consider (1) alone. Since opposite angles of a parallelogram are equal, $\angle ABC = \angle ADC$. Further, since there are 360° in a parallelogram,

$$\angle ABC + \angle ADC + \angle BAD + \angle BCD = 360$$

$$\angle ABC + \angle ADC + 140 = 360$$

$$\angle ABC + \angle ABC = 220$$

$$2\angle ABC = 220$$

$$\angle ABC = 110$$

Hence, (1) is sufficient.

From $\angle BAD = 140$ and the fact that consecutive angles of a parallelogram are supplementary, we get $\angle ABC = 40$. Hence, (2) is also sufficient. The answer is D.

16. What is the value of $p^3 + 2p$?

    (1) $p^2 - 5p + 4 = 0$.

    (2)   The value of $p^2 + \dfrac{1}{p}$ is –2.

Factoring the equation $p^2 - 5p + 4 = 0$ gives

$$(p - 1)(p - 4) = 0$$

$$p - 1 = 0 \quad \text{or} \quad p - 4 = 0$$

Hence, $p = 1$ or $p = 4$. However, $1^3 + 2 \cdot 1 \neq 4^3 + 2 \cdot 4$. Therefore, (1) is not sufficient.

Translating (2) into an equation gives $p^2 + \dfrac{1}{p} = -2$

Multiplying by p gives $p^3 + 1 = -2p$

Rearranging gives $p^3 + 2p = -1$

Hence, (2) is sufficient to answer the question. The answer is B.

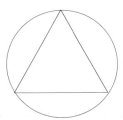

17.   An equilateral triangle is inscribed in a circle, as shown above. What is the area of the triangle?

(1)   The radius of the circle is 2.

(2)   The ratio of the radius of the circle to a side of the triangle is $1 : \sqrt{3}$.

Adding radii to the diagram yields

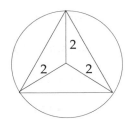

Now, viewing the bottom triangle in isolation yields

Recall, in a 30°–60°–90° triangle, the side opposite the 30° angle is $1/2$ the length of the hypotenuse, and the side opposite the 60° angle is $\dfrac{\sqrt{3}}{2}$ times the length of the hypotenuse. Hence, the altitude of the above triangle is 1, and the base is $\sqrt{3} + \sqrt{3} = 2\sqrt{3}$. Thus, the area of the triangle is $A = \dfrac{1}{2} \cdot 2\sqrt{3} \cdot 1$. By symmetry, the area of the inscribed triangle is $3A$. Therefore, (1) is sufficient.

(2) is not sufficient, as the following diagrams show:

Ratio: $\dfrac{r}{s} = \dfrac{1}{\sqrt{3}}$ *Ratio:* $\dfrac{r}{s} = \dfrac{4}{4\sqrt{3}} = \dfrac{1}{\sqrt{3}}$

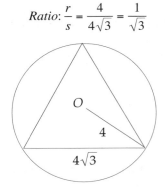

The answer is A.

18. If $2x + y = -31$, what is the value of x?

    (1) $(y - 2) \cdot (y - 2) - 4 = 0$

    (2) $y = 2$

Since we are given one equation in two variables, we need at least one other equation or the value of y itself in order to determine the value of x. (2) gives a value for y. Hence, (2) is sufficient. Although (1) gives another equation, it still is not sufficient:

$$(y - 2) \cdot (y - 2) - 4 = 0$$

$$(y - 2) \cdot (y - 2) = 4$$

$$(y - 2)^2 = 4$$

$$y - 2 = \pm 2$$

$$y = 2 \pm 2$$

$$y = 0 \quad \text{or} \quad y = 4$$

Since there are two values for y, we cannot uniquely determine the value of x. The answer is B.

19. The symbol Θ denotes one of the operations: addition, subtraction, multiplication, or division. What is the value of $\pi \Theta \sqrt{2}$?

    (1) $1 \Theta 1 = 1$

    (2) $0 \Theta 0 = 0$

Consider (1) alone. Now, $1 \cdot 1 = 1$ and $1 \div 1 = 1$, so Θ could denote multiplication or division. But, $\pi \cdot \sqrt{2} \neq \pi \div \sqrt{2}$. Therefore, the value of $\pi \Theta \sqrt{2}$ cannot be uniquely determined from (1) alone.

Consider (2) alone. Now, $0 \cdot 0 = 0$, $0 + 0 = 0$, and $0 - 0 = 0$. So in this case, Θ could denote multiplication, addition, or subtraction. But, $\pi \cdot \sqrt{2} \neq \pi + \sqrt{2} \neq \pi - \sqrt{2}$. Therefore, the value of $\pi \Theta \sqrt{2}$ cannot be uniquely determined from (2) alone.

Consider (1) and (2) together. From (1), we know that Θ must denote multiplication or division; from (2), we know that Θ must denote multiplication, addition, or subtraction. The only operation common to these two groups is multiplication. Hence, the value of $\pi \Theta \sqrt{2}$ can be uniquely determined:

$$\pi \Theta \sqrt{2} = \pi \cdot \sqrt{2}$$

The answer is C.

20. Let ∇ denote a mathematical operation. Is it true that $x \nabla y = y \nabla x$ for all x and y?

    (1) $x \nabla y = \dfrac{1}{x} + \dfrac{1}{y}$

    (2) $x \nabla y = x - y$

$$x \nabla y = \frac{1}{x} + \frac{1}{y}$$

$$= \frac{1}{y} + \frac{1}{x} \qquad \text{(By the commutative property of addition)}$$

$$= y \nabla x$$

Hence, (1) is sufficient. (2) is also sufficient. For example, let $x = 2$ and $y = 1$. Then $x \nabla y = 2 \nabla 1 = 2 - 1 = 1$, but $y \nabla x = 1 \nabla 2 = 1 - 2 = -1$. Hence in this case, the response is "**no**, it's not true that $x \nabla y = y \nabla x$ for all x and y." The answer is D.

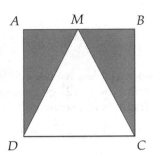

21. The triangle above has side *DC* of the square as its base. What is the area of the shaded region?

    (1) $DM = 5$

    (2)   *M* is the midpoint of side *AB*.

(1) is not sufficient to determine the area since the position of *M* is not known:

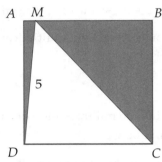
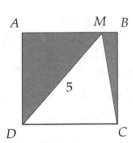

(2) is not sufficient since no dimensions are given. However, together (1) and (2) are sufficient:

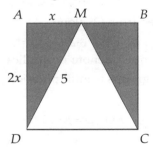

Applying the Pythagorean Theorem yields

$$x^2 + (2x)^2 = 5^2$$

$$x^2 + 4x^2 = 5^2$$

$$5x^2 = 5^2$$

$$x^2 = 5$$

$$x = \sqrt{5}$$

Since the height of the unshaded triangle is the same as the length of a side of the square, the area of the triangle is

$$A = \frac{1}{2}\left(2\sqrt{5}\right)\left(2\sqrt{5}\right) = 10$$

Subtracting this from the area of the square will give the area of the shaded region. The answer is C.

22. If p and q are consecutive even integers, is $p > q$?

    (1) $p - 2$ and $q + 2$ are consecutive even integers.

    (2) p is prime.

Consider (1) alone. First, check whether p can be larger than q. Place p and q on a number line:

Then, place $p - 2$ and $q + 2$ on the number line:

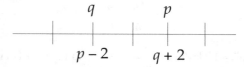

This diagram shows that $p - 2$ and $q + 2$ are also consecutive even integers. Hence, p can be larger than q.

    Next, we check whether p can be less than q. Place p and q on a number line:

Then, place $p - 2$ and $q + 2$ on the number line:

On this diagram, $p - 2$ and $q + 2$ are not consecutive even integers. Hence, p cannot be less than q. Thus, (1) is sufficient.

    Next, consider (2) alone. Since p is now both prime and even, $p = 2$—the only even prime. Now, q could be either 0 or 4. Hence, we cannot determine whether $p > q$, and (2) is insufficient. The answer is A.

23. S is a set of integers such that

    I)   If x is in S, then $-x$ is in S.

    II)   If both x and y are in S, then so is $x + y$.

    Is -2 in S?

    (1)   1 is in S.

    (2)   0 is in S.

Suppose 1 is in S. Then by Property I, -1 is in S. Now, by Property II, $-1 + (-1) = -2$ is in S. Hence, (1) is sufficient.

    Next, suppose 0 is in S. Then by Property I, $-0 = 0$, which does not give us another element. Further, by Property II, $0 + 0 = 0$, which again does not give us another element. Thus, (2) is not sufficient. The answer is A.

24.   If $m = 3^{n-1}$, what is the value of $\dfrac{m}{n}$?

   (1) $3^{4n-1} = 27$
   (2) $m = 3^{3n+1}$

Consider (1) alone:

$$3^{4n-1} = 27$$
$$3^{4n-1} = 3^3$$
$$4n - 1 = 3$$
$$4n = 4$$
$$n = 1$$

Since $n = 1$, $m = 3^{n-1} = 3^{1-1} = 3^0 = 1$. Hence, $\dfrac{m}{n} = \dfrac{1}{1} = 1$, and (1) is sufficient.

Consider (2) alone. Since 3^{n-1} and 3^{3n+1} are both equal to m, they must equal each other:

$$3^{n-1} = 3^{3n+1}$$
$$n - 1 = 3n + 1$$
$$-2n = 2$$
$$n = -1$$

Since $n = -1$, $m = 3^{n-1} = 3^{-1-1} = 3^{-2} = \dfrac{1}{3^2} = \dfrac{1}{9}$. Hence, $\dfrac{m}{n} = \dfrac{\frac{1}{9}}{-1} = -\dfrac{1}{9}$, and (2) is also sufficient. The answer is D.

25.   If x is an integer, is $\sqrt{x^2 + y^2}$ an integer?

   (1) $x^2 - y^2 = 0$
   (2) $x^2 - k^2 = -y^2$ for some positive integer k.

From $x^2 - y^2 = 0$, we get $x^2 = y^2$. Plug this into the expression $\sqrt{x^2 + y^2}$:

$$\sqrt{x^2 + x^2} =$$
$$\sqrt{2x^2} =$$
$$\sqrt{2} \cdot x$$

Since $\sqrt{2}$ is not an integer, $\sqrt{x^2 + y^2}$ is not an integer. Hence, (1) is sufficient to answer the question.

Adding k^2 and y^2 to both sides of $x^2 - k^2 = -y^2$ yields

$$x^2 + y^2 = k^2$$

Plugging this into the expression $\sqrt{x^2 + y^2}$ yields

$$\sqrt{k^2} =$$
$$k$$

Since k is an integer, $\sqrt{x^2 + y^2}$ is an integer. Hence, (2) is also sufficient to answer the question. The answer is D.

Part Two
VERBAL

Format of the Verbal Portion

The verbal portion of the test consists of three types of questions: *Reading Comprehension*, *Arguments*, and *Sentence Correction*. They are designed to test your ability to reason using the written word. There is roughly the same number of each type of question, for a total of 41 questions.

READING COMPREHENSION

- **INTRODUCTION**
  The Source for the Passages

- **READING METHODS**
  Why Speed Reading Doesn't Work
  Pre-reading the Topic Sentences

- **THE SIX QUESTIONS**
  Main Idea Questions
  Description Questions
  Writing Technique Questions
  Extension Questions
  Application Questions
  Tone Questions

- **PIVOTAL WORDS**

- **THE THREE STEP METHOD**
  1. (Optional) Preview the First Sentences
  2. Note the Six Questions
  3. Note the Pivotal Words

- **EXTRA READING**

Introduction

The GMAT reading comprehension passages are about 200 to 400 words long. The subject matter of a passage can be almost anything, but the most common themes are politics, history, culture, science, and business.

Most people find the passages difficult because the subject matter is dry and unfamiliar. Obscure subject matter is chosen so that your reading comprehension will be tested, not your knowledge of a particular subject. Also the more esoteric the subject the more likely everyone taking the test will be on an even playing field. However, because the material must still be accessible to laymen, you won't find any tracts on subtle issues of philosophy or abstract mathematics. In fact, if you read books on current affairs and the Op/Ed page of the newspaper, then the style of writing used in the GMAT passages will be familiar and you probably won't find the reading comprehension section particularly difficult.

The passages use a formal, compact style. They are typically taken from articles in academic journals, but they are rarely reprinted verbatim. Usually the chosen article is heavily edited until it is honed down to about 200 to 400 words. The formal style of the piece is retained but much of the "fluff" is removed. The editing process condenses the article to about one-third its original length. Thus, a GMAT passage contains about three times as much information for its length as does the original article. This is why the passages are similar to the writing on the Op/Ed page of a newspaper. After all, a person writing a piece for the Op/Ed page must express all his ideas in about 500 words, and he must use a formal (grammatical) style to convince people that he is well educated.

In addition to being dry and unfamiliar, GMAT passages often start in the middle of an explanation, so there is no point of reference. Furthermore, the passages are untitled, so you have to hit the ground running.

The passages presented depend on how well you are performing on the test. However, unlike other parts of the test, the questions presented do not depend on your performance.

The longer passages will require you to scroll through the passage.

Reading Methods

Reading styles are subjective—there is no best method for approaching the passages. There are as many "systems" for reading the passages as there are test-prep books—all "authoritatively" promoting their method, while contradicting some aspect of another. A reading technique that is natural for one person can be awkward and unnatural for another person. However, I find it hard to believe that many of the methods advocated in certain books could help anyone. Be that as it may, I will throw in my own two-cents worth—though not so dogmatically.

Some books recommend speed-reading the passages. This is a mistake. Speed reading is designed for ordinary, nontechnical material. Because this material is filled with "fluff," you can skim over the nonessential parts and still get the gist—and often more—of the passage. As mentioned before, however, GMAT passages are dense. Some are actual quoted articles (when the writers of the GMAT find one that is sufficiently compact). Most often, however, they are based on articles that have been condensed to about one-third their original length. During this process no essential information is lost, just the "fluff" is cut. This is why speed reading will not work here—the passages contain too much information. You should, however, read somewhat faster than you normally do, but not to the point that your comprehension suffers. You will have to experiment to find your optimum pace.

One technique that you may find helpful is to preview the passage by reading the first sentence of each paragraph. Generally, the topic of a paragraph is contained in the first sentence. Reading the first sentence of each paragraph will give an overview of the passage. The topic sentences act in essence as a summary of the passage. Furthermore, since each passage is only three or four paragraphs long, previewing the topic sentences will not use up an inordinate amount of time. (I don't use this method myself, however. I prefer to see the passage as a completed whole, and to let the passage unveil its main idea to me as I become absorbed in it. I find that when I try to pre-analyze the passage it tends to become disjointed, and I lose my concentration. Nonetheless, as mentioned before, reading methods are subjective, so experiment—this may work for you.)

Points to Remember

1.   Reading styles are subjective—there is no best method for approaching the passages.

2.   Don't speed read, or skim, the passage. Instead, read at a faster than usual pace, but not to the point that your comprehension suffers.

3.   (Optional) Preview the first sentence of each paragraph before you read the passage.

The Six Questions

The key to performing well on the passages is not the particular reading technique you use (so long as it's not speed reading). Rather the key is to become completely familiar with the question types—there are only six—so that you can anticipate the questions that *might* be asked as you read the passage and answer those that *are* asked more quickly and efficiently. As you become familiar with the six question types, you will gain an intuitive sense for the places from which questions are likely to be drawn. Note, the order in which the questions are asked <u>roughly</u> corresponds to the order in which the main issues are presented in the passage. Early questions should correspond to information given early in the passage, and so on.

The following passage and accompanying questions illustrate the six question types. Read the passage slowly to get a good understanding of the issues.

There are two major systems of criminal procedure in the modern world—the adversarial and the inquisitorial. The former is associated with common law tradition and the latter
5 with civil law tradition. Both systems were historically preceded by the system of private vengeance in which the victim of a crime fashioned his own remedy and administered it privately, either personally or through an agent.
10 The vengeance system was a system of self-help, the essence of which was captured in the slogan "an eye for an eye, a tooth for a tooth." The modern adversarial system is only one historical step removed from the private
15 vengeance system and still retains some of its characteristic features. Thus, for example, even though the right to institute criminal action has now been extended to all members of society and even though the police department
20 has taken over the pretrial investigative functions on behalf of the prosecution, the adversarial system still leaves the defendant to conduct his own pretrial investigation. The trial is still viewed as a duel between two adversaries,
25 refereed by a judge who, at the beginning of the trial has no knowledge of the investigative background of the case. In the final analysis the adversarial system of criminal procedure symbolizes and regularizes the punitive
30 combat.

By contrast, the inquisitorial system begins historically where the adversarial system stopped its development. It is two historical steps removed from the system of private
35 vengeance. Therefore, from the standpoint of legal anthropology, it is historically superior to the adversarial system. Under the inquisitorial system the public investigator has the duty to investigate not just on behalf of the prosecutor
40 but also on behalf of the defendant. Additionally, the public prosecutor has the duty to present to the court not only evidence that may lead to the conviction of the defendant but also evidence that may lead to his ex-
45 oneration. This system mandates that both parties permit full pretrial discovery of the evidence in their possession. Finally, in an effort to make the trial less like a duel between two adversaries, the inquisitorial system mandates
50 that the judge take an active part in the conduct of the trial, with a role that is both directive and protective.

Fact-finding is at the heart of the inquisitorial system. This system operates on the
55 philosophical premise that in a criminal case the crucial factor is not the legal rule but the facts of the case and that the goal of the entire procedure is to experimentally recreate for the court the commission of the alleged crime.

MAIN IDEA QUESTIONS

All authors have a point they want to make in their writing. Main idea questions test your ability to identify and understand an author's intent. The main idea is usually stated in the last— occasionally the first—sentence of the first paragraph. If it's not there, it will probably be the last sentence of the entire passage. Main idea questions are usually the first questions asked.

Some common main idea questions are

☐ Which one of the following best expresses the main idea of the passage?

☐ The primary purpose of the passage is to . . .

☐ In the passage, the author's primary concern is to discuss . . .

Main idea questions are rarely difficult; after all the author wants to clearly communicate her ideas to you. If, however, after the first reading, you don't have a feel for the main idea, review the first and last sentence of each paragraph; these will give you a quick overview of the passage.

Because main idea questions are relatively easy, the GMAT writers try to obscure the correct answer by surrounding it with close answer-choices ("detractors") that either overstate or understate the author's main point. Answer-choices that stress specifics tend to understate the main idea; choices that go beyond the scope of the passage tend to overstate the main idea.

 Note! The answer to a main idea question will summarize the author's argument, yet be neither too specific nor too broad.

In most GMAT passages the author's primary purpose is to persuade the reader to accept her opinion. Occasionally, it is to describe something.

Example: (Refer to passage on page 348.)

The primary purpose of the passage is to

(A) explain why the inquisitorial system is the best system of criminal justice
(B) explain how the adversarial and the inquisitorial systems of criminal justice both evolved from the system of private vengeance
(C) show how the adversarial and inquisitorial systems of criminal justice can both complement and hinder each other's development
(D) show how the adversarial and inquisitorial systems of criminal justice are being combined into a new and better system
(E) analyze two systems of criminal justice and deduce which one is better

✗ check for key words when answers seem similar.

The answer to a main idea question will summarize the passage without going beyond it. (A) violates these criteria by *overstating* the scope of the passage. The comparison in the passage is between two specific systems, not between *all* systems. (A) would be a good answer if "best" were replaced with "better." **Beware of extreme words**. (B) violates the criteria by *understating* the scope of the passage. Although the evolution of both the adversarial and the inquisitorial systems is discussed in the passage, it is done to show why one is superior to the other. As to (C) and (D), both can be quickly dismissed since neither is mentioned in the passage. Finally, the passage does two things: it presents two systems of criminal justice and shows why one is better than the other. (E) aptly summarizes this, so it is the best answer.

Following is a mini-passage. These exercises are interspersed among the sections of this chapter and are written to the same specifications as actual GMAT passages. Because the mini-passages are short and designed to test only one issue, they are more tractable than a full passage.

Application: *(Mini-passage)*

As Xenophanes recognized as long ago as the sixth century before Christ, whether or not God made man in His own image, it is certain that man makes gods in his. The gods of Greek mythology first appear in the writings of Homer and Hesiod, and, from the character and actions of these picturesque and, for the most part, friendly beings, we get some idea of the men who made them and brought them to Greece.

But ritual is more fundamental than mythology, and the study of Greek ritual during recent years has shown that, beneath the belief or skepticism with which the Olympians were regarded, lay an older magic, with traditional rites for the promotion of fertility by the celebration of the annual cycle of life and death, and the propitiation of unfriendly ghosts, gods or demons. Some such survivals were doubtless widespread, and, prolonged into classical times, probably made the substance of Eleusinian and Orphic mysteries. Against this dark and dangerous background arose Olympic mythology on the one hand and early philosophy and science on the other.

In classical times the need of a creed higher than the Olympian was felt, and Aeschylus, Sophocles and Plato finally evolved from the pleasant but crude polytheism the idea of a single, supreme and righteous Zeus. But the decay of Olympus led to a revival of old and the invasion of new magic cults among the people, while some philosophers were looking to a vision of the uniformity of nature under divine and universal law.

From Sir William Cecil Dampier, *A Shorter History of Science*, ©1957, Meridian Books.

The main idea of the passage is that

(A)   Olympic mythology evolved from ancient rituals and gave rise to early philosophy
(B)   early moves toward viewing nature as ordered by divine and universal law coincided with monotheistic impulses and the disintegration of classical mythology
(C)   early philosophy followed from classical mythology
(D)   the practice of science, i.e., empiricism, preceded scientific theory

Most main idea questions are rather easy. This one is not—mainly, because the passage itself is not an easy read. Recall that to find the main idea of a passage, we check the last sentence of the first paragraph; if it's not there, we check the closing of the passage. Reviewing the last sentence of the first paragraph, we see that it hardly presents a statement, let alone the main idea. Turning to the closing line of the passage, however, we find the key to this question. The passage describes a struggle for ascendancy amongst four opposing philosophies: (magic and traditional rites) vs. (Olympic mythology) vs. (monotheism [Zeus]) vs. (early philosophy and science). The closing lines of the passage summarize this and add that Olympic mythology lost out to monotheism (Zeus), while magical cults enjoyed a revival and the germ of universal law was planted. Thus the answer is (B).

As to the other choices, (A) is false. "Olympic mythology [arose] on one hand and early philosophy and science on the other" (closing to paragraph two); thus they initially developed in parallel. (C) is also false. It makes the same type of error as (A). Finally, (D) is not mentioned in the passage.

* look immediately before & immediately after.

DESCRIPTION QUESTIONS

Description questions, as with main idea questions, refer to a point made by the author. However, description questions refer to a minor point or to incidental information, not to the author's main point.

Again, these questions take various forms:

- ☐   According to the passage . . .
- ☐   In line 37, the author mentions . . . for the purpose of . . .
- ☐   The passage suggests that which one of the following would . . .

The answer to a description question must refer <u>directly</u> to a statement in the passage, not to something implied by it. However, the correct answer will paraphrase a statement in the passage, not give an exact quote. In fact, exact quotes ("Same language" traps) are often used to bait wrong answers.

Caution: When answering a description question, you must find the point in the passage from which the question is drawn. Don't rely on memory—too many obfuscating tactics are used with these questions.

Not only must the correct answer refer directly to a statement in the passage, it must refer to the relevant statement. The correct answer will be surrounded by wrong choices which refer directly to the passage but don't address the question. These choices can be tempting because they tend to be quite close to the actual answer.

Once you spot the sentence to which the question refers, you still must read a few sentences before and after it, to put the question in context. If a question refers to line 20, the information needed to answer it can occur anywhere from line 15 to 25. Even if you have spotted the answer in line 20, you should still read a couple more lines to make certain you have the proper perspective.

Example: (Refer to passage on page 348.)

According to the passage, the inquisitorial system differs from the adversarial system in that

was explicitly stated not implied or probably true!

- (A)   it does not make the defendant solely responsible for gathering evidence for his case
- (B)   it does not require the police department to work on behalf of the prosecution
- (C)   it does not allow the victim the satisfaction of private vengeance
- (D)   it requires the prosecution to drop a weak case
- (E)   a defendant who is innocent would prefer to be tried under the inquisitorial system

This is a description question, so the information needed to answer it must be stated in the passage—though not in the same language as in the answer. The needed information is contained in lines 37–40, which state that the public prosecutor has to investigate on behalf of both society and the defendant. Thus, the defendant is not solely responsible for investigating his case. Furthermore, the paragraph's opening implies that this feature is not found in the adversarial system. This illustrates why you must determine the context of the situation before you can safely answer the question. The answer is (A).

The other choices can be easily dismissed. (B) is the second best answer. Lines 19–21 state that in the adversarial system the police assume the work of the prosecution. Then lines 31–33 state that the inquisitorial system begins where the adversarial system stopped; this implies that in both systems the police work for the prosecution. (C) uses a false claim ploy. The passage states that both systems are removed from the system of private vengeance. (D) is probably true, but it is neither stated nor directly implied by the passage. Finally, (E) uses a reference to the passage to make a true but irrelevant statement. People's attitude or preference toward a system is not a part of that system.

Application: *(Mini-passage)*

If dynamic visual graphics, sound effects, and automatic scorekeeping are the features that account for the popularity of video games, why are parents so worried? All of these features seem quite innocent. But another source of concern is that the games available in arcades have, almost without exception, themes of physical aggression.... There has long been the belief that violent content may teach violent behavior. And yet again our society finds a new medium in which to present that content, and yet again the demand is nearly insatiable. And there is evidence that violent video games breed violent behavior, just as violent television shows do....

The effects of video violence are less simple, however, than they at first appeared. The same group of researchers who found negative effects [from certain video games] have more recently found that two-player aggressive video games, whether cooperative or competitive, reduce the level of aggression in children's play....

It may be that the most harmful aspect of the violent video games is that they are solitary in nature. A two-person aggressive game (video boxing, in this study) seems to provide a cathartic or releasing effect for aggression, while a solitary aggressive game (such as Space Invaders) may stimulate further aggression. Perhaps the effects of television in stimulating aggression will also be found to stem partly from the fact that TV viewing typically involves little social interaction.

From Patricia Marks Greenfield, *Mind and Media: The Effects of Television, Video Games, and Computers.* © 1984 by Harvard University Press.

According to the passage, which of the following would be likely to stimulate violent behavior in a child playing a video game?

  I. Watching the computer stage a battle between two opponents
  II. Controlling a character in battle against a computer
  III. Challenging another player to a battle in a non-cooperative two-person game

(A) II only
(B) III only
(C) I and II only
(D) II and III only

Item I, True: Stimulation would occur. This choice is qualitatively the same as passively watching violence on television. **Item II, True:** Stimulation would also occur. This is another example of solitary aggression (implied by the second sentence of the last paragraph). **Item III, False:** No stimulation would occur. Two-player aggressive games are "cathartic" (again the needed reference is the second sentence of the last paragraph). The answer is (C).

Often you will be asked to define a word or phrase based on its context. For this type of question, again you must look at a few lines before and after the word. <u>Don't</u> assume that because the word is familiar you know the definition requested. Words often have more than one meaning. And the GMAT often asks for a peculiar or technical meaning of a common word. For example, as a noun *champion* means "the winner," but as a verb *champion* means "to be an advocate for someone." You must consider the word's context to get its correct meaning.

On the GMAT the definition of a word will not use as simple a structure as was used above to define *champion*. One common way the GMAT introduces a defining word or phrase is to place it in <u>apposition</u> to the word being defined.

Don't confuse "apposition" with "opposition": they have antithetical [exactly opposite] meanings. Words or phrases in <u>apposition</u> are placed next to each other, and the second word or phrase defines, clarifies, or gives evidence for the first word or phrase. The second word or phrase will be set off from the first by a comma, semicolon, hyphen, or parentheses. (Note: If a comma is not followed by a linking word—such as *and, for, yet*—then the following phrase is probably appositional.)

Example:

The discussions were acrimonious, frequently degenerating into name-calling contests.

After the comma in this sentence, there is no linking word (such as *and, but, because, although*, etc.). Hence the phrase following the comma is in apposition to *acrimonious*—it defines or further clarifies the word. Now acrimonious means bitter, mean-spirited talk, which would aptly describe a name-calling contest.

Application: *(Mini-passage)*

The technical phenomenon, embracing all the separate techniques, forms a whole.... It is useless to look for differentiations. They do exist, but only secondarily. The common features of the technical phenomenon are so sharply drawn that it is easy to discern that which is the technical phenomenon and that which is not.

... To analyze these common features is tricky, but it is simple to grasp them. Just as there are principles common to things as different as a wireless set and an internal-combustion engine, so the organization of an office and the construction of an aircraft have certain identical features. This identity is the primary mark of that thoroughgoing unity which makes the technical phenomenon a single essence despite the extreme diversity of its appearances.

As a corollary, it is impossible to analyze this or that element out of it—a truth which is today particularly misunderstood. The great tendency of all persons who study techniques is to make distinctions. They distinguish between the different elements of technique, maintaining some and discarding others. They distinguish between technique and the use to which it is put. These distinctions are completely invalid and show only that he who makes them has understood nothing of the technical phenomenon. Its parts are ontologically tied together; in it, use is inseparable from being.

From Jacques Ellul, *The Technological Society*, ©1964 by Alfred A. Knopf, Inc.

The "technical phenomenon" referred to in the opening line can best be defined as

(A)   all of the machinery in use today
(B)   the abstract idea of the machine
(C)   a way of thinking in modern society
(D)   what all machines have in common

(A): No, it is clear from the passage that the technical phenomenon is more abstract than that, since it is described in the opening paragraph as uniting all the separate "techniques" (not machines) and as comprising the "features" that such things as an office and an aircraft have in common. (B): No, the passage states that the technical phenomenon is something that includes both techniques and their use (See closing lines of the passage); it is thus broader that just the idea of machinery. **(C): Yes**, this seems to be the best answer; it is broad enough to include both techniques and their uses and abstract enough to go beyond talking only about machines. (D): No, the passage suggests that it is something that techniques have in common and techniques can include airplanes or offices.

Strategy:
★ closely related
to main idea
re-read TS of
each ¶

WRITING TECHNIQUE QUESTIONS

All coherent writing has a superstructure or blueprint. When writing, we don't just randomly jot down our thoughts; we organize our ideas and present them in a logical manner. For instance, we may present evidence that builds up to a conclusion but intentionally leave the conclusion unstated, or we may present a position and then contrast it with an opposing position, or we may draw an extended analogy.

There is an endless number of writing techniques that authors use to present their ideas, so we cannot classify every method. However, some techniques are very common to the type of explanatory or opinionated writing found in GMAT passages.

A.   Compare and contrast two positions.

This technique has a number of variations, but the most common and direct is to develop two ideas or systems (comparing) and then point out why one is better than the other (contrasting).

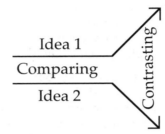

Some common tip-off phrases to this method of analysis are

- By contrast

- Similarly

Some typical questions for these types of passages are

- According to the passage, a central distinction between a woman's presence and a man's presence is:

- In which of the following ways does the author imply that birds and reptiles are similar?

Writing-technique questions are similar to main idea questions; except that they ask about how the author <u>presents</u> his ideas, not about the ideas themselves. Generally, you will be given only two writing methods to choose from, but each method will have two or more variations.

Example: (Refer to passage on page 348.)

Which one of the following best describes the organization of the passage?

(A)   Two systems of criminal justice are compared and contrasted, and one is deemed to be better than the other.
(B)   One system of criminal justice is presented as better than another. Then evidence is offered to support that claim.
(C)   Two systems of criminal justice are analyzed, and one specific example is examined in detail.
(D)   A set of examples is furnished. Then a conclusion is drawn from them.
(E)   The inner workings of the criminal justice system are illustrated by using two systems.

B is wrong b/c it doesn't start out saying one method the other.

Clearly the author is comparing and contrasting two criminal justice systems. Indeed, the opening to paragraph two makes this explicit. The author uses a mixed form of comparison and contrast. He opens the passage by developing (comparing) both systems and then shifts to developing just the adversarial system. He opens the second paragraph by contrasting the two criminal justice systems and then further develops just the inquisitorial system. Finally, he closes by again contrasting the two systems and implying that the inquisitorial system is superior.

Only two answer-choices, (A) and (B), have any real merit. They say essentially the same thing—though in different order. Notice in the passage that the author does not indicate which system is better until the end of paragraph one, and he does not make that certain until paragraph two. This contradicts the order given by (B). Hence the answer is (A). (Note: In (A) the order is not specified and therefore is harder to attack, whereas in (B) the order is definite and therefore is easier to attack. Remember that a measured response is harder to attack and therefore is more likely to be the answer.)

B.   Show cause and effect.

In this technique, the author typically shows how a particular cause leads to a certain result or set of results. It is not uncommon for this method to introduce a sequence of causes and effects. A causes B, which causes C, which causes D, and so on. Hence B is both the effect of A and the cause of C. For a discussion of the fallacies associated with this technique see Causal Reasoning (page 467). The variations on this rhetorical technique can be illustrated by the following schematics:

Example: *(Mini-passage)*

Thirdly, I worry about the private automobile. It is a dirty, noisy, wasteful, and lonely means of travel. It pollutes the air, ruins the safety and sociability of the street, and exercises upon the individual a discipline which takes away far more freedom than it gives him. It causes an enormous amount of land to be unnecessarily abstracted from nature and from plant life and to become devoid of any natural function. It explodes cities, grievously impairs the whole institution of neighborliness, fragmentizes and destroys communities. It has already spelled the end of our cities as real cultural and social communities, and has made impossible the construction of any others in their place. Together with the airplane, it has crowded out other, more civilized and more convenient means of transport, leaving older people, infirm people, poor people and children in a worse situation than they were a hundred years ago. It continues to lend a terrible element of fragility to our civilization, placing us in a situation where our life would break down completely if anything ever interfered with the oil supply.

George F. Kennan

Which of the following best describes the organization of the passage?

(A)   A problem is presented and then a possible solution is discussed.
(B)   The benefits and demerits of the automobile are compared and contrasted.
(C)   A topic is presented and a number of its effects are discussed.
(D)   A set of examples is furnished to support a conclusion.

This passage is laden with effects. Kennan introduces the cause, the automobile, in the opening sentence and from there on presents a series of effects—the automobile pollutes, enslaves, and so on. Hence the answer is (C). Note: (D) is the second-best choice; it is disqualified by two flaws. First, in this context, "examples" is not as precise as "effects." Second, the order is wrong: the conclusion, *"I worry about the private automobile"* is presented first and then the examples: it pollutes, it enslaves, etc.

C.   State a position and then give supporting evidence.

This technique is common with opinionated passages. Equally common is the reverse order. That is, the supporting evidence is presented and then the position or conclusion is stated. And sometimes the evidence will be structured to build up to a conclusion which is then left unstated. If this is done skillfully the reader will be more likely to arrive at the same conclusion as the author.

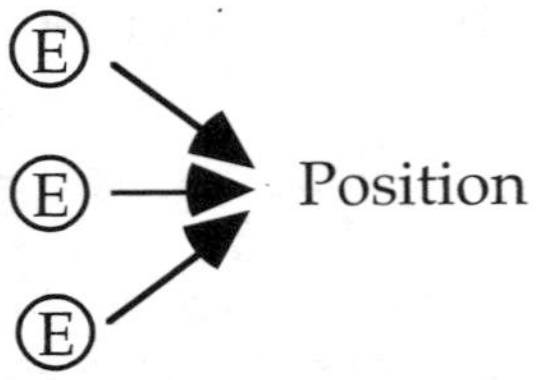

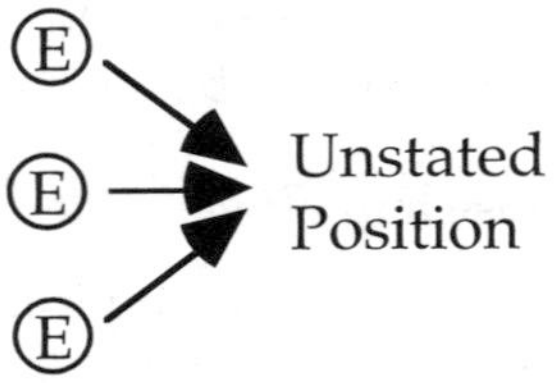

Following are some typical questions for these types of passages:

- According to the author, which of the following is required for one to become proficient with a computer?

- Which of the following does the author cite as evidence that the bald eagle is in danger of becoming extinct?

[handwritten: make an analogy that isn't explicitly stated.]

EXTENSION QUESTIONS → *[handwritten]*

[handwritten in left margin: Apply what you read to something not stated.]

Extension questions are the most common. They require you to go beyond what is stated in the passage, asking you to draw an inference from the passage, to make a conclusion based on the passage, or to identify one of the author's tacit assumptions.

You may be asked to draw a conclusion based on the ideas or facts presented:

☐   It can be inferred from the passage that . . .

☐   The passage suggests that . . .

Since extension questions require you to go beyond the passage, the correct answer must say *more* than what is said in the passage. Beware of same language traps with these questions: the correct answer will often both paraphrase and extend a statement in the passage, but it will not directly quote it.

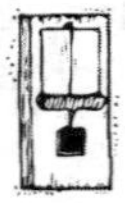

Trap!

"Same Language" traps: For extension questions, any answer-choice that explicitly refers to or repeats a statement in the passage will probably be wrong.

The correct answer to an extension question will not require a quantum leap in thought, but it will add significantly to the ideas presented in the passage.

Example: (Refer to passage on page 348.)

[handwritten in left margin: lines 37-44]

The author views the prosecution's role in the inquisitorial system as being

(A)   an advocate for both society and the defendant   → *[handwritten: not an advocate, just needs to consider both sides.]*
(B)   solely responsible for starting a trial
(C)   a protector of the legal rule
(D)   an investigator only
(E)   an aggressive but fair investigator

This is an extension question. So the answer will not be explicitly stated in the passage, but it will be strongly supported by it.

The author states that the prosecutor is duty bound to present any evidence that may prove the defendant innocent and that he must disclose all pretrial evidence (i.e., have no tricks up his sleeve). This is the essence of fair play. So the answer is probably (E).

However, we should check all the choices. (A) overstates the case. Although the prosecutor must disclose any evidence that might show the defendant innocent, the prosecutor is still advocating society's case against the defendant—it must merely be measured advocacy. This is the second-best answer. As for (B), although it is implied that in both systems the right to initiate a case is extended to all people through the prosecutor, it is not stated or implied that this is the only way to start a case. Finally, neither (C) nor (D) is mentioned or implied in the passage. The answer, therefore, is (E).

Application: *(Mini-passage)*

Often, the central problem in any business is that money is needed to make money. The following discusses the sale of equity, which is one response to this problem.

Sale of Capital Stock: a way to obtain capital through the sale of stock to individual investors beyond the scope of one's immediate acquaintances. Periods of high interest rates turn entrepreneurs to this equity market. This involves, of necessity, a dilution of ownership, and many owners are reluctant to take this step for that reason. Whether the owner is wise in declining to use outside equity financing depends upon the firm's long-range prospects. If there is an opportunity for substantial expansion on a continuing basis and if other sources are inadequate, the owner may decide logically to bring in other owners. Owning part of a larger business may be more profitable than owning all of a smaller business.

Small-Business Management, 6th Ed., © 1983 by South-Western Publishing Co.

The passage implies that an owner who chooses not to sell capital stock despite the prospect of continued expansion is

(A)   subject to increased regulation
(B)   more conservative than is wise under the circumstances
(C)   likely to have her ownership of the business diluted
(D)   sacrificing security for rapid growth

(A): No. This is not mentioned in the passage. **(B): Yes.** The passage states that *"the owner may decide logically to bring in other owners"*; in other words, the owner would be wise to sell stock in this situation. (C): No. By NOT selling stock, the owner retains full ownership. (D) No. Just the opposite: the owner would be sacrificing a measure of security for growth if she did sell stock.

[handwritten: extend what you read.]

APPLICATION QUESTIONS

[handwritten margin note: similar to extension]

Application questions differ from extension questions only in degree. Extension questions ask you to apply what you have learned from the passage to derive new information about the same subject, whereas application questions go one step further, asking you to apply what you have learned from the passage to a different or hypothetical situation.

The following are common application questions:

☐   Which one of the following is the most likely source of the passage?

☐   Which one of the following actions would be most likely to have the same effect as the author's actions?

You may be asked to complete a thought for the author:

☐   The author would most likely agree with which one of the following statements?

☐   Which one of the following sentences would the author be most likely to use to complete the last paragraph of the passage?

To answer an application question, take the author's perspective. Ask yourself: what am I arguing for? what might make my argument stronger? what might make it weaker?

Because these questions go well beyond the passage, they tend to be the most difficult. Furthermore, because application questions and extension questions require a deeper understanding of the passage, skimming (or worse yet, speed-reading) the passage is ineffective. Skimming may give you the main idea and structure of the passage, but it is unlikely to give you the subtleties of the author's attitude.

Example: (Refer to passage on page 348.)

Based on the information in the passage, it can be inferred that which one of the following would most logically begin a paragraph immediately following the passage?

(A)   Because of the inquisitorial system's thoroughness in conducting its pretrial investigation, it can be concluded that a defendant who is innocent would prefer to be tried under the inquisitorial system, whereas a defendant who is guilty would prefer to be tried under the adversarial system.
(B)   As the preceding analysis shows, the legal system is in a constant state of flux. For now the inquisitorial system is ascendant, but it will probably be soon replaced by another system.
(C)   The accusatorial system begins where the inquisitorial system ends. So it is three steps removed from the system of private vengeance, and therefore historically superior to it.
(D)   Because in the inquisitorial system the judge must take an active role in the conduct of the trial, his competency and expertise have become critical.
(E)   The criminal justice system has evolved to the point that it no longer seems to be derivative of the system of private vengeance. Modern systems of criminal justice empower all of society with the right to instigate a legal action, and the need for vengeance is satisfied through a surrogate—the public prosecutor.

The author has rather thoroughly presented his position, so the next paragraph would be a natural place for him to summarize it. The passage compares and contrasts two systems of criminal justice, implying that the inquisitorial system is superior. We expect the concluding paragraph to sum up this position. Now all legal theory aside, the system of justice under which an innocent person would choose to be judged would, as a practical matter, pretty much sum up the situation. Hence the answer is (A).

Application: *(Mini-passage)*

The idea of stuff expresses no more than the experience of coming to a limit at which our senses or our instruments are not fine enough to make out the pattern.

Something of the same kind happens when the scientist investigates any unit or pattern so distinct to the naked eye that it has been considered a separate entity. He finds that the more carefully he observes and describes it, the more he is *also* describing the environment in which it moves and other patterns to which it seems inseparably related. As Teilhard de Chardin has so well expressed it, the isolation of individual, atomic patterns "is merely an intellectual dodge."

...Although the ancient cultures of Asia never attained the rigorously exact physical knowledge of the modern West, they grasped in principle many things which are only now occurring to us. Hinduism and Buddhism are impossible to classify as religions, philosophies, sciences, or even mythologies, or again as amalgamations of all four, because departmentalization is foreign to them even in so basic a form as the separation of the spiritual and the material.... Buddhism ... is not a culture but a critique of culture, an enduring nonviolent revolution, or "loyal opposition," to the culture with which it is involved. This gives these ways of liberation something in common with psychotherapy beyond the interest in changing states of consciousness. For the task of the psychotherapist is to bring about a reconciliation between individual feeling and social norms without, however, sacrificing the integrity of the individual. He tries to help the individual to be himself and to go it alone in the world (of social convention) but not of the world.

From Alan W. Watts, *Psychotherapy East and West*, © 1961 by Pantheon Books, a division of Random House.

What does the passage suggest about the theme of the book from which it is excerpted?

(A) The book attempts to understand psychotherapy in the context of different and changing systems of thought.
(B) The book argues that psychotherapy unites elements of an exact science with elements of eastern philosophy.
(C) The book describes the origins of psychotherapy around the world.
(D) The book compares psychotherapy in the West and in the East.

(A): Yes, this is the most accurate inference from the passage. The passage discusses how the more carefully a scientist views and describes something the more he describes the environment in which it moves, and the passage traces similarities between psychotherapy and Eastern systems of (evolving) thought. (B): No, this is too narrow an interpretation of what the whole book would be doing. (C): No, too vague; the passage is too philosophical to be merely a history. (D): No, also too vague, meant to entrap those of you who relied on the title without thinking through the passage.

which is the author's attitude?
tone is typically negative & never extreme.

TONE QUESTIONS

Tone questions ask you to identify the writer's attitude or perspective. Is the writer's feeling toward the subject positive, negative, or neutral? Does the writer give his own opinion, or does he objectively present the opinions of others?

SKEPTICAL → pick doubtful or cautious.

Before you read the answer-choices, decide whether the writer's tone is positive, negative, or neutral. It is best to do this without referring to the passage.

However, if you did not get a feel for the writer's attitude on the first reading, check the adjectives that he chooses. Adjectives and, to a lesser extent, adverbs express our feelings toward subjects. For instance, if we agree with a person who holds strong feelings about a subject, we may describe his opinions as impassioned. On the other hand, if we disagree with him, we may describe his opinions as excitable, which has the same meaning as "impassioned" but carries a negative connotation.

Example: (Refer to passage on page 348.)

The author's attitude toward the adversarial system can best be described as

(A) encouraged that it is far removed from the system of private vengeance
(B) concerned that it does not allow all members of society to instigate legal action
(C) pleased that it does not require the defendant to conduct his own pretrial investigation
(D) hopeful that it will be replaced by the inquisitorial system
(E) doubtful that it is the best vehicle for justice

The author does not reveal his feelings toward the adversarial system until the end of paragraph one. Clearly the clause "the adversarial system of criminal procedure symbolizes and regularizes the punitive combat" indicates that he has a negative attitude toward the system. This is confirmed in the second paragraph when he states that the inquisitorial system is historically superior to the adversarial system. So he feels that the adversarial system is deficient.

The "two-out-of-five" rule is at work here: only choices (D) and (E) have any real merit. Both are good answers. But which one is better? Intuitively, choice (E) is more likely to be the answer because it is more measured. To decide between two choices attack each: the one that survives is the answer. Now a tone question should be answered from what is directly stated in the passage—not from what it implies. Although the author has reservations toward the adversarial system, at no point does he say that he hopes the inquisitorial system will replace it, he may prefer a third system over both. This eliminates (D); the answer therefore is (E).

The remaining choices are not supported by the passage. (A), using the same language as in the passage, overstates the author's feeling. In lines 13–15, he states that the adversarial system is only *one* step removed from the private vengeance system—not *far* removed. Remember: Be wary of extreme words. (A) would be a better choice if "far" were dropped. (B) makes a false claim. In lines 16–19, the author states that the adversarial system *does* extend the right to initiate legal action to all members of society. Finally, (C) also makes a false claim. In lines 21–23, the author states that the defendant in the adversarial system is still left to conduct his own pretrial investigation.

Application: *(Mini-passage)*

An elm in our backyard caught the blight this summer and dropped stone dead, leafless, almost overnight. One weekend it was a normal-looking elm, maybe a little bare in spots but nothing alarming, and the next weekend it was gone, passed over, departed, taken....

The dying of a field mouse, at the jaws of an amiable household cat, is a spectacle I have beheld many times. It used to make me wince.... Nature, I thought, was an abomination.

Recently I've done some thinking about that mouse, and I wonder if his dying is necessarily all that different from the passing of our elm. The main difference, if there is one, would be in the matter of pain. I do not believe that an elm tree has pain receptors, and even so, the blight seems to me a relatively painless way to go. But the mouse dangling tail-down from the teeth of a gray cat is something else again, with pain beyond bearing, you'd think, all over his small body. There are now some plausible reasons for thinking it is not like that at all.... At the instant of being trapped and penetrated by teeth, peptide hormones are released by cells in the hypothalamus and the pituitary gland; instantly these substances, called endorphins, are attached to the surfaces of other cells responsible for pain perception; the hormones have the pharmacologic properties of opium; there is no pain. Thus it is that the mouse seems always to dangle so languidly from the jaws, lies there so quietly when dropped, dies of his injuries without a struggle. If a mouse could shrug, he'd shrug....

Pain is useful for avoidance, for getting away when there's time to get away, but when it is end game, and no way back, pain is likely to be turned off, and the mechanisms for this are wonderfully precise and quick. If I had to design an ecosystem in which creatures had to live off each other and in which dying was an indispensable part of living, I could not think of a better way to manage.

From Lewis Thomas, *On Natural Death*, © 1979 by Lewis Thomas.

Which one of the following would best characterize the author's attitude toward the relationship between pain and death?

(A)   Dismay at the inherent cruelty of nature
(B)   Amusement at the irony of the relationship between pain and death
(C)   Admiration for the ways in which animal life functions in the ecosystem

(D)   A desire to conduct experiments on animals in order to discover more about the relationship between pain and death

The author's attitude toward the relationship between pain and death evolves through three stages. First, he expresses revulsion at the relationship. This is indicated in the second paragraph by the words *"wince"* and *"abomination."* Then in the third paragraph, he adopts a more analytical attitude and questions his previous judgment. This is indicated by the clause, *"I wonder if his dying is necessarily all that different from the passing of our elm."* And in closing the paragraph, he seems resigned to the fact the relationship is not all that bad. This is indicated by the sentence, *"If a mouse could shrug, he'd shrug."* Finally, in the last paragraph, he comes to express admiration for the relationship between pain and death. This is indicated by the phrase *"wonderfully precise and quick,"* and it is made definite by the closing line, *"If I had to design an ecosystem . . . in which dying was an indispensable part of living, I could not think of a better way to manage."* Thus, the answer is (C).

The other choices are easily ruled out. Choice (A) is perhaps superficially tempting. In the second paragraph the author does express dismay at the ways of nature, but notice that his concerns are in the past tense. He is *now* more understanding, wiser of the ways of nature. As to (B), the author is subtly reverential, never ironical, toward nature. Finally, (D) is not mentioned or alluded to in the passage.

Beware of answer-choices that contain extreme emotions. Remember the passages are taken from academic journals. In the rarefied air of academic circles, strong emotions are considered inappropriate and sophomoric. The writers want to display opinions that are considered and reasonable, not spontaneous and off-the-wall. So if an author's tone is negative, it may be disapproving—not snide. Or if her tone is positive, it may be approving—not ecstatic.

Furthermore, the answers must be indisputable. If the answers were subjective, then the writers of the GMAT would be deluged with letters from angry test takers, complaining that their test-scores are unfair. To avoid such a difficult position, the writers of the GMAT never allow the correct answer to be either controversial or grammatically questionable.

Let's use these theories to answer the following questions.

Example:

Which one of the following most accurately characterizes the author's attitude with respect to Phillis Wheatley's literary accomplishments?

(A)   enthusiastic advocacy
(B)   qualified admiration
(C)   dispassionate impartiality
(D)   detached ambivalence
(E)   perfunctory dismissal

Even without reference to the passage, this is not a difficult question to answer.

Scholars may advocate each other's work, but they are unlikely to be enthusiastic advocates. Furthermore, the context stretches the meaning of advocacy—to defend someone else's cause or plight. So (A) is unlikely to be the answer.

(B) is the measured response and therefore is probably the answer.

"Dispassionate impartiality" is a rather odd construction; additionally, it is redundant. It could never be the answer to a GMAT question. This eliminates (C).

"Detached ambivalence" is not as odd as "dispassionate impartiality," but it is unusual. So (D) is unlikely to be the answer.

Remember, scholars want their audience to consider their opinions well thought out, not off-the-wall. But *perfunctory* means "hasty and superficial." So (E) could not be the answer.

Hence, even without the passage we can still find the answer, (B).

Example:

Which one of the following best describes the author's attitude toward scientific techniques?

(A) critical
(B) hostile
(C) idealistic
(D) ironic
(E) neutral

(A) is one of two measured responses offered. Now a scholar may be critical of a particular scientific technique, but only a crackpot would be critical of *all* scientific techniques—eliminate (A).

"Hostile" is far too negative. Scholars consider such emotions juvenile—eliminate (B).

"Idealistic," on the other hand, is too positive; it sounds pollyannaish—eliminate (C).

"Ironic" seems illogical in this context. It's hard to conceive of a person having an ironic attitude toward scientific techniques—eliminate (D).

(E) is the other measured response, and by elimination it is the answer.

Description, extension, and application questions make up about 80% of the reading comprehension questions, main idea questions about 10%, and tone and writing technique questions about 5% each.

Points to Remember

1.   The order of the passage questions <u>roughly</u> corresponds to the order in which the issues are presented in the passage.

2.   The six questions are

  Main Idea
  Description
  Writing Technique
  Extension
  Application
  Tone

3.   The main idea of a passage is usually stated in the last, sometimes the first, sentence of the first paragraph. If it's not there, it will probably be the last sentence of the entire passage.

4.   If after the first reading, you don't have a feel for the main idea, review the first and last sentence of each paragraph.

5.   The answer to a description question must refer directly to a statement in the passage, not to something implied by it. However, the correct answer will paraphrase a passage statement, not quote it exactly. In fact, exact quotes are used with these questions to bait wrong answers.

6.   When answering a description question, you must find the point in the passage from which the question is drawn.

7.   If a description question refers to line 20, the information needed to answer it can occur anywhere from line 15 to 25.

8.   Some writing techniques commonly used in the GMAT passages are

   A.   Compare and contrast two positions.

   B.   Show cause and effect.

   C.   State a position; then give supporting evidence.

9.   For extension questions, any answer-choice that refers explicitly to or repeats a statement in the passage will probably be wrong.

10.   Application questions differ from extension questions only in degree. Extension questions ask you to apply what you have learned from the passage to derive new information about the same subject, whereas application questions go one step further, asking you to apply what you have learned from the passage to a different or hypothetical situation.

11.   To answer an application question, take the perspective of the author. Ask yourself: what am I arguing for? what might make my argument stronger? what might make it weaker?

12.   Because application questions go well beyond the passage, they tend to be the most difficult.

13.   For tone questions, decide whether the writer's tone is positive, negative, or neutral before you look at the answer-choices.

14.   If you do not have a feel for the writer's attitude after the first reading, check the adjectives that she chooses.

15.   Beware of answer-choices that contain extreme emotions. If an author's tone is negative, it may be disapproving—not snide. Or if her tone is positive, it may be approving—not ecstatic.

16.   The answers must be indisputable. A correct answer will never be controversial or grammatically questionable.

17.   Description, extension, and application questions make up about 80% of the reading comprehension questions, main idea questions about 10%, and tone and writing technique questions about 5% each.

Mentor Exercise

Directions: This passage is followed by a group of questions to be answered based on what is <u>stated</u> or <u>implied</u> in the passage. Choose the <u>best</u> answer; the one that most accurately and completely answers the question. Hints, insights, and answers immediately follow the questions.

From Romania to Germany, from Tallinn to Belgrade, a major historical process—the death of communism—is taking place. The German Democratic Republic no longer exists as a sepa-
5   rate state. And the former German Democratic Republic will serve as the first measure of the price a post-Communist society has to pay for entering the normal European orbit. In Yugoslavia we will see whether the federation
10   can survive without communism.

One thing seems common to all these countries: dictatorship has been defeated and freedom has won, yet the victory of freedom has not yet meant the triumph of democracy.
15   Democracy is something more than freedom. Democracy is freedom institutionalized, freedom submitted to the limits of the law, freedom functioning as an object of compromise between the major political forces on the scene.

20   We have freedom, but we still have not achieved the democratic order. That is why this freedom is so fragile. In the years of democratic opposition to communism, we supposed that the easiest thing would be to introduce changes in
25   the economy. In fact, we thought that the march from a planned economy to a market economy would take place within the framework of the bureaucratic system, and that the market within the Communist state would explode the totali-
30   tarian structures. Only then would the time come to build the institutions of a civil society; and only at the end, with the completion of the market economy and the civil society, would the time of great political transformations finally
35   arrive.

The opposite happened. First came the big political change, the great shock, which either broke the monopoly and the principle of Communist Party rule or simply pushed the
40   Communists out of power. Then came the creation of civil society, whose institutions were created in great pain, and which had trouble negotiating the empty space of freedom. Only then, as the third moment of change, the final

45   task was undertaken: that of transforming the totalitarian economy into a normal economy where different forms of ownership and different economic actors will live one next to the other.

50   Today we are in a typical moment of transition. No one can say where we are headed. The people of the democratic opposition have the feeling that we won. We taste the sweetness of our victory the same way the Communists, only
55   yesterday our prison guards, taste the bitterness of their defeat. Yet, even as we are conscious of our victory, we feel that we are, in a strange way, losing. In Bulgaria the Communists have won the parliamentary elections and will govern
60   the country, without losing their social legitimacy. In Romania the National Salvation Front, largely dominated by people from the old Communist bureaucracy, has won. In other countries democratic institutions seem shaky,
65   and the political horizon is cloudy. The masquerade goes on: dozens of groups and parties are created, each announces similar slogans, each accuses its adversaries of all possible sins, and each declares itself representative of the na-
70   tional interest. Personal disputes are more important than disputes over values. Arguments over values are fiercer than arguments over ideas.

1. The author originally thought that the order of events in the transformation of communist society would be represented by which one of the following?

    (A) A great political shock would break the totalitarian monopoly, leaving in its wake a civil society whose task would be to change the state-controlled market into a free economy.
    (B) The transformation of the economy would destroy totalitarianism, after which a new and different social and political structure would be born.
    (C) First the people would freely elect political representatives who would transform the economy, which would then undermine the totalitarian structure.
    (D) The change to a democratic state would necessarily undermine totalitarianism, after which a new economic order would be created.
    (E) The people's frustration would build until it spontaneously generated violent revolution, which would sentence society to years of anarchy and regression.

1. This is a description question, so you should locate the point in the passage from which it was drawn. It is the third paragraph. In lines 25–30, the author recalls his expectation that, by introducing the market system, the communist system would topple from within.

Trap!   Be careful not to choose (A). It chronicles how the events actually occurred, not how they were *anticipated* to occur. (A) is baited with the words "great shock," "monopoly," and "civil society."

The answer is (B).

2. Beginning in the second paragraph, the author describes the complicated relationship between "freedom" and "democracy." In the author's view, which one of the following statements best reflects that relationship?

    (A) A country can have freedom without having democracy.
    (B) If a country has freedom, it necessarily has democracy.
    (C) A country can have democracy without having freedom.
    (D) A country can never have democracy if it has freedom.
    (E) If a country has democracy, it cannot have freedom.

2. This is an extension question, so the answer must say more than what is said in the passage, without requiring a quantum leap in thought. The needed reference is *"Democracy is something more than freedom"* (line 15). Since freedom can exist without democracy, freedom alone does not insure democracy.

The answer is (A).

3. From the passage, a reader could conclude that which one of the following best describes the author's attitude toward the events that have taken place in communist society?

    (A) Relieved that at last the democratic order has surfaced.
    (B) Clearly wants to return to the old order.
    (C) Disappointed with the nature of the democracy that has emerged.
    (D) Confident that a free economy will ultimately provide the basis for a true democracy.
    (E) Surprised that communism was toppled through political rather than economic means.

3. This is a tone question. The key to answering this question is found in the closing comments. There the author states *"The masquerade goes on,"* referring to nascent democracies. So he has reservations about the newly emerging democracies.

Watch out! Watch out for (E). Although it is supported by the passage, it is in a supporting paragraph. The ideas in a concluding paragraph take precedence over those in a supporting paragraph.

The answer is (C).

4. A cynic who has observed political systems in various countries would likely interpret the author's description of the situation at the end of the passage as

    (A) evidence that society is still in the throws of the old totalitarian structure.
    (B) a distorted description of the new political system.
    (C) a necessary political reality that is a prelude to "democracy."
    (D) a fair description of many democratic political systems.
    (E) evidence of the baseness of people.

4. This is an application question. These are like extension questions, but they go well beyond what is stated in the passage. In this case we are asked to interpret the author's comments from a cynic's perspective. Because application questions go well beyond the passage, they are often difficult, as is this one.

Hint! A cynic looks at reality from a negative perspective, usually with a sense of dark irony and hopelessness.

Don't make the mistake of choosing (E). Although a cynic is likely to make such a statement, it does not address the subject of the passage—political and economic systems. The passage is not about human nature, at least not directly.

The answer is (D).

5. Which one of the following does the author imply may have contributed to the difficulties involved in creating a new democratic order in eastern Europe?

    I.   The people who existed under the totalitarian structure have not had the experience of "negotiating the empty space of freedom."
    II.   Mistaking the order in which political, economic, and social restructuring would occur.
    III. Excessive self-interest among the new political activists.

    (A) I only
    (B) II only
    (C) I and III only
    (D) II and III only
    (E) I, II, and III

5. This is an extension question. Statement I is true. In lines 40–43, the author implies that the institutions of the new-born, free society were created in great pain because the people lacked experience. Statement II is true. Expectations that the market mechanisms would explode totalitarianism and usher in a new society were dashed, and having to readjust one's expectations certainly makes a situation more difficult. Finally, statement III is true. It summarizes the thrust of the passage's closing lines.

The answer is (E).

6. By stating "even as we are conscious of our victory, we feel that we are, in a strange way, losing" (lines 56–58) the author means that

    (A) some of the old governments are still unwilling to grant freedom at the individual level.
    (B) some of the new governments are not strong enough to exist as a single federation.
    (C) some of the new democratic governments are electing to retain the old political parties.
    (D) no new parties have been created to fill the vacuum created by the victory of freedom.
    (E) some of the new governments are reverting to communism.

6. This is a hybrid extension and description question. Because it refers to a specific point in the passage, you must read a few sentences before and after it. The answer can be found in lines 58–70.

The answer is (C).

Exercise

Directions: This passage is followed by a group of questions to be answered based on what is <u>stated</u> or <u>implied</u> in the passage. Choose the <u>best</u> answer; the one that most accurately and completely answers the question.

In the United States the per capita costs of schooling have risen almost as fast as the cost of medical treatment. But increased treatment by both doctors and teachers has shown
5 steadily declining results. Medical expenses concentrated on those above forty-five have doubled several times over a period of forty years with a resulting 3 percent increase in the life expectancy of men. The increase in educa-
10 tional expenditures has produced even stranger results; otherwise President Nixon could not have been moved this spring to promise that every child shall soon have the "Right to Read" before leaving school.

15   In the United States it would take eighty billion dollars per year to provide what educators regard as equal treatment for all in grammar and high school. This is well over twice the $36 billion now being spent. Independent
20 cost projections prepared at HEW and at the University of Florida indicate that by 1974 the comparable figures will be $107 billion as against the $45 billion now projected, and these figures wholly omit the enormous costs
25 of what is called "higher education," for which demand is growing even faster. The United States, which spent nearly eighty billion dollars in 1969 for "defense," including its deployment in Vietnam, is obviously too poor
30 to provide equal schooling. The President's committee for the study of school finance should ask not how to support or how to trim such increasing costs, but how they can be avoided.

35   Equal obligatory schooling must be recognized as at least economically unfeasible. In Latin America the amount of public money spent on each graduate student is between 350 and 1,500 times the amount spent on the me-
40 dian citizen (that is, the citizen who holds the middle ground between the poorest and the richest). In the United States the discrepancy is smaller, but the discrimination is keener. The richest parents, some 10 percent, can af-
45 ford private education for their children and

help them to benefit from foundation grants. But in addition they obtain ten times the per capita amount of public funds if this is compared with the per capita expenditure made
50 on the children of the 10 percent who are poorest. The principal reasons for this are that rich children stay longer in school, that a year in a university is disproportionately more expensive than a year in high school, and that
55 most private universities depend—at least indirectly—on tax-derived finances.

Obligatory schooling inevitably polarizes a society; it also grades the nations of the world according to an international caste sys-
60 tem. Countries are rated like castes whose educational dignity is determined by the average years of schooling of its citizens, a rating which is closely related to per capita gross national product, and much more painful.

1. Which one of the following best expresses the main idea of the passage?

    (A) The educational shortcomings of the United States, in contrast to those of Latin America, are merely the result of poor allocation of available resources.
    (B) Both education and medical care are severely underfunded.
    (C) Defense spending is sapping funds which would be better spent in education.
    (D) Obligatory schooling must be scrapped if the goal of educational equality is to be realized.
    (E) Obligatory education does not and cannot provide equal education.

2. The author most likely would agree with which one of the following solutions to the problems presented by obligatory education?

(A) Education should not be obligatory at all.

(B) Education should not be obligatory for those who cannot afford it.

(C) More money should be diverted to education for the poorest.

(D) Countries should cooperate to establish common minimal educational standards.

(E) Future spending should be capped.

3. According to the passage, education is like health care in all of the following ways EXCEPT:

(A) It has reached a point of diminishing returns, increased spending no longer results in significant improvement.

(B) It has an inappropriate "more is better" philosophy.

(C) It is unfairly distributed between rich and poor.

(D) The amount of money being spent on older students is increasing.

(E) Its cost has increased nearly as fast.

4. Why does the author consider the results from increased educational expenditures to be "even stranger" than those from increased medical expenditures?

(A) The aging of the population should have had an impact only on medical care, not on education.

(B) The "Right to Read" should be a bare minimum, not a Presidential ideal.

(C) Educational spending has shown even poorer results than spending on health care, despite greater increases.

(D) Education has become even more discriminatory than health care.

(E) It inevitably polarizes society.

5. Which one of the following most accurately characterizes the author's attitude with respect to obligatory schooling?

(A) qualified admiration
(B) critical
(C) neutral
(D) ambivalent
(E) resentful

6. By stating "In Latin America the amount of public money spent on each graduate student is between 350 and 1,500 times the amount spent on the median citizen" and "In the United States the discrepancy is smaller" the author implies that

(A) equal education is possible in the United States but not in Latin America.

(B) equal education for all at the graduate level is an unrealistic ideal.

(C) educational spending is more efficient in the United States.

(D) higher education is more expensive than lower education both in Latin America and in the United States, but more so in Latin America.

(E) underfunding of lower education is a world-wide problem.

Answers and Solutions to Exercise

1. The answer to a main idea question will summarize the passage, without going beyond it.

(A) fails to meet these criteria because it makes a false claim. Lines 36–42 imply that the discrepancy in allocation of funds is greater in Latin America. Besides, Latin America is mentioned only in passing, so this is not the main idea.

(B) also makes a false claim. The author implies that increased funding for education is irrelevant, if not counterproductive. In fact, the sentence *"The President's committee for the study of school finance should ask not how to support or how to trim such increasing costs, but how they can be avoided"* implies that he thinks an increase in funding would be counterproductive.

(C) is implied by the sentence *"The United States . . . is obviously too poor to provide equal schooling,"* but the author does not fully develop this idea. Besides, he implies that the problem is not financial.

(D) is the second-best answer-choice. The answer to a main idea question should sum up the passage, not make a conjecture about it. Clearly the author has serious reservations about obligatory schooling, but at no point does he state or imply that it should be scrapped. He may believe that it can be modified, or he may be resigned to the fact that, for other reasons, it is necessary. We don't know.

Finally, (E) aptly summarizes the passage, without going beyond it. The key to seeing this is the opening to paragraph three, *"Equal obligatory schooling must be recognized as at least economically unfeasible."* In other words, regardless of any other failings, it cannot succeed economically and therefore cannot provide equal education.

2. This is an application question. These questions tend to be rather difficult, though this one is not. To answer an application question, put yourself in the author's place. If you were arguing his case, which of the solutions would you advocate?

As to (A), although we rejected the recommendation that obligatory education be eliminated as Question 1's answer, it is the

answer to Question 2. The author does not merely imply that obligatory education has some shortcomings; he suggests that it is fundamentally flawed. Again this is made clear by the opening to paragraph three, *"Equal obligatory schooling must be recognized as at least economically unfeasible."* Still, there is a possible misunderstanding here: perhaps the author believes that obligatory education is a noble but unrealistic idea. This possibility, however, is dispelled by the closing paragraph in which he states that obligatory education polarizes society and sets up a caste system. Obviously, such a system, if this is true, should be discarded. The answer is (A).

The other choices can be easily dismissed. (B) is incorrect because nothing in the passage suggests that the author would advocate a solution that would polarize society even more. Indeed, at the end of paragraph three, he suggests that the rich already get more than their fair share.

(C) is incorrect because it contradicts the author. Paragraph two is dedicated to showing that the United States is too poor to provide equal schooling. You can't divert money you don't have.

(D) is incorrect. It reads too much into the last paragraph.

Finally, (E) is the second-best answer-choice. Although the author probably believes that future spending should be restrained or capped, this understates the thrust of his argument. However, he might offer this as a compromise to his opponents.

3. This is a description question, so we must find the place from which it is drawn. It is the first paragraph. The sentence *"But increased treatment by both doctors and teachers has shown steadily declining results"* shows that both have reached a point of diminishing returns. This eliminates (A) and (B). Next, the passage states *"Medical expenses concentrated on those above forty-five have doubled several times"* (lines 5–7) and that the demand and costs of higher education are growing faster than the demand and costs of elementary and high school education. This eliminates (D). Next, the opening to the passage states that the costs of education *"have risen almost as fast as the cost of medical*

treatment." This eliminates (E). Hence, by process of elimination, the answer is (C). We should, however, verify this. In paragraph three, the author does state that there is a "keen" discrepancy in the funding of education between rich and poor, but a survey of the passage shows that at no point does he mention that this is also the case with health care.

4. This is an extension question. We are asked to interpret a statement by the author. The needed reference is the closing sentence to paragraph one. Remember: extension questions require you to go beyond the passage, so the answer won't be explicitly stated in the reference—we will have to interpret it.

The implication of President Nixon's promise is that despite increased educational funding many children cannot even read when they graduate from school. Hence the answer is (B).

Don't make the mistake of choosing (C). Although at first glance this is a tempting inference, it would be difficult to compare the results of education and medical care directly (how would we do so?). Regardless, the opening line to the passage states that educational costs have risen "almost as fast" as medical costs, not faster.

(A) is incorrect because the passage never mentions the aging of the population. The same is true for (D).

Many students who cannot solve this question choose (E)—don't. It uses as bait language from the passage, *"inevitably polarizes a society."* Note: The phrase "Right to Read" in (B) is not a same language trap; it is merely part of a paraphrase of the passage. The correct answer to an extension question will often both paraphrase and extend a passage statement but will not quote it directly, as in (E).

5. Like most tone questions this one is rather easy. Although choice (A) is a measured response, the author clearly does not admire the obligatory school system. This eliminates (A); it also eliminates (C) and (D). Of the two remaining choices, (B) is the measured response, and it is the answer. Although the author strongly opposes obligatory schooling, "resentful" is too strong and too personal. A scholar would never directly express resentment or envy, even if that is his true feeling.

6. This is another extension question. By stating that the amount of funding spent on graduate students is more than 350 times the amount spent on the average citizen, the author implies that it would be impossible to equalize the funding. Hence the answer is (B).

None of the other choices have any real merit. (A) is incorrect because the import of the passage is that the rich get better schooling and more public funds in the United States and therefore discrimination is "keener" here (lines 42–43).

(C) and (D) are incorrect because they are neither mentioned nor implied by the passage.

(E) is the second-best choice. Although this is implied by the numbers given, it has little to do with the primary purpose of the passage—to show that obligatory education is perhaps not such a good idea.

Pivotal Words

As mentioned before, each passage contains about 300 words and only a few questions, so you will <u>not</u> be tested on most of the material in the passage. Your best reading strategy, therefore, is to identify the places from which questions will most likely be drawn and concentrate your attention there.

Pivotal words can help in this regard. Following are the most common pivotal words.

PIVOTAL WORDS

But	**Although**
However	**Yet**
Despite	**Nevertheless**
Nonetheless	**Except**
In contrast	**Even though**

making a key turn = exception will draw questions here!

As you may have noticed, these words indicate contrast. Pivotal words warn that the author is about to either make a U-turn or introduce a counter-premise (concession to a minor point that weakens the argument).

Example: (Counter-premise)

I submit that the strikers should accept the management's offer. Admittedly, it is less than what was demanded. But it does resolve the main grievance—inadequate health care. Furthermore, an independent study shows that a wage increase greater than 5% would leave the company unable to compete against Japan and Germany, forcing it into bankruptcy.

The conclusion, "the strikers should accept the management's offer," is stated in the first sentence. Then "Admittedly" introduces a concession (counter-premise); namely, that the offer was less than what was demanded. This weakens the speaker's case, but it addresses a potential criticism of his position before it can be made. The last two sentences of the argument present more compelling reasons to accept the offer and form the gist of the argument.

Pivotal words mark natural places for questions to be drawn. At a pivotal word, the author changes direction. The GMAT writers form questions at these junctures to test whether you turned with the author or you continued to go straight. Rarely do the GMAT writers let a pivotal word pass without drawing a question from its sentence.

 As you read a passage, note the pivotal words and refer to them when answering the questions.

Strategy

Let's apply this theory to the passage on criminal justice. For easy reference, the passage is reprinted here in the left-hand column, with explanations in the right-hand column. The pivotal words are marked in bold.

There are two major systems of criminal procedure in the modern world—the adversarial and the inquisitorial. The former is associated with common law tradition and the latter with civil law tradition. Both systems were historically preceded by the system of private vengeance in which the victim of a crime fashioned his own remedy and administered it privately, either personally or through an agent. The vengeance system was a system of self-help, the essence of which was captured in the slogan "an eye for an eye, a tooth for a tooth." The modern adversarial system is only one historical step removed from the private vengeance system and still retains some of its characteristic features. Thus, for example, **even though** the right to institute criminal action has now been extended to all members of society and **even though** the police department has taken over the pretrial investigative functions on behalf of the prosecution, the adversarial system still leaves the defendant to conduct his own pretrial investigation. The trial is still viewed as a duel between two adversaries, refereed by a judge who, at the beginning of the trial has no knowledge of the investigative background of the case. In the final analysis the adversarial system of criminal procedure symbolizes and regularizes the punitive combat.

By contrast, the inquisitorial system begins historically where the adversarial system stopped its development. It is two historical steps removed from the system of private vengeance. Therefore, from the standpoint of legal anthropology, it is historically superior to the adversarial system. Under the inquisitorial system the public investigator has the duty to investigate not just on behalf of the prosecutor **but also** on behalf of the defendant. Additionally, the public prosecutor has the duty to present to the court not only evidence that may lead to the conviction of the defendant **but also** evidence that may lead to his exoneration. This system mandates that both parties permit full pretrial discovery of the evidence in their possession. Finally, in an effort to make the trial less like a duel between two adversaries, the inquisitorial system mandates that the judge take an active part in the conduct of the trial, with a role that is both directive and protective.

Fact-finding is at the heart of the inquisitorial system. This system operates on the philosophical premise that in a criminal case the crucial factor is not the legal rule but the facts of the case and that the goal of the entire procedure is to experimentally recreate for the court the commission of the alleged crime.

Even though—Here "even though" is introducing a concession. In the previous sentence, the author stated that the adversarial system is only one step removed from the private vengeance system. The author uses the two concessions as a hedge against potential criticism that he did not consider that the adversarial system has extended the right to institute criminal action to all members of society and that police departments now perform the pretrial investigation. But the author then states that the adversarial system still leaves the defendant to conduct his own pretrial investigation. This marks a good place from which to draw a question. Many people will misinterpret the two concessions as evidence that the adversarial system is two steps removed from the private vengeance system.

By contrast—In this case the pivotal word is not introducing a concession. Instead it indicates a change in thought: now the author is going to discuss the other criminal justice system. This is a natural place to test whether the student has made the transition and whether he will attribute the properties soon to be introduced to the inquisitorial system, not the adversarial system.

But also—In both places, "but also" indicates neither concession nor change in thought. Instead it is part of the coordinating conjunction "not only . . . but also . . . ." Rather than indicating contrast, it emphasizes the second element of the pair.

Let's see how these pivotal words can help answer the questions in the last section. The first is from the Description Section:

Example:

According to the passage, the inquisitorial system differs from the adversarial system in that

(A)   it does not make the defendant solely responsible for gathering evidence for his case
(B)   it does not require the police department to work on behalf of the prosecution
(C)   it does not allow the victim the satisfaction of private vengeance
(D)   it requires the prosecution to drop a weak case
(E)   a defendant who is innocent would prefer to be tried under the inquisitorial system

The pivotal phrase "by contrast" flags the second paragraph as the place to begin looking. The pivotal phrase "but also" introduces the answer—namely that the prosecutor must also investigate "on behalf of the defendant." The answer is (A).

The next question is from the Writing Techniques Section:

Example:

Which one of the following best describes the organization of the passage?

(A)   Two systems of criminal justice are compared and contrasted, and one is deemed to be better than the other.
(B)   One system of criminal justice is presented as better than another. Then evidence is presented to support that claim.
(C)   Two systems of criminal justice are analyzed, and one specific example is examined in detail.
(D)   A set of examples is presented. Then a conclusion is drawn from them.
(E)   The inner workings of the criminal justice system are illustrated by using two systems.

The pivotal phrase "by contrast" gives this question away. The author is comparing and contrasting two criminal justice systems, which the opening pivotal word introduces. Hence the answer is (A).

For our final example, consider the question from the Extension Section:

Example:

The author views the prosecution's role in the inquisitorial system as being

(A)   an advocate for both society and the defendant
(B)   solely responsible for starting a trial
(C)   a protector of the legal rule
(D)   an investigator only
(E)   an aggressive but fair investigator

The information needed to answer this question is introduced by the pivotal phrase, "but also." There it is stated that the prosecutor must present evidence that may exonerate the defendant; that is, he must act fairly. The answer is (E).

Points to Remember

1. Pivotal words indicate that the author is about to make a U-turn in thought or introduce a counter-premise (concession to a minor point that weakens the argument).

2. The following are the most common pivotal words:

But	**Although**
However	**Yet**
Despite	**Nevertheless**
Nonetheless	**Except**
In contrast	**Even though**

3. Pivotal words mark natural places for questions to be drawn. At a pivotal word, the author changes direction. The GMAT writers form questions at these junctures to test whether you made the turn with the author or whether you continued to go straight. Rarely do the GMAT writers pass a pivotal word without drawing a question from its sentence.

4. As you read each passage, note the pivotal words.

Mentor Exercise

The premise with which the multiculturalists begin is unexceptional: that it is important to recognize and to celebrate the wide range of cultures that exist in the United States. In what sounds like a reflection of traditional American pluralism, the multiculturalists argue that we must recognize difference, that difference is legitimate; in its kindlier versions, multicultural-ism represents the discovery on the part of minority groups that they can play a part in molding the larger culture even as they are molded by it. And on the campus multicultural-ism, defined more locally as the need to recog-nize cultural variations among students, has tried with some success to talk about how a racially and ethnically diverse student body can enrich everyone's education.

Phillip Green, a political scientist at Smith and a thoughtful proponent of multiculturalism, notes that for a significant portion of the students the politics of identity is all-consuming. Students he says "are unhappy with the thin gruel of rationalism. They require a therapeutic cur-riculum to overcome not straightforward racism but ignorant stereotyping."

(1) But multiculturalism's hard-liners, who seem to make up the majority of the movement, damn as racism any attempt to draw the myriad of American groups into a common American culture. For these multiculturalists, differences are absolute, irreducible, intractable—occasions not for understanding but for separation. The multiculturalist, it turns out, is not especially interested in the great American hyphen, in the syncretistic (and therefore naturally tolerant) identities that allow Americans to belong to more than a single culture, to be both particularists and universalists.

The time-honored American mixture of assimilation and traditional allegiance is denounced as a danger to racial and gender authenticity. This is an extraordinary reversal of the traditional liberal commitment to a "truth" that transcends parochialisms. In the new race/class/gender formation, universality is replaced by, among other things, feminist science Nubian numerals (as part of an Afro-centric science), and what Marilyn Frankenstein of the University of Massachusetts-Boston describes as "ethno-mathematics," in which the cultural basis of counting comes to the fore.

There are two critical pivotal words in this passage—(1) **But**, and (2) **however**.

(1) **But**. Until this point, the author did not reveal his feeling toward multiculturalism. He presented an objective, if not positive, view of the movement. However, "**But**" introduced an abrupt change in direction (a U-turn). Before he talked about the "kindlier" multiculturalism—to which he appears to be sympathetic. Now he talks about "hard-line" multiculturalism, which he implies is intolerant and divisive.

The pivotal word "**but**" doesn't just change the direction of the passage, it introduces the main idea: that multiculturalism has become an extreme and self-contradictory movement.

The multiculturalists insist on seeing all perspectives as tainted by the perceiver's particular point of view. Impartial knowledge, they argue, is not possible, because ideas are simply the expression of individual identity, or of the unspoken but inescapable assumptions that are inscribed in a culture or a language. The problem, **(2) however,** with this warmed-over Nietzscheanism is that it threatens to leave no ground for anybody to stand on. So the multiculturalists make a leap, necessary for their own intellectual survival, and proceed to argue that there are some categories, such as race and gender, that do in fact embody an unmistakable knowledge of oppression. Victims are at least epistemologically lucky. Objectivity is a mask for oppression. And so an appalled former 1960s radical complained to me that self-proclaimed witches were teaching classes on witchcraft. "They're not teaching students how to think," she said, "they're telling them what to believe."

(2) however. This is the second critical pivotal word. The author opened this paragraph by presenting the multiculturalist's view; now he will criticize their positions.

1. Which one of the following ideas would a multiculturalist NOT believe?

   (A) That we should recognize and celebrate the differences among the many cultures in the United States.

   (B) That we can never know the "truth" because "truth" is always shaped by one's culture.

   (C) That "difference" is more important than "sameness."

   (D) That a school curriculum should be constructed to compensate for institutionalized racism.

   (E) That different cultures should work to assimilate themselves into the mainstream culture so that eventually there will be no excuse for racism.

1. The sentence introduced by the pivotal word "**But**" gives away the answer to this question.

The answer is (E).

2. According to a hard-line multiculturalist, which one of the following groups is most likely to know the "truth" about political reality?

   (A) Educated people who have learned how to see reality from many different perspectives.

   (B) A minority group that has suffered oppression at the hands of the majority.

   (C) High government officials who have privileged access to secret information.

   (D) Minorities who through their education have risen above the socioeconomic position occupied by most members of their ethnic group.

   (E) Political scientists who have thoroughly studied the problem.

2. This is a rather hard extension question.

 Hint! A subjugated minority group has at least the "unmistakable knowledge of oppression" (last paragraph).

Watch out! Don't make the mistake of choosing (D). Upper class minorities have simply exchanged one tainted point of view for another—and probably a more tainted one since the adopted position does not allow for knowledge of "oppression."

The answer is (B).

3. The author states that in a "kindlier version" of multiculturalism, minorities discover "that they can play a part in molding the larger culture even as they are molded by it." If no new ethnic groups were incorporated into the American culture for many centuries to come, which one of the following would be the most probable outcome of this "kindlier version"?

    (A)   At some point in the future, there would be only one culture with no observable ethnic differences.
    (B)   Eventually the dominant culture would overwhelm the minority cultures, who would then lose their ethnic identities.
    (C)   The multiplicity of ethnic groups would remain but the characteristics of the different ethnic groups would change.
    (D)   The smaller ethnic groups would remain, and they would retain their ethnic heritage.
    (E)   The minority cultures would eventually overwhelm the dominant culture, which would then lose its identity.

3. This application question clearly goes well beyond the passage.

    If no new ethnic groups were incorporated into the American culture, then the interplay between the larger and smaller groups would continue, with both groups changing, until there would be only one common (and different from any original) group.

The answer is (A).

4. The author speaks about the "politics of identity" that Phillip Green, a political scientist at Smith, notes is all-consuming for many of the students. Considering the subject of the passage, which one of the following best describes what the author means by "the politics of identity"?

    (A)   The attempt to discover individual identities through political action
    (B)   The political agenda that aspires to create a new pride of identity for Americans
    (C)   The current obsession for therapy groups that help individuals discover their inner selves
    (D)   The trend among minority students to discover their identities in their ethnic groups rather than in their individuality
    (E)   The increased political activism of minorities on college campuses

4. This is an extension question. You may find the classification of the these problems as "application" or "extension" to be somewhat arbitrary or even disagree with a particular classification. As mentioned before, application and extension questions differ only in degree. Question 3 is clearly an application question; by asking you to make a conjecture about the future, it goes well beyond the passage. How to classify Question 4, however, is not so clear. I classified it as an extension question because it seems to be asking merely for the author's true meaning of the phrase "the politics of identity." That is, it stays within the context of the passage.

Trap!   Don't be led astray by (B); it uses the word "political" to tempt you. Although it is perhaps a good description, it is not within the context of the passage, which focuses on ethnic politics, not national identities through "roots."

The answer is (D).

5. Which one of the following best describes the attitude of the writer toward the multicultural movement?

   (A) Tolerant. It may have some faults, but it is well-meaning overall.
   (B) Critical. A formerly admirable movement has been taken over by radical intellectuals.
   (C) Disinterested. He seems to be presenting an objective report.
   (D) Enthusiastic. The author embraces the multiculturalist movement and is trying to present it in a favorable light.
   (E) Ambivalent. Like a moth to a flame he is simultaneously attracted and repulsed by the movement.

5. Like most tone questions this one is rather easy.

   To get a feel for the author's attitude, check the adjectives he chooses. The author starts by introducing the "kindlier" version of multiculturalism and describes a proponent of multiculturalism, Phillip Green, as "thoughtful." Then he introduces the "hard liners" who "damn" any attempt at cultural assimilation. He feels that the movement has changed; that it has gone bad.

The answer is (B).

6. "Multiculturalist relativism" is the notion that there is no such thing as impartial or objective knowledge. The author seems to be grounding his criticism of this notion on

   (A) the clear evidence that science has indeed discovered "truths" that have been independent of both language and culture.
   (B) the conclusion that relativism leaves one with no clear notions of any one thing that is true.
   (C) the absurdity of claiming that knowledge of oppression is more valid than knowledge of scientific facts.
   (D) the agreement among peoples of all cultures as to certain undeniable truths— e.g., when the sky is clear, day is warmer than night.
   (E) the fact that "truth" is not finitely definable and therefore that any discussion of impartial or objective truth is moot.

6. This is an another extension question.

Hint!

   The answer can be derived from the pivotal sentence containing "however" (2).

The answer is (B).

Exercise

According to usage and conventions which are at last being questioned but have by no means been overcome, the social presence of a woman is different in kind from that
5   of a man. A man's presence is dependent upon the promise of power which he embodies. If the promise is large and credible his presence is striking. If it is small or incredible, he is found to have little presence. The
10   promised power may be moral, physical, temperamental, economic, social, sexual—but its object is always exterior to the man. A man's presence suggests what he is capable of doing to you or for you. His presence may
15   be fabricated, in the sense that he pretends to be capable of what he is not. But the pretense is always toward a power which he exercises on others.

By contrast, a woman's presence ex-
20   presses her own attitude to herself, and defines what can and cannot be done to her. Her presence is manifest in her gestures, voices, opinions, expressions, clothes, chosen surroundings, taste—indeed there is nothing
25   she can do which does not contribute to her presence. Presence for a woman is so intrinsic to her person that men tend to think of it as an almost physical emanation, a kind of heat or smell or aura.

30   To be born a woman has been to be born, within an allotted and confined space, into the keeping of men. The social presence of women has developed as a result of their ingenuity in living under such tutelage within
35   such a limited space. But this has been at the cost of a woman's self being split into two. A woman must continually watch herself. Whilst she is walking across a room or whilst she is weeping at the death of her father, she
40   can scarcely avoid envisaging herself walking or weeping. From earliest childhood she has been taught and persuaded to survey herself continually.

And so she comes to consider the *surveyor*
45   and the *surveyed* within her as the two

constituent yet always distinct elements of her identity as a woman.

She has to survey everything she is and everything she does because how she appears
50   to others, and ultimately how she appears to men, is of crucial importance for what is normally thought of as the success of her life. Her own sense of being in herself is supplanted by a sense of being appreciated as
55   herself by another. Men survey women before treating them. Consequently how a woman appears to a man can determine how she will be treated. To acquire some control over this process, women must contain it and
60   internalize it. That part of a woman's self which is the surveyor treats the part which is the surveyed so as to demonstrate to others how her whole self would like to be treated. And this exemplary treatment of herself by
65   herself constitutes her presence. Every woman's presence regulates what is and is not "permissible" within her presence. Every one of her actions—whatever its direct purpose or motivation—is also read as an indication of
70   how she would like to be treated. If a woman throws a glass on the floor, this is an example of how she treats her own emotion of anger and so of how she would wish to be treated by others. If a man does the same, his action
75   is only read as an expression of his anger. If a woman makes a good joke this is an example of how she treats the joker in herself and accordingly of how she as joker-woman would like to be treated by others. Only a man can
80   make a good joke for its own sake.

1. According to "usage and conventions," appearance is NECESSARILY a part of reality for

    (A) men
    (B) women
    (C) both men and women
    (D) neither men nor women
    (E) men always and women occasionally

2. In analyzing a woman's customary "social presence," the author hopes to

    (A) justify and reinforce it.
    (B) understand and explain it.
    (C) expose and discredit it.
    (D) demonstrate and criticize it.
    (E) sanction and promote it.

3. It can be inferred from the passage that a woman with a Ph.D. in psychology who gives a lecture to a group of students is probably MOST concerned with

    (A) whether her students learn the material.
    (B) what the males in the audience think of her.
    (C) how she comes off as a speaker in psychology.
    (D) finding a husband.
    (E) whether a man challenges her.

4. The passage portrays women as

    (A) victims
    (B) liars
    (C) actresses
    (D) politicians
    (E) ignorant

5. Which one of the following is NOT implied by the passage?

    (A) Women have split personalities.
    (B) Men are not image-conscious.
    (C) Good looks are more important to women than to men.
    (D) A man is defined by what he does, whereas a woman is defined by how she appears.
    (E) A man's presence is extrinsic, whereas a woman's is intrinsic.

6. The primary purpose of the passage is to

    (A) compare and contrast woman's presence and place in society with that of man's.
    (B) discuss a woman's presence and place in society and to contrast it with a man's presence and place.
    (C) illustrate how a woman is oppressed by society.
    (D) explain why men are better than women at telling jokes.
    (E) illustrate how both men and women are hurt by sexism.

Answers and Solutions to Exercise

This passage is filled with pivotal words, some of which are crucial to following the author's train of thought. We will discuss only the critical pivotal words. The first pivotal word, "but" (line 16), introduces a distinction between a man's presence and a woman's: a man's is external, a woman's internal. The second pivotal word, "by contrast," introduces the main idea of the passage. The author opened the passage by defining a man's presence; now she will define a woman's presence. The last pivotal word, "but" (lines 35–36), also introduces a change in thought. Now the author discusses how a woman's presence has split her identity into two parts—the *surveyor* and the *surveyed*. By closing with, *"Only a man can make a good joke for its own sake,"* the author is saying a man can concentrate on the punch line, whereas a woman must concentrate on its delivery.

1. This is a description question. The needed reference is contained in lines 24–27: *"there is nothing [a woman] can do which does not contribute to her presence. Presence for a woman is intrinsic to her person . . ."* If something is intrinsic to you, then it necessarily is part of your reality. Hence the answer is (B).

Note the question refers to "usage and conventions" discussed in the passage, not to any other way of viewing the world—such as your own!

2. Although the author opens the passage with a hint that she doesn't like the customary sex roles (*"conventions which are at last being questioned"*), the rest of the passage is explanatory and analytical. So (C) and (D) are too strong. The answer is (B).

3. This is an application question; we are asked to apply what we have learned from the passage to a hypothetical situation.

The best way to analyze this question is to compare the speaker to a joke-teller. The passage paints a portrait of a woman as most concerned with the image she presents to the world. She is not concerned with the speech or joke, *per se*, rather with how she delivers it. *"Only a man can make a good joke for its own sake."* The answer is (C).

Don't make the mistake of choosing (B). Although men have, in the main, molded her self-image, she has gone beyond that; she now measures herself in the abstract: "how will I come off to the ultimately critical audience?" and not "how will actual audience members see me?"

4. This description question is a bit tricky because the second-best choice is rather good. Women are concerned with the image they present, so they cannot be themselves—they must act their part. Hence the answer is (C).

You may have been tempted by (A). According to the passage, women are thrown into the role of an actress, "into the keeping of men." So, like victims, they are not responsible for their social position. However, nothing in the passage directly suggests that it is wrong for women to be in this position or that women attempt to refuse this role. According to the passage, therefore, women are not, strictly speaking, victims. (*Victim* means "someone not in control of something injurious happening to him or her.")

5. This is an extension question. The passage discusses the fact that a man may fabricate his image (lines 14–16). This suggests that men *are* conscious of their images, but the passage also states that image is not intrinsic to their personalities, as it is for women. The answer is (B).

6. This is a rather hard main idea question because the second-best choice, (A), is quite good.

The passage does open with a discussion of a man's presence. But in paragraph two the pivotal phrase "by contrast" introduces a woman's presence; from there the discussion of a man's presence is only in regard to how it affects a woman's. So a woman's presence is the main idea; contrasting it with a man's presence is secondary. (B) gives the proper emphasis to these two purposes.

The Three Step Method

Now we apply all the methods we have learned to another passage. First let's summarize the reading techniques we have developed and express them in a three-step attack strategy for reading GMAT passages:

THE THREE STEP METHOD

1. **(Optional) Preview the first sentence of each paragraph.**

2. **Read the passage at a faster than usual pace (but not to the point that comprehension suffers). Stay alert to places from which any of the six questions might be drawn:**

   a.) **Main Idea**
   b.) **Description**
   c.) **Writing Technique**
   d.) **Extension**
   e.) **Application**
   f.) **Tone**

3. **Annotate the passage and note any pivotal words. Then use them as reference points when answering the questions. Following are some common annotation marks (you may want to add to this list):**

   A = **A**uthor's Attitude
   C = **C**omplex point
   ? = **Question?** I don't understand this part (you can bet that this area will be important to *at least* one question)
   SP = **S**ignificant **p**oint
   ! = **Exclamation!** Strong opinion
   W = **W**eak, questionable or unsupported argument or premise

Notice how the three-step process proceeds from the general to the specific. The **first step**, previewing the first sentences, gives you an overview of the passage. This will help you answer main idea questions. The **second step**, reading the passage at a slightly faster than usual pace, brings out the passage's structure (i.e., does the author compare and contrast, show cause and effect, etc.). Further, it will clue you into the author's attitude (positive, negative, objective, indifferent, etc.). Finally, the **third step**, noting pivotal words and annotating, will solidify your understanding of the passage and highlight specific details.

The three step method should be viewed as a dynamic, and not a static, process. The steps often overlap and they are not performed in strict order. Comprehending a passage is an ebb and flow process. Analyzing a passage to understand how it is constructed can be compared to dismantling an engine to understand how it was built—you may stop occasionally and reassemble parts of it to review what you just did; then proceed again to dismantle more. Likewise, when reading a passage, you may first read and annotate a paragraph (disassembling it) and then go back and skim to reassemble it. During this process, comprehension proceeds from the global to the specific. This can be represented by an inverted pyramid:

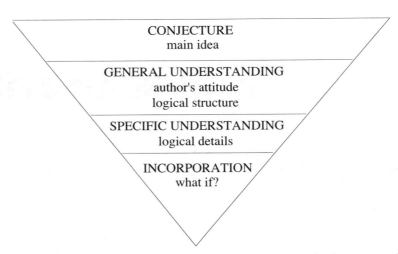

In the conjecture stage, we form a tentative main idea—one which we may have to modify or even reject as we read more deeply into the passage. In the general understanding stage, we develop a feel for the author's tone and discover the schema that she uses to present her ideas. In the specific understanding stage, we fill in the minor gaps in our understanding. Finally, in the incorporation stage, we integrate the ideas presented in the passage into our own thought process. We now understand the ideas sufficiently to defend them, apply them to other situations, or evaluate their validity in a hypothetical situation. Only with complete understanding of the passage can this be done.

Let's apply the three step method to the passage on the next page. Begin by previewing the first sentence of each paragraph:

The sentence *"That placebos can cure everything from dandruff to leprosy is well known"* implies that the passage is about placebos and that they are perhaps cure-alls.

The sentence *"Every drug tested would prove effective if special steps were not taken to neutralize the placebo effect"* gives the first bit of evidence supporting the topic sentence.

The sentence *"Most people feel that the lucky patients in a drug test get the experimental drug because the real drug provides them a chance to be cured"* might be introducing a counter-premise or pivotal point; we won't know until we read the passage.

The sentence *"Placebos regularly cure more than five percent of the patients and would cure considerably more if the doubts associated with the tests were eliminated"* provides more support for the topic sentence.

The sentence *"The actual curing power of placebos probably stems from the faith of the patient in the treatment"* explains why the topic sentence is true.

The sentence *"It may take a while to reach the ten percent level of cure because any newly established program will not have cultivated the word-of-mouth advertising needed to insure its success"* is hard to interpret. This does not help us.

The sentence *"Unfortunately, placebo treatment centers cannot operate as nonprofit businesses"* seems to be off the subject. Again, this does not help us.

In summary, although the last two sentences were not useful, we now have a good idea of what the passage is about: *how* and *why* placebos are effective. We now read the passage—looking for places from which any of the six questions might be drawn, noting the pivotal words, and annotating key points.

Passage begins on the next page.

That placebos can cure everything from dandruff to leprosy is well known. They have a long history of use by witch doctors, faith healers, and even modern physicians, all of whom refuse to admit their efficacy. Modern distribution techniques can bring this most potent of medicines to the aid of everyone, not just those lucky enough to receive placebos in a medical testing program.

Every drug tested would prove effective if special steps were not taken to neutralize the placebo effect. This is why drug tests give half the patients the new medication and half a harmless substitute. These tests prove the value of placebos because approximately five percent of the patients taking them are cured even though the placebos are made from substances that have been carefully selected to be useless.

Most people feel that the lucky patients in a drug test get the experimental drug because the real drug provides them a chance to be cured. **(1) Yet** analysis shows that patients getting the placebo may be the lucky ones because they may be cured without risking any adverse effects the new drug may have. Furthermore, the drug may well be found worthless and to have severe side effects. No harmful side effects result from placebos.

Placebos regularly cure more than five percent of the patients and would cure considerably more if the doubts associated with the tests were eliminated. Cures are principally due to the patient's faith, **(2) yet** the patient must have doubts knowing that he may or may not be given the new drug, which itself may or may not prove to be an effective drug. Since he knows the probability of being given the true drug is about fifty percent, the placebo cure rate would be more than doubled by removing these doubts if cures are directly related to faith.

The actual curing power of placebos probably stems from the faith of the patient in the treatment. This suggests that cure rates in the ten percent range could be expected if patients are given placebos under the guise of a proven cure, even when patients know their problems are incurable.

It may take a while to reach the ten percent level of cure because any newly established program will not have cultivated the word-of-mouth advertising needed to insure its success. One person saying "I was told that my problem was beyond medical help, but they cured me," can direct countless people to the treatment with the required degree of faith. Furthermore, when only terminal illnesses are treated, those not cured tell no one of the failure.

Unfortunately, placebo treatment centers cannot operate as nonprofit businesses. The nonprofit idea was ruled out upon learning that the first rule of public medicine is never to give free medicine. Public health services know that medicine not paid for by patients is often not taken or not effective because the recipient feels the medicine is worth just what it cost him. **(3) Even though** the patients would not know they were taking sugar pills, the placebos cost so little that the patients would have no faith in the treatment. Therefore, though it is against higher principles, treatment centers must charge high fees for placebo treatments. This sacrifice of principles, however, is a small price to pay for the greater good of the patients.

1. Which one of the following best expresses the main idea of the passage?

(A) Placebo treatment is a proven tool of modern medicine and its expanded use would benefit society's health.

(B) Because modern technology allows for distribution of drugs on a massive scale, the proven efficacy of the placebo is no longer limited to a privileged few.

(C) The curative power of the placebo is so strong that it should replace proven drugs because the patients receiving the placebo will then be cured without risking any adverse side effects.

(D) The price of placebo treatment must be kept artificially high because patients have little faith in inexpensive treatments.

(E) Semi-placebos—drugs that contain only a small amount of the usual dosage—are even more effective curatives than either the placebo or the full-strength drug.

2. Which one of the following is most analogous to the idea presented in the last paragraph?

   (A) Buying a television at a discount house
   (B) Making an additional pledge to charity
   (C) Choosing the most expensive dish-washer in a manufacturer's line
   (D) Waiting until a book comes out in paperback
   (E) Contributing one dollar to the Presidential Campaign fund on your tax return

3. According to the passage, when testing a new drug medical researchers give half of the subjects the test drug and half a placebo because

   (A) proper statistical controls should be observed.
   (B) this method reduces the risk of maiming too many subjects if the drug should prove to be harmful.
   (C) all drugs which are tested would prove to be effective otherwise.
   (D) most drugs would test positively otherwise.
   (E) the cost of dispensing drugs to all the patients is prohibitive.

4. It can be inferred from the passage that the author might

   (A) believe that the benefits of a placebo treatment program which leads patients to believe they were getting a real drug would outweigh the moral issue of lying.
   (B) support legislation outlawing the use of placebos.
   (C) open up a medical clinic that would treat patients exclusively through placebo methods.
   (D) believe that factors other than faith are responsible for the curative power of the placebo.
   (E) believe that placebo treatment centers should be tax-exempt because they are nonprofit businesses.

5. Which one of the following best describes the organization of the material presented in the passage?

   (A) A general proposition is stated; then evidence for its support is given.
   (B) Two types of drug treatment—placebo and non-placebo—are compared and contrasted.
   (C) A result is stated, its cause is explained, and an application is suggested.
   (D) A dilemma is presented and a possible solution is offered.
   (E) A series of examples is presented; then a conclusion is drawn from them.

6. Which one of the following most accurately characterizes the author's attitude toward placebo treatment?

   (A) reserved advocacy
   (B) feigned objectivity
   (C) summary dismissal
   (D) perplexed by its effectiveness
   (E) zealous promotion

The first item is a main idea question:

1. Which one of the following best expresses the main idea of the passage?

    (A) Placebo treatment is a proven tool of modern medicine and its expanded use would benefit society's health.
    (B) Because modern technology allows for distribution of drugs on a massive scale, the proven efficacy of the placebo is no longer limited to a privileged few.
    (C) The curative power of the placebo is so strong that it should replace proven drugs because the patients receiving the placebo will then be cured without risking any adverse side effects.
    (D) The price of placebo treatment must be kept artificially high because patients have little faith in inexpensive treatments.
    (E) Semi-placebos—drugs that contain only a small amount of the usual dosage—are even more effective curatives than either the placebo or the full-strength drug.

As we found by previewing the topic sentences, the passage is about the efficacy of placebo treatment. Careful reading shows that the passage also promotes expanded use of placebos. Hence the answer is (A).

The other choices can be quickly dismissed. (B) is the second-best choice: the author *does* mention that modern distribution techniques can bring the curative power of placebos to everyone, but he does <u>not</u> fully develop that idea. This answer-choice is tempting because it is contained in the topic paragraph. As to (C), it overstates the author's claim. Although in the third paragraph, the author states that those who receive the placebos may be the lucky ones, this is referring to new, unproven drugs, not to established drugs. As to (D), it, like (B), is mentioned in the passage but is not fully developed. It's tempting because it appears in the last paragraph—a natural place for the conclusion. Finally, (E) is neither mentioned nor implied by the passage.

The second item is an application question.

2. Which one of the following is most analogous to the idea presented in the last paragraph?

    (A) Buying a television at a discount house
    (B) Making an additional pledge to charity
    (C) Choosing the most expensive dishwasher in a manufacturer's line
    (D) Waiting until a book comes out in paperback
    (E) Contributing one dollar to the Presidential Campaign fund on your tax return

The information needed to answer this question is heralded by the pivotal phrase "Even though" (lines 69–72). The implication of that sentence is "you get what you pay for." This would motivate one to buy the most expensive item in a manufacturer's line. Hence the answer is (C).

The third item is a description question.

3. According to the passage, when testing a new drug medical researchers give half of the subjects the test drug and half a placebo because

    (A) proper statistical controls should be observed.
    (B) this method reduces the risk of maiming too many subjects if the drug should prove to be harmful.
    (C) all drugs which are tested would prove to be effective otherwise.
    (D) most drugs would test positively otherwise.
    (E) the cost of dispensing drugs to all the patients is prohibitive.

Since this is a description question, you must refer to the passage to answer it. The opening sentence to paragraph two contains the needed information. That sentence states "<u>Every</u> drug would prove effective if special steps were not taken to neutralize the placebo effect." Hence the answer is (C).

Choice (D) illustrates why you must refer directly to the passage to answer a description question: unless you have a remarkable memory, you will be unsure whether the statement was that **all** or that **most** drugs would prove effective.

The fourth item is an extension question.

4.   It can be inferred from the passage that the author might

(A)   believe that the benefits of a placebo treatment program that lead patients to believe they were getting a real drug would outweigh the moral issue of lying.
(B)   support legislation outlawing the use of placebos.
(C)   open up a medical clinic that would treat patients exclusively through placebo methods.
(D)   believe that factors other than faith are responsible for the curative power of the placebo.
(E)   believe that placebo treatment centers should be tax-exempt because they are nonprofit businesses.

The answer is (A). One of the first clues to the author's view on this issue is contained in the pivotal clause "yet the patient . . . effective drug" (lines 34–37). Later, in paragraph six, the author nearly advocates that the patient should not be told that he or she might be receiving a placebo. Finally, the closing line of the passage cinches it. There, the author implies that certain principles *can be* sacrificed for the greater good of the patients.

The fifth item is a writing technique question.

5.   Which one of the following best describes the organization of the material presented in the passage?

(A)   A general proposition is stated; then evidence for its support is given.
(B)   Two types of drug treatment—placebo and non-placebo—are compared and contrasted.
(C)   A result is stated, its cause is explained, and an application is suggested.
(D)   A dilemma is presented and a possible solution is offered.
(E)   A series of examples is presented; then a conclusion is drawn from them.

In the first paragraph the author claims that placebos can cure everything from dandruff to leprosy—this is a result. Then in paragraphs two, three, four, and five, he explains the causes of the result. Finally, he alludes to an application—the placebo treatment centers. The answer is (C).

The sixth item is a tone question.

6.   Which one of the following most accurately characterizes the author's attitude toward placebo treatment?

(A)   reserved advocacy
(B)   feigned objectivity
(C)   summary dismissal
(D)   perplexed by its effectiveness
(E)   zealous promotion

This question is a little tricky. Only choices (A) and (B) have any real merit. Although the passage has a detached, third-person style, the author nonetheless *does* present his opinions—namely that placebos work and that their use should be expanded. However, that advocacy is reserved, so the answer is (A).

The other choices can be quickly eliminated:

"Summary dismissal" is not supported by the passage. Besides, a scholar would never summarily dismiss something; he would consider it carefully—or at least give the impression that he has—before rejecting it. This eliminates (C).

Given the human ego, we are unlikely to admit that we don't understand the subject we are writing about. This eliminates (D).

"Zealous promotion" is too strong; "promotion" itself is probably too strong. This eliminates (E).

Points to Remember

1. UNDERLINE THE THREE STEP METHOD

    1.   (Optional) Preview the first sentence of each paragraph.

    2.   Read the passage at a faster than usual pace (but not to the point that comprehension suffers), being alert to places from which any of the six questions might be drawn:

        a.)   Main Idea
        b.)   Description
        c.)   Writing Technique
        d.)   Extension
        e.)   Application
        f.)   Tone

    3.   Annotate the passage and note any pivotal words. Then use these as reference points for answering the questions. Following are some common annotation marks (you may want to add to this list):

        A = Author's Attitude
        C = Complex point
        ? = Question? I don't understand this part (you can bet that this area will be important to *at least* one question)
        SP = Significant point
        ! = Exclamation! Strong opinion
        W = Weak, questionable or unsupported argument or premise

Mentor Exercise

Following the Three Step Method, we preview the first sentence of each paragraph in the passage: (The body of the passage will be presented later.)

The enigmatic opening sentence *"Many readers, I suspect, will take the title of this article [Women, Fire, and Dangerous Things] as suggesting that women, fire, and dangerous things have something in common—say, that women are fiery and dangerous"* does not give us much of a clue to what the passage is about.

The sentence *"The classical view that categories are based on shared properties is not entirely wrong"* is more helpful. It tells us the passage is about categorization and that there are at least two theories about it: the classical view, which has merit, and the modern view, which is apparently superior.

The sentence *"Categorization is not a matter to be taken lightly"* merely confirms the subject of the passage.

Although only one sentence was helpful, previewing did reveal a lot about the passage's subject matter—categorization. Now we read the passage, noting pivotal words, annotating, and noting likely places from which any of the six questions might be drawn. After each paragraph, we will stop to analyze and interpret what the author has presented:

> Many readers, I suspect, will take the title of this article [*Women, Fire, and Dangerous Things*] as suggesting that women, fire, and dangerous things have something in common—say, that women are fiery and dangerous. Most feminists I've mentioned it to have loved the title for that reason, though some have hated it for the same reason. But the chain of inference—from conjunction to categorization to commonality—is the norm. The inference is based on the common idea of what it means to be in the same category: things are categorized together on the basis of what they have in common. The idea that categories are defined by common properties is not only our everyday folk theory of what a category is, it is also the principle technical theory—one that has been with us for more than two thousand years.

In this paragraph, the author introduces the subject matter of the passage—categorization. And the pivotal sentence, introduced by "but," explains the classical theory of categorization, albeit rather obtusely. Namely, like things are placed in the same category.

Now we consider the second paragraph:

> The classical view that categories are based on shared properties is not entirely wrong. We often do categorize things on that basis. But that is only a small part of the story. In recent years it has become clear that categorization is far more complex than that. A new theory of categorization, called *prototype theory*, has emerged. It shows that human categorization is based on principles that extend far beyond those envisioned in the classical theory. One of our goals is to survey the complexities of the way people really categorize. For example, the title of this book was inspired by the Australian aboriginal language Dyirbal, which has a category, *balan*, that actually includes women, fire, and dangerous things. It also includes birds that are *not* dangerous, as well as exceptional animals, such as the platypus, bandicoot, and echidna. This is not simply a matter of categorization by common properties.

In this paragraph, the second pivotal word—but—is crucial. It introduces the main idea of the passage—the prototype theory of categorization. Now everything that is introduced should be attributed to the prototype theory, <u>not</u> to the classical theory. Wrong answer-choices are likely to be baited with just the opposite.

The author states that the prototype theory goes "far beyond" the classical theory. Although he does not tell us what the prototype theory *is*, he does tell us that it *is not* merely categorization by common properties.

Now we turn to the third paragraph:

Categorization is not a matter to be taken lightly. There is nothing more basic than categorization to our thought, perception, action and speech. Every time we see something as a *kind* of thing, for example, a tree, we are categorizing. Whenever we reason about *kinds* of things—chairs, nations, illnesses, emotions, any kind of thing at all—we are employing categories. Whenever we intentionally perform any *kind* of action, say something as mundane as writing with a pencil, hammering with a hammer, or ironing clothes, we are using categories. The particular action we perform on that occasion is a *kind* of motor activity, that is, it is in a particular category of motor actions. They are never done in exactly the same way, yet despite the differences in particular movements, they are all movements of a kind, and we know how to make movements of that kind. And any time we either produce or understand any utterance of any reasonable length, we are employing dozens if not hundreds of categories: categories of speech sounds, of words, of phrases and clauses, as well as conceptual categories. Without the ability to categorize, we could not function at all, either in the physical world or in our social and intellectual lives.

Though the author does not explicitly state it, this paragraph defines the theory of prototypes. Notice the author likes to use an indirect, even cryptic, method of introducing or switching topics, which makes this a classic GMAT type passage. The GMAT writers have many opportunities here to test whether you are following the author's train of thought.

Now we attack the questions.

1. The author probably chose *Women, Fire, and Dangerous Things* as the title of the article because
    I. he thought that since the Dyirbal placed all three items in the same category, women, fire, and dangerous things necessarily had something in common.
    II. he was hoping to draw attention to the fact that because items have been placed in the same category doesn't mean that they necessarily have anything in common
    III. he wanted to use the Dyirbal classification system as an example of how primitive classifications are not as functional as contemporary Western classification systems.
    (A) I only
    (B) II only
    (C) III only
    (D) II and III only
    (E) I, II, and III

1. This is an extension question. The second paragraph contains the information needed to answer it. There the author states that women, fire, and dangerous things belong to a category called *balan* in an Australian aboriginal language, which is <u>not</u> simply based on common properties. This eliminates Statement I and confirms Statement II.

The answer is (B).

2. According to the author,
    I. categorizing is a fundamental activity of people.
    II. whenever a word refers to a kind of thing, it signifies a category.
    III. one has to be able to categorize in order to function in our culture.
    (A) I only
    (B) II only
    (C) I and II only
    (D) II and III only
    (E) I, II, and III

2. This is a description question, so we must find the points in the passage from which the statements were drawn.

Remember! Remember, the answer to a description question will not directly quote a statement from the passage, but it will be closely related to one—often a paraphrase.

The needed references for Statements I, II, and III are all contained in the closing paragraph.

The answer is (E).

3. Which one of the following facts would most weaken the significance of the author's title?
    (A) The discovery that all the birds and animals classified as *balan* in Dyirbal are female
    (B) The discovery that the male Dyirbal culture considers females to be both fiery and dangerous
    (C) The discovery that all items in the *balan* category are considered female
    (D) The discovery that neither fire nor women are considered dangerous
    (E) The discovery that other cultures have categories similar to the *balan* category

3. To weaken an argument, attack one or more of its premises. Now the implication of the title is that *women, fire,* and *dangerous things* <u>do not</u> have anything in common. To weaken this implication, the answer should state that all things in the *balan* category <u>have</u> something in common.

The answer is (C).

4. If linguistic experts cannot perceive how women, fire, and dangerous things in the category *balan* have at least one thing in common, it follows that
    (A) there probably is something other than shared properties that led to all items in *balan* being placed in that category.
    (B) the anthropologists simply weren't able to perceive what the items had in common.
    (C) the anthropologists might not have been able to see what the items had in common.
    (D) the items do not have anything in common.
    (E) the Australian aboriginal culture is rather mystic.

4. This is an extension question; we are asked to draw a conclusion based on the passage.

Hint!

The thrust of the passage is that commonality is not the only way to categorize things.

The answer is (A).

5. Which one of the following sentences would best complete the last paragraph of the passage?
    (A) An understanding of how we categorize is central to any understanding of how we think and how we function, and therefore central to an understanding of what makes us human.
    (B) The prototype theory is only the latest in a series of new and improved theories of categorization; undoubtedly even better theories will replace it.
    (C) The prototype theory of categories has not only unified a major branch of linguistics, but it has applications to mathematics and physics as well.
    (D) An understanding of how the prototype theory of categorization evolved from the classical theory is essential to any understanding of how we think and how we function in society.
    (E) To fully understand how modern Australian society functions, we must study how it is influenced by aboriginal culture—most specifically how aborigines organize and classify their surroundings.

5. This is an application question; we are asked to complete a thought for the author.

Most of the third paragraph is introducing the prototype theory of categorization. But in the last sentence the author changes direction somewhat—without any notice, as is typical of his style. Now he is discussing the importance of the ability to categorize. The clause *"Without the ability to categorize, we could not function at all"* indicates that this ability is fundamental to our very being.

Watch out!

Be careful not to choose (D). Although it is probably true, it is too specific: in the final sentence the author is discussing categorization in general.

The answer is (A).

Exercise

Directions: This passage is followed by a group of questions to be answered based on what is stated or implied in the passage. Choose the best answer; the one that most accurately and completely answers the question.

Global strategies to control infectious disease have historically included the erection of barriers to international travel and immigration. Keeping people with
5 infectious diseases outside national borders has reemerged as an important public health policy in the human immunodeficiency virus (HIV) epidemic. Between 29 and 50 countries are reported to have introduced border
10 restrictions on HIV-positive foreigners, usually those planning an extended stay in the country, such as students, workers, or seamen.

Travel restrictions have been
15 established primarily by countries in the western Pacific and Mediterranean regions, where HIV seroprevalence is relatively low. However, the country with the broadest policy of testing and excluding foreigners is
20 the United States. From December 1, 1987, when HIV infection was first classified in the United States as a contagious disease, through September 30, 1989, more than 3 million people seeking permanent residence
25 in this country were tested for HIV antibodies. The U.S. policy has been sharply criticized by national and international organizations as being contrary to public health goals and human-rights principles.
30 Many of these organizations are boycotting international meetings in the United States that are vital for the study of prevention, education, and treatment of HIV infection.

The Immigration and Nationality Act
35 requires the Public Health Service to list "dangerous contagious diseases" for which aliens can be excluded from the United States. By 1987 there were seven designated diseases—five of them sexually transmitted
40 (chancroid, gonorrhea, granuloma inguinale, lymphog-ranuloma venereum, and infectious syphilis) and two non-venereal (active tuberculosis and infectious leprosy). On June 8, 1987, in response to a
45 Congressional direction in the Helms Amendment, the Public Health Service

added HIV infection to the list of dangerous contagious diseases.

A just and efficacious travel and immi-
50 gration policy would not exclude people because of their serologic status unless they posed a danger to the community through casual transmission. U.S. regulations should list only active tuberculosis as a contagious
55 infectious disease. We support well-funded programs to protect the health of travelers infected with HIV through appropriate immunizations and prophylactic treatment and to reduce behaviors that may transmit
60 infection.

We recognize that treating patients infected with HIV who immigrate to the United States will incur costs for the public sector. It is inequitable, however, to use cost
65 as a reason to exclude people infected with HIV, for there are no similar exclusionary policies for those with other costly chronic diseases, such as heart disease or cancer.

Rather than arbitrarily restrict the
70 movement of a subgroup of infected people, we must dedicate ourselves to the principles of justice, scientific cooperation, and a global response to the HIV pandemic.

1. According to the passage, countries in the western Pacific have

(A) a very high frequency of HIV-positive immigrants and have a greater reason to be concerned over this issue than other countries.

(B) opposed efforts on the part of Mediterranean states to establish travel restrictions on HIV-positive residents.

(C) a low HIV seroprevalence and, in tandem with Mediterranean regions, have established travel restrictions on HIV-positive foreigners.

(D) continued to obstruct efforts to unify policy concerning immigrant screening.

(E) joined with the United States in sharing information about HIV-positive individuals.

2. The authors of the passage conclude that

   (A) it is unjust to exclude people based on their serological status without the knowledge that they pose a danger to the public.

   (B) U.S. regulations should require more stringent testing to be implemented at all major border crossings.

   (C) it is the responsibility of the public sector to absorb costs incurred by treatment of immigrants infected with HIV.

   (D) the HIV pandemic is largely over-stated and that, based on new epidemiological data, screening immigrants is not indicated.

   (E) only the non-venereal diseases active tuberculosis and infectious leprosy should be listed as dangerous and contagious diseases.

3. It can be inferred from the passage that

   (A) more than 3 million HIV-positive people have sought permanent residence in the United States.

   (B) countries with a low seroprevalence of HIV have a disproportionate and unjustified concern over the spread of AIDS by immigration.

   (C) the United States is more concerned with controlling the number of HIV-positive immigrants than with avoiding criticism from outside its borders.

   (D) current law is meeting the demand for prudent handling of a potentially hazardous international issue.

   (E) actions by countries in the western Pacific and Mediterranean regions to restrict travel are ineffective.

4. Before the Helms Amendment in 1987, seven designated diseases were listed as being cause for denying immigration. We can conclude from the passage that

   (A) the authors agree fully with this policy but disagree with adding HIV to the list.

   (B) the authors believe that sexual diseases are appropriate reasons for denying immigration but not non-venereal diseases.

   (C) the authors disagree with the amendment.

   (D) the authors believe that non-venereal diseases are justifiable reasons for exclusion, but not sexually transmit-ted diseases.

   (E) the authors believe that no diseases should be cause for denying immigration.

5. In referring to the "costs" incurred by the public (line 63), the authors apparently mean

   (A) financial costs.
   (B) costs to the public health.
   (C) costs in manpower.
   (D) costs in international reputation.
   (E) costs in public confidence.

Answers and Solutions to Exercise

Previewing the first sentence of each paragraph shows that the passage is about restricting travel of HIV-positive persons and that the authors feel there should be no restrictions. There are two pivotal words: "however" (line 18), and "Rather than" (line 69), which introduces the concluding paragraph.

1. This is a description question, so we must find the point in the passage from which the question is drawn. It is the opening sentence to paragraph two. There it is stated that countries in the western Pacific and Mediterranean regions have a low incidence of HIV infection and have introduced border restrictions. The answer, therefore, is (C).

2. This is another description question. The answer is (A). This is directly supported by the opening sentence of paragraph four. Note that (A) is a paraphrase of that sentence.

   Be careful with (Ċ). Although this is hinted at in paragraph five, it is never directly stated that the public sector is <u>responsible</u> for these costs, only that it would in fact pick up these costs. Remember: A description question must be answered from what is directly stated in the passage, not from what it implies.

3. This is an extension question. Lines 26–28 state *"U.S. policy has been sharply criticized by national and international organizations."* Given that this criticism has not caused the United States to change its policies, it must be more concerned with controlling the number of HIV-positive immigrants than with avoiding criticism. The answer, therefore, is (C).

   Don't be tempted by (A); it's a same language trap. Every word in it is taken from the passage. However, the passage states that over 3 million people were tested for HIV antibodies (lines 23–26), <u>not</u> that they were tested "positive" for HIV antibodies.

4. This is another extension question. In lines 53–55, the authors state that only active tuberculosis should be listed as a dangerous contagious disease. · We expect that they would oppose adding HIV to the list. The answer is (C).

5. Although governments have ostensibly restricted the immigration of HIV-positive persons out of fear that they may spread the disease, the authors apparently are referring to financial costs, not costs to public health. This is indicated by lines 64–68, where they describe heart disease and cancer as non-contagious and costly, yet still admissible. The answer, therefore, is (A).

Directions: Each passage in this group is followed by questions based on its content. After reading a passage, choose the best answer to each question. Answer all questions following a passage on the basis of what is <u>stated</u> or <u>implied</u> in that passage. Answers and solutions begin on page 405.

Most students arrive at [college] using "discrete, concrete, and absolute categories to understand people, knowledge, and values." These students live with a *dualistic* view, seeing "the
5 world in polar terms of we-right-good vs. other-wrong-bad." These students cannot acknowledge the existence of more than one point of view toward any issue. There is one "right" way. And because these absolutes are assumed
10 by or imposed on the individual from external authority, they cannot be personally substantiated or authenticated by experience. These students are slaves to the generalizations of their authorities. An eye for an eye! Capital punish-
15 ment is apt justice for murder. The Bible says so.

Most students break through the dualistic stage to another equally frustrating stage—*multiplicity*. Within this stage, students see a variety of ways to deal with any given topic or problem.
20 However, while these students accept multiple points of view, they are unable to evaluate or justify them. To have an opinion is everyone's right. While students in the dualistic stage are unable to produce evidence to support what
25 they consider to be self-evident absolutes, students in the multiplistic stage are unable to connect instances into coherent generalizations. Every assertion, every point, is valid. In their democracy they are directionless. Capital pun-
30 ishment? What sense is there in answering one murder with another?

The third stage of development finds students living in a world of *relativism*. Knowledge is relative: right and wrong depend on the con-
35 text. No longer recognizing the validity of each individual idea or action, relativists examine everything to find its place in an overall framework. While the multiplist views the world as unconnected, almost random, the relativist seeks
40 always to place phenomena into coherent larger patterns. Students in this stage view the world analytically. They appreciate authority for its expertise, using it to defend their own generaliza-

tions. In addition, they accept or reject ostensi-
45 ble authority *after systematically* evaluating its validity. In this stage, however, students resist decision making. Suffering the ambivalence of finding several consistent and acceptable alternatives, they are almost overwhelmed by diver-
50 sity and need means for managing it. Capital punishment is appropriate justice—in some instances.

In the final stage students manage diversity through individual *commitment*. Students do not
55 deny relativism. Rather they assert an identity by forming commitments and assuming responsibility for them. They gather personal experience into a coherent framework, abstract principles to guide their actions, and use these princi-
60 ples to discipline and govern their thoughts and actions. The individual has chosen to join a particular community and agrees to live by its tenets. The accused has had the benefit of due process to guard his civil rights, a jury of peers
65 has found him guilty, and the state has the right to end his life. This is a principle my community and I endorse.

1. It can be inferred from the passage that the author would consider which of the following to be good examples of "dualistic thinking"?

    I.   People who think "there is a right way and a wrong way to do things"
    II. Teenagers who assume they know more about "the real world" than adults do
    III. People who back our country "right or wrong" when it goes to war

    (A) I only
    (B) II only
    (C) III only
    (D) I and II only
    (E) I and III only

2. Students who are "dualistic" thinkers may not be able to support their beliefs convincingly because

   (A) most of their beliefs *cannot* be supported by arguments.
   (B) they have accepted their "truths" simply because authorities have said these things are "true."
   (C) they half-believe and half-disbelieve just about everything.
   (D) their teachers almost always think that "dualistic" thinkers are wrong.
   (E) they are enslaved by their authorities.

3. Which one of the following assertions is supported by the passage?

   (A) *Committed* thinkers are not very sure of their positions.
   (B) *Relativistic* thinkers have learned how to make sense out of the world and have chosen their own positions in it.
   (C) *Multiplicity* thinkers have difficulty understanding the relationships between different points of view.
   (D) *Dualistic* thinkers have thought out the reasons for taking their positions.
   (E) *Dualistic* thinkers fear the power of authority.

4. In paragraph two, the author states that in their "democracy" students in the *multiplicity* stage are directionless. The writer describes *multiplicity* students as being in a "democracy" because

   (A) there are so many different kinds of people in a democracy.
   (B) in an "ideal" democracy, all people are considered equal; by extension, so are their opinions.
   (C) Democrats generally do not have a good sense of direction.
   (D) although democracies may grant freedom, they are generally acknowledged to be less efficient than more authoritarian forms of government.
   (E) in a democracy the individual has ultimate authority over himself, not the state.

5. Which one of the following kinds of thinking is NOT described in the passage?

   (A) People who assume that there is no right or wrong in any issue
   (B) People who make unreasoned commitments and stick by them
   (C) People who believe that right or wrong depends on the situation
   (D) People who commit themselves to a particular point of view after having considered several alternative concepts
   (E) People who think that all behavior can be accounted for by cause and effect relationships

6. If students were asked to write essays on the different *concepts* of tragedy as exemplified by Cordelia and Antigone, and they all responded by showing how each character exemplified a traditional definition of tragedy, we could, according to the passage, hypothesize which one of the following about these students?

   (A) The students were locked into the relativist stage.
   (B) The students had not advanced beyond the dualist stage.
   (C) The students had at least achieved the multiplicity stage.
   (D) The students had reached the commitment stage.
   (E) We have no indication of which cognitive stage the students were in.

7. Which one of the following best describes the organization of the passage?

   (A) Four methods of thought are compared and contrasted.
   (B) It is shown how each of four types of thought evolved from each other.
   (C) Four methods of thought are presented, and each is shown to complement the other.
   (D) The evolution of thought from simplistic and provincial through considered and cosmopolitan is illustrated by four stages.
   (E) The evolution of thought through four stages is presented, and each stage is illustrated by how it views capital punishment.

A growing taste for shark steaks and shark-fin soup has for the first time in 400 million years put the scourge of the sea at the wrong end of the food chain. Commercial land-
5 ings of this toothsome fish have doubled every year since 1986, and shark populations are plunging. It is hardly a case of good riddance. Sharks do for gentler fish what lions do for the wildebeest: they check populations by feeding
10 on the weak. Also, sharks apparently do not get cancer and may therefore harbor clues to the nature of that disease.

Finally, there is the issue of motherhood. Sharks are viviparous. That is, they bear their
15 young alive and swimming (not sealed in eggs) after gestation periods lasting from nine months to two years. Shark mothers generally give birth to litters of from eight to twelve pups and bear only one litter every other year.

20 This is why sharks have one of the lowest fecundity rates in the ocean. The female cod, for example, spawns annually and lays a few million eggs at a time. If three quarters of the cod were to be fished this year, they could be
25 back in full force in a few years. But if humans took that big of a bite out of the sharks, the population would not recover for 15 years.

So, late this summer, if all goes according to plan, the shark will join the bald eagle and
30 the buffalo on the list of managed species. The federal government will cap the U.S. commercial catch at 5,800 metric tons, about half of the 1989 level, and limit sportsmen to two sharks per boat. Another provision discourages
35 finning, the harvesting of shark fins alone, by limiting the weight of fins to 7 percent of that of all the carcasses.

Finning got under the skin of environmentalists, and the resulting anger helped to mobi-
40 lize support for the new regulations. Finning itself is a fairly recent innovation. Shark fins contain noodle-like cartilaginous tissues that Chinese chefs have traditionally used to thicken and flavor soup. Over the past few years rising
45 demand in Hong Kong has made the fins as valuable as the rest of the fish. Long strands are prized, so unusually large fins can be worth considerably more to the fisherman than the average price of about $10 a pound.

50 But can U.S. quotas save shark species that wander the whole Atlantic? The blue shark, for example, migrates into the waters of something like 23 countries. John G. Casey, a biologist with the National Marine Fisheries Service
55 Research Center in Narragansett, R.I., admits that international co-ordination will eventually be necessary. But he supports U.S. quotas as a first step in mobilizing other nations. Meanwhile the commercial fishermen are not
60 waiting for the new rules to take effect. "There's a pre-quota rush on sharks," Casey says, "and it's going on as we speak."

8. According to the passage, shark populations are at greater risk than cod populations because

(A) sharks are now being eaten more than cod.
(B) the shark reproduction rate is lower than that of the cod.
(C) sharks are quickly becoming fewer in number.
(D) sharks are now as scarce as bald eagles and buffalo.
(E) sharks are scavengers and therefore more susceptible to disease.

9. According to the passage, a decrease in shark populations

I. might cause some fish populations to go unchecked.
II. would hamper cancer research.
III. to one-quarter the current level would take over a decade to recover from.

(A) II only
(B) III only
(C) I and III only
(D) I and II only
(E) I, II, and III

10. If the species *Homo logicus* was determined to be viviparous and to have extremely low fecundity rates on land, we might expect that

   (A)   *Homo logicus* could overpopulate its niche and should be controlled.
   (B)   *Homo logicus* might be declared an endangered species.
   (C)   *Homo logicus* would pose no danger to other species and would itself be in no danger.
   (D)   *Homo logicus* would soon become extinct.
   (E)   None of these events would be expected with certainty.

11. Which one of the following best describes the author's attitude toward the efforts to protect shark populations?

   (A)   strong advocate
   (B)   impartial observer
   (C)   opposed
   (D)   perplexed
   (E)   resigned to their ineffectiveness

12. It can be inferred from the passage that

   I.   research efforts on cancer will be hindered if shark populations are threatened.
   II.   U.S. quotas on shark fishing will have limited effectiveness in protecting certain species.
   III. some practices of Chinese chefs have angered environmentalists.

   (A)   I only
   (B)   II only
   (C)   I and II only
   (D)   II and III only
   (E)   I, II, and III

13. An irony resulting from the announcement that sharks will be placed on the managed list is

   (A)   we will now find out less about cancer, so in effect by saving the sharks, we are hurting ourselves.
   (B)   sharks are far more dangerous to other fish than we are to them.
   (C)   more chefs are now using the cartilaginous tissues found in shark fins.
   (D)   more sharks are being killed now than before the announcement.
   (E)   man will now protect a creature that he has been the victim of.

"A writer's job is to tell the truth," said Hemingway in 1942. No other writer of our time had so fiercely asserted, so pugnaciously defended or so consistently exemplified the writer's obligation to speak truly. His standard of truth-telling remained, moreover, so high and so rigorous that he was ordinarily unwilling to admit secondary evidence, whether literary evidence or evidence picked up from other sources than his own experience. "I only know what I have seen," was a statement which came often to his lips and pen. What he had personally done, or what he knew unforgettably by having gone through one version of it, was what he was interested in telling about. This is not to say that he refused to invent freely. But he always made it a sacrosanct point to invent in terms of what he actually knew from having been there.

The primary intent of his writing, from first to last, was to seize and project for the reader what he often called "the way it was." This is a characteristically simple phrase for a concept of extraordinary complexity, and Hemingway's conception of its meaning subtly changed several times in the course of his career—always in the direction of greater complexity. At the core of the concept, however, one can invariably discern the operation of three aesthetic instruments: the sense of place, the sense of fact, and the sense of scene.

The first of these, obviously a strong passion with Hemingway, is the sense of place. "Unless you have geography, background," he once told George Antheil, "you have nothing." You have, that is to say, a dramatic vacuum. Few writers have been more place-conscious. Few have so carefully charted out the geographical ground work of their novels while managing to keep background so conspicuously unobtrusive. Few, accordingly, have been able to record more economically and graphically the way it is when you walk through the streets of Paris in search of breakfast at a corner café . . . Or when, at around six o'clock of a Spanish dawn, you watch the bulls running from the corrals at the Puerta Rochapea through the streets of Pamplona towards the bullring.

"When I woke it was the sound of the rocket exploding that announced the release of the bulls from the corrals at the edge of town. Down below the narrow street was empty. All the balconies were crowded with people. Suddenly a crowd came down the street. They were all running, packed close together. They passed along and up the street toward the bullring and behind them came more men running faster, and then some stragglers who were really running. Behind them was a little bare space, and then the bulls, galloping, tossing their heads up and down. It all went out of sight around the corner. One man fell, rolled to the gutter, and lay quiet. But the bulls went right on and did not notice him. They were all running together."

This landscape is as morning-fresh as a design in India ink on clean white paper. First is the bare white street, seen from above, quiet and empty. Then one sees the first packed clot of runners. Behind these are the thinner ranks of those who move faster because they are closer to the bulls. Then the almost comic stragglers, who are "really running." Brilliantly behind these shines the "little bare space," a desperate margin for error. Then the clot of running bulls—closing the design, except of course for the man in the gutter making himself, like the designer's initials, as inconspicuous as possible.

14. According to the author, Hemingway's primary purpose in telling a story was

(A) to construct a well-told story that the reader would thoroughly enjoy.

(B) to construct a story that would reflect truths that were not particular to a specific historical period.

(C) to begin from reality but to allow his imagination to roam from "the way it was" to "the way it might have been."

(D) to report faithfully reality as Hemingway had experienced it.

(E) to go beyond the truth, to "create" reality.

15. From the author's comments and the example of the bulls (paragraph 4), what was the most likely reason for which Hemingway took care to include details of place?

   (A) He felt that geography in some way illuminated other, more important events.
   (B) He thought readers generally did not have enough imagination to visualize the scenes for themselves.
   (C) He had no other recourse since he was avoiding the use of other literary sources.
   (D) He thought that landscapes were more important than characters to convey "the way it was."
   (E) He felt that without background information the readers would be unable to follow the story.

16. One might infer from the passage that Hemingway preferred which one of the following sources for his novels and short stories?

   (A) Stories that he had heard from friends or chance acquaintances
   (B) Stories that he had read about in newspapers or other secondary sources
   (C) Stories that came to him in periods of meditation or in dreams
   (D) Stories that he had lived rather than read about
   (E) Stories adapted from myths

17. It has been suggested that part of Hemingway's genius lies in the way in which he removes himself from his stories in order to let readers experience the stories for themselves. Which of the following elements of the passage support this suggestion?

   I. The comparison of "the designer's initials" to the man who fell and lay in the gutter (lines 61–62) during the running of the bulls
   II. Hemingway's stated intent to project for the reader "the way it was" (line 21)
   III. Hemingway's ability to invent fascinating tales from his own experience

   (A) I only
   (B) II only
   (C) I and II only
   (D) I and III only
   (E) I, II, and III

18. From the passage, one can assume that which of the following statements would best describe Hemingway's attitude toward knowledge?

   (A) One can learn about life only by living it fully.
   (B) A wise person will read widely in order to learn about life.
   (C) Knowledge is a powerful tool that should be reserved only for those who know how to use it.
   (D) Experience is a poor teacher.
   (E) One can never truly "know" anything.

19. The author calls "the way it was" a "characteristically simple phrase for a concept of extraordinary complexity" (lines 21–23) because

   (A) the phrase reflects Hemingway's talent for obscuring ordinary events.
   (B) the relationship between simplicity and complexity reflected the relationship between the style and content of Hemingway's writing.
   (C) Hemingway became increasingly confused about "the way it was" throughout the course of his career.
   (D) Hemingway's obsession for geographic details progressively overshadowed the dramatic element of his stories.
   (E) it typifies how Hemingway understated complex issues.

Imagine that we stand on any ordinary seaside pier, and watch the waves rolling in and striking against the iron columns of the pier. Large waves pay very little attention to the columns—they divide
5 right and left and re-unite after passing each column, much as a regiment of soldiers would if a tree stood in their way; it is almost as though the columns had not been there. But the short waves and ripples find the columns of the pier a much
10 more formidable obstacle. When the short waves impinge on the columns, they are reflected back and spread as new ripples in all directions. To use the technical term, they are "scattered." The obstacle provided by the iron columns hardly affects the long
15 waves at all, but scatters the short ripples.

We have been watching a working model of the way in which sunlight struggles through the earth's atmosphere. Between us on earth and outer space the atmosphere interposes innumerable obstacles in
20 the form of molecules of air, tiny droplets of water, and small particles of dust. They are represented by the columns of the pier.

The waves of the sea represent the sunlight. We know that sunlight is a blend of lights of many
25 colors—as we can prove for ourselves by passing it through a prism, or even through a jug of water, or as Nature demonstrates to us when she passes it through the raindrops of a summer shower and produces a rainbow. We also know that light con-
30 sists of waves, and that the different colors of light are produced by waves of different lengths, red light by long waves and blue light by short waves. The mixture of waves which constitutes sunlight has to struggle through the obstacles it meets in the atmo-
35 sphere, just as the mixture of waves at the seaside has to struggle past the columns of the pier. And these obstacles treat the light waves much as the columns of the pier treat the sea-waves. The long waves which constitute red light are hardly affected,
40 but the short waves which constitute blue light are scattered in all directions.

Thus, the different constituents of sunlight are treated in different ways as they struggle through the earth's atmosphere. A wave of blue light may be
45 scattered by a dust particle, and turned out of its course. After a time a second dust particle again turns it out of its course, and so on, until finally it enters our eyes by a path as zigzag as that of a flash of lightning. Consequently, the blue waves of the
50 sunlight enter our eyes from all directions. And that is why the sky looks blue.

20. We know from experience that if we look directly at the sun, we will see red light near the sun. This observation is supported by the passage for which one of the following reasons?

(A) It seems reasonable to assume that red light would surround the sun because the sun is basically a large fireball.

(B) It seems reasonable to assume that the other colors of light would either cancel each other or combine to produce red.

(C) It seems reasonable to assume that red light would not be disturbed by the atmospheric particles and would consequently reach us by a relatively direct path from the sun to our eyes.

(D) It is not supported by the passage. The author does not say what color of light should be near the sun, and he provides no reasons that would allow us to assume that the light would be red.

(E) Gazing directly at the sun forces the eye to focus on the longer red waves.

21. Scientists have observed that shorter wavelength light has more energy than longer wavelength light. From this we can conclude that

(A) red light will exert more energy when it hits the surface of the earth than will blue light.

(B) lightning is caused by the collision of blue light with particles in the air.

(C) red light will travel faster than blue light.

(D) blue light has more energy than red light.

(E) blue light has less energy than red light.

22. A scientist makes new observations and learns that water waves of shorter wavelengths spread in all directions not only because they scatter off piers but also because they interact with previously scattered short water waves. Drawing upon the analogy between water waves and light waves, we might hypothesize which of the following?

   (A) Blue light waves act like ripples that other blue light waves meet and scatter from.
   (B) Red light waves will be scattered by blue light waves like incoming long water waves are scattered by outgoing ripples.
   (C) Red light waves can scatter blue light waves, but blue light waves cannot scatter red.
   (D) The analogy between water and light waves cannot be extended to include the way in which short water waves become ripples and scatter one another.
   (E) The scattering effect of blue light waves is canceled by that of red.

23. Which one of the following is a reason for assuming that sunlight is constituted of waves of many colors?

   (A) The mixture of waves that make up sunlight has to struggle through a variety of obstacles in the atmosphere.
   (B) When passing through water in the atmosphere, sunlight is sometimes broken down into an array of colors.
   (C) Many different wavelengths of light enter our eyes from all directions.
   (D) The mere fact that light waves can be scattered is a reason for assuming that sunlight is constituted of waves of different colors.
   (E) When passing through dust in the atmosphere, sunlight is sometimes broken down into an array of colors.

24. From the information presented in the passage, what can we conclude about the color of the sky on a day with a large quantity of dust in the air?

   (A) The sky would be even bluer
   (B) The sky would be redder
   (C) The sky would not change colors
   (D) We do not have enough information to determine a change in color
   (E) The sky would assume a violet hue

25. We all know that when there is a clear sky, the western sky appears red as the sun sets. From the information presented in the passage, this phenomenon would seem to be explained by which of the following?

   I. Light meets more obstacles when passing parallel to the earth's surface than when traveling perpendicular. Consequently, even red light is diffused.
   II. The blue light may not make it through the denser pathway of the evening sky, leaving only the long light waves of red.
   III. The short red light waves have more energy and are the only waves that can make it through the thick atmosphere of the evening sky.

   (A) I only
   (B) II only
   (C) I and II only
   (D) II and III only
   (E) I, II, and III

26. Which one of the following does the author seem to imply?

   (A) Waves of light and waves of water are identical.
   (B) Waves of light have the same physical shape as waves of water.
   (C) Waves of light and waves of water do not have very much in common.
   (D) Waves of water are only models of waves of light.
   (E) There are colors of light waves just as there are colors of water waves.

Answers and Solutions

Answers to Questions

1.	E	8.	B	15.	A	22.	D
2.	B	9.	C	16.	D	23.	B
3.	C	10.	E	17.	C	24.	D
4.	B	11.	B	18.	A	25.	C
5.	E	12.	B	19.	B	26.	D
6.	B	13.	D	20.	C		
7.	E	14.	D	21.	D		

Before we turn to the answers, three pivotal words in the first passage should be noted: "However" (line 20), "however" (line 46), and "Rather" (line 55).

Questions 1–7

1. This is an extension question. Statement I is true. This is the essential characteristic of dualistic (right/wrong) thinkers (lines 3–9). This eliminates (B) and (C). Statement II is false. Dualistic thinkers grant authority (right thinking) to adults and adult figures. This is clear from the sentence, *"These students are slaves to the generalizations of their authorities."* This eliminates (D). Unfortunately, we have to check Statement III. It is true since Dualistic thinkers believe *their* group is right and the *other* group is wrong. (Again, see lines 3–9.) The answer, therefore, is (E).

2. This is another extension question. Dualistic thinkers probably cannot give cogent arguments for their beliefs since they have adopted them unquestioningly from authority figures; dualistic thinkers do not know (have never thought of) the reasons for which their beliefs are right or wrong. Hence the answer is (B).

3. This is a description question. (A) is false. After carefully thinking through their reasons, committed thinkers are reasonably sure of their position. (B) is also false. Relativistic thinkers make sense of the world, but they have not chosen their position; indeed they cannot even choose a position. (C) is true. Multiplicity thinkers see the world as randomly organized; they can't see the relationships that connect different positions. (See the first pivotal word, "however" [line 20].)

4. This is an extension question. Multiplicity students view all opinions as equally valid. They have yet to learn how to rank opinions (truths)—all votes (thoughts) count equally. The answer is (B).

Note, (C) is offered to humor Republicans. The test-makers sometimes run out of tempting wrong choices. Don't dwell on such humorous nonsense.

5. This is another description question. (A): No, these are the Multiplists. (B): No, Dualists think this way. (C): No, this describes Relativists. Don't confuse (A) and (C). Multiplists acknowledge no right or wrong; whereas Relativists acknowledge a morality, but one that is context dependent. (D): No, Committed thinkers fit this description rather nicely. Hence, by process of elimination, we have learned the answer is (E).

6. This is an application question. Since all the students showed how the characters exemplified the *same* concept of "tragedy," they must be working from a common definition of tragedy (the traditional one). They have accepted "authority's" definition of tragedy and have shown how each character fits it. It never occurred to them that there may be other ways to view a tragedy. Hence they are all dualistic thinkers. The answer is (B).

7. This is a writing technique question. In each paragraph the author shows how a stage of thought evolved from a previous stage—except the dualistic stage, which starts the analysis. Further, the thought process in each stage is illustrated by how it views capital punishment. Hence the answer is (E).

Be careful not to choose (D). Although dualistic thinking certainly is simplistic and provincial, and committed thinking seems to be considered and cosmopolitan, neither of these judgments is stated nor implied by the passage.

Questions 8–13

8. This is a description question. Paragraph 3 contains the information needed to answer it. There it is stated that the cod population can replenish itself in a few years, but the shark population would take 15 years. Hence the answer is (B).

   Don't make the mistake of choosing (C). Although it is certainly supported by the passage, it does not state how this relates to cod—they too may be decreasing in number. (C) uses the true-but-irrelevant ploy.

9. This is a description question. Statement I is true. It is supported by the analogy drawn between lions and sharks (lines 8–10). This eliminates (A) and (B). Statement II is false. It is too strong an inference to draw from the information in lines 10–12. If sharks were on the verge of extinction, this "could hamper" research. But given that the author does not claim or imply that sharks are near extinction, "would hamper" is too strong. Besides, the author does not state that sharks are being used in research, just that they may be useful in that regard. This eliminates (D) and (E). Hence, by process of elimination, we have learned the answer is (C).

10. This is an application question; we are asked to apply what we have learned in the passage to a hypothetical situation. A review of the passage shows that only (B) and (E) have any real merit. But sharks have survived for 400 million years with an extremely low fecundity rate. This eliminates (B). Hence the answer is (E).

11. This is a rather easy tone question. The passage has a matter-of-fact or journalistic tone to it. So the answer is (B).

12. This is an extension question. Statement I is incorrect. Like Statement II in Question 9, it overstates the case. Statement II is correct. We know from lines 51–53 that some species of sharks migrate into the waters of over 20 countries. U.S. quotas alone cannot "protect" these sharks, even if the quotas reduce the rate of killing in U.S. waters. Statement III is incorrect. The environmentalists are angry at the finning fishermen who are over-fishing the waters, there is nothing in the passage to suggest that this anger is also directed towards the chefs. The answer is (B).

13. By announcing the impending classification, the federal government ironically encourages fishermen to kill as many sharks as they can before the regulations go into effect—stimulating the opposite of what was intended, i.e., the saving of sharks. The answer is (D).

Questions 14–19

14. This is a description question. (A) is false. The enjoyment of the reader was incidental to Hemingway's primary purpose—truth-telling. (B) is false, though very tempting. The first half of this item "*to construct a story that would reflect truths*" looks very good. The second half, however, spoils it by adding the qualifier "*not particular to a specific historical period.*" Reviewing the passage reveals no indication that Hemingway is trying to create any kind of "general truth." In fact, one can argue that Hemingway's emphasis on developing a strong "sense of place" (lines 30–34), and his belief that when trying to tell the truth "I only know what I have seen" (line 10) support the inference that Hemingway sees truth as subjective, not objective. (C) is also false. The passage gives no indication that Hemingway was interested in the way things "might have been." (D) is true. This is clearly the author's interpretation of Hemingway's purpose. Look at the first few sentences of both the first and the second paragraphs. Notice that this question item emphasizes subjective truth, or the truth "as Hemingway had experienced it."

   Strategy: In this question, you have two choices—(B) and (D)—which at first glance seem very close. Let's assume you don't understand exactly why a "close second" is wrong. When confronted with this situation, it's a good idea to take a few seconds and try to get into the *Question-Writer's* mindset. What are you missing that the Question-Writer thinks is an important point in this passage? In this case, the Question-Writer is focusing on the subtle point that Hemingway sees his perspective as "subjective," that certain things, true in some places or to some people, may not be true in other places or to other people. In other words, there is no "objective reality."

   If intuition is the only way to distinguish between the two close choices, then you should mark them in your test booklet as *close*, perhaps like this $\left\{\begin{array}{l}\nearrow \textbf{(B)} \\ \textbf{(C)} \\ \searrow \textbf{(D)}\end{array}\right.$, to show that you had to choose between them, and move on. If you have trouble with later questions on the same passage, you may want to go back, analyze the passage, and determine the real difference between the earlier "close pair." The Question-Writer may be testing the same question from a different angle, in which case time is well spent pondering the issue.

15. This is an extension question. In lines 31–33, Hemingway effectively equates geography with background, and says that without them "you have nothing." In lines 35–38, the author refers to the "geographical groundwork" of Hemingway's novels. Both of these statements imply that details of place set the stage for other, more important events. Hence the answer is (A). Don't try to draw a distinction between "geography," "background," and "landscape." The author uses them interchangeably when referring to details of place. Such latitude with labels is often mimicked by the Question-Writers.

Choice (D) is a close second-best. The author indicates that geography, background, and landscape are quite important to Hemingway. In fact, "first" in the opening to paragraph 3 almost indicates that details of place are the most important aspect of his writing. Looking closely, however, we see that the passage gives no indication of Hemingway's perspective on characters. So no comparison can be made.

16. Hemingway's primary intent was to project for the reader "the way it was," as seen through his eyes. The answer is (D).

17. This is an extension question. Statement I is true. The last line of the passage states that the designer's initials (i.e., the writer's presence) are made as inconspicuous as possible. Statement II is also true. Readers cannot see "the way it was" if they are looking through another medium (the author). Hemingway appears to say, in effect: *"I'm striving to report exactly what happened (and not my opinions about it). The readers must draw their own conclusions."* Statement III is false. In fact, a good case could be made that writing only from personal experience would tend to increase, not decrease, the presence of the writer in his writings. The answer is (C).

18. This is an application question; we are asked to put ourselves in Hemingway's mind. From Hemingway's statement "I only know what I have seen" and from the author's assertion that Hemingway refused to honor secondary sources, we can infer that he believed one can "know" only through experience. Hence the answer is (A).

19. This is an extension question. The answer is (B). There is a great parallel here. *Phrase* (in the passage) corresponds to *style* (in the answer-choice), and *concept* corresponds to *content*.

Questions 20–26

20. This is an extension question. According to the passage, red light would not be significantly deflected and consequently would pass through a relatively direct route from the sun to our eyes. Hence the answer is (C).

21. This is another extension question. Since the passage is a science selection, we should expect a lot of extension questions. (A): No, if anything, blue light would exert more energy. (B): No. We can not infer this. The collision of blue light with particles in the air is the reason for a blue sky, not for lightning. (C): No. Speed of light is not mentioned in the passage. **(D): Yes.** Blue light has a shorter wavelength, consequently it has more energy than red light.

22. This is an application question since it introduces new information about water waves and asks us to conclude how the behavior of light waves might be similarly affected. Given this information, however, we can justify no conclusion about whether light waves imitate water waves in this new regard. The analogy might hold or it might break down. We don't yet know. (To find out we would have to do an experiment using light.) The answer is (D).

23. (A): No. We do not know anything about a "variety" of obstacles; even if we did, we would have no reason to assume that light is constituted of different colors. **(B): Yes.** See lines 24–29. Rainbows occur because light is constituted of many colors. (C): No. This is a distortion of lines 49–51, and it sounds illogical to boot. (D): No. This gives no reason to assume that light is constituted of many colors. (E): No. Water vapor in the atmosphere causes rainbows, not dust.

24. (A): No. Although dust is mentioned as one of the three important obstacles (lines 20–21), we simply do not have enough information to conclude how dust density would change sky color. (B): No. While this idea may fit with the common lore that a lot of dust in the air creates great, red sunsets, the passage itself gives no basis to any conclusion regarding color change. (C): No. Same reason as in (A) and (B). **(D): Yes**. There is not enough information in the passage to determine a relationship between color change and dust density. The dust may give off a certain color of its own—we can't say for certain.

25. Statement I is true. There are obviously more particles on a horizontal than a vertical path. The glowing red sky is reasonable evidence for some diffusion. Note that Question 24 asks "what can we *conclude*" while this question asks what seems *plausible* (what "would seem to be explained"). So, while we are attempting to make very similar inferences in both questions, what we can do with the data depends, among other things, on the degree of certainty requested. Statement II is true. The path of evening light probably has a greater average density, since it spends more time passing through a zone of thicker atmosphere. It is reasonable to assume this significantly greater density, or the absolute number of particles, might present an obstacle to blue light. Statement III is false. There are two things wrong with this answer: (1) red light waves are not short, relative to blue; (2) we do not know that waves with more energy will more readily pass through obstacles. The passage, in fact, implies just the opposite. The answer is (C).

26. (A): No. Water waves offer only a model for light waves. As a model, they are identical in some ways but not in others. (B): No. This is not implied by the passage. What they have in common is the way they act when they impinge on obstacles. (C): No. Waves of water are used as a model because they have much in common with waves of light. **(D): Yes.** See explanation for (A).

ARGUMENTS

- **INTRODUCTION**

- **OBFUSCATION**

- **LOGIC I**
  Conclusions
  Premises
  > Suppressed Premises
  > Counter-Premises

- **LOGIC II (Diagramming)**
  If..., then...
  Embedded *If-Then* Statements
  Affirming the Conclusion Fallacy
  Denying the Premise Fallacy
  Transitive Property
  DeMorgan's Laws
  A unless B
  Game-like Arguments

- **CLASSIFICATION**
  Generalization
  Analogy
  Causal Reasoning
  Common Fallacies
  1. Contradiction
  2. Equivocation
  3. Circular Reasoning
  4. Shifting the Burden of Proof
  5. Unwarranted Assumptions
  6. True but Irrelevant
  7. Appeal to Authority
  8. Personal Attack

- **EXTRA ARGUMENTS**

Introduction

An argument, as used on the GMAT, is a presentation of facts and opinions in order to support a position. In common jargon, an argument means a heated debate between two people. While the GMAT will offer a few of these arguments, most will be formal presentations of positions. The arguments come from disparate sources—including sociology, philosophy, science, and even popular culture. The richest source, however, is the Op/Ed page of newspapers.

Many arguments will be fallacious. And many correct answers will be false! This often causes students much consternation; they feel that the correct answer should be *true*. But the arguments are intended to test your ability to think logically. Now logic is the study of the relationships between statements, <u>not</u> of the truth of those statements. Being overly concerned with finding the truth can be ruinous to your GMAT logic score.

Many books recommend reading the question before reading the argument. This method, however, does not work for me; I find it distracting and exhausting. Reading the questions twice can use up precious time and tax your concentration. I get the feeling that many books recommend this method because it gives the readers a feeling that they are getting the "scoop" on how to beat the test. Nevertheless, you may want to experiment—it may work for *you*.

We will analyze the arguments from four different perspectives. First, we will study how the answer-choices are constructed to obscure the correct answer. The GMAT writers rely heavily on obfuscation for argument questions. Next, we will study the structure of an argument—the premises, conclusions, counter-premises, etc. Although the questions are designed so that they can be answered without reference to formal logic, some knowledge of the foundations of logic will give you a definite advantage. Then, we will study how to diagram certain arguments. Finally, we will classify the major types of reasoning used in arguments and their associated fallacies.

OBFUSCATION

In most arguments, the writer is trying to convince you of the validity of her position, so she has a vested interest in presenting the point as clearly as possible. Of course, the point may be complex or subtle or both. Nevertheless, she wants to express it clearly and simply. To obscure this underlying simplicity, the writers of the GMAT cannot change the wording of the statement much because that would leave it vague and poorly written. Their only option, therefore, is to camouflage the answer-choices.

Creating a good but incorrect answer-choice is much harder than developing the correct answer. For this reason, usually only one attractive wrong answer-choice is presented. This is called the "2 out of 5" rule. That is, only two of the five answer-choices will have any real merit. Hence, even if you don't fully understand an argument, you probably can still eliminate the three fluff choices, thereby greatly increasing your odds of answering the question correctly.

Logic I

Although in theory argument questions are designed to be answered without any reference to formal logic, some knowledge of the fundamentals of logic will give you a definite advantage. Armed with this knowledge, you should quickly notice that the arguments are fundamentally easy and that most of them fall into a few basic categories. In this section, we will study the logical structure of arguments. In Logic II, we will symbolize and diagram arguments.

Conclusions

Most argument questions hinge, either directly or indirectly, on determining the conclusion of the argument. The conclusion is the main idea of the argument. It is what the writer tries to persuade the reader to believe. Most often the conclusion comes at the end of the argument. The writer organizes the facts and his opinions so that they build up to the conclusion. Sometimes, however, the conclusion will come at the beginning of an argument, rarely does it come in the middle, and occasionally, for rhetorical effect, the conclusion is not even stated.

Example:

> The police are the armed guardians of the social order. The blacks are the chief domestic victims of the American social order. <u>A conflict of interest exists, therefore, between the blacks and the police.</u>—Eldridge Cleaver, *Soul on Ice*

Here the first two sentences anticipate or set up the conclusion. By changing the grammar slightly, the conclusion can be placed at the beginning of the argument and still sound natural:

> <u>A conflict of interest exists between the blacks and the police</u> because the police are the armed guardians of the social order and the blacks are the chief domestic victims of the American social order.

The conclusion can also be forced into the middle:

> The police are the armed guardians of the social order. <u>So a conflict of interest exists between the blacks and the police</u> because the blacks are the chief domestic victims of the American social order.

It is generally awkward, as in the previous paragraph, to place the conclusion in the middle of the argument because then it cannot be fully anticipated by what comes before nor fully explained by what comes after. On the rare occasion when a conclusion comes in the middle of an argument, most often either the material that comes after it or the material that comes before it is not essential.

> Summary: To find the conclusion, check the last sentence of the argument. If that is not the conclusion, check the first sentence. Rarely does the conclusion come in the middle of an argument.

When determining the meaning of a conclusion, be careful not to read any more into it than what the author states. You must read arguments with more care than you would use in your everyday reading.

For example, many people will interpret the sentence

> "Every Republican is not a conservative"

to mean that some Republicans are not conservative.[*] The writers of the GMAT do not use grammar (logic) that loosely. On the GMAT, the above sentence would mean what it literally states—that no Republican is a conservative.

> Read the words and sentences of an argument precisely, and use their **literal** meaning.

---

[*] To give the sentence that meaning, reword it as "Not every Republican is a conservative".

To illustrate further, consider the meaning of *some* in the sentence

"Some of Mary's friends went to the party."

It would be unwarranted, based on this statement, to assume that some of Mary's friends did not go to the party. Although it may seem deceiving to say that *some* of Mary's friends went to the party when in fact *all* of them did, it is nonetheless technically consistent with the meaning of *some*.

> *Some* means "at least one and perhaps <u>all</u>."

As mentioned before, the conclusion usually comes at the end of an argument, sometimes at the beginning, and rarely in the middle. Writers use certain words to indicate that the conclusion is about to be stated. Following is a list of the most common conclusion indicators:

CONCLUSION INDICATORS

hence	**therefore**	**conclude that**
so	**accordingly**	**as a result**
thus	**consequently**	**implies**
follows that	**shows that**	**means that**

These conclusion flags are very helpful, but you must use them cautiously because many of these words have other functions.

Example:

All devout Muslims abstain from alcohol. Steve is a devout Muslim. <u>Thus</u>, he abstains from alcohol.

In this example, "thus" anticipates the conclusion that necessarily follows from the first two sentences. Notice the different function of *thus* in the following argument.

Example:

The problem is simple when the solution is <u>thus</u> stated.

In this example, *thus* means "in that manner."

Most often the conclusion of an argument is put in the form of a statement (as with every example we have considered so far). Sometimes, however, the conclusion is given as a command or obligation.

Example:

All things considered, you ought to vote.

Here, the author implies that you are obliged to vote.

Example:

Son, unless you go to college, you will not make a success of yourself. No Carnegie has ever been a failure. So you will go to college.

Here the conclusion is given as an imperative command.

The conclusion can even be put in the form of a question. This rhetorical technique is quite effective in convincing people that a certain position is correct. We are more likely to believe something if we feel that we concluded it on our own, or at least if we feel that we were not told to believe it. A conclusion put in question form can have this result.

Example:

The Nanuuts believe that they should not take from Nature anything She cannot replenish during their lifetime. This assures that future generations can enjoy the same riches of Nature that they have. At the current rate of destruction, the rain forests will disappear during our lifetime. Do we have an obligation to future generations to prevent this result?

Here the author trusts that the power of her argument will persuade the reader to answer the question affirmatively.

Taking this rhetorical technique one step further, the writer may build up to the conclusion but leave it unstated. This allows the reader to make up his own mind. If the build-up is done skillfully, the reader will be more likely to agree with the author, without feeling manipulated.

Example:

He who is without sin should cast the first stone. There is no one here who does not have a skeleton in his closet.

The unstated but obvious conclusion here is that none of the people has the right to cast the first stone.

When determining the conclusion's scope be careful not to read any more or less into it than the author states. GMAT writers often create wrong answer-choices by slightly overstating or understating the author's claim. Certain words limit the scope of a statement. These words are called quantifiers—pay close attention to them. Following is a list of the most important quantifiers:

Quantifiers

all	except	likely
some	most	many
only	could	no
never	always	everywhere
probably	must	alone

Example:

Whether the world is Euclidean or non-Euclidean is still an open question. However, if a star's position is predicted based on non-Euclidean geometry, then when a telescope is pointed to where the star should be it will be there. Whereas, if the star's position is predicted based on Euclidean geometry, then when a telescope is pointed to where the star should be it won't be there. This strongly indicates that the world is non-Euclidean.

Which one of the following best expresses the main idea of the passage?

(A) The world may or may not be Euclidean.
(B) The world is probably non-Euclidean.
(C) The world is non-Euclidean.
(D) The world is Euclidean.
(E) The world is neither Euclidean nor non-Euclidean.

Choice (A) understates the main idea. Although the opening to the passage states that we don't know whether the world is non-Euclidean, the author goes on to give evidence that it is non-Euclidean. Choice (C) overstates the main idea. The author doesn't say that the world is non-Euclidean, just that evidence strongly indicates that it is. In choice (B), the word "probably" properly limits the scope of the main idea, namely, that the world is probably non-Euclidean, but we can't yet state so definitively. The answer is (B).

<u>Warm-Up Drill</u> I

> Directions: Find, then underline, the conclusion to each of the following arguments. If an argument does not state the conclusion, complete it with the most natural conclusion. Answers and solutions begin on the next page.

1.   When a man is tired of London, he is tired of life; for there is in London all that life can afford.—Samuel Johnson

2.   Some psychiatrists claim that watching violent movies dissipates aggression. Does watching pornography dissipate one's libido?

3.   By the age of 10 months, purebred golden retrievers display certain instinctive behaviors. Because this 11-month-old golden retriever does not display these instinctive behaviors, it is not a purebred.

4.   Most people would agree that it is immoral to lie. But if a kidnaper accosts you on the street and asks which way his escaped victim went, would it be immoral to point in the opposite direction?

5.   Beware, for I am fearless, and therefore, powerful.—Mary Shelley, *Frankenstein*

6.   The continuous stream of violent death depicted on television has so jaded society that murder is no longer shocking. It's hardly surprising, then, that violent crime so permeates modern society.

7.   Where all other circumstances are equal, wages are generally higher in new than in old trades. When a projector attempts to establish a new manufacture, he must at first entice his workmen from other employments by higher wages than they can either earn in their old trades, or than the nature of his work would otherwise require, and a considerable time must pass away before he can venture to reduce them to the common level.—Adam Smith, *The Wealth of Nations*

8.   Existentialists believe that our identity is continually evolving, that we are born into this world without an identity and do not begin to develop one until the act of retrospection. So one's identity is always trailing oneself like the wake of a boat. As one goes through life, the wake becomes wider and wider defining him more and more precisely.

9.   In time I began to recognize that all of these smaller complaints about rigidity, emotional suffocation, the tortured logic of the law were part of a more fundamental phenomenon in the law itself. Law is at war with ambiguity, with uncertainty. In the courtroom, the adversary system—plaintiff against defendant—guarantees that someone will always win, someone loses. No matter if justice is evenly with each side, no matter if the issues are indefinite and obscure, the rule of law will be declared.—Scott Turow, *One L*

10. Either God controls all of man's behavior or God does not control any of man's behavior. God must not control man's behavior since there is so much evil in the world.

11. The more deeply I understand the central role of caring in my own life, the more I realize it to be central to the human condition.—Milton Mayeroff, *On Caring*

Solutions to Warm-Up Drill I

1. <u>When a man is tired of London, he is tired of life</u>; for there is in London all that life can afford.—Samuel Johnson

2. The conclusion is not stated, but the arguer implies that watching violent movies does *not* dissipate aggression.

3. By the age of 10 months, purebred golden retrievers display certain instinctive behaviors. Because this 11 month-old golden retriever does not display these instinctive behaviors, <u>it is not a purebred.</u>

4. No conclusion is stated. But the author implies that to lie is not always immoral.

5. Beware, for I am fearless, and therefore, <u>powerful</u>.—Mary Shelley, *Frankenstein*

6. The implied conclusion is that violence depicted on television contributes to society's high rate of violence.

7. Where all other circumstances are equal, <u>wages are generally higher in new than in old trades</u>. When a projector attempts to establish a new manufacture, he must at first entice his workmen from other employments by higher wages than they can either earn in their old trades, or than the nature of his work would otherwise require, and a considerable time must pass away before he can venture to reduce them to the common level.—Adam Smith, *The Wealth of Nations*

8. Existentialists believe that our identity is continually evolving, that we are born into this world without an identity and do not begin to develop one until the act of retrospection. So <u>one's identity is always trailing oneself</u> like the wake of a boat. As one goes through life, the wake becomes wider and wider defining him more and more precisely.

9. In time I began to recognize that all of these smaller complaints about rigidity, emotional suffocation, the tortured logic of the law were part of a more fundamental phenomenon in the law itself. <u>Law is at war with ambiguity, with uncertainty</u>. In the courtroom, the adversary system—plaintiff against defendant—guarantees that someone will always win, someone loses. No matter if justice is evenly with each side, no matter if the issues are indefinite and obscure, the rule of law will be declared.—Scott Turow, *One L*

10. Either God controls all of man's behavior or God does not control any of man's behavior. <u>God must not control man's behavior</u> since there is so much evil in the world.

11. The more deeply I understand the central role of caring in my own life, the more I realize <u>it to be central to the human condition</u>.—Milton Mayeroff, *On Caring*

Premises

Once you've found the conclusion, most often everything else in the argument will be either premises or "noise." The premises provide evidence for the conclusion; they form the foundation or infrastructure upon which the conclusion depends. To determine whether a statement is a premise, ask yourself whether it supports the conclusion. If so, it's a premise. Earlier we saw that writers use certain words to flag conclusions; likewise writers use certain words to flag premises. Following is a partial list of the most common premise indicators:

PREMISE INDICATORS

because	for
since	is evidence that
if	in that
as	owing to
suppose	inasmuch as
assume	may be derived from

Premise indicators are very helpful. As with conclusion indicators, though, you must use them cautiously because they have other functions. For example, *since* can indicate a premise, or it can merely indicate time.

Example:

Since the incumbent's views are out of step with public opinion, he probably will not be reelected.

Here "since" is used to flag the premise that the incumbent's positions are unpopular. Contrast this use of "since" with the following example.

Example:

Since the incumbent was elected to office, he has spent less and less time with his family.

In this case, "since" merely expresses a passage of time. The statement as a whole expresses an observation, rather than an argument.

SUPPRESSED PREMISES

Most arguments depend on one or more unstated premises. Sometimes this indicates a weakness in the argument, an oversight by the writer. More often, however, certain premises are left tacit because they are too numerous, or the writer assumes that his audience is aware of the assumptions, or he wants the audience to fill in the premise themselves and therefore be more likely to believe the conclusion.

Example:

Conclusion: I knew he did it.
Premise: Only a guilty person would accept immunity from prosecution.

The suppressed premise is that he did, in fact, accept immunity. The speaker assumes that his audience is aware of this fact or at least is willing to believe it, so to state it would be redundant and ponderous. If the unstated premise were false (that is, he did not accept immunity), the argument would not technically be a lie; but it would be very deceptive. The unscrupulous writer may use this ploy if he thinks that he can get away with it. That is, his argument has the intended effect and the false premise, though implicit, is hard to find or is ambiguous. Politicians are not at all above using this tactic.

Example:

Politician: A hawk should not be elected President because this country has seen too many wars.

The argument has two tacit premises—one obvious, the other subtle. Clearly, the politician has labeled his opponent a hawk, and he hopes the audience will accept that label. Furthermore, although he does not state it explicitly, the argument rests on the assumption that a hawk is likely to start a war. He hopes the audience will fill in that premise, thereby tainting his opponent as a warmonger.

A common question on the GMAT asks you to find the suppressed premise of an argument. Finding the suppressed premise, or assumption, of an argument can be difficult. However, on the GMAT you have an advantage—the suppressed premise is listed as one of the five answer-choices. To test whether an answer-choice is a suppressed premise, ask yourself whether it would make the argument more plausible. If so, then it is very likely a suppressed premise.

Example:

American attitudes tend to be rather insular, but there is much we can learn from other countries. In Japan, for example, workers set aside some time each day to exercise, and many corporations provide elaborate exercise facilities for their employees. Few American corporations have such exercise programs. Studies have shown that the Japanese worker is more productive than the American worker. Thus it must be concluded that the productivity of American workers will lag behind their Japanese counterparts, until mandatory exercise programs are introduced.

The conclusion of the argument is valid if which one of the following is assumed?

(A) Even if exercise programs do not increase productivity, they will improve the American worker's health.
(B) The productivity of all workers can be increased by exercise.
(C) Exercise is an essential factor in the Japanese worker's superior productivity.
(D) American workers can adapt to the longer Japanese work week.
(E) American corporations don't have the funds to build elaborate exercise facilities.

The unstated essence of the argument is that exercise is an integral part of productivity and that Japanese workers are more productive than American workers because they exercise more. The answer is (C).

Example:

Steve Cooper, senior sales officer, has trained many top salespeople in this company, including 14 who have become the top salespersons in their regions and 3 who have won the top salesperson award. Although there is an art to selling, Mr. Cooper's success at training top salespeople shows that the skills required to become a top salesperson can be both taught and learned.

The argument depends on which one of the following assumptions?

(A)   Mr. Cooper does not teach the hard-sell method. Nor does he teach the I'll-be-your-pal method. Instead, he stresses the professional-client relationship.
(B)   More than 50% of the people trained by Mr. Cooper went on to become successful salespeople.
(C)   One of the successful salespeople who trained under Mr. Cooper was not an accomplished salesperson before learning the Cooper Method.
(D)   There is a large and expanding industry dedicated to training salespeople.
(E)   There is no one method with which to approach sales; a method that works for one person may not for another person.

If the salespeople trained by Mr. Cooper were successful before studying under him, then clearly the argument would be specious. On the other hand, if none of the salespeople were successful before studying under him, then the argument would be strong. However, the argument does not require this strong of a statement in order to be valid. All it needs is one person who profited from the tutelage of Mr. Cooper. The answer is (C).

Many students have problems with this type of question. They read through the answer-choices and find no significant statements. They may pause at (C) but reject it—thinking that the argument would be deceptive if only one person out of 17 profited from the tutelage of Mr. Cooper. However, the missing premise doesn't have to make the argument good, just valid.

Example:

The petrochemical industry claims that chemical waste dumps pose no threat to people living near them. If this is true, then why do they locate the plants in sparsely populated regions. By not locating the chemical dumps in densely populated areas the petrochemical industry tacitly admits that these chemicals are potentially dangerous to the people living nearby.

Which of the following, if true, would most weaken the author's argument?

(A)   Funding through the environmental Super Fund to clean up poorly run waste dumps is reserved for rural areas only.
(B)   Until chemical dumps are proven 100% safe, it would be imprudent to locate them were they could potentially do the most harm.
(C)   Locating the dumps in sparsely populated areas is less expensive and involves less government red tape.
(D)   The potential for chemicals to leach into the water table has in the past been underestimated.
(E)   People in cities are more likely to sue the industry if their health is harmed by the dumps.

The suppressed *false* premise of the argument is that all things being equal there is no reason to prefer locating the sites in sparsely populated areas. To weaken the argument, we need to show it is <u>not</u> true that all things are equal. In other words, there are advantages other than safety in locating the sites in sparsely populated areas. Choice (C) gives two possible advantages—cost and ease. Hence (C) is the answer.

Warm-Up Drill II

> **Directions:** For each of the following arguments, identify the suppressed premise and state whether it is a reasonable assumption for the author to make. Answers and solutions begin on the next page.

1.   Sacramento is the capital of California; thus it is located northeast of San Francisco.

2.   I read it in a book, so it must be true.

3.   Any government action that intrudes on the right of privacy is unconstitutional. Therefore, requiring government employees to take a drug test is unconstitutional.

4.   After studying assiduously for three months, Sean retook the SAT and increased his score by more than four hundred points. Therefore, the Educational Testing Service canceled his score.

5.   When explorers arrived in the Americas in the 1500s A.D., they observed the natives hunting with bronze tipped arrows. Archaeological evidence shows that bronze was not smelted in the Americas until the 1200s A.D. Therefore, native Americans must have begun hunting with arrows sometime between 1200 and 1500 A.D.

6.   Fiction is truer than history, because it goes beyond the evidence.—E. M. Forster

7.   In Knox's theory of military strategy, all decisions about troop deployment must be made by a committee of generals. If, however, his model of command were in effect during World War II, then daring and successful operations—such as Patton's unilateral decision to land paratroopers behind enemy lines during the Battle of the Bulge—would not have been ordered.

8.   In recent years many talented and dedicated teachers have left the public school system for the private sector because the public school system's salary scale is not sufficient for a family to maintain a quality standard of living. To lure these dedicated teachers back to the public schools, we must immediately raise the pay scale to a level comparable to that of the private sector, and thereby save our schools.

Solutions to Warm-Up Drill II

1. The suppressed premise is that the capital of California is located northeast of San Francisco. This is a reasonable assumption because it is true!

2. The suppressed premise is that only the truth is published. Clearly this is not a reasonable assumption.

3. The suppressed premise is that being forced to take a drug test is an invasion of privacy. This is a reasonable assumption.

4. ETS's suppressed premise is that extremely high score improvements indicate cheating. This is arguably a reasonable assumption, but it is not consistent with the tradition of assuming one innocent until proven otherwise. (By the way, this is a true story. Sean sued ETS and the courts ordered them to release his score.)

5. The suppressed premise is that hunting with arrows did not begin until the arrows were tipped with bronze. This seems to be a questionable assumption.

6. The suppressed premise is that what goes beyond the evidence is truer that what does not. This is a questionable assumption; arguably just the opposite is the case.

7. The suppressed premise is that only decisions made by a single individual can be daring. This assumption has some truth to it, but it's a bit extreme.

8. The suppressed premise is that comparable pay would be sufficient to entice the teachers to change their careers again. This is probably a reasonable assumption since the teachers were described as dedicated.

COUNTER-PREMISES

When presenting a position, you obviously don't want to argue against yourself. However, it is often effective to concede certain minor points that weaken your argument. This shows that you are open-minded and that your ideas are well considered. It also disarms potential arguments against your position. For instance, in arguing for a strong, aggressive police department, you may concede that in the past the police have at times acted too aggressively. Of course, you will then need to state more convincing reasons to support your position.

Example:

I submit that the strikers should accept the management's offer. Admittedly, it is less than what was demanded. But it does resolve the main grievance—inadequate health care. Furthermore, an independent study shows that a wage increase greater than 5% would leave the company unable to compete against Japan and Germany, forcing it into bankruptcy.

The conclusion, "the strikers should accept the management's offer," is stated in the first sentence. Then "Admittedly" introduces a concession; namely, that the offer was less than what was demanded. This weakens the speaker's case, but it addresses a potential criticism of his position before it can be made. The last two sentences of the argument present more compelling reasons to accept the offer and form the gist of the argument.

Following are some of the most common counter-premise indicators:

COUNTER-PREMISE INDICATORS

but	**despite**
admittedly	**except**
even though	**nonetheless**
nevertheless	**although**
however	**in spite of the fact**

As you may have anticipated, the GMAT writers sometimes use counter-premises to bait wrong answer-choices. Answer-choices that refer to counter-premises are very tempting because they refer directly to the passage and they are *in part* true. But you must ask yourself "Is this the main point that the author is trying to make?" It may merely be a minor concession.

In the following argument, notice how the counter-premise is used as bait.

Example:

Nature constantly adjusts the atmospheric carbon level. An increase in the level causes the atmosphere to hold more heat, which causes more water to evaporate from the oceans, which causes increased rain. Rain washes some carbon from the air into the oceans, where it eventually becomes part of the seabed. A decrease in atmospheric carbon causes the atmosphere to hold less heat, which causes decreased evaporation from the oceans, which causes less rain, and thus less carbon is washed into the oceans. Yet some environmentalists worry that burning fossil fuels may raise atmospheric carbon to a dangerous level. It is true that a sustained increase would threaten human life. But the environmentalists should relax— nature will continually adjust the carbon level.

Which one of the following, if true, would most weaken the argument in the passage?

(A)   Plant life cannot survive without atmospheric carbon.

(B)   It is not clear that breathing excess carbon in the atmosphere will have a negative effect on human life.

(C)   Carbon is part of the chemical "blanket" that keeps the Earth warm enough to sustain human life.

(D)   Breathing by animals releases almost 30 times as much carbon as does the burning of fossil fuels.

(E)   The natural adjustment process, which occurs over millions of years, allows wide fluctuations in the carbon level in the short term.

The counter-premise in this argument is the sentence "It is true that a sustained increase [in atmospheric carbon] would threaten human life." By making this concession, the author shows that he is aware of the alternatives and the potential seriousness of situation; it also provides a hedge against potential criticism that the situation is too important to risk following his advice.

The question asks us to weaken the argument. As mentioned before, to weaken an argument typically you attack a premise (either expressed or suppressed) of the argument. Now, someone who did not fully understand the author's main point might mistake the counter-premise for a premise. Look at answer-choice (B); it directly attacks the counter-premise by implying that it may not be true. Choice (B) is offered as bait. Some people will fall for it because it attacks a statement in the argument, as should the answer. The best answer, however, will attack the main premise.

One possibility the author did not account for is that the natural adjustment process may require many years and that in the short run dangerous levels of carbon could accumulate. This directly attacks the main premise of the argument, "Nature *constantly* adjusts the atmospheric carbon level." Hence the answer is (E).

It is often clarifying to outline an argument's logical structure. An outline can make clear the argumentative strategy the author is using. The above argument has the following structure:

Main Premise
Explanation of Main Premise
Secondary Premise
Counter-Premise
Conclusion

The first sentence introduces the main premise that nature constantly adjusts the atmospheric carbon level. The next three sentences explain that premise. Then in the fifth sentence, the secondary premise is introduced that environmentalists are concerned that burning fossil fuels may increase atmospheric carbon to dangerous levels. Then the penultimate (next to last) sentence introduces the counter-premise that an increase in the carbon level would be a threat to human life. This measures the conclusion that environmentalists should relax because nature will adjust the carbon level.

Points to Remember

1. Most argument questions hinge on determining the conclusion of the argument.

2. To find the conclusion, check the final sentence of the argument. If the last sentence is not the conclusion, check the first sentence. Rarely does the conclusion come in the middle of the argument.

3. Take the words and sentences in an argument literally.

4. *Some* means "at least one and perhaps <u>all</u>."

5. Some of the most common conclusion flags are

hence	**therefore**
so	**accordingly**
thus	**consequently**
follows that	**shows that**
conclude that	**implies**
as a result	**means that**

6. While conclusions are usually presented as statements, they can also be expressed as commands, obligations, questions, or even left unstated.

7. The premises provide evidence for the conclusion; they form the foundation or infrastructure upon which the conclusion depends. To determine whether a statement is a premise, ask yourself whether it supports the conclusion. If so, it's a premise.

8. The following is a partial list of the most common premise indicators:

because	**for**
since	**is evidence that**
if	**in that**
as	**owing to**
suppose	**inasmuch as**
assume	**may be derived from**

9. Often a key premise to an argument will be suppressed.

10. To test whether an answer-choice is a suppressed premise, ask yourself whether it would make the argument more plausible. If so, then it is very likely a suppressed premise.

11. A common argument question asks you to either strengthen or weaken an argument. Typically, these questions pivot on suppressed premises: to strengthen an argument, show that a suppressed premise is true; to weaken an argument, show that a suppressed premise is false.

12. A counter-premise is a concession to a minor point that weakens your argument.

13. The following are some of the most common counter-premise indicators.

but	**despite**
admittedly	**except**
even though	**nonetheless**
nevertheless	**although**
however	**in spite of the fact**

Exercise

1. Two prestigious fine art schools are located in New England, Central and Northeast. Talented vocal students attend each school. At Central, voice students are required to take voice lessons twice each week and to practice their singing at least one hour each day. At Northeast, voice students are required to take voice lessons only once per week, and they are required to practice only three times each week. The voice students from both schools were recently tested on a variety of vocal techniques, including breath control. Voice students at Central were able to hold a single note for 60 seconds, which was 15 seconds longer than the Northeast voice students. Thus, one must conclude that Northeast voice students will improve their breath control only if they increase their voice lessons to twice per week and their practice to one hour each day.

   The paragraph assumes which one of the following?

   (A) All students would be able to hold a note for 60 seconds if they take frequent voice lessons and practice their singing at least one hour per day.

   (B) All students can have the same quality singing voices if they take voice lessons and practice one hour per day.

   (C) Students with better breath control appreciate music more.

   (D) Taking voice lessons twice per week and practicing one hour each day are essential factors in the ability of Central voice students to hold notes longer than the Northeast voice students.

   (E) If students practice singing regularly, they will prefer voice to other forms of musical expression.

2. Gasoline-powered boat engines manufactured in the a North American country prior to 1990 contribute significantly to the pollution found in the world's oceans. In 1990, however, the government imposed stricter pollution controls on gasoline engines manufactured for boats, and beginning in 1995, the government imposed a program of inspections for pre-1990 boat engines with increasingly rigorous pollution standards. As the older boat engines fail to pass inspection, boat owners are increasingly retiring their old engines in favor of newer, less-polluting boat engines. As a result, the amount of pollution these older boat engines emit into the world's oceans will steadily decrease over the next ten years.

   Which one of the following statements, if true, most seriously undermines the argument?

   (A) Water from the various oceans cannot be accurately divided among nations because ocean currents travel thousands of miles and cross numerous national boundary lines.

   (B) Even as they become older, boat engines manufactured after 1990 will never pollute as much as boat engines manufactured prior to 1990.

   (C) When boat owners retire their older boat engines in favor of newer ones, the older engines are frequently sent overseas to countries with less stringent pollution standards, where they are in high demand.

   (D) The government's pollution control standards for boat engines are increasingly stricter up until 1998; then they level off.

   (E) If demand for new fishing and pleasure boats increases significantly every year, then pollution of the world's oceans will continue to increase, regardless of the fact that older boat engines are being retired.

3. Plants that exhibit certain leaf diseases tend to measure extremely high in the amount of zinc in their leaf and stem tissue. Botanists have discovered that phosphorus of the type typically used in a phosphorus-high fertilizer reacts with the zinc in such a way as to prevent treated plants from exhibiting the leaf diseases. Thus, plants can be cured from these leaf diseases by the use of a fertilizer high in phosphorus.

The passage's conclusion is based upon which one of the following premises?

(A) Plants with certain leaf diseases contain the same high level of zinc in their leaf and stem tissue.

(B) Zinc is the cause and not merely an effect of the leaf diseases.

(C) Treating the plants with a fertilizer high in phosphorus will have no negative effect on the plants.

(D) The amount of phosphorus-high fertilizer which should be used depends upon the size and location of the plants.

(E) Normal plant tissue does not contain zinc.

4. To be accepted as a member at the Brown Country Club, one must have a net worth of over ten million dollars and must not have any connections to the entertainment industry. Robert Chase, the publishing magnate, has a net worth of 5 billion dollars and has been accepted as a member at the Brown Country Club.

Given the statements above, which one of the following conclusions must be true?

(A) Chase's membership was preapproved.

(B) Chase does not know anyone who has connections to the entertainment industry.

(C) Chase's ex-business partner is a major concert promoter, has a net worth of 100 million dollars, and is a member of the Brown Country Club.

(D) Chase's brother, who has also petitioned for membership at Brown, has a net worth of 10 billion dollars and considers it beneath his dignity to associate with anyone in the entertainment industry. Hence, his petition will be accepted.

(E) Chase has not financed any Hollywood movies.

5. Explorers of the northern regions in the early 1700s observed the natives playing an instrument similar to the mandolin. The instrument was strung with horse hair. Horses were not introduced into the New World until the 1500s. Thus, we can conclude that natives developed the instrument sometime between the introduction of horses to the New World and the time of the explorers in the early 1700s.

Which one of the following assumptions is critical to the passage's conclusion?

(A) Natives used the mandolin-like instrument in all their religious events.

(B) Using horse hair in the mandolin-like instrument was one of the natives' earliest uses of horse hair.

(C) This instrument was used by natives throughout North America.

(D) Since it was first developed, the instrument was made with horse hair.

(E) Explorers in the 1700s were the first to document natives' use of horse hair.

6. The math professor's goals for classroom honesty and accurate student assessment were founded upon his belief that the fear of punishment and corresponding loss of privileges would make students think twice or even three times before cheating on exams, thus virtually eliminating cheating in his classroom. In order for this atmosphere to prevail, the students had to believe that the consequences for cheating were severe and that the professor had the means to discover cheaters and enforce the punishment against them.

If the statements contained in the preceding passage are true, which one of the following can be properly inferred?

(A) A student would only be deterred from cheating if he knew he would be discovered and punished.
(B) A student will not cheat on an exam if he feels he is well prepared for the exam.
(C) A student who cheats on an exam believes that he will not be able to pass the exam without cheating.
(D) If the professor wants to achieve his goals, he should make his students aware of his policy on cheating and the consequences that would befall those who cheat on his exams.
(E) If the professor wants never to have an incident of cheating in his classroom, his policy on cheating must be stronger than any other professor's policy on cheating.

7. The survival of the publishing industry depends upon the existence of a public who will buy the printed word in the form of newspapers, books and magazines. Over the past several years, however, the advance of electronic media, particularly CD-ROMs, online computer services, and the Internet, has made information available to the public electronically without the need for printed materials. As the availability of electronic media increases and as it is more easily accessible, the public has less need for printed materials.

Which one of the following statements flows logically from the passage?

(A) Teachers and libraries must promote the importance of books and other written materials.
(B) The publishing industry is threatened by the advance of the computer information age.
(C) Every member of the public has a duty to become informed about the Internet.
(D) Tabloids will most successfully compete with computers.
(E) The publishing industry will survive if the educated members of the public continue to purchase written materials.

8. Pharmacists recently conducted a study with respect to the reasons their customers purchased eye drops to soothe eye dryness. Dry eyes were more frequently experienced by customers who wore contact lenses than by customers who did not wear contact lenses. The pharmacists concluded that wearing contact lenses, by itself, can cause contact wearers to have dry eyes.

Which one of the following statements, if true, most seriously undermines the pharmacists' conclusion?

(A) An inherited condition can cause both weak eyesight and dry eyes.
(B) Physical exertion causes dry eyes in many people who wear contact lenses.
(C) Most people who have dry eyes do not wear contact lenses.
(D) Most people who wear contact lenses do not have dry eyes.
(E) Both weak vision and dry eyes cause headaches.

9. Kirkland's theory of corporate structure can be represented by a truncated pyramid. There are workers, middle management, and executive management, but no head of the corporation. Instead, all major decisions are made by committee. As a consequence, in Kirkland's structure, risky, cutting-edge technologies cannot be developed.

Which one of the following is an assumption on which the argument depends?

(A) Cutting-edge technologies are typically developed by entrepreneurs, not by big corporations.

(B) Only single individuals will make risky decisions.

(C) An individual is more likely to take a gamble on his own than in a group.

(D) All heads of corporations reached their positions by taking risks.

(E) All cutting-edge technologies involve some risk.

10. Advertisers are often criticized for their unscrupulous manipulation of people's tastes and wants. There is evidence, however, that some advertisers are motivated by moral as well as financial considerations. A particular publication decided to change its image from being a family newspaper to concentration on sex and violence, thus appealing to a different readership. Some advertisers withdrew their advertisements from the publication, and this must have been because they morally disapproved of publishing salacious material.

Which one of the following, if true, would most strengthen the argument?

(A) The advertisers switched their advertisements to other family newspapers.

(B) Some advertisers switched from family newspapers to advertise in the changed publication.

(C) The advertisers expected their product sales to increase if they stayed with the changed publication, but to decrease if they withdrew.

(D) People who generally read family newspapers are not likely to buy newspapers that concentrate on sex and violence.

(E) It was expected that the changed publication would appeal principally to those in a different income group.

11. Some people believe that witnessing violence in movies will discharge aggressive energy. Does watching someone else eat fill one's own stomach?

In which one of the following does the reasoning most closely parallel that employed in the passage?

(A) Some people think appropriating supplies at work for their own personal use is morally wrong. Isn't shoplifting morally wrong?

(B) Some people think nationalism is defensible. Hasn't nationalism been the excuse for committing abominable crimes?

(C) Some people think that boxing is fixed just because wrestling usually is. Are the two sports managed by the same sort of people?

(D) Some people think that economists can control inflation. Can meteorologists make the sun shine?

(E) Some people think workaholics are compensating for a lack of interpersonal skills. However, aren't most doctors workaholics?

12. The Agricultural Board of a western European country determines when and under what conditions new food-producing plants and seeds can be sold to the public. As a result, the Agricultural Board plays an important part in improving agricultural production in western Europe. Individual farmers and farm research centers are involved in the time-consuming task of discovering and testing new varieties of fruits and vegetables. But the Agricultural Board is responsible for verifying the qualities of the new products and for approving their sale and distribution to the public. New plants and seeds are not available to improve agricultural production until after they have been approved by the Agricultural Board.

The passage implies which one of the following statements?

(A)   The Agricultural Board requires that new varieties of fruits and vegetables be regulated.
(B)   Before new varieties of fruits and vegetables are made available to the public, they do not improve agricultural production.
(C)   Researchers who develop new varieties of fruits and vegetables are responsible for the long period of time before such products are released to the public, not the Agricultural Board.
(D)   The Agricultural Board should work more closely with farm research centers to guarantee the quality of new fruit and vegetable varieties.
(E)   If the discovery of a new variety of apple has progressed from the research center to the public, it will improve agricultural production.

13. It has been suggested that with the continued advance of technology, robots will be able to replace skilled craftsmen who currently assemble and test sophisticated manufactured goods, such as musical instruments. This suggestion is based on the belief that the assembly and testing of musical instruments consists of learning a series of techniques and processes, which can be programmed automatically without any understanding of how the various parts are supposed to work together to produce a high quality musical instrument. If this were the case, then robots could be programmed to follow the techniques and processes, and craftsmen would not be needed to assemble and test the instruments. But to do their jobs, skilled craftsmen must also understand the principles of sound production, together with the nuances of tone quality and the other criteria of a high quality musical instrument. Therefore, the idea that robots will replace people in the production of musical instruments is seriously flawed.

Which one of the following selections, if true, would most seriously weaken the author's conclusion that robots will not replace skilled craftsmen in the production of musical instruments?

(A)   Not as many musical instruments are being produced today, so the industry cannot afford to pay skilled craftsmen.
(B)   Musical instruments are not produced individually any more, but are mass produced in factories.
(C)   Robots can be programmed to understand the principles of sound production, the nuances of tone quality and the other criteria of a high quality musical instrument.
(D)   Robots can accomplish mundane assembly tasks much more cost-effectively than skilled craftsmen can.
(E)   Skilled craftsmen are responsible for ensuring that musical instruments meet high quality standards.

14. Over the past two decades, a wide gap in pay has arisen between medical professionals who practice in the public health arena as opposed to those who practice privately. As a result, many doctors, nurses and other health professionals employed by public and nonprofit agencies have left their public health jobs in favor of private clinics and hospitals. Public and nonprofit agencies will be able to entice these professionals to return to public health jobs if salaries are made commensurate with those paid in the private sector. The quality of medical care provided by public and nonprofit agencies will thus be improved.

Which one of the following is presumed in the position stated above?

(A) The experience obtained by medical professionals in private clinics and hospitals will be especially important in the public health arena.

(B) How well public and nonprofit health agencies perform depends for the most part upon the experience level of their health professionals.

(C) Unless public and nonprofit health agencies act, the salaries paid to medical professionals in private practice will continue to outpace those paid in the public health arena.

(D) Medical health professionals who moved from the public sector to the private sector would change jobs again.

(E) If the pay disparity between the public and private medical sectors continues to increase, many doctors and nurses will move from private practice to the public health area.

15. Diseases have always plagued the earth's living organisms. Scientists believe that huge numbers of plant and animal diseases have developed and been eradicated naturally over time. This ongoing emergence and disappearance of diseases is ignored by those who blame the widespread incidence of cancer entirely upon man's alteration of naturally occurring substances to, for instance, produce bigger and better food sources. For example, some claim that the use of hormones to increase meat production heightens the risk of cancer in people who eat meat. People who hold this view need to accept the fact that even if cancer was not such a prevalent disease, another disease would have arisen naturally to take its place.

Which one of the following identifies a flaw in the passage's reasoning?

(A) The writer wrongly assumes that the use of hormones in meat production never has an effect upon people who eat meat.

(B) The writer ignores the fact that scientists are developing cures for some types of cancer.

(C) The writer does not consider the fact that a number of diseases have not yet been discovered.

(D) While the writer identifies a group that believes cancer is caused by man's interference with natural forms of food production, he does not identify or recognize scientists who disagree with this contention.

(E) The author does not acknowledge that man's alteration of naturally occurring substances might trigger the emergence of new diseases.

Answers and Solutions to Exercise

1.	D	6.	D	11.	D
2.	C	7.	B	12.	B
3.	B	8.	A	13.	C
4.	E	9.	B	14.	D
5.	D	10.	C	15.	E

1. The implied premise of the first question is that Central voice students have better breath control than Northeast voice students because the Central students take more frequent voice lessons and are required to practice more often. Further, it is assumed that more lessons and practice are indispensable factors to this result. (D) is the correct answer.

Selection (A) is the second best answer. The conclusion in the first question states that Northeast students *"will improve their breath control only if they increase"* their lessons and practice. Put another way, more frequent voice lessons and practice are required for greater breath control. Selection (A) says that all students who take frequent lessons and practice often would have good breath control, but (A) does not imply that such a schedule of lessons and practice are necessary.

2. Typically, to weaken an argument, one of its premises must be shown to be false or flawed. The argument implies that when boat owners buy new engines for their boats, their old engines will be discarded or destroyed. Selection (C) contradicts this assumption by explaining that old boat engines are in high demand in countries with less rigorous pollution standards and that old engines are often sent overseas to satisfy that demand. Thus these old engines may still be in use. Selection (C) is the right answer.

3. In this question, the premise has been suppressed. If the high level of zinc found in diseased plants is merely a symptom of the diseases, and zinc does not actually cause the diseases, then the fact that a fertilizer high in phosphorus causes plants not to exhibit the diseases, is irrelevant. So the question is based upon the assumption set forth in choice (B). The answer is (B).

4. The argument states that two criteria must be met before the Brown Country Club will accept a person:

I. He or she must have a net worth of over ten million dollars.

II. He or she must not have any connections to the entertainment industry.

Since the Chase was accepted as a member, he must not have any connections to the entertainment industry and therefore could not have financed a Hollywood movie. The answer is (E).

5. Natives could have initially developed their mandolin-like instrument with strings made from something other than horse hair, perhaps tree bark. In order for the conclusion in the argument to be valid, we must assume that the instrument was first developed with horse hair. Selection (D) is the assumption upon which the conclusion is based. The answer is (D).

6. A conclusion for this argument is requested. In order to accurately assess his students on exams, the professor desires to eliminate cheating from his classroom. He believes that a tough policy on cheating will deter students from cheating. Therefore, he is more likely to reach his goal if he announces his policy on cheating and makes it known that he will track down cheaters and punish them. The answer is (D).

7. The first sentence is critical to this question—publishers depend upon people who buy books and other printed materials. If the advance of the computer information age eliminates the need for printed information, then the publishing industry is threatened by the public's wide-spread use of computers and the Internet. The answer is (B).

8. This argument does not consider that an outside factor may cause some people to have both poor vision and dry eyes. Selection (A) provides an outside factor for both conditions. It is the correct answer.

Selection (D) is tempting, but don't be misled. Even if most people who wear contact lenses do not have dry eyes, this does not weaken the argument because it is based on the incidence of dry eyes between people who wear contact lenses and those who do not. Secondly, the author does not argue that wearing contact lenses *must* cause dry eyes, only that it *can* cause dry eyes.

9.   The link that allows the conclusion to be drawn is the assumption that <u>only</u> individuals make risky decisions. The answer is (B).

Both (A) and (C) are close second-best choices (a double-detractor pair). Both are supported by the passage, but each understates the scope of the suppressed premise. The argument states that in Kirkland's model of corporate structure cutting-edge technologies <u>cannot</u> be developed, not that they are less likely to be developed.

10.   The suppressed premise in this argument is that the advertisers hurt themselves financially by withdrawing their advertisements, or at least did not help themselves. To strengthen the argument, we need to show that this assumption is true. Choice (C) implies that this is the case by stating that the advertisers expected to lose sales if they withdrew their advertisements. Hence the answer is (C).

11.   To answer this question, we need to identify the argument's structure and the author's tone. The argument has two parts. First, a statement is made. Then it is questioned by drawing an extreme analogy. By putting the conclusion in question form, the author hopes you will be more likely to come to the same conclusion she did. It's important to note the sarcasm in the analogy. Obviously, watching someone else eat doesn't fill your own stomach. The author implies it is equally unlikely that watching violent movies will dissipate aggressive energy, or satisfy one's need for violence.

In the argument, the writer throws out a statement and then ridicules it by drawing an extreme analogy. Look at choice (D). It presents a statement: *"Some people think that economists can control inflation."* Then ridicules it with an extreme analogy: *"Can meteorologists make the sun shine?"* Hence the answer is (D).

(B) is somewhat tempting. It does have the same basic structure as the original argument—a statement is offered and then questioned. However, the tone in (B) is not sarcastic. Furthermore, the question *"Hasn't nationalism*

been the excuse for committing abominable crimes?" isn't in analogy form.

12.   This question is fairly simple; students should not agonize over it. Clearly, before a new variety of fruit or vegetable can improve agricultural production, it must be made available to the public. Selection (B) is the correct answer.

Answers such as (B) often cause students much difficulty. Students may hesitate to mark such a clear and simple answer because they believe they must have missed something. Sometimes they have. But sometimes the simple answer is the correct answer. Caution: Students should attempt to distinguish the <u>simple</u> answer from the <u>simplistic</u> answer. While the simple answer may more often be the correct answer over a complex answer, rarely is the simplistic answer correct.

Don't be misled by answer (C). Even though the argument supports (C), the question asks for a statement that is inferred from the passage. Thus, the answer must go beyond what is divulged in the passage.

13.   Remember that in order to weaken or undermine an argument, one of the premises of the argument must be disproved. The implied premise of this passage is that robots cannot be programmed to understand the principles of sound production and the other criteria of a quality musical instrument, and thus they will not replace skilled craftsmen.

(A) No. Whether or not the industry can afford to pay skilled craftsmen is irrelevant to the question of whether robots could be programmed to perform the craftsmen's work at the same skill level.

(B) No. This selection is also irrelevant to the argument, which considers whether robots can perform the skilled work of craftsmen.

(C) Yes. The implied premise of the argument is that robots cannot understand the workings of musical instruments or how to produce a high quality musical instrument. If robots can be programmed with these understandings, the author's conclusion would be seriously undermined.

(D) No. This statement is true, but the tasks in issue are not mundane assembly tasks. Rather, they involve the more sophisticated understandings and nuances of musical instruments.

(E) No. This statement does not weaken the argument. Instead, it reinforces it.

14. Don't ponder too long over this question. The answer is fairly simple. The question presumes that medical professionals who left their jobs in the public health sector for higher paying private jobs would return to the public health sector if salaries go up enough. (D) is the correct choice.

15. The author seems to consider the emergence of new diseases as entirely independent of man's use of technological advances. However, the implementation of scientific advances might impact the "ongoing emergence and disappearance of diseases." Therefore, the flaw in the writer's reasoning stems from his refusal to consider the possible impact of man's alteration of naturally occurring substances upon the emergence of new diseases. The correct answer is (E).

Selection (A) is tempting. However, the author disagrees with those who argue that man's conduct is "entirely" responsible for the high incidence of cancer. Thus, he implies that man's actions might have some role in the prevalence of cancer. There is nothing in the passage to indicate whether or not (B) is true, even though it is common knowledge that scientists are continually conducting cancer research. The test is designed so that outside knowledge is not needed to answer the questions. Rather, the questions should be answered solely on the basis of what is stated or implied in the passage. Inadvertently, the test authors might include a question that can be more readily answered with outside knowledge, but they make every effort to avoid that situation. With respect to (C), whether or not diseases have been discovered or not is irrelevant to the passage, and (D) is similarly irrelevant.

Logic II (Diagramming)

Most arguments are based on some variation of an *if-then* statement. However, the *if-then* statement is often embedded in other equivalent structures. Diagramming brings out the superstructure and the underlying simplicity of arguments.

If-Then

If the premise of an *if-then* statement is true, then the conclusion must be true as well. This is the defining characteristic of a conditional statement; it can be illustrated as follows:

$$A \longrightarrow B$$
$$\underline{A}$$
$$\therefore \quad B \qquad \text{(Where the symbol } \therefore \text{ means "therefore")}$$

This diagram displays the *if-then* statement "A—>B," the affirmed premise "A," and the necessary conclusion "B." Such a diagram can be very helpful in showing the logical structure of an argument.

There are three statements that can be derived from the implication "if A, then B"; two are invalid, and one is valid.

From "if A, then B" you *cannot* conclude "if B, then A." For example, if it is cloudy, you cannot conclude that it is raining. From experience, this example is obviously true; it seems silly that anyone could commit such an error. However, when the implication is unfamiliar to us, this fallacy can be tempting.

Another, and not as obvious, fallacy derived from "if A, then B" is to conclude "if not A, then not B." Again, consider the weather example. If it is not raining, you cannot conclude that it is not cloudy—it may still be overcast. This fallacy is popular with students.

Finally, there is one statement that *is* logically equivalent to "if A, then B." Namely, **"if not B, then not A."** This is called the **contrapositive**.

To show the contrapositive's validity, we once again appeal to our weather example. If it is not cloudy, then from experience we know that it cannot possibly be raining.

We now know two things about the implication "if A, then B":

1)   If A is true, then B must be true.
2)   If B is false, then A must be false.

If you assume no more than these two facts about an implication, then you will not fall for the fallacies that trap many students.

Example: *(If-then)*

If Jane does not study for the GMAT, then she will not score well. Jane, in fact, did not study for the GMAT; therefore she scored poorly on the test.

When symbolizing arguments we may let a letter stand for an element, a phrase, a clause, or even an entire sentence. The clause *"Jane does not study for the GMAT"* can be symbolized as ~S, and the clause *"she will not score well"* can be symbolized as ~W. Substituting these symbols into the argument yields the following diagram:

$$\sim S \longrightarrow \sim W$$
$$\sim S$$
$$\therefore \quad \sim W$$

This diagram shows that the argument has a valid *if-then* structure. A conditional statement is presented, ~S—>~W; its premise affirmed, ~S; and then the conclusion that necessarily follows, ~W, is stated.

Most of the arguments that you will have to diagram are more complex than this one—but not much more. In fact, once you master diagramming, you will find these arguments rather routine.

Embedded *If-Then* Statements

Usually, arguments involve an *if-then* statement. Unfortunately, the *if-then* thought is often embedded in other equivalent structures. In this section, we study how to spot these structures.

Example: *(Embedded If-then)*

John and Ken cannot both go to the party.

At first glance, this sentence does not appear to contain an *if-then* statement. But it essentially says:

> *"if John goes to the party, then Ken does not."*

Note, the statement "if Ken goes to the party, then John does not" expresses the same thing. So we don't need to state both.

Example: *(Embedded If-then)*

Danielle will be accepted to business school only if she does well on the GMAT.

Given this statement, we know that *if* Danielle is accepted to business school, *then* she must have done well on the GMAT. Note: Students often wrongly interpret this statement to mean:

> *"If Danielle does well on the GMAT, then she will be accepted to business school."*

There is no such guarantee. The only guarantee is that if she does not do well on the GMAT, then she will not be accepted to business school.

> ### "A only if B" is logically equivalent to "if A, then B."

Embedded If-Then Drill

Directions: Each of the following sentences contains an embedded *if-then* statement. Translate each sentence into an equivalent *if-then* form. Solutions are on page 450.

Sentence	*If-Then* Form
1. Only if John is allowed to go will Ken go.	
2. Give a talented teacher academic freedom, and she will excel.	
3. No Montague is a Rothschild.	
4. Anyone who is not a Montague cannot be a Rothschild.	
5. All Montagues are Rothschilds.	
6. Only Montagues are Rothschilds.	
7. A Montague will not attend a party hosted by a Rothschild.	
8. Men and women cannot understand one another.	
9. There is no God but Allah.	
10. None but the worthy are saved.	
11. For a Montague to attend a party it is necessary for a Rothschild to attend.	

Affirming the Conclusion Fallacy

Remember that an *if-then* statement, **A—>B**, tells us only two things:

(1)   If A is true, then B is true as well.
(2)   If B is false, then A is false as well (contrapositive).

If, however, we know the conclusion is true, the *if-then* statement tells us *nothing* about the premise. And if we know that the premise is false (we will consider this next), then the *if-then* statement tells us *nothing* about the conclusion.

Example: *(Affirming the Conclusion Fallacy)*

If he is innocent, then when we hold him under water for sixty seconds he will not drown. Since he did not die when we dunked him in the water, he must be innocent.

The logical structure of the argument above is most similar to which one of the following?

(A)   To insure that the remaining wetlands survive, they must be protected by the government. This particular wetland is being neglected. Therefore, it will soon perish.

(B)   There were nuts in that pie I just ate. There had to be, because when I eat nuts I break out in hives, and I just noticed a blemish on my hand.

(C)   The president will be reelected unless a third candidate enters the race. A third candidate has entered the race, so the president will not be reelected.

(D)   Every time Melinda has submitted her book for publication it has been rejected. So she should not bother with another rewrite.

(E)   When the government loses the power to tax one area of the economy, it just taxes another. The Supreme Court just overturned the sales tax, so we can expect an increase in the income tax.

To symbolize this argument, let the clause *"he is innocent"* be denoted by I, and let the clause *"when we hold him under water for sixty seconds he will not drown"* be denoted by ~D. Then the argument can be symbolized as

$$
\begin{array}{c}
\text{I—>~D} \\
\text{~D} \\
\hline
\therefore \quad \text{I}
\end{array}
$$

Notice that this argument is fallacious: the conclusion *"he is innocent"* is also a premise of the argument. Hence the argument is circular—it proves what was already assumed. The argument affirms the conclusion then invalidly uses it to deduce the premise. The answer will likewise be fallacious.

We start with answer-choice (A). The sentence

"To insure that the remaining wetlands survive, they must be protected by the government"

contains an embedded *if-then* statement:

"If the remaining wetlands are to survive, then they must be protected by the government."

This can be symbolized as S—>P. Next, the sentence

"This particular wetland is being neglected"

can be symbolized as ~P. Finally, the sentence

"It will soon perish"

can be symbolized as ~S. Using these symbols to translate the argument gives the following diagram:

$$
\begin{array}{c}
\text{S—>P} \\
\text{~P} \\
\hline
\therefore \quad \text{~S}
\end{array}
$$

The diagram clearly shows that this argument does not have the same structure as the given argument. In fact, it is a valid argument by contraposition.

Turning to (B), we reword the statement

> *"when I eat nuts, I break out in hives"*

as

> *"If I eat nuts, then I break out in hives."*

This in turn can be symbolized as N—>H.

Next, we interpret the clause

> *"there is a blemish on my hand"*

to mean *"hives,"* which we symbolize as H. Substituting these symbols into the argument yields the following diagram:

$$N \longrightarrow H$$
$$H$$
$$\overline{\therefore \quad N}$$

The diagram clearly shows that this argument has the same structure as the given argument. The answer, therefore, is (B).

Denying the Premise Fallacy

$$A \longrightarrow B$$
$$\sim A$$
$$\overline{\therefore \quad \sim B}$$

The fallacy of denying the premise occurs when an *if-then* statement is presented, its premise denied, and then its conclusion wrongly negated.

Example: *(Denying the Premise Fallacy)*

The senator will be reelected only if he opposes the new tax bill. But he was defeated. So he must have supported the new tax bill.

The sentence *"The senator will be reelected only if he opposes the new tax bill"* contains an embedded *if-then* statement: *"If the senator is reelected, then he opposes the new tax bill."** This in turn can be symbolized as

$$R \longrightarrow \sim T$$

The sentence *"But the senator was defeated"* can be reworded as *"He was not reelected,"* which in turn can be symbolized as

$$\sim R$$

Finally, the sentence *"He must have supported the new tax bill"* can be symbolized as

$$T$$

Using these symbols the argument can be diagrammed as follows:

---

* "A only if B" is equivalent to "If A, then B."

$$R \longrightarrow \sim T$$
$$\sim R$$
$$\therefore \quad T$$

[Note: Two negatives make a positive, so the conclusion ~(~T) was reduced to T.] This diagram clearly shows that the argument is committing the fallacy of denying the premise. An *if-then* statement is made; its premise is negated; then its conclusion is negated.

Transitive Property

$$A \longrightarrow B$$
$$B \longrightarrow C$$
$$\therefore A \longrightarrow C$$

These arguments are rarely difficult, provided you step back and take a bird's-eye view. It may be helpful to view this structure as an inequality in mathematics. For example, $5 > 4$ and $4 > 3$, so $5 > 3$.

Notice that the conclusion in the transitive property is also an *if-then* statement. So we don't know that C is true unless we know that A is true. However, if we add the premise "A is true" to the diagram, then we <u>can</u> conclude that C is true:

$$A \longrightarrow B$$
$$B \longrightarrow C$$
$$A$$
$$\therefore \quad C$$

As you may have anticipated, the contrapositive can be generalized to the transitive property:

$$A \longrightarrow B$$
$$B \longrightarrow C$$
$$\sim C$$
$$\therefore \quad \sim A$$

Example: *(Transitive Property)*

If you work hard, you will be successful in America. If you are successful in America, you can lead a life of leisure. So if you work hard in America, you can live a life of leisure.

Let W stand for *"you work hard,"* S stand for *"you will be successful in America,"* and L stand for *"you can lead a life of leisure."* Now the first sentence translates as W—>S, the second sentence as S—>L, and the conclusion as W—>L. Combining these symbol statements yields the following diagram:

$$W \longrightarrow S$$
$$S \longrightarrow L$$
$$\therefore W \longrightarrow L$$

The diagram clearly displays the transitive property.

DeMorgan's Laws

> ~(A & B) = ~A or ~B
> ~(A or B) = ~A & ~B

If you have taken a course in logic, you are probably familiar with these formulas. Their validity is intuitively clear: The conjunction **A&B** is false when either, or both, of its parts are false. This is precisely what **~A or ~B** says. And the disjunction **A or B** is false only when both A and B are false, which is precisely what **~A and ~B** says.

You will rarely get an argument whose main structure is based on these rules—they are too mechanical. Nevertheless, DeMorgan's laws often help simplify, clarify, or transform parts of an argument.

Example: *(DeMorgan's Law)*

It's not the case that the senator will be both reelected and not acquitted of campaign fraud.

Let R stand for *"the senator will be reelected,"* and let A stand for *"acquitted of campaign fraud."* Using these symbol statements to translate the argument yields

$$~(R\ \&\ ~A),$$

which by the first of DeMorgan's laws is equivalent to

$$~R\ or\ ~(~A).$$

This in turn can be reduced to

$$~R\ or\ A.$$

This final diagram tells us that the senator either will not be reelected or will be acquitted, or both.

Example: *(DeMorgan's Law)*

It is not the case that either Bill or Jane is going to the party.

This argument can be diagrammed as ~(B or J), which by the second of DeMorgan's laws simplifies to (~B and ~J). This diagram tells us that neither of them is going to the party.

A unless B

> ~B—>A

"A unless B" is a rather complex structure. Though surprisingly we use it with little thought or confusion in our day-to-day speech.

To see that "A unless B" is equivalent to "~B—>A," consider the following situation:

Biff is at the beach unless it is raining.

Given this statement, we know that if it is not raining, then Biff is at the beach. Now if we symbolize "Biff is at the beach" as B, and "it is raining" as R, then the statement can be diagrammed as

$$~R—>B.$$

Example: *(A unless B)*

Melinda can earn an MBA unless she does poorly on the GMAT or does not get a scholarship.

Which one of the following statements cannot be validly drawn from the above statements?

(A)   Melinda received an MBA. So she must have both done well on the GMAT and gotten a scholarship.

(B)   Melinda received an MBA and she did well on the GMAT. So she must have gotten a scholarship.

(C)   Melinda did poorly on the GMAT. So she will not earn an MBA.

(D)   If Melinda does not earn an MBA, then she did poorly on the GMAT or could not get a scholarship.

(E)   If Melinda does poorly on the GMAT and does not get a scholarship, then she will not earn an MBA.

This argument says that two things stand in Melinda's way—performing poorly on the GMAT and not getting a scholarship. That is, if Melinda does well on the GMAT and gets a scholarship, then she *can* earn an MBA.

Since Melinda received an MBA in choice (A), she must have overcome the two obstacles—the GMAT and the scholarship. Hence (A) is valid. This eliminates (A). Next, (B) essentially expresses the same thought as (A). This eliminates (B). Next, (C) says that Melinda didn't meet one of the two criteria, so she won't earn an MBA. Hence (C) is valid. This eliminates (C). You should notice that the conclusion in (D) is too strong. Melinda may do well on the GMAT *and* get a scholarship yet decide not to pursue an MBA. The answer, therefore, is (D).

Game-Like Arguments

Although they do not occur frequently, game-like arguments are common enough to warrant study.

Example: *(Game)*

No one will be admitted to Yale Business School unless he or she studies hard for the GMAT. No one studied hard for the GMAT unless he or she was not a graduate from Tri-State University.

Which one of the following conclusions necessarily follows from the above statements?

(A)   No graduate of Tri-State University was admitted to Yale Business School.

(B)   Some graduates of Tri-State University were admitted to Yale Business School.

(C)   All graduates of Tri-State University studied hard for the GMAT.

(D)   Only graduates of Tri-State University did well on the GMAT.

(E)   Only college graduates did well on the GMAT.

We begin by symbolizing the statements. *"No one will be admitted to Yale Business School unless he or she studies hard for the GMAT"* can be symbolized as

$$\sim\!SH \longrightarrow \sim\!Y,$$

where SH stands for *"he or she studies hard for the GMAT,"* and Y stands for *"admitted to Yale Business School."*

The second condition appears confusing at first but is actually straightforward once we get around the obfuscating tactics. *"No one studied hard for the GMAT unless he or she was not a graduate from Tri-State University"* can be symbolized as

$$\sim(\sim G)\longrightarrow\sim SH,$$

where G indicates *"a graduate of Tri-State University."* Recalling that two negatives make a positive, we simplify this to

$$G\longrightarrow\sim SH$$

Using the transitive property to combine this with the first premise, $\sim SH\longrightarrow\sim Y$, yields

$$G\longrightarrow\sim Y$$

In other words, if a person graduated from Tri-State University, he or she was not admitted to Yale. The answer is (A).

Points to Remember

1.   Look for embedded *if-then* statements.

2.   An *if-then* statement, A—>B, tells us only two things:
   - (1)   If A is true, then B is true as well.
   - (2)   If B is false, then A is false as well (contrapositive).

3.   Affirming the conclusion fallacy:

$$\begin{array}{l} A\longrightarrow B \\ B \\ \hline \therefore \quad A \end{array}$$

4.   Denying the premise fallacy:

$$\begin{array}{l} A\longrightarrow B \\ \sim A \\ \hline \therefore \quad \sim B \end{array}$$

5.   Transitive property:

$$\begin{array}{l} A\longrightarrow B \\ B\longrightarrow C \\ \hline \therefore \ A\longrightarrow C \end{array}$$

6.   DeMorgan's Laws:

$$\begin{array}{l} \sim(A \ \& \ B) = \sim A \text{ or } \sim B \\ \sim(A \text{ or } B) = \sim A \ \& \ \sim B \end{array}$$

7.   A unless B:

$$\boxed{\sim B\longrightarrow A}$$

Exercise

Directions: The questions in this section are based on the reasoning contained in brief statements or passages. For some questions, more than one of the choices could conceivably answer the question. However, you are to choose the <u>best</u> answer; that is, the response that most accurately and completely answers the question. You should not make assumptions that are by common sense standards implausible, superfluous, or incompatible with the passage. Answers and solutions begin on page 451.

1. To avoid economic collapse, Russia must increase its GNP by 20%. However, due to the structure of its economy, if the 20% threshold is reached, then a 40% increase in GNP is achievable.

   Assuming that the above statements are true, which one of the following must also be true?

   (A) If ethnic strife continues in Russia, then a 20% increase in GNP will be unattainable.
   (B) If a 40% increase in Russia's GNP is impossible, its economy will collapse.
   (C) If Russia's GNP increases by 40%, its economy will not collapse.
   (D) If the 20% threshold is reached, then a 40% increase in GNP is achievable and a 60% increase is probable.
   (E) If Russia's economy collapses, then it will not have increased its GNP by 40%.

2. Some folks who live in the hills belong to the Hatfield clan; others belong to the McCoy clan.
   No Hatfields can farm.
   All McCoys can farm.
   Therefore, McCoys are not Hatfields.
   Everyone who is not a Hatfield is a horseback rider.

   Assume that each one of the above statements is true. Which of the following must be true if it is also true that no Hatfields ride horses.

   (A) The only people who can farm are horseback-riding McCoys.
   (B) Anyone who does not belong to the McCoy clan belongs to the Hatfield clan.
   (C) All horseback riders can farm.
   (D) All horseback riders must be McCoys.
   (E) All McCoys are horseback riders.

3. When a region is in a drought, the water level of rivers and streams is seriously reduced. When water levels are down, food is also scarce for wildlife. Therefore, if food is not scarce for wildlife, then the region is not in a drought.

   In which one of the following selections does the reasoning most closely follow the reasoning in the above passage?

   (A) If the dirty clothes hamper is full, the sock drawer is empty, and if the sock drawer is empty, the dirty clothes hamper is full, so if the sock drawer is not empty, the clothes hamper is not full.
   (B) If the temperature falls below freezing, the petunias will die, and if the petunias die, they will not flower any more, so if the petunias still produce flowers, the temperature is not below freezing.
   (C) If raccoons bear live young, they must be mammals, so if they are amphibians, they must lay eggs to reproduce, if they reproduce at all.
   (D) If you want to fix an omelet, you will have to use six eggs, and you will have no eggs left for pancakes, so if you make the omelet, you won't be able to fix pancakes.
   (E) If earth scientists are correct, global temperatures are warming, and if the earth's temperature increases, ocean levels will rise, so if ocean levels rise, earth scientists were correct.

4. If the dog is a collie, it will shed its downy undercoat only in the spring. The dog shed in the spring, so it must be a collie.

Which one of the following selections demonstrates the same reasoning presented in the passage?

(A) In the winter time in the mountains, it frequently snows. Three inches of snow fell last night, so it must be winter.

(B) When the wind sweeps down from the mountains, a cold front will follow right behind. Right now the winds are gusting up to 40 mph, so a cold front must be on its way.

(C) The crystal paperweights in Sharon's paperweight collection are always dusted very carefully. The red paperweight is not handled carefully when dusted, so it must not be a crystal paperweight.

(D) One more hard frost would kill the tomato plants. But a week later, the tomato plants were still alive. Therefore, a hard frost must not have occurred within the last week.

(E) One must be very coordinated like Franklin to be a good drummer. However, Franklin's inability to read music will prevent him from being a good drummer.

5. If a person studies four hours a day for the GMAT , he will score in the top 10 percent. Every student at Harvard Business School scored in the top 10 percent. Thus, Sarah who is studying at Harvard Business School must have studied at least four hours a day.

The reasoning in the argument above is flawed because it

(A) fails to consider that many students at Harvard studied more than four hours a day.

(B) fails to consider that studies have shown that studying one subject more than three hours a day can be counterproductive.

(C) fails to consider that studying less than four hours a day may be sufficient for some people to score in the top 10 percent.

(D) fails to consider that people who studied less than three hours a day did not get into Harvard.

(E) fails to consider that an additional eight hours a week of studying is an impossible burden for most college students.

6. If the rebels truly want a political settlement, they will stop shelling the Capitol. They did stop shelling the Capitol. Hence, the rebels sincerely want peace.

Which one of the following uses reasoning that is most similar to that used in the above argument?

(A) There's a cat in this house. There must be, because I'm allergic to cats; and I just sneezed.

(B) In order for a bill to pass, it must be supported by the President. The Crime Bill is not being supported by the President. Therefore, it will not pass.

(C) The flood of refugees will continue unless the U.N. sends in peace keepers. The U.N. has announced that peace-keeping troops will not be sent, so the flood of refugees will continue.

(D) Every time the United States attempts to mediate between two warring parties, it becomes the target of both. So the same will occur with the civil war in Girunda.

(E) If you want dessert, you must eat your vegetables. You did not eat your vegetables, so there will be no dessert for you.

7. Any person who scores poorly on the GMAT will not get into business school unless he bribes the admissions officers or has a relative on the board of regents.

Based on the above statements, all of the following statements can be made EXCEPT.

(A)   If a person who did poorly on the GMAT has neither the money to bribe the admissions officers nor a relative on the board of regents, then he will not get into business school.

(B)   If a person did poorly on the GMAT, is in business school, and does not have a relative on the board of regents, then he must have bribed the admissions officers.

(C)   If a person does not take the GMAT but has a relative on the board of regents, then he will get into business school.

(D)   If a person is in business school and does not have relatives on the board of regents nor has ever committed bribery, then he must have done well on the GMAT.

(E)   If a person did poorly on the GMAT, is in business school, and did not bribe anyone, then he must have a relative on the board of regents.

8. Magazine commentary: If the major television networks acted responsibly, they would commit their most talented writers, directors and actors to create quality programs suitable for family viewing during "prime time" viewing hours each weekday evening. Instead, television programming is full of sex, violence, and adult situations and language. In fact, the most-watched programs are a situation comedy full of degrading and sexual humor and a police show with frequent violence and adult language. At present, only a few networks carry quality programs that are suitable for family viewing.

If you assume that the statements in the commentary are true, then which one of the following statements must also be true?

(A)   Children are being exposed to adult situations and language at a younger age.

(B)   Networks that carry programs unsuitable for family viewing are only concerned with the bottom line financially and do not act responsibly toward their viewing public.

(C)   Only a minority of families watch programs carried on public television stations.

(D)   Advertisers must put pressure on the major networks to carry more programs suitable for family viewing.

(E)   Most of the major networks are not meeting their responsibility to bring the public high quality programs suitable for family viewing.

9. If you make good grades in high school, you will get into a good college. If you get into a good college, you will find a good job. So, if you make good grades in high school, you will find a good job.

Which one of the following selections most closely follows the reasoning in the passage?

(A) If you brush your teeth twice every day, you will keep your teeth clean. If you keep your teeth clean, you will not get cavities. So, if you brush your teeth twice every day, you will have low dental bills.

(B) If you vacuum your room on Fridays, it will stay clean. If your room stays clean, you can invite your friends over. So, if you invite your friends over, your room will stay clean.

(C) If you plant your garden in healthy soil, your vegetable plants will grow well. If your vegetable plants grow well, you will have a high vegetable yield. So, if you plant your garden in healthy soil, you will have a high vegetable yield.

(D) If you invest in the stock market, you are optimistic that the market will go up. If you have a good attitude about things in general, then you are optimistic that the market will go up. So, if you invest in the market, you have a good attitude about things in general.

(E) If you study hard for the math exam, you will make an A on the exam. If you study hard for the math exam, you will not get enough sleep. So if you make an A on the math exam, you will not get enough sleep.

10. The art jury will select either Fillmore's or Clivestone's sculptures, but not both, for the midwest art show to be held next spring. If Fillmore's sculptures are chosen, then the show will contain bronze works. If Clivestone's sculptures are selected, the show will contain sculptures made from stainless steel.

Assuming the statements in the passage are true, which one of the following statements must also be true?

(A) The art show might contain no bronze or stainless steel sculptures.

(B) If the art show contains bronze sculptures, then it is certain that Fillmore's sculptures were chosen for the show.

(C) The art show will certainly contain either bronze or stainless steel sculptures, and the art show will most certainly not contain both types of sculptures.

(D) If the art show contains stainless steel sculptures, it is possible, but not certain, that Clivestone's sculptures were selected by the jury for the show.

(E) If the art show contains neither bronze nor stainless steel sculptures, it is certain that neither Fillmore's nor Clivestone's sculptures were selected for the show.

11. Senator Janice White is quietly lobbying to become chairman of one of the Senate's most prestigious committees. However, that post currently belongs to Senator Dan Smith. If Senator Smith already has twenty senators committed to his continued chairmanship of the committee, then Senator White will consider another committee. If Senator Smith does not have that much support lined up yet, then Senator White will study Senator Smith's past committee voting record for inconsistent and unpopular votes. If Senator White finds that Smith's voting record is out of favor with today's voter and publicizes it, then her chances of capturing the chairmanship would be increased, and she would publicly announce her interest in the chairmanship. If Senator Smith's committee voting record is in keeping with current public sentiment and contains no inconsistencies, then Senator White will focus her attention on another committee chairmanship.

Based upon the information provided in the passage, which one of the following statements must be false?

(A) Senator Smith has lined up only five votes, and Senator White drops her interest in the committee chairmanship.

(B) A number of inconsistencies are found in Senator Smith's voting record, and Senator White publicly announces her interest in the committee chairmanship.

(C) Several of Senator Smith's past committee votes would find disfavor with today's voting public, and Senator White does not pursue the committee chairmanship.

(D) Senator Smith's past committee voting record contains nothing that would increase Senator White's chances of obtaining the chairmanship, and Senator White publicly announces her interest in being named chairman.

(E) Senator Smith already has the support of thirty of his fellow senators, and Senator White focuses her interest on another committee.

12. People who do well in the sled pull competition have tremendous upper body strength. Caleb has tremendous upper body strength. Therefore, Caleb performed well in the sled pull competition.

Which one of the following contains the same reasoning that is presented in the passage?

(A) People who are anemic cannot donate blood. Mary donates blood regularly. Therefore, she must not be anemic.

(B) People who swim competitively are thin and muscular. Ben is thin and muscular Therefore, Ben is a competitive swimmer.

(C) People who volunteer at the trauma center must handle being on their feet all day. Casey is a frequent volunteer at the trauma center. Therefore, he must handle being on his feet all day.

(D) People who are overly sensitive to the cold cannot work at the Arctic substation. John is overly sensitive to the cold. Therefore John cannot work at the Arctic substation.

(E) People who have ulcers cannot eat spicy hot food. Kevin has recurrent ulcers. Therefore Kevin is on a bland diet.

13. If the City Parks Department receives the same allocation in next year's municipal budget, it is expected to raise admission fees to the indoor recreation center by fifty cents. If the City Parks Department announces a higher admission fee increase, then its budget allocation for next year must have been reduced.

Which of the following selections expresses a reasoning pattern most similar to the pattern expressed in the passage?

(A) If the mountains continue to receive snow at the rate experienced for the past two weeks, ski areas would have a record snow base this winter. Instead, snow fall diminished, and ski areas have a normal ski base this winter.

(B) If urban neighborhoods wish to reduce crime in their neighborhoods, they should implement neighborhood crime watch programs. If neighborhoods experience higher burglary and theft rates, it must mean that they have not have implemented crime watch programs.

(C) If the price of raw plastic pellets remains the same, companies that manufacture molded plastic parts such as fishing bobbers can be expected to keep their wholesale prices at last year's levels. Thus, if these wholesalers raise their prices on fishing bobbers, it will be because raw material costs increased.

(D) If major league baseball teams wish to increase attendance at home games, they should not increase their ticket prices. If they do increase ticket prices, they should be expected to provide better seating and concessions at the stadiums.

(E) If television networks want to broadcast quality programming, they should recruit programs with good writers and actors. Thus, if the networks recruit poorly written and poorly acted programs, it is likely their television viewership will decline.

14. A movie publicist accompanied a new movie release with the following endorsement:

This movie is a must-see for men and women who are in or want to have a committed relationship in the Nineties. While the leading actor in the movie has unrefined edges, he eventually becomes sensitive and caring. The leading actress begins to understand and appreciate her lover's uniquely male characteristics without booting him out the door. If you are a true Nineties man or woman—self-reliant, yet perceptive and caring—you must see this movie!

If the publicist's claims about the movie are true, which one of the following is also true?

(A) Men and women who are perceptive and caring are also self-reliant.

(B) A man who has seen the movie but is still not perceptive and caring misrepresents himself as a true Nineties man.

(C) People who go to the movie described in the passage are more sensitive than people who go to action thriller movies.

(D) No other movie recognizes true Nineties men and women.

(E) Most everyone would recognize the type of man or woman who would go to see the movie described in the passage.

15. A manufacturer can only recoup its retooling costs for redesigning a product if it sells enough of the product to its distributors to pass its break-even point. Unless retail companies believe the product will sell well, however, they will not buy enough of the product from distributors to enable the manufacturer to recoup its costs. Manufacturers are more likely to retool products if the products have scored favorably in market studies or if large advance orders for the redesigned products have come in before the retooling process is started, or both.

Of the following selections, which one can be appropriately inferred from the above passage?

(A) If a manufacturer receives large advance orders for the redesigned product from its distributors, it will recoup its retooling costs.

(B) Retail companies that stock products based on favorable market studies will sell a lot of products.

(C) A manufacturer that has recouped its retooling costs has sold enough of the redesigned product to pass its break-even point.

(D) A manufacturer that did not get many advance orders for a redesigned product did not make a profit.

(E) A manufacturer that had enough sales of a redesigned product to pass its break-even point by a wide margin did not make a profit on its sale of the product.

16. If Joan was growing marijuana plants in her home, she would not allow police investigators to search her home without a warrant. As a result, allowing the police to search her home without a warrant shows that Joan does not grow marijuana plants in her home.

Which one of the following contains an argument logically most similar to the argument presented in the passage?

(A) If Justin were playing golf at the city golf course, he would not be home until dinner. Therefore, the fact that he gets home by mid-afternoon shows that he is not playing golf at the city course.

(B) If Paul were stingy, he would not buy Dorian a birthday present. Therefore, Paul's buying Francis a birthday present shows that he is stingy.

(C) If Jason were over 30, he would not want to listen to rap music. Therefore, the fact that Jason does not like to listen to rap music shows that he is over 30.

(D) If Sandra were a good seamstress, she would not buy cheap fabric. Therefore, the fact that Sandra is not a good seamstress shows that she bought cheap fabric.

(E) If Kevin were hungry, he would not skip breakfast. Therefore, the fact that Kevin is hungry shows that he did not skip breakfast.

17. Students at Lincoln High School will boycott graduation ceremonies unless the administration allows the band director to keep his teaching position rather than forcing him to retire at the end of the school year. If the band director continues to teach at the high school, however, then the administration will have to eliminate one of the new coaching positions it planned for next year. So, the new coaching position will be eliminated.

The conclusion stated in the passage above is properly drawn if which one of the following assumptions is made?

(A) Students will drop out of the band program.

(B) The administration will insist that the high school band director retire.

(C) The students will not boycott graduation ceremonies.

(D) The administration has the authority to allow the band director to keep his teaching position.

(E) The high school students will not drop their threat to boycott graduation ceremonies if other student benefits are offered.

18. A lawyer who does not return phone calls from her clients cannot be a skillful, experienced lawyer. I feel comfortable with the skill and experience of my attorney because she returns all of my phone calls, even when she is busy.

Which of the following selections presents a reasoning pattern most similar to the flawed pattern presented in the passage?

(A) Anyone who plays on a baseball team has had to make sacrifices for the good of the team. Ted is used to making sacrifices, so he might play on a baseball team.

(B) Anyone who is opposed to the city bond issue has not received the city's information packet on the issue. Sandy says she will vote against the city bond issue, so she hasn't received the city information packet.

(C) No one who likes science fiction movies will miss seeing the second release of the Star Wars trilogy in movie theaters. Jimmy loves the Star Wars movies, but he did not see the second movie of the trilogy when it was released recently.

(D) A school-age child who spends three afternoons a week at gymnastics practice does not have a proper balance between school work and gymnastics. Tom spends only one afternoon per week at gymnastics practice, so he has a proper balance between school and gymnastics.

(E) A person who is jumpy and impatient will not work well with animals. Janice is impatient, so she would not be a good animal trainer.

19. Rebecca: When I went hiking in the mountains the other day, every bird that scolded me was a Steller's Jay, and every Steller's Jay I saw scolded me.

Which one of the following statements can be inferred from Rebecca's observations?

(A) The only jays that Rebecca saw while hiking were Steller's Jays.

(B) There were no Gray Jays in the area where Rebecca hiked.

(C) While she was hiking, no Gray Jays scolded Rebecca.

(D) All the jays that Rebecca saw scolded her.

(E) Rebecca did not see any Gray Jays while she was hiking.

Solutions to Embedded If-Then Drill

Sentence	*If-Then* Form
1. Only if John is allowed to go will Ken go.	If Ken goes, then John is allowed to go.
2. Give a talented teacher academic freedom, and she will excel.	If a talented teacher is given academic freedom, she will excel.
3. No Montague is a Rothschild.	If Montague, then not Rothschild.
4. Anyone who is not a Montague cannot be a Rothschild.	If not a Montague, then not Rothschild.
5. All Montagues are Rothschilds.	If Montague, then Rothschild.
6. Only Montagues are Rothschilds.	If Rothschild, then Montague.
7. A Montague will not attend a party hosted by a Rothschild.	If a Rothschild hosts a party, then a Montague will not attend.
8. Men and women cannot understand each other.	If Pat is a man, then he can't understand women. If Pat is a woman, then she can't understand men.
9. There is no God but Allah.	If G is God, then G is Allah.
10. None but the worthy are saved.	If X is saved, then X is worthy.
11. For a Montague to attend a party it is necessary for a Rothschild to attend.	If a Montague attends a party, then a Rothschild attends.

Answers and Solutions to Exercise

1.	B	6.	A	11.	D	16.	A
2.	E	7.	C	12.	B	17.	C
3.	B	8.	E	13.	C	18.	D
4.	A	9.	C	14.	B	19.	C
5.	C	10.	D	15.	C		

1. Diagramming will show this seemingly difficult problem to be simply an application of the contrapositive. The sentence *"To avoid economic collapse, Russia must increase its GNP by 20%"* can be reworded as *"if Russia does not increase its GNP by 20%, its economy will collapse."* This in turn can be symbolized as

~20%—>Collapse.

Next, symbolize the clause *"if the 20% threshold is reached, then a 40% increase is achievable"* as

20%—>40%.

Applying the contrapositive to this statement yields

~40%—>~20%.

Using the transitive property to combine this with the first symbol statement yields

~40%—>Collapse.

In other words, if a 40% increase in GNP is unattainable, the economy will collapse. This is precisely what choice (B) states. The answer is (B).

2. This problem looks rather complicated at first glance. But only the last two statements of the passage are necessary to solve the problem. The statement, *"Therefore, McCoys are not Hatfields"* contains an embedded if-then statement. *"If a person belongs to the McCoy clan, they he does not belong to the Hatfield clan."* This statement can be diagrammed as follows:

M—>~H

The next statement, *"Everyone who is not a Hatfield is a horseback rider"* also contains an embedded if-then statement: *"If a person is not a Hatfield, then he is a horseback rider."* This can be diagrammed as:

~H—>R

If you use the transitive property to combine these two diagrams, the following diagram results:

M—>R

This diagram is translated to read that if a person belongs to the McCoy clan, then he is a horseback rider. This is the same as saying that all McCoys are horseback riders. Thus, selection (E) is the correct answer.

3. The statement, *"When a region is in a drought, the water level of rivers and streams is seriously reduced,"* can be pictured as:

D—>WR

The statement, *"When water levels are down, food is also scarce for wildlife,"* can be pictured as:

WR—>FS

The statement *"if food is not scarce for wildlife, then the region is not in a drought"* can be pictured as:

~FS—>~D

The diagram for the entire passage looks like this:

D—>WR
WR—>FS
~FS—>~D

The diagram shows the argument to be a valid application of the transitive and contrapositive properties.

Take a minute to diagram the five possible answers. In choice (B), the statement, *"If the temperature falls below freezing, the petunias will die"* can be pictured as:

F—>PD

The clause *"if the petunias die, they will not flower any more"* can be pictured as:

PD—>NF

Finally, the clause *"if the petunias still produce flowers, the temperature is not below freezing"* can be pictured as:

$$\sim NF \longrightarrow \sim F$$

If you diagram the entire petunia passage, it looks like this:

$$F \longrightarrow PD$$
$$\underline{PD \longrightarrow NF}$$
$$\sim NF \longrightarrow \sim F$$

The diagram follows the same sequence as the diagram for the passage. Thus the argument in selection (B) is also a valid application of the transitive and contrapositive properties. The answer is selection (B).

4. This question presents an example of faulty reasoning. *"If the dog is a collie, it will shed its downy undercoat only in the spring"* can be pictured as $C \longrightarrow S$. The next clause, *"The dog shed in the spring,"* can be pictured as S. The conclusion of the passage, *"so it must be a collie,"* can be pictured as $\therefore C$. The entire passage can be diagrammed as follows:

$$C \longrightarrow S$$
$$\underline{S}$$
$$\therefore \quad C$$

This diagram shows that the argument mistakenly affirms the conclusion. One of the selections makes the same mistake. Briefly diagram the answer selections to see which argument mistakenly affirms the conclusion the same way the collie example does.

In selection (A), the first sentence, *"In the winter time in the mountains, it frequently snows,"* can be pictured as $W \longrightarrow S$. The next clause, *"Three inches of snow fell last night,"* can be diagrammed as S. Finally, the conclusion, *"so it must be winter,"* can be diagrammed as $\therefore W$. The entire argument in diagram form is pictured as

$$W \longrightarrow S$$
$$\underline{S}$$
$$\therefore \quad W$$

The argument in selection (A) presents the same diagram as the argument in the passage. Both commit the fallacy of affirming the conclusion. Selection (A) is the correct answer.

5. We begin by symbolizing the argument. The sentence *"If a person studies four hours a day for the GMAT, he will score in the top 10 percent"* can be symbolized as

$$\textbf{4hrs} \longrightarrow \textbf{10\%}$$

The sentence *"Every student at Harvard Business School scored in the top 10 percent"* can be reworded as an if-then statement: *"If a person is a student at Harvard Business School, then he scored in the top 10 percent."* This in turn can be symbolized as

$$\textbf{H} \longrightarrow \textbf{10\%},$$

where H stands for *"a student at Harvard Business School."* Now, the phrase *"Sarah who is studying at Harvard Business School"* affirms the premise in the conditional $\textbf{H} \longrightarrow \textbf{10\%}$. Hence, we know she scored in the top 10%. This affirms the conclusion in the conditional $\textbf{4hrs} \longrightarrow \textbf{10\%}$. Up to here the argument is valid. But it then commits the fallacy of affirming the conclusion by stating than she must have studied 4 hours a day. This ignores the possibility that Sarah may be gifted and hence for her studying only two hours a day may be sufficient. The answer is (C).

6. Let T stand for *"the rebels truly want a political settlement,"* and let S stand for *"they will stop shelling the Capitol."* Now the argument can be symbolized as

$$T \longrightarrow S$$
$$\underline{S}$$
$$\therefore \quad T$$

This diagram clearly shows that the argument is committing the fallacy of affirming the conclusion. The answer will commit the same fallacy.

Begin with choice (A). The clause *"I'm allergic to cats"* contains an embedded *if-then* statement: *"If there is a cat around, I start sneezing."* This in turn can be symbolized as $C \longrightarrow Sn$, where C stands for *"there is a cat around,"* and Sn stands for *"I start sneezing."* Substituting these symbols into the argument yields

$$C \longrightarrow Sn$$
$$\underline{Sn}$$
$$\therefore \quad C$$

The diagram shows that this argument has the same structure as the original argument. The answer is (A).

7. Let's start by symbolizing the argument. Symbolize the phrase "will get into business school" as S.* Next, symbolize the phrase "he bribes an admission officer" as B. Finally, symbolize the phrase "has a relative on the board of regents" as R. Substituting the symbols into the argument, we get the following diagram:

$$\sim(B \text{ or } R) <—> \sim S$$

which simplifies to

$$(B \text{ or } R) <—> S$$

(Note: We'll add the phrase "any person who scored poorly on the GMAT" to the diagram later.)

We now use this diagram to analyze each of the answer-choices. As for choice (A), from ~S we can conclude, by applying the contrapositive to the diagram, ~(B or R). From DeMorgan's laws, we know that this is equivalent to ~B & ~R. This is the premise of (A). That is, (A) is a valid argument by contraposition. This eliminates (A).

Since choice (B) affirms S, we know from the diagram that B or R must be true. But choice (B) denies R. So from the meaning of "or," we know that B must be true. This is the conclusion of choice (B). Hence choice (B) is a valid deduction. This eliminates choice (B).

For simplicity we did not diagram the entire argument. But for choice (C), we need to complete the diagram. The premise of the argument is "any person who scores poorly on the GMAT." This clause can be reworded as "If a person does poorly on the GMAT," which can be symbolized as P. Affixing this to the original diagram gives

$$P—>[(B \text{ or } R)<—>S].$$

Recall that if the premise of an *if-then* statement is true then the conclusion must be true as well. But if the premise is false, then we cannot determine whether the conclusion is true or false. Now (C) negates the premise, ~P. So its conclusion—that a person will get into business school, S—is a non sequitur. Hence (C) is the answer.

---

* Note that we dropped the "not" from the original phrase.

8. (A) No. The commentator argues that the <u>networks</u> are not acting responsibly. While the author could perhaps place some of the blame on the viewing audience, he does not.

(B) No. The commentator does not tell us why the networks don't broadcast more family programs, so this statement does not follow from the passage.

(C) No. Again, we do not know from the passage anything about the programming on public television stations or what the viewership is for those stations.

(D) No. The commentator is concerned that the networks are not acting responsibly; he does not elicit help from television advertisers in this passage.

(E) **Yes.** The commentator states that <u>if</u> networks acted responsibly, they would broadcast more family programming. The passage strongly implies that the networks are not currently meeting their responsibility to the viewing public.

Selection (E) is an application of the contrapositive. The commentator's argument can be diagrammed as follows:

$$R—> \sim SVL$$

R stands for *"If the major television networks acted responsibly,"* and ~**SVL** stands for *"they would commit their most talented writers, directors and actors to create quality programs suitable for family viewing during "prime time" viewing hours each weekday evening."* The next statement in the passage negates both sides of this diagram, changing the **R** to ~**R** and ~**SVL** to **SVL**. *"Instead, television programming is full of sex, violence, and adult situations and language."* The diagram would look like the following:

$$\sim R—>SVL$$

Selection (E) also applies the contrapositive to the author's initial conclusion. The networks are <u>not</u> acting responsibly, so "prime time" television is still full of sex, adult language and violence. ~**R**—>**SVL**. Thus, (E) follows from the commentator's position. Most major networks are not meeting their responsibility to provide high quality programs suitable for family viewing.

9. This passage applies the transitive property, just like the preceding passage did. *"If you make good grades in high school, you will get into a good college"* can be diagrammed as:

GG—>GC

The next statement, *"If you get into a good college, you will find a good job,"* can be diagrammed as follows:

GC—>GJ

Finally, if you combine these two statements using the transitive property, your diagram will look like the following:

GG—>GJ

The author concludes that good grades in high school will result in a good job.

Quickly diagram out the statements contained in each of the five possible answers. Notice that selection (C) also makes use of the transitive property. The first statement, *"If you plant your garden in healthy soil, your vegetable plants will grow well,"* can be diagrammed as follows:

HS—>PG

The next statement, *"If your vegetable plants grow well, you will have a high vegetable yield,"* looks like the following:

PG—>HY

If you combine these two statements using the transitive property, your conclusion will be: *"If you plant your garden in healthy soil, you will have a high vegetable yield"* and your diagram will look like:

HS—>HY

This is the same reasoning followed in the passage. As a result, selection (C) is correct. The other selections do not follow the same reasoning presented in the passage.

10. The passage indicates that the sculptures of Fillmore or Clivestone will be selected for the art show, but not both. The diagram would look like (**F—>B**) or (**C—>SS**). Each of the selections can be considered against this diagram.

Selection (A) states that the show will not contain bronze or stainless steel sculptures. It is obviously false because the passage says that one or the other type sculptures will be selected for the show. Selection (B) is flawed because the conclusion is used to affirm the premise. Instead of **F—>B**, selection (B) concludes **B—>F**. But we don't know if the reverse is true. Bronze sculptures by another artist might have been selected for the show. The first part of selection (C) is correct because we know that either Fillmore's or Clivestone's works will be selected for the show. But we do not have enough information to know whether the second part of (C) is true. As with (B), perhaps other artists will be featured whose work includes bronze or stainless steel sculptures. Selection (E) sounds true, but it contradicts the passage. The author tells us that one or the other will be selected. So (E) is not correct.

Selection (D) is the best answer. Since Clivestone's sculptures might be chosen over Fillmore's, it is certainly possible that the show would contain his stainless steel sculptures. (D) begins by affirming the conclusion to the diagram **C—>SS**. But unlike the flawed selection (B), (D) does not rule out other possibilities. In fact, selection (D) is perhaps too weak to be untrue. It states that the stainless steel sculptures in the show might be Clivestone's sculptures. This is true.

11. The question asks which one of the selections is <u>false</u> based upon the information provided in the passage below. Selection (A) might be true because Senator Smith's voting record might be unchallengeable. The scenario in selection (B) could certainly happen. If Senator Smith hasn't lined up enough support, and if his voting record isn't perfect, Senator White will challenge him for the chairmanship. Selection (C) does not consider the amount of support behind Senator Smith. If twenty-five senators are already lined up behind him, then his voting record is irrelevant. Selection (E) is correct because if Senator Smith has the support of thirty senators, Senator White will not challenge him.

Selection (D) is the correct answer. It is inconsistent with the passage that Senator White would strive for the chairmanship if Senator Smith's voting record is good. The passage indicates that *"If Senator White finds that Smith's voting record is out of favor with today's voter and publicizes it, then her chances of capturing the chairmanship would be increased."* This can diagrammed as follows:

$$BV \longrightarrow I$$

If you apply the contrapositive to this statement, your diagram will look like this:

$$\sim I \longrightarrow \sim BV$$

The next sentence in the passage, *"If Senator Smith's committee voting record is in keeping with current public sentiment and contains no inconsistencies, then Senator White will focus her attention on another committee chairmanship,"* can be reworded to say that *"If Senator Smith has a good committee voting record, then Senator White will not seek the chairmanship."* This can be diagrammed as follows:

$$\sim BV \longrightarrow \sim CH$$

If you use the transitive property to combine this with the statement $\sim I \longrightarrow \sim BV$, your diagram will look like the following:

$$\sim I \longrightarrow \sim CH$$

In selection (D), the clause *"Senator Smith's past committee voting record contains nothing that would increase Senator White's chances of obtaining the chairmanship"* — $\sim I$ — affirms the premise of the last diagram. Hence, we conclude that Senator White does not seek the chairmanship — $\sim CH$. But Selection (D) negates this conclusion. It states that despite Senator Smith's good voting record, Senator White publicly announces her interest in being named chairman — CH. Thus, the statement in Selection (D) is false and is the correct answer.

12. The error in this passage is that it affirms the conclusion. The first sentence, *"People who do well in the sled pull competition have tremendous upper body strength,"* is represented by the following:

$$SP \longrightarrow UBS$$

The next sentence, *"Caleb has tremendous upper body strength,"* affirms the conclusion. But the last sentence, *"Therefore, Caleb performed well in the sled pull competition,"* invalidly affirms the premise that leads to the conclusion. This fallacy is diagrammed below.

$$\begin{array}{l} SP \longrightarrow UBS \\ \underline{UBS \qquad\qquad} \\ \therefore \qquad SP \end{array}$$

This diagram clearly displays the fallacy in affirming the conclusion.

In selection (B), the same fallacy exists. It can be demonstrated by diagramming the sentences in selection (B). *"People who swim competitively are thin and muscular. Ben is thin and muscular. Therefore, Ben is a competitive swimmer."*

$$\begin{array}{l} SC \longrightarrow TM \\ \underline{TM \qquad\qquad} \\ \therefore \qquad SC \end{array}$$

Diagramming one of the other answer choices shows why the flaw exists in both the passage and selection (B). For example, take selection (D). *"People who are overly sensitive to the cold cannot work at the Arctic substation"* can be diagrammed as:

$$OS \longrightarrow \sim AS$$

The last part of selection (D), *"John is overly sensitive to the cold. Therefore John cannot work at the Arctic substation,"* adds to the diagram as follows:

$$\begin{array}{l} OS \longrightarrow \sim AS \\ \underline{OS \qquad\qquad} \\ \therefore \qquad \sim AS \end{array}$$

In selection (D), the premise and conclusion are merely repeated in the last two sentences. In contrast, in the last part of the passage and in selection (B), the conclusion is used to affirm the premise. By diagramming these two different selections, the fallacy in the passage and in selection (B) becomes clear.

13. Diagramming this problem helps to simplify it. The sentence, *"If the City Parks Department receives the same allocation in next year's municipal budget, it is expected to raise admission fees to the indoor recreation center by fifty cents,"* can be diagrammed as:

SA—>50¢

SA stands for "receives the same allocation in next year's municipal budget" and **50¢** stands for "raise admission fees to the indoor recreation center by fifty cents." The next sentence, *"If the City Parks Department announces a higher admission fee increase, then its budget allocation for next year must have been reduced,"* can be diagrammed as:

~50¢—>~SA

This diagram can be recognized as the contrapositive. Thus, in finding the answer to this problem, you should look for an "if, then" statement and its contrapositive. In selection (C), the sentence, *"If the price of raw plastic pellets remains the same, companies that manufacture molded plastic parts such as fishing tackles and other plastic fishing bobbers can be expected to keep their wholesale prices at last year's levels,"* can be diagrammed as follows:

P$—>W$

P$** stands for "the price of raw plastic pellets remains the same" and **W$ stands for "keep their wholesale prices at last year's levels." The sentence, *"Thus, if these wholesalers raise their prices on fishing bobbers, it will be because raw material costs increased."* can be diagrammed as follows:

~W$—>~P$

This is the contrapositive of **P$—>W$**. The reasoning is the same as that expressed in the passage. The answer is selection (C).

14. The passage contains an embedded *if-then* statement. If you go to the movie, then you must be a true Nineties man or woman and have the three qualities listed—self-reliance, perceptiveness and a caring disposition. The selections should be considered with this *if-then* statement in mind.

(A). No. The passage states that if you are a Nineties man or woman and see the movie, you are self-reliant, perceptive and caring. But nothing in the passage makes these three characteristics interdependent upon each other.

(B). **Yes**. Again, as the passage recites, if you see the movie, you are a true Nineties man or woman—self-reliant, perceptive and caring. If a man sees the movie but he doesn't have all three characteristics, then he is not a true Nineties man and he misrepresents himself by going to the movie with that in mind.

(C). No. The passage doesn't tell us anything about the type of people who go see action thriller movies.

(D). No. The passage doesn't tell us anything about what claims have been made about other movies.

(E). No. The passage doesn't tell us how to make this determination.

15. The first sentence is all that is needed to determine the answer to this question. *"A manufacturer can only recoup its retooling costs for redesigning a product if it sells enough of the product to its distributors to pass its break-even point."* We can conclude from this statement that if a manufacturer has recouped its retooling costs on a product, it had enough sales to pass its break-even point. This can be symbolized as **RC—>BEP**. **R C** stands for "recoup costs" and **BEP** stands for "break-even point." Selection (C) affirms this hypothesis. It states that a manufacturer that has recouped its retooling costs, or **RC**, has sold enough product to pass its break-even point, **BEP**. The answer is (C).

Selection (A) is not correct because we are not told how many orders it will take for the manufacturer to recoup its retooling costs. Selection (B) is irrelevant to the issue. Selection (D) is not correct because again, we are not told how many orders were necessary for the manufacturer to pass its break-even point. Maybe its retooling costs for the particular product were not high and not many sales would be needed to reach the break-even point.

We aren't given enough information in (D) to know if it can be correctly inferred from the passage. Finally, (E) would appear to be contradictory and thus not properly inferred from the passage.

16.   In order to find the solution to this question, you should diagram the arguments presented in the passage and in the answer selections. The first clause, *"If Joan were growing marijuana plants in her home,"* can be symbolized as **MP**. The second clause, *"she would not allow police investigators to search her home without a warrant,"* can be symbolized as **~S**. The entire argument can be diagrammed as follows:

$$M\text{—>}{\sim}S$$
$$\underline{S\qquad\qquad}$$
$$\therefore\quad {\sim}MP$$

This diagram shows that the argument is a valid application of the contrapositive.

Diagram each of the answer selections. For instance, selection (C) can be diagrammed as follows, where **>30** represents *"If Jason were over 30,"* and **~RM** represents *"he would not want to listen to rap music."* Diagramming the entire selection would look like this:

$$>30\text{—>}{\sim}RM$$
$$\underline{RM\qquad\qquad}$$
$$\therefore\qquad >30$$

As can be seen from the diagram, it does not correspond to the logic in the passage. Now, let's diagram selection (A). The first clause, *"If Justin were playing golf at the city golf course,"* can be represented as **G**, and the second clause, *"he would not be home until dinner,"* can be represented as **~H**. The rest of the argument can be represented as follows:

$$G\text{—>}{\sim}H$$
$$\underline{H\qquad\qquad}$$
$$\therefore\quad {\sim}G$$

As you can see, the logic is the same in selection (A) as it is in the passage. It is a valid application of the contrapositive. You should also diagram the remaining selections to see how their logic patterns differ from the logic presented in the passage. The answer is (A).

17.   Remember, "A unless B" is the equivalent of ~B—>A. The first sentence in the passage can be depicted as

$$\sim BD\text{—>}BG$$

where **B D** stands for "the administration allows the band director to keep his teaching position" and **BG** stands for "Students at Lincoln High School will boycott graduation ceremonies." The second sentence contains an implied if-then statement. It can be stated as follows: "If the administration allows the band director to keep his teaching position, then it will have to eliminate one of the new coaching positions." This can be depicted as

$$BD\text{—>}EC$$

Of course, **EC** stands for *"it will have to eliminate one of the new coaching positions."* As presented, the two diagrammed statements cannot be connected. However, let's suppose the high school students do not boycott graduation ceremonies, which is selection (C). If we apply the contrapositive to the first diagram, ~BD—>BG, the statement becomes

$$\sim BG\text{—>}BD$$

Then we can use the transitive property to combine **~BG—>BD** with **BD—>EC** to yield the following diagram:

$$\sim BG\text{—>}EC$$

That is, if the students don't boycott graduation ceremonies, then a new coaching position will be eliminated. Thus, the correct assumption is that the students will not boycott graduation ceremonies. The answer is selection (C).

18. The first part of the passage contains an implied if-then statement. It can be restated as, *"If a lawyer does not return phone calls from her clients, then she cannot be a skillful, experienced lawyer."* This can be pictured as

$$\sim PC \longrightarrow \sim SE$$

Part of the next sentence in the passage, *"she returns all of my phone calls,"* negates the premise in the "if-then" statement. From this, the author concludes that her lawyer is skillful and experienced. This can be summarized as follows:

$$\sim PC \longrightarrow \sim SE$$
$$\underline{PC \hspace{3.5cm}}$$
$$\therefore \hspace{2cm} SE$$

Remember that an *if-then* statement tells us only two things: First, it tells us that if the premise is true, then the conclusion is also true. Second, if the conclusion is false, then we know that the premise is also false. (This is the contrapositive.).

Thus, the diagram presents an *if-then* statement, and then denies the premise of the statement. Thus, we cannot say anything about the conclusion, not based upon what we know generally about *if-then* statements. If the conclusion were denied, then we would know the premise is false. But if the premise is false, we can go no further. We do not know the effect of a false premise upon the conclusion. This passage is an example of the fallacy of denying the premise.

Look at the structure of the answer selections. Selection (D) contains an implied *if-then* statement as follows: *"If a school-age child spends three afternoons a week at gymnastics practice, then he does not have a proper balance between school work and gymnastics."* This can be depicted as

$$3G \longrightarrow \sim B$$

The next part of (D) negates the premise because it states that Tom does not spend three afternoons at gymnastics practice; he only spends one afternoon there. But the argument erroneously concludes that denying the premise also denies the conclusion. Denying that Tom does not have a proper balance (or concluding that Tom does have a proper balance between school work and gymnastics) does not necessarily follow from denying the premise. Thus, selection (D) presents the same erroneous reasoning presented in the passage and it is the correct answer. The answer is (D).

19. The passage contains an embedded if-then statement. "Every bird that scolded me was a Steller's Jay" can be transformed into: If the bird scolded me, then it was a Steller's Jay. This can be diagrammed as

$$BS \longrightarrow SJ$$

Now we turn to the answer-choices.

(A). No. The passage indicates that every bird that scolded Rebecca was a Steller's Jay. Stating it another way, a bird scolded Rebecca if and only if it was a Steller's Jay. The passage doesn't preclude the possibility that Rebecca saw other types of jays that didn't scold her.

(B) No. Remember the diagram above, **BS—>SJ**. Gray Jays are not in the equation, but the equation indicates that if Rebecca saw any Gray Jays, they didn't scold her.

(C) **Yes**. Review the diagram, **BS—>SJ**. If a particular bird scolded Rebecca, then it must have been a Steller's Jay, not a Gray Jay. Let's apply the contrapositive to the diagram:

$$\sim SJ \longrightarrow \sim BS$$

A Gray Jay is not a Steller Jay. The hypothesis of the *if-then* contrapositive statement, **~SJ—>~BS**, is thus supported. As a result, the conclusion ~**BS**, must follow. No Gray Jays scolded Rebecca.

(D) No. Unless all the jays Rebecca saw were Steller's Jays (which we do not know), this statement does not follow. This statement is not supported by the diagram, which is limited to Steller Jays.

(E) No. Again, consider the diagram, **BS—>SJ**. It does not exclude Gray Jays, but it does not allow them to scold Rebecca. So again, Rebecca could have seen Gray Jays, but they didn't scold her as she hiked.

Classification

In Logic II, we studied deductive arguments. However, the bulk of arguments on the GMAT are *inductive*. In this section we will classify and study the major types of inductive arguments.

An argument is deductive if its conclusion *necessarily* follows from its premises—otherwise it is inductive. In an inductive argument, the author presents the premises as evidence or reasons for the conclusion. The validity of the conclusion depends on how compelling the premises are. Unlike deductive arguments, the conclusion of an inductive argument is never certain. The *truth* of the conclusion can range from highly likely to highly unlikely. In reasonable arguments, the conclusion is likely. In fallacious arguments, it is improbable. We will study both reasonable and fallacious arguments.

First, we will classify the three major types of inductive reasoning—generalization, analogy, and causal—and their associated fallacies. Next, we will study common fallacies.

Generalization

Generalization and analogy, which we consider in the next section, are the main tools by which we accumulate knowledge and analyze our world. Many people define *generalization* as "inductive reasoning." In colloquial speech, the phrase "to generalize" carries a negative connotation. To argue by generalization, however, is neither inherently good nor bad. The relative validity of a generalization depends on both the context of the argument and the likelihood that its conclusion is true. Polling organizations make predictions by generalizing information from a small sample of the population, which hopefully represents the general population. The soundness of their predictions (arguments) depends on how representative the sample is and on its size. Clearly, the less comprehensive a conclusion is the more likely it is to be true.

Example:

During the late seventies when Japan was rapidly expanding its share of the American auto market, GM surveyed owners of GM cars and asked them whether they would be more willing to buy a large, powerful car or a small, economical car. Seventy percent of those who responded said that they would prefer a large car. On the basis of this survey, GM decided to continue building large cars. Yet during the '80s, GM lost even more of the market to the Japanese.

Which one of the following, if it were determined to be true, would best explain this discrepancy.

(A) Only 10 percent of those who were polled replied.
(B) Ford which conducted a similar survey with similar results continued to build large cars and also lost more of their market to the Japanese.
(C) The surveyed owners who preferred big cars also preferred big homes.
(D) GM determined that it would be more profitable to make big cars.
(E) Eighty percent of the owners who wanted big cars and only 40 percent of the owners who wanted small cars replied to the survey.

The argument generalizes *from* the survey *to* the general car-buying population, so the reliability of the projection depends on how representative the sample is. At first glance, choice (A) seems rather good, because 10 percent does not seem large enough. However, political opinion polls are typically based on only .001 percent of the population. More importantly, we don't know what percentage of GM car owners received the survey. Choice (B) simply states that Ford made the same mistake that GM did. Choice (C) is irrelevant. Choice (D), rather than explaining the discrepancy, gives even more reason for GM to continue making large cars. Finally, choice (E) points out that part of the survey did not represent the entire public, so (E) is the answer.

Analogy

To argue by analogy is to claim that because two things are similar in some respects, they will be similar in others. Medical experimentation on animals is predicated on such reasoning. The argument goes like this: the metabolism of pigs, for example, is similar to that of humans, and high doses of saccharine cause cancer in pigs. Therefore, high doses of saccharine probably cause cancer in humans.

Clearly, the greater the similarity between the two things being compared the stronger the argument will be. Also the less ambitious the conclusion the stronger the argument will be. The argument above would be strengthened by changing "probably" to "may." It can be weakened by pointing out the dissimilarities between pigs and people.

The following words usually indicate that an analogy is being drawn:

ANALOGY INDICATORS

like	**likewise**
similar	**also**
too	**compared to**
as with	**just as . . . so too . . .**

Often, however, a writer will use an analogy without flagging it with any of the above words.

Example:

Just as the fishing line becomes too taut, so too the trials and tribulations of life in the city can become so stressful that one's mind can snap.

Which one of the following most closely parallels the reasoning used in the argument above?

(A)   Just as the bow may be drawn too taut, so too may one's life be wasted pursuing self-gratification.

(B)   Just as a gambler's fortunes change unpredictably, so too do one's career opportunities come unexpectedly.

(C)   Just as a plant can be killed by over watering it, so too can drinking too much water lead to lethargy.

(D)   Just as the engine may race too quickly, so too may life in the fast lane lead to an early death.

(E)   Just as an actor may become stressed before a performance, so too may dwelling on the negative cause depression.

The argument compares the tautness in a fishing line to the stress of city life; it then concludes that the mind can snap just as the fishing line can. So we are looking for an answer-choice that compares two things and draws a conclusion based on their similarity. Notice that we are looking for an argument that uses similar reasoning, but not necessarily similar concepts. In fact, an answer-choice that mentions either tautness or stress will probably be a same-language trap.

Choice (A) uses the same-language trap—notice "too taut." The analogy between a taut bow and self-gratification is weak, if existent. Choice (B) offers a good analogy but no conclusion. Choice (C) offers both a good analogy and a conclusion; however, the conclusion, "leads to lethargy," understates the scope of what the analogy implies. Choice (D) offers a strong analogy and a conclusion with the same scope found in the original: "the engine blows, the person dies"; "the line snaps, the mind snaps." This is probably the best answer, but still we should check every choice. The last choice, (E), uses language from the original, "stressful," to make its weak analogy more tempting. The *best* answer, therefore, is (D).

Causal Reasoning

Of the three types of inductive reasoning we will discuss, causal reasoning is both the weakest and the most prone to fallacy. Nevertheless, it is a useful and common method of thought.

To argue by causation is to claim that one thing causes another. A causal argument can be either weak or strong depending on the context. For example, to claim that you won the lottery because you saw a shooting star the night before is clearly fallacious. However, most people believe that smoking causes cancer because cancer often strikes those with a history of cigarette use. Although the connection between smoking and cancer is virtually certain, as with all inductive arguments it can never be 100 percent certain. Cigarette companies have claimed that there may be a genetic predisposition in some people to both develop cancer and crave nicotine. Although this claim is highly improbable, it is conceivable.

There are two common fallacies associated with causal reasoning:

1. **Confusing <u>Correlation</u> with <u>Causation</u>.**

   To claim that A caused B merely because A occurred immediately before B is clearly questionable. It may be only coincidental that they occurred together, or something else may have caused them to occur together. For example, the fact that insomnia and lack of appetite often occur together does not mean that one necessarily causes the other. They may both be symptoms of an underlying condition.

2. **Confusing Necessary Conditions with Sufficient Conditions.**

   A is necessary for B means "B cannot occur without A." *A is sufficient for B* means "A causes B to occur, but B can still occur without A." For example, a small tax base is sufficient to cause a budget deficit, but excessive spending can cause a deficit even with a large tax base. A common fallacy is to assume that a necessary condition is sufficient to cause a situation. For example, to win a modern war it is necessary to have modern, high-tech equipment, but it is not sufficient, as Iraq discovered in the Persian Gulf War.

All Things Being Equal

This rather amorphous category is the source of many GMAT questions. Usually, two situations are given that appear similar in all important aspects. From these two apparently similar situations, a conclusion will be drawn that may be surprising or contradictory. Your task in these problems is to show or speculate that there is a critical dissimilarity between the two situations (i.e., <u>Not All Things Are Equal</u>). The following example is a classic all-things-being-equal question.

Example:

The Blane County District Attorney claims that her senior assistant, Tom Feather, is the best criminal prosecutor in Blane County. Inexplicably, a much lower percentage of the criminal defendants Mr. Feather prosecutes are convicted of serious crimes than criminal defendants tried by other prosecutors.

Which one of the following selections goes farthest in crediting both the district attorney's confidence in Mr. Feather and Mr. Feather's low conviction rate?

(A) Since the Blane County District Attorney appointed Mr. Feather as her senior assistant, her judgment would be questioned if she didn't claim that Mr. Feather is the best.

(B) The district attorney followed established procedure in promoting Mr. Feather to senior assistant from among the ranks of assistant district attorneys.

(C) Several years ago, Mr. Feather was involved in training attorneys new to the district attorney's office, and he trained a number of the assistant district attorneys currently on the staff.

(D) In the district attorney's office, the weakest, most difficult cases are usually assigned to Mr. Feather.

(E)   Mr. Feather's conviction record is much better than the conviction record of the previous senior assistant district attorney.

In finding the best answer to this question, we are asked to pick an explanation for why not all things are equal. For only if things are not equal can both seemingly contradictory statements in the passage be supported. If cases are randomly assigned in the district attorney's office, then Mr. Feather's low conviction rate discredits the district attorney's claim. However, if Mr. Feather is assigned the cases that are the most difficult to prove, then it is reasonable that his conviction rate will be lower than the conviction rates of other prosecutors in the office. Perhaps a less skillful prosecutor would have an even lower conviction rate if given the weakest cases to take to trial. Selection (D) is the correct answer.

Selection (A) is the second best answer because it provides an explanation for the district attorney's claim. Obviously, the district attorney will want her staff and the public to think that she has chosen the best person for the job of first assistant district attorney. She might exaggerate Mr. Feather's capabilities to bolster her own image. But the answer doesn't explain why even if Mr. Feather is quite talented, he has such a low conviction record.

Selection (B) doesn't really explain either of the positions in the passage. Explaining that Mr. Feather was promoted from within the ranks doesn't support the district attorney's claim about Mr. Feather's prosecuting abilities or explain why Mr. Feather has such a low conviction record.

Neither does selection (C) explain why the district attorney touts Mr. Feather as the best. Selection (C) also does not explain Mr. Feather's poor conviction record.

Selection (E) just compares Mr. Feather's record with that of his predecessor. It doesn't support the claims contained in the passage.

Common Fallacies

Contradiction

Contradiction is the most glaring type of fallacy. It is committed when two opposing statements are simultaneously asserted. For example, saying "it is raining *and* it is not raining" is a contradiction. If the contradictions on the GMAT were this basic, the test would be significantly easier. Typically, however, the arguer obscures the contradiction to the point that the argument can be quite compelling. Take, for instance, the following argument:

We cannot know anything, because we intuitively realize that our thoughts are unreliable.

This argument has an air of reasonableness to it. But "intuitively realize" means "to know." Thus the arguer is in essence saying that we *know* that we don't know anything. This is self-contradictory.

Example:

In the game of basketball, scoring a three-point shot is a skill that only those with a soft shooting touch can develop. Wilt Chamberlain, however, was a great player, so even though he did not have a soft shooting touch he would have excelled at scoring three point shots.

Which one of the following contains a flaw that most closely parallels the flaw contained in the passage?

(A)   Eighty percent of the freshmen at Berkeley go on to get a bachelor's degree. David is a freshman at Berkeley, so he will probably complete his studies and receive a bachelor's degree.

(B)   If the police don't act immediately to quell the disturbance, it will escalate into a riot. However, since the police are understaffed, there will be a riot.

(C)   The meek shall inherit the earth. Susie received an inheritance from her grandfather, so she must be meek.

    (D)   During the Vietnam War, the powerful had to serve along with the poor. However, Stevens' father was a federal judge, so Stevens was able to get a draft deferment.

    (E)   All dolphins are mammals and all mammals breathe air. Therefore, all mammals that breathe air are dolphins.

The argument clearly contradicts itself. So look for an answer-choice that contradicts itself in like manner. Choice (A) is not self-contradictory. In fact, it's a fairly sound argument—eliminate it. Choice (B), on the other hand, is not a very sound argument. The police, though understaffed, may realize the seriousness of the situation and rearrange their priorities. Nevertheless, (B) does not contain a contradiction—eliminate it. Choice (C), though questionable, does not contain a contradiction—eliminate it. Choice (D), however, does contain a contradiction. It begins by stating that both the powerful and the poor had to serve in Vietnam and ends by stating that some powerful people—namely, Stevens—did not have to serve. This is a contradiction, so (D) is probably the answer. Choice (E), like the original argument, is invalid but does not contain a contradiction—eliminate it. The answer is (D).

Equivocation

Equivocation is the use of a word in more than one sense during an argument. It is often done intentionally.

Example:

Individual rights must be championed by the government. It is right for one to believe in God. So government should promote the belief in God.

In this argument, *right* is used ambiguously. In the phrase "individual rights" it is used in the sense of a privilege, whereas in the second sentence *right* is used to mean correct or moral. The questionable conclusion is possible only if the arguer is allowed to play with the meaning of the critical word *right*.

Example:

Judy: Traditionally, Republican administrations have supported free trade. But the President must veto the North American Free Trade Act because it will drain away American jobs to Mexico and lead to wholesale exploitation of the Mexican workers by international conglomerates.

Tina: I disagree. Exploitation of workers is the essence of any economic system just like the exploitation of natural resources.

Judy and Tina will not be able to settle their argument unless they

    (A)   explain their opinions in more detail
    (B)   ask an expert on international trade to decide who is correct
    (C)   decide whose conclusion is true but irrelevant
    (D)   decide whose conclusion is based on a questionable premise
    (E)   define a critical word

Clearly, Judy and Tina are working with different definitions of the word *exploitation*. Judy is using the meaning that most people attribute to exploitation—abuse. We can't tell the exact meaning Tina intends, but for her exploitation must have a positive, or at least neutral, connotation, otherwise she would be unlikely to defend it as essential. Their argument will be fruitless until they agree on a definition for *exploitation*. Hence the answer is (E).

Circular Reasoning

Circular reasoning involves assuming as a premise that which you are trying to prove. Intuitively, it may seem that no one would fall for such an argument. However, the conclusion may appear to state something additional, or the argument may be so long that the reader may forget that the conclusion was stated as a premise.

Example:

The death penalty is appropriate for traitors because it is right to execute those who betray their own country and thereby risk the lives of millions.

This argument is circular because "right" means essentially the same thing as "appropriate." In effect, the writer is saying that the death penalty is appropriate because it is appropriate.

Shifting the Burden of Proof

As mentioned before, it is incumbent upon the writer to provide evidence or support for her position. To imply that a position is true merely because no one has disproved it is to shift the burden of proof to others.

Example:

Since no one has been able to prove God's existence, there must not be a God.

There are two major weaknesses in this argument. First, the fact that God's existence has yet to be proven does not preclude any future proof of existence. Second, if there is a God, one would expect that his existence is independent of any proof by man.

Reasoning by shifting the burden of proof is not always fallacious. In fact, our legal system is predicated on this method of thought. The defendant is *assumed* innocent until proven guilty. This assumption shifts the onus of proof to the state. Science can also validly use this method of thought to better understand the world—so long as it is not used to claim "truth." Consider the following argument: "The multitude of theories about our world have failed to codify and predict its behavior as well as Einstein's theory of relativity. Therefore our world is probably Einsteinian." This argument is strong so long as it is qualified with "probably"—otherwise it is fallacious: someone may yet create a better theory of our world.

Unwarranted Assumptions

We talked about unwarranted assumptions in connection with analyzing a problem. Now we will discuss it as a method of fallacious thought. The *fallacy of unwarranted assumption* is committed when the conclusion of an argument is based on a premise (implicit or explicit) that is false or unwarranted. An assumption is unwarranted when it is false—these premises are usually suppressed or vaguely written. An assumption is also unwarranted when it is true but does not apply in the given context—these premises are usually explicit. The varieties of unwarranted assumptions are too numerous to classify, but a few examples should give you the basic idea.

Example: *(False Dichotomy)*

Either restrictions must be placed on freedom of speech or certain subversive elements in society will use it to destroy this country. Since to allow the latter to occur is unconscionable, we must restrict freedom of speech.

The conclusion above is unsound because

(A)   subversives do not in fact want to destroy the country
(B)   the author places too much importance on the freedom of speech
(C)   the author fails to consider an accommodation between the two alternatives
(D)   the meaning of "freedom of speech" has not been defined
(E)   subversives are a true threat to our way of life

The arguer offers two options: either restrict freedom of speech, or lose the country. He hopes the reader will assume that these are the only options available. This is unwarranted. He does not state how the so-called "subversive elements" would destroy the country, nor for that matter why they would want to destroy it. There may be a third option that the author did not mention; namely, that society may be able to tolerate the "subversives"; it may even be improved by the diversity of opinion they offer. The answer is (C).

Example:

Of course Steve supports government sponsorship of the arts. He's an artist.

Which one of the following uses reasoning that is most similar to the above argument?

(A)   Of course if a person lies to me, I will never trust that person again.

(B)   Conservatives in the past have prevented ratification of any nuclear arms limitation treaties with the Soviet Union (or Russia), so they will prevent the ratification of the current treaty.

(C)   Mr. Sullivan is the police commissioner, so it stands to reason that he would support the NRA's position on gun control.

(D)   Following her conscience, Congresswoman Martinez voted against the death penalty, in spite of the fact that she knew it would doom her chances for reelection.

(E)   You're in no position to criticize me for avoiding paying my fair share of taxes. You don't even pay your employees a fair wage.

This argument is fallacious—and unfair—because it assumes that all artists support government sponsorship of the arts. Some artists, however, may have reasons for not supporting government sponsorship of the arts. For example, they may believe that government involvement stifles artistic expression. Or they may reject government involvement on purely philosophical grounds. The argument suggests a person's profession taints his opinion. Choice (C) does the same thing, so it is the answer.

True But Irrelevant

This tactic is quite simple: the arguer bases a conclusion on information that is true but not germane to the issue.

Example:

This pain relief product can be bought over the counter or in a stronger form with a prescription. But according to this pamphlet, for the prescription strength product to be effective it must be taken at the immediate onset of pain, it must be taken every four hours thereafter, and it cannot be taken with any dairy products. So it actually doesn't matter whether you use the prescription strength or the over-the-counter strength product.

Which one of the following best identifies the flaw in the above argument?

(A)   The fact that many people could not live a full life without the prescription strength product cannot be ignored.

(B)   It cannot be concluded that just because the prescription strength product has certain guidelines and restrictions on its use that it is not more effective.

(C)   It does not consider that complications may arise from the prescription strength product.

(D)   It fails to consider that other products may be more effective in relieving pain.

(E)   It is unreasonable to assume that the over-the-counter strength product does not have similar restrictions and guidelines for its use.

It is unreasonable to reject the effectiveness of a product merely because it has modest requirements for use. All medications have directions and restrictions. Hence the answer is (B). Don't make the mistake of choosing (A). Although it is a good rebuttal, it does not address the flaw in the argument. Interestingly, it too is true but irrelevant.

Appeal to Authority

To appeal to authority is to cite an expert's opinion as support for one's own opinion. This method of thought is not necessarily fallacious. Clearly, the reasonableness of the argument depends on the "expertise" of the person being cited and whether he or she is an expert in a field relevant to the argument. Appealing to a doctor's authority on a medical issue, for example, would be reasonable; but if the issue is about dermatology and the doctor is an orthopedist, then the argument would be questionable.

Example:

The legalization of drugs is advocated by no less respectable people than William F. Buckley and federal judge Edmund J. Reinholt. These people would not propose a social policy that is likely to be harmful. So there is little risk in experimenting with a one-year legalization of drugs.

In presenting her position the author does which one of the following?

(A)   Argues from the specific to the general.
(B)   Attacks the motives of her opponents.
(C)   Uses the positions of noted social commentators to support her position.
(D)   Argues in a circular manner.
(E)   Claims that her position is correct because others cannot disprove it.

The only evidence that the author gives to support her position is that respected people agree with her. She is appealing to the authority of others. Thus, the answer is (C).

Personal Attack

In a personal attack (ad hominem), a person's character is challenged instead of her opinions.

Example:

Politician: How can we trust my opponent to be true to the voters? He isn't true to his wife!

This argument is weak because it attacks the opponent's character, not his positions. Some people may consider fidelity a prerequisite for public office. History, however, shows no correlation between fidelity and great political leadership.

Example:

A reporter responded with the following to the charge that he resorted to tabloid journalism when he rummaged through and reported on the contents of garbage taken from the home of Henry Kissinger.

"Of all the printed commentary . . . only a few editorial writers thought to express the obvious point that when it comes to invasion of privacy, the man who as National Security Advisor helped to bug the home phones of his own staff members is one of our nation's leading practitioners."—Washington Monthly, October 1975

In defending his actions, the reporter does which one of the following?

(A)   Attacks the character of Henry Kissinger.
(B)   Claims Henry Kissinger caused the reporter to act as he did.
(C)   Claims that "bugging" is not an invasion of privacy.
(D)   Appeals to the authority of editorial writers.
(E)   Claims that his actions were justified because no one was able to show otherwise.

The reporter justifies his actions by claiming that Kissinger is guilty of wrong doing. So, instead of addressing the question, he attacks the character of Henry Kissinger. The answer is (A).

Points to Remember

1. Most GMAT arguments are inductive, not deductive.

2. An argument is inductive if its conclusion does not necessarily follow from its premises—otherwise it is deductive.

3. Unlike with deductive arguments, the conclusion of an inductive argument is never certain.

4. The three major types of inductive reasoning are

    ☐ Generalization

    ☐ Analogy

    ☐ Causal
        a. Confusing Correlation with Causation
        b. Confusing Necessary Conditions with Sufficient Conditions

5. The most common fallacies are

    1. Contradiction
    2. Equivocation
    3. Circular Reasoning
    4. Shifting the Burden of Proof
    5. Unwarranted Assumptions
    6. True but Irrelevant
    7. Appeal to Authority
    8. Personal Attack

Exercise

Directions: The questions in this section are based on the reasoning contained in brief statements or passages. For some questions, more than one of the choices could conceivably answer the question. However, you are to choose the <u>best</u> answer; that is, the response that most accurately and completely answers the question. You should not make assumptions that are by common sense standards implausible, superfluous, or incompatible with the passage. Answers and solutions begin on page 480.

1. That the policy of nuclear deterrence has worked thus far is unquestionable. Since the end of the Second World War, the very fact that there were nuclear armaments in existence has kept major powers from using nuclear weapons, for fear of starting a worldwide nuclear exchange that would make the land of the power initiating it uninhabitable. The proof is that a third world war between superpowers has not happened.

   Which one of the following, if true, indicates a flaw in the argument?

   (A) Maintaining a high level of nuclear armaments represents a significant drain on a country's economy.
   (B) From what has happened in the past, it is impossible to infer with certainty what will happen in the future, so an accident could still trigger a third world war between superpowers.
   (C) Continuing to produce nuclear weapons beyond the minimum needed for deterrence increases the likelihood of a nuclear accident.
   (D) The major powers have engaged in many smaller-scale military operations since the end of the Second World War, while refraining from a nuclear confrontation.
   (E) It cannot be known whether it was nuclear deterrence that worked, or some other factor, such as a recognition of the economic value of remaining at peace.

2. A medical journal used a questionnaire survey to determine whether a particular change in its format would increase its readership. Sixty-two percent of those who returned the questionnaire supported that change. On the basis of this outcome, the decision was made to introduce the new format.

   Which one of the following, if it were determined to be true, would provide the best evidence that the journal's decision will have the desired effect?

   (A) Of the readers who received questionnaires, 90 percent returned them.
   (B) Other journals have based format changes on survey results.
   (C) The percentage of surveyed readers who like the format change was almost the same as the percentage of the entire potential readership who would like the format change.
   (D) It was determined that the new format would be less costly than the old format.
   (E) Ninety percent of the readers who were dissatisfied with the old format and only 50 percent of the readers who liked the old format returned their questionnaires.

3. In Brazil, side-by-side comparisons of Africanized honeybees and the native honeybees have shown that the Africanized bees are far superior honey producers. Therefore, there is no reason to fear that domestic commercial honey production will decline in the United States if local honeybees are displaced by Africanized honeybees.

Each of the following, if true, would weaken the argument EXCEPT:

(A) The honeybees native to Brazil are not of the same variety as those most frequently used in the commercial beekeeping industry in the United States.

(B) Commercial honey production is far more complicated and expensive with Africanized honeybees than it is with the more docile honeybees common in the United States.

(C) If Africanized honeybees replace local honeybees, certain types of ornamental trees will be less effectively pollinated.

(D) In the United States a significant proportion of the commercial honey supply comes from hobby beekeepers, many of whom are likely to abandon beekeeping with the influx of Africanized bees.

(E) The area of Brazil where the comparative study was done is far better suited to the foraging habits of the Africanized honeybees than are most areas of the United States.

4. For a television program about astrology, investigators went into the street and found twenty volunteers born under the sign of Gemini who were willing to be interviewed on the program and to take a personality test. The test confirmed the investigators' personal impressions that each of the volunteers was more sociable and extroverted than people are on average. This modest investigation thus supports the claim that one's astrological birth sign influences one's personality.

Which one of the following, if true, indicates the most serious flaw in the method used by the investigators?

(A) The personality test was not administered or scored personally by the investigators.

(B) People born under astrological signs other than Gemini have been judged by astrologers to be much less sociable than those born under Gemini.

(C) The personal impressions the investigators first formed of other people have tended to be confirmed by the investigators' later experience of those people.

(D) There is not likely to be a greater proportion of people born under the sign of Gemini on the street than in the population as a whole.

(E) People who are not sociable and extroverted are not likely to agree to participate in such an investigation.

5. Democracy is the best form of government yet created. Therefore, we must be vigilant in its defense; that is, we must be prepared to defend the right to freedom. Because this right is fundamental to any progressive form of government, it is clear that democracy is better than any other form of government.

Which one of the following illustrates the same flawed reasoning as found in the passage?

(A) I never get a headache when I eat only Chinese food, nor when I drink only wine. But when I eat Chinese food and drink wine, I get a headache. So the combination of the two must be the cause of my headaches.

(B) The two times I have gone to that restaurant something bad has happened. The first time the waiter dropped a glass and it shattered all over the table. And after the second time I went there, I got sick. So why should I go there again—something bad will just happen again.

(C) I would much rather live a life dedicated to helping my fellow man than one dedicated to gaining material possessions and seeing my fellow man as a competitor. At the end of each day, the satisfaction of having helped people is infinitely greater than the satisfaction of having achieved something material.

(D) I'm obsessed with volleyball; that's why I play it constantly. I train seven days a week, and I enter every tournament. Since I'm always playing it, I must be obsessed with it.

(E) In my academic studies, I have repeatedly changed majors. I decide to major in each new subject that I'm introduced to. Just as a bee lights from one flower to the next, tasting the nectar of each, I jump from one subject to the next getting just a taste of each.

6. A survey of alumni of the class of 1960 at Aurora University yielded puzzling results. When asked to indicate their academic rank, half of the respondents reported that they were in the top quarter of the graduating class in 1960.

Which one of the following most helps account for the apparent contradiction above?

(A) A disproportionately large number of high-ranking alumni responded to the survey.

(B) Few, if any, respondents were mistaken about their class rank.

(C) Not all the alumni who were actually in the top quarter responded to the survey.

(D) Almost all of the alumni who graduated in 1960 responded to the survey.

(E) Academic rank at Aurora University was based on a number considerations in addition to average grades.

7. Astronomers have created a mathematical model for determining whether life exists outside our solar system. It is based on the assumption that life as we know it can exist only on a planet such as our own, and that our sun, which has nine planets circling it, is the kind of star commonly found throughout the universe. Hence it is projected that there are billions of planets with conditions similar to our own. So astronomers have concluded that it is highly probable, if not virtually certain, that life exists outside our solar system. Yet there has never been detected so much as one planet beyond our solar system. Hence life exists only on planet Earth.

Which one of the following would most weaken the above argument?

(A) Thousands of responsible people, people with reputations in the community to protect, have claimed to have seen UFOs. Statistically, it is virtually impossible for this many people to be mistaken or to be lying.

(B) Recently it has been discovered that Mars has water, and its equatorial region has temperatures in the same range as that of northern Europe. So there may be life on Mars.

(C) Only one percent of the stars in the universe are like our sun.

(D) The technology needed to detect planets outside our solar system has not yet been developed.

(E) Even if all the elements for life as we know it are present, the probability that life would spontaneously generate is infinitesimal.

8. To score in the ninetieth percentile on the GMAT, one must study hard. If one studies four hours a day for one month, she will score in the ninetieth percentile. Hence, if a person scored in the top ten percent on the GMAT, then she must have studied at least four hours a day for one month.

Which one of the following most accurately describes the weakness in the above argument?

(A) The argument fails to take into account that not all test-prep books recommend studying four hours a day for one month.

(B) The argument does not consider that excessive studying can be counterproduc-tive.

(C) The argument does not consider that some people may be able to score in the ninetieth percentile though they studied less than four hours a day for one month.

(D) The argument fails to distinguish between how much people should study and how much they can study.

(E) The author fails to realize that the ninetieth percentile and the top ten percent do not mean the same thing.

9. Advertisement: Anyone who exercises knows from firsthand experience that exercise leads to better performance of such physical organs as the heart and the lungs, as well as to improvement in muscle tone. And since your brain is a physical organ, your actions can improve its performance, too. Act now. Subscribe to *Stimulus*: read the magazine that exercises your brain.

The advertisement employs which one of the following argumentative strategies?

(A) It cites experimental evidence that subscribing to the product being advertised has desirable consequences.

(B) It ridicules people who do not subscribe to *Stimulus* by suggesting that they do not believe that exercise will improve brain capacity.

(C) It explains the process by which the product being advertised brings about the result claimed for its use.

(D) It supports its recommendation by a careful analysis of the concept of exercise.

(E) It implies that brains and muscle are similar in one respect because they are similar in another respect.

10. When workers do not find their assignments challenging, they become bored and so achieve less than their abilities would allow. On the other hand, when workers find their assignments too difficult, they give up and so again achieve less than what they are capable of achieving. It is, therefore, clear that no worker's full potential will ever be realized.

Which one of the following is an error of reasoning contained in the argument?

(A) mistakenly equating what is actual and what is merely possible

(B) assuming without warrant that a situation allows only two possibilities

(C) relying on subjective rather than objective evidence

(D) confusing the coincidence of two events with a causal relation between the two

(E) depending on the ambiguous use of a key term

11. The senator has long held to the general principle that no true work of art is obscene, and thus that there is no conflict between the need to encourage free artistic expression and the need to protect the sensibilities of the public from obscenity. When well-known works generally viewed as obscene are cited as possible counterexamples, the senator justifies accepting the principle by saying that if these works really are obscene then they cannot be works of art.

The senator's reasoning contains which one of the following errors?

(A) It seeks to persuade by emotional rather than intellectual means.

(B) It contains an implicit contradiction.

(C) It relies on an assertion of the senator's authority.

(D) It assumes what it seeks to establish.

(E) It attempts to justify a position by appeal to an irrelevant consideration.

12. The 1980s have been characterized as a period of selfish individualism that threatens the cohesion of society. But this characterization is true of any time. Throughout history all human actions have been motivated by selfishness. When the deeper implications are considered, even the simplest "unselfish" acts prove to be instances of selfish concern for the human species.

Which one of the following is a flaw in the argument?

(A) The claim that selfishness has been present throughout history is not actually relevant to the argument.

(B) No statistical evidence is provided to show that humans act selfishly more often than they act unselfishly.

(C) The argument assumes that selfishness is unique to the present age.

(D) The argument mentions only humans and does not consider the behavior of other species.

(E) The argument relies on two different uses of the term "selfish."

13. The true scientific significance of a group of unusual fossils discovered by the paleontologist Charles Walcott is more likely to be reflected in a recent classification than it was in Walcott's own classification. Walcott was, after all, a prominent member of the scientific establishment. His classifications are thus unlikely to have done anything but confirm what established science had already taken to be true.

Which one of the following most accurately describes a questionable technique used in the argument?

(A) It draws conclusions about the merit of a position and about the content of that position from evidence about the position's source.

(B) It cites two pieces of evidence, each of which is both questionable and unverifiable, and uses this evidence to support its conclusions.

(C) It bases a conclusion on two premises that contradict each other and minimizes this contradiction by the vagueness of the terms employed.

(D) It attempts to establish the validity of a claim, which is otherwise unsupported, by denying the truth of the opposite of that claim.

(E) It analyzes the past on the basis of social and political categories that properly apply only to the present and uses the results of this analysis to support its conclusion.

14. Giselle: The government needs to ensure that the public consumes less petroleum. When things cost more, people buy and use less of them. Therefore, the government should raise the sales tax on gasoline, a major petroleum product.

Antoine: The government should not raise the sales tax on gasoline. Such an increase would be unfair to gasoline users. If taxes are to be increased, the increases should be applied in such a way that they spread the burden of providing the government with increased revenues among many people, not just the users of gasoline.

As a rebuttal of Giselle's argument, Antoine's response is ineffective because

(A) he ignores the fact that Giselle does not base her argument for raising the gasoline sales tax on the government's need for increased revenues

(B) he fails to specify how many taxpayers there are who are not gasoline users

(C) his conclusion is based on an assertion regarding unfairness, and unfairness is a very subjective concept

(D) he mistakenly assumes that Giselle wants a sales tax increase only on gasoline

(E) he makes the implausible assumption that the burden of increasing government revenues can be more evenly distributed among the people through other means besides increasing the gasoline sales tax

15. All intelligent people are nearsighted. I am very nearsighted. So I must be a genius.

Which one of the following exhibits both of the logical flaws exhibited in the argument above?

(A) I must be stupid because all intelligent people are nearsighted and I have perfect eyesight.

(B) All chickens have beaks. This bird has a beak. So this bird must be a chicken.

(C) All pigs have four legs, but this spider has eight legs. So this spider must be twice as big as any pig.

(D) John is extremely happy, so he must be extremely tall because all tall people are happy.

(E) All geniuses are very nearsighted. I must be very nearsighted since I am a genius.

16. Susan has been collecting unemployment compensation for a long time. She always applies for jobs that require more education than she has—and is always turned down. She tells her friends, "There aren't any jobs for me."

What is the error in Susan's reasoning?

(A) she hasn't gone to a job guidance center
(B) assuming what it seeks to establish
(C) assuming that she only has two choices
(D) equating the actual and the possible
(E) confusing coincidence with a relationship

17. Cats used to be characterized as independent animals who do not need contact with other animals or humans. Dogs, on the other hand, previously were thought of as animals who are devoted to other animals and humans. When experiments on feline and canine behavior are examined, however, what was thought of as unstereotypical behavior proves to be instances of stereotypical behavior of all animals, including humans.

Which one of the following is a flaw in the argument?

(A) The claim that what stereotypical behavior used to be believed to be is not actually relevant.
(B) No evidence is provided to show that animals ever act in stereotyped ways more than unstereotyped ways, or vice versa.
(C) The argument relies on two different uses of the term "stereotypical."
(D) The argument assumes that some stereotyped behavior is unique to all animals.
(E) The argument does not mention specific human behavior.

18. Computers have solved many problems for us, but they create some problems too. Say, for example, that you are writing a novel. After you are done with your first draft you decide to change your heroine's name from Linda to Lydia. With a typewriter you would have to retype every page containing the heroine's name. With word processing software, on a computer, you press just a few keys and the computer takes care of all the work. But technology hasn't solved all our problems. While many of Shakespeare's original documents survive, it takes only misplaced keystrokes to wipe out your next masterpiece.

Which of the following propositions is illustrated by this passage?

(A) All you really need is a typewriter.
(B) All you really need is some parchment paper, a quill pen, and some ink.
(C) New technology can improve our lives and cause some problems.
(D) Always make backup copies of your documents.
(E) Most computers are good, some computers are bad.

19. On several Native American reservations, comparisons of buffalo herds versus domesticated cattle herds have shown that the buffalo herds are far superior meat producers. In addition, native tribes use every part of the buffalo as they did before wild buffalo were almost destroyed on this continent. Therefore, domesticated cattle herds should be replaced with buffalo herds as soon as possible.

Each of the following, if true, would weaken the argument EXCEPT:

(A) Only Native American tribes use part of the buffalo other than the meat.
(B) Not everyone likes the taste of buffalo as much as they like the taste of regular beef.
(C) Cattle ranchers may not know how to raise buffalo.
(D) Professional chefs need time to develop meals that include buffalo.
(E) Cattle ranches may not have the type of grazing land required for buffalo.

20. The United States has experienced a big growth in job creation. This trend has continued for several years and will soon eliminate the problem of joblessness.

Which one of the answers below is an error in the reasoning that leads to the above prediction?

(A) It does not quote numbers showing how jobs are growing in comparison to the population.
(B) Some people will never have jobs because they lack the skills to hold a simple job.
(C) It fails to quote government reports comparing pay rates of new jobs to minimum wage.
(D) Some people will have to hold two or even three jobs to live at a minimum level.
(E) It fails to consider tax rates.

21. The idea that parents should be given choices in the material taught to their children in nursery school should be dropped. The parents who want to control the information presented to their young children in pre-school and nursery school are never happy. For example, last year, one set of parents was angry that their 5-year old twins were not piano prodigies by the time they started public kindergarten. Their pre-school class had been exposed to some basic music classes and the parents said that those classes should have made their children piano prodigies.

There is a problem with the above argument. The flaw is that it:

(A) Misrepresents ideas advocated by opponents.
(B) Assumes the conclusion is true in stating the premise.
(C) Does not discuss the idea being argued but instead attacks parents who support the idea.
(D) Does not define "happy."
(E) Summarizes a position the argument is directed toward discrediting.

22. Until she was given tenure at the college, Susan was considered an average teacher. It is clear that if her receiving tenure was justified, then Susan was much better than average or very loyal. Soon after she was awarded tenure, however, it was shown that she was not better than average. Thus, one is forced to conclude that Susan must have been very loyal.

Which one of the following states an assumption upon which the argument depends?

(A) Susan being given tenure was justified.
(B) Susan was a teacher at a college.
(C) Giving tenure to someone who is very loyal would be justified.
(D) Anyone who gets tenure is very loyal.
(E) If someone is an above average teacher or very loyal, then they deserve tenure.

23. The significance of Monet's work is reflected in a recent discussion of art more than it was in his own descriptions. He is, usually, considered a founding member of French impressionists. Thus, his descriptions are unlikely to do more than confirm what he thought to be true.

Which one of the following most accurately describes a questionable technique used in the argument?

(A) It cites two pieces of evidence, each of which is both questionable and unverifiable, and uses this evidence to support its conclusions.

(B) It uses the descriptions from a famous artist to support its conclusions.

(C) It attempts to establish the validity of a claim, which is otherwise unsupported, by denying the truth of the opposite of that claim.

(D) It bases a conclusion on two premises that contradict each other and minimize this contradiction by the vagueness of the terms employed.

(E) It draws conclusions about the merit of a position from evidence about the position's source.

24. Senator: Some economists believe that our country's continued growth requires a higher level of homeownership than we currently have. A recent proposal would allow individuals to remove as much as $20,000 from an IRA, SEP IRA, and Keogh without penalty if the money went to the purchase of a primary residence. Supporters of this proposal claim that its implementation would increase revenues for the construction industry as well as tax revenues for city, county, and state governments.

The passage as a whole provides the most support for which one of the following conclusions?

(A) The proposed incentive is likely to attract additional money into the homebuying market.

(B) Supporters of this proposal have some motive other than their expressed aim.

(C) The government has no effective means of influencing the amount of money that people are willing to put into savings accounts.

(D) A program that resulted in an increase of tax revenues would be greeted negatively by city, county, and state officials.

(E) The economy is in danger unless some incentive to increased homeownership can be found to stimulate growth.

25. Researchers believe that we will ultimately be able to explain all "psychic" phenomena. Achieving this goal requires knowledge of how mental images are "sent" and "received" over distance and how senders and receivers interact at a biological level. At present, there is a substantial amount of fundamental knowledge about receiving images and sending images. Thus, as researchers claim, psychic phenomena will soon be explainable.

Which one of the following indicates an error in the reasons in the passage?

(A) The conclusion contradicts researchers.

(B) The passage fails to describe what is currently known about senders and receivers.

(C) The passage does not indicate that any knowledge has been achieved about how senders and receivers interact at a biological level.

(D) The argument does not indicate whether this information will be useful.

(E) The passage is not specific about what psychic phenomena are being researched.

26. Rev. Hayes says that an action is right if it benefits one or more other people and an action is wrong if it harms anyone. Rev. Hayes says the action is wrong if the harm could have been seen with reasonable thought or whether or not harm was intended to anyone.

Which one of the following most clearly conforms to the principle cited above?

(A) Frank wrote a proposal attempting to cause trouble between Linda and Jane; this action was morally bad, even though, in fact, it had an opposite effect than the one intended.

(B) Giving a homeless man a ride to a local shelter, Fred was in a serious car accident that was not his fault. The homeless man, injured in the accident, received a settlement from the other driver's insurance company. The settlement allowed him to get an apartment for him and his family; thus showing that a right action can have both bad and good consequences.

(C) Giving a homeless man a ride to a local shelter, George was in a serious car accident that was his fault. The homeless man, injured in the accident, received a settlement from George's insurance company. The settlement allowed him to get an apartment for him and his family; thus showing that a right action can have both bad and good consequences.

(D) Linda agreed to watch her friend's cat for two weeks at her home. Everything went fine for 10 days. Then, on the next day, when Linda opened the window and sat down to watch television, the cat fell out of the window and was injured. She took the cat to a local vet, paid the bill, and the cat was almost recovered by the time Linda's friend returned. Even though she intended no harm, Linda's action was wrong.

(E) Mary, a trained social worker, was asked by a homeless man for food. She walked with the man to the local shelter that runs a soup kitchen. There, the man choked while eating lunch and died. Thus, Mary performed a wrong action.

27. An author writing a book about birth order advertised in his local paper for people who were first born. Fifty people consented to be interviewed and assessed for certain personality traits. As the writer suspected, the interview results and personality assessments showed that first-borns were more goal-oriented and serious-minded than random samples of the general public. These findings support the conclusion that people are affected by their birth order.

Which one of the following selections, if true, points out the most critical weakness in the method used by the author to investigate birth order characteristics?

(A) Last born children are typically more laid-back and calm than their older siblings.

(B) The interviews and assessments were performed by an outside firm, not by the author.

(C) People who saw the newspaper ad were not more likely to be first born than the number of first-born people in the population in general.

(D) The author's subsequent contact with people who were middle children or last born tended to reinforce his initial impression of the character traits of people who were not first born.

(E) People who are not goal-oriented and serious-minded were not as likely to respond to the author's newspaper ad nor were they as likely to agree to participate in the study.

28. Heavy snow fall in the Sierra Nevada Mountains is usually preceded by subzero temperatures in northwestern Canada. When snow fall is high in Canada's northwestern provinces, the same storm typically produces heavy snows in the Sierra Nevadas. Therefore, subzero temperatures cause winter snow storms to rebuild as they move down from Canada to the Sierra Nevadas.

Which selection contains the same type flaw as that contained in the passage above?

(A) Professional golfers tend to have lean builds. Therefore, professional golfers typically have healthy eating habits.

(B) People tend to write larger when they use wide-ruled notebook paper than when they use narrow-ruled paper. Therefore, people write more neatly on the wide-ruled paper.

(C) Students who participate in debate in high school often end up as trial lawyers. Therefore, participating in high school debate must somehow influence students to attend law school.

(D) During the hottest part of the day, song birds do not visit unshaded feeders. Therefore, song birds must visit the feeders before dawn.

(E) The kind of shows on Broadway can impact the type of shows premiered during new television seasons. Therefore, if the new Broadway shows feature aliens as characters in their productions, then the new television shows will also feature alien characters.

29. Ten years after graduation, men and women who had participated in the Thompson High School basketball program were surveyed with regard to their individual playing records for their teams. Some of the results of the survey were curious. Seventy-five percent of those responding reported that they had started for their respective boys' or girls' teams, when the actual number of boys and girls who had started for their teams was only 50%.

Which one of the following provides the most helpful explanation for the apparent contradiction in these survey results?

(A) A very small number of those responding were incorrect in reporting that they held starting positions.

(B) A disproportionately high number of players who started for their teams responded to the survey.

(C) Not all starting players responded to the survey.

(D) Almost all men and women who played basketball for Thompson High School ten years earlier responded to the survey.

(E) Not all good basketball players started for their teams; some good players were deliberately held out to play later in the game.

30. Magazine ad: Men and women who run competitively learn that at least two of their human capabilities—physical stamina and breath control—can be stretched to higher and higher levels. The vigorous conditioning runners undergo is critical to their performance. Proper conditioning can also stretch another human capability—our minds. If you rigorously condition your mind, it can also attain higher and higher levels. Stretch and stimulate your mind! Join your local Puzzlemaster Club.

This magazine ad uses which one of the following strategies in its approach?

(A) The ad relies on the results of experiments to suggest that joining a Puzzlemaster Club will have the effect of improving mental abilities.

(B) The ad ridicules people who don't join a Puzzlemaster Club by suggesting that they don't want to improve their minds.

(C) The ad explains why becoming a member of a Puzzlemaster Club will stretch and stimulate your mind.

(D) The ad supports or justifies its goal, i.e., that people join a Puzzlemaster Club, by carefully documenting the benefits of competitive running.

(E) The ad implies that because physical stamina, breath control and the mind are all human capabilities, our minds can be stretched to higher levels just as stamina and breath control can be stretched.

31. Participants at a continuing legal education seminar were asked to evaluate the seminar schedule, location and topic selection to determine whether changes would increase attendance at next year's seminar. A majority of the evaluations recommended that the seminar schedule be changed so that the sessions would be held from 8:00 a.m. to 4:00 p.m. instead of the current 9:00 a.m. to 5:00 p.m. schedule. Based upon the results of the evaluations, the sponsors of the seminar decided to change to an earlier schedule for next year's program.

Which of the following selections, if true, would most prove the sponsors right in their decision to change to an earlier schedule next year?

(A) Approximately 85% of the people who received evaluation forms completed their forms and handed them in.

(B) Other seminar sponsors have made changes in their programs based on comments they have received in evaluation forms.

(C) About the same percentage of people attending the seminar wanted the earlier schedule as those who returned their evaluation forms.

(D) An earlier seminar schedule would make commuting easier for the participants.

(E) A significantly larger percentage of people who preferred the earlier schedule returned their evaluation forms than people who preferred the 9:00 a.m. to 5:00 p.m. schedule.

32. Psychologists have studied the impact a person's attitude has on his ability to accomplish tasks. In one study, a group of college students was outfitted with contraptions designed to administer soothing heat pulses to the students' neck and shoulder muscles. The students were told that the pulses would enhance their performance of in-class assignments. Only half of these contraptions worked, but neither the students nor the psychologists were told which students would actually receive these pulses. This component of the experiment is often frustrated, however, because ___

Which one of the following selections, if it is true, completes the sentence most appropriately?

(A) frequently the faces of the students who actually receive the pulses become a little flushed.

(B) students who believe they are receiving the warm pulses do better on their class assignments.

(C) students who participate in the studies are volunteers who must told that some of them will not receive the heat pulses.

(D) many students will not complete the experiment if the sessions last too long.

(E) many of the participating students suffer from tension headaches which readily respond to the heat pulses.

33. In a suburban community in the Southeast, neighborhood security guards have their residents' permission to call local police if anyone is observed entering the home of a resident who is out of town. When residents leave town, they report their departure and return dates to the neighborhood security office. If guards observe someone entering the home of a resident who is out of town, they will immediately call the police. The residential burglary rate for that community has decreased since the implementation of this reporting procedure.

If it is true that the burglary rate has decreased in this community since the reporting procedure was implemented, then which of the following would be most important to know to make sure the conclusion is valid?

(A) Are residents who report their travel plans to the security office also taking other precautions to protect their homes while they are away?

(B) How many other communities utilize this reporting procedure with their neighborhood security offices?

(C) Will residents be harassed by security guards or the police if they return home early from their travels?

(D) Is this community similar to other guarded suburban communities in the Southeast?

(E) Are homes in this community sometimes burglarized even when residents are in town?

34. The number of citations issued to convenience stores for selling tobacco products to minors has dramatically decreased in recent years. Between the years 1985-1990, a total of 5,511 citations were issued to convenience stores for this infraction. For the period 1990-1995, however, only 3,189 citations were issued. These statistics prove that local enforcement agencies have seriously neglected their inspection and surveillance of tobacco sales practices since 1990.

Which one of the following does the author assume in reaching his conclusion?

(A) Monitoring and enforcement of tobacco violations became more lax due to a change in the political climate in Washington, D.C.

(B) The decrease in the number of citations was not due to a reduction in the number of tobacco sales actually made to minors.

(C) Authorities focused more on enforcing the ban on liquor sales to minors than the ban on the sale of tobacco products to minors.

(D) Local enforcement agencies suffered from a reduction in personnel during the period 1990-1995.

(E) For several years prior to 1985, in excess of 1,500 citations per year were issued in connection with tobacco sales to minors.

35. County building inspectors report that almost fifty percent of the homes they inspect are equipped with gauges that monitor carbon monoxide levels. Fifteen years ago, only twenty-five percent of inspected homes were equipped with these gauges. However, even though more homes are now monitored for poisonous carbon monoxide fumes, the total number of homes with confirmed dangerous fume levels is no higher now than it was fifteen years ago because a large proportion of gauges produce false readings.

Which one of the following assumptions must be made in order for the author to be correct in drawing the conclusion stated in the passage?

(A) Thirty percent of the residential carbon monoxide gauges have been installed within the last fifteen years.

(B) The number of confirmed dangerous fume readings per year in homes with carbon monoxide gauges has increased in recent years.

(C) Not all carbon monoxide gauges report false carbon monoxide fume levels.

(D) The percentage of malfunctioning carbon monoxide gauges has increased in the last fifteen years.

(E) Properly functioning gauges do not, in themselves, decrease the risk that dangerous carbon monoxide fumes will enter people's homes.

36. Clearly, the strict policy adopted by prestigious Central University against cheating has worked. Since the university implemented its "no tolerance for cheating" policy two years ago, no student has dared to risk the harsh consequences for cheating. Central University has threatened to immediately shut down all competitive athletic activities if any student is caught cheating on an exam. Because students don't want to incur the wrath of the university and their fellow students, no has been caught cheating on an exam since the policy was implemented. This proves that the policy works.

Which of the following selections points out a flaw in the author's reasoning?

(A) Central University's athletic programs account for a significant percentage of the university's annual budget.

(B) Considering the problems Central University experienced in the years preceding the "no tolerance for cheating" policy, it is impossible to predict that students will never again cheat on exams at Central University.

(C) A teacher could accuse a student of cheating who is innocent, for instance, if a student's examination on computer disk was inadvertently copied onto another student's disk during the grading process; this could trigger a shut-down of athletic activities.

(D) Students have cheated in more sneaky ways outside of classroom exams, for example, by students paraphrasing their classmates' book reports.

(E) It is impossible to tell whether cheating incidents disappeared due to another reason, i.e., perhaps teachers implemented classroom testing procedures which made it extremely difficult to cheat on classroom tests.

Answers and Solutions to Exercise

1.	E	7.	D	13.	A	19.	A	25.	C	31.	C
2.	C	8.	C	14.	A	20.	B	26.	D	32.	A
3.	C	9.	E	15.	D	21.	C	27.	E	33.	A
4.	E	10.	B	16.	C	22.	A	28.	C	34.	B
5.	D	11.	D	17.	C	23.	E	29.	B	35.	D
6.	A	12.	E	18.	C	24.	A	30.	E	36.	E

1. The argument commits the fallacy of false correlation. The argument assumes the fear of the destructive affects of nuclear war has prevented a nuclear exchange. It does not take into account that other factors may have affected events, such as the economic value of remaining at peace. The answer is (E).

2. The argument generalizes *from* the survey *to* the general readership, so the reliability of the projection depends on how representative the sample is. At first glance, choice (A) seems rather good; 90% is an excellent return for any survey. However, it has a flaw—we don't know what percentage of the readers received the survey. Perhaps only a few questionnaires were sent out. Choice (B) is irrelevant since we don't know whether the decisions had the desired effect. Choice (C) points out that the survey *is* representative of the potential readership. Hence, it should be accurate. The answer is (C).

3. The answer is (C), which commits the true-but-irrelevant fallacy. The passage is about the commercial production of honey, not about pollination, nor for that matter about ornamental trees.

4. The argument generalizes from a sample to the general population. To weaken it, we must show that the sample is not representative of the general population. Now if only sociable and extroverted people are likely to submit to an interview, then the sample would not represent the general population. The answer, therefore, is (E).

  Don't make the mistake of choosing (D). Although it addresses the issue of the representativeness of the sample, it actually strengthens the argument by showing that the sample is typical of the general public.

5. The argument in the passage is circular (and filled with non-sequiturs). It is incumbent on the writer to give evidence or support for the conclusion. In this argument, though, the writer first states that democracy is the best government, the rest is merely "noise," until he restates the conclusion.

  Choice (A) is a reasonably valid causation argument—eliminate. (B) argues by generalization. Although it is of questionable validity, it is not circular because the conclusion, "it will happen again," is not stated, nor is it implicit in the premises—eliminate. (C) is not circular because the conclusion is mentioned only once—eliminate. (D) begins by stating, "I'm obsessed with volleyball." It does not, however, provide compelling evidence for that claim: training seven days a week, rather than indicating obsession, may be required for, say, members of the Olympic Volleyball Team. Further, the argument repeats the conclusion at the end. So it is circular in the same manner as the original. Hence (D) is our answer.

6. If all the alumni responded, the result would be a true contradiction. Suppose, however, only two alumni responded—one who scored in the top quarter of the class and one who did not. Then half of the respondents would have been in the top quarter of the class. The answer is (A).

7. This argument implies that since no planet has been discovered outside our solar system, none exist and therefore no life exists elsewhere in the universe. Hence the burden of proof is shifted from the arguer to the astronomers.

Although choice (A) weakens the argument, it has a flaw: the UFOs may not be life forms. Choice (B) is irrelevant. Although the argument states that the only life in the universe is on Earth, it is essentially about the possibility of life beyond our solar system. Choice (C) also weakens the argument. However, one percent of billions is still a significant number, and it is not clear whether one percent should be considered "common." Since a GMAT answer must be indisputable, there is probably a better answer-choice. The underlying premise of the argument is that since no other planets have been detected, no others exist. Choice (D) attacks this premise directly by stating that no planets outside our solar system have been discovered because we don't yet have the ability to detect them. This is probably the best answer, but we must check all the choices. Choice (E) strengthens the argument by implying that even if there were other planets it would be extremely unlikely that they would contain life. The answer, therefore, is (D).

At this time, I would like to discuss the relative difficulty of the problems we have been studying. You may feel that the arguments have been fairly easy. However, they have the same level of difficulty as those on the GMAT. When arguments are classified by the method of reasoning used, their underlying simplicity becomes apparent, and with sufficient study, everyone can master them.

8. You may have noticed that this argument uses the converse of the fallacy *"Confusing Necessary Conditions with Sufficient Conditions"* mentioned earlier. In other words, it assumes that something which is sufficient is also necessary. In the given argument, this is fallacious because some people may still score in the ninetieth percentile, though they studied less than four hours a day for one month. Therefore the answer is (C).

9. The argument draws an analogy between muscles and brains, and it concludes that since exercise improves the performance of one's muscles it will also improve the performance of one's brain. The answer is (E).

10. This argument commits the fallacy of false dichotomy. It assumes that workers have only two reactions to their work—either it's not challenging or it's too challenging. Clearly, there is a wide range of reactions between those two extremes. The answer is (B).

11. The opening sentence *"The senator has long held to the general principle that no true work of art is obscene"* is the premise of the senator's argument. It contains an embedded if-then statement: *If it is a work of art, then it is not obscene.* This can be diagrammed as follows:

$$A \longrightarrow \sim O$$

where A stands for "it is a work of art" and O stands for "it is obscene." Now, the senator justifies this principle by stating *"if these works really are obscene then they cannot be works of art,"* which can be symbolized as

$$O \longrightarrow \sim A$$

Applying the contrapositive to this diagram yields

$$A \longrightarrow \sim O$$

Now, we have already established that this is the premise of the argument. Hence the senator's argument is circular—he assumes what he seeks to establish. The answer is (D).

12. The argument starts out using the word "selfish" in the usual sense—self-centered. But in the phrase *"even the simplest 'unselfish' acts prove to be instances of selfish concern for the human species"* it uses the term to mean altruistic. Thus, the argument is equivocating. The answer is (E).

13. The argument unfairly assumes that Walcott's background prevents him from being objective. The answer is (A).

14. The argument commits the true-but-irrelevant fallacy. In this context, it is often called the *straw-man* fallacy. Instead of addressing Giselle's statement, Antoine sets up a statement that Giselle did not make and then attacks that straw-man. Arguing with someone who employs this tactic can be quite infuriating. Giselle's argument is that taxes should be increased to cut consumption of gasoline, <u>not</u> to raise revenue. Antoine ignores this fact and argues that if the government needs additional revenue (which Giselle does not claim) then the burden should be distributed evenly. The answer is (A).

15. This argument commits two errors. First, it takes a necessary condition to be sufficient. The statement *"All intelligent people are nearsighted"* means that for a person to be intelligent he or she must *necessarily* be nearsighted. But being nearsighted is not sufficient to make one intelligent. Second, the argument overstates the claim made in the premise. The premise is about intelligent people in general, not a subgroup of intelligent people—geniuses. Now in choice (D), the statement *"all tall people are happy"* has the same form as *"All intelligent people are nearsighted"*; the statement *"John is extremely happy"* has the same form as *"I am very nearsighted"*; and the statement *"so he must be extremely tall"* has the same form as *"So I must be a genius."* This shows a one-to-one correspondence between choice (D) and the given argument. Hence the answer is (D).

Choices (A) and (E) are eye-catchers because they mention nearsightedness. Remember the answer to a logical structure (logical flaw) argument will have the same structure as the given argument but will be in a different context.

(B) is second-best. It does commit the fallacy of taking a necessary condition to be sufficient, but it does not overstate the claim.

It's hard to give choice (C) any meaning.

16. The argument commits the fallacy of false dichotomy. It assumes that Susan has only two possibilities—a job that requires more education or no job. Clearly, there is a wide choice between these extremes. The answer is (C).

17. In the phrase "unstereotypical behavior" the word "stereotypical" is being used with the usual meaning. But in the phrase "stereotypical behavior" the word is being used with a different meaning. Thus, the argument equivocates. The answer is (C).

18. This is a straightforward question. It uses the example to illustrate how new technologies can both liberate us, by increasing productivity and therefore increasing the range of choices, and exposing us to danger. The answer is (C).

19. The answer is (A). The fact that Native American tribes use parts of the buffalo other than the meat is true but does not figure into this argument. The passage is about the production of meat from buffalo, not using parts of the buffalo other than the meat.

20. It is unwarranted to assume that all people can hold a job. Some people, because of a lack of education or training, or because of physical or mental handicap, will never be able to hold a job. These people may be considered chronically unemployed. The answer is (B).

21. Instead of discussing the proposal, the passage attacks the people supporting the proposal. The answer is (C).

22. The statement "It is clear that if her receiving tenure was justified, then Susan was much better than average or very loyal" can be symbolized as

$$T \rightarrow (BA \text{ or } VL)$$

where T stands for "tenure was justified," BA stands for "better than average," and VL stands for "very loyal." Now, the statement "it was shown that she was not better than average"—~BA—reduces the diagram to

$$T \rightarrow VL$$

The diagram tells us that if we assume that T is true, then, as the argument concludes, VL must be true. Hence, the argument assumes that Susan's tenure was justified. The answer is (A).

23. The argument unfairly assumes Monet's background prevents him from being objective. The answer is (E).

24. **(A) Yes.** Since one of the most difficult problems for many new homeowners is getting the down payment, this would solve that problem.

(B) No. This is speculation.

(C) No. The claim is too broad. The passage does not imply that the government has no means of influencing the savings rate. In fact, this proposal might increase savings.

(D) No. On the contrary, the opposite is likely true.

(E) No. The claim that the economy will be endangered is too strong.

25. Two conditions are introduced as necessary for achieving the goal of explaining psychic phenomena:

1) how mental images are sent and received over distance

2) how senders and receivers interact at a biological level

The first is partially fulfilled. The passage states that we know a substantial amount about receiving images and sending images. However, it does not mention anything about how senders and receivers interact. Hence the passage does not meet the very conditions it requires—this is an error in reasoning. The answer is (C).

26. The argument claims that an action is right only if it meets *both* the following criteria:

(1) It benefits another person.
(2) It is performed with that intent.

The argument also claims that an action that harms another person is wrong if it meets *either one* of the following criteria:

(1) The harm was intended.
(2) Reasonable thought would show that the action was likely to cause harm.

In choice (D), Linda should have realized that if she was watching television and the window was open, the cat might jump out. This satisfies the second criteria for a wrong action. Reasonable thought would have shown Linda the error of this choice. The answer is (D)[*].

As for the other choices, (A) is second best. The first part of (A), *"Frank wrote a proposal attempting to cause trouble between Linda and Jane,"* meets the first criterion for a wrong action. But, the remainder of the sentence doesn't relate to the second criterion.

In (B), even though the homeless man was injured, both criteria of the right action are satisfied. Who was at fault in the accident is besides the point.

In (C), even though the homeless man was injured, both criteria of the right action are satisfied. Again, who was at fault in the accident is besides the point. Both Fred (in (B)) and George performed actions that eventually met both criteria of a right action.

Choice (E) satisfies only the second criterion for a right action. However, since no harm was intended and could not be foreseen, this choice does not satisfy either criteria for a wrong action.

---

[*] Remember: Only one of the statements is an *either-or* construction need be true for the whole structure to be true.

27. The argument generalizes from a small sample to the population as a whole. If the sample is shown not to be representative of the general population, then the author's conclusion is weakened. If goal-oriented and serious-minded people were more likely to respond to the author's newspaper ad and agree to be studied, then this shows that the sample was not representative of the general population. Selection (E) points out this weakness and is the correct answer. If first-born people who were not serious-minded and goal-oriented simply didn't respond to the newspaper ad, then the sample studied by the author was not representative of first-borns in the general population. Rather, his sample consisted heavily of first-borns who had those two personality traits, and thus his conclusion would be seriously flawed.

Selection (C) is tempting. Although it goes to the core of the question, that is, how representative is the study sample of the general public, it actually strengthens the writer's argument. Selection (C) suggests that the newspaper ad was exposed to the general public as opposed to a more limited audience.

28. The author of this passage uses a false correlation in his argument. He assumes that subzero temperatures lead to heavy snow storms in the Sierra Nevada Mountains. The author doesn't recognize that some other weather condition might lead to both the subzero temperatures and the heavy snow storms. As you look over the answer selections, it appears that selection (C) makes the same mistake. In (C), it is assumed that participation in high school debate must influence students to attend law school. Instead, perhaps a student's interest in public affairs or some other subject *causes* her to take high school debate classes *and* go to law school. The argument doesn't contemplate another possible cause. Thus, selection (C) is the correct answer. The other selections also contain flaws, but they do not pattern the same defect contained in the passage.

29. If all of the men and women who had played basketball for Thompson High School ten years earlier had responded to the survey, then the results would indeed contradict the facts. However, if a disproportionately higher number of starting players responded to the survey, then the apparent contradiction can be easily explained. If only four people responded to the survey and three of them were in fact starting players, then 75% of those responding were starters. This would explain the apparent contradiction. The answer is Selection (B).

Selection (A) does not explain the contradiction; in fact, it seems to support the contradiction because it states that people reported their starting positions correctly. If instead Selection (A) had indicated that people's faulty memories accounted for inaccurate responses, then it would help explain the contradiction.

Selection (C) is too vaguely worded to be of much help. Perhaps only two starting players failed to respond while all the other starting players responded to the survey. This might help explain the contradiction if a larger percentage of non-starters failed to respond.

If Selection (D) were true, then it would not help resolve the contradiction. Rather, it would make the contradiction more inexplicable, particularly if we assume that the people who responded were correct in their responses.

Finally, Selection (E) might help explain the contradiction if good players who played later in the game were confused about whether they were classified as starters or not. But this answer is not the best answer. Selection (B) is by far the best answer.

30. This magazine ad draws parallels between one human capability—the mind—and two other human capabilities—physical stamina and breath control. It suggests that because competitive runners who condition properly can stretch their stamina and breath control, proper conditioning can also stretch this third capability—the mind. Selection (E) is the correct answer.

Selection (A) is incorrect because the ad doesn't discuss experiment results. Rather, the ad describes some general observations about competitive runners. Selection (B) is incorrect because the ad does not ridicule anyone. Selection (C) doesn't provide any details of what activities occur in a Puzzlemaster Club, so we don't know how club members might stretch their minds. Finally, selection (D) does not carefully document the benefits of competitive running. Like (A), selection (D) only makes general statements about men and women who run competitively.

31. The argument presumes that the comments in the evaluation forms are representative of all the people who attended the seminar. So the reliability of the preferences expressed in the evaluation forms depends upon how representative they are of all seminar participants. If the evaluation comments were representative of all participants, then reliance upon them would be warranted in determining the schedule for next year.

Upon first glance, selection (A) looks correct. But a close reading of selection (A) suggests there might be a problem with how many people actually received the evaluation forms. If the evaluation forms were handed out only at every other table, then the comments might be representative of only half of the participants. Selections (B) and (D) are irrelevant to the argument here. Selection (E) weakens the reliability of the results rather than strengthens them because it appears that a rather small number of people would have a big impact on the results. Selection (C) is correct because it strengthens the connection between the sample and the general population. It states that the percentage results would be the same for the sample who returned evaluation forms and for all people who attended the seminar.

32. One of the purposes of these studies, of course, is to find out whether or not students who think they are receiving the soothing heat pulses do better on their assignments than they would otherwise. If the psychologists knew ahead of time which students were receiving the pulses, they might subconsciously evaluate the students' assignments based on the results they anticipated. Only if both students and psychologists are shielded from knowing who is receiving the pulses can the students' assignments be graded and the results fairly tallied and analyzed. Selection (A) states that often students who receive the heat pulses become flushed in the face. This condition would be observable by both students and psychologists and would definitely frustrate one of the purposes of the experiment. Thus (A) is the correct answer. The other answer selections do not indicate how either students or psychologists would learn which students were actually receiving the heat pulses. Selection (C) is tempting, but it does not suggest that students know which of them will actually receive the pulses and which will not.

33. This passage is an example of an argument that generalizes from the purported success the reporting program has had in reducing burglary rates. In order for the conclusion to be valid, it must be based upon all other things being the same. If some other factor is instrumental in reducing the burglary rate, then concluding that the reporting program is responsible for the reduced crime rate would be weakened. Look at selection (A). If people who travel take additional precautions, for instance, if they installed motion detector lights on the outside of their homes, then perhaps increased lighting is responsible for lowering the burglary rate rather than the new travel reporting procedure.

The other selections are irrelevant to determining what caused the lower burglary rate in the community under study. What happens in other communities doesn't impact results in the subject community. Selection (C) is a tempting choice because the answer might suggest that the security guards and police are observant and taking action as a result of the reporting procedure. But (C) does not suggest a reason that might weaken the validity of the conclusion. Selection (A) does, and it is the correct answer.

34. Based on the conclusion of the passage, the author believes that convenience stores continued to sell tobacco products to minors but that they just weren't caught as often during the years 1990-1995. He places the blame for this at the feet of local enforcement agencies. Thus, selection (B) is assumed in the author's conclusion and is the correct selection. The author assumes that the number of tobacco sales to minors did not decrease. However, if in fact the number of tobacco sales to minors decreased from 1990-1995, then the author's conclusion is flawed. But that isn't the question here. Rather, the question asks about the assumptions the author has made in reaching his conclusion, valid or not. This question points out the importance of reading the specific question asked about the test passage.

Selections (A), (C) and (D) would perhaps explain why fewer citations were issued during 1990- 1995. But they are not assumptions the author has necessarily made in reaching his conclusion. The basic underpinning of the author's conclusion is his belief or assumption that convenience stores continued to sell tobacco products to minors at the same levels sold during the preceding five year period. Selection (E) is irrelevant to the conclusion because it has no bearing on why the number of citations decreased during 1990-1995.

35. If the percentage of malfunctioning carbon monoxide gauges is the same now as it was fifteen years ago, then the number of homes with confirmed dangerous fume levels would be twice as high today as it was then because there are twice as many gauges in homes now (50% is twice as high as 25%). But if the percentage of defective gauges has increased within the last fifteen years, then the number of confirmed dangerous readings would decrease, perhaps even to the numbers experienced fifteen years ago. But this would occur only if the proportion of defective gauges increased dramatically within the last fifteen years. Thus, selection (D) is the correct answer.

Since the assumption is based on the proportion of gauges that accurately read fume levels, selection (A) is irrelevant. Selection (B) is inconsistent with the author's conclusion. Selection (C) does not provide us with any information as to how many gauges are flawed. This statement would be true if even one gauge works properly. Selection (E) might be true, but it has no bearing on the author's conclusion and the assumptions upon which it is based.

36. The author makes a false correlation. He assumes that the only reason Central University has had no cheating incidents in the last two years is due to the new strict "no tolerance for cheating" policy. The author should have checked to see if other factors might have had an impact on cheating. Perhaps the faculty is so supportive of the university's athletic programs that they refused to report suspected cheating. Choice (E) provides another possible explanation why cheating has disappeared, the faculty's implementation of procedures which make it virtually impossible to cheat on a classroom exam. The correct answer is (E).

Choice (A) is irrelevant to the problem. While choice (B) might be true, it doesn't answer the question. It doesn't point out a flaw in the author's explanation for why no cheating occurred for two years. Choice (C) might also be true, but like (B), it doesn't explain why the author's reasoning is faulty. Finally, choice (D) contradicts the author's conclusion that no cheating occurred, but it doesn't point out a problem with the author's reasoning.

EXTRA ARGUMENTS

1. A prestigious golf association hosts a special tournament every year over the Labor Day weekend. It accepts into the tournament only those golfers who pay the entry fee by June 1 and who have won a major tournament during the previous calendar year. Fred Smith, a successful professional golfer for many years, paid the entry fee by June 1 to be in the Labor Day tournament. The golf association accepted Smith to play in the tournament.

Which one of the following conclusions flows logically from the paragraph?

(A) Smith won a major golf tournament the previous calendar year.

(B) Smith has played in the Labor Day tournament in previous years.

(C) Smith is well know for his professional golfing career.

(D) The golf association asked Smith to enter the tournament.

(D) Television coverage of the Labor Day tournament will focus on Smith's participation.

2. One theory of school governance can be pictured as an upside-down triangle. Students, teachers and the faculty/parent committee make up the body of the triangle, but the triangle has no point, that is, it has no school principal. Schools are run by the faculty/parent committee, which makes all significant decisions concerning academic standards, curriculum, discipline, extra-curricular activities, etc. As a result, under this theory, innovative teaching methods and progressive academic programs cannot be implemented.

The argument depends upon which one of the following assumptions?

(A) Innovative teaching methods and progressive academic programs are usually implemented by individual private schools, not by public school systems.

(B) Only principals will try new methods and programs.

(C) A person acting by himself is more likely to direct that new methods be tried than if he is acting as part of a committee.

(D) All school principals achieved their positions by taking academic risks.

(E) All innovative teaching methods and progressive academic programs encompass some risk.

3. Based upon studies conducted over the last two decades that show head injuries can be reduced if children wear bicycle helmets, some jurisdictions have passed laws requiring that children under the age of 12 wear helmets when they ride their bicycles. A surprising result has been observed, however. Even though a large number of children do wear bicycle helmets, more head injuries than expected are continuing to occur. And this is the result even though the studies have shown that wearing a helmet reduces the incidence of head injuries.

Which one of the following statements, if true, might suitably explain the unexpected finding?

(A) A large number of parents are not making their children wear bicycle helmets.
(B) More children are riding bicycles now than before bicycle helmets were introduced.
(C) Because bicycle helmets are quite expensive, many parents don't buy them for their children.
(D) Bicycle helmets were not designed to prevent all head injuries, so it is not surprising that head injuries still occur.
(E) Bicycle helmets do not work properly if they are not properly secured with the chin strap, and many children and their parents do not secure the chin strap properly.

4. Automobiles use 50 percent of all energy consumed in the United States. Since Congress has passed legislation requiring all cars built after 2002 to be twice as energy-efficient, eventually automobiles will consume only 25 percent.

The argument makes which of the following assumptions?

(A) Electric cars will not become widely available before 2002.
(B) The public will not be buying twice as many cars in 2002 as it is currently.
(C) As cars become more energy-efficient, the public does not increase its use of cars.
(D) Cars will actually be three times as energy-efficient in 2002.
(E) Cars will not be significantly more expensive in 2002.

5. Donna: For the most part, medical researchers agree that someone who regularly consumes large amounts of alcohol will probably have serious health problems.

Steve: Heavy drinking does not adversely impact one's health. My great uncle drank heavily for years and seemed in perfect health. In fact, he lived to be 87 years old.

Which one of the following is a major flaw in Steve's argument?

(A) Steve's argument uses only one example to attempt to refute a probable, not a foregone, result.
(B) Steve cites an example that medical researchers did not study.
(C) Steve's argument implies that there can be no correlation between heavy drinking and poor health.
(D) Steve's argument fails to acknowledge the possibility that his great uncle may not have been in good health after all.
(E) Steve doesn't indicate how long ago his great uncle lived so that different medical treatments can be taken into account.

6. Government take-over of foreign private industry in developing countries is generally regarded as an example by which the profits and benefits of a foreign enterprise can be redirected to improve the lot of native populations. The government's take-over of a large foreign mining operation in a fledgling African country a few years ago is a poor example of this principle, however. The government ousted the corporation in name, but the management team and workforce, most of whom were foreign, remained to operate the facility and were given a large pay increase. Profits from the operation were thus severely reduced. As a result, native projects did not receive large profits from the operation, nor were natives hired to replace foreign workers.

Which one of the following describes the type of argument used in the passage?

(A) The author supplies an example that supports the general principle.
(B) The author compares and contrasts two divergent examples of the same principle.
(C) The author weakens the argument by supplying evidence which undermines the argument.
(D) The author disproves the argument with one compelling example.
(E) The author explains why all general principles have flaws.

7. Edward Grieg: Your gallery is biased against my paintings. I have submitted twenty canvases in the last three years and you have not accepted any of them for display. You are punishing me because I won the Western Art award three years ago and your manager thought the award should have gone to his artist son.

Gallery owner: You are wrong! Our acceptance standards and display policies do not discriminate against you. Our staff covers the painters' names, so the review board does not know who the artist is when it determines which pieces of art will be accepted for display and sale. The review board would not know which paintings you submitted.

Which one of the following assumptions does the gallery owner make in his reply?

(A) The gallery manager holds no bad feelings about Edward Grieg winning the Western Art award over his artist son.

(B) Many artists submit their work to galleries without having any pieces accepted for display.

(C) The review board cannot recognize Edward Grieg's paintings without seeing his name on the canvases.

(D) The gallery accepts only nature studies, and Edward Grieg's paintings frequently portray people and interior settings.

(E) The review board has tended to favor oil paintings over the last several years and Edward Grieg more typically paints water colors.

8. Scientists have studied the effects of electromagnetic fields associated with high voltage power lines upon people whose homes are located within 300 yards of the lines. They have compared the growth rate of children who live near the lines with the growth rate of children who live elsewhere. Because they found no significant differences in the growth rates in the two study areas, they have concluded that electromagnetic fields are harmless.

Which one of the following, if true, would most seriously jeopardize the scientists' conclusion?

(A) The scientists did not consider other possible impacts upon growth rates.

(B) In studying people who lived near high voltage power lines, the scientists did not consider what type of housing those people lived in.

(C) The growth rates of children have changed considerably since the 1920s.

(D) People who live near electromagnetic fields suffer health problems that are not reflected in the growth rates of their children.

(E) As children get older, their activities tend to occur away from home more often.

9. Scientists used to think that pepper plants had the ability to produce an unlimited number of peppers. So long as the plant was properly fertilized and pollinated, and temperature, water and sunlight controlled, they believed pepper plants would continue to produce indefinitely. However, scientists have now learned that a pepper plant will not produce more than 200 peppers in its lifetime. If a pepper plant goes dormant due to a deficiency of light or water, for example, when reinvigorated, it will start producing peppers where it left off. But a normal pepper plant will produce no more than 200 peppers.

Assume the information in the passage is true, and assume that a pepper plant has been discovered that has produced 225 peppers and is still producing. If so, the still-producing pepper plant CANNOT fit which one of the following categories?

(A) An abnormal pepper plant flourishing under ideal temperature, humidity, water and light conditions.

(B) A normal pepper plant that went into a dormancy stage and then was revived.

(C) An abnormal pepper plant grown organically.

(D) A normal pepper plant grown from the seed of an abnormal pepper plant.

(E) A abnormal pepper plant grown in the lab without soil.

10. In the last decade, the use of bicycle helmets has increased tremendously, particularly among young children. Although bicycle helmets appear to be as sturdy and safe as football helmets, they are exempt from the safety standards the government has imposed upon the manufacture of football helmets. As a result, a child involved in a bicycle accident is more likely to suffer a serious head injury than is a child injured in a football game.

The argument depends upon which one of the following assumptions:

(A) Youngsters ride their bicycles less carefully when they wear helmets.

(B) The government has mandated a set of safety standards for manufacturers of bicycle helmets.

(C) Children are more likely to be injured riding their bicycles than playing football.

(D) More children ride bicycles than play football.

(E) Bicycle helmets are less likely to meet the government's helmet safety standards than are football helmets, which are subject to the safety standards.

11. Because of winter storm damage, the cost of a pound of apples at the local supermarket has increased 40 percent while the cost of a pound of oranges has increased 20 percent. Therefore, apples are now more expensive than oranges.

The argument's reasoning is questionable because the argument fails to rule out the possibility that

(A)   before the storm, apples had increased in price less than oranges

(B)   before the storm, apples had already been more expensive than oranges

(C)   before the storm, oranges were significantly more expensive than apples

(D)   apples will fall back to their normal price more quickly than oranges will

(E)   consumers will reduce their purchases of apples until the price falls to below that of oranges

12. Ten years ago, the total share of federal, state, and local taxes was 23 percent of the nation's Gross National Product. Now, that share has decreased to 21 percent.

Which one of the following can be properly inferred from the facts given above?

(A)   The total amount of federal, state, and local taxes paid now is less than the amount paid ten years ago.

(B)   On average, people now have a better standard of living than they did ten years ago.

(C)   The average taxpayer keeps a greater percentage of income for his own use than he did ten years ago.

(D)   Federal, state, and local governments have reduced the level of services they offer to constituents.

(E)   Inefficiency and fraud have been reduced in government services.

13. This past holiday weekend, the number of traffic accidents that occurred on a particular stretch of Highway 79 was 25 percent lower than the corresponding number of accidents last year in the same location over the same holiday weekend. This is good evidence that the Highway Patrol's publicity campaign against speeding has resulted in safer driving habits among motorists.

Which of the following is assumed in reaching the conclusion above?

(A)   Traffic accident rates on the particular stretch of Highway 79 will continue to drop as long as the Highway Patrol's publicity campaign continues.

(B)   The two holiday weekends cover exactly the same calendar dates.

(C)   Highway Patrol cars are patrolling the particular stretch of Highway 79 more frequently.

(D)   The total number of miles driven on the particular stretch of Highway 79 has not decreased 25% or more since last year.

(E)   A reduction in speeding is the only driving habit that has improved since last year.

14. Those who prepare a nation's armed forces can learn much from the world of college athletics. In athletic competition, winning teams are generally those whose members are well-trained as individuals and as a team, who are inspired by their coach, and who learn from mistakes made in games they lose. Similarly, a military that is successful needs well-trained soldiers who are confident about their capabilities, with each and every soldier learning from his mistakes in order to constantly improve his abilities.

Which of the following expresses the most serious weakness in the comparison drawn between athletes and soldiers?

(A) Coaches of athletic teams are often chosen for their ability to teach young adults, while admirals and generals often lack this capability.

(B) Not all college athletics are team sports. In sports such as tennis or gymnastics, competitors play as individuals.

(C) College athletic teams that lose games can review mistakes to improve each member's performance, but soldiers who make significant errors in battle may not survive to learn from their mistakes.

(D) Even those teams from the wealthiest colleges do not have the resources that a nation can marshal in developing its armed forces.

(E) Both men and women serve in modern armed forces, but there is no college athletic event in which men and women compete on the same team.

15. *Advertisement*: Do you want to be more energetic, vigorous, and physically fit? Take a daily supplement of Vita-plus, a vitamin combination containing additional proprietary ingredients. Our studies using hundreds of volunteers show that after just one week of taking 2 capsules daily, participants report being more energetic and alert on average than the average level reported by the National Institutes of Health survey of all Americans.

Which of the following would most strengthen the advertisement's claim that Vita-Plus supplements make one more energetic and alert?

(A) Those who voluntarily chose to take more than 2 capsules daily reported energy levels even greater than those who took only 2 capsules.

(B) The volunteers were randomly selected from all those who answered a newspaper advertisement and were willing to pay for the cost of the Vita-Plus capsules.

(C) At the beginning of the study, the volunteers' reports on alertness showed levels on average no different from the average level reported by the National Institutes of Health.

(D) Some of the volunteers were given capsules that solely contained cellulose, an inert substance with no vitamins or other health-inducing substances. Those volunteers also reported increased levels of alertness and energy.

(E) Some of the volunteers were given capsules that solely contained cellulose, an inert substance with no vitamins or other health-inducing substances. Those volunteers reported no increase in alertness or energy.

16. Over the last 20 years, psychologists have studied the effect of television viewing on the subsequent levels of violent behavior by young adults. The researchers studied children between the ages of 10 and 15 and found that those children who viewed an average of 6 hours or more of television daily were over four times as likely to be arrested for violent crimes when they were young adults than those young adults who as children watched less than 2 hours of television daily. Therefore, researchers concluded that television viewing causes increased levels of violent activity in young adults.

Which of the following would indicate a flaw in the researcher's conclusion?

(A) The researchers did not establish that those who watched more than six hours of television were watching shows that featured violence.

(B) The researchers did not establish that those who watched more violent shows were even more likely to be arrested than those who watched less violent shows.

(C) The researchers did not establish that some other reason, such as parental style, was not a factor for both the differences in television viewing and later arrest levels between the two groups.

(D) The researchers did not carry out their study long enough to determine if television viewing influences arrest records for those over the age of 40.

(E) The researchers did not establish that those who were arrested for violent crimes had actually caused serious injury to other people.

17. Here-and-There Import Company has always shown a quarterly loss whenever the value of the dollar falls 7% or more against the yen in the previous fiscal quarter. The company had a loss this quarter. Therefore, the dollar must have fallen at least 7% against the yen last quarter.

Which of the following exhibits a parallel pattern of reasoning as the argument above?

(A) Every Fourth of July weekend, the police strictly enforce parking regulations. I just received a parking ticket. Therefore, today must be July 4th.

(B) Whenever the circus comes to town, schoolchildren become very hard to control. Since little Susie is behaving very properly, the circus must not be in town.

(C) C & D bakery shows a profit whenever the local factory hires overtime workers. Because the factory has hired overtime workers, C & D bakery will show a profit.

(D) Whenever it has been sunny, Biff has gone to the beach, Therefore it must be sunny, because Biff has just left for the beach.

(E) Everybody who is somebody went to the awards banquet. Since Steve did not go to the awards banquet, he must not be anybody.

18. The news media is often accused of being willing to do anything for ratings. However, recent action by a television network indicates that the news media is sometimes guided by moral principle. This network had discovered through polling voters on the east coast that the Republican candidate for President had garnered enough votes to ensure victory before the polls closed on the west coast. However, the network withheld this information until the polls on the west coast closed so that the information would not affect the outcome of key congressional races.

Which one of the following most strengthens the argument?

(A) The network had endorsed the Republican candidate for President.

(B) The network expected its ratings to increase if it predicted the winner of the presidential race, and to decrease if did not predict the winner.

(C) A rival network did predict a winner of the presidential race before the polls on the west coast closed.

(D) The network believed that it would receive higher ratings by not predicting the winner of the presidential race.

(E) The network feared that predicting the winner of the presidential race could so anger Congress that it might enact legislation preventing all future polling outside of voting centers.

19. An oligarchy is a government run by a small, conservative faction. Often, oligarchies consist of families such as the Royal family in Saudi Arabia. Like the Royal family in Saudi Arabia, no one person in an oligarchy has the power to make a particular investment. Therefore, risky investments are never made by oligarchies.

The conclusion of the argument is valid if which one of the following is assumed?

(A) Not all oligarchies are run by families.

(B) The Royal family in Saudi Arabia has never made a risky investment.

(C) Conservative governments rarely make risky investments.

(D) Only liberal governments make risky investments.

(E) Only individuals make risky investments.

20. The first African slaves were brought to the Americas in the early 1600s, where their labor was used primarily for agricultural and household purposes. The institution of slavery in the New World presupposes not only the existence of slaves and owners, but also a system of laws in place which recognized and protected the practice of slavery. However, laws were not enacted, for example, declaring slaves the personal property of their owners and imposing punishments upon those who aided slaves in escape, until many years later.

If the sentences in the passage above are true, then they support which one of the following statements?

(A) Arguing that laws needed to be enacted recognizing and protecting the institution of slavery before the practice of slavery could have existed in the New World is to ignore historical fact.

(B) Prior to 1700, some of the Europeans who came to the New World enslaved native Indian populations.

(C) Slavery was practiced in many parts of the world before Africans were first brought to the New World as slaves.

(D) The prior existence of a supportive legal system is needed before an institutional practice can develop.

(E) One of the reasons slavery developed in the New World was the tremendous need for manual labor.

21. It is certain that at least as many migratory birds fly through Hilden every fall as fly through Paluska.

The conclusion above follows logically from which one of the following statements?

(A)   Paluska's average snowfall exceeds Hilden's by eight inches.

(B)   Residents of Paluska have been warned not to use bird feeders this fall to avoid spreading a disease diagnosed in dead birds found at a few feeders in Paluska.

(C)   Hilden is the county in which Paluska is located.

(D)   More natural predators have been reported in Hilden than in Paluska.

(E)   Hilden's population exceeds Paluska's population by 25,000.

22. The football coach at a midwestern college noticed that some of his players were frequently late to morning football practices and seemed somewhat lethargic after they did arrive. He directed his assistant coach to look into the matter. The assistant coach reported back that most of the late and less active players belonged to fraternities on campus which were renowned for their frequent and late-night parties. The head coach then prohibited all of his football players from being members of fraternities. He reported that this would ensure that his players would get to practice on time and that they would have more productive practice sessions.

The head coach's reasoning is not sound because he fails to establish which one of the following:

(A)   He fails to establish a system to monitor his players' fraternity membership and to impose penalties for those who do not follow his new rule.

(B)   He fails to establish that his players are physically big and strong enough to be successful football players.

(C)   He fails to establish that his new policy will ensure that at least some of his football players will go to bed at a more reasonable hour.

(D)   He fails to establish that his best football players did not belong to fraternities anyway.

(E)   He fails to establish that the success of the fraternity system will not suffer if the football players are precluded from becoming members.

Answers and Solutions

1.	A	7.	C	13.	D	19.	E
2.	B	8.	D	14.	C	20.	A
3.	E	9.	B	15.	E	21.	C
4.	C	10.	E	16.	C	22.	C
5.	A	11.	C	17.	D		
6.	C	12.	C	18.	B		

1. The golf association requires two conditions to be met before a golfer will be admitted into the Labor Day tournament. First, the golfer must pay the entry fee by June 1st. Second, the golfer must have won a major tournament during the previous calendar year. Since Smith was accepted to play in the Labor Day tournament, he must have won a major tournament the previous year. Selection (A) is correct.

2. The link that allows the conclusion to be drawn in this problem is the assumption that <u>only</u> principals will try new methods and programs. Under this theory of governance by committee, new methods and programs cannot be implemented. Thus, the theory assumes that only individuals will try new ideas. Selection (B) is the correct answer.

Selection (C) is a close second. It is supported by the argument, but it understates the breadth of the implied premise. The question states that in this theory of school governance, new methods and programs <u>cannot</u> be implemented, not that they are less likely to be implemented.

3. Before looking at the possible answers, take a few seconds to think about what might be causing the unexpected result. What could explain the continuing incidence of head injuries? Perhaps children's bicycle helmets were not designed properly or perhaps children are not using the helmets properly.

Now look at the possible selections. (A) and (C) are not correct because they are possible explanations for why children do not wear helmets. The passage asks why injuries still occur in children who do wear helmets. (B) is irrelevant; it does not explain why head injuries occur in children who wear bicycle helmets. The passage implies that bicycle helmets reduce the total incidence of head injuries, not that they eliminate all head injuries. Selection (D) contradicts this implication because it states that the same injuries occur that bicycle helmets help prevent. Selection (E) remains, and it is the correct selection. It also fits an explanation we thought of before reviewing the selections.

4. The answer is (C). Although cars may be twice as efficient in 2002 if the public uses cars more than twice as much as currently, then automobiles could use more (not less) than 50 percent of energy consumed in the United States.

5. Selection (A) is correct. Donna's argument does not state that people who drink heavily will necessarily have serious health problems, only that they will <u>probably</u> have serious health problems. Providing only one example to attempt to disprove a probable result is a serious flaw.

We do not know whether medical researchers considered the case of Steve's great uncle, so (B) is not correct. Steve's argument does not imply that there is no correlation between drinking and health. He is unequivocal that there is no correlation. Therefore, (C) is not correct. Steve's great uncle clearly didn't have any serious health problems because he appeared to be in good health and he lived to be 87, so selection (D) cannot be correct. Finally, (E) is irrelevant to the arguments presented. What type medical treatments were used is irrelevant to whether or not Steve's great uncle was affected by his heavy drinking.

6. (A) is not the correct answer. The example does not support the general principle—that government take-over of foreign business benefits native populations.

(B) is not correct, because the author presents only one example of the principle, not two divergent examples.

(C) is the correct selection. The author challenges the general principle by identifying a situation in which the native population did not benefit by government's take-over of a foreign business.

(D) is not correct. The author didn't completely disprove of the argument; he only provided one example that didn't follow the general principle.

(E) is not correct. In the passage, the author points out why this principle is not borne out by every situation, but he does not argue that all general principles have flaws.

7. (A) No. The gallery owner's argument attempts to directly refute this charge; it is not an assumption in his argument.

(B) No. The gallery owner's argument is based on the quality and style of Grieg's paintings, not the number of pieces of artwork Grieg or any other artist submits.

(C) Yes. The gallery owner states that the artists' names are covered so the review board could not know who the artists are. He or she assumes that the members of the review board will not be able to recognize Grieg's paintings if his name is not disclosed. But the review board could recognize Grieg's paintings based on his style, medium, subject matter, and other things.

(D) No. We have no information as to the type of artwork displayed in the gallery.

(E) No. Again, we have no information as to what type of art the review board has favored in the gallery in recent years.

8. (A) No. The study is concerned only with the effects of electromagnetic fields. Determining what other factors might impact children's growth rates would be irrelevant to determining the effects of electromagnetic fields.

(B) No. Since the growth rate for both groups of children was the same, it does not appear that the type of housing was important in determining the effects of exposure to electromagnetic fields.

(C) No. The growth rate of children in the 1920s is insignificant to the purpose of this study—to determine whether proximity to electromagnetic fields has any harmful effects.

(D) Yes. The scientists assume that the only negative effect from living near electromagnetic fields would be a lower growth rate in children. Perhaps adults and children who live near the lines suffer from other ailments. These would not be reflected in a study of children's growth rates and thus, this statement, if true, would seriously jeopardize the scientists' conclusion.

(E) No. Children's growth rates were the same, so how much time children who lived near the power lines spent at home would appear to be irrelevant.

9. The question asks us to find the category that COULD NOT APPLY to the plant. So if the passage could describe the high-bearing pepper plant, then it is not the correct choice.

(A) No. If the pepper plant has already produced 225 peppers and is still producing, it is not a normal pepper plant. So the high-bearing plant could be an abnormal pepper grown under ideal conditions.

(B) Yes. The high producing plant cannot be a normal pepper plant, even one that went into a dormancy stage and then was revived. The passage tells us that normal plants cannot produce more than 200 peppers, even those that go through a dormancy period. We know that the plant will "start producing peppers where it left off" and produce no more than 200 peppers.

(C) No. We know from the passage that no normal pepper plant can produce more than 200 peppers. If the plant is abnormal in any way, it cannot be a normal plant. So the high-bearing plant could be an abnormal plant grown organically.

(D) No. This plant was grown from the seed of an abnormal plant, so it could have produced the abnormal results reported.

(E) No. Again, we know that a plant that produces more than 200 peppers is abnormal. Therefore, the high-bearing plant could be an abnormal plant grown in the lab without soil.

10. (A) No. Nothing in the argument suggests that the incidence of accidents has gone up with the increased use of bicycle helmets.

(B) No. In fact, the argument states just the opposite—that bicycle helmets are exempt from the safety standards the government requires for football helmets.

(C) No. This argument concerns the incidence of <u>head</u> injuries in children who ride bicycles contrasted with children who play football. This selection encompasses all types of injuries, not merely head injuries. We have no information about the incidence of other types of injuries sustained in these activities, i.e., broken bones, sprained ankles, etc.

(D) No. Again, the author provides no information as to how many children play football and ride bicycles. And the conclusion in the passage deals with the probability of head injuries in children who participate in both activities, not the number of children who participate in these activities.

(E) Yes. The argument implies that because bicycle helmets are exempt from the government safety standards for football helmets, children will more likely be injured in bicycle accidents. However, bicycle helmets might be exempt from the standards because the government believes bicycle helmets already meet the safety standards applicable to football helmets. We don't know the reason bicycle helmets are not covered by the standards. The implication in this argument is that bicycle helmets are not as safe as football helmets, and therefore, they are less likely to meet the football helmet safety standards.

11. By concluding that apples are more expensive than oranges because the cost of apples went up a greater percentage, we implicitly assume that oranges were not much more expensive initially. For example, if apples were initially $1 per pound and increased 40% to $1.40 per pound while oranges were originally $2 per pound and increased 20% to $2.40 per pound, apples would not be more expensive. The answer is (C).

As for (A), whatever increase in prices occurred before the storm has no effect on the results after the storm. With (B), if apples were previously more expensive and increased in price a greater percentage than oranges, they would be even more expensive. Finally, choices (D) and (E) have no impact on the current prices of apples and oranges.

12. If the various levels of government collect a smaller share of the GNP through taxes, then the average taxpayer keeps a larger share. The answer is (C).

Be careful of choice (A): it commits an error by failing to distinguish between percentage and amount. While the percentage share of taxes has decreased, the overall amount of tax revenue could have increased if the GNP is larger than it was ten years ago.

The other choices can not be logically inferred from the passage. Each choice offers a possible cause or effect of the tax reduction, but none of these must occur.

13. This is a case of All-Things-Being-Equal. In order to attribute the reduction in accidents to the Highway Patrol's Publicity campaign, we must remove the possibility of alternative explanations. Choice (D) removes one such explanation—that the decrease in accidents could have been due to a decrease in driving on the highway. The answer is (D).

14. The passage draws an analogy between armed forces and college athletic teams, and concludes that training methods which work in college sports will be effective in the military as well. There are three training methods listed for a successful sports team:

1) trained as individuals and as team
2) inspired by their coach
3) learn from their mistakes

Reasoning by analogy is not made invalid by minor differences between the two items being compared. Choices (A), (B), (D), and (E) point out such differences but do not detract from the essence of the analogy. However, choice (C) states that it may not be possible for soldiers to learn from their mistakes, a definite distinction between sports and the military, and one that weakens the argument. The answer is (C).

15. To strengthen a claim that a substance has a certain health effect, we often test the substance against a placebo, an inert substitute. If the substance tested produces results that the placebo does not, we attribute these differences to the action of the substance. In choice (E), some of the volunteers were given cellulose instead of Vita-plus, and these volunteers did not show the same increased energy as those who received Vita-plus. This strengthens the conclusion that Vita-plus increased one's energy. The answer is (E).

Choice (A) suffers from the weakness that those who believe in the efficacy of Vita-plus and take increased doses may convince themselves that it truly has an effect. Choice (B) shows the same weakness: maybe only "true believers" are willing to pay for the cost of the capsules.

As for (C), this choice is required to properly compare the two levels, but it is not sufficient to show Vita-plus caused any differences. Finally, choice (D) weakens the claim by stating that another substance shows the same results as Vita-plus.

16. This argument claims that a causal relationship exists between television viewing and arrest levels of young adults because the two situations are correlated. However, the argument does not rule out the possibility that both of these situations may be caused by a third, independent event. The answer is (C).

The other choices may all be true, but they do not impact the researchers' conclusion.

17. With parallel pattern of reasoning questions, we first identify the structure and validity of the passage, and then consider each answer-choice in turn.

The argument in the passage may be diagrammed as follows:

Dollar drops —> Quarterly loss
Quarterly loss _____
∴ Dollar dropped

This argument is invalid since it commits the fallacy of affirming the conclusion.

Consider choice (D):

Sunny —> Biff goes to beach
Biff goes to beach _____
∴ Sunny

The answer is (D).

As for (A), a diagram shows:

4th of July weekend —> Parking enforced
Parking enforced _____
∴ July 4th

This appears to have the same structure as the original passage, but it is in fact much stronger. While the premise in (A) discusses the 4th of July weekend, the choice concludes the day is July 4th itself.

Choices (B) and (C) exhibit valid reasoning and therefore can not be parallel to the original argument. Finally, it's hard to know exactly what choice (E) is saying.

18. The suppressed premise in this argument is that the network hurt itself by not predicting the winner of the presidential race, or at least did not help itself. To strengthen the argument, we need to show that this assumption is true. Choice (B) implies that this is the case by stating that the network expected to lose ratings if it did not predict a winner. Hence the answer is (B).

19. If risky investments are never made by oligarchies because no one person has the power to make a particular investment, then it must be the case that only individuals make risky investments. The answer is (E).

20. (A) **Yes.** According to the passage, the practice of slavery began much sooner than laws were enacted to protect its practice. Thus, to argue that laws needed to be in place *first* is to ignore historical fact.

(B) No. The passage is concerned with the importation of African slaves and when laws were first enacted concerning slavery. We don't know the timing of slavery laws relative to when Europeans enslaved native Indian populations, so this statement is not supported by the passage.

(C) No. Whether or not slavery was practiced elsewhere prior to the importation of African slaves is irrelevant to the question—which statement is supported by the passage with respect to the institution of slavery in the New World?

(D) No. This statement is directly contradicted by the passage. The facts set forth in the passage prove just the opposite—that slavery was practiced long before a supportive legal system developed.

(E) No. Again, this statement is irrelevant to the question. The reasons slavery developed in the New World are not significant to the timing of a legal system supportive of slavery.

21. (A) No. We are not given any information as to how average snowfall might impact migratory bird flight patterns.

(B) No. We don't know whether migratory birds are susceptible to the disease or if they might in fact be carriers of the disease. If they are carriers of the disease, then the fact that the disease has been diagnosed in Paluska would not necessarily affect the levels of migratory birds flying through either Hilden or Paluska.

(C) Yes. If Paluska is a town in Hilden County, then birds that fly through Paluska are also flying through Hilden County. So at least as many birds fly through Hilden as fly through Paluska. The following diagram might be helpful in conceptualizing this problem.

(D) No. Knowing that more natural predators have been reported in Hilden does not verify that there actually are more predators in Hilden. Furthermore, we don't know the sizes of Hilden and Paluska. If Paluska is very small and Hilden is very large, the fact that more predators have been sighted in Hilden would not be significant to this passage.

(E) No. Again, while population density might impact migratory bird patterns, we don't know how big Paluska and Hilden are. If Hilden's area exceeds Paluska's area significantly, the fact that Hilden has a bigger population might not affect the numbers of migratory birds that fly through each place.

22. (A) No. This answer deals with enforcement of the new policy, not whether the new policy is likely to change the unwanted behavior in the first place.

(B) No. This answer is irrelevant to the issue—behavior the coach wishes to change.

(C) Yes. The coach assumes that if his players do not belong to fraternities, they will not have other distractions at night to keep them from getting a reasonable night's sleep. Many other reasons may keep the players up late at night—non-fraternity parties, library research, part time jobs, etc.

(D) No. We know from the passage that only some of the football players were late and lethargic at practice and that many of these later players were fraternity members. Perhaps his best players were fraternity members who showed up to practice on time, but we cannot tell this from the passage.

(E) No. This answer is also irrelevant to the issue. The impact of the coach's rule upon the fraternity system is unimportant in this scenario.

SENTENCE CORRECTION

- **INTRODUCTION**

- **PRONOUN ERRORS**

- **SUBJECT-VERB AGREEMENT**

- **MISPLACED AND REDUNDANT MODIFIERS**   *read by*

- **FAULTY PARALLELISM**

- **FAULTY VERB TENSE**

- **IDIOM & USAGE**

Introduction

The field of grammar is huge and complex—tomes have been written on the subject. This complexity should be no surprise since grammar deals with the process of communication.

GMAT grammar tests only a small part of standard written English. Grammar can be divided into two parts: Mechanics and Usage.

Mechanics concerns punctuation, capitalization, etc. It is not tested on the GMAT nearly as often as is usage. So don't spend too much time worrying whether the comma is in the right place or whether a particular word should be capitalized. (For a thorough discussion of punctuation, see the Analytical Writing Assessment chapter.)

Usage concerns how we choose our words and how we express our thoughts. In other words, are the connections between the words in a sentence logically sound, and are they expressed in a way that conforms to standard idiom? This is the part of grammar that is most important on the GMAT. Six major categories of usage are tested:

> Pronoun Errors
> Subject-Verb Agreement
> Misplaced and Redundant Modifiers
> Faulty Parallelism
> Faulty Verb Tense
> Faulty Idiom

To do well on this portion of the test, you need to know certain basic components of English grammar and usage. The more familiar you are with the parts of speech (nouns, verbs, pronouns, adjectives, adverbs, and so forth) and how they function in a sentence, the easier the test will be for you.

Pronoun Errors

A pronoun is a word that stands for a noun, known as the antecedent of the pronoun. The key point for the use of pronouns is this:

 Pronouns must agree with their antecedents in both number (singular or plural) and person (1st, 2nd, or 3rd).

must be in sentence

Example:

Steve has yet to receive his degree.

Here, the pronoun *his* refers to the noun *Steve*.

Following is a list of the most common pronouns:

PRONOUNS

Singular	Plural	Both Singular and Plural
I, me	we, us	any
she, her	they	none
he, him	them	all
it	these	most
anyone	those	more
either	some	who
each	that	which
many a	both	what
nothing	ourselves	you
one	any	
another	many	
everything	few	
mine	several	
his, hers	others	
this		
that		

Reference

 A pronoun should be plural when it refers to two nouns joined by *and*.

Example:

Jane and Katarina believe *they* passed the final exam.

The plural pronoun *they* refers to the compound subject, *Jane and Katarina*.

504

Note! **A pronoun should be singular when it refers to two nouns joined by *or* or *nor*.**

Faulty Usage

Incorrect: Neither Jane *nor* Katarina believes *they* passed the final.

Correct: Neither Jane *nor* Katarina believes *she* passed the final.

 Note! **A pronoun should refer to one and only one noun or compound noun.**

This is probably the most common error on the GMAT. If a pronoun follows two nouns, it is often unclear which of the nouns the pronoun refers to.

Faulty Usage

The breakup of the Soviet Union has left *nuclear weapons* in the hands of unstable, nascent *countries*. It is imperative to world security that *they* be destroyed.

Although one is unlikely to take the sentence to mean that the countries must be destroyed, that interpretation is possible from the structure of the sentence. It is easily corrected:

The breakup of the Soviet Union has left *nuclear weapons* in the hands of unstable, nascent *countries*. It is imperative to world security that ***these weapons*** be destroyed.

Faulty Usage

In Somalia, *they* have become jaded by the constant warfare.

This construction is faulty because *they* does not have an antecedent. The sentence can be corrected by replacing *they* with *people*:

In Somalia, *people* have become jaded by the constant warfare.

Better:

The people of Somalia have become jaded by the constant warfare.

 Note! **In addition to agreeing with its antecedent in number, a pronoun must agree with its antecedent in person.**

Faulty Usage

One enters this world with no responsibilities. Then comes school, then work, then marriage and family. No wonder *you* look longingly to retirement.

In this sentence, the subject has changed from *one* (third person) to *you* (second person). To correct the sentence either replace *one* with *you* or vice versa:

You enter this world with no responsibilities. Then comes school, then work, then marriage and family. No wonder *you* look longingly to retirement.

One enters this world with no responsibilities. Then comes school, then work, then marriage and family. No wonder *one* looks longingly to retirement.

Warm-Up Drill I

> In each of the following sentences, part or all of the sentence is underlined. The answer-choices offer five ways of phrasing the underlined part. If you think the sentence as written is better than the alternatives, choose A, which merely repeats the underlined part; otherwise choose one of the alternatives. Answers and solutions begin on page 532.

1.   Had the President's Administration not lost the vote on the budget reduction package, his first year in office would have been rated an A.

   (A)   Had the President's Administration not lost the vote on the budget reduction package, his first year in office would have been rated an A.
   (B)   If the Administration had not lost the vote on the budget reduction package, his first year in office would have been rated an A.
   (C)   Had the President's Administration not lost the vote on the budget reduction package, it would have been rated an A.
   (D)   Had the President's Administration not lost the vote on its budget reduction package, his first year in office would have been rated an A.
   (E)   If the President had not lost the vote on the budget reduction package, the Administration's first year in office would have been rated an A.

2.   The new law requires a manufacturer to immediately notify their customers whenever the government is contemplating a forced recall of any of the manufacturer's products.

   (A)   to immediately notify their customers whenever the government is contemplating a forced recall of any of the manufacturer's products.
   (B)   to immediately notify customers whenever the government is contemplating a forced recall of their products.
   (C)   to immediately, and without delay, notify its customers whenever the government is contemplating a forced recall of any of the manufacturer's products.
   (D)   to immediately notify whenever the government is contemplating a forced recall of any of the manufacturer's products that the customers may have bought.
   (E)   to immediately notify its customers whenever the government is contemplating a forced recall of any of the manufacturer's products.

3.   World War II taught the United States the folly of punishing a vanquished aggressor; so after the war, they enacted the Marshall Plan to rebuild Germany.

   (A)   after the war, they enacted the Marshall Plan to rebuild Germany.
   (B)   after the war, the Marshall Plan was enacted to rebuild Germany.
   (C)   after the war, the Marshall Plan was enacted by the United States to rebuild Germany.
   (D)   after the war, the United States enacted the Marshall Plan to rebuild Germany.
   (E)   after the war, the United States enacted the Marshall Plan in order to rebuild Germany.

4. In the 1950's, integration was an anathema <u>to most Americans; now, however, most Americans accept it as desirable.</u>

    (A) to most Americans; now, however, most Americans accept it as desirable.
    (B) to most Americans, now, however, most Americans accept it.
    (C) to most Americans; now, however, most Americans are desirable of it.
    (D) to most Americans; now, however, most Americans accepted it as desirable.
    (E) to most Americans. Now, however, most Americans will accept it as desirable.

5. Geologists in California have discovered a fault near the famous San Andreas Fault, <u>one that they believe to be a trigger for</u> major quakes on the San Andreas.

    (A) one that they believe to be a trigger for
    (B) one they believe to be a trigger for
    (C) one that they believe triggers
    (D) that they believe to be a trigger for
    (E) one they believe acts as a trigger for

6. A bite from the tsetse fly invariably paralyzes <u>its victims unless an antidote is administered</u> within two hours.

    (A) its victims unless an antidote is administered
    (B) its victims unless an antidote can be administered
    (C) its victims unless an antidote was administered
    (D) its victims unless an antidote is administered to the victims
    (E) its victims unless they receive an antidote

Subject-Verb Agreement

Within a sentence, there are certain requirements for the relationship between the subject and the verb.

 The subject and verb must agree both in number and person.

Example:

> We have surpassed our sales goal of one million dollars.

Here, the first person plural verb *have* agrees with its first person plural subject *we*.

Note: ironically, third person <u>singular</u> verbs often end in *s* or *es*:

> He *seems* to be fair.

 Intervening phrases and clauses have no effect on subject-verb agreement.

Example:

> Only one of the President's nominees was confirmed.

Here, the singular verb *was* agrees with its singular subject *one*. The intervening prepositional phrase *of the President's nominees* has no effect on the number or person of the verb.

Collective nouns followed by intervening phrases are particularly easy to miss.

Example:

> The *content* of the boxes *is* what she wants.
>
> The *meaning* of her sentences *is* not clear.
>
> A *group* of lions *is* called a "pride."

Be careful when a simple subject is followed by a phrase beginning with *as well as, along with, together with, in addition to,* or a similar expression. Be sure to make the verb agree with the simple subject, not with a noun in the intervening phrase.

Example:

> Our *Senator*, along with most congressmen, *opposes* the bill.

Here, the singular verb *opposes* agrees with its singular subject *Senator*. The intervening phrase *along with most congressmen* has no effect on the number or person of the verb.

508

When the subject and verb are reversed, they still must agree in both number and person.

Example:

Attached are copies of the contract.

Here, the plural verb *are attached* agrees with its plural subject *copies*. The sentence could be rewritten as

Copies of the contract *are attached.*

Although it may seem obvious that when reversing the normal order of the subject and the verb their agreement must be preserved, this *obvious* error is easy to miss.

Example (wrong):

Attached to the email *is* the graphic file and the agreement.

This ungrammatical sentence sounds natural perhaps because its error is committed so often. The compound subject of the sentence is *the graphic file and the agreement*, which must take a plural verb:

Attached to the email *are* the graphic file and the agreement.

With the natural order of the subject first and then the verb in this sentence, one would be unlikely to mistakenly choose a singular verb:

The graphic file and the agreement *are attached* to the email.

Be careful when an inverted subject verb order is introduced by construction such as *there is, there are, here is, here are*. In these constructions, the actual subject follows the verb.

Example:

There *is* much *disagreement* between the parties.

The word *there* introduces the singular verb *is*, which agrees with the singular subject of the sentence *disagreement*.

In these constructions, it tempting to mistakenly use a singular verb before the plural subject.

Example (wrong):

There *is a wallet and a key* on the dresser.

The compound (plural) subject of this sentence is *a wallet and a key*. It requires a plural verb:

There *are a wallet and a key* on the dresser.

This error occurs often in daily speech because the verb has to be chosen before we fully form the subject in our minds. Since the first part of the compound subject *a wallet* is singular, we naturally introduce it with the singular verb *is*.

Warm-Up Drill II

Answers and solutions begin on page 535.

1. <u>The rising cost</u> ~~of government bureaucracy~~ have made it all but impossible to reign in the budget deficit.

    (A)   The rising cost
    (B)   Since the rising costs
    (C)   Because of the rising costs
    (D)   The rising costs
    (E)   Rising cost

    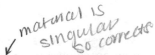
    add in extra words

2. In a co-publication agreement, ownership ~~of both the material and~~ <u>its means of distribution are equally shared by the parties.</u>

    material is singular so correct

    (A)   its means of distribution are equally shared by the parties.
    (B)   its means of distribution are shared equally by each of the parties.
    (C)   its means of distribution is equally shared by the parties.
    (D)   their means of distribution is equally shared by the parties.
    (E)   the means of distribution are equally shared by the parties.

3. The rise in negative attitudes ~~toward foreigners~~ <u>indicate that the country is becoming less tolerant, and therefore that</u> the opportunities are ripe for extremist groups to exploit the illegal immigration problem.

    (A)   indicate that the country is becoming less tolerant, and therefore that
    (B)   indicates that the country is becoming less tolerant, and therefore
    (C)   indicates that the country is becoming less tolerant, and therefore that
    (D)   indicates that the country is being less tolerant, and therefore
    (E)   indicates that the country is becoming less tolerant of and therefore that

4. <u>The harvest</u> ~~of grapes in the local valleys~~ decreased ~~in 1990~~ for the third straight year but <u>were</u> still ~~at a robust level.~~

    (A)   The harvest of grapes in the local valleys decreased in 1990 for the third straight year but were
    (B)   The harvest of grapes in the local valleys began to decrease in 1990 for the third straight year but were
    (C)   In 1990, the harvest of grapes in the local valleys decreased for the third straight year but were
    (D)   The harvest of grapes in the local valleys decreased for the third straight year in 1990 but was
    (E)   The harvest of grapes in the local valleys began decreasing in 1990 for the third straight year but was

subject (handwritten annotation)

5. Each of the book's protagonists—Mark Streit, Mary Eby, and Dr. Thomas—has a powerful, dynamic personality.

    (A) Each of the book's protagonists—Mark Streit, Mary Eby, and Dr. Thomas—has
    (B) Each of the book's protagonists—Mark Streit, Mary Eby, and Dr. Thomas—have
    (C) All the book's protagonists—Mark Streit, Mary Eby, and Dr. Thomas—has
    (D) Mark Streit, Mary Eby, and Dr. Thomas—the book's protagonists—each has
    (E) Each of the book's protagonists—Mark Streit, Mary Eby, and Dr. Thomas—could have had

plural. (handwritten annotation)

6. More important than winning is developing the ability to work with others and developing leadership skills.

    (A) More important than winning is developing the ability to work with others and developing leadership skills.
    (B) More important than winning are the ability to work with others and leadership skills.
    (C) Developing the ability to work with others and developing leadership skills is more important than winning.
    (D) More important than winning are developing the ability to work with others and developing leadership skills.
    (E) More important than winning has been the development of the ability to work with others and the development leadership skills.

7. There is a number of solutions to the problem of global warming that have not been considered by this committee.

    (A) There is a number of solutions
    (B) There are a number of solutions
    (C) There was a number of solutions
    (D) There were a number of solutions
    (E) There have been a number of solutions

Misplaced and Redundant Modifiers

A modifier is a phrase or a clause that describes something. A misplaced modifier, therefore, is one that describes the wrong item in a sentence, often creating an illogical statement.

 As a general rule, a modifier should be placed as close as possible to what it modifies.

Example:

Following are some useful tips for protecting your person and property from the FBI.

As written, the sentence implies that the FBI is a threat to your person and property. To correct the sentence put the modifier *from the FBI* next to the word it modifies, *tips*:

Following are some useful tips from the FBI for protecting your person and property.

Example:

I saw the senators debating while watching television.

As written, the sentence implies that the senators were debating and watching television at the same time. To improve the sentence, put the modifier *while watching television* next to the word it modifies, *I*:

While watching television, I saw the senators debating.

The sentence can be made even clearer and more direct without the modifier:

I saw the senators debating on television.

 When a phrase begins a sentence, make sure that it modifies the subject of the sentence.

Example:

Coming around the corner, a few moments passed before I could recognize my old home.

As worded, the sentence implies that the moments were coming around the corner. The sentence can be corrected as follows:

As I came around the corner, a few moments passed before I could recognize my old home.
or
Coming around the corner, I paused a few moments before I could recognize my old home.

Example:

When at summer camp, my family moved.

As worded, the sentence implies that the family was at summer camp. The sentence can be corrected as follows:

When I was at summer camp, my family moved.

When a prepositional phrase begins a sentence, make sure that it modifies the *true* subject of the phrase.

This error is easy to miss.

Example:

> As the top programmer, I feel that only Steve can handle this project.

Who is the top programmer in this sentence, I or Steve? Since only Steve can handle the project, it's likely that he is the top programmer. The sentence can be corrected as follows:

> As the top programmer, only Steve can handle this project.

or

> I feel that as the top programmer only Steve can handle this project.

 When a verbal phrase ends a sentence, make sure that it cannot modify more than one idea in the main clause.

This error can be rather subtle.

Example:

> Oddly, the senator known to be a strong closer performed poorly in the final two debates, causing a drop in his poll numbers.

There are two conflicting ideas expressed in the main clause of this sentence: the senator is a strong closer and he did poorly in the final debates. As written, it is not clear which one caused the drop in his poll numbers (though logically the drop was caused by his poor performance). The sentence can be made clearer as follows:

> Though known to be a strong closer, the senator's poor performance in the final two debates caused his poll numbers to drop.

or

> The senator's poor performance in the final two debates caused his poll numbers to drop. Oddly, he is known to be a strong closer.

REDUNDANT MODIFIERS

Be careful not to modify a word with a word that means the same thing.

Example:

> The old heirlooms are priceless.

By definition, heirlooms (valuables handed down from generation to generation) are old. The sentence can be corrected by dropping the word "old":

> The heirlooms are priceless.

Warm-Up Drill III

Answers and solutions begin on page 538.

1. By focusing on poverty, the other causes of crime—such as the breakup of the nuclear family, changing morals, the loss of community, etc.—have been overlooked by sociologists.

   (A) the other causes of crime—such as the breakup of the nuclear family, changing morals, the loss of community, etc.—have been overlooked by sociologists.
   (B) the other causes of crime have been overlooked by sociologists—such as the breakup of the nuclear family, changing morals, the loss of community, etc.
   (C) there are other causes of crime that have been overlooked by sociologists—such as the breakup of the nuclear family, changing morals, the loss of community, etc.
   (D) crimes—such as the breakup of the nuclear family, changing morals, the loss of community, etc.—have been overlooked by sociologists.
   (E) sociologists have overlooked the other causes of crime—such as the breakup of the nuclear family, changing morals, the loss of community, etc.

2. Using the Hubble telescope, previously unknown galaxies are now being charted.

   (A) Using the Hubble telescope, previously unknown galaxies are now being charted.
   (B) Previously unknown galaxies are now being charted, using the Hubble telescope.
   (C) Using the Hubble telescope, previously unknown galaxies are now being charted by astronomers.
   (D) Using the Hubble telescope, astronomers are now charting previously unknown galaxies.
   (E) With the aid of the Hubble telescope, previously unknown galaxies are now being charted.

3. The bitter cold the Midwest is experiencing is potentially life threatening to stranded motorists unless well-insulated with protective clothing.

   (A) stranded motorists unless well-insulated
   (B) stranded motorists unless being insulated
   (C) stranded motorists unless they are well-insulated
   (D) stranded motorists unless there is insulation
   (E) the stranded motorist unless insulated

4. Traveling across and shooting the vast expanse of the Southwest, in 1945 Ansel Adams began his photographic career.

   (A) Traveling across and shooting the vast expanse of the Southwest, in 1945 Ansel Adams began his photographic career.
   (B) In 1945, Ansel Adams began his photographic career, traveling across and shooting the vast expanse of the Southwest.
   (C) Having traveled across and shooting the vast expanse of the Southwest, in 1945 Ansel Adams began his photographic career.
   (D) Ansel Adams, in 1945 began his photographic career, traveling across and shooting the vast expanse of the Southwest.
   (E) Traveling across and shooting the vast expanse of the Southwest, Ansel Adams began his photographic career in 1945.

5. The Harmony virus will destroy <u>a computer system unless inoculated</u> by an anti-harmony program.

    (A) a computer system unless inoculated
    (B) a computer system unless the system is inoculated
    (C) a computer system unless it is inoculated → unclear
    (D) a computer system unless inoculation occurred
    (E) a system unless it's being inoculated

6. <u>As head of the division, we believe</u> you should make the decision whether to retake the rebel stronghold.

    (A) As head of the division, we believe
    (B) Seeing as you are the head of the division, we believe
    (C) Being the head of the division, we believe
    (D) As head of the division, we are inclined to believe
    (E) We believe that as head of the division

7. <u>It is well established that the death of a parent during childhood can cause insecurity in adults.</u>

    (A) It is well established that the death of a parent during childhood can cause insecurity in adults.
    (B) It is well established that the death of a parent when a child can cause insecurity in adults.
    (C) It is well established that the death of a parent occurring when a child can cause insecurity in adults.
    (D) It is well established that people who during childhood experience the death of a parent can be insecure as adults.
    (E) That people who during childhood experience the death of a parent can be insecure as adults is well established.

8. <u>Based on the yarns of storytellers, linguistic archeologists are compiling a written history of Valhalla and are realizing</u> that much of what was considered myth is in fact true.

    (A) Based on the yarns of storytellers, linguistic archeologists are compiling a written history of Valhalla and are realizing
    (B) Basing on the yarns of storytellers, linguistic archeologists are compiling a written history of Valhalla and are realizing
    (C) Using the yarns of storytellers, linguistic archeologists are compiling a written history of Valhalla and are realizing
    (D) Based on the yarns of storytellers, linguistic archeologists are compiling a written history of Valhalla and are coming to the realization
    (E) Deriving it from the yarns of storytellers, linguistic archeologists are compiling a written history of Valhalla and are realizing

Faulty Parallelism

Faulty parallelism occurs when units with similar functions in a sentence are not written with similar structures. For example, the verbs in a sentence should have the same tense if the subject performs the actions simultaneously.

 For a sentence to be parallel, similar elements must be expressed in similar form.

 When two adjectives modify the same noun, they should have similar forms.

Example:

The topology course was both *rigorous* and *a challenge*.

Since both *rigorous* and *a challenge* are modifying *course*, they should have the same form:

The topology course was both *rigorous* and *challenging*.

 When a series of adjectives modify the same noun, they should have similar forms.

Example:

The interim Prime Minister is *strong, compassionate,* and *wants* to defeat the insurgency with a minimum of civilian casualties.

The adjectives *strong* and *compassionate* begin a series of adjectives modifying the Prime Minister. Hence, the verb clause *wants to defeat . . .* is out of balance. The sentence can be corrected by turning the verb clause into an adjective clause:

The interim Prime Minister is *strong, compassionate,* and *determined* to defeat the insurgency with a minimum of civilian casualties.

Notice that the clause *determined to defeat . . .* has much more structure and information than the single word modifiers *strong* and *compassionate*. Often, this imbalance in complexity can make a sentence stilted and the lesser adjectives will need to be subordinated:

The interim Prime Minister, who is *strong* and *compassionate, wants* to defeat the insurgency with a minimum of civilian casualties.

However, the first rewrite is natural and more powerful. We will discuss these structures in detail later.

When a series of clauses is listed, the verbs in each clause must have the same form.

Example:

During his trip to Europe, the President will *discuss* ways to stimulate trade, *offer* economic aid, and *trying* to forge a new coalition with moderate forces in Russia.

In this example, the first two verbs, *discuss* and *offer*, are simple future tense. But the third verb in the series, *trying*, is progressive. *Trying* should be in the simple future tense *try*:

During his trip to Europe, the President will *discuss* ways to stimulate trade, *offer* economic aid, and *try* to forge a new coalition with moderate forces in Russia.

 When a series of clauses with different verbs is listed, make sure the verb in each clause is included.

Although this may seem obvious, this error of omission can be surprisingly subtle to detect.

Example:

Your battlefield debriefing should *include enemy troop strength* and *why you believe the objective is necessary.*

Notice that the second clause is missing its verb. This forces the reader to assume that the writer just elected not to repeat the verb *include*. However, using the verb *include* in the second clause would be at best imprecise. The second clause would be more balanced and clearer with the verb *explain*:

Your battlefield debriefing should *include enemy troop strength* and *explain why you believe the objective is necessary.*

 When the first half of a sentence has a certain structure, the second half should preserve that structure.

Example:

To acknowledge that one is an alcoholic is *taking* the first and hardest step to recovery.

The first half of the above sentence has an infinitive structure, *to acknowledge*, so the second half must have a similar structure:

To acknowledge that one is an alcoholic is *to take* the first and hardest step to recovery.

 To correct an unparallel structure, first try giving the similar terms the same structure. For instance, change an adjective and a noun to two adjectives. However, this can make the sentence awkward. In these cases, you may need to subordinate one term to another.

Example:

He *ranks* as one of the top volleyball players in the country and is often *solicited* by clothing companies for his endorsement.

The first clause in this sentence uses the active verb *ranks*, and the second clause uses the passive verb *solicited*. The sentence can be made parallel by making the first clause passive:

> He is *ranked* as one of the top volleyball players in the country and is often *solicited* by clothing companies for his endorsement.

However, this sentence is plodding. Let's try making both clauses active:

> He ranks as one of the top volleyball players in the country, and clothing companies often solicit him for his endorsement.

This sentence is both plodding and awkward. Instead of forcing a parallel structure here, let's just subordinate the first clause to the second clause:

> As one of the top volleyball players in the country, he is often solicited by clothing companies for his endorsement.

 Note!   **Make sure the elements of correlative conjunctions are balanced.**

Following are some common correlative conjunctions:

> both . . . and . . .
> either . . . or . . .
> neither . . . nor . . .
> not only . . . but also . . .
> whether . . . or . . .

Example:

> Agreeing to modest cuts in health benefits is a tacit admission by the union leadership *both* of its decreased influence *and* the increased influence of workers.

Here, the prepositional phrase *of its decreased influence* and the adjective phrase *increased influence of workers* are not balanced. This can be corrected by placing the preposition *of* before the conjunction *both*:

> Agreeing to modest cuts in health benefits is a tacit admission by the union leadership of *both* its decreased influence *and* the increased influence of workers.

Example:

> In criticizing the team, the coach was *not only* referring to the poor shooting *but also* to the numerous turnovers.

Here, the phrase *referring to the poor shooting* and the phrase *to the numerous turnovers* are not balanced. This can be corrected by moving the word *referring* before the word *not*:

> In criticizing the team, the coach was referring *not only* to the poor shooting *but also* to the numerous turnovers.

Warm-Up Drill IV
Answers and solutions begin on page 541.

1. Common knowledge tells us that sensible exercise and <u>eating properly will result</u> in better health.

   (A)   eating properly will result
   (B)   proper diet resulted
   (C)   dieting will result
   (D)   proper diet results
   (E)   eating properly results

2. This century began with <u>war brewing in Europe, the industrial revolution well-established, and a nascent communication age.</u>

   (A)   war brewing in Europe, the industrial revolution well-established, and a nascent communication age.
   (B)   war brewing in Europe, the industrial revolution surging, and a nascent communication age.
   (C)   war in Europe, the industrial revolution well-established, and a nascent communication age.
   (D)   war brewing in Europe, the industrial revolution well-established, and the communication age beginning.
   (E)   war brewing in Europe, the industrial revolution well-established, and saw the birth of the communication age.

3. It is often better <u>to try repairing an old car than to junk it.</u>

   (A)   to try repairing an old car than to junk it.
   (B)   to repair an old car than to have it junked.
   (C)   to try repairing an old car than to junking it.
   (D)   to try and repair an old car than to junk it.
   (E)   to try to repair an old car than to junk it.

4. <u>Jurassic Park, written by Michael Crichton, and which was first printed in 1988,</u> is a novel about a theme park of the future in which dinosaurs roam free.

   (A)   Jurassic Park, written by Michael Crichton, and which was first printed in 1988,
   (B)   Jurassic Park, written by Michael Crichton and first printed in 1988,
   (C)   Jurassic Park, which was written by Michael Crichton, and which was first printed in 1988,
   (D)   Written by Michael Crichton and first printed in 1988, Jurassic Park
   (E)   Jurassic Park, <u>which</u> was written by Michael Crichton and first printed in 1988,

Faulty Verb Tense

A verb is usually defined as

a word that expresses action or state of being

Oddly, this definition is simultaneously both nebulous and too precise: "state of being" is vague, and words other than verbs can carry the weight of action in a sentence. However, any attempt to better define the concept of the verb will lead us into far more detail than we have room to discuss. Let's just use the above definition to reinforce our intuitive understanding of the meaning and function of a verb in a sentence.

A verb has four principal forms:

1. **Present Tense**
    a. Used to express present tense.

    He studies hard.

    b. Used to express general truths.

    During a recession, people are cautious about taking on more debt.

    c. Used with *will* or *shall* to express future time.

    He will take the GMAT next year.

2. **Past Tense**
    a. Used to express past tense.

    He took the GMAT last year.

3. **Past Participle**
    a. Used to form the *present perfect tense*, which indicates that an action was started in the past and its effects are continuing in the present. It is formed using *have* or *has* and the past participle of the verb.

    He has prepared thoroughly for the GMAT.

    b. Used to form the *past perfect tense*, which indicates that an action was completed before another past action. It is formed using *had* and the past participle of the verb.

    He had prepared thoroughly before taking the GMAT.

    c. Used to form the *future perfect tense*, which indicates that an action will be completed before another future action. It is formed using *will have* or *shall have* and the past participle of the verb.

    He will have prepared thoroughly before taking the GMAT.

4. **Present Participle (-*ing* form of the verb)**

a. Used to form the *present progressive tense*, which indicates that an action is ongoing. It is formed using *is, am,* or *are* and the present participle of the verb.

He is preparing thoroughly for the GMAT.

b. Used to form the *past progressive tense*, which indicates that an action was in progress in the past. It is formed using *was* or *were* and the present participle of the verb.

He was preparing for the GMAT.

c. Used to form the *future progressive tense*, which indicates that an action will be in progress in the future. It is formed using *will be* or *shall be* and the present participle of the verb.

He will be preparing thoroughly for the GMAT.

If similar answers — choose shorter option.

PASSIVE VOICE

Note! **The passive voice removes the subject from the sentence. It is formed with the verb *to be* and the past participle of the main verb.**

Passive: *The bill was resubmitted by the Senator.*

Active: *The Senator resubmitted the bill.*

Unless you want to de-emphasize the doer of an action, you should favor the active voice. Passive sentences are usually considered loose. Notice in the above example that the sentence with the active verb is more lively, more powerful.

Note! **Be alert to passive constructions that point to the wrong doer of an action.**

Example:

The head of the insurgency of *was reported killed* in the first day of action by the press.

The passive structure seems to imply that the press killed the head of the insurgency. In the construction *killed in the first day of action by the press* drop the intervening phrase *in the first day* and you get *killed by the press.* The sentence is better expressed at least partially in the active voice:

The press *reported* that the head of the insurgency *was killed* in the first day of action.

Here, the subject *press* uses the active verb *reported*, and presumably the army is alluded to by the passive verb *was killed*.

Warm-Up Drill V

Answers and solutions begin on page 542.

1. In the past few years and to this day, many teachers of math and science <u>had chosen to return to the private sector.</u>

    (A) had chosen to return to the private sector.
    (B) having chosen to return to the private sector.
    (C) chose to return to the private sector.
    (D) have chosen to return to the private sector.
    (E) have chosen returning to the private sector.

2. <u>Most of the homes that were destroyed in last summer's brush fires were</u> built with wood-shake roofs.

    (A) Most of the homes that were destroyed in last summer's brush fires were
    (B) Last summer, brush fires destroyed most of the homes that were
    (C) Most of the homes that were destroyed in last summer's brush fires had been
    (D) Most of the homes that the brush fires destroyed last summer's have been
    (E) Most of the homes destroyed in last summer's brush fires were being

3. Although World War II ended nearly a half century ago, Russia and Japan still <u>have not signed a formal peace treaty; and both countries have been</u> reticent to develop closer relations.

    (A) have not signed a formal peace treaty; and both countries have been
    (B) did not signed a formal peace treaty; and both countries have been
    (C) have not signed a formal peace treaty; and both countries being
    (D) have not signed a formal peace treaty; and both countries are
    (E) are not signing a formal peace treaty; and both countries have been

4. The Democrats have accused the Republicans of resorting to dirty tricks by planting a mole on the Democrat's planning committee and then <u>used the information obtained to sabotage</u> the Democrat's campaign.

    (A) used the information obtained to sabotage
    (B) used the information they had obtained to sabotage
    (C) of using the information they had obtained to sabotage
    (D) using the information obtained to sabotage
    (E) to have used the information obtained to sabotage

Idiom & Usage

Idioms are figures of speech that convey messages which are peculiar to a language. If taken literally, the message would not have the same meaning as the speaker intended.

Accept/Except

Accept means to receive something that is offered or agree to something. *Except* means leave out or exclude something.

> The European powers would have *accepted* Iran's offer if it had included on-site and unrestricted inspections.

> All the world's industrial powers signed the treaty to reduce global warming *except* the United States.

Account for / +o

When explaining something, the correct idiom is *account for*.

> We had to *account for* all the missing money.

When receiving blame or credit, the correct idiom is *account to*:

> You will have to *account to* the state for your crimes.

Adapted to/for/from

Adapted to means "naturally suited for." *Adapted for* means "created to be suited for." *Adapted from* means "changed to be suited for." Consider these examples:

> The polar bear is *adapted to* the subzero temperatures.

> For any "New Order" to be successful, it must be *adapted for* the continually changing world power structure.

> Lucas' latest release is *adapted from* the 1950 B-movie "Attack of the Amazons."

Affect/Effect

Affect, usually a verb, means to influence something or the act upon something. *Effect*, usually a noun, means the result.

> The anti-venom had the desired *effect*, and the boy fully recovered.

Here, *effect* is a noun meaning result.

> The negotiators were not *affected* by the large, violent street protests.

Here, *affected* is a verb meaning *influence*.

All ready vs. Already

All ready means "everything is ready."

Already means "earlier."

Alot vs. A lot

Alot is nonstandard; *a lot* is the correct form.

Among/Between

Between should be used when referring to <u>two things</u>, and *among* should be used when referring to more than two things. For example,

The young lady must choose *between* two suitors.

The fault is spread evenly *among* the three defendants.

As/Like

A frequent mistake is to use *like* when *as* is needed. If you are connecting a clause to its subject, use *as*. If you merely need a preposition to introduce a noun, use *like*.

It appears *as* though the peace plan has failed.
(*As* is introducing the clause "the peace plan has failed.")

It looks *like* rain.
(*Like* is introducing the noun "rain.")

As to

This construction is usually imprecise or vacuous. In almost all cases, you should replace it with a more precise preposition or delete it.

(Poor)	The prosecuting attorney left little doubt *as to* the defendant's motive for the murder.
(Better)	The prosecuting attorney left little doubt *about* defendant's motive for the murder.
(Poor)	The question *as to whether* it's better to let the bill die in committee or be voted down on the floor of the house is purely political.
(Better)	The question *whether* it's better to let the bill die in committee or be voted down on the floor of the house is purely political.

[handwritten marginal note: Subtle]

Being that vs. Since

Being that is nonstandard and should be replaced by *since*.

(Faulty)	*Being that* darkness was fast approaching, we had to abandon the search.
(Better)	*Since* darkness was fast approaching, we had to abandon the search.

Beside/Besides

Adding an *s* to *beside* completely changes its meaning: *Beside* means "next to." *Besides* means "in addition."

> We sat *beside* (next to) the host.

> *Besides* (in addition), money was not even an issue in the contract negotiations.

Center on vs. Center around *= slang = BAD*

Center around is colloquial. It should not be used in formal writing.

> *(Faulty)* The dispute *centers around* the effects of undocumented workers.
>
> *(Correct)* The dispute *centers on* the effects of undocumented workers.

Conform to (not *with*)

> Stewart's writing does not *conform to* standard literary conventions.

Consensus of opinion

Consensus of opinion is redundant: *consensus* means "general agreement."

Correspond to/with

Correspond to means "in agreement with."

> The penalty does not *correspond to* the severity of the crime.

Correspond with means "to exchange letters."

> He *corresponded with* many of the top European leaders of his time.

Double negatives

> *(Faulty)* *Scarcely nothing* was learned during the seminar.
>
> *(Better)* *Scarcely anything* was learned during the seminar.

Doubt that vs. Doubt whether

Doubt whether is nonstandard.

> *(Faulty)* I *doubt whether* his new business will succeed.
>
> *(Correct)* I *doubt that* his new business will succeed.

Farther/Further

Use *farther* when referring to distance, and use *further* when referring to degree.

> They went no *further* (degree) than necking.

> He threw the discs *farther* (distance) than the top seated competitor.

Fewer/Less

Use *fewer* when referring to a number of items. Use *less* when referring to a continuous quantity.

> In the past, we had *fewer* options.

> The impact was *less* than what was expected.

Identical with (not *to*)

> This bid is *identical with* the one submitted by you.

In contrast to (not *of*)

> In *contrast to* the conservative attitudes of her time, Mae West was quite provocative.

Independent of (not *from*)

> The judiciary is *independent of* the other branches of government.

It's/Its

It's is a contraction of *it is*. *Its* is the possessive form of *it*. To check whether the apostrophe is needed, merely read the sentence replacing *its* or *it's* with *it is*. If the sentence reads well, then the apostrophe is needed; otherwise it's not.

> *It's* [it is] too early to determine *its* [possession] cause.

Likely vs. Liable

Likely simply means something will probably occur. *Liable* means vulnerability to legal responsibility or to something unpleasant.

> If we don't pay the bill on time, we are *liable* to damage our credit with the company; and if we don't pay it at all, we are *liable* to be sued.

A common mistake is use *liable* to mean *likely*:

> (Faulty)   The top-rated team is *liable* to win the tournament.
> (Correct)   The top-rated team is *likely* to win the tournament.

Not only . . . but also

In this construction, *but* cannot be replaced with *and*.

> (Faulty)   Peterson is *not only* the top salesman in the department *and also* the most proficient.

> (Correct)   Peterson is *not only* the top salesman in the department *but also* the most proficient.

On account of vs. Because

Because is always better than the circumlocution *on account of*.

> (Poor)   *On account of* his poor behavior, he was expelled.

> (Better)   *Because* he behaved poorly, he was expelled.

One another/Each other

Each other should be used when referring to two things, and *one another* should be used when referring to more than two things.

> The members of the basketball team (more than two) congratulated *one another* on their victory.

> The business partners (two) congratulated *each other* on their successful first year.

Plus vs. And

Do not use *plus* as a conjunction meaning *and*.

> (Faulty)   His contributions to this community are considerable, *plus* his character is beyond reproach.

> (Correct)   His contributions to this community are considerable, *and* his character is beyond reproach.

Note: *Plus* can be used to mean *and* as long as it is not being used as a conjunction.

> (Acceptable)   His generous financial contribution *plus* his donated time has made this project a success.

In this sentence, *plus* is being used as a preposition. Note, the verb *has* is singular because an intervening prepositional phrase (*plus* his donated time) does not affect subject verb agreement.

Regard vs. Regards

Unless you are giving best wishes to someone, you should use *regard*.

> (Faulty)   In *regards* to your letter, we would be interested in distributing your product.

> (Correct)   In *regard* to your letter, we would be interested in distributing your product.

Regardless vs. Irregardless

Regardless means "not withstanding." Hence, the "ir" in *irregardless* is redundant. *Regardless* is the correct form.

Retroactive to (not *from*)

The correct idiom is *retroactive to*:

> The tax increase is *retroactive to* February.

Speak to/with

To *speak to* someone is to tell them something.

> We *spoke to* Jennings about the alleged embezzlement.

To *speak with* someone is to discuss something with them.

> Steve *spoke with* his friend Dave for hours yesterday.

The reason is because

This structure is redundant. Equally common and doubly redundant is the structure *the reason why is because*.

(Poor)	The *reason why* I could not attend the party *is because* I had to work.
(Better)	I could not attend the party *because* I had to work.

Whether vs. As to whether

The circumlocution *as to whether* should be replaced by *whether*.

(Poor)	The United Nations has not decided *as to whether* to authorize a trade embargo.
(Better)	The United Nations has not decided *whether* to authorize a trade embargo.

Whether vs. If

Whether introduces a choice; *if* introduces a condition. A common mistake is to use *if* to present a choice.

(Faulty)	He inquired *if* we had decided to keep the gift.
(Correct)	He inquired *whether* we had decided to keep the gift.

Warm-Up Drill VI

Answers and solutions begin on page 543.

1. Regarding legalization of drugs, I am not concerned so much by its potential impact on middle class America <u>but instead</u> by its potential impact on the inner city.

   (A) but instead
   (B) so much as
   (C) rather
   (D) but rather
   (E) as

2. Unless you maintain at least a 2.0 GPA, <u>you will not graduate medical school.</u>

   (A) you will not graduate medical school.
   (B) you will not be graduated from medical school.
   (C) you will not be graduating medical school.
   (D) you will not graduate from medical school.
   (E) you will graduate medical school.

3. <u>The studio's retrospective art exhibit refers back to</u> a simpler time in American history.

   (A) The studio's retrospective art exhibit refers back to → redundant .
   (B) The studio's retrospective art exhibit harkens back to
   (C) The studio's retrospective art exhibit refers to
   (D) The studio's retrospective art exhibit refers from
   (E) The studio's retrospective art exhibit looks back to

4. <u>Due to the chemical spill, the commute into the city will be delayed by as much as 2 hours.</u>

   (A) Due to the chemical spill, the commute into the city will be delayed by as much as 2 hours.
   (B) The reason that the commute into the city will be delayed by as much as 2 hours is because of the chemical spill.
   (C) Due to the chemical spill, the commute into the city had been delayed by as much as 2 hours.
   (D) Because of the chemical spill, the commute into the city will be delayed by as much as 2 hours.
   (E) The chemical spill will be delaying the commute into the city by as much as 2 hours.

Points to Remember

1. A pronoun should be plural when it refers to two nouns joined by *and*.

2. A pronoun should be singular when it refers to two nouns joined by *or* or *nor*.

3. A pronoun should refer to one, and only one, noun or compound noun.

4. A pronoun must agree with its antecedent in both number and person.

5. The subject and verb must agree both in number and person.

6. Intervening phrases and clauses have no effect on subject-verb agreement.

7. When the subject and verb are reversed, they still must agree in both number and person.

8. As a general rule, a modifier should be placed as close as possible to what it modifies.

9. When a phrase begins a sentence, make sure that it modifies the subject of the sentence.

10. For a sentence to be parallel, similar elements must be expressed in similar form.

11. When two adjectives modify the same noun, they should have similar forms.

12. When a series of clauses is listed, the verbs must be in the same form.

13. When the first half of a sentence has a certain structure, the second half should preserve that structure.

14. An adverb modifies a verb, an adjective, or another adverb.

15. A verb has four principal forms:

   I.   Present Tense
       a. Used to express something that is occurring now.
       b. Used to express general truths.
       c. Used with *will* or *shall* to express future time.

   II. Past Tense
       a. Used to express something that occurred in the past.

   III. Past Participle
       a. Used to form the *present perfect tense*, which indicates that an action was started in the past and its effects are continuing in the present. It is formed using *have* or *has* and the past participle of the verb.
       b. Used to form the *past perfect tense*, which indicates that an action was completed before another past action. It is formed using *had* and the past participle of the verb.
       c. Used to form the *future perfect tense*, which indicates that an action will be completed before another future action. It is formed using *will have* or *shall have* and the past participle of the verb.

IV. Present Participle (-*ing* form of the verb)

    a. Used to form the *present progressive tense*, which indicates that an action is ongoing. It is formed using *is*, *am*, or *are* and the present participle of the verb.

    b. Used to form the *past progressive tense*, which indicates that an action was in progress in the past. It is formed using *was* or *were* and the present participle of the verb.

    c. Used to form the *future progressive tense*, which indicates that an action will be in progress in the future. It is formed using *will be* or *shall be* and the present participle of the verb.

16. Unless you want to de-emphasize the doer of an action, you should favor the active voice.

17. Attack strategy for identifying misplaced modifiers:

    I. Find the subject and the verb.

    II. Isolate the subject and the verb by deleting intervening phrases.

    III. Follow the rule of proximity: Modifiers should describe the closest units.

    IV. Check the punctuation. Any punctuation should create coherence and not confusion.

<u>Solutions to Warm-Up Drill I</u>

1.   <u>Had the President's Administration not lost the vote on the budget reduction package, his first year in office would have been rated an A.</u>

(A)   Had the President's Administration not lost the vote on the budget reduction package, his first year in office would have been rated an A.

(B)   If the Administration had not lost the vote on the budget reduction package, his first year in office would have been rated an A.

(C)   Had the President's Administration not lost the vote on the budget reduction package, it would have been rated an A.

(D)   Had the President's Administration not lost the vote on its budget reduction package, his first year in office would have been rated an A.

(E)   If the President had not lost the vote on the budget reduction package, the Administration's first year in office would have been rated an A.

The answer is (E).

Choice (A) is incorrect because *his* appears to refer to *the President*, but the subject of the subordinate clause is *the President's Administration*, not *the President*.

Choice (B) changes the structure of the sentence, but retains the same flawed reference.

In choice (C), *it* can refer to either *the President's Administration* or *the budget reduction package*. Thus, the reference is ambiguous.

Choice (D) adds another pronoun, *its*, but still retains the same flawed reference.

Choice (E) corrects the flawed reference by removing all pronouns.

2.   The new law requires a manufacturer <u>to immediately notify their customers whenever the government is contemplating a forced recall of any of the manufacturer's products.</u>

(A)   to immediately notify their customers whenever the government is contemplating a forced recall of any of the manufacturer's products.

(B)   to immediately notify customers whenever the government is contemplating a forced recall of their products.

(C)   to immediately, and without delay, notify its customers whenever the government is contemplating a forced recall of any of the manufacturer's products.

(D)   to immediately notify whenever the government is contemplating a forced recall of any of the manufacturer's products that the customers may have bought.

(E)   to immediately notify its customers whenever the government is contemplating a forced recall of any of the manufacturer's products.

The answer is (E).

Choice (A) is incorrect because the plural pronoun *their* cannot have the singular noun *a manufacturer* as its antecedent.

Although choice (B) corrects the given false reference, it introduces another one. *Their* can now refer to either *customers* or *government*, neither of which would make sense in this context.

Choice (C) also corrects the false reference, but it introduces a redundancy: *immediately* means "without delay."

Choice (D) corrects the false reference, but its structure is very awkward. The direct object of a verb should be as close to the verb as possible. In this case, the verb *notify* is separated from its direct object *customers* by the clause "*that the government is contemplating a forced recall of any of the manufacturer's products that.*"

Choice (E) is correct because the singular pronoun *its* has the singular noun *a manufacturer* as its antecedent.

3. World War II taught the United States the folly of punishing a vanquished aggressor; so <u>after the war, they enacted the Marshall Plan to rebuild Germany.</u>

    (A) after the war, they enacted the Marshall Plan to rebuild Germany.
    (B) after the war, the Marshall Plan was enacted to rebuild Germany.
    (C) after the war, the Marshall Plan was enacted by the United States to rebuild Germany.
    (D) after the war, the United States enacted the Marshall Plan to rebuild Germany.
    (E) after the war, the United States enacted the Marshall Plan in order to rebuild Germany.

The answer is (D).

Choice (A) is incorrect. Since *United States* is denoting the collective country, it is singular and therefore cannot be correctly referred to by the plural pronoun *they*.

Choice (B) is not technically incorrect, but it lacks precision since it does not state who enacted the Marshall Plan. Further, it uses a passive construction: *"was enacted."*

Choice (C) states who enacted the Marshall Plan, but it retains the passive construction *"was enacted."*

Choice (D) corrects the false reference by replacing *they* with *the United States*. Further, it uses the active verb *enacted* instead of the passive verb *was enacted*.

Choice (E) is second-best. The phrase *"in order"* is unnecessary.

4. In the 1950's, integration was an anathema <u>to most Americans; now, however, most Americans accept it as desirable.</u>

    (A) to most Americans; now, however, most Americans accept it as desirable.
    (B) to most Americans, now, however, most Americans accept it.
    (C) to most Americans; now, however, most Americans are desirable of it.
    (D) to most Americans; now, however, most Americans accepted it as desirable.
    (E) to most Americans. Now, however, most Americans will accept it as desirable.

The answer is (A).

Choice (A) is correct as written.

Choice (B) creates a run-on sentence by replacing the semicolon with a comma. Without a connecting word—*and, or, but*, etc.—two independent clauses must be joined by a semicolon or written as two separate sentences. Also, deleting *"as desirable"* changes the meaning of the sentence.

Choice (C) uses a very awkward construction: *are desirable of it*.

Choice (D) contains an error in tense. The sentence progresses from the past to the present, so the verb in the second clause should be *accept*, not *accepted*.

Choice (E) writes the two clauses as separate sentences, which is allowable, but it also changes the tense of the second clause to the future: *will accept*.

5. Geologists in California have discovered a fault near the famous San Andreas Fault, <u>one that they believe to be a trigger for</u> major quakes on the San Andreas.

    (A) one that they believe to be a trigger for
    (B) one they believe to be a trigger for
    (C) one that they believe triggers
    (D) that they believe to be a trigger for
    (E) one they believe acts as a trigger for

The answer is (B).

Choice (A) is incorrect since the relative pronoun *that* is redundant: the pronoun *one*, which refers to the newly discovered fault, is sufficient.

Choice (B) has both the correct pronoun and the correct verb form.

Although choice (C) reads more smoothly, it still contains the double pronouns.

Choice (D) is incorrect. Generally, relative pronouns such as *that* refer to whole ideas in previous clauses or sentences. Since the second sentence is about the fault and not its discovery, the pronoun *that* is appropriate.

Choice (E) is very tempting. It actually reads better than choice (A), but it contains a subtle flaw. *One* is the direct object of the verb *believes* and therefore cannot be the subject of the verb *acts*. Since *they* clearly is not the subject, the verb *acts* is without a subject.

6. A bite from the tsetse fly invariably paralyzes <u>its victims unless an antidote is administered</u> within two hours.

    (A) its victims unless an antidote is administered
    (B) its victims unless an antidote can be administered
    (C) its victims unless an antidote was administered
    (D) its victims unless an antidote is administered to the victims
    (E) its victims unless they receive an antidote

The answer is (E).

Choice (A) is incorrect since it is unclear whether the victim or the fly should receive the antidote.

Choice (B) is incorrect since *is* is more direct than *can be*.

Choice (C) is incorrect. A statement of fact should be expressed in the present tense, not the past tense.

Choice (D) is wordy. A pronoun should be used for the phrase *the victims*.

Choice (E) is the answer since *they* correctly identifies who should receive the antidote.

Solutions to Warm-Up Drill II

1. <u>The rising cost</u> of government bureaucracy have made it all but impossible to reign in the budget deficit.

    (A)   The rising cost
    (B)   Since the rising costs
    (C)   Because of the rising costs
    (D)   The rising costs
    (E)   Rising cost

The answer is (D).

Choice (A) is incorrect because the plural verb *have* does not agree with its singular subject *the rising cost*.

Both (B) and (C) are incorrect because they turn the sentence into a fragment.

Choice (D) is the correct answer since now the plural verb *have* agrees with its plural subject *the rising costs*.

Choice (E) is incorrect because *rising cost* is still singular.

2. In a co-publication agreement, ownership of both the material and <u>its means of distribution are equally shared by the parties.</u>

    (A)   its means of distribution are equally shared by the parties.
    (B)   its means of distribution are shared equally by each of the parties.
    (C)   its means of distribution is equally shared by the parties.
    (D)   their means of distribution is equally shared by the parties.
    (E)   the means of distribution are equally shared by the parties.

The answer is (C).

Choice (A) is incorrect. Recall that intervening phrases have no effect on subject-verb agreement. In this sentence, the subject *ownership* is singular, but the verb *are* is plural. Dropping the intervening phrase clearly shows that the sentence is ungrammatical:

> *In a co-publication agreement, ownership are equally shared by the parties.*

Choice (B) is incorrect. Neither adding *each of* nor interchanging *shared* and *equally* addresses the issue of subject-verb agreement.

Choice (C) is correct since the singular verb *is* agrees with its singular subject *ownership*.

Choice (D) contains a faulty pronoun reference. The antecedent of the plural pronoun *their* would be the singular noun *material*.

Choice (E) is incorrect since it still contains the plural verb *are*.

3.   The rise in negative attitudes toward foreigners <u>indicate that the country is becoming less tolerant, and therefore that</u> the opportunities are ripe for extremist groups to exploit the illegal immigration problem.

   (A)   indicate that the country is becoming less tolerant, and therefore that
   (B)   indicates that the country is becoming less tolerant, and therefore
   (C)   indicates that the country is becoming less tolerant, and therefore that
   (D)   indicates that the country is being less tolerant, and therefore
   (E)   indicates that the country is becoming less tolerant of and therefore that

The answer is (B).

   Choice (A) has two flaws. First, the subject of the sentence *the rise* is singular, but the verb *indicate* is plural. Second, the comma indicates that the sentence is made up of two independent clauses, but the relative pronoun *that* immediately following *therefore* forms a subordinate clause.

   Choice (B) is the answer because it both corrects the verb's number and removes the subordinating relative pronoun *that*.

   Choice (C) corrects the number of the verb, but retains the subordinating relative pronoun *that*.

   Choice (D) corrects the number of the verb and eliminates the subordinating relative pronoun *that*. However, the verb *being* is less descriptive than the verb *becoming*: "As negative attitudes toward foreigners increase, the country becomes correspondingly less tolerant." *Being* does not capture this notion of change.

   Choice (E) corrects the verb's number, and by dropping the comma, makes the subordination allowable. However, it introduces the preposition *of* which does not have an object: less tolerant of what?

4.   <u>The harvest of grapes in the local valleys decreased in 1990 for the third straight year but were</u> still at a robust level.

   (A)   The harvest of grapes in the local valleys decreased in 1990 for the third straight year but were
   (B)   The harvest of grapes in the local valleys began to decrease in 1990 for the third straight year but were
   (C)   In 1990, the harvest of grapes in the local valleys decreased for the third straight year but were
   (D)   The harvest of grapes in the local valleys decreased for the third straight year in 1990 but was
   (E)   The harvest of grapes in the local valleys began decreasing in 1990 for the third straight year but was

The answer is (D).

   Choice (A) is incorrect since the singular subject *the harvest* requires a singular verb, not the plural verb *were*.

   Choice (B) is illogical since it states that the harvest began to decrease in 1990 and then it states that it was the third straight year of decrease.

   In choice (C), the plural verb *were* still does not agree with its singular subject *the harvest*.

   Choice (D) has the singular verb *was* agreeing with its singular subject *the harvest*. Further, it places the phrase *in 1990* more naturally. The answer is (D).

   Choice (E) contains the same flaw as choice (B).

5.   <u>Each of the book's protagonists—Mark Streit, Mary Eby, and Dr. Thomas—has</u> a powerful, dynamic personality.

  (A)   Each of the book's protagonists—Mark Streit, Mary Eby, and Dr. Thomas—has
  (B)   Each of the book's protagonists—Mark Streit, Mary Eby, and Dr. Thomas—have
  (C)   All the book's protagonists—Mark Streit, Mary Eby, and Dr. Thomas—has
  (D)   Mark Streit, Mary Eby, and Dr. Thomas—the book's protagonists—each has
  (E)   Each of the book's protagonists—Mark Streit, Mary Eby, and Dr. Thomas—could have had

The answer is (A).

Choice (A) is correct as written.

In choice (B) the plural verb *have* is incorrect. When *each*, *every*, or *many a* precedes two or more subjects linked by *and*, they separate the subjects and the verb is singular.

Choice (C) is incorrect since the singular verb *has* does not agree with the plural subject *all*.

In choice (D) the singular verb *has* is incorrect. When *each* follows a plural subject, it does not separate the subjects and the verb remains plural.

Choice (E) also changes the meaning of the original sentence, which states that the protagonist <u>do</u> have powerful, dynamic personalities.

6.   <u>More important than winning is developing the ability to work with others and developing leadership skills.</u>

  (A)   More important than winning is developing the ability to work with others and developing leadership skills.
  (B)   More important than winning are the ability to work with others and leadership skills.
  (C)   Developing the ability to work with others and developing leadership skills is more important than winning.
  (D)   More important than winning are developing the ability to work with others and developing leadership skills.
  (E)   More important than winning has been the development of the ability to work with others and the development leadership skills.

The answer is (D).

Choice (A) is incorrect since the compound subject *developing the ability to work with others and developing leadership skills* requires a plural verb, not the singular verb *is*.

Choice (B) uses the correct plural verb *are*, but deleting the word *developing* makes the meaning of the sentence less clear.

Choice (C) uses a the natural order of subject then verb, but it is incorrect since the compound subject *developing the ability to work with others and developing leadership skills* requires a plural verb, not the singular verb *is*.

Choice (D) has the plural verb *are* agreeing with its compound subject *developing the ability to work with others and developing leadership skills*. The answer is (D).

Choice (E) is incorrect since the compound subject *the development of the ability to work with others and the development leadership skills* requires a plural verb, not the singular verb *has*.

7.　<u>There is a number of solutions</u> to the problem of global warming that have not been considered by this committee.

    (A)　There is a number of solutions
    (B)　There are a number of solutions
    (C)　There was a number of solutions
    (D)　There were a number of solutions
    (E)　There have been a number of solutions

The answer is (B).

    Choice (A) is incorrect since the plural subject *a number* requires a plural verb, not the singular verb *is*.

    Choice (B) is the answer because it correctly uses the plural verb *are* with the plural subject *a number*.

    Choice (C) is incorrect since the plural subject *a number* requires a plural verb, not the singular verb *was*. Further, the shift in verb tense from *was* to *have not been* is awkward.

    Choice (D) is incorrect because the shift in verb tense from *were* to *have not been* is awkward.

    Choice (E) is incorrect because it is awkward and changes the meaning of the sentence.

Solutions to Warm-Up Drill III

1.　The answer is (E).

    Choice (A) is incorrect since it implies that *the other causes of crime* are doing the focusing.

    Choice (B) has the same flaw as Choice (A).

    Choice (C) is incorrect. The phrase *by focusing on poverty* must modify the subject of the sentence, but *there* cannot be the subject since the construction *there are* is used to introduce a subject.

    Choice (D) implies that *crimes* are focusing on poverty.

    Choice (E) correctly puts the subject of the sentence *sociologists* immediately next to its modifying phrase *by focusing on poverty*.

2.　The answer is (D).

    Choice (A) is incorrect because the phrase *using the Hubble telescope* does not have a noun to modify.

    Choice (B) is incorrect because the phrase *using the Hubble telescope* still does not have a noun to modify.

    Choice (C) offers a noun, *astronomers*, but it is too far from the phrase *using the Hubble telescope*.

    Choice (D) offers a noun, *astronomers*, and correctly places it immediately after the modifying phrase *using the Hubble telescope*.

    In choice (E), the phrase *with the aid of the Hubble telescope* does not have a noun to modify.

3.　The answer is (C).

    Choice (A) is incorrect. As worded, the sentence implies that the cold should be well-insulated.

    Choice (B) is awkward; besides, it still implies that the cold should be well-insulated.

    Choice (C) is the answer since it correctly implies that the stranded motorists should be well-insulated with protective clothing.

    Choice (D) does not indicate what should be insulated.

    Choice (E), like choices (A) and (B), implies that the cold should be well-insulated.

4. The answer is (E).

Choice (A) has two flaws. First, the introductory phrase is too long. Second, the subject Ansel Adams should immediately follow the introductory phrase since it was Ansel Adams—not the year 1945—who was traveling and shooting the Southwest.

Choice (B) is incorrect because the phrase *traveling across . . . Southwest* is too far from its subject Ansel Adams. As written, the sentence seems to imply that the photographic career was traveling across and shooting the Southwest.

Choice (C) is inconsistent in verb tense. Further, it implies that Adams began his photographic career after he traveled across the Southwest.

Choice (D) is awkward.

Choice (E) is the best answer.

5. The answer is (B).

Choice (A) is incorrect because it implies that the Harmony virus should be inoculated when it's the computer system that needs to be protected.

Choice (B) is the answer since it correctly implies that the computer system should be inoculated, not the virus.

Choice (C) sounds better, but it is not clear what the pronoun "it" is referring to, the virus or the computer. Hence, it is not clear whether it's the virus or the computer that needs to be inoculated.

Choice (D) is awkward, and it implies that the Harmony virus should be inoculated when it's the computer system that needs to be protected.

Choice (E) is awkward, and it implies that the Harmony virus should be inoculated when it's the computer system that needs to be protected.

6. The answer is (E).

Choice (A) is incorrect because it implies that *we* are the head of the division instead of the actual head of the division *you*.

Although Choice (B) makes clear who is the head of the division (*you* not *we*), the structure "Seeing as you . . ." is too lose and informal.

Choice (C) makes the same mistake as the original sentence: It implies that *we* are the head of the division instead of the actual head of the division *you*.

Choice (D) is incorrect because it merely adds unnecessary words "are inclined to" which does not correct the flaw in the original sentence: It still implies that *we* are the head of the division instead of the actual head of the division *you*.

Choice (E) is the answer because the clause "that as head of the division" correctly modifies the head of the division *you*.

7. The answer is (D).

Choice (A) is incorrect because the phrase "during childhood" modifies "parent" illogically implying that the parent died during childhood.

Choice (B) is incorrect because the phrase "when a child" modifies "parent" illogically implying that the parent died during childhood.

Choice (C) is incorrect because the phrase "occurring when a child" modifies "parent" illogically implying that the parent died during childhood.

Choice (D) is the answer. Now, the phrase "during childhood" correctly modifies "people."

Choice (E) is very awkward. The long clause "That people who . . . as adults" is the subject of the sentence. Although perhaps not ungrammatical, Choice (E) is very hard to read.

8. The answer is (C).

Choice (A) is incorrect because the phrase "Based on the yarns of storytellers" modifies "linguistic archeologists" illogically implying that the archeologists are based on the yarns of storytellers.

Choice (B) is incorrect because the phrase "Basing on the yarns of storytellers" modifies "linguistic archeologists" illogically implying that the archeologists are based on the yarns of storytellers. Further, the phrase "Basing on the yarns of storytellers" is very awkward.

Choice (C) is the answer. The clause "Using the yarns of storytellers" correctly modifies "linguistic archeologists," showing how they are using the yarns. The clause can also be placed after the subject it modifies: Linguistic archeologists using the yarns of storytellers . . . . Notice that the same transposition in the original sentence will make the illogical modification of the subject, linguistic archeologists, even more pronounced: Linguistic archeologists based on the yarns of storytellers . . . . Here, "based on the yarns of storytellers" modifies "Linguistic archeologists" illogically implying that the archeologists are based on the yarns of storytellers.

Choice (D) is incorrect because the phrase "coming to the realization" is wordy. Further, the phrase "Based on the yarns of storytellers" modifies "linguistic archeologists" illogically implying that the archeologists are based on the yarns of storytellers.

Choice (E) is incorrect because it is awkward and vague: what is "it" referring to?

<u>Solutions to Warm-Up Drill IV</u>

1. The answer is (D).

Choice (A) is incorrect since *eating properly* (verb-adverb) is not parallel to *sensible exercise* (adjective-noun).

Choice (B) offers two parallel nouns, *exercise* and *diet*. However, a general truth should be expressed in the present tense, not in the past tense.

Choice (C) is not parallel since it pairs the noun *exercise* with the gerund (a verb acting as a noun) *dieting*.

Choice (D) offers two parallel nouns—*exercise* and *diet*—and two parallel verbs—*tells* and *results*.

Choice (E) contains the same mistake as choice (A).

2. The answer is (D).

Choice (A) is incorrect. Although the first two phrases, *war brewing in Europe* and *the industrial revolution well-established*, have different structures, the thoughts are parallel. However, the third phrase, *and a nascent communication age,* is not parallel to the first two.

Choice (B) does not make the third phrase parallel to the first two.

Choice (C) changes the meaning of the sentence: the new formulation states that war already existed in Europe while the original sentence states that war was only developing.

Choice (D) offers three phrases in parallel form.

Choice (E) is not parallel since the first two phrases in the series are noun phrases, but *saw the birth of the communication age* is a verb phrase. When a word introduces a series, each element of the series must agree with the introductory word. You can test the correctness of a phrase in a series by dropping the other phrases and checking whether the remaining phrase agrees with the introductory word. In this series, each phrase must be the object of the preposition *with*:

> This century began *with* <u>war brewing in Europe</u>
> This century began *with* <u>the industrial revolution well-established</u>
> This century began *with* <u>saw the birth of the communication age</u>

In this form, it is clear the verb *saw* cannot be the object of the preposition *with*.

3. The answer is (E).

Choice (A) is incorrect since the verb *repairing* is not parallel to the verb *junk*.

In choice (B), the construction *have it junked* is awkward. Further, it changes the original construction from active to passive.

Choice (C) offers a parallel construction (*repairing/junking*), but it is awkward.

Choice (D) also offers a parallel construction (*repair/junk*), but the construction *try and* is not idiomatic.

Choice (E) offers a parallel construction (*repair/junk*), and the correct idiom—*try to*.

4. The answer is (B).

Choice (A) is incorrect since the verb *written* is not parallel to the construction *which was . . . printed*.

Choice (B) is the correct answer since the sentence is concise and the verb *written* is parallel to the verb *printed*.

Choice (C) does offer a parallel structure (*which was written/which was printed*); however, choice (B) is more concise.

Choice (D) rambles. The introduction *Written by . . . 1988* is too long.

Choice (E) also offers a parallel structure (*which was written/[which was] printed*); however, Choice (B) again is more concise. Note: *which was* need not be repeated for the sentence to be parallel.

Solutions to Warm-Up Drill V

1. The answer is (D).

   Choice (A) is incorrect because it uses the past perfect *had chosen*, which describes an event that has been completed before another event. But the sentence implies that teachers have and are continuing to return to the private sector. Hence, the present perfect tense should be used.

   Choice (B) is incorrect because it uses the present progressive tense *having chosen*, which describes an ongoing event. Although this is the case, it does not capture the fact that the event began in the past.

   Choice (C) is incorrect because it uses the simple past *chose*, which describes a past event. But again, the sentence implies that the teachers are continuing to opt for the private sector.

   Choice (D) is the correct answer because it uses the present perfect *have chosen* to describe an event that occurred in the past and is continuing into the present.

   Choice (E) is incorrect because it leaves the thought in the sentence uncompleted.

2. The answer is (C).

   Choice (A) is incorrect because the simple past *were* does not express the fact that the homes had been built before the fire destroyed them.

   Choice (B) merely rearranges the wording while retaining the simple past *were*.

   Choice (C) is the correct answer because it uses the past perfect *had been* to indicate that the homes were completely built before they were destroyed by the fires.

   Choice (D) is incorrect because it uses the present perfect *have been*, which implies that the homes were destroyed before being built.

   Choice (E) is incorrect. Although dropping the phrase *that were* makes the sentence more concise, the past progressive *were being* implies that the homes were destroyed while being built.

3. The answer is (A).

   Choice (A) is correct as written. The present perfect verb *have . . . signed* correctly indicates that they have not signed a peace treaty and are not on the verge of signing one. Further, the present perfect verb *have been* correctly indicates that in the past both countries have been reluctant to develop closer relations and are still reluctant.

   In choice (B), the simple past *did* does not capture the fact that they did not sign a peace treaty immediately after the war and still have not signed one.

   Choice (C) is very awkward, and the present progressive *being* does not capture the fact that the countries have been reluctant to thaw relations since after the war up through the present.

   In choice (D), the present tense *are* leaves open the possibility that in the past the countries may have desired closer relations but now no longer do.

   In choice (E), the present progressive tense *are . . . signing*, as in choice (D), leaves open the possibility that in the past the countries may have desired closer relations but now no longer do.

4. The answer is (C).

   Choice (A) is incorrect because the simple past *obtained* does not express the fact that the information was gotten before another past action—the sabotage.

   Choice (B) is incorrect because *used* is not parallel to *of resorting*.

   Choice (C) is correct because the phrase *of using* is parallel to the phrase *of resorting*. Further, the past perfect *had obtained* correctly expresses that a past action—the spying—was completed before another past action—the sabotage.

   Choice (D) is incorrect because *using* is not parallel to *of resorting* and the past perfect is not used.

   Choice (E) is incorrect because *to have used* is not parallel to *of resorting* and the past perfect is not used.

Solutions to Warm-Up Drill VI

1. The answer is (E).

    The correct structure for this type of sentence is *not so much by _____ as by _____*.

2. The answer is (D).

    Choice (A) is incorrect. In this context, *graduate* requires the word *from*: "you will not *graduate from* medical school."

    The use of the passive voice in choices (B) and (C) weakens the sentence.

    Choice (D) is the answer since it uses the correct idiom *graduate from*.

    Choice (E) changes the meaning of the sentence and does not correct the faulty idiom.

3. The answer is (C).

    Choice (A) is incorrect. *Retrospective* means looking back on the past. Hence, in the phrase *refers back*, the word *back* is redundant.

    Choice (B) is incorrect because *harkens back* is also redundant.

    Choice (C) is correct. Dropping the word *back* eliminates the redundancy.

    Choice (D) is incorrect because the preposition *from* is non-idiomatic.

    Choice (E) is incorrect because *looks back* is also redundant.

    Note: One could argue that the phrase *American history* also makes the sentence redundant. However, it is not underlined in the sentence. It is not at all uncommon to find questionable structures in parts of the sentence that are not underlined. In fact, you may even find questionable structures in the underlined part of the sentence that are not corrected by any of the answer choices because the writers are testing a different mistake. Concern yourself with correcting only the underlined part of the sentence.

4. The answer is (D).

    Choice (A) is incorrect. Although many educated writers and speakers begin sentences with *due to*, it is almost always incorrect.

    Choice (B) is incorrect: it is both redundant and awkward.

    Choice (C) is incorrect. The past perfect *had been delayed* implies the delay no longer exists. Hence, the meaning of the sentence has been changed.

    Choice (D) is correct. In general, *due to* should not be used as a substitute for *because of, owing to, by reason of*, etc.

    Choice (E) is incorrect. The future progressive *will be delaying* is unnecessary and ponderous. Had choice (E) used the simple future *will delay*, it would have been better that choice (D) because then it would be more direct and active.

ANALYTICAL
WRITING
ASSESSMENT

Format of the Analytical Writing Assessment

The Analytical Writing Assessment (AWA) is the first section of the GMAT. It is 60 minutes long and requires you to respond to two essay questions: the *Analysis of an Issue* essay followed by the *Analysis of an Argument* essay. You will be given 30 minutes to complete each essay.

FORMAT
Analysis of an Issue
Analysis of an Argument

How to Get a "Top-Half" Score

Writing essays for standardized exams can raise anxieties in people who are poised when answering other kinds of test questions. Perhaps this is because critical and creative skills are being tested and evaluated in a more subjective manner than they are within the objective multiple-choice format. Performance anxiety can lead to a host of problems, from having a difficult time understanding exactly what is being asked to having debilitating uncertainties about how to begin an answer.

The best way to reduce such anxieties, and therefore increase your chance of obtaining a top-half score, is through *rehearsal*, which encompasses four activities that need to take place before taking the GMAT:

1) understanding the two writing tasks and how they differ
2) knowing what the evaluators expect to find in top-half essays
3) anticipating an organizational scheme for each of the two essays
4) writing out at least one answer for each of the two question types

Having completed these four steps, you will be in an excellent position to approach the Analytical Writing Assessment with confidence and competency.

ANALYTICAL WRITING

- **INTRODUCTION**

- **PUNCTUATION**
  Commas
  Semicolons
  Colons
  Dashes
  Apostrophes
  Sentence Fragments
  Run-On Sentences

- **GENERAL TIPS ON WRITING YOUR ESSAYS**
  Structure
  Style

- **ANALYSIS OF AN ISSUE**
  Patterns of Development
  Writing Your Issue Essay
  Sample Issues & Essays
  Practice
  More Sample Issue Essays

- **ANALYSIS OF AN ARGUMENT**
  Writing Your Argument Essay
  Sample Arguments & Essays
  Practice
  More Sample Argument Essays

Introduction

The Analytical Writing Assessment requires you to respond to two essay questions within 60 minutes. The first section, *Analysis of an Issue* (30 minutes), asks that you discuss the complexities of an issue and take a position on the problem. The second section, *Analysis of an Argument* (30 minutes), asks that you evaluate an argument or critique a line of reasoning. You are not required to agree or disagree with the argument, but you must clearly point out the strengths and weaknesses in the argument.

The issue and argument topics that you will be asked to write about may or may not pertain to business. You can visit the Web site www.mba.com to download a comprehensive list of sample topics. It is helpful to review this list of topics, but do not try to write a sample essay for each one because the list is much too extensive. Moreover, the wording of the question on the test may be altered, so it is best just to become familiar with the kind of issues and arguments you will be required to address. The more familiar you are with the material that will be on the test, the more prepared and confident you'll be on test day.

You will type your essay on a computer using a very basic word processor. The Analytical Writing Assessment starts with a tutorial that shows how the word processor works. You may write your essay on the computer or on paper supplied at the center. However, handwritten essays can take up to four weeks to be scored. After completing the Issue section, you may move on to the Argument section. There is no break between sections, and, once you exit either section, you cannot return, even if you finish with time remaining.

Scoring the Analytical Writing Section

Your Issue and Argument scores are combined into one average score that is reported to the colleges. Although you can view your math and verbal scores at the test center shortly after the test, your analytical writing score will not be available until 10–15 days after the test.

Each of your two essays will be graded holistically, receiving a score between 0 and 6, with half-point intervals possible. Each paper will be read by two readers, one of which may be E-rater®. E-rater is an electronic evaluation that will examine the organization and variety of your essay as well as the clarity with which you have analyzed the given topic. The two readers' scores will be averaged to give one score per essay. These scores, when averaged, represent the total score awarded for the Analytical Writing Assessment. Papers awarded 6's are considered to be *outstanding*, 5's are *strong*, 4's are *adequate*, 3's are *limited*, 2's are *seriously flawed*, and 1's are *fundamentally deficient*. Notice that papers graded with "top-half" scores—4, 5, or 6—are described as having positive attributes, whereas papers receiving "bottom-half" scores—1, 2, or 3—are described as being problematic.

Before we begin studying particular essays, we need to review some fundamentals of sentence structure and punctuation. No matter how inspired an essay is, its score may be hurt by punctuation errors that make the essay difficult to read or inadvertently change its intended meaning.

Punctuation

Although you can receive a high score on the Analytical Writing Assessment even if your essays contain some grammatical errors, the official guidelines indicate that grammar is given some weight in the scoring. Knowing the rules that govern punctuation will reduce your error rate dramatically. Moreover, knowledge of grammar and punctuation will be invaluable in your graduate writing, where mistakes can be costly. In this section, we will discuss the most commonly used punctuation marks: commas, semicolons, colons, dashes, apostrophes, and quotation marks. We will also discuss the use of punctuation to correct run-on sentences and sentence fragments.

Commas

Use a comma:
- (Rule 1) in series and lists.
- (Rule 2) after an introductory phrase.
- (Rule 3) to set off nonrestrictive clauses.
- (Rule 4) to set off interjections and transitional phrases.
- (Rule 5) with a coordinating conjunction to separate two independent clauses.

- **Rule 1** – Use a comma to separate each item in a series or list of three or more words, phrases, or clauses. Also, use commas with descriptive words where two or more adjectives modify the same noun.

   Example:

   I <u>made the beds, swept the floors, vacuumed the carpet, and scrubbed the bathtub</u> to get ready for our guests. Then I went shopping to stock the refrigerator with <u>drinks, vegetables, and fruit</u>. I hope I'm ready to welcome them into our home and to have a great visit.

In this example, the four underlined clauses in the opening series are separated by commas, and the three underlined words in the list are separated by commas. Notice that the concluding sentence does not contain any commas. In this sentence, the clause *to welcome them into our home* and the clause *to have a great visit* are part of a series of only two elements and are simply separated by the conjunction *and*. Note that a series of words or phrases is marked by a relationship between the elements, whereas a list is simply a notation of two or more words that may or may not be related. For instance, in the example above, the first sentence contains a series of clauses. Each clause is related because they are all actions that the person took. The second sentence contains a list of items such as you would take to the grocery store.

Commas are also used with descriptive words. Use a comma in a series of two or more adjectives that modify the same noun.

   Example:

   The <u>long, narrow, winding road</u> lead to a <u>beautiful, serene lake</u>.

In this example, *long*, *narrow*, and *winding* are adjectives that all modify the noun *road*. Thus, they are separated by commas. Likewise, *beautiful* and *serene* modify *lake* and are separated by commas. Note that no comma follows the last adjective in the series; also be careful in determining the function of the last word of the series. You must make sure that all the adjectives equally modify the noun. For example,

Before you watch TV, I want you to clean the <u>dirty, grimy kitchen sink</u>.

In this example, *kitchen sink* acts as a single noun because without *kitchen*, *sink* is not adequately identified. Therefore, *grimy* is the last adjective before the noun in the series and no comma should be placed after it.

✔ <u>Check your work</u>

Look through your work for any series of words, phrases or clauses. If there are two or more of these elements, place a comma after all but the last one.

Example (without punctuation):

He thought taking a road trip would <u>help him feel rejuvenated</u> <u>allow him to work through his feelings</u> and <u>provide some much needed solitude in which to get his studying done</u>.

Here the three clauses are underlined. Once you have identified these clauses, you should place commas after each clause except the last one:

He thought taking a road trip would help him feel rejuvenated, allow him to work through his feelings, and provide some much needed solitude in which to get his studying done.

This example contains a list of adjectives:

She looked longingly through the window at the lovely elegant pearl necklace.

First, identify the list of words: *lovely*, *elegant*, and *pearl* modify *necklace*. Now confirm that each adjective equally modifies the noun *necklace*. To do this, insert the word *and* in between each adjective:

She looked longingly through the window at the lovely *and* elegant *and* pearl necklace.

Clearly, the sentence does not make sense with the *and* between *elegant* and *pearl*. Therefore, you should place the commas appropriately:

She looked longingly through the window at the lovely, elegant pearl necklace.

➢ **Rule 2** – Use a comma to set off an introductory word, phrase, or clause from the independent clause that follows. Introductory elements that require a comma are prepositional phrases, subordinating clauses, transitional words or phrases, and verbal phrases.

A *prepositional phrase* begins with a preposition and includes any modifiers or objects. Prepositional phrases usually signal a relationship, particularly a relationship of time or location.

Examples:

<u>In the movie *Titanic*</u>, Leonardo di Caprio's character Jack dies.

<u>Since the accident last year</u>, she has been afraid to drive on the highway.

Both introductory clauses in these examples begin with prepositions. The clauses indicate a relationship of location (<u>*In the movie*</u>...) and time (<u>*Since the accident*</u>...) between the introductory phrases and the independent clauses that follow. Therefore, they must be set off by commas.

A *subordinating clause* begins with a *subordinator*, which is a word that indicates a relationship—usually a relationship of time or location—between the clause it begins and the independent clause that follows. This relationship makes a subordinating clause similar to a prepositional phrase. However, unlike a prepositional phrase, a subordinating clause can also be referred to as a dependent clause because it has both a subject and a verb. It is a dependent clause, not an independent clause, because it cannot stand alone as a sentence.

Example:

<u>When I first entered the workforce</u>, we didn't have all the modern technological conveniences that make today's business world move at such a rapid pace.

Here the phrase *When I first entered the workforce* begins with the subordinator *When*, which signals a time relationship between the subordinating clause and the independent clause that follows. Although this clause has a subject (*I*) and a verb (*entered*), it cannot stand alone as a sentence and requires the independent clause to complete the thought. Here is another example:

<u>Before I had a chance to answer</u>, he snatched the paper out of my hands and threw it in the fire.

Here again an introductory subordinating clause requires the independent clause to complete the sentence. In both examples, a comma is required to set off the subordinating clause from the independent clause.

Transitional words and phrases add coherence to your writing. They help connect one sentence to the next. A comprehensive list of transitional words and phrases appears later in this chapter, but here are some of the most commonly used transitions: *finally, furthermore, moreover,* and *next* indicate sequence; *again, likewise,* and *similarly* indicate comparison; *although, but, however, by contrast,* and *on the other hand* indicate contrast; *for example, in fact,* and *specifically* indicate examples; *accordingly, as a result, consequently,* and *therefore* indicate cause and effect.

Example:

Dear Employees,

I am writing to tell you about a new incentive program we are beginning here at ABC Company. <u>Specifically,</u> this incentive program will focus on rewarding sales. Our customer base has dropped drastically this year. <u>Consequently,</u> we must look for new ways to increase sales. <u>Although we have offered incentives in the past</u>, this program will be different because it will reward you for improvement in sales rather than for your sales numbers. <u>Furthermore,</u> you will not only be able to earn monetary rewards, but you may also be awarded with extra vacation days.

Happy selling,
Mr. Smith

In this example, transitional words and phrases are used to make the text flow more smoothly. A comma is required after each transitional word or phrase.

Verbal phrases contain verb elements but function as nouns, adjectives or adverbs rather than verbs. There are two kinds of verbal phrases that can act as introductory phrases and therefore must be set off by commas: participial phrases and infinitive phrases.

Participial phrases are made up of a present participle (the *–ing* form of a verb) or a past participle (the *–ed* form of a verb) as well as any modifiers or objects. Participial phrases act as adjectives because they describe, or modify, the subject in the independent clause.

Examples:

<u>Standing alone by the door</u>, Ricky watched the rest of the boys dance with their dates.

<u>Angered by the kids' cutting remarks</u>, Naomi stormed out of the room and then burst into tears.

The first example contains a participial phrase that contains the present participle *Standing*. The introductory phrase *Standing alone by the door* describes Ricky. In the second example, the past participle *Angered* makes up the participial phrase, and the full introductory phrase describes Naomi.

Infinitive phrases are made up of an infinitive as well as any modifiers or objects.

Examples:

<u>To win a gold medal</u>, you must work very hard.

<u>To earn a high score on the GMAT</u>, you must study this guide thoroughly.

To win is the infinitive in the first sentence, and *To earn* is the infinitive in the second sentence. Both infinitives serve as part of the introductory phrase, which must be set off by commas.

✔ <u>Check your work</u>

To find introductory phrases that should be set off with a comma, first look for the subject and verb of the independent clause. Then note any words that precede the subject and verb. Other than articles and adjectives, any words or phrases that precede the subject and verb make up the introductory phrase. You can then confirm this by identifying the introductory phrase.

Example:

The strongest qualities of a teacher are patience and understanding.

Here *qualities* is the subject (don't be thrown off by *of a teacher*) and *are* is the verb. *The* and *strongest* precede the subject in this sentence. *The* is an article and *strongest* is an adjective, so there is no need for a comma here. Now look at this example:

Knowing that the strongest qualities of a teacher are patience and understanding, Beth highlighted these qualities on her résumé.

Here *Beth* is the subject and *highlighted* is the verb. The phrase *Knowing that the strongest qualities of a teacher are patience and understanding* is a participial phrase and therefore should be set off with a comma.

Many writers do not place a comma after a short introductory clause.

Example:

This morning I stopped at the bagel shop for coffee.

Here a comma is acceptable after *This morning*; however, it is not necessary. You can use your ear to make a decision in cases like these. Often commas may be placed where there would be a pause if the sentence is spoken. When in doubt, however, use a comma.

➤ **Rule 3** – Use a comma to set off nonrestrictive clauses and phrases, clauses and phrases that are not essential in identifying the words they modify. Adjectival clauses and appositives (words that rename a noun) are most often nonrestrictive.

Adjectival clauses are phrases that begin with *who*, *whom*, *whose*, *which*, *that*, *when*, *where*, or *why*. In many cases, an adjectival clause is nonrestrictive such as in the following example:

The heart, <u>which pumps the body's blood</u>, is necessary to sustain life.

In this sentence, the adjectival clause *which pumps the body's blood* is set off by commas because it is not essential to the sentence. The sentence would have the same meaning without the clause. By contrast, the adjectival clause in the next sentence is restrictive because it is necessary to convey the meaning of the sentence:

The police who are investigating the murders in Maryland are using geographic profiling to aid in their search for the perpetrator.

The adjectival clause *who are investigating the murders in Maryland* is necessary to provide the reader with full details about the police and the murderer for whom they are searching. Without this phrase, the reader would not know that the police are in Maryland and that they are investigating a murderer.

Appositives act as nouns or noun substitutes by modifying the noun that precedes the appositive. Just as with adjectival clauses, nonrestrictive appositives are set off by commas, whereas restrictive appositives are not.

Nonrestrictive examples:

My high school English teacher, Mr. Roper, taught me how to use commas properly.
She drove her new car, a Honda Accord, to the senior center to pick up her grandmother.
The book club will be meeting this Wednesday to discuss the latest book, Grisham's *Rainmaker*.

In these examples, the underlined phrases are nonrestrictive appositives, which rename the noun preceding them. These phrases add interesting description to the sentences, but they are not necessary to make the sentences complete and understandable. On the other hand, some appositives are essential to capture the full meaning of the sentence. Such restrictive appositives should not be set off with commas as shown in the following examples:

My son Michael is two years old, and my other son Jacob is five months old.
Meet me at 6:00 at the new restaurant *Vinny's Vittles* that just opened on Main Street.
My friend Tammy met me at the beach yesterday.

The appositives in these examples are necessary in specifying the subjects. This information is necessary so the reader has a clear understanding of the subject involved in the text.

✓ Check your work

Review each sentence in your writing. Identify the adjectival phrases and appositives and the nouns they modify. For each adjectival phrase or appositive, ask yourself if the phrase provides important identifying information about the noun, or if it just provides "extra" information. If you are still unsure, read the sentence without the adjectival phrase or appositive. Does the sentence still have its full meaning? If so, set the phrase off with commas. If not, omit the commas.

➢ **Rule 4** – Use a comma to set off interjections and transitional phrases.

An *interjection* is usually one or two words that interrupt the flow of a sentence and give extra information about the content of the sentence. Although an interjection provides added detail that enhances the reader's knowledge, generally the information provided by an interjection could be omitted with little or no effect on the meaning of the sentence. Therefore, most interjections should be set off by commas as in the following examples:

I could probably take, say, five people in my van for the carpool.
She was, oddly enough, the only one who entered the contest.
I was thinking, by the way, that we could stop by the store on the way home.

A *transitional phrase* directs the flow of an essay. Often, transitional phrases are helpful in leading to a conclusion and therefore should not be set off with commas such as in these two examples:

His strategy was to impress the boss and thus receive the promotion.
I was tired and therefore did not want to go to the party.

In these examples, the transitional words serve to fully define the meaning of the sentences. There are instances, however, where a transitional word could be omitted without affecting the meaning of the sentence.

Examples:

I was not confident, however, that he knew the answer.
The message when on to say, furthermore, that he would not be coming home for dinner.

The transitional words in these examples enhance the text by emphasizing the direction in which the meaning of the sentence is moving. However, the meaning of the sentences would be the same without the transitional words.

✓ Check your work

To double-check your use of commas with interjections, identify any word or words that interrupt your sentence and have little or no effect to the meaning of the sentence. Set these words off with commas. Next, check for transitional words, keeping in mind the list of common transitional phrases we discussed earlier. Once you have identified the transitional words, ask yourself if the words are necessary to convey the meaning of the sentence. If they are necessary, don't set them off with commas; if they aren't, use commas.

➢   **Rule 5** – Use a comma and a coordinating conjunction to join two independent clauses.

An *independent clause* is a group of words that contain both a subject and a verb and can stand alone as a sentence.

Example:

I drove my car to work. (*I* is the subject, and *drove* is the verb.)

A *coordinating conjunction* is a word that serves as a link between a word or group of words. These conjunctions are easy to remember by using the acronym BOYFANS:

> **B**ut
> **O**r
> **Y**et
> **F**or
> **A**nd
> **N**or
> **S**o

Short, choppy sentences can make your writing tedious to read. To provide some interest and variety to your writing, you will want to join some of the sentences in your essays. To do so, you will need to use a comma and a coordinating conjunction. Let's look at some examples:

Too choppy:

I took a long lunch. I went back to work. I got behind on my work. I had to stay late.

Better:

I took a long lunch, <u>and</u> I went back to work. I got behind on my work, <u>so</u> I had to stay late.

Too choppy:

My guests were arriving in an hour. I wanted to throw a memorable New Year's Eve party. I made the punch and hors d'oeuvres ahead of time. I found that I still had a lot to get done to get ready. I decided to put the ice in the punch. Then I discovered that my icemaker was broken. I didn't have time to go to the store. I wasn't prepared to serve anything else either. I hurried to the pantry to view my options. All I had were some tea bags. I decided to throw a New Year's Eve tea party instead.

Better:

My guests were arriving in an hour, <u>and</u> I wanted to throw a memorable New Year's Eve party. I made the punch and hors d'oeuvres ahead of time, <u>yet</u> I found that I still had a lot to get done to get ready. I decided to put the ice in the punch, <u>but</u> then I discovered that my icemaker was broken. I didn't have time to go to the store, <u>nor</u> was I prepared to serve anything else. I hurried to the pantry to view my options. All I had were some tea bags, <u>so</u> I decided to throw a New Year's Eve tea party instead.

In both examples, combining sentences with commas and conjunctions make them more interesting and easier to read. We will learn more ways to create interest in your writing when we discuss writing style later on. For now, let's make sure we can apply Rule 5 correctly.

✔ Check your work

To properly combine two independent clauses with a comma and a conjunction, you must check to make sure that the clauses joined by the comma and conjunction are indeed independent clauses. To do this, first find all the conjunctions. Then look at the clauses on either side of each conjunction. Does each clause have a subject and a verb? Can each clause stand alone as sentences? If so, the conjunction is properly placed and a comma should precede the conjunction.

Incorrect:

We went to the mall last night, and bought some new dresses for work.

Correct:

We went to the mall last night and bought some new dresses for work.

Correct:

We went to the mall last night, and Terri bought some new dresses for work.

In the first example, *and* is the conjunction. *We went to the mall last night* is an independent clause (*we* is the subject, *went* is the verb). However, *bought some new dresses for work* is not an independent clause because there is no subject. Therefore, the sentence can be corrected by simply omitting the comma as seen in the second example. Or, if there is a possible subject for the sentence, it can be added and the comma can stay as seen in the third example. Here is another example where the same guidelines apply:

Incorrect:

He committed the crime, but didn't think the judge's ruling was fair.

Correct:

He committed the crime but didn't think the judge's ruling was fair.

Correct:

He committed the crime, but he didn't think the judge's ruling was fair.

Using a semicolon is another way to correctly join two independent clauses, and we will discuss it next.

Semicolons

Use a semicolon
➢   (Rule 1) to join two independent clauses.
➢   (Rule 2) to join more than two independent clauses.
➢   (Rule 3) to separate items in a series.

➢   **Rule 1** – Use a semicolon to join two independent clauses that are closely related. You may also use a semicolon in coordination with a transitional word and in place of a comma and a conjunction.

Sometimes a period seems like too strong of a mark to use to separate two closely related sentences, but a comma does not emphasize both sentences adequately. In cases like this, you can use a semicolon to join two independent clauses. Using a semicolon to join two independent clauses gives you as the writer a subtle way of showing a relationship between two clauses. You might use a semicolon, for example, if your second sentence restates your first. Or perhaps your second sentence more clearly defines your first sentence by giving an example or by presenting a contrast. Finally, you may want to link two clauses with a semicolon if they have a cause and effect relationship.

Example:

Loyalty is the foundation upon which relationships are built; without loyalty, friendships and marriages crumble.

In this example, the second sentence restates the first sentence. A semicolon is appropriate here and functions to convey the close relationship between the two sentences.

Example:

The puppy scooted blindly across the floor; his eyes hadn't opened yet leaving him totally dependent on his mother.

The second sentence in this example more clearly defines why the puppy is moving around blindly. The semicolon ties the explanation of the first clause to the description in the second clause. A semicolon is also functional in this last example:

Of course it's pouring down rain on the day of the picnic; it was sunny the day we were inside roller-skating!

The semicolon here emphasizes the irony that is portrayed in this sentence by connecting the two contrasting sentences.

Contrasting clauses may also be joined by using a semicolon along with a transitional word.

Example:

These days there is a cure for every ailment; however, the side effects of many medications are worse than the condition for which the medication is prescribed.

Here two independent clauses are joined with a semicolon and the transitional word *however*. The second clause shows that medicines don't always produce positive effects in contrast with the first clause, which indicates that almost every ailment can be cured. The transitional word *however* further defines this contrasting relationship. A transitional word may also serve to emphasize a cause-effect relationship such as in this example:

The drought has greatly affected many farmers; therefore, the price of produce is expected to rise.

You may choose to use semicolons to portray a close relationship between two clauses as seen in the examples above. In other cases, you may recognize that using a variety of punctuation marks adds interest to your writing. Based on this recognition, the choice to join two clauses with a semicolon and a transitional word may be a stylistic choice rather than a grammatical one. Likewise, adding variety to your writing may be the purpose when it comes to replacing a comma and conjunction with a semicolon.

Example:

The slippery rock presented the climbers with a challenge, <u>so</u> they watched their footing very closely.

Becomes:
The slippery rock presented the climbers with a challenge; they watched their footing very closely.

In the first example, the two independent clauses are joined with a comma and a conjunction, and in the second sentence, a semicolon replaces the comma and the conjunction. While both sentences are correct and function equally well, you may choose to use the semicolon this way to add variety. Sometimes, however, it is necessary to replace the comma with a semicolon in order to provide clarity. In these cases, you may or may not omit the conjunction. For example,

> From such a great distance, the man could not make out the faces of the evil, crafty conspirators, but, if he moved any closer, he would be taking an unnecessary, careless risk of being seen.

Because this sentence contains so much punctuation, it is a bit tedious to read and can be confusing. To remedy this, a semicolon can be used to join the two clauses. In this case, the conjunction *but* is important in enhancing the cause and effect relationship in the sentence and therefore it should remain:

> From such a great distance, the man could not make out the faces of the evil, crafty conspirators; but, if he moved any closer, he would be taking an unnecessary, careless risk of being seen.

The semicolon in the example above provides much needed clarity to the sentence by separating the two independent clauses.

✔ Check your work

To use a semicolon to join two independent clauses, analyze the two clauses carefully to make sure there is a close relationship between the two before placing the semicolon. Be careful not to misuse semicolons, especially when you use them with a transitional word or in place of a comma and conjunction. For example:

Incorrect:

I was forced; therefore, to take the detour around the construction site.

Correct:

I was forced, therefore, to take the detour around the construction site.

In this example, *therefore* is a transitional word and should be set off with commas. Furthermore, the clause *I was forced* is an independent clause and *to take the detour around the construction site* is not, so the clauses cannot be set apart by a semicolon.

Take the same caution when replacing a comma and conjunction with a semicolon. Remember that, to join two clauses with a comma and a conjunction, both clauses must be independent. That is, each clause must be able to stand alone as a separate sentence. For example,

Incorrect:

He completed the yard work, and then enjoyed a lemonade break with his mom.

Incorrect:

He completed the yard work; and then enjoyed a lemonade break with his mom.

Correct:

He completed the yard work and then enjoyed a lemonade break with his mom.

The subject in this sentence is *He* and the compound verb is *completed* and *enjoyed*. There is no subject in the second part of the sentence, so it is incorrect to use a comma and conjunction in the sentence. Likewise, a semicolon cannot be used.

➢ **Rule 2** – Use a semicolon to join more than two independent clauses.

In Rule 1, we discussed using a semicolon to join two independent clauses. Semicolons can also be used to join multiple independent clauses in more complex sentences:

Example:

Over the past few years, violence has adopted a new calling card; it is more random, gruesome and sinister than ever. In this country of freedom, violence has made its presence known in all areas of life. In schools, students take the lives of other students before taking their own; a close knit community is gripped by fear because of random shootings by a sniper; a father kills another father over their sons' hockey game.

This example could be written as a few separate sentences; however, since the independent clauses are all closely related, it is acceptable to link them with semicolons. Joining multiple independent clauses is often a stylistic choice and an effective one because it makes an impact by more closely connecting the sentences. When not serving just a stylistic choice, joining more than two independent clauses with a semicolon adds clarity such as in the following example:

Confusing:

The Thompsons spent two exciting weeks on safari in Africa and returned with wild tales of their trip. They saw all the sights anyone who goes on safari dreams of: They saw zebras, rhinoceroses, and giraffes grazing on the savanna, they witnessed a lion chasing after an antelope, a herd of elephants stomped across the road in front of their truck, and some curious, chattering monkeys came up to their truck and took food out of their hands.

Better:

The Thompsons spent two exciting weeks on safari in Africa and returned with wild tales of their trip. They saw all the sights anyone who goes on safari dreams of: They saw zebras, rhinoceroses, and giraffes grazing on the savanna; they witnessed a lion chasing after an antelope; a herd of elephants stomped across the road in front of their truck; and some curious, chattering monkeys came up to their truck and took food out of their hands.

In the first example, the writer uses commas to separate the series of clauses. However, because the clauses themselves contain lists of words separated by commas, the sentence is confusing; the semicolons in the second example provide clarity by dividing the clauses.

✓ Check your work

To join multiple independent clauses with a semicolon, make sure the clauses you are joining are related. Also consider using a semicolon instead of a comma to join clauses. To do this, check for commas within the clauses. Too many commas cause confusion and can be eliminated by using semicolons instead. Be careful, however, not to use semicolons too often because overuse can make a writer sound pedantic. When used conservatively, semicolons can add a great deal of impact. To avoid overusing semicolons, reread your text and make sure your use of semicolons is sporadic; semicolons should never appear as often as commas or periods.

Too many semicolons:

My next interviewee came in and sat across from me; she tried to put on a confident face; she maintained eye contact throughout the interview; I could tell she was nervous, though; she played anxiously with her ring; she shifted positions every few seconds; her voice quivered a bit.

Better:

My next interviewee came in and sat across from me. She tried to put on a confident face by maintaining eye contact throughout the interview. I could tell she was nervous, though; she played anxiously with her ring, shifted positions every few seconds and her voice quivered a bit.

Semicolons are used in place of periods and almost all of the commas in the first example. In the rewrite of the example, all but one semicolon is replaced with a period. The remaining semicolon is placed after *I could tell she was nervous, though.* The clause that follows gives a description that further defines the assumption that the interviewee was nervous.

> ➤ **Rule 3** – Use a semicolon to separate items in a series when the items themselves contain commas.

Just as you should use semicolons to join independent clauses when the clauses contain commas, you should also use semicolons to separate words and phrases in a series when those words and phrases contain commas. For example,

> **Confusing:**
>
> I boarded a flight in Los Angeles, California, had a two-hour layover in Detroit, Michigan, and finally landed in London, England.

> **Better:**
>
> I boarded a flight in Los Angeles, California; had a two-hour layover in Detroit, Michigan; and finally landed in London, England.

This sentence contains a series of clauses, which must be separated. However, each clause contains the name of a city and a state, which also must be separated. Using only commas in this example causes confusion because it is difficult to tell which commas separate clauses and which ones separate the elements within each clause. Separating the clauses with semicolons clarifies the meaning. Here is another example:

> All employees must bring a pen, paper, and a notebook to the first day of training; a laptop, highlighter and paperclips to day two; and a sample report, pie chart and three markers to the last day.

Here again, too many commas creates confusion, so in order to simplify the sentence and make it more clear, the clauses in the series are separated by semicolons.

✔ <u>Check your work</u>

Check each of the independent clauses you have joined with commas. Do any of the independent clauses contain commas? If so, joining the independent clauses with a semicolon instead of a comma will probably make the sentence clearer.

> **Confusing:**
>
> My pottery class is on Mondays, Wednesdays, and Fridays, and I baby sit my nephew, niece, and neighbor's son on Tuesdays and Thursdays.

> **Better:**
>
> My pottery class is on Mondays, Wednesdays, and Fridays; and I baby sit my nephew, niece and neighbor's son on Tuesdays and Thursdays.

Again, be careful not to overuse semicolons. If, after you review your writing, you feel you have used semicolons too often, consider using other methods to join phrases. For example, you might use a period to divide clauses into separate sentences. Remember that semicolons can make a big impact but only when used conservatively and correctly.

Colons

Use a colon:
> ➤ (Rule 1) to introduce an explanation or example.
> ➤ (Rule 2) to introduce a series, list, or quotation.

> ➤ **Rule 1** – Use a colon to relate two independent clauses when introducing an explanation or example.

When a comma does not place adequate emphasis on the relationship between two independent clauses, you can use a semicolon. When a semicolon does not provide adequate emphasis, you can use a colon. A colon joins two independent clauses to emphasize the relationship between the two clauses and is often used to introduce an explanation or an example.

Example:

When I picture my dream house, it is set in beautiful scenery: the beach or mountains, for example, would provide an ideal setting for a home.

In this sentence, the colon serves to introduce two examples of a dream home. The colon in this example strengthens the relationship between the idea of a beach or mountain home and the subject of dream homes in the first clause. A colon can also introduce an explanation such as in the following example:

Dave and Stephanie's presentation lacked the usual enthusiasm: this could be because they were at the office all night working on the ad campaign.

The second clause in this example explains the first clause and therefore may be introduced with a colon.

✓ Check your work

Just as with semicolons, the choice to use colons can be a stylistic one. If you do choose to use a colon to introduce an explanation or example, make sure that both the preceding clause and the clause that follows are independent clauses.

Capitalize the clause that follows a colon if it is a formal statement or if the content that is introduced contains more than one sentence.

Example (formal statement):

Our club bylaws shall set forth the following: Rules for meetings, code of conduct, and membership procedures.

Example (more than one clause):

When thinking of a future career, there are many choices: Becoming a lawyer would be a good financial decision. On the other hand, teaching may provide more personal satisfaction.

➢ **Rule 2** – Use a colon after an independent clause to introduce a series, list, or quotation.

Use a colon to introduce a series or list such as in the following examples:

We need to get several things done before our trip: pay the bills, water the plants, and take the dog to the kennel.

Before we can take off, you must do the following: fasten your seat belt, turn off your cell phone, and return your tray table to its upright position.

The names of the people who made the volleyball team are as follows: Ruth, Mary Lynn, Amy, Sarah, Alicia, and Elizabeth.

Note that when the word *following* or *follows* is used to introduce a list or series you must use a colon. You should also use a colon to introduce a quotation.

Example:

As people seek to build relationships and, in so doing, break down the walls of racism, they should remember Martin Luther King, Jr.'s famous words: "I have a dream that [we] will one day live in a nation where [we] will not be judged by the color of [our] skin but by the content of [our] character."

✓ Check your work

Use a colon to introduce a series or list. Always use a colon if the clause that introduces the list or series contains the term *follows* or *following*.

Example:

The following improvements need to be made to your house before you try to sell it: new carpet should be installed, the outside trim should be painted, and the fixtures in the downstairs bathroom should be replaced.

Do not use a colon if the list or series is introduced by phrases such as *especially*, *such as*, *namely*, *for instance*, *for example*, or *that is* unless the series is made up of one or more independent clauses.

Incorrect (colon introducing a series of phrases):

Some of my life goals, for example: to ski in the Alps, bungee jump from Victoria Falls, and visit the Great Wall of China.

Correct (colon introducing a series of independent clauses):

I have set some goals that I wish to achieve before I get too old to do so. For example: I want to ski in the Alps, bungee jump from Victoria Falls, and visit the Great Wall of China.

Note that a comma would work in this sentence as well. The colon following *For example* places more emphasis on the text that follows.

Do not use a colon to introduce a series that is the object of the verb in the sentence. For example,

Incorrect:

After the maitre d' seated us, I ordered: French onion soup, a Caesar salad, and filet mignon.

Correct:

After the maitre d' seated us, I ordered French onion soup, a Caesar salad, and filet mignon.

You may use a colon to introduce a quotation and, in this instance, you must capitalize the first word of the quotation.

Example:

The principles of this country are founded on the *Declaration of Independence* and its famous words: "We hold these truths to be self-evident, that all men are created equal, that they are endowed by their Creator with certain unalienable Rights, that among these are Life, Liberty and the pursuit of Happiness."

Dashes

Use dashes
➤   (Rule 1) to interrupt a sentence.
➤   (Rule 2) to emphasize parenthetical or explanatory information.

➤   **Rule 1** – Use a dash to interrupt the normal word order of a sentence.

Example:

If you are interested in martial arts—and who wouldn't be interested in such a disciplined art?—there are many centers for instruction.

The dashes in this example allow you to break into the sentence in an informal way. Here is another example:

I was unable—unwilling, really—to head up the new committee at the office.

✓ <u>Check your work</u>

Although commas may be used to set off phrases that interrupt a sentence, dashes add emphasis to the clause that is set off. In addition, dashes set an informal tone in your writing. Because of their informality, dashes should be used sparingly, if ever, in graduate writing. When you do choose to use dashes, you may include question marks and exclamation points in the clauses that are set off by dashes (as in the first example above).

➢ **Rule 2** – Use dashes to set off parenthetical or explanatory information.

    Example:

    The editor of the *Banner Herald* often employs hyperbole—deliberate exaggeration or overstatement to show special emphasis or create humor—to express his political views.

Here dashes set apart the definition of *hyperbole*. Though not necessary to the meaning of the sentence, the definition adds useful information. Again, dashes are an informal way of setting off information; a comma would serve the same purpose here.

✓ <u>Check your work</u>

Review each sentence in your writing and identify any information that is parenthetical or that explains a topic in the sentence. You may set this information off with dashes. Remember, though, that dashes should seldom be used in formal writing. In formal writing, you should use commas to set off these elements from the rest of the sentence.

Apostrophes

Use an apostrophe
➢   (Rule 1) in contractions.
➢   (Rule 2) to show possession.

➢ **Rule 1** – Use an apostrophe in a contraction, a word that is a shortened combination of two words.

Contractions are used in informal writing and serve to shorten two words by leaving out some letters and joining the two words with an apostrophe. Following is a chart that lists some common contractions and the words that form them:

Words that combine to form a contraction	Contractions
it is	it's
I am	I'm
he will	he'll
they are	they're
you are	you're
we will	we'll
could not	couldn't
would not	wouldn't
cannot	can't
does not	doesn't
do not	don't
will not	won't
let us	let's
I would	I'd
they would	they'd
was not	wasn't
I will	I'll
should not	shouldn't
we had	we'd
they will	they'll

✓ <u>Check your work</u>

The use of contractions is quite simple: if you wish to shorten two words into one and it is appropriate to do so using an apostrophe, you simply replace the words with the correct contraction. There are, however, some common mistakes people make when using contractions. There are a few contractions that sound like possessive words, and these are often confused. For example, the contraction *they're* sounds like the possessive *their*, but the two words have very different meanings.

Example (they're):
I don't know where they think *they're* going, but *they're* going to end up at a dead end.

Example (their):
When I saw them heading toward the dead end, I assumed they did not know *their* way.

Example (they're and their):
They're going to run into a dead end because they don't know *their* way.

Remember that *they're* is short for *they are. Their* is the third person plural possessive. The next pair of words to watch out for is the contraction *you're* and the possessive *your*.

Example (you're):
You're not going to succeed in school if you don't study hard.

Example (your):
Your success in school is dependent upon hard work.

Example (you're and your):
You're not going to succeed in school if you don't try *your* best in all that you do.

You're is short for *you are*, and *your* is the second person singular possessive. The final pair of words that can be confusing are *it's* and *its*.

Example (it's):
It's seemingly impossible for a cat to travel that far to get home.

Example (its):
A cat will travel a long way to find *its* home and the family it loves.

Example (it's and its):
It's amazing the distance a cat will travel to find *its* way back home.

Be careful when you use *it's* or *its*; remember that *it's* is the contraction for *it is* and *its* is the third person singular possessive.

To check for proper use of a contraction, especially those that can be tricky, substitute the words that have been replaced by the contraction. If the full-length word makes sense, the contraction is correct. If not, you need to check your spelling. Once again, though, keep in mind that contractions are more appropriate for use in informal writing.

➢   **Rule 2** – Use an apostrophe to show possession.

To show the possessive form of singular nouns, add an apostrophe and an *–s*

Examples:

Teddy cleaned the *dog's* house before he and his family went on vacation.
The teacher used *Julia's* homework as an example because it was exceptional.
She didn't feel comfortable borrowing *Harris's* car.

To show the possessive form of plural nouns, add an *–s* and an apostrophe:

Examples:

Coach Hannigan distributed the *girls'* uniforms at soccer practice.

Some plural nouns, however, do not end in *–s*. In these instances, add an apostrophe and an *–s*.

Examples:

The *women's* meeting will be held in the gymnasium on Thursday night.
All of the *children's* bikes were parked in the driveway.
Competition between *men's* sports teams is fierce.

✓ Check your work
Check for the correct use of apostrophes with possessives by first identifying the nouns that show possession. Then identify whether the noun is singular or plural. If the noun is singular, add an apostrophe and an *–s*. If the noun is plural, add an *–s* and an apostrophe. Finally, take note of any irregular plural nouns that do not end in *–s*. Add an apostrophe and an *–s* to irregular nouns.

Quotation Marks

Use quotation marks to set off quotations and dialogue.

Example (quotation):

In his famous inaugural address, President John F. Kennedy implored, "My fellow Americans, ask not what your country can do for you: Ask what you can do for your country."

Example (dialog):

"Where are you going tonight?" asked Greg.
"Beth and I are going to the library to get some research done," Susan replied. "Then we're heading to the mall to do some shopping."

When using quotation marks
➤   (Rule 1) commas and periods go inside the quotation marks.
➤   (Rule 2) semicolons and colons go outside the quotation marks.
➤   (Rule 3) question marks and exclamation points go outside the quotation marks.

➤   **Rule 1** – Commas and periods should be placed inside quotation marks.

Example:

"I don't understand what you're trying to say," Glen said. "You need to speak up."

Don't use a comma and quotation marks for indirect quotes.

Example (direct quote):

He said, "I don't have time to take the car for an oil change today."

Example (indirect quote):

He said that he didn't have time to take the car for an oil change today.

✓ Check your work
Place commas and periods inside quotation marks. To determine if a quote is a direct or indirect quote, ask yourself if the quote comes directly from the speaker and if the quote contains the exact words of the speaker. If so, place quotation marks around the quote. If not, there should be no comma or quotation marks.

➢ **Rule 2** – Place semicolons and colons outside quotation marks.

Example (semicolon):

My mom always used to say, "A stitch in time saves nine"; I always remember that quote when I am tempted to procrastinate.

Example (colon):

Patrick Henry made a strong statement when he said, "Give me liberty or give me death": he felt that it would be better to die than to live in a country without freedom.

✓ Check your work

When you use quotation marks with a semicolon or colon, first determine whether you are using the semicolon or colon correctly. Then make sure you place the semicolon or colon outside the quotation marks.

➢ **Rule 3** – Place question marks and exclamation points outside quotation marks unless they are a part of the quotation.

Examples (question mark):

Did you hear Professor Johnston say, "You must read the first 500 pages for a quiz on Monday"?

Stunned, she implored, "Why didn't you tell me you were leaving for good?"

In the first example, the quotation is a statement that does not require a question mark; however, the overall sentence that contains the quotation is a question. Therefore, the question mark goes outside the quotation marks. In the second example, though, the quotation is a question, so the question mark goes inside the quotation marks.

Examples (exclamation point):

I can't believe she finally said, "I love you"!

The woman ran after the thief yelling, "Hey, come back with my purse!"

Overall, the first sentence is an exclamatory sentence, but the phrase *I love you* is not; therefore, the exclamation point goes outside the quotation marks. *Hey, come back with my purse* in the second sentence, however, is an exclamation, so the exclamation point goes inside the quotation marks.

✓ Check your work

Examine all quotations in your writing. If the quotation itself is a question or exclamation, place the appropriate punctuation mark inside the quotation marks. If, however, the overall sentence is a question or exclamation but the actual quote is not, the punctuation should be placed outside the quotation marks.

Sentence Fragments

A *sentence fragment* is a clause that is punctuated like an independent clause, but it lacks a grammatical element required to make it a complete sentence. As we discussed before, an independent clause must have a subject and a verb. Without both a subject and a verb, a clause is a sentence fragment because it cannot function alone.

Example (independent clause):

I ran down the road.

Examples (sentence fragments):

Ran down the road.

Running down the road.

The independent clause above has both a subject (*I*) and a verb (*ran*). The first example of a sentence fragment, however, has only a verb (*ran*). The last example contains the participle *Running*, which needs a helping verb like *was* as well as a subject like *He*: He <u>was running</u> down the road.

To correct sentence fragments in your writing
➢   (Step 1) identify them.
➢   (Step 2) revise them.

➢   **Step 1** – Identify sentence fragments in your writing.

To find sentence fragments in your writing, first analyze each sentence. In your analysis, mark the subject and verb by underlining the subject once and the verb twice. Following are some examples:

On our way to the store tomorrow, <u>we</u> <u>need</u> to stop at the bank.
Sprinting toward the finish line, <u>Dan</u> <u>took</u> a deep breath and pressed on.
<u>Providing</u> equal opportunity to all citizens <u>is</u> of utmost importance.

The first two examples begin with introductory phrases, which can be confusing so take care in identifying these types of clauses and isolating them from the independent clause. The third example contains a gerund, *providing*, which acts as a noun. Now let's analyze each sentence of a paragraph. First, we will underline each subject and each verb. Then we will flag each sentence that is a fragment with a star.

<u>Dan</u> always <u>has</u> busy days at his law office. *In the morning, <u>stops</u> for breakfast at a coffee shop near the office. *Upon entering the office. <u>Dan</u> <u>gets</u> his messages from his secretary. For the rest of the day <u>Dan</u> <u>keeps</u> busy. *Reviewing briefs and preparing witnesses. Usually <u>Dan</u> <u>does</u> not <u>have</u> time to go out to lunch, but his <u>secretary</u> generally <u>has</u> something delivered to him. Dan's <u>afternoon</u> <u>progresses</u> in much the same way as his morning. *When he gets home. <u>He</u> <u>is</u> exhausted. *Because he is so tired. <u>He</u> <u>goes</u> to bed at 8:00.

Clearly, many of the sentences in this paragraph need to be revised. Before we can complete the revisions, though, we need to analyze what the problem is in each of the identified sentence fragments. Let's look at each sentence:

<u>Dan</u> always <u>has</u> busy days at his law office. (This sentence is fine.)

*In the morning, <u>stops</u> for breakfast at a coffee shop near the office. (The introductory phrase here can make the sentence tricky because you may be tempted to identify *morning* as the subject. Although *stops* is the verb, the subject is missing.)

*Upon entering the office. (This introductory phrase has been set off by itself.)

<u>Dan</u> <u>gets</u> his messages from his secretary. (This sentence is fine.)

For the rest of the day, <u>Dan</u> <u>keeps</u> busy. (This sentence is fine, but again there is an introductory phrase, which can be deceiving.)

*Reviewing briefs and preparing witnesses. (This clause should act as the object of the sentence and therefore is missing both the subject and the verb.)

Usually <u>Dan</u> <u>does</u> not <u>have</u> time to go out to lunch, but his <u>secretary</u> generally <u>has</u> something delivered to him. (Two independent clauses are correctly joined here with a comma and a conjunction. In a sentence like this, identifying the subject and verb can be confusing. In the second clause, for example, it would be easy to mistake *his* as the subject when *his* is actually an adjective modifying the subject *secretary*.)

Dan's <u>afternoon</u> <u>progresses</u> in much the same way as his morning. (This sentence is fine, but again, *Dan's* could be confused as the subject when *afternoon* is actually the subject.)

*When he gets home. (The subject here is *he*, and the verb is *gets*. However, the subordinator *when* makes the sentence a dependent clause and it therefore cannot stand alone as a sentence.)

<u>He</u> <u>is</u> exhausted. (This sentence is fine.)

*Because he is so tired. (The subject here is *he*, and the verb is *is*. However, the subordinator *because* makes the sentence a dependent clause and it therefore cannot stand alone as a sentence.)

<u>He</u> <u>goes</u> to bed at 8:00. (This sentence is fine.)

> **Step 2** – After you have identified the sentences that are fragments, you must revise them. There are two ways to revise sentence fragments:

- Combine sentences to make them complete.

Example:

(Fragments) Because I was at the office working. I didn't make it to dinner.

(Revised) Because I was at the office working, I didn't make it to dinner.

- Add the necessary elements to the fragment to make it complete.

Example:

(Fragments) From the beginning. Wanted to practice law in a small town.

(Revised) From the beginning, he wanted to practice law in a small town.

Now, let's revise our example from Step 1:

Dan always has busy days at his law office. In the morning, he stops for breakfast at a coffee shop near the office. Upon entering the office, Dan gets his messages from his secretary. For the rest of the day Dan keeps busy reviewing briefs and preparing witnesses. Usually Dan does not have time to go out to lunch, but his secretary generally has something delivered to him. Dan's afternoon progresses in much the same way as his morning. When he gets home, he is exhausted. Because he is so tired, he goes to bed at 8:00.

*In the morning, stops for breakfast at a coffee shop near the office. (We corrected this sentence by adding the subject *he* after the introductory phrase.)

*Upon entering the office. (We corrected this sentence by replacing the period after *office* with a comma and thereby making it an introductory phrase and combining it with the next sentence.)

*Reviewing briefs and preparing witnesses. (We corrected this fragment by simply combining it with the complete clause that preceded it.)

*When he gets home. (We corrected this sentence by replacing the period after *home* with a comma and thereby making it an introductory phrase and combining it with the next sentence.)

*Because he is so tired. (We corrected this sentence by replacing the period after *tired* with a comma and thereby making it an introductory phrase and combining it with the next sentence.)

Once you have made your revisions, make sure you reread your writing. Identify the subject and verb in each sentence once again to make sure your revisions corrected the fragments.

Run-On Sentences

A *run-on sentence* contains one or more independent clauses but does not have all the proper words and marks of punctuation that are required to join independent clauses.

Example:

David went on a field trip to an aquarium with his classmates and they saw a large variety of fish.

In this example, two independent clauses are joined with a coordinating conjunction, but there is no comma. This type of run-on sentence is called a *fused* sentence. A fused sentence can also lack both a comma and a conjunction such as in the following example:

The debate over alien existence will probably continue for years some are sure they have seen aliens.

This next sentence contains a comma but no coordinating conjunction:

Many people believe in the powers of a psychic, sometimes even detectives depend on psychics to help solve crimes.

Because this sentence contains a comma but no coordinating conjunction, it is called a *comma splice*.

To correct run-on sentences in your writing
➢   (Step 1) identify them.
➢   (Step 2) revise them.

➢   **Step 1** – Identify run-on sentences in your writing.

To find run-on sentences in your writing, first analyze each sentence. In your analysis, mark the subject and verb by underlining the subject once and the verb twice. Following are some examples:

Osteoporosis is very common among women but drinking milk and taking calcium supplements can help prevent it.

This example is a fused sentence because it contains two independent clauses linked by a coordinating conjunction but no comma.

History provides us with interesting stories, it also helps us in the future because we can learn from mistakes made in history.

This example is a comma splice because it contains two independent clauses linked by a comma but no coordinating conjunction. These examples contain only two independent clauses that are not combined correctly. Many writers also link multiple clauses incorrectly. If you are prone to this error, it is important that you take the time to go through each sentence and identify the subjects and verbs. From there, you can revise your sentences accurately.

➢   **Step 2** – Revise your run-on sentences by using one of five methods:

•   Separate the clauses in to complete sentences.

Example:

(Run-on) Working together as a team is more productive than working individually, a team can get more accomplished than one person.

(Revised) Working together as a team is more productive than working individually. A team can get more accomplished than one person.

- Link the clauses with a semicolon.

Example:

(Run-on) Writing is great therapy letting off steam through the written word is a good way to work through frustration.

(Revised) Writing is great therapy; letting off steam through the written word is a good way to work through frustration.

- Link the clauses with a comma and a coordinating conjunction.

Example:

(Run-on) I went to Florida last week to go to Disney World with a friend but it rained the whole time that I was there.

(Revised) I went to Florida last week to go to Disney World with a friend, but it rained the whole time that I was there.

- Rewrite the clauses to form just one independent clause.

Example:

(Run-on) This summer has been a very hot one, it has been humid also.

(Revised) This summer has been a very hot and humid one.

- Rewrite the clauses to form one independent clause with an introductory dependent clause.

Example:

(Run-on) We re-painted our house, the old paint was peeling and fading.

(Revised) Because the old paint was peeling and fading, we re-painted our house.

Make sure you review your work after making revisions to ensure that all run-on sentences have indeed been corrected. In addition, try to use all five methods of revision in your writing; don't correct each run-on with the same method. Using different forms of revision will result in varying sentence patterns, which will enhance your writing style. We will discuss writing style shortly as well as strengthening the structure of your essay. First, however, let's make sure you know how to apply the rules of punctuation we just covered.

Warm-Up Drill I

> Directions: Read each sentence and then make necessary punctuation and spelling corrections. Pay special attention to sentence fragments and run-on sentences and re-write them so that they are grammatically correct. Answers and solutions begin on the next page.

1.   Dana is a foster mother. Takes care of newborns. When babies are put up for adoption a social worker places the baby in Dana's house where the baby stays until the adoption is completed usually the baby stays no longer than six weeks unless there is no adoptee lined up yet.

2.   Buying a new car is a big decision their are many factors to consider dependability for example is a key factor in choosing the car to suit your needs.

3.   The energetic boisterous boy climbed the jungle gym hung from the monkey bars jumped down and then ran to the merry-go-round.

4.   What do you think he meant when he said, "Your going to have to figure that one out on you're own"

5.   A cool sparkling stream meandered through the peaceful forest and some deer stopped to take a drink and glanced up for a moment to look at me they disappeared into the trees.

6.   Some people claim even boast that they've never read an entire book. This is there loss because reading leads to knowledge knowledge leads to power power enables people to influence those around them.

7.   That Halloween night can't have been spookier if it had come out of a story a horror story. Patches of fog enveloped the trees in some places and the trees cast dark eerie shadows in others. Because of the full moon.

8.   The mens' group did charity work this weekend they completed the following projects they helped rebuild a church that had been damaged in a tornado they completed some of the landscaping on the church grounds and they began repairs to the pastors home nearby the church.

9.   Many people suffer from "diet fatigue" they try diet after diet only to meet failure with each one. What they should be focusing on instead is nutritional eating and fitness nutritional eating consists of eating well-balanced servings of meats vegetables fruits and grains drinking lots of water and indulging in junk food sparingly. Proper fitness can come in the form of aerobic exercise walking sports or weight training making just a few adjustments in daily eating and exercise habits can make all the difference in a persons physical and emotional well-being.

10. The beautiful grand stain-glassed windows added a majestic feeling to the old cathedral.

Solutions to Warm-Up Drill I

1. Dana is a foster <u>mother who takes</u> care of newborns. When babies are put up for <u>adoption,</u> a social worker places the baby in Dana's house where the baby stays until the adoption is <u>completed. Usually</u> the baby stays no longer than six weeks unless there is no adoptee lined up yet.

    Takes care of newborns is a fragment; it was corrected by joining it to the first clause *Dana is a foster mother. When babies are put up for adoption* is an introductory dependent clause and should be followed by a comma. The last clause is a run-on sentence, and it was corrected by placing a period after *completed.*

2. Buying a new car is a big <u>decision. There</u> are many factors to <u>consider: dependability, for example,</u> is a key factor in choosing the car to suit your needs.

    The first clause is a run-on sentence and should be divided into two sentences; thus, a period was placed between *decision* and *There*. Moreover, *their* was replaced with the correct word *there*. Once you have divided the sentence into two separate clauses, notice that *dependability* is an example. Therefore, a colon should follow *consider*. In addition, *for example* should be set off by commas because it is an interjection.

3. The <u>energetic, boisterous</u> boy climbed the jungle <u>gym, hung</u> from the monkey <u>bars, jumped down, and</u> then ran to the merry-go-round.

    Energetic and *boisterous* are adjectives that modify *boy*. Because there are two adjectives modifying the same noun, they should be separated by a comma. In addition, a set of four phrases follows—*climbed the jungle gym, hung from the monkey bars, jumped down,* and *then ran to the merry-go-round*—and should also be separated by commas.

4. What do you think he meant when he said, "<u>You're</u> going to have to figure that one out on <u>your own</u>"?

    Your and *you're* are misspelled. The contraction *you're* should be the first word in the quotation, and the possessive *your* should precede *own*. The question mark in the sentence should be placed outside the quotation marks because the quotation itself is not a question; however, the complete sentence is a question.

5. A <u>cool, sparkling</u> stream meandered through the peaceful <u>forest. Some</u> deer stopped to take a drink. <u>Before they disappeared into the trees, they glanced up for a moment to look at me.</u>

    First, a comma should separate the series of adjectives *cool* and *sparkling*. Second, this clause is a run-on sentence and was corrected by dividing it into two independent clauses by placing a period between *forest* and *Some*. Finally, a third clause was created by converting the sentence fragment into an introductory clause.

6. Some people <u>claim, even boast, that they have</u> never read an entire book. This is <u>their</u> loss because reading leads to <u>knowledge; knowledge</u> leads to <u>power; power</u> enables people to influence those around them.

    Even boast is an interjection and should be set apart by commas. You should use commas instead of dashes because the topic of the sentences is formal. The contraction *they've* should be changed to *they have* to maintain the formality. The next sentence should contain the possessive *their*. Finally, the last clause is a run-on sentence. Because the clauses are closely related, they should be separated by semicolons.

7. That Halloween night <u>couldn't</u> have been spookier if it had come out of a <u>story—a</u> horror story. Patches of fog enveloped the trees in some <u>places. Because of the full moon, the trees cast dark, eerie shadows in others.</u>

    Can't is the wrong contraction here. You can test it by plugging in the full-length words—*That Halloween night cannot have been spookier. A horror story* at the end of the sentence provides further explanation of *story* and thus can be set apart with a dash. A dash was used instead of a comma because of the informal topic. A comma should separate the adjectives *dark* and *eerie*. Finally, *Because of the full moon* is a sentence fragment and was converted into an introductory phrase for the last independent clause.

8. The <u>men's</u> group did charity work this <u>weekend. They</u> completed the following <u>projects: they</u> helped rebuild a church that had been damaged in a <u>tornado, they</u> completed some of the landscaping on the church <u>grounds, and</u> they began repairs to the <u>pastor's</u> home nearby the church.

    Because the word *men* is a plural noun that does not end in *–s*, its possessive should be spelled with an apostrophe and then an *–s*. Also, the first clause is a run-on, so there should be a period between *weekend* and *They*. Next, there should be a colon after *projects* in order to introduce the series of clauses that follow. The word *following* is your clue to use a colon in this instance. Each clause in the series should be separated by a comma. Finally, *pastor's* is possessive and should contain an apostrophe.

9. Many people suffer from "diet <u>fatigue";</u> they try diet after diet only to meet failure with each one. What they should be focusing on instead is nutritional eating and <u>fitness. Nutritional</u> eating consists of eating well-balanced servings of <u>meats, vegetables, fruits, and</u> <u>grains; drinking</u> lots of <u>water; and</u> indulging in junk food sparingly. Proper fitness can come in the form of aerobic <u>exercise, walking, sports, or</u> weight <u>training. Making</u> just a few adjustments in daily eating and exercise habits can make all the difference in a <u>person's</u> physical and emotional well-being.

    The first clause is a run-on and should be divided into two separate sentences; since they're closely related, you may use a semicolon. The semicolon should be placed outside the quotation marks around *diet fatigue*. A period should follow *fitness* in order to separate the next run-on sentence into separate sentences. In the third sentence, you are presented with a series of clauses; one of the clauses contains a list of words that require commas to separate them. Because so many commas can be confusing, the series of clauses should be separated by semicolons. The series of words in the sentence that follows should be separated by commas as well. A final sentence should be set off starting at *Making*. Finally, the possessive of *person's* must contain an apostrophe.

10. The <u>beautiful, grand</u> stain-glassed windows added a majestic feeling to the old cathedral.

    A comma should separate *beautiful* and *grand*. Notice that there is no comma after *grand*. You can double-check this by placing *and* between each adjective: *The beautiful and grand and stain-glassed window*. The *and* between *grand* and *stain-glassed* does not make sense; therefore, there should be no comma preceding *stain-glassed*.

General Tips on Writing Your Essays

Structure

Now that you know when to use a semicolon instead of a comma, how do you get started writing your essay? Learning the rules that govern written English is one thing; putting your knowledge to use is another. We will discuss some specific tips in each of the essay sections later, but for now, we will look at some general techniques to make your essay the best it can be. We begin by looking at the proper structure for your introduction and for your conclusion.

Introduction

Your introduction should serve two structural purposes: It should restate your topic so that the reader need not review the given question, and it should offer a clear thesis so the reader knows what your purpose is. Simply defined, a thesis states the main idea of your essay. Because the strategy you need to employ for developing your thesis differs for each type of essay, however, we will discuss it in further detail later on in this chapter.

Your introduction should, in effect, restate the given topic. In other words, your reader should be able to ascertain the issue or argument without reading the given topic. Suppose the GMAT gives you this argument:

> *The following letter was sent by a group of homeowners from the Rivermill Subdivision to all homeowners in that subdivision.*

> "Providence Golf Community down the street has a homeowner's association. Part of the role of this association is to develop bylaws, which dictate the outside appearance of all homes in the community. For example, according to the rules set forth in the covenant, homeowners may only build privacy fences around their yard; no chain link is permitted. Property values in this community are double property values in our subdivision. In order to raise our property values, we need to improve the look of our neighborhood. Therefore, we should start an association and develop a covenant."

Your initial reaction to this prompt may be to begin your essay with a direct response such as *This letter presents a faulty argument.* However, this introductory sentence does not provide adequate information because it does not specify *which* letter and therefore it would leave the reader confused. Following is the beginning of an introduction that does give adequate information to the reader:

> Does the adoption of covenants in housing communities result in rising property values? In a letter to the residents of Rivermill Subdivision, a small group of homeowners stated that property values in nearby Providence were double the property values in Rivermill because of such a covenant.

Not only should you restate the topic, but you should also do so in a way that will spark interest. It may seem like a tall order to restate your topic, create a thesis, AND make it captivating, but if you don't grab your reader's attention in the introduction, it doesn't matter how interesting the body of your essay is because he won't feel compelled to read on. Think of your introduction as the worm on a fishhook, just dangling there enticing the fish to bite. There are several techniques you can employ to get your reader to "bite" and, thus, read on.

- Begin your introduction with a question. Naturally, when a question is posed to your reader, he or she will want to keep reading to find out the answer.
- Begin your introduction with a quote. Because you will not have time to research your topic for the GMAT, this may not be as feasible as, say, on a term paper for a graduate class; however, if you can remember a specific quote pertinent to your topic, use it.
- Begin with an anecdote. An anecdote is entertaining and will thus draw in the reader.
- Begin with an illustration or a hypothetical example based on the topic you are going to discuss.
- Begin with a true-to-life example.
- Begin with vivid description of something pertaining to your topic.

It is particularly important that, in the context of the GMAT, you make a concerted effort to create a captivating introduction. Keep in mind that the scorers of your essays are the scorers of everyone else's essays. They read hundreds of responses to the same issues and arguments. You must make your essay stand out. What better way to make it stand out than to make it exceptional from the beginning?

Conclusion

The conclusion of your essay is just as important as the introduction because it wraps up your thoughts and evidence and should leave your reader satisfied that a convincing discussion has just taken place. Your conclusion should include a restatement of your thesis and then end with a more general statement, perhaps a warning or a call for action. Tip: If time is running out and you get stuck trying to formulate a conclusion, try beginning with "In conclusion" or "In summary." Then continue by restating your thesis.

Style

We have examined the rules that govern the English language, and we have learned some techniques on structure. But how does a writer make a piece of writing his own? And how does a writer add interest to his essays? The way a writer uses words and phrases to add personality to his writing is called *style*. A writer is to style as a figure skater is to skating. A writer can learn all the rules that make his writing correct, just as a figure skater can learn how to accomplish her jumps and footwork. But just learning the rules of grammar is not enough to create a well-written essay; learning just the rules of skating is not enough to earn a gold medal. The writer must bring his own methods and personality to his writing just as a skater must invest her own personality and flair in her performance.

Many elements combine to form a writer's style, and, even though many of these elements can be identified, each is unique to a writer. Moreover, a good writer does not allow any elements of his style to stagnate. Rather, he continues to practice writing in order to continually improve and develop his style. We will touch briefly on how you can develop your writing style, but first let's look at some specific elements of style.

Transitions

Transitional phrases are an important element of style because they create coherence. They guide the reader from point A to point B. On the GMAT, the reader will read through your essay quickly, scoring according to his first impression of what you wrote. If your essay is choppy and does not flow well, the reader will not gain a good first impression. Therefore, it is imperative that your essay exhibits solid cohesiveness. Look at the lists below for some examples of transitional words and phrases that will help you write a smooth, coherent essay.

Agreement: also, plus, in addition, further, furthermore, moreover, additionally, to add to that, next, in accordance with, accordingly, in agreement, finally, for instance, for example, in exemplification, exemplifying that, in fact, factually speaking, in terms of, and so forth, in coordination with, along those lines, collectively speaking, generally speaking, indeed, undoubtedly, obviously, to be sure, equally

Contrast: however, in contrast, on the contrary, on the other hand, from a different angle, nonetheless, nevertheless, but, yet, a catch to this is, sadly enough, as a hindrance, oddly enough, instead, in direct opposition, still, rather

Result: as a result, as a consequence, consequently, thus, therefore, hence, thereby, resulting in, ultimately, in the end, finally, in the overall analysis, in hindsight, in retrospect, retrospectively, vicariously, the long term effect, as a short term result, significantly, as a major effect, effectively, heretofore, hereafter, thereafter, in short, generally, over all, concluding

Transitional words and phrases are helpful not only in linking your ideas between sentences, but also in providing cohesiveness from paragraph to paragraph. Each paragraph of your essay should include a topic sentence, which can also act as a transitional sentence. This transitional sentence should link your paragraphs by relating to some element in the preceding paragraph. Take a look at the following example:

> The size of your house will probably be a factor in how you decide to decorate. If you have a large house, you may opt for a grand, sophisticated look. Over-sized furniture and ornate fixtures will complement solid-colored walls accented with artwork. On the other hand, a cozy look suits a smaller home. This look can be achieved by choosing less formal furniture, simple accents and warm colors. Equally, patterned wall-coverings add a lovely touch to a small home.
>   <u>Regardless of the size of your house, your financial situation will also likely play a large role in the style of décor you choose.</u> Limited funds may force you to make some of your own decorations, like curtains and knick knacks. However, unlimited funds may offer the option of hiring an interior decorator to do all the work for you.

The first sentence of the second paragraph is not only the topic sentence of the paragraph (it lets the reader know what the paragraph will be about), but also the transitional sentence that links the two paragraphs. Notice that the phrase "Regardless of the size of your house" refers to the topic of the first paragraph, thereby tying together the topics of both paragraphs. In addition, the word "also" in this sentence indicates that a second factor of decorating is being introduced.

Other more subtle transitions occur in the first paragraph. For example, "over-sized furniture" in the third sentence refers to the "large house" in the preceding sentence. This provides a transition without using a transitional word. Notice further that "large" is part of the subordinate clause in the second sentence but "over-sized" is part of the main subject in the third sentence, thus providing transition while also giving the reader some variety in sentence pattern. (We will discuss varying your sentences later on.)

More obvious are the transitional words we discussed previously. In the first paragraph, for example, the phrase "On the other hand" depicts the contrast between a large and a small house while "equally" continues the thoughts pertaining to a cozy home. In the second paragraph, "However" is used to show contrast in a pattern much like in the first paragraph.

Using transitions, both subtle and obvious, in your sentences and between paragraphs is essential in creating cohesiveness in your essay. Without this clarity, your essay will likely be choppy and difficult for the scorer to read and understand. A word of caution, however, before we move on: Since time is limited on the writing assessment sections, you must be concise and to the point. Be careful not to overuse transitional words and phrases because overuse can make you sound like a pedantic writer rather than an intelligent one.

<u>Varying Your Sentences</u>

No matter how well your essay flows, the reader will easily get bored if your essay consists only of sentences that contain the same words and follow the same structure. Consider this paragraph:

> Dogs are smarter than cats. They are often used to help handicapped people. Dogs help blind people. Dogs also help epileptic people. Dogs can sense when an epileptic person is about to have a seizure. Dogs are also used in rescue work. They help rescue skiers. They also help in catastrophic events. They rescue people after earthquakes.

There are several things wrong with this paragraph:

- Almost every sentence is the same length.
- The structure in each sentence is almost identical: Subject + Verb + Direct Object.
- The same words are used over and over: "dogs," "they," "also," "help," "rescue."
- No description is used to further illustrate the writer's points.

To add more interest to your writing, you need to vary your sentence length and structure. Try different beginnings for your sentences. Employ a variety of words and use these words to paint a vivid picture of your subject. Let's apply these tips to the paragraph above:

> Dogs are more intelligent than your average feline. A cat cannot, for example, guide a blind person across busy streets and along crowded sidewalks. Amazingly enough, a dog is also a perfect companion for a person with epilepsy because a dog seems to be able to sense when a seizure is coming on. While dogs help keep the handicapped away from danger, they also aid in rescuing people who have fallen victim to dangerous situations, like skiers trapped in an avalanche. Moreover, when catastrophic events, like earthquakes, leave victims pinned beneath debris and rubble, a canine team often comes to the rescue.

A good way to vary your sentences is to begin them in different ways. For example, you could begin your sentence with the subject and predicate and then build on them using various words and phrases. This type of sentence is called a *cumulative sentence.* By contrast, in a *periodic sentence,* you use words and phrases to build up to the subject and the predicate at the end of the sentence. Here are some examples:

Cumulative sentence:

The energetic children played hard, chasing each other in all directions, occasionally falling and then scrambling to their feet, giggling at each other's antics and never stopping for even a moment to catch their breath.

Periodic sentence:

With flour in her hair, dough in between her fingers and sauce all over her face, she attempted to make a gourmet pizza.

Both types of sentences not only add variety, but also bring rhythm and cadence to writing. This rhythm creates interest and is pleasant to the reader. Additionally, descriptive words paint a clear picture for the reader.

Figurative Language

Another excellent way to paint vivid pictures for your reader is to use figures of speech. Figures of speech—like similes, metaphors, analogies, personification, hyperbole, irony, and allusion—when used correctly, add extra flair to your writing. They add to your style of writing an element that takes your writing from ordinary to extraordinary.

Similes show a marked comparison between two things by using the phrases "like," "as," or "as if."

Example:

The cat stood poised and still as a statue, waiting for the opportune moment to pounce.

Here the cat is described "as a statue" because it is standing so still.

Metaphors show absolute comparison by omitting "like," "as," or "as if."

Example:

She is Mother Theresa when it comes to her generosity and compassion.

Here the comparison is absolute because the writer states that this person *is* Mother Theresa; the writer does not say that this person is just *like* Mother Theresa.

Analogies compare the similar features of two dissimilar things. Analogies often bring clarity to writing by showing a reader another way of seeing something. Analogies are not limited to a sentence; sometimes an analogy streams its way through an entire piece of writing.

Example:

Office cooperation is like a soccer game. Each employee has a position on the playing field, and each position dictates an employee's function. Working together, the office completes passes by communicating well within each department. Shots on goal are taken when employees meet with prospective clients to pitch ideas. And the whole office triumphs when a goal is scored and a prospect becomes a client.

Here one element, an office working together, is compared to another, a soccer team playing a game. Although an office and a soccer team are two very unrelated things, the writer sees similarities in some aspects between the two and uses these similarities to show more clearly how an office works together.

Personification gives human characteristics to animals, inanimate objects and ideas in order to make them more real and understandable.

Example:

The rusty car groaned, coughed, then gave one last sputter and died.

The car in this sentence comes to life even as it "dies" because of the human characteristics it is given.

Hyperbole uses deliberate exaggeration or overstatement to show special emphasis or create humor.

Example:

Fat-free foods have become so popular that soon all vendors will want to give it a shot. Before you know it, Kentucky Fried Chicken will have fat-free fried chicken. Big Macs will contain 0 grams of fat. And the amount of fat in a Pizza Hut cheese pizza? You guessed it—none!

In order to show how far out of hand peoples' obsession with fat-free foods has become, this description purposefully exaggerates a world where the most unlikely things are fat-free.

Irony uses language that makes a suggestion that directly contrasts with the literal word or idea. It can offer humor to writing, or a bitter tone when it is used in sarcasm.

Example:

Scientists have worked hard to develop ways to decrease infant mortality rates and increase longevity. As a result, more people are living longer and scientists will soon have to develop some methods with which to control overpopulation.

This sentence uses irony by predicting that, because scientists have now discovered ways to increase a person's life span, they will soon have to deal with another problem—overpopulation. This is because, with everyone living longer, there will soon be too many people for the earth to support.

Allusion makes indirect reference to known cultural works, people or events. The familiarity allusions bring to writing helps the writer make connections with the reader.

Example:

I have so much to do today, I feel like David must have felt as he approached Goliath.

Most people are familiar with the Bible story of David and Goliath. David is a small shepherd who slays the giant, Goliath, with a slingshot and one stone after the army's best soldiers fail. Even through his feat, however, David must have felt a bit intimidated when facing Goliath, a feeling this writer intimates when thinking about everything that needs to be done.

Figures of speech to avoid

Clichés are overused phrases that prevent your writing from being fresh and original, so don't use clichés like "Cute as a button" or "Busy as a bee."

Mixed metaphors are comparisons that are not consistent; they only cause confusion. For example, "The infant was like a baby bird, opening his cavernous well for food." Here the simile that an infant is like a baby bird holds true, but the following words that equate the baby's mouth to a cavernous well are not consistent.

Tone

The words you choose will greatly affect the tone of your essay. Likewise, the tone you wish to achieve will depend on your audience. In this case, you know your audience will consist of men and women who will be quickly reading your essay and then assigning a score based on their impression and how well you handled the topic. Knowing this, you will want to use a professional, formal tone, the kind you will probably use in most of your graduate work. Using a formal tone means that you will want to keep some distance between you, the writer, and your audience, the scorer. Be courteous and polite but avoid being chummy or intimate in any way. Furthermore, you should avoid all colloquialisms and slang.

Diction

While tone defines the overall language you use, diction deals with the specific kinds of words and phrases you choose for your essay. Since you have already determined your audience and thus ascertained that you need to portray a formal tone in your essay, you must be consistent with your diction, or word choice. Diction may be classified as technical (*homo sapien* rather than *human*), formal (*Please inform me when you are ready to depart.*), informal or colloquial (*Give me a buzz when you're ready to go.*), or slang (*She's a real couch potato and watches the tube from early morning 'til the cows come home.*) Knowing that your audience dictates a formal tone, you must also be consistent in maintaining formal diction. Look at the following example of inconsistent diction:

> Violence in schools has become an epidemic problem. School shootings occur regularly, and fights erupt daily in the nation's classrooms. Even with the addition of metal detectors at school entrances, violence will never be eradicated because the jocks are always ganging up on the geeks. If only we could just all get along.

This example begins with a formal tone and formal diction; however, it takes a quick turn when the writer uses slang words like "jocks" and "geeks." The paragraph is concluded informally with "If only we could just all get along."

As you write your essay, and later when you proofread it, you will want to make sure that you preserve the formality your audience requires.

Person

It is important to maintain consistency in person. For example, if you begin your essay in second person (*you*) do not shift to third person (*he*, *she*, *it*, *one*, or *they*). Let's look at a couple of examples illustrating a shift in person:

Example:

<u>One</u> can get excellent grades in school if <u>you</u> study hard.

The switch from "one" to "you" is confusing and awkward.

Example:

Off the coast of Puerto Rico, on the island of Vieques, is an old French mansion turned hotel. Here one can enjoy spacious guest rooms and a cozy library. One can lounge around the pool and indulge in the honorary pool bar. Because the hotel is not far from the ocean, you can also take a leisurely walk down to the white sandy beach where one can spend a lazy day basking in the sun.

The switch from *one* to *you* is confusing in this paragraph and detracts from the imagery. Decide from the beginning of your essay what person you wish to employ and make a conscious effort to stick to it.

Developing Your Style

Your goal as a writer is to create interest and coherence through your unique writing style. Using figures of speech and maintaining consistent use of tone, diction and person are effective ways to create interest. Using transitions creates coherence. Also remember that part of creating coherence is being concise. Use only the details that are necessary to support your topic and avoid tedious description. This is not to say that you should avoid vivid imagery, but that you should take care to ensure that your information adds to your writing rather than detracts from your writing.

In taking all of these elements of style into account, the most important aspect to remember about developing your style is that it only comes through practice. Practice your writing and proofread, proofread, proofread. If you do all of these things, you will be well on your way to becoming an effective, skillful writer. Are you ready to start practicing? Let's move on and discuss the two different essays you will be asked to write.

Warm-Up Drill II

Directions: Read each paragraph in the following essay and rewrite it, making necessary changes in order to enhance the effectiveness of the essay. Pay close attention to all of the elements you learned about writing style. Answers and solutions begin on the next page.

Issue prompt:

It is more beneficial to complete independent study than to attend college.

1. This opinion is not valid and is clearly not based on any evidence that would prove its validity. One can't gain more knowledge by completing independent study instead of attending college. It is necessary to look at some evidence to prove this.

2. Some people think that there are too many distractions at college because there are so many other students who take up class time. Interaction with other students can provide valuable insight into topics you study in college. Other people's backgrounds and experience add differences in perspectives and, in some cases, valuable expertise. Professors add expertise as well since they are the experts in the areas they are teaching. When a student studies on his own, he is dependent only on what he knows. He is also dependent on what he can read about. He is also dependent on his own background and experiences. This is very limiting to the value he can obtain from his education.

3. Some people think that students can learn more discipline by studying independently at home instead of going to college. College students learn a lot of discipline. They are held accountable by their college professors. They are held accountable by fellow students too. They depend upon them to contribute to the class. Students who study on their own are only accountable to themselves. Many times, studies get set aside when life gets too busy. Studies get the boot when a student encounters a subject they're not too excited about.

4. Studying at home independently is not as beneficial as attending college because the degree you get, if you get a degree at all, will not carry as much weight with potential employers as will a college degree from an accredited college or university. Employers place more weight on someone whose expertise they can depend on. Employers feel they can depend more on the expertise of someone who has been trained at a college or university.

5. People should go to college. You can't depend on your own motivation to finish your studies at home. A student gains a lot more from the interaction they receive between other students and professors in college. Students who get a degree from a college may have a better chance of getting a good job after college.

Solutions to Warm-Up Drill II

1. The opening sentence in this paragraph does not make an effective introduction. It does not restate the topic but rather makes a direct address to the topic question. A good introduction should not require the reader to read the topic. The second sentence of the paragraph gives a concise thesis statement but should be elaborated on a bit. Also, the contraction *can't* does not fit with the formal tone of the essay. The last sentence serves as a transition to the next paragraph, but it does not show much sophistication or subtlety.

    Better:
    Should a student give up a college education in order to complete an independent study at home? Although the financial savings of independent study may be substantial, one can gain more benefits by obtaining a college or university education. Studying at a college or university can give a student a broader education, can help him learn discipline through accountability, and can pay off in the long run.

    This introduction begins with a question, which is more effective than directly addressing the question/topic. The thesis statement concisely lists three reasons a formal education is better than independent study; this sentence gives the reader a clear idea of what the essay will be about.

2. The first sentence serves as a topic sentence for the paragraph; however, it should be reworded to act as a better transitional sentence, one that would tie in with the last sentence of the preceding paragraph. The second sentence would function better with a transitional phrase like *On the contrary* to introduce it. Also in this sentence, the use of second person *you* is inconsistent with the rest of the essay. The fourth sentence uses the same two words *add* and *expertise* that were used in the preceding sentence. These should be changed to add some variety. The next three sentences are repetitive and should be combined.

    Better:
    Some people think that distractions at college from other students who take up class time results in a narrow education. On the contrary, interaction with other students can provide valuable insight into the topics one studies in college. Other people's backgrounds and experience add different perspectives and, in some cases, valuable expertise. Professors offer much value as well since they are the experts in the areas they are teaching. When a student studies on his own, he is dependent only on what he knows or can read about and on his own background and experiences. This severely limits the value he can obtain from his education.

    The first sentence works as a transition because it uses the word *narrow*, which contrasts with the word *broader* from the thesis statement in the preceding paragraph.

3. The first sentence works well as a topic sentence, but it uses the same wording as the topic sentence for the preceding paragraph. In the fifth sentence, the use of *they* and *them* is confusing because it is unclear whether the pronoun reference is to the student or fellow students. The remaining sentences are all the same length and therefore choppy. The last sentence strays from the formal tone of the essay. In addition, the word *they* does not agree in person with *a student*.

    Better:
    One valuable lesson students can learn at college is discipline. College students learn a lot of discipline because they are held accountable by their professors. Moreover, they are often held accountable by fellow students who depend upon them to contribute to the class. Students who study on their own are accountable only to themselves. Many times, studies get set aside when life gets too busy or when a student encounters a subject for which he is not enthusiastic.

    The word *valuable* ties in well with the word *value* in the last sentence of the preceding paragraph. Thus, this sentence serves not only as a topic sentence but also as a transitional sentence.

4.   Again, the first sentence provides a good topic sentence but not a good transition from the preceding paragraph. The second sentence unnecessarily repeats the word *weight* from the first sentence. In the third sentence, the text shifts to second person *you*. The last sentence repeats the word *depend* from the preceding sentence.

Better:
Studying at a college or university may not make every topic seem scintillating; however, when a student is held accountable, he is more driven. As he is driven to succeed, he will eventually earn a degree. Studying at home independently is not as beneficial as attending college because the degree a student gets, if he gets a degree at all, will not carry as much weight with potential employers as will a degree from an accredited college or university. Employers place more confidence in someone whose expertise they can rely on. Employers feel they can depend more on the expertise of someone who has been trained at a college or university.

The topic sentence in this paragraph provides transition because it refers to the preceding paragraph by relating *scintillating* courses to being *enthusiastic* about subjects.

5.   The first sentence does not act as a thorough topic sentence, nor does it provide a good transition. The second sentence uses *you* and *your*, which is an inconsistent use of person. In addition, the contraction *can't* takes away from the formal tone of the essay. Overall, this last paragraph is not effective; it has short, choppy sentences and does not adequately conclude the subject by restating the topic and giving final remarks.

Better:
Whether one is trained at a university or opts to stay home to study independently, an education is extremely important; however, it is clear that a student can benefit more from a formal education than from independent study. Students should not depend on their own motivation to finish their studies, nor should they miss out on the opportunity to benefit from the interaction they will receive from other students and professors in college. Despite any financial savings a student may earn by studying independently, the rewards of a college education will pay off in the long run.

The transition here works well because the first sentence uses the word *trained*, which is used in the sentence before it. This final paragraph functions effectively as a conclusion because it restates the topic. It also brings the writing full circle by once again mentioning the monetary aspect of education, which, as you recall, was mentioned in the introductory paragraph.

Analysis of an Issue

The *Analysis of an Issue* section of the test asks you to do just that—analyze an issue, present your perspective on the given issue, and provide solid evidence to support your position. You will have 30 minutes to plan and write your essay. Following is the grading scale for the Issue essay. Remember that the highest possible score is a 6.

SCORE

6   OUTSTANDING

A 6 essay presents a cogent, well-articulated discussion of the issue and demonstrates mastery of the elements of effective writing.

A typical paper in this category

—explores ideas and develops a position on the issue with insightful reasons and/or persuasive examples
—sustains a well-focused, well-organized discussion of the subject
—expresses ideas with language that is clear and precise
—varies sentence structure and vocabulary appropriate to the subject
—demonstrates superior facility with the conventions (grammar, usage, and mechanics) of standard written English but may have minor flaws

5   STRONG

A 5 essay presents a well-developed discussion of the issue and demonstrates a strong control of the elements of effective writing.

A typical paper in this category

—develops a position on the issue with well-chosen reasons and/or examples
—is focused and generally well organized
—uses language fluently, with varied sentence structure and appropriate vocabulary
—demonstrates facility with the conventions of standard written English but may have minor flaws

4   ADEQUATE

A 4 essay presents a competent discussion of the issue and demonstrates adequate control of the elements of writing.

A typical paper in this category

—develops a position on the issue with relevant reasons and/or examples
—is adequately organized
—expresses ideas clearly
—demonstrates adequate control of language, including diction and syntax, but may lack sentence variety
—demonstrates adequate control of the conventions of standard written English but may have some flaws

3   LIMITED

A 3 essay presents some competence in its discussion of the issue and in its control of the elements of writing but is clearly flawed.

A typical paper in this category exhibits <u>one or more</u> of the following characteristics:

—is vague or limited in developing a position on the issue
—is poorly focused and/or poorly organized
—is weak in the use of relevant reasons and/or examples
—has problems expressing ideas clearly
—has problems in fluency, with poorly formed sentences or inappropriate vocabulary
—has occasional major errors or frequent minor errors in grammar, usage, and mechanics

2   SERIOUSLY FLAWED

A 2 essay presents a weak discussion of the issue and demonstrates little control of the elements of writing.

A typical paper in this category exhibits <u>one or more</u> of the following characteristics:

—is unclear or seriously limited in presenting and developing a position on the issue
—is unfocused and/or disorganized
—provides few, if any, relevant reasons or examples
—has serious and frequent problems in the use of language and sentence structure
—contains frequent errors in grammar, usage, or mechanics that interfere with meaning

1   FUNDAMENTALLY DEFICIENT

A 1 essay is seriously deficient in basic writing skills.

A typical paper in this category exhibits <u>one or more</u> of the following characteristics:

—provides little evidence of the ability to organize or develop a coherent response on the issue
—has severe and persistent errors in language and sentence structure
—contains a pervasive pattern of errors in grammar, usage, and mechanics that interfere with meaning

0   Any paper that is blank, totally illegible, or obviously not written on the assigned topic receives a score of zero.

Using the scoring criteria for the *Analysis of an Issue* essay, make sure that your writing demonstrates that you can:

• develop a position (which is different from merely stating a position)
• organize to present a focused discussion
• use standard written English and appropriate vocabulary
• express ideas in clear and precise language

Patterns of Development

Just as there is no universal answer to every question, there are many ways to write a persuasive Issue essay. There are specific strategies that you can use to more effectively respond to different types of Issue topics. These strategies, or methods, are called patterns of development. The type of pattern you choose to employ in writing your essay is dependent upon the question or prompt to which you are responding. Usually, an essay question will contain certain clues, which enable you to determine which pattern of development to use. After choosing a method to use, you will find it much easier to develop a clear, concise thesis, which, in turn, will affect the way you organize your essay.

There are three main patterns of development. Let's examine them now so we have a better understanding of how to apply them. For each, we will discuss clues in an Issue question that prompt the use of a particular pattern of development, we will look at an example of such a question, and we will determine what your job as a writer will be in applying this method.

Comparison – Contrast

An Issue question that commands the use of the Comparison – Contrast pattern of development:

- will use words that suggest similarity or difference.
- will seek to persuade the reader that one item is superior to another.

Example:

"American cars are better than foreign cars."

The author uses the word *than* to compare the two cars, and he seeks to persuade the reader that an American car is a wiser choice than a foreign one.

Your job: By employing the Comparison – Contrast pattern of development, you will portray similarities and differences between two items to prove which one is superior, either in agreement or disagreement with the author's opinion.

Cause – Effect

An Issue question that requires the use of the Cause – Effect method of response:

- may include an "If…then" statement.
- may lack an effect.

Example (if…then):

"If college and university faculty spent time outside the academic world working in professions relevant to the courses they teach, then the overall quality of higher education would greatly increase."

The author argues that if a certain action is taken, a desirable effect is achieved.

Your job: In your essay, you must prove that a particular cause results in a particular effect, either in agreement or disagreement with the author.

Example (lack of effect):

"More restrictions should be set on teenage drivers."

In this "call for action" statement, the author offers no effects that will result if the action is taken, but surely it is implied that, if the author feels the action should be taken, he assumes something positive will result.

Your job: In your responsive essay, it would be your responsibility to support your position in agreement with this statement or against it, thus proving the implied effect.

Definition

An Issue question that dictates the use of the Definition pattern of development:

- will attempt to show that, by definition, a particular idea or concept is of great value.
- may portray a very limited definition of an idea or concept.

Example (great value):

"Patriotism breaks down the walls of division."

The author believes that a concept can do a great thing.

Your job: Define the idea or concept and show that, because of its attributes and qualities, it has value or it lacks value.

Example (limited definition):

"A person's generosity can be determined by examining what he or she has given to charity."

In this example, the author seeks to provide a very limited definition of a particular concept.

Your job: Support the author's definition with evidence, or show that the definition is much broader.

Writing Your Issue Essay

Now that you are familiar with the different methods you can employ to write your essay, let's get down to the nitty gritty of organizing your thoughts by using these patterns of development. Remember, you are aiming for a 6 essay, one that presents clear, concise evidence to support your view. Writing a 6 essay doesn't have to be a difficult task. All you have to do is follow seven simple steps, some of which will ask you to plug information into formulas. Note that some steps may include specific formulas for each pattern of development. Also note that you need not enter complete, descriptive sentences into the formulas; simple notes and phrases will suffice.

➢ **Step 1 – Understanding the Issue**

In order to properly present your perspective on an issue, you must first understand the issue you are being asked to discuss. Understanding the issue allows you to fully develop your position, presenting your evidence in a way that is most effective and appropriate for the topic. There are two steps that will help you understand the issue.

First, take a couple of minutes to read the given question carefully. Second, ask yourself the following questions:

- What does the statement mean?
- What is the issue at hand?
- What is implied by the statement?
- What is the writer's stand on the issue?
- What, if any, evidence does the writer use to support his position?

➢ **Step 2 – Choosing Your Pattern of Development**

Keeping in mind our discussion of the three patterns of development, look for the necessary criteria in your question. If you think the question requires more than one method, choose the one you think works the best. On a timed writing assignment, your essay will be fairly short and therefore you cannot adequately utilize two methods.

➢ **Step 3 – Developing Your Thesis**

The next, and perhaps the most important, step is to develop your thesis. Your thesis states the purpose of your essay. Without a thesis statement, your reader does not know what you are setting out to prove. And without a thesis statement, it would be very difficult to organize your essay with clarity and coherence. Don't be intimidated by the task of formulating what is to be the crux of your essay. It can be quite simple. Just use the formulas below:

THESIS FOR COMPARISON – CONTRAST ESSAY (*formula 1-1*):

I believe that Item A, _____, is better than Item B, _____, because
1) _____, 2) _____, 3) _____.

THESIS FOR CAUSE – EFFECT ESSAY (*formula 1-2*):

If _____, then _____, because
1) _____, 2) _____, 3) _____.

THESIS FOR DEFINITION ESSAY (*formula 1-3*):

By definition, _____ possess(es) these qualities: 1) _____,
2) _____, 3) _____ which have a positive effect because
A) _____, B) _____, C) _____.

➢ Step 4 – Understanding Counter Arguments

Have you ever been in an argument and find that you're just not getting very far very fast? This could be because you are failing to see things from the other person's point of view. Being able to see the "flip side of the coin" can go a long way in proving your point and disarming your opponent's objections. By showing that you are aware, though perhaps not understanding, of the opposing side you are adding credibility to your argument because it is clear that you have viewed the issue from all angles. To write an effective position essay, you must present your knowledge of a counter argument. In other words, you must show that you have considered the other side of the argument. Organize your counter argument this way:

COMPARISON – CONTRAST COUNTER CLAIM (*formula 2-1*):

Others may think Item B is better than Item A because 1) _____,
2) _____, 3) _____.
(Note that these three points should contrast directly with the three points of your thesis. (see *formula 1-1*))

CAUSE – EFFECT COUNTER CLAIM (*formula 2-2*):

Some may feel that _____ would cause _____ based on _____.
(Note that this point should contrast directly with point #1 of your thesis. (see *formula 1-2*))

DEFINITION (*formula 2-3*):

By definition some may feel that _____ exhibits or is defined by _____ which could be positive / negative.
(Note that this point should contrast directly with point #1 of your thesis. (see *formula 1-3*))

➢ Step 5 – Organizing Your Thoughts

Now let's organize all of our information so that writing the essay will be quick and simple. Following are formulas specific to each pattern of development. These formulas will prompt you to plug in your thesis and counter argument points. (Note that the following formulas require you to plug in the three numbered items from your thesis in succession. Although it is not necessary that you discuss them in this order, we will label it that way for simplicity.) In addition, there are spaces in the formula for you to insert 1 or 2 pieces of supporting evidence.

COMPARISON – CONTRAST ESSAY FORMULA (*formula 3-1*):
I.   Introduction – Paragraph 1
    A. Restate your topic
    B. Thesis statement (*formula 1-1*)
II. Support – Paragraph 2
    A. Counter Claim point #1 (*formula 2-1*)
    B. Thesis point #1 (*formula 1-1*)
        1. Support for thesis point #1
        2. Support for thesis point #1

   III. Support – Paragraph 3
      A. Counter Claim point #2 *(formula 2-1)*
      B. Thesis point #2 *(formula 1-1)*
         1. Support for thesis point #2
         2. Support for thesis point #2
   IV. Support – Paragraph 4
      A. Counter Claim point #3 *(formula 2-1)*
      B. Thesis point #3 *(formula 1-1)*
         1. Support for thesis point #3
         2. Support for thesis point #3
   V. Conclusion – Paragraph 5
      A. Restate thesis
      B. Issue a warning or a call for action

CAUSE - EFFECT ESSAY FORMULA *(formula 3-2)*:
   I. Introduction – Paragraph 1
      A. Restate your topic
      B. Thesis statement *(formula 1-2)*
   II. Support – Paragraph 2
      A. Counter Claim *(formula 2-2)*
      B. Thesis point #1 *(formula 1-2)*
         1. Support for thesis point #1
         2. Support for thesis point #1
   III. Support – Paragraph 3 – Thesis point #2 *(formula 1-2)*
      A. Support for thesis point #2
      B. Support for thesis point #2
   IV. Support – Paragraph 4 – Thesis point #3 *(formula 1-2)*
      A. Support for thesis point #3
      B. Support for thesis point #3
   V. Conclusion – Paragraph 5
      A. Restate thesis
      B. Issue a warning or a call for action

DEFINITION ESSAY FORMULA *(formula 3-3)*:
   I. Introduction – Paragraph 1
      A. Restate your topic
      B. Thesis statement *(formula 1-3)*
   II. Support – Paragraph 2
      A. Counter Claim *(formula 2-3)*
      B. Thesis point #1 *(formula 1-3)*
         1. Support by using thesis point A *(formula 1-3)*
         2. Support by using thesis point A *(formula 1-3)*
   III. Support – Paragraph 3 – Thesis point #2 *(formula 1-3)*
      A. Support by using point B *(formula 1-3)*
      B. Support by using point B *(formula 1-3)*
   IV. Support – Paragraph 4 – Thesis point #3 *(formula 1-3)*
      A. Support by using point C *(formula 1-3)*
      B. Support by using point C *(formula 1-3)*
   V. Conclusion – Paragraph 5
      A. Restate thesis
      B. Issue a warning or a call for action

➢ <u>Step 6 – Writing Your Essay</u>

Now that you have organized your thoughts and support, it is time to write! The best strategy under the pressure of a time restraint is to just begin writing—as quickly as you can while still being careful. (You should allow yourself 20-25 of the 30 minutes for writing.) Organization should not be difficult with the help of your formulas. In following your formula, don't forget to add transitional words, phrases and sentences to help give your essay coherence. As you write, remember the mechanical rules you learned at the beginning of this chapter and keep in mind the techniques we discussed in the section *General Tips on Writing Your Essays*. The key to successful timed writings is to reserve a bit of time at the end so that you can go back and proofread and add finishing touches that will make your essay flow well and that will present your ideas clearly.

➤ Step 7 – Revising Your Essay

Because you have written quickly, you must spend some time, about 5-8 minutes, at the end of the section reviewing your essay, making necessary changes to enhance the clarity, coherence and grammatical accuracy of your writing. You must look for misspellings and mechanical errors while at the same time keeping in mind the following questions:

- Is my introduction captivating?
- Is my thesis statement concise?
- Do my body paragraphs clearly support my thesis?
- Have I used logical transitions that help the text flow smoothly between sentences and between paragraphs?
- Have I maintained a formal tone and diction throughout my essay?
- Have I maintained consistent use of person (i.e., first, second, third)?
- Is there a word, or are there words, which I have employed too often throughout the essay?
- Do my sentences vary in length and structure?

As you ask yourself these questions, make the necessary changes. If you still have time left after you have completed the initial revision, go back and read your essay again. A writer makes many, many revisions to his manuscript before it is ready to be published, so you can never proofread too many times!

Sample Issues & Essays

Now let's apply the 7 steps to three examples.

Example 1: Comparison – Contrast Essay

Prompt: "A new custom home is a much better purchase than an older, run-down home."

➤ Step 1 – Understanding the Issue

- What does the statement mean? *If you are in the market to buy a house, a new home would be a better value.*
- What is the issue at hand? *What kind of home is the best to buy?*
- What is implied by the statement? *That one who purchases an old home is not making a wise choice. Also implied is that an older home is run-down.*
- What is the writer's stand on the issue? *He believes a new home is superior to an old one.*
- What, if any, evidence does the writer use to support his position? *Old houses are run-down, new homes can be custom built.*

➤ Step 2 – Choosing My Pattern of Development

This prompt requires me to employ the Comparison – Contrast pattern of development because the statement uses the word "than," a contrasting word. Moreover, the author is trying to convince me that it is better to buy a new home than an old one.

➤ Step 3 – Developing My Thesis

THESIS FOR COMPARISON – CONTRAST ESSAY *(formula 1-1)*:

I believe that Item A, an old home, is better than Item B, a new home, because 1) an old home exemplifies old-style motifs that are unique in today's market, 2) foundations are stronger in older homes, 3) can remodel an old home in any way.

> Step 4 – Understanding Counter Argument

COMPARISON – CONTRAST COUNTER CLAIM *(formula 2-1)*:

Others may think Item B is better than Item A because 1) you can "keep up with the Joneses" with your modern décor, 2) new homes may be built quickly for easy occupancy, 3) new homes can be custom-built. (Note that these three points should contrast directly with the three points of your thesis. (see *formula 1-1*))

> Step 5 – Organizing My Thoughts

COMPARISON – CONTRAST ESSAY FORMULA *(formula 3-1)*:

I.   Introduction – Paragraph 1
   A.   Some people feel that the purchase of a new home is a smarter investment choice than the purchase of an older home.
   B.   For anyone who puts stock in the aged and unique, the traditional home may be the choice of a lifetime with its old-fashioned motifs, its strong foundations, and its versatility to become the house its owner designs.
II.   Support – Paragraph 2
   A.   keeping up with the Joneses – modern décor
   B.   bring back old-time motifs
      1.   More choices – can choose from different time periods
      2.   More unique versus "cookie cutter" homes of today
III.   Support – Paragraph 3
   A.   Homes can be built quicker
   B.   As a result, foundations not as strong in new homes
      1.   Mass production of homes – builder doesn't establish good foundation
      2.   Older homes in better condition over long period of time because built more solidly
IV.   Support – Paragraph 4
   A.   Custom-built
   B.   Can remodel any way owner wants
      1.   No allowance restrictions placed on owner by builder
V.   Conclusion – Paragraph 5
   A.   Modern homes just don't offer the old-fashioned charm an older well-built, unique home can offer.
   B.   When it comes to such an important decision as purchasing a home, the choice is clear: an older home has much more to offer and will last for many years to come.

> Step 6 – Writing My Essay

Modern-day housing developments are springing up everywhere, dotting hills and filling in every open space available. Characterized by "cookie cutter" homes, houses all cut from the same mold, the look of these communities lacks distinctiveness. For anyone who puts stock in the aged and unique rather than the new and ordinary, the traditional house may be the choice of a lifetime with its old-fashioned motifs, its strong foundations, and its versatility to become the home of its owner's design.

Many homeowners do not feel the need to be the designer behind their home. Rather, they strive to "keep up with the Joneses" by filling their houses with the same modern décor that fills the homes of their neighbors. On the flip side, when seeking to invest in a traditional home, the buyer has a plethora of options because older homes offer so much uniqueness. This uniqueness can be seen in the motifs of style, which are almost non-existent in today's market of prefabricated homes but are powerful reminders of days gone by in older structures. These are the structures that offer a homeowner an admirable individuality.

Clearly, modern-day homes, which lack individuality, are built more quickly than homes of the past, a fact that seems to fit today's hurried society. But what does a homeowner have to show for this efficiency years down the road? There is much value added to a home constructed by a builder who takes time and pays attention to detail instead of putting up as many homes as possible in the shortest amount of time possible. For example, in the past when builders did take extra time and care, the foundations and overall structures were, and still are, much stronger. This is because many builders today, eager to make a quick buck, do not give homes ample time to "settle" on their foundation before continuing with the construction. Overall, older houses are in better condition, even over the course of time, because they were more solidly built.

Many prospective buyers today overlook the quality of a home's structure and are compelled to purchase by the alluring idea of "custom building" their house. These homebuyers enjoy the process of choosing paint colors, fixtures and floor coverings. Consider an older home, however. Here the possibilities are endless, and traditional buyers may even negotiate remodeling into the price of the house. What is more, there are no spending restrictions which contemporary builders often impose on their buyers.

Spending restrictions represent just one of many ways that freedom is limited when purchasing a new home instead of an older home. Whether one prefers an elegant, plantation-style mansion or a peaceful, rustic country getaway, the distinctive older home has much more to offer than the commonplace modern home set in communities of houses that all look the same. Simply put, it comes down to whether the prospective buyer is willing to trade quality and originality for expediency.

➢   Step 7 – Revising My Essay

When critiquing other essays, you often learn a lot about the strengths and weaknesses in your own writing. So here's an assignment: Let's take our revision questions; your job is to complete the task required for each question.

- Is the introduction captivating? Why or why not? Do you recognize a certain method the author employed to make the introduction interesting?

- Is the thesis statement concise? Does it clearly show the purpose of the essay?

- Do the body paragraphs clearly support each point made in the thesis? If not, where does the essay lack necessary support?

- Are there logical transitions that make the text flow smoothly between sentences and between paragraphs? Underline each word, phrase or sentence that acts as a transition.

- Is the tone and diction consistent throughout the essay? If not, point out the places where consistency breaks down.

- Is the use of person consistent? If not, point out the places where consistency is not maintained.

- Is there a word, or are there words, which have been used too often in the essay? List these words. Also list the words that have been used to provide variety in the essay.

- Do the sentences vary in length and structure?

Example 2: Cause – Effect Essay

Prompt: "Students should not be required to take courses outside their field of study."

➤ Step 1 – Understanding the Issue

- **What does the statement mean?** *Colleges should not make students take courses, like General Education courses, if they do not pertain to their area of study.*
- **What is the issue at hand?** *Whether or not students benefit from taking college courses that don't pertain to their major.*
- **What is implied by the statement?** *That a student will be adequately prepared for the "real world" without taking a wide range of classes.*
- **What is the writer's stand on the issue?** *That students should not be required to take these classes.*
- **What, if any, evidence does the writer use to support his position?** *The writer does not give any evidence to support his view.*

➤ Step 2 – Choosing My Pattern of Development

This prompt is a "call for action" statement, and, although no effect is discussed, the writer implies that his recommended course of action would result in a positive effect.

➤ Step 3 – Developing My Thesis

THESIS FOR CAUSE-EFFECT ESSAY *(formula 1-2)*:

If <u>students are not required to take courses outside their field of study</u>, then <u>they will not be prepared</u>, because 1) <u>they will be ill-prepared if they fail to get a job in their field</u>, 2) <u>they will be lacking in important skills – communication or thinking/reasoning skills</u>, 3) <u>they will be close-minded and ignorant to things happening in the world around them</u>.

➤ Step 4 – Understanding Counter Argument

CAUSE – EFFECT COUNTER CLAIM *(formula 2-2)*:

Some may feel that <u>requiring students to take courses only in their field of study</u> would cause <u>students to be more knowledgeable in their field</u> because <u>they would have more thoroughly studied this area</u>. (Note that this point should contrast directly with point #1 of your thesis. (see *formula 1-2*))

➤ Step 5 – Organizing My Thoughts

CAUSE - EFFECT ESSAY FORMULA *(formula 3-2)*:

I.   Introduction – Paragraph 1
  A.   Some feel students should not be required to take courses outside their field of study.
  B.   If students are not required to take courses outside their field of study, they will be ill-prepared should they fail to get a job in their field, they will lack important skills, and they will be close-minded and ignorant to things happening in the world around them.
II. Support – Paragraph 2
  A.   Some may feel that requiring students to take courses only in their field of study would cause students to be more knowledgeable in their field because they would have more thoroughly studied this area.
  B.   Many people are unable to get a job in their field after they graduate.
    1.   Without some knowledge of other fields, these highly trained people will be stuck working menial jobs.
III. They will be lacking in important skills.
  A.   Students studying the sciences will lack communication skills.
  B.   Students studying the arts will lack critical thinking and reasoning skills.
IV. They will be close-minded and ignorant of things happening in the world around them.
  A.   Lack of familiarity with certain fields promotes disinterest in these topics as they pertain to current events (politics, scientific research).
  B.   This disinterest promotes apathy in participating in or supporting causes that result from these current events.

V. Conclusion – Paragraph 5
   A. Students must take a well-rounded schedule of classes in order to be prepared for work outside their field and so they will have adequate skills to use toward a common interest in society.
   C. Students should welcome an opportunity to learn about all areas of study.

➤ Step 6 – Writing My Essay

Colleges and universities require students, regardless of their majors, to complete General Education courses, basic courses that cover general subject areas. These classes include basic literature and writing courses, basic science and math courses, and basic arts classes like music and drama. Some feel students should not be required to take these General Education classes. However, if students are not required to take courses outside their major, they will be ill-prepared should they fail to get a job in their field, they will lack important skills, and they will be close-minded and ignorant of things happening in the world around them.

Many opponents of General Education classes are themselves unaware of the advantages of a well-rounded education. They focus only on the theory that students will be more fully prepared to enter their field as a result of more extensive study in their area. What they fail to see, however, is that many graduates are not able to find jobs in their field of expertise. So, without a broad range of knowledge, these highly trained graduates would be stuck in menial jobs.

Even if graduates do get jobs within their field, such a wide range of skills are required in the workplace in order to be successful that, without a diverse educational background, a graduate will not be fully competent in any job. For example, when a graduate begins looking for a job, she will discover that excellent communication skills are invaluable in the workplace, both in dealing with customers and with colleagues. Without some base of communication knowledge, such as a student would receive in a basic English class, the candidate will be overlooked for someone who does show strength in communication. Moreover, most jobs require strong problem-solving skills, skills that develop from learning how to think and reason critically. These skills are reinforced in math and science classes.

Lack of familiarity in certain educational arenas, like math and science, results in a provincial attitude. This lack of familiarity leads to disinterest in the areas where a student has not gained knowledge. Likewise, this disinterest leads to apathy in participating or supporting any causes that are linked to these fields of study. For example, a student who has not studied science will be indifferent to scientific ideas, ideas which could become theories and could help all of mankind. A student who does not study politics and government will likely be apathetic toward participating in important political events such as elections.

It is important that a country's citizens take part in supporting causes and concepts that generate a common interest in society. Without a well-rounded schedule of classes in college, however, the citizen base will soon be filled with people who are unprepared and indifferent to anything that does not directly pertain to their area of interest. Instead of complaining about an opportunity to gain a broad range of knowledge, students should consider it a privilege and an asset.

➤ Step 7 – Revising My Essay

Read over the essay above and then answer the following questions.

- Is the introduction captivating? Why or why not? Do you recognize a certain method the author employed to make the introduction interesting?

- Is the thesis statement concise? Does it clearly show the purpose of the essay?

- Do the body paragraphs clearly support each point made in the thesis? If not, where does the essay lack necessary support?

- Are there logical transitions that make the text flow smoothly between sentences and between paragraphs? Underline each word, phrase or sentence that acts as a transition.

- Is the tone and diction consistent throughout the essay? If not, point out the places where consistency breaks down.

- Is the use of person consistent? If not, point out the places where consistency is not maintained.

- Is there a word, or are there words, which have been used too often in the essay? List these words. Also list the words that have been used to provide variety in the essay.

- Do the sentences vary in length and structure?

Example 3: Definition Essay

   Prompt: "The positive effects of competition in a society far outweigh the negative effects."

➢   Step 1 – Understanding the Issue

   • What does the statement mean? *Competition affects society in a good way, not a bad way.*
   • What is the issue at hand? *Whether or not competition is good for society.*
   • What is implied by the statement? *That a society benefits from competition amongst its members.*
   • What is the writer's stand on the issue? *That competition is good and provides benefits.*
   • What, if any, evidence does the writer use to support his position? *The writer does not give any evidence to support his view.*

➢   Step 2 – Choosing My Pattern of Development

Although the comparison between a society driven by competition and one where competition plays little or no role seems to hint that the Comparison-Contrast method should be used, the Definition pattern of development is a better fit because it is necessary to look at the qualities of *competition* that make it a positive influence rather than a negative one.

➢   Step 3 – Developing My Thesis

THESIS FOR DEFINITION ESSAY *(formula 1-3)*:

   By definition, <u>competition</u> possesses these qualities: 1) <u>gives everyone the same chance at the beginning</u>, 2) <u>drives people to succeed</u>, 3) <u>provides a way to recognize people who advance</u> which have a positive effect because A) <u>no one can use the excuse that they didn't have the same opportunities; everyone has a chance to succeed</u>, B) <u>people want to be the best, and gives everyone their "place" in life</u>, C) <u>gives self-worth to those who are recognized for their accomplishments</u>.

➢   Step 4 – Understanding Counter Argument

DEFINITION *(formula 2-3)*:

   By definition, some may feel that <u>competition helps only a few/pushing only a few to the top, leaving others feeling left out or insignificant</u> which could be positive or **negative**.
   (Note that this point should contrast directly with point #1 of your thesis. (see *formula 1-3*))

➢   Step 5 – Organizing My Thoughts

DEFINITION ESSAY FORMULA *(formula 3-3)*:

I.   Introduction – Paragraph 1
   A.   Competition benefits a society.
   B.   Everyone is given a chance to succeed in a society where competition drives people to be the best and recognizes the accomplishments of the many who advance.
II.   Support – Paragraph 2
   A.   Some feel that competition helps only a few, leaving others feeling left out or insignificant. There is a push to eliminate salutatorian/valedictorian recognition speeches at graduation.
   B.   Competition gives everyone the same chance at the beginning.
       1.   Just like a marathon – everyone begins at the same starting line.
       2.   No one has an excuse – it is up to each individual to decide how to run the race. Some want to work harder than others and therefore deserve recognition.
III.   Competition drives people to be their best
   A.   Everyone's "best" is different.
   B.   Gives everyone their place in life – if no competition, we'd have a world full of custodians, no CEO's or vice versa.
IV.   With competition comes the chance to recognize winners.
   A.   Gives self-worth to those recognized, causing them to set even greater goals.
   B.   Encourages those who were not recognized to try harder so that they too may be recognized.

V. Conclusion – Paragraph 5
   A. Competition is vital to a growing and thriving society.
   B. How will you run the race? Will you strive to be the best?

➢ Step 6 – Writing My Essay

On your mark! All the runners are at the starting line. *Get set!* The runners are poised, in position. *Go!* The runners take off. The spirit of competition is the driving force behind these runners' desire to win. And, as an integral part of a society, competition brings many benefits. Everyone is given a chance to succeed in a society where competition drives people to be their best, and competition recognizes the accomplishments of those who advance.

Some feel that, although competition recognizes winners, there are so few winners that many are left feeling insignificant and alienated. This attitude has, for example, lead to a movement to eliminate salutatorian and valedictorian recognition and speeches at graduation ceremonies. Those in the movement claim that acknowledging salutatorian and valedictorian students for their scholastic achievements causes other students to feel slighted. This is a misguided assumption. Government gives everyone equal opportunity to attend school and to excel. Some students work harder than others and deserve special honors at graduation. Just like in a race, everyone begins at the same starting line and therefore has the same chance to succeed. Each person makes his own decision about how he will run the race. No one has an excuse, then, for not trying his best to succeed.

Competition drives people to achieve a goal. For most, this goal represents a person's best. Since everyone's concept of "best" is different, achievement differs for each person. Therefore, when an individual reaches his goal, this gives him a certain status. This status is different for each person, depending on the goal that was attained. This is extremely important because if competition did not place people at different positions in life, the resulting equality would be stultifying to society. For example, the work force would consist of only custodians and no CEO's or vice versa.

CEO's get to where they are only through competition. As an employee works hard and competes within a company, he is rewarded for his accomplishments with promotions. Not only does competition award people through tangible benefits like promotions, but competition also gives long-lasting psychological awards such as a feeling of self-worth or pride. This recognition encourages people who succeed to raise their personal goals even higher. Recognition also drives those who were not recognized to do better so that they too may be rewarded.

Because competition results in rewards, both tangible and emotional, it is essential for a growing and thriving society. Everyone begins at the same starting line and is given the same chance to succeed. When the starting gun fires, it is up to each runner to decide how he will run the race. This decision will ultimately determine who will become the winners. Driven by competition, these winners, along with the losers, comprise a successful society.

➢ Step 7 – Revising My Essay

Read over the essay above and then answer the following questions:

- Is the introduction captivating? Why or why not? Do you recognize a certain method the author employed to make the introduction interesting?

- Is the thesis statement concise? Does it clearly show the purpose of the essay?

- Do the body paragraphs clearly support each point made in the thesis? If not, where does the essay lack necessary support?

- Are there logical transitions that make the text flow smoothly between sentences and between paragraphs? Underline each word, phrase or sentence that acts as a transition.

- Is the tone and diction consistent throughout the essay? If not, point out the places where consistency breaks down.

- Is the use of person consistent? If not, point out the places where consistency is not maintained.

- Is there a word, or are there words, which have been used too often in the essay? List these words. Also list the words that have been used to provide variety in the essay.

- Do the sentences vary in length and structure?

Practice

Now it's your turn to practice some Issue essays. Consider the five prompts below and write your responsive essays, making sure you follow the 7 steps we discussed.

Prompts:

"Museums should have the liberty to exhibit whatever displays they want without the interference of government censorship."

"When people work in teams, they are more productive than when they work individually."

"If everyone would closely examine their past, they would realize that only a few individuals have played a role in shaping their behavior and their way of thinking."

"Success is easily obtained but difficult to maintain."

"Society is governed by two types of laws, just and unjust. People must obey just laws but are at liberty to defy those laws which they determine are frivolous or unjust."

More Sample Issue Essays

Issue prompt:

"There is little need for books today because one can learn just as much or more from television."

When I was little, I would line up my stuffed animals and "read" to them. Although I was not old enough to know the letters formed words and the words formed sentences, I knew there was a story to tell, and I knew there was an audience who would be interested in hearing the story. Now I watch my two-year-old daughter do the same thing. In this media age, books often take a back seat to television, which is unfortunate because books offer so much more. Books are a better tool with which to build imagination. Moreover, readers can gain much more knowledge from the wide variety of books that are available.

Satellite dishes and improved cable offer hundreds of channels, a variety that some TV viewers argue is sufficient to replace reading. However, libraries and bookstores offer thousands, not hundreds, of titles from which to choose. Among these choices, a reader can find books on any theme he chooses, from topics of today to stories of every era in the past. Television, unfortunately, is controlled mostly by popular trends. Aside from a handful of specialty channels like *The History Channel*, there is little on TV about historical events. Furthermore, TV viewers' choices are limited since the television broadcasting companies choose what they will offer on each channel.

A limited choice of TV channels results in limited knowledge. The written word offers much more detail than television. Most TV shows are limited to two hours or less, and because of this time restriction, fewer details can be included in shows like movies and documentaries. For example, a TV documentary on orangutans would most likely be a one hour program which would offer some basic knowledge about orangutans, their habitat and their way of life. A book about orangutans, on the other hand, would educate the reader far beyond the basic knowledge he would gain from watching a television program.

In addition to offering more information on a greater number of subjects, the added description included in books helps readers improve vocabulary. In books, readers see unfamiliar words in context, enabling them to decipher the meaning. For TV viewers, unfamiliar words in conversation usually go unnoticed. In fact, many people watch TV simply to "veg," or, in other words, to sit and do nothing but be vaguely aware of the images flickering across the screen. Watching television requires little of the concentration that is required for reading books; consequently the viewer overlooks many details.

Because watching TV does not require active participation, the imagination suffers. Television programs take the viewer quickly from one scene to the next, prohibiting the viewer from taking notice of the details of the setting. Books inspire imagination, allowing the reader to picture for herself the setting and characters of the story. A book's character may be described as tall, dark complected, and wearing a bright purple robe; it is up to the reader to imagine exactly what the character looks like. Is the character Italian or perhaps Native American? Is the bright purple robe rather gaudy looking, or does it give the character an air of sophistication? Television makes those decisions for the viewer by placing in the program a specific actor in garb chosen by costume designers, thus leaving little room for imagination.

Imagination is the key to forward thinking, thinking that brings a person success in what he does. Without imagination, problems go unsolved and new and inventive ideas never make it to the drawing board. Imagination produces creativity, which inspires dreamers. I hope my daughter will continue to be a dreamer, allowing her imagination to blossom. And when the letters, then words, then sentences take form for her, she will have the added benefit of gaining boundless knowledge from books.

Issue prompt:

> *"Many of today's technological conveniences were developed to save time. Ironically, these developments have created an even more hurried, fast-paced society, where people actually have less leisure time."*

Ah, the good ol' days! When people sat on their front porch talking and watching the world go by instead of finishing up last-minute work on their laptops. When letters took a week to spread the latest news instead of a few seconds through e-mail. In a world of pagers, faxes, cell phones, and computers, a very hurried society is characterized by impatient workaholics whose nerves are on edge and whose lives are unknowingly empty.

Many of today's conveniences were developed to meet growing impatience with the speed it took to spread information. Through the development of such things as faxes, cell phones and e-mail, however, a new impatience was born. This new impatience is characterized by frustration with the sophistication and complexity of modern technology. Office workers grit their teeth in frustration when an e-mail takes too long to download. In annoyance, they may shut down their computer assuming there is something wrong with the machine. This wastes even more time while restarting the computer and finally retrieving the culprit e-mail. Overnight delivery services emerged to meet this all-consuming impatience as well. Oftentimes, however, even this speedy service is not expedient enough. Some find it necessary to rush a package to the airport so that it may arrive at its destination just a few hours earlier.

This annoyance with our more efficient world has thrown society into a frenzy where even the most technologically advanced equipment is unsatisfactorily slow. The resulting annoyance and impatience can turn into rage in the office and on the highway, with stressed out employees who "go postal," losing all rationale and even causing injury to colleagues. Preventable injuries occur on highways as road rage consumes drivers who are eager to get to their next destination.

In a world where people are eager to pass information ever more quickly and get to their next destination ever more quickly, this has truly become a society of workaholics. Because the transfer of information is so much more efficient with modern technologies, workers find they can accomplish much more in a given day. Driven by this fact, they work more hours. There is always time to make that last call or send a quick e-mail at the end of the day. And portable conveniences like laptops and palm pilots make it possible for people to work essentially anywhere; work is no longer confined to the office and is often completed at home.

Perhaps the most detrimental aspect of our more hurried society lies at home. Because many people spend more time working, and because work is transportable, many spouses discover that their partners spend more time with their computers and cell phones than with their family. Additionally, other conveniences like microwave meals encourage quick meals on-the-go. Rushed families rarely spend quality time together around the dinner table. Rather, they all go their separate ways to eat in front of the TV, at the computer, or at a desk reviewing reports.

At home, in the office and on the streets, a fast-paced society continues to become more hurried as technology continues to match a perpetually growing impatience. Is all of this annoyance, frustration, and rage worth the added convenience that technology has brought to our society? It hardly seems so. In fact, in looking back at the good 'ol days, it seems that in a world with far less vexation and anger, there was more happiness.

Issue prompt:

"Character is created in a crisis."

In 1992, Hurricane Andrew slammed into Florida causing millions of dollars of damage. Many residents lost everything, including their homes. Those houses that had the strongest foundations withstood the storm most favorably. Additionally, the homes that had been adequately prepared to face the storm fared better than those whose windows were not boarded. Character is like a house. If your character has a strong foundation and displays traits of preparedness, you can weather a storm well. In this light, it is clear that character is not born from crisis, but rather, it merely emerges during difficult times.

It is not adversity but the small moments of life that create character. Poor decisions, regardless of how insignificant, break down your character. Anytime you are inconsistent in following your principles, no matter how small the compromise, cracks in your foundation undoubtedly weaken your character. On the positive side, though, you can learn a lot from your mistakes. In fact, lessons learned from failures are indispensable in building character. To discern the lesson to be learned, however, takes conscious effort. If you are unwilling to put effort into developing character, you will continue to repeat your mistakes, and your life will stagnate.

Part of building character and thus avoiding stagnation is building on your strengths. Taking what is good and making it exceptional is what character building is all about. Continued improvement in life makes you stronger. This too takes a conscious effort in using strengths to positively affect others around you. Channeling the positive to help others results in personal growth, which in turn builds character.

Only when you are willing to learn from your mistakes and make a conscious effort to grow can you face a crisis successfully. It is during this adversity that character comes to light. If you have learned from past failures, you will have the strength to face a crisis head on. You will have adequate problem-solving skills to overcome obstacles set before you. If you have made the conscious effort to build on your positive traits, you will have the means with which to get through the crisis positively with the will to move ahead.

The will and ability to move forward from crisis is the defining moment of your character. As you move forward, though, you should never stop working to improve, because the stronger your foundation is, the better it will weather any type of storm. What kind of storm can the foundation of your character withstand?

Issue prompt:

"People should pursue careers that provide financial security even if they do not enjoy the work."

"I want to be a fireman when I grow up!" A simple dream from a young child in response to the question every youngster faces at one point or another: What do you want to be when you grow up? The innocence of a child, however, protects him from the world of finances; something everyone is forced to face later on in life. And when that realization hits, what path is best for a person to take: the path that leads to a career with large financial promises, or the one that leads to a career that provides more personal satisfaction? Because contentment has so many rewards, it is better for a person to choose the job that will provide happiness even if it does not pay as well as other jobs.

Some people find it necessary to get the best paying job to make financial ends meet. Often someone in financial dire straits will stick with a good paying job just long enough to get ahead and then, because they are unhappy at the job, they quit to find work elsewhere. This has several negative effects. First, the transition to a new job is difficult, and it can be made worse for a new employee if they are followed by negativity. Company officers are reluctant to invest training time and money in employees only to have them leave after a short time and therefore may not be willing to provide favorable references. Second, workers who leave jobs after short periods of time are not with a company long enough to advance within the company. These workers may find that they would have done just as well to begin in a job that they like even if it did not pay as well, because by the time they start all over, they could have already been promoted. The increase in salary that comes with most promotions could equal the wages they were earning at the job they did not enjoy.

The potential for promotion should be a major consideration when deciding between the high paying job and the job that provides satisfaction. Employees in positions they do not enjoy often work with a poor attitude. This promotes laziness and apathy. Managers quickly pick up on this and likely pass up these types of employees for promotions. On the other hand, workers who enjoy their job greet each workday with enthusiasm, fresh creativity and perseverance. Bosses commend this type of work ethic and reward such employees with promotions.

Careers that offer promotions and, most importantly, job satisfaction stimulate self-respect and pride. These characteristics are priceless and have an enormously positive impact on a person and their job performance. The employee who has pride in what he does takes ownership. He is empowered to take charge of the position he holds and give it 110 percent. This attitude has a domino effect and soon colleagues begin to take more pride in their work as well. Managers notice this natural leadership and reward it with promotions.

Taking pride in a job leads to success, not just monetarily, but also personally. Personal success and satisfaction far outweigh monetary gain. So if the little boy still wants to be a fireman when he grows up, he should be a fireman, even if it means he will live in a modest home instead of a mansion. He will never regret the happiness and contentment he will feel by following his dream instead of following the green.

Issue prompt:

"The idea that individuals should focus on personal self-improvement assumes that there is something inherently wrong with people."

A best-selling book offers "Seven Ways to Become a Better Person." A radio ad promises you will feel great in 30 days or less just by taking some pills. "If you buy our exercise equipment," a TV ad guarantees, "you'll have the body you've always wanted." And don't miss that talk show today because the guest speaker will teach you how to have confidence. In today's society, we are continually bombarded with the latest techniques of how to better ourselves, a focus which some feel is unhealthy. On the contrary, a focus on self-improvement is very important in helping people grow in character.

Although some may believe that focusing on the need for self-improvement assumes that there is something inherently wrong with people, this focus maintains quite the opposite. In fact, self-improvement helps build character. Building character involves taking a person's strengths and building on them. Such strengths as unselfishness can be developed into a lifelong habit of generosity, a positive spirit into an unfailing compassion for others. Everyone has strength in character and the ability to build on these strengths through self-improvement.

Everyone also has weaknesses. Weaknesses are not flaws, but rather negative traits that, through self-improvement, can be developed into more positive traits. For example, impatience can be turned into determination to accomplish goals. Strong will can be turned into perseverance. If a person can just find a way to capitalize on a weakness, it can be turned into a strength. Self-improvement is the best way to do this.

Recent focus on self-improvement is valuable because of the wealth of resources such a focus offers. There is a plethora of different ways a person can work on self-improvement. Groups offer support for improvement, and individual strategies are available in many different forms. Books and videos offer plans for developing a positive attitude. Gyms and health stores offer ways to build self-esteem by building better health.

No matter the method a person chooses for self-improvement, every individual has room to improve. Even when a person reaches a specific goal of improvement, there are still ways to build on character and become a person with more positive traits. Those who grow in character, grow in self-esteem, which then breeds confidence. Confidence and a feeling of self-worth give people the power to positively influence those around them. Positive influences are invaluable in our society, so we should never stop making an effort to improve ourselves.

Issue prompt:

Public figures should expect their private lives to be scrutinized.

Television shows, newspapers, books, magazines and tabloids delve into the lives of singers, actors, athletes and politicians on a daily basis. Should these public figures expect to lose some of their privacy? Whether they want to or not, people who are in positions that will sometimes place them in the spotlight open themselves to scrutiny from their audience, because people have a natural curiosity and interest in those who have achieved fame.

Although public figures should expect some scrutiny in their lives, there is a point where it can become dangerous. For example, it was reported in 1997 that the driver of Princess Diana's car was driving recklessly to get away from aggressive Paparazzi. As a result, the car spun out of control killing Diana. Other similar stories report stalkers and "Peeping Toms" who take too much liberty in examining the private lives of stars, athletes and politicians. While these are extreme cases of obsession, public figures must realize that there is a natural human desire to more intimately know the familiar faces on TV or on the sports field. This is especially true of actors and actresses. Television and movie viewers get to know their favorite characters on screen and therefore have a desire to "get to know" the actors behind these characters.

Not only do people want to get to know those whom they look up to, but they also strive to be like their favorite stars. Ads on TV encourage viewers to "Be like Mike [Michael Jordan]." On Halloween, teenage girls can emulate their favorite pop singer by obtaining a Britney Spears costume. Although many people admittedly would not choose a life of glamour and fame, there is something alluring about the lifestyle, and therefore admirers of people in the limelight are driven to discover personal facts about those whom they admire. Knowing these intimate details makes a famous person seem more down-to-earth and thus allows the ordinary person to feel like they have something in common with the rich and famous.

The media makes a concerted effort to give viewers a chance to become acquainted with public figures. They splash familiar stars' faces on the cover of magazines. Channels like *E!* and *VH1* feature behind the scenes stories about singers and actors, their highs and lows and how they became famous. Tabloids are a huge business supported by readers who hungrily devour the latest gossip about their favorite star. Even the news capitalizes on human interest stories that feature public figures. For example, although long and drawn-out, OJ Simpson's murder trial dominated the news, yet no one seemed to complain.

The news often highlights human interest stories that uncover the blunders of politicians. Former President Clinton's escapades with Monica Lewinsky, for example, made headlines for months. Many public figures, especially politicians, anticipate the scrutinizing eye under which they will find themselves and proactively confess to past mistakes. This takes some of the media pressure off them. Sadly, others find themselves on the front cover of every magazine and newspaper and in every headline when marital infidelity or an encounter with drugs is exposed.

Politicians are of deep interest to the public because they are the nation's leaders. Since people must place some trust in political figures to run the country effectively, politicians should expect their private lives to be examined. Not only should they expect ordinary citizens to dig into their lives, but they should also anticipate other political figures to look closely at their lives. Political campaigns, unfortunately, often focus on tearing apart the opponent. To do this, a politician must find a way to attack his opponent, which requires investigating the personal life of the candidate. This comes with the territory. If a would-be politician cannot stomach having some negative aspect of his life exposed, he should not enter the world of politics.

Although many people work hard to achieve the fame of a popular singer, actor, athlete, or politician, some become bitterly disenchanted with the lifestyle when they realize they may lose much of their privacy. This should certainly be a matter of consideration before pursuing any career that places a person in the spotlight. It is, after all, natural that admirers will be interested in the details of the life of public figures. Public figures should consider this admiration flattery rather than an intrusion on their privacy.

Issue prompt:

"It is necessary for a leader to compromise his principles if compromising them is favorable to a greater number of people."

This nation has seen many outstanding leaders, like George Washington and Abraham Lincoln. Have you ever wondered what separates great leaders from ineffective leaders? Contrary to popular belief, great leaders are not born. Rather, if you want to be an effective leader, you must realize that it takes a lot of work and perseverance. Furthermore, of all the character traits that can be cultivated to make a good leader, the ability to stick to your principles is the most important; to be a great leader, you should never compromise your principles, no matter how high the price.

As a leader, you may sometimes pay a price by losing favor with the majority because of a decision you have made. At these times, it may be tempting for you to give in to the demands of your followers. However, remember that, regardless of the capacity in which you lead, you are in a position of leadership because there are people who thought your ideas were good, and therefore they made a conscious decision to follow you. Knowing this, you should be encouraged to stick to your decisions since, in the end, even if your followers still disagree with your decision, they will respect you for standing firm on your principles. If you possess honor in your word, your followers will entrust you with more responsibility knowing that, since you did not compromise your beliefs in one decision, you are not likely to go back on your word in other situations.

As followers take note that you refuse to give in by compromising your principles, they will come to the realization that they made an excellent choice in a leader, and they will gain a deeper respect for you as their leader. As people gain new respect for you, they will be more willing to follow you in all of your decisions, even if they do not fully agree with all of them. This type of respect is important for your leadership because it creates an atmosphere conducive to cooperation and teamwork. In this cooperative environment, your followers will be willing to step up and take on some of the responsibility if they believe in you and what you stand for.

With you as their guide, your team's confidence will grow. As their confidence grows, your self-confidence will flourish. A confident leader is much more effective than one who is unsure of himself. If you do not portray confidence in what you do, others will not feel confident in your decisions either. Moreover, if you lack confidence in your ability as a leader, you will likely at some point give in to others' wishes over your own principles. Your followers will perceive you as weak and will recede from your leadership. If you believe in yourself, however, you will benefit from lifelong supporters who respect your confidence and the consistency of your principles.

Unwillingness to compromise principles breeds the stalwart leader within you. Becoming an effective leader requires this confidence in the actions that you take and the decisions that you make. The respect you will earn by standing firm in what you believe will take your leadership farther than you ever thought possible.

Issue prompt:

"Parents must be involved in their children's education in order to make them successful."

Sally is a Sophomore in high school. Although she is a bright girl and has the potential to excel in school, she lacks the ability to apply herself and therefore is not doing well. As a result, she does not enjoy school and often cuts classes to hang out at the mall with friends who share her same ethic. Sally enjoys athletics and earned a spot on the Girls' Softball team. She competed in six matches, but when progress reports were issued, she was forced to leave the team because her grades were not up to par. Sally's father is a lawyer and often works so late, the family rarely sees him. Sally's mother works in an office, but after work, she enjoys going out with her colleagues. Often, Sally is on her own when she gets home and must prepare dinner for herself and her 12-year-old sister. Sally's parents have missed countless parent-teacher conferences and have yet to meet most of her teachers. They are aware of only one instance of Sally's truancy; usually she gets home in time to erase the school's message from the answering machine. When her parents heard about her "first" unexcused absence from school, they did nothing but tell her not to do it again.

Tommy is also a Sophomore. He is intelligent and works hard to obtain near-perfect grades. He enjoys school and enthusiastically participates in all of his classes. Tommy is the goalie on the Boys' Soccer team and can be depended upon to maintain his important position on the team. Tommy's parents are divorced, and Tommy and his twin 10-year-old brothers live with their mother. She works in an office and gets home promptly by 5:30. Although she must rely on Tommy to watch the twins after school, she always prepares dinner when she gets home. After dinner, Tommy and his brothers must finish their homework before they are permitted to do anything else. Tommy's mom checks everyone's homework when they are done and helps them with work they do not understand. Although Tommy's father lives an hour away, he often meets Tommy's mother for parent-teacher conferences, and he consistently makes it to Tommy's games. Tommy has never considered skipping school because he knows the consequences at home would be great.

Two students, two very different results at school and two opposite attitudes about life. The difference? Parental involvement. Although teachers can equip a student with the tools he needs to succeed in life, it is up to parents to instill in their children the motivation and determination to use these tools to be successful. To do this, parents must be willing to be involved in every aspect of their children's lives, particularly in their education. It is unfair for parents to expect teachers and school administrators to take sole responsibility for the complete education and training that prepares a student for his adult life.

Some parents feel inadequate to help their children in school because they are unfamiliar with their children's school subjects, or because they did not do well in school themselves. No matter how little academic knowledge parents have, however, they can play an integral part in her child's education. For example, there are many opportunities to volunteer in schools. Parents can become a part of the school's Parent-Teacher Association or Parent-Teacher-Student Organization. Parents can help with sports' teams or at the very least, make an effort to support the athletes by coming to the games. If parents' jobs hinder them from attending school functions, they can play an important role at home by keeping their children accountable in school matters like homework. They can help their children with things the children do not understand or get a tutor if they do not understand it either.

Although parents cannot always help a child scholastically, they can teach their children lifelong lessons in motivation and determination. If a man wants to learn how to fish, he can obtain a net and a boat and learn how to cast the net. But he is not a fisherman simply because he has the right tools and knowledge. Someone must instill in him the motivation and determination to sit on a boat day after day performing the tedious task of casting a net that does not always produce a big catch. In the same way, a teacher can give their students the book knowledge they need to be experts in various fields; however, it is the parents who must empower their children to use the knowledge to be successful. This requires parents to teach their children the value of education and thus inspire motivation; parents must teach their children never to give up and thus inspire determination.

Only motivated learners have the determination to gain the knowledge and responsibility that will enable them to succeed in life. It is the responsibility of parents to instill in their children these qualities. One of the most effective ways parents can teach their children the importance of such qualities is by modeling them in their own lives. Parents should make an effort to model responsibility through motivation and determination in their own lives. Such examples provide the best lessons a student will ever learn.

Analysis of an Argument

The *Analysis of an Argument* section of the test requires you to critique an argument and discuss the logical soundness of it. You are not required to agree or disagree with it. You have 30 minutes to plan and write your critique. Following is the grading scale for the Argument essay. Remember that the highest possible score is a 6.

SCORE

6   OUTSTANDING

A 6 essay presents a cogent, well-articulated discussion of the issue and demonstrates mastery of the elements of effective writing.

A typical paper in this category

— clearly identifies and insightfully analyzes important features of the argument
— develops ideas cogently, organizes them logically, and connects them smoothly with clear transitions
— effectively supports the main points of the critique
— demonstrates superior control of language, including diction and syntactic variety
— demonstrates superior facility with the conventions (grammar, usage, and mechanics) of standard written English but may have minor flaws

5   STRONG

A 5 paper presents a well-developed critique of the argument and demonstrates a good control of the elements of effective writing.

A typical paper in this category

— clearly identifies important features of the argument and analyzes them in a generally thoughtful way
— develops ideas clearly, organizes them logically, and connects them with appropriate transitions
— sensibly supports the main points of the critique
— demonstrates clear control of language, including diction and syntactic variety
— demonstrates facility with the conventions of standard written English but may have minor flaws

4   ADEQUATE

A 4 essay presents a competent critique of the argument and demonstrates adequate control of the elements of writing.

A typical paper in this category

— identifies and capably analyzes important features of the argument
— develops and organizes ideas satisfactorily but may not always connect them with transitions
— supports the main points of the critique
— demonstrates adequate control of language, including diction and syntax, but may lack syntactic variety
— displays control of the conventions of standard written English but may have some flaws

3   LIMITED

A 3 paper demonstrates competence in its critique of the argument and in its control of the elements of writing but is clearly flawed.

A typical paper in this category exhibits <u>one or more</u> of the following characteristics:

—does not identify or analyze most of the important features of the argument, although some analysis is present
—is limited in the logical development and organization of ideas
—offers support of little relevance and value for points of the critique
—uses language imprecisely and/or lacks sentence variety
—has occasional major errors or frequent minor errors in grammar, usage, and mechanics

2   SERIOUSLY FLAWED

A 2 paper demonstrates serious weaknesses in analytical writing skills.

A typical paper in this category exhibits <u>one or more</u> of the following characteristics:

—does not understand, identify, or analyze main features of the argument
—does not develop ideas or is disorganized
—provides little, if any, relevant reasonable support
—has serious and frequent problems in the use of language and sentence structure
—contains frequent errors in grammar, usage, or mechanics that interfere with meaning

1   FUNDAMENTALLY DEFICIENT

A 1 paper demonstrates fundamental deficiencies in analytical writing skills.

A typical paper in this category exhibits <u>one or more</u> of the following characteristics:

—provides little evidence of the ability to understand and analyze the argument or to develop an organized response to it.
—has severe and persistent errors in language and sentence structure
—contains a pervasive pattern of errors in grammar, usage, and mechanics, thus resulting in incoherence

0   Any response totally illegible, or obviously not written on the assigned topic receives a score of zero.

Using the scoring criteria for the *Analysis of an Argument* essays, make sure that your writing demonstrates that you can:

• identify and analyze important features of an argument
• develop ideas clearly and logically, using appropriate transitions
• support ideas
• express ideas in standard written English, using appropriate diction

Writing Your Argument Essay

Now that you are familiar with techniques for analyzing an argument, it is time to discuss techniques that will help you write an effective critique. Again, you will have 30 minutes to complete this portion of the test and, luckily, there are only 5 steps you need to take. As with the *Analysis of an Issue* section, we will create some formulas to simplify the task. Plugging information into these formulas will help you organize your ideas and prepare you for your critique.

➢   Step 1 – Understanding the Argument

Remember that your goal in the Argument section is to analyze the given argument. You cannot effectively analyze the argument until you completely understand it. To understand the argument, first read it and then answer the following questions. Keep in mind that you have a short amount of time, so spend more time mulling over the questions than jotting down notes. If you do write notes, make sure they are just short words and phrases that will help you formulate a plan, not long notations that will take time to write and then review.

- Identify the conclusion.
- What premises does the author offer to support the conclusion?
- What fallacies or flaws do you recognize in the argument?
- What assumptions are made in the argument?
- What does the argument fail to address?
- What necessary evidence is omitted from the argument?

➢   Step 2 – Developing Your Thesis

Your thesis statement will set up your entire essay by letting the reader know what direction your critique will take. It will also provide you with a blueprint by which you can organize your essay.

ANALYSIS OF AN ARGUMENT THESIS *(formula 1)*:
The argument that _____ creates several problems because 1) it assumes that _____, 2) it fails to address _____, 3) it omits the following important evidence: _____.

➢   Step 3 – Organizing Your Thoughts

Once you have formulated a thesis, it is time to organize the information that you will present in your essay. This is now a simple task since you have already developed a thesis. You only need to plug in the correct information in the formula below. (Note that the following formula requires you to plug in the three numbered items from your thesis in succession. Although it is not necessary to discuss them in this order, we will label it that way for simplicity.) In addition, there are spaces in the formula for you to insert 1 or 2 pieces of supporting evidence.

ANALYSIS OF AN ARGUMENT ESSAY FORMULA *(formula 2)*:
I.   Introduction
  A.   Restate topic
  B.   Thesis *(formula 1)*
II.   The argument assumes that … (thesis point #1)
  A.   Support
  B.   Support
III.   The argument never addresses … (thesis point #2)
  A.   Support
  B.   Support
IV.   The argument omits important evidence … (thesis point #3)
  A.   Support
  B.   Support
V.   Conclusion
  A.   Restate thesis
  B.   Offer solution to strengthen argument

➤ Step 4 – Writing Your Essay

Writing your essay should not be difficult now that you have organized your points and the support for each point. Paying close attention to the general tips you learned earlier and the more specific techniques in this section, start writing. Following your essay formula, make sure you include transitional words and phrases, which will enhance the flow of your critique. You should spend about 20 minutes writing, reserving about 5 minutes at the end for proofreading and revising.

➤ Step 5 – Revising Your Essay

You should spend about 5 minutes proofreading and revising your essay. Look for misspellings and grammatical errors while keeping in mind the following questions:

- Is my introduction captivating?
- Does my thesis clearly tell the reader what my essay will be about?
- Have I thoroughly, yet concisely, proven my points?
- Do my body paragraphs support my thesis?
- Have I used logical transitions that help the text flow smoothly between sentences and between paragraphs?
- Have I maintained a formal tone and diction throughout my essay?
- Have I maintained consistent use of person (i.e., first, second, third)?
- Is there a word, or are there words, which I have used too often in the essay?
- Do my sentences vary in length and structure?

If time is still remaining after you have made any necessary changes, go back and revise your essay again. You may catch more errors the second time around.

Sample Arguments & Essays

Following is an example of an *Analysis of an Argument* essay. Let's complete each of the five steps to illustrate the process.

Argument:

The following appeared in a memo from a human resources manager at Presto Products.

"Over the past year, we have had 25 percent more on-the-job accidents than Mega Manufacturing, which is just down the street. Mega Manufacturing's employees begin work at 9:00 instead of 8:00, like Presto Products, and they end at 5:30 just like we do. This means that their employees work one hour less than our employees do. We should adopt the same working hours as Mega Manufacturing so our employees are more rested. This would decrease the number of on-the-job accidents since it would take away the fatigue factor."

➤ Step 1 – Understanding the Argument

- Identify the conclusion. *Presto has had more on-the-job accidents than Mega, and the HR manager feels this is caused by fatigue since Presto employees work one hour longer than Mega employees.*
- What premises does the author offer to support the conclusion? *Mega employees begin work later and have fewer on-the-job accidents.*
- What fallacies or flaws do you recognize in the argument? *The author makes a hasty generalization, comparing the two companies as if they are identical.*
- What assumptions are made in the argument? *That fatigue is the main factor in accidents. Also that Presto's employees are suffering from fatigue just because of one extra hour of work. Also assumes that break times at both companies are the same.*
- What does the argument fail to address? *What each company does. (Maybe one company's employees spend more time working with hazardous equipment.)*
- What necessary evidence is omitted from the argument? *What each company does. Also, the size of each company – size both of the actual building and of the number of employees (more people in a smaller space could lead to more accidents).*

➤ Step 2 – Developing My Thesis

The argument that <u>Presto's occurrences of on-the-job accidents would be less if the employees worked an hour less</u> creates several problems because 1) it assumes that <u>fatigue is the main factor in on-the-job accidents and that breaks are the same at both companies,</u> 2) it fails to address <u>what each company does,</u> 3) it omits the following important evidence: <u>What the companies do and the size of the companies</u>.

➤ Step 3 – Organizing My Thoughts

ANALYZING AN ARGUMENT ESSAY FORMULA *(formula 2)*:
I.   Introduction
     A.   A memo recently went out to Presto employees regarding on-the-job accidents. It seems that Presto's rate of accidents is 25 percent higher than that of nearby Mega Manufacturing. The memo suggested that Presto employees' workdays should be shortened by one hour by starting work at 9:00 instead of 8:00.
     B.   The argument that Presto's occurrences of on-the-job accidents would be less if the employees worked an hour less creates several problems because it assumes fatigue is the main factor in the accidents, it fails to address what each company does, and it does not discuss the size of the companies.
II. The argument assumes that … (thesis point #1)
     A.   Fatigue is the main factor in on-the-job accidents
     B.   Both companies give their employees the same time for breaks
III. The argument never addresses … (thesis point #2)
     A.   What the companies do
     B.   How the companies' industries differ
IV. The argument omits important evidence … (thesis point #3)
     A.   What the companies do
     B.   The size of the companies, both in actual building size and number of employees
V.   Conclusion
     A.   Restate thesis
     B.   Presto should examine other elements in the location where the majority of the accidents occur. Such things as machinery, workspace and employee experience may be important factors to consider.

➤ Step 4 – Writing My Essay

On-the-job accidents are a major concern to companies. Every year, workplace injuries cost companies thousands of dollars in medical expenses and wages paid to recovering employees. Naturally, these companies look for ways to reduce risks and make the workplace safer. Recently, a memo went out to Presto Product employees regarding on-the-job accidents. It seems that Presto's rate of accidents is 25 percent higher than that of nearby Mega Manufacturing. The memo suggested that Presto employees' workdays should be shortened by one hour by starting work at 9:00 instead of 8:00. However, this argument has several flaws: Based on an assumption that Presto employees work more hours than Mega Manufacturing, it offers fatigue as the main factor in these accidents, and it does not discuss the size of the companies or describe what each company does.

   By not taking into account what each company does, the Presto memo fails to accurately identify the cause of on-the-job accidents. For example, perhaps Presto Products uses forklifts and Mega Manufacturing does not. If this were the case, Presto could have a higher rate of accidents involving those workers who operate the heavy machinery. In addition, the type of work Presto employees do could be more of a contributing factor to fatigue than the number of hours worked. If workers at Presto Products spend a majority of the day on their feet, they would clearly be more affected by fatigue than a company whose employees spend much of their time at desks.

   In addition to the misguided assumptions the Presto memo makes about fatigue, it also fails to consider break times during a workday. By law, companies are required to give their employees a certain number of timed breaks. The number of breaks required is dependent upon the number of hours an employee is required to work. Therefore, it is possible that at Mega Manufacturing employees get fewer breaks than Presto employees do. Moreover, perhaps lunch time at Mega Manufacturing is shorter than at Presto. Over the course of a day, then, Presto employees may work the same number of hours as the workers at Mega Manufacturing.

Besides failing to consider break times during the workday, the Presto memo also omits important information. The memo should address various concrete factors such as the size of the Presto's building and the number of employees working there. By comparing this information to the same type of information from Mega Manufacturing, it may be possible to draw an accurate comparison. For example, perhaps Presto's staff has outgrown their facility while Mega Manufacturing's small staff enjoys the luxury of private offices and a large spacious warehouse. For Presto, a crowded building could become a hazard.

There are many potential hazards at the workplace. A company like Presto cannot validly assume that fatigue is the main cause of on-the-job accidents without supplying solid evidence to support such a finding. If they wish to prove that fatigue is the primary cause of on-the-job accidents, they must rule out other potential causes. Discussing other potentially hazardous factors with their employees would also go a long way toward finding a solution.

➢   Step 5 – Revising My Essay

Just like in *Analysis of an Issue*, here is your chance to revise an essay. Answer the following questions regarding the essay above.

- Is the introduction captivating? Why or why not? Do you recognize a certain method the author employs to make the introduction interesting?

- Is the thesis statement concise? Does it clearly show the purpose of the essay?

- Do the body paragraphs clearly support each point made in the thesis? If not, where does the essay lack necessary support?

- Are there logical transitions that make the text flow smoothly between sentences and between paragraphs? Underline each word, phrase or sentence that acts as a transition.

- Is the tone and diction consistent throughout the essay? If not, point out the places where consistency breaks down.

- Is the use of person consistent? If not, point out the places where consistency is not maintained.

- Is there a word, or are there words, which have been used too often in the essay? List these words. Also list the words that have been used to provide variety in the essay.

- Do the sentences vary in length and structure?

Practice

Consider the Argument prompts below and, using the five steps we have discussed, practice analyzing some arguments.

Arguments:

The manager at WKAM radio station recently sent out a memo that included the following:

"At the beginning of this past year, we removed 'Fred Kalin's Sports Talk' from the 11:00 news. Since then, our ratings have gone down. Therefore, we will reinstate Fred's spot so that our ratings will be revived."

The following is from a letter from the Barrow County School Board:

"Two years ago, we formed a committee whose sole purpose is to examine area schools and identify potential problems. This year, the committee's study noted that the 10 worst schools were run by principals with the least experience. Next year, these principals will be replaced by people with more experience so that the schools will begin to improve."

The following appeared in a letter from Smiler Toothpaste's marketing department to its CEO:

"Glamour Teeth just introduced Mr. Tooth in their new advertising campaign. Mr. Tooth is a cute cartoon tooth who encourages everyone to try the new Glamour Teeth toothpaste. Since the new ad campaign began, sales of the new Glamour Teeth toothpaste have risen 67%. We should develop our own cartoon mascot to star in a new ad campaign. This would give our sales the boost they need to compete with or even surpass Glamour Teeth's sales."

The following appeared in a business plan for ABC Company, located in Hankville:

"All of the successful small businesses in the neighboring town of Sharpston are family-owned. Since we are a small business, if we want to be successful, we should offer employment to family members of any employees we hire. This will create a more family-oriented atmosphere."

Health stores get most of their business from people who are into fitness. Therefore, when considering where to locate, a health store should open only in towns where sports equipment stores flourish and fitness centers are full.

More Sample Argument Essays

Argument

A national news station recently reported the following:

> *"Over the past few years, the number of women leaving the workforce to stay at home with their children has increased by 47%. More mothers are exploring this option because they dislike dropping their children off at daycare. Therefore, if companies wish to retain these mothers as employees, they should build onsite daycare centers."*

Analysis

Over the last two decades, women have made great strides in improving the equality between men and women in the workforce. However, although women are climbing the corporate ladder faster and more frequently than ever, a new trend has evolved. A national news station discussed this trend citing the results of a recent survey, which shows a dramatic increase in the number of women who are leaving their careers to stay at home with their children. The news report suggested that mothers are quitting their jobs because they dislike leaving their children at daycare. Therefore, they implored, if companies wish to retain these mothers as employees, they should build onsite daycare centers. Although the survey results in this argument are valid, they are not fully developed and the suggested solution makes generalized assumptions and omits other important avenues companies could explore to retain employees.

The news station was accurate in reporting that many women are opting to stay home with their children rather than to go to work. Basing this claim on a survey adds credibility to the report. However, the writers at the news station should have considered investigating the matter more thoroughly and thus fully developing the story. In addition to obtaining the results from the survey that indicated the increase in the number of homemakers, they should have requested more detailed results that would explain the reasons more women are leaving their jobs to stay at home. If these results were not readily available, the station should have considered conducting their own survey to obtain these answers.

Had the station obtained more details about the reasons so many women are leaving the workforce, they would not have made the mistaken assumption that mothers' dislike of daycare is the main reason behind the trend. Perhaps they would have realized that, although it is true that mothers do not like having to drop their children off at daycare, there are more specifics to the dilemma. For example, some families discover that the cost of daycare, commuting, and a work wardrobe surpasses the cost to a one-income family where the father works and the mother saves on the added expense that comes from holding a job. Many mothers are staying home simply because they feel more comfortable being the one to raise their children. They realize that they are missing many important aspects of their children's lives and make the necessary monetary adjustments to become a one-income family.

Clearly, there are many reasons some families are opting to live on one salary, and these reasons go beyond the daycare factor. If the news station had discussed these reasons, they would probably have made several other suggestions to companies who wish to retain these women as employees. For example, companies could explore alternate scheduling options such as flex schedules and part-time work. Flex schedules would allow mothers to take part in important events in their children's lives by scheduling their workday around their children's schedules. An employee on a flex schedule could, for example, come in earlier than other employees and leave in time to catch her child's baseball game. Part-time opportunities not only give mothers more time with their children, but they also help alleviate the cost of daycare and commuting. A part-timer may choose to just work three days a week, spending the other two at home. Many women would likely stay with their company if they were given an opportunity to telecommute. This would be an excellent option for companies to offer to mothers whose jobs require excessive computer work or research as this can easily be done from a remote location.

Although the news station's suggestion that companies should build onsite daycare centers was a viable one, the station should certainly have taken more time to fully address the issue. They should consider giving a follow-up report in which they discuss other reasons women are returning home to be with their children. These details will likely lead to further suggestions they can give to companies struggling with the popular trend of women giving up their careers to be homemakers.

Argument

The following is from a speech by the president of the Best Charity Club to her club members:

> *"Three months ago, the Charity for Youth Club held a bake sale at the annual Fourth of July Bash in town. They raised over $2,000. Our club budget currently has a deficit of $1,000, and we have some pending purchases and contributions which total over $1,000. This brings our monetary need to $2,000. We should hold a bake sale at the annual Christmas Party at the civic center in order to raise the funds we need to cover these costs."*

Analysis

Every year, charities raise thousands of dollars for good causes. Recently in a speech to her club members, the president of the Best Charity Club mentioned that at the last Fourth of July Bash, the Charity for Youth Club raised over $2,000 by conducting a bake sale. To meet monetary needs of $2,000, the president stated that it would be in the best interest of the Best Charity Club to hold a similar fundraiser at the annual Christmas Party. Although the president was probably correct in recounting the profit the Charity for Youth Club made at the Fourth of July Bash, she is too quick to assume that her club can make similar profits; she has failed to analyze specific details about the Charity for Youth Club's fundraiser to confirm that her club can duplicate the bake sale and its favorable results.

The president of the Best Charity Club assumes that her club can duplicate the results of the Charity for Youth Club's summer bake sale. However, along with this assumption is the presumption that charitable givers will be as willing to donate to her club's charity as to the cause of the Charity for Youth Club. She does not discuss either cause, so we do not have a reference from which to judge. Perhaps the Charity for Youth Club raises money for children who have cancer. Perhaps the Best Charity Club donates money to political causes. Clearly, children with cancer pull at peoples' heartstrings more strongly than do politicians. Causes that tug at a person's heart are more likely to get people to open their wallets as well. Regardless of the specific cause, however, the president of Best Charity assumes that people will be just as likely to give at the Christmas party as at the Fourth of July event. Since people often spend a lot of money on Christmas gifts, they may not be as willing to give to charity as during the summer months.

Not only will the Best Charity Club need to plan for a bake sale at a different time of year than the Charity for Youth's sale, but they will also need to project how many baked goods to prepare and what kinds. The president of the Best Charity Club failed to address these specifics of the Charity for Youth Club's bake sale. For example, it would be helpful for the Best Charity Club to be knowledgeable about what types of baked goods sold well at the Charity for Youth's bake sale and what pricing was set for each item. If the president does not address these details, her club's bake sale may not be as successful.

The president must look even further than the pricing her club should set for the baked goods. She must also look at the costs that her club will incur. She has omitted these costs from her speech, but without some knowledge of a budget for baking products and rent for a selling space at the Christmas party, she cannot accurately calculate the profit her club can make. Without this calculation, she will have a difficult time setting goals with her club members.

Many specifics still need to be discussed with all club members. The president of Best Charity Club should not assume that her club can hold a bake sale that will add the necessary profit of $2,000 to their bank ledger. Even though another charity has been successful in this way, she cannot guarantee to her club members that they can equal this effort. She must give her club members more details from the Charity for Youth Club's bake sale such as items sold, pricing, and cost to the club. From there, she should brainstorm with her club about other fundraising ideas in case their bake sale does not ring up the necessary number of sales to meet the deficit in her club's budget.

Argument

The following is from a television campaign ad:

> *"Residents of Lawrence County should elect Thornton Campbell as school superinten-dent in the next election. Thornton Campbell has served as superintendent for 16 years in neighboring Downs County. Since he became superintendent, Downs County Schools have improved their test scores by 43%. If we elect Campbell, Lawrence County School test scores will improve."*

Analysis

You've seen them on TV around election time—political ads, one after another, bombarding you with the accomplishments of one candidate and the "dirt" on another. Knowing what to believe and what to dismiss as mere drivel can be difficult. It is easy to believe things that are stated as fact. For example, in a recent television political ad, supporters of Superintendent Thornton Campbell suggested that he should be elected superintendent of Lawrence County. The ad offered support by reviewing Campbell's past record as superintendent of neighboring Downs County. Apparently, test scores in this county went up by 43%. The ad suggested, then, that if Campbell were elected superintendent of Lawrence County, their test scores would improve as well. Although the ad states a positive statistic, it does not provide enough information for voters to make a well-informed decision to vote for Campbell as superintendent.

The ad does not provide adequate information because its assumptions are misleading. The ad assumes that the improvement in test scores is a direct result of Campbell's efforts; however, there are other factors that could have played a vital role in the higher scores. For example, perhaps the test has changed. Standardized tests are under continual revision. Revisions over a number of years could result in higher scores as students adapt to the test. This improvement could have coincidentally corresponded with Campbell's term as superintendent of Down's County Schools making it seem as though it was a result of Campbell's service as superintendent.

Even if the ad did prove that the improved test scores at Downs County were a direct result of Campbell's work, it assumes that he can duplicate the results in a different county. The most significant element of any county is its people. There is no mention of the population that makes up each county. For example, suppose Lawrence County is more ethnically diverse than Downs County. Campbell's strengths may not lie in dealing with a diverse student body and work staff; he may not be as successful in such a situation.

Perhaps the ad should have focused on other positive efforts that made Campbell successful when he served as superintendent of Downs County. Many voters may be more interested in knowing how the candidate dealt with violence in Downs County School, for example, than they are in test scores. In addition, if the ad gave voters more information about Campbell's past, they would be able to compare him more intelligently with other candidates.

Voters need many details to make good decisions when they cast their vote. This ad does not provide enough details about Thornton Campbell. Campbell's supporters should submit another ad that cites examples of programs that Campbell instituted that played a direct role in improving the students' test scores. In addition, they should expand the ad to include details about other positive efforts that made a difference during Campbell's term as superintendent in Downs County. From these details, voters can get an idea of what Campbell could bring to Lawrence County Schools that would benefit students and teachers. Voters not only want a superintendent who can help a school system raise test scores, but they also want to be assured that he will effectively combat violence in school, make it a priority to get graduates in to college, improve athletic programs and institute a quality curriculum. Voters must see more details about Thornton Campbell in order to cast a well-informed vote.

Software

(Windows and Mac Classic)

INSTALLATION DIRECTIONS FOR GMAT PREP COURSE SOFTWARE

Windows:
1. Insert the disk into the CD-ROM drive.
2. From the Start menu, select Run and then select Browse.
3. Select your CD-ROM drive from the Browse menu.
4. Select the file gmat.exe
5. Click Open and then click OK.

Macintosh Classic:
1. Insert the disk into the CD-ROM drive.
2. If necessary, double click the disk icon.
3. Double click the icon: gmat.sea
4. Select a folder into which you would like to place the file.
5. Click Save.

SOFTWARE ORIENTATION

If you are familiar with computers and software, you are unlikely to need to read this orientation: We put considerable thought into making the software as simple and intuitive as possible.

A. **Main Menu**

You start a test by clicking either the Mentor Mode or Test Mode button of the test you want to take. In Mentor Mode, you can immediately see a solution to each problem and you will not be timed. Select this mode for studying. In Test Mode, you will not see solutions of the problems and you will be timed. Select this mode for practice at taking timed GMATs.

1. **Select Section Screen**

When you click Mentor Mode, the Select Section Screen appears. On this screen, click the section of the test you want to study. If you have chosen Test Mode instead of Mentor Mode, this screen will not appear and you will be taken directly to the first section of the test.

2. **Section/Direction Screen**

After clicking the section you want to study, the program takes you to the first page of the section—the Directions page. To see the first question, click Next.

3. **Selecting an Answer**

You select an answer by clicking its letter (or typing its letter). This highlights the letter, and, if you are in Mentor Mode, presents a feedback box that explains why your selection is correct or incorrect. You can change your answers as often as you like. Some solutions to the questions are too long to display all at once in the feedback box. In these cases, use the scroll bar to scroll through the solution. When there is more text to be viewed, the scroll bar will be highlighted.

B. **Navigation**

There are three ways to reach other questions.

1. **Questions Near By**

If the question is near by, merely click Next (or Back) the appropriate number of times.

2. **Questions Moderately Far Away**

If the question is farther away, press the Right Arrow Key on the keyboard the appropriate number of times (this is available only on extended keyboards). If you are on Question 3 and want to go to Question 7, then press the Right Arrow Key four times

3. **Questions Far Away**

If the question is far away, click the Status Button, which takes you to the Status Display. From there, you can go to any question by merely clicking the question. If you are on Question 3 and want to go to Question 26, click the Status Button and then click Question 26.

C. The Navigation Strip

The Navigation Strip is present at the bottom of the screen when questions are present.

1. **Status Button**

    Clicking the Status Button takes you to the Status Display which lists the questions you have answered correctly or incorrectly (in Test Mode, it states only whether the questions have been answered). The Status Display is also a convenient and fast way to reach far away questions. If you are on Question 21 and want to go to Question 2, then click the Status Button and then click Question 2.

2. **Time Button**

    The Time Button displays the time you have been working on a section and the time you have remaining.

3. **Stop Button**

    The Stop Button gives you access to your current score (and from there access to the Score Conversion Chart). It also allows you to navigate to other sections of the test or to return to the Main Menu.

    A. **Return to the Section Button**

    The Return to the Section Button takes you back to the question you were working on.

    B. **Switch Sections (Go to Next Section)**

    The Switch Sections Button takes you to the Switch Sections Screen from which you can choose another section of the test.

    In Test Mode, the Switch Sections Button is labeled Go to Next Section, and it takes you directly to the next section. If you want to skip that section, just click the Stop Button and then click the Go to Next Section Button. By doing this, you will be unable to return to the skipped section.

    C. **Return to Main Menu Button**

    The Return to Main Menu Button takes you back to the Main Menu. When you select this option, the Are You Sure dialog box will appear reminding you that your current score and status will be erased. (Note, changing sections within a test does not erase your score or status.)

    D. **Show Score Button**

    The Show Score Button takes you to the Score Display which shows your current score for the entire test and for each section.

Online Course

To register for your Personal Online GMAT Course, go to

examville.com/novapress

Then click the SignUp button. After selecting a Username and Password, click the Register button. You will then be taken to the Welcome Screen:

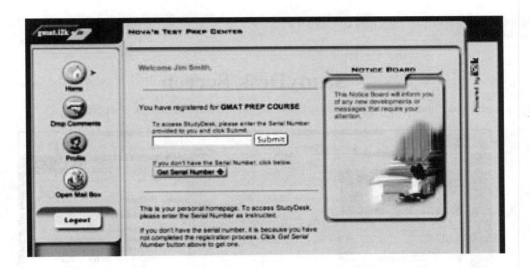

This is your gateway to all the interactive features of your Personal Online GMAT Course.

StudyDesk Tour

The StudyDesk presents short chapters of text along with exercises like a prep book does. But it also offers many powerful, interactive features. Such as,

Ask Questions!

We respond within 24 hours. During regular business hours, questions are usually answered in real time. At the bottom of every page of text, there is a button titled "Tool Box." Use this button to Search, Take Notes, and Ask Questions. If there is a specific sentence or paragraph that you don't fully understand, just drag it to the Feedback screen and click Submit Question. StudyDesk will first search its database of questions that have been asked by students in the course. It will then present any answers that may have been previously written on the issue, and it will relay the question to us.

Monitoring

StudyDesk monitors your progress and directs you to weak areas that you need to study more.

Feedback

When you answer a question, you are told immediately whether you answered it correctly and you can elect to return to the question, view a solution, or proceed to the next question.

Take Notes

You can take notes at nearly every place in the course. Your notes are stored, and you may search them at any time.

Search

You can search every part of your course, including text, notes, questions and answers. This is convenient when you need to quickly review a term or concept.

Rank

You can compare your performance in the course to other students who are taking the course.

The following illustrated tour will give you a good idea of what expect from your Personal Online GMAT Course.

StudyDesk Screen

This is where you choose an activity: Study a lesson, take an exercise, check a report, etc.

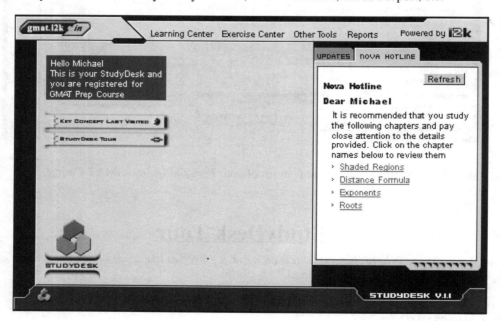

Learning Center

This is where you study the lessons or chapters. It is the core of the course. You can also review our answers to your questions and view the course details.

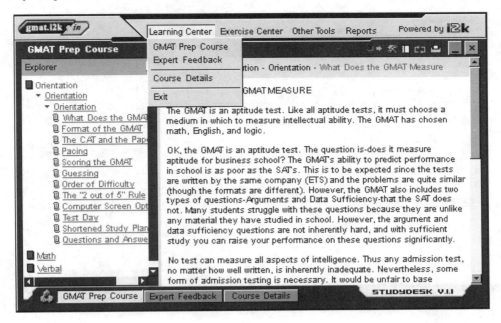

Exercise Center

This is where you access the exercises. These exercises are also presented in the core of the course; but they are collected here so that you may conveniently and quickly find an exercise.

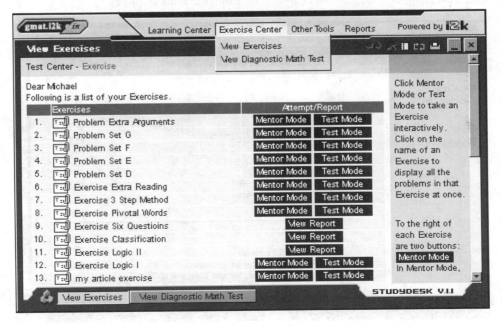

Other Tools

This is where you can access some of the tools, such as, the search function. These tools are usually available in the core of the course as well.

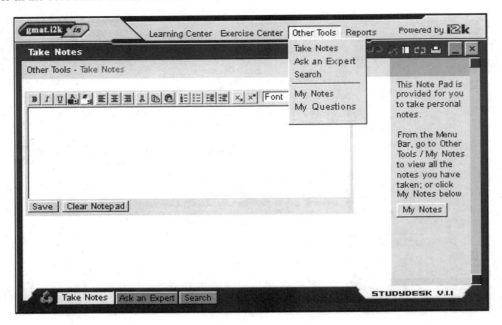

Reports

This is where you can view your rank. Your Rank is calculated by evaluating your performance on StudyDesk and comparing it with other students using StudyDesk. You can view your rank at every level of the course. That is, on course, topic, or chapter level using the Rank Explorer.

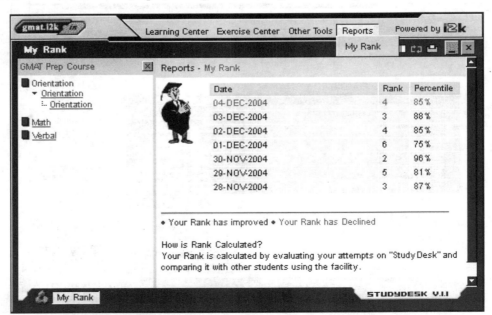